Praise for *Turning Ju*

"Wonderfully written as well as intensely thought provoking, *Turning Judaism Outward* is the most in-depth treatment of the life of the Rebbe ever written. The author has managed to successfully reconstruct the history of one of the most important Jewish religious leaders of the 20th century, whose life has up to now been shrouded in mystery. A compassionate, engaging biography, this magnificent work will open up many new avenues of research."

—Dana Evan Kaplan, author, *Contemporary American Judaism: Transformation and Renewal;* editor, *The Cambridge Companion to American Judaism*

"In contrast to other recent biographies of the Rebbe, Chaim Miller has availed himself of all the relevant textual sources and archival documents to recount the details of one of the more fascinating religious leaders of the twentieth century. Through the voice of the author, even the most seemingly trivial aspect of the Rebbe's life is teeming with interest.... I am confident that readers of Miller's book will derive great pleasure and receive much knowledge from this splendid and compelling portrait of the Rebbe."

—Elliot R. Wolfson, Abraham Lieberman Professor of Hebrew and Judaic Studies, New York University

"Only truly great biographers have been able to accomplish what Chaim Miller has with this book... I am awed by his work, and am now even more awed than ever before by the Rebbe's personality and prodigious accomplishments."

—Rabbi Dr. Tzvi Hersh Weinreb, Executive Vice President Emeritus, Orthodox Union; Editor-in-Chief, *Koren-Steinsaltz Talmud*

"A fascinating account of the life and legacy of a spiritual master. The author's meticulous scholarship is matched by his love of Torah. This book will inspire many who already know about the seventh Lubavitcher Rebbe and many others who don't yet have that privilege."

—Daniel Matt, author of the multi-volume annotated translation of the Zohar, *The Zohar: Pritzker Edition*

"This well researched and thoroughly documented biography by a leading Chabad scholar presents an integrated account of the life and teachings of the Lubavitcher Rebbe, Rabbi Menachem Mendel Schneerson. Innumerable details are integrated into an account that brings to life the Rebbe's teachings and influence, without hiding the paradoxes and controversies that were raised by his career."

—Lawrence H. Schiffman, Edelman Professor Emeritus of Hebrew and Judaic Studies, Skirball Department of Hebrew and Judaic Studies, New York University; Vice Provost for Undergraduate Education, Yeshiva University

"A masterful work of scholarship, beautifully written, with new insight into the life of an introverted, brilliant scholar who created the largest and most influential outreach program in Jewish history."

—Rabbi Menachem Genack, CEO Orthodox Union Kosher

"A masterful and erudite biography of the 'Rebbe'.... All who are interested in the life of this remarkable man and leader will profit and be captivated by the work of Rabbi Miller!"

—Chancellor David Ellenson, Hebrew Union College–Jewish Institute of Religion

"Though two decades have passed since the death of Rabbi Menachem Mendel Schneerson, his messages of love of Torah and for his people continue to inspire so many in the Jewish world. Chaim Miller's meticulous and heartfelt examination of the "Rebbe's" indomitable quests and profound successes will be eagerly read by all those desirous of learning about the life, learning, leadership and legacy of this remarkable rabbinic figure."

—Jeffrey S. Gurock, Libby M. Klaperman Professor of Jewish History, Yeshiva University; author, *Orthodox Jews in America*

"A desperately needed framework that can help anyone who heard about the Rebbe but had too many wrong mental models (and too many literary hindrances) to approach him culturally and spiritually."

—Dr. Domenico Lepore, founder, *Intelligent Management*; author, *Sechel: Logic, Language and Tools to Manage any Organization as a Network*

"There are *tzadikim* whose lives are like the *Song of Songs*. The words and events are explicit and clear, but the mystery, the secret remains unsolved. Rabbi Chaim Miller has written a masterpiece depicting the remarkable life and times of the Lubavitcher Rebbe *z'ya*. While honest and bold, it respects the *sod*, the secret of the towering *tzadik* whose life's song changed the world."

—Rabbi Moshe Weinberger, Congregation Aish Kodesh, Woodmere, NY;
mashpia at Yeshiva University

"Chaim Miller's biography *Turning Judaism Outward*... is not afraid to engage the more complex and difficult questions about "the Rebbe's" life. Using hundreds, perhaps thousands, of documents carefully footnoted, including sermons, official records, and letters, some only published in the past few years, Miller reconstructs the life of a somewhat iconoclastic Hasidic master.... In lucid, loving (but not overly apologetic) prose, Miller tells the very compelling story of a complicated life. I highly recommend it even for those who know little or nothing about the person or the world it describes."

—Shaul Magid, Jay and Jeannie Schottenstein Chair in
Jewish Studies, Indiana University/Bloomington

"An important contribution about an individual who inspired an extremely great number of people. This volume should be widely read."

—Rabbi Aaron Rakeffet, Professor of Rabbinic Literature, Yeshiva University;
author, *The Rav – the World of Rabbi Joseph Ber Soloveitchik*

"Miller's new biography of the Rebbe combines several methods of description, testimony, and analysis. He offers a nuanced view of a complex and unique phenomenon in the Jewish religious world."

—Dov Schwartz, Chair, the Interdisciplinary Unit and the
department of Jewish Philosophy, Bar-Ilan University;
author, *Habad's Thought: From Beginning to End*

Also by Chaim Miller

The Kol Menachem Chumash – Gutnick Edition

Rambam: Principles of Faith – Slager Edition

The Kol Menachem Haggadah – Slager Edition

The Kol Menachem Megillah – Slager Edition

The Five Books of Moses, Lifestyle Books – Slager Edition

The Kol Menachem Tehillim – Schottenstein Edition

The Kol Menachem Chumash (Hebrew) – Leviev Edition

TURNING JUDAISM OUTWARD

a biography of rabbi

MENACHEM MENDEL SCHNEERSON

the seventh lubavitcher rebbe

by rabbi

CHAIM MILLER

KOL MENACHEM · GUTNICK LIBRARY OF JEWISH CLASSICS

ISBN-13: 978-1-934152-36-2
ISBN-10: 1-934152-36-6

Library of Congress Control Number: 2014906880

Available from:

Kol Menachem
827 Montgomery Street,
Brooklyn, NY 11213
1-888-580-1900
1-718-951-6328
1-718-953-3346 (Fax)

www.kolmenachem.com
info@kolmenachem.com

Contact the author at:
chaimmiller@gmail.com

First Edition — June 2014

Picture of Heinrich Maier courtesy of: Atelier Balassa - ullstein bild / The Granger Collection.

to

David & Lara Slager

Contents

FOREWORD

There is a reason why, twenty years after the passing of Rabbi Menachem Mendel Schneerson (1902-1994), the Seventh Lubavitcher Rebbe, few have attempted to paint his full biographical portrait. Given the tremendous influence of the Rebbe, which continues to be potent and inspiring to a vast number of his admirers today, the omission seems bizarre. Rabbi Schneerson's life is unusual on so many accounts: the huge following he amassed after the Chabad movement was almost decimated by the Holocaust; the remarkable success of his devotees in building Jewish institutions around the world; his wide appeal beyond the ranks of the faithful, among politicians, academics, and intellectuals; his vast knowledge of Judaic texts alongside training in the sciences and a familiarity with Western thought; his deeply inclusive vision that embraced religious Jews and their secular brethren, Jews and non Jews, and sought to dismantle the barriers separating one race from another; his phenomenal energy and dedication to his goals, even into his ninth decade; his enigmatic, mystical personality, deeply influenced by Jewish esoteric wisdom; and his fascinating life history, beginning with the pogroms and the Russian Revolution, to the halls of academia in Berlin and Paris, to the escape from Nazi occupied France; and then the radical shift from a quiet, introverted intellectual to a global personality who could swing thousands into action with his mere word.

Such a man would seem to be an excellent subject for a biographical sketch. Why, then, is there such a paucity of material in this area?

The answer to this question is complex, but I will attempt to address briefly some of the obstacles in painting an authentic picture of the Rebbe's life, and how I have sought to navigate them. I do not claim, by any means, to have fully resolved these concerns, but I have grappled with them—in an attempt to render a narrative which is at least a true portrait of Menachem Mendel Schneerson, although inevitably an inadequate one.

1. *Problems with primary sources*

During most of his lifetime, almost no information was available about the Rebbe's early life, before his arrival in the United States in 1941. By the time interest in the field began to gain momentum around a decade ago, there was almost no one alive who personally remembered the Rebbe from this period, except for a few individuals who were small children at the time.

What *has* emerged over the last two decades are many documents relating to his early life: his personal notebooks (*Reshimot*) from the period, extensive correspondence with his father-in-law and father, his academic records, his mother's personal diaries, his Russian passport, and some memoirs of Chasidim from this period who observed him closely. When this is all pieced together, along with numerous other fragments of documentary information, we can make a reasonable attempt to locate exactly where the Rebbe was and what he was doing for the first four decades of his life, the impressions that he made on others, as well as some of his inner thoughts.

Chronicling the latter fifty years of his life, in the U.S.A., poses its own set of challenges. The Rebbe was an extremely private person and did not share his inner world with anybody, except perhaps his wife. While he was an extremely public figure, corresponding and meeting with thousands of individuals personally each year and spending much time sharing his ideas in long sermons, information about his inner thoughts and struggles is sorely lacking. I have attempted to compensate for this by drawing on the many accounts of private, often candid, conversations with the Rebbe penned by visitors. Although, of course, these lack the reliability of documentary evidence, by drawing from a vast range of such testimonies, especially from sources outside of the Lubavitch movement, I hope that the contours of his temperament, charisma and humanity will come more closely into focus.

2. *Prevalence of Hagiography*

With internal accounts of Chasidic history crafted by followers and devotees, hagiography is the norm, not the exception. Historian David Assaf has summed up the concerns of dealing with such accounts which are often "lost in their adulation and veneration....selective range of sources, deliberate concealment, obfuscation, and even distortion."[1] The hagiographic author blurs the line between testimony and interpretation, such that the text is rearranged according to the writer's own values. As Immanuel Etkes has similarly noted, "What all have in common is the effort to paint a picture of the past with which they can identify."[2]

In preparing this work I have been acutely aware of these pitfalls, and have sought to render the narrative with as much scrupulous objectivity as possible. While it is almost inevitable that personal bias will influence an author in some way or another, my goal has been to offer a detached and dispassionate account of events as they transpired. The reader, of course, will be the judge of how successful I have been.

Even with these concerns sharply in focus, the task of separating the man from the myth is fraught with difficulty. A historian who finds aggrandizement of the Rebbe distasteful may tend to overcompensate, deflating his image too much. Scholar Nehemia Polen has observed one recent attempt to view the Rebbe through the lens of secular historiography, that it is

> so intent on deflating Schneerson's aggrandized image, bringing him down to earth, that one is at a loss to understand how his followers were inspired to spread his message to every corner of the earth.... A hermeneutic of suspicion is called for, but one must know of what to be suspicious.[3]

In attempting to address this concern, I have aimed to render what Polen describes as "a robust portrait that takes seriously the imaginative reach of a great thinker," seeking to "capture both the possibilities and perils of religious leadership."

3. *Complexity of Character*

By his own admission, the Rebbe was a man who fell into the category of those "for whom the central, overwhelming focus of their lives is in the world of thought, the world of ideas, and their main activities... focused inwards, to *'the world set in their hearts'* (Ecc. 3:11), and not to the outside world surrounding them" (see p. 99). His sermons and discourses are evidence of an extremely rich inner life, a man who inhabited a universe of elevated patterns of thought. Even his mundane actions and other this-wordly activities were guided by the unrelenting application of rigorously deduced principles. An electrical engineer by training, whose profession was to check wiring against blueprint, the Rebbe spent his entire life clarifying what he understood to be the Torah's blueprint for our times, and implementing it with consistency.

Rabbi Menachem Mendel Schneerson is therefore a person who cannot be grasped by anecdotes and glimpses from his interaction with people alone; there is a pressing need to see his activities in the context of the ideas that motivated him. Polen describes this as "the limits of a journalistic portrayal of a person of spirit that observes externals but vacates considerations of interiority."

Elliot Wolfson, too, has elaborated on the point:

> If we are honest, we must admit that any attempt to speak of the Seventh Rebbe will be fraught with the danger of providing a hermeneutical lens that is too narrow to view the many facets of the phenomenon at hand....
>
> When we attempt to gauge the life and impact of the Seventh Rebbe, we are indeed reaching for the Infinite; there is always a surplus that we cannot know and about which we cannot speak.... there is no manner of beholding him that is not beholding through a garment.[4]

I believe it is due to these formidable challenges, among others, that there has been so little effort towards producing a full biography of the late Rebbe, despite his extraordinary life and sustained interest in his teachings. No work, to my knowledge, recounts the story of the Rebbe's whole life in accurate detail, while at the same time demonstrating an intimate understanding of his published sermons and discourses. To be sure, there are many collections of anecdotes, personal reflections, and collages of his life and teachings; but if you will follow the narrative here from beginning to end, you can decide for yourself whether my presumption has been correct: that there is an immeasurable advantage in seeing the *entire story* of the Rebbe's life amid the intricate world of ideas which he inhabited.

Whatever your existing views of the Seventh Lubavitcher Rebbe, if any, I invite you to join me in the following pages on a journey of a man through historical turmoil, on an insatiable quest for knowledge; a story of immense personal tragedy, but of deep faith both in G-d and in humanity. It is the biography of a man who did much to reorientate his co-religionists in America from a defensive position to an expansive one—turning Judaism outwards.

Chaim Miller

28th *Nissan* 5774 / 28th April 2014

Acknowledgments

First and foremost I extend my gratitude to David and Lara Slager whose outstanding generosity has made this book possible, as well as most of my other works throughout the last decade. The Slager family have set a fine example to the Jewish community, both in their personal lives and with their outstanding philanthropic efforts towards an impressive array of causes across the globe. I wish David, Lara, and their precious children Hannah and Sara Malka, all the abundant blessings that they deserve.

I extend my heartfelt wishes to Rabbi Meyer Gutnick, co-founder and director of Kol Menachem publishing, who had the courage to invest in an unknown author, and since then has been an unfailing source of material support and moral encouragement for my work. Motivated by a great love for the Rebbe, and recognizing the urgency of spreading his Torah teachings, Rabbi Gutnick has chosen to invest his own natural talent at "getting things done" into a very worthy cause. In the merit of this, and all his many other impressive philanthropic efforts, may G–d bless him, together with his dear wife Shaindy, and all their wonderful children and grandchildren, with *chasidishe nachat* and only revealed and open goodness.

In particular, I extend my thanks to Rabbi Chaim Rapoport who dedicated much of his time to a careful review of the manuscript, offering many helpful emendations and suggestions; and to Rabbi Yisroel Newman for his helpful edits after reading the text, and for his ongoing assistance. I also thank Rabbi Michoel Seligson for answering my questions at short notice, and Rabbi Menachem Kirschenbaum for stimulating my interest in Chabad history.

My dear friend Eli Shear has been instrumental in this work for a number of reasons. He is the one who introduced me to the world of Chabad, without which this book, or any of my other works, would never had transpired. And through a meticulous edit he has immeasurably transformed the original manuscript of this book into something eminently more readable and enjoyable.

For assistance with proofreading I thank: Rebbetzin Sarah Nechama Yarmush, Chaya Sarah Cantor, Rochelle Ginsburg and Sara Shear.

And finally, to my greatest support, my wife Chani, who sees me through moments of despondence and self-doubt, and to my wonderful children: Leah, Mendel, Mushka, Levi, Esther Miriam, Ariella and Menucha, my greatest pride and joy.

CHAPTER ONE

LIFE AT HOME

1902–1922

Menachem Mendel Schneerson, aged 2

The tides of fortune turned against the Russian Jewish community in 1881, with the assassination of Czar Alexander II, as widescale pogroms were officially sanctioned. In less than a year, one hundred and sixty localities went up in flames, with Jews maimed and killed indiscriminately, and countless Jewish properties destroyed. These unrivaled episodes of ethnic violence, which continued sporadically over the next decades, resulted in a panic among the Jewish population, and they fled in huge numbers.[1]

It was at this time and place in history that Menachem Mendel Schneerson was born, on Friday 18th April (11th *Nissan*) 1902, in Nikolayev, Russia. Ostensibly he was named after his paternal ancestor, the Third Lubavitcher Rebbe, Rabbi Menachem Mendel Schneerson (1789–1866), but the name also connoted the pain and constraints of the times. Menachem means "one who comforts," a derivative of the Biblical name Noah (Noach), whose birth gave humanity hope that "this one will comfort us (*yenachamenu*) from pain" (Gen. 5:29).

Already at the tender age of three, when he was exposed to brutal violence with the 1905 pogrom in his home town, Menachem Mendel's talents as a comforter began to emerge. As mobs roamed the streets shouting "kill the Jews," attacking innocent victims and setting Jewish homes and businesses on fire, the young Menachem Mendel huddled with his mother, Chana, along with other Jewish women and children at a hidden location in a local pharmacy. Due to the cramped conditions and palpable fear, many of the children began to cry loudly, endangering everybody's safety. Menachem Mendel instinctively shifted into "comforter" mode. The young boy circulated the room and, one by one, soothed each of the children until they had calmed down. The pharmacy owner, who obviously had been worried for his own safety, was taken aback.[2]

Unfortunately, much more comforting was going to be needed. In his childhood and youth alone, Menachem Mendel was to live through subsequent pogroms, blood libels, the First World War, a typhus epidemic, the Bolshevik Revolution and the rise of Communism. "I had to look at things in a positive light," he recalled years later to confidante and Chasid, Rabbi Berel Junik (1927-2005), "otherwise I would have never been able to go on living."

His coping mechanism, it seems, was to stay aloof and immerse his head in books. He possessed natural genius and a penchant for study, and the detached, idealistic world of the mind must have offered some inner peace amid the external fear and turmoil. As his community faced constant violence, threatened and actual, the young boy dreamed of a time of undisturbed tranquility. In a rare autobiographical glimpse from this period, he later wrote, "from the day I went to *cheder* (primary school), and even before then, an image of the future redemption began to form in my imagination, the redemption of the Jewish people from this final exile, such a redemption that would explain the sufferings of exile, the harsh decrees and genocides... *'On that day you will say, "I will praise You, G-d, although You were angry with me"'* (Isaiah 12:1)."[3]

Even before the 1905 pogrom erupted, Menachem Mendel had

already absorbed the atmosphere of unrest. As anti-Czarist protests were taking place outside their home in the wake of the revolution, Menachem Mendel's mother found him on the balcony of their apartment, joining the demonstration. He was screaming out loud in Russian *daloy samadershzavye,* "An end to the autocracy!" Fearing for their safety, the family took the boy inside and quietened him.[4]

It is often repeated how, upon Menachem Mendel's birth, six telegrams were received by his parents from Rabbi Shalom Dov Ber Schneersohn (1860-1920), the Fifth Lubavitcher Rebbe; and how Menachem Mendel's mother was careful to ritually wash her infant's hands each time before he ate, a highly unusual practice for a child of that age.[5] The Schneerson name itself instantly brings to mind the long illustrious dynasty of Lubavitcher Rebbes.

In reality, though, Menachem Mendel was only a distant cousin of the prevailing Lubavitch dynasty—his paternal great-great-great grandfather had been the Rebbe—and there were hundreds of Schneersohn descendents scattered around Russia.[6] The five-generation gap since the last Rebbe in Menachem Mendel's family, represented a considerable ancestral distance from the Lubavitch dynasty.

Menachem Mendel was raised in the household of a Rav, an ordained, communal Rabbi, not a Rebbe. Rabbi Levi Yitzchak ("Levik") Schneerson (1878-1944) stemmed from a distinguished line of Rabbis, from both his mother and father's side, all of them Chabad Chasidim, but the office of Rebbe differs considerably from a traditional, congregational Rabbi. A Rebbe is perceived as the head of the community's organic hierarchy, a unique soul which contains a splinter of the soul of every Chasid (disciple). Through a Rebbe, energy is infused into the world and reaches his followers by means of their utter devotion (*bitul*) to his every word. From an exalted spiritual viewpoint, which cannot be reached by other souls, the Rebbe acts as a guide in the worship of G-d and offers a higher intuition even in worldly matters, such as finance, health and relationships. His word is accepted unquestioningly, forming an unbreakable bond (*hitkashrut*) between Rebbe and Chasid. "To question the Rebbe is worse than sin; it is absurd," wrote Nobel laureate Elie Wiesel, "for it destroys the very relationship that binds you to him."[7] A Rebbe's blessing is considered to shatter heavenly decrees, heal the sick and, in the eyes of some, to work miracles. He will also have a proclivity for saving souls and easing the path of repentance.[8]

A Rabbi (Rav), on the other hand, will be responsible for the traditional ecclesiastic duties of his congregation—to ensure that Jewish law is adhered to in the synagogue, in areas of *kashrut* (kosher food preparation) and in the construction of *mikvaot* (ritual baths). He will officiate at weddings and funerals and will be consulted by congregants on *halachic* issues. A more advanced Rabbi may also rule in financial disputes, conduct divorces and conversions, and will be consulted by junior colleagues about the finer points of Jewish law. Every city, even small towns, would typically have their own Rav, but in an entire movement of Chasidim, there would be just one Rebbe.

A further unique feature of Rebbehood is the phenomenon of a regal "court," a physical-social epicenter of activity. A court would consist of the Rebbe, his personal secretaries, administrators and other functionaries, a small group of close Chasidim (*mekuravim*) who accompanied the Rebbe everywhere; the "residents" (*yoshevim*), who would live close to the Rebbe and droves of other Chasidim who would visit for advice and pilgrimage. Physically, a court would usually have living quarters for the Rebbe and his immediate family, a synagogue/study hall, and, most importantly, an inner sanctum where the Rebbe would receive visitors for *yechidut* (private consultation). The court would be funded by a voluntary tax, *ma'amad,* given by all Chasidim to the Rebbe, according to their willingness and ability. For a Chasid, to be in the Rebbe's presence at his court would be an exhilarating experience; and from a typical pilgrimage, where the Chasid would pray several times in the Rebbe's synagogue and hear him deliver Torah thoughts, the Chasid would be energized for months, if not years.[9]

This experience of coming into personal contact with the stately and mystical persona of a Rebbe, and witnessing the passion at his court, was entirely absent from Menachem Mendel's childhood and youth. He never met the Fifth Lubavitcher Rebbe, whose "reign" continued until 1920, nor did he see the celebrated court in Lubavitch (Lyubavichi), which ran from 1813 to 1915, the home of four successive generations of Chabad Rebbes. (As we shall see, he was only introduced to the Sixth Rebbe, Rabbi Yosef Yitzchak Schneersohn (1880-1950), when it was suggested in 1923 that he marry Rabbi Yosef Yitzchak's second daughter, Moussia.)

From a contemporary point of view, it seems bizarre that Menachem Mendel never visited Lubavitch or met the reigning Rebbe in his childhood and youth, because in recent decades Chasidim would fly to the Rebbe's court regularly, often one or more times in a year, and they would nearly always bring along their children at some point. But a century ago, such pilgrimages were less frequent, due to the difficulties and expenses of travel (railways in Russia were poorly developed before the Revolution). Menachem Mendel's father, Rabbi Levi Yitzchak, was an important figure: from 1909 onwards, the Rav of a major city with the largest Jewish population in southern Ukraine. With demanding Rabbinic duties, it would have been difficult for him to leave his home town for a five-hundred mile pilgrimage to Lubavitch, especially with young children. We also need to bear in mind the many years of social and political unrest in the area during the first two decades of the Twentieth Century, which would have ruled out many windows of opportunity for extended travel.[10]

Still, the omission is striking. The fact remains that Menachem Mendel Schneerson, who was later to become one of the most influential and celebrated Rebbes in the history of Chasidut, did not have a direct encounter with a Chabad Rebbe until the age of twenty-one.[11] In fact, his closest personal connection to a Rebbe up to that point was with his namesake and paternal ancestor five generations earlier, the Third Rebbe of Chabad, Menachem Mendel Schneerson (also known by the title of his voluminous responsa *Tzemach Tzedek*).[12]

Tzemach Tzedek had been one of the most successful of the Chabad Rebbes, transforming the movement from what was initially perceived by some outsiders as a deviant sect, to win widespread acceptance among the Orthodox community. During his long tenure as Rebbe, from 1831 to 1866, he attracted a huge following of a reputed one hundred-thousand Chasidim;[13] but after his passing, the movement splintered, and five of his six surviving sons each succeeded in setting up their own courts in different locations.[14] The only son of *Tzemach Tzedek* who did *not* become a Rebbe was the oldest son—and paternal ancestor of the Seventh Rebbe—Rabbi Baruch Shalom Schneerson (1806-1869).[15] Baruch Shalom did not establish a dynastic branch of Chabad, like his brothers, but he did compose his own Chasidic discourses, and left behind an ethical will which was found after his death.[16]

Baruch Shalom's oldest son, Rabbi Levi Yitzchak (1834-1878), was appointed as Rav in Podobranka and later Beshenkowitz, but tragically passed away at the tender age of forty-four.[17] His son, Baruch Shneur Zalman (d. 1926), married Zelda Rachel Chaikin, daughter of a wealthy Chasid from his home town, Podobranka.[18] We know that Baruch Shneur *was* a regular attendee at the court of the Fifth Lubavitcher Rebbe, since his extensive journals of experiences there between 1911 and 1916 have survived.[19]

Baruch Shneur and Zelda Rachel's oldest son, Rabbi Levi Yitzchak Schneerson, was the father of the future Seventh Rebbe, Menachem Mendel.[20] "Reb Levik," as he was affectionately known, was born in 1878 in Podobranka, Russia, and studied under the tutelage of his great-uncle Yoel Chaikin, the town's Rabbi. Reb Levik earned a reputation as a brilliant Talmudic scholar, even outside the Chabad community. He was an extremely close devotee of the Fifth Lubavitcher Rebbe, Rabbi Shalom Dov Ber (*Rashab*), who later described Levik as one of just three disciples of whom he would be proud "in this world and the next." As early as 1896, when Reb Levik was just eighteen, he was sent by the Rebbe Rashab to Germany to perform a Rabbinic inspection of *mikvaot*, a task which demanded mastery of a highly complex area of Jewish law. Reb Levik probably studied in Rashab's *Tomchei Temimim*, the first Lubavitcher Yeshivah, as soon as it opened its doors in 1897;[21] and in the summer of 1900, following the suggestion of Rashab, he married Chana Yanovsky (b. 1880), daughter of Chabad Chasid Meir Shlomo Yanovsky, Chief Rabbi of Nikolayev.[22] (Yanovsky had inherited the position from his illustrious grandfather Rabbi Avraham David Lavut (1814-1890), a disciple of *Tzemach Tzedek* and author of a number of important Rabbinic texts).[23]

Supported by his father-in-law, who was extremely benevolent but not wealthy,[24] Reb Levik spent the next nine years of married life in his wife's childhood home, and was reputed to have been immersed in study for as much as eighteen hours a day. In 1901, tragedy hit the family when Chana's youngest and only brother, Yisrael Leib, contracted a fatal bout of typhus, and passed away at the tender age of fifteen. Her father, Meir Shlomo, slipped into a deep depression which paralyzed him from all activity, prompting a letter of consolation from Rashab, who advised studying certain inspirational passages of Chasidic texts together with his son-in-law, Levik.[25]

From 1902 onwards, Reb Levik conducted regular missions for Rashab, attending Rabbinic meetings on his behalf, and he organized the distribution of *matzah* to Jewish soldiers during the Russian-Japanese war of 1904-5. While they were residing at the Yanovsky's, three sons were born to Levik and Chana: Menachem Mendel, in 1902; Dov Ber (Berel) in 1904,[26] and Yisrael Aryeh Leib (Leibel) in May 1906.[27]

II.

By 1905, pressure was already mounting for Reb Levik to find his own source of income—the Schneersons were cramped together with their infants, parents-in-law, and Chana's two younger sisters, Miriam Gittel and Ettel, in one apartment—and Rashab began efforts to find Levik a rabbinic position.[28] In 1906 a job became available in another city, but it required a diploma equivalent to five years of college study. While prolonged secular study did not appeal to Reb Levik, for the sake of supporting his family he spent several months studying Russian, in preparation for examinations. After travelling three hundred miles to register in Kiev, he discovered that the curriculum required study of Old Church Slavonic and Christian scriptures, leading him to promptly abandon the entire project and return home without registering.

At the end of 1906, another Rabbinic position became available, and Rashab sent a letter to the community suggesting that they accept Reb Levik as their Rav.[29] The community insisted that for Reb Levik to be considered a candidate, he would have to obtain a prestigious *semicha* (Rabbinic ordination) from one of the leading non-Chasidic giants of the day, Rabbi Chaim Soloveitchik of Brisk (1853-1918). Confident that Reb Levik would impress the Brisker Rav, Rashab advised Levik to make the trip, encouraging him that the Brisker was "genuinely G-d fearing."[30]

In a 1951 sermon, the Seventh Rebbe recalled what had transpired at the *semicha* test.

> Since my father dressed like a Chasid of those times, and Reb Chaim Brisker knew he was from the [Schneerson] family, he tested him painstakingly, hoping to find a justification not to give him *semicha.* After exhaustive testing, he was forced to award him *semicha,* lamenting, "Oh my goodness, Reb Levik! You have such a good mind,

> and look where you have placed it." He was referring to the fact that my father put his scholarly energies into Chasidut and Kabbalah.[31]

Despite a further letter of support from Rashab, shortly before the community's elections for Rav, the position did not materialize for Reb Levik.[32]

On 1st January (27th *Tevet*) 1908, the much loved Chabad Rabbi of Yekatrinoslav (now Dnipropetrovsk), a major center some two hundred miles north-east of Nikolayev, passed away. Rabbi Dov Zev ("Bere Volf") Kozevnikov (b. 1839), had been a disciple of the Third Chabad Rebbe, *Tzemach Tzedek*. He was a short man, extremely humble, and, like many Chasidim of that era, he preferred not to display his substantial Talmudic knowledge except when necessary. Well versed in Chasidut and Kabbalah, he was cherished by Chasidim as one of the *yechidei segulah* (unique individuals) of their times. Reb Volf would regularly be wrapped in *tallit* and *tefilin*, busy with prayer and study, until four o'clock in the afternoon. He gave so much of his money to the poor that the community was forced to pay his salary directly to his wife so as to ensure the family's livelihood. His passing left a huge void, and Rashab perceived Reb Levik as an ideal successor. The position was an extremely coveted one: Yekatrinoslav was one of the largest cities in Southern Ukraine, and was home to the largest Jewish populations in the district.[33]

During the same period, the community of Yekatrinoslav sustained two further losses: Baruch Zaslovsky, Rabbi of the industrial district, passed away two days before Passover; and then the young, energetic Rabbi Eliyahu Shmuel Levin passed away less than two months later, aged forty-two. (The doctor who had treated Kozevnikov, Zaslovsky and Levin vowed never to treat a Rabbi again!) The only remaining Rav was head of the Rabbinic court, the esteemed Rabbi Binyamin Zakheim, who was too old and frail to service the needs of such a large community.[34]

In the eyes of the community, Reb Levik had two huge drawbacks: he was too young, a mere thirty years old; and he was perceived as being "old-school," appealing only to elderly traditionalists. The candidate supported by the *mitnagdim, maskilim,* Zionists and the wealthy was Lithuanian-educated Rabbi Pinchas Gelman (1880-1921). A handsome, charismatic, well dressed man, Rabbi Gelman enjoyed much popularity. He was learned, gifted as a Hebrew writer and delivered fiery sermons in Russian.[35]

"The dispute escalated to the heavens," recalled Rabbi Yehudah Leib Levin (1894-1971), who was Rav in Yekatrinoslav (then Dnipropetrovsk) and Moscow after the Second World War. "There was fighting and *chilul Hashem* (desecration of G-d's name) in all the synagogues for several months." Even though it was against his nature, Reb Levik became embroiled in the dispute, since he had been instructed to seek the position by his Rebbe, Rashab.[36]

In her memoir of the period, Chana recalled the irony of Sergei Pavlovitch, a prominent non-religious Jew who was impressed with Reb Levik, rising to his cause. Amid the heat of the dispute, Pavlovitch "could be sitting on the boulevard on Shabbat afternoon, smoking a cigarette, while considering ways to get the Chasidic Rabbi appointed."[37]

Eventually, a compromise was decided, and both Rabbis were appointed over different parts of the town: Rabbi Gelman over the area close to the Dnieper River, which had been Rabbi Kozevnikov's province, and Rabbi Schneerson was assigned to the area which was previously presided over by Rabbi Eliyahu Shmuel Levin.[38]

So, in 1909, Reb Levik, his wife Chana and their three sons relocated to Yekatrinoslav, where Levik would commence what would be a perpetual struggle as the city's Rabbi. But it was these difficult years which would mold the personality of Menachem Mendel Schneerson, the future Rebbe of Lubavitch, as a fiercely independent, unashamedly traditional but culturally aware Jew.

Even after the Schneerson's arrival in town, the political heat took a while to subside. In the press, *maskilim* denounced the new Rabbi, pointing to his descent from *Tzemach Tzedek*, who had been outspoken against intellectual "enlightenment."[39] Every Jew who cherished civilized culture was called upon to ensure that Schneerson should have no influence in the city, for he represented a danger to progress.[40]

When diplomatic methods failed, Reb Levik's opponents resorted to dubious methods. As the Seventh Rebbe himself recalled at a Purim gathering some seventy-five years later:

> One fine day the Police Chief showed up at our house and asked to speak with the Rabbi in a private place. It's not difficult to imagine how frightening this was for us all. In those days, under Czar Nicholas, a personal visit from the Chief of Police was no small matter.
>
> After he had left, we asked my father what had happened. He said that a complaint had been leveled against him with the authorities. My father was unfit to be Rav of an important city, the informants argued, since he had been seen drinking liquor, and dancing arm-in-arm with a shoemaker![41]

While the allegations might seem humorous, we need to bear in mind that the authorities, who were often deeply anti-Semitic, did not need much enticement to bring charges against a Rabbi. A number of the Chabad Rebbes had, in the past, been imprisoned for seemingly minor allegations, significantly endangering their lives, and this brush with the authorities must have been quite traumatic for the Schneerson family. Resorting to informing the police (*mesirah*) is an especially dirty act of foul-play in Jewish communal politics, and it gives us some sense of the deep factions that had developed.

We begin to see, however, a pattern emerging in how Reb Levik defended himself from his critics. While "on paper" he was an "old-school" Rabbi with uncompromisingly traditional values, it seems that when secular Jews, and even the non-Jewish police, met Rabbi Schneerson they were impressed with his intelligence and humanity. Here, and on a number of subsequent occasions, Reb Levik was received positively by academics, intellectuals, and Jews from a diverse range of backgrounds.[42] We can imagine, then, the parental image in which Menachem Mendel was reared: a Rabbi deeply committed to Chasidic values and yet worldly enough to make an impression on the most secular Jews.

These were times when traditional edifices had already been crumbling for a generation, and there was a rapid hemorrhaging of Chasidic youth to competing ideologies. Nowhere was this more evident than in the story of Rebbetzin Chana's own first cousin, Tziporah (b. 1878)—daughter of Meir Yanovsky's younger sister, Chana—and her husband Tuvia Shlonsky. Tziporah, like thousands of others, was influenced by the strong intellectual currents of the times; already as a teenager, her enthusiasm for observant Judaism had eroded as she became increasingly involved with the Social Democrat movement. She was attracted to Tuvia, who seemed to be an ideally "modern" Lubavitcher: well learned in Torah, but also secularly knowledgeable and polished; not at all sheltered from modern ideologies.

While Tziporah's emotional detachment from traditional Judaism was all but complete, Tuvia remained torn, and the issue plagued their marriage. Tuvia had been fascinated by the writings of the secular author Ahad Ha'am, who was popular among intellectuals of the day; but he remained, at heart, a Chabad Chasid and desired to educate his six children in that path. The spirit of their home ended up as a sort of compromise: proudly Jewish, Zionist, traditional but not particularly observant. On one wall hung a painting of Maimonides, and on another, a picture of Russian anarchist, Michael Bakunin (1814-1876).[43]

The Shlonskys moved to Yekatrinoslav in 1905, and as soon as their cousins, the Schneersons, arrived, the two families became extremely close, living next door to each other from around 1909 to 1913. While the adults would pass from one apartment to the next through the doorways, the children simply entered and left through the windows. The youngest of the six Shlonsky children, Verdina (1905-1990), later a prominent Israeli composer and pianist, recalled her memories of Levik and Chana Schneerson in an interview in 1977. "They were so beautiful, aesthetic, musical and pure. Really pure. Chana was a very beautiful woman, always dressed elegantly. She was very sociable. Reb Levik was a tall and handsome man with a striking beard, like Hertzl."[44] Verdina's older brother, Avraham (1900-1973), who later became a significant Israeli poet, recalled of the Schneerson household, "I was influenced by this peculiar climate: filled with stringency, fear, nuances and mystery. It was immensely charming to me."[45]

In addition to Chana's close friendship with her cousin and neighbor Tzipora, Reb Levik also shared a warm relationship with Tuvia. The two men would spend hours in conversation about religion, faith and even literature. Tuvia would sometimes lend Reb Levik some of his secular books, including volumes of *Hashiloach,* a journal of Hebrew literature influenced by Ahad Ha'am, and Reb Levik would read them in the only location sanctioned for a Chasidic Rabbi to read such material—the bathroom.[46]

III.

What education did Menachem Mendel receive in his childhood years? The popular form of Jewish education in that period was the *cheder metukan,* or "improved school," an attempt to modernize the traditional *cheder* to the prevailing conditions. The major emphasis of the *cheder metukan* was still Torah, but the curriculum was expanded to include some secular subjects and new pedagogic methods. Everything was taught in Hebrew.

In Yekatrinoslav a successful *cheder metukan* and *yeshivah* had been founded by the non-Chasidic Rabbi, Pinchas Gelman; but Reb Levik preferred that his children study according to traditional methods, in Yiddish, so he hired the services of a private *melamed* (teacher) for his sons and a handful of other local children.

The *melamed,* Menachem Mendel's only significant pedagogue besides his father, was Rabbi Zalman Vilenkin (1878-1963), a childhood friend of Reb Levik. In 1909 a possible job opportunity for a *shochet* had arisen in Yekatrinoslav and Reb Levik was instrumental in Reb Zalman's relocation to the city to take the position. When the job failed to materialize immediately, Reb Levik suggested that, in the meantime, Reb Zalman could teach his sons and a few other students.

For the next five years, from the age of seven until twelve, Menachem Mendel learned under Reb Zalman's tutelage along with his brothers Berel and Leibel, and a few other Yekatrinoslav boys. Reb Zalman was known to be a *masmid,* a person who devoted virtually all his available time to Torah study. He knew all Six Orders of the *Mishnah* by heart, and numerous Chasidic discourses. He was considered to be a clear, effective speaker and also gave classes for adults in the community.

Reb Zalman recalled in later years, that Menachem Mendel—or "Mekka" as he was known to his friends—was always engrossed in his studies; and that he was introverted, generally not mingling or socializing with the other children.[47] "He was quiet. He loved to think," Verdina Shlonsky recalled. "He didn't play children's games with us."[48]

Even at this young age, Menachem Mendel had broader interests, particularly in astronomy. On his bedroom walls hung charts of the skies.[49] He also devoured dictionaries in his spare time, and by the age of ten was busy acquiring a knowledge of Russian, English and Italian.[50] "He was interested in everything," Verdina remembered. "The adults used to speak about the interest he showed in science."[51]

Avraham Shlonsky also attended the *cheder*, and soon became zealously observant, refusing to eat in his own mother's kitchen which was not sufficiently kosher. (He ate next door at the Schneersons' instead). On the fast of *Tisha B'Av*, Avraham even followed the pietistic practice of sleeping with a hard rock under his head.

"During the time we were in Yekatrinoslav," the Rebbe later wrote to Avraham, "you always sought out the audacious. You went against the grain."[52] After Avraham's bar mitzvah in 1915, his father, Tuvia wanted to send the boy to study in Lubavitch to continue in the path of a dedicated Chasid, but his mother, Tzipora, would hear nothing of it. She insisted that her son get a good secular education in a local Russian school. As a compromise, Avraham was sent to a Hebrew-speaking Gymnasium in Israel. While Avraham Shlonsky did not retain his orthodoxy, his poetry was later influenced by the Messianism and dreams for the future which he had absorbed in the Schneerson home.[53]

Reb Levik's *cheder* was also attended by the two younger Schneerson boys, who were known by their friends as "Belka" (Berel) and "Luba" (Leibel). Berel was a blonde boy, more lively than his older brother. (It is unclear whether the health condition which plagued him in later life affected him during his youth.[54]) The youngest son, Leibel, was described by Verdina Shlonsky as "an unusual child. In physical appearance he was very similar to his oldest brother."

Rabbi Yitzchak Goldshmidt, a Chernobeler Chasid and *shochet* from Yekatrinoslav who had been a strong supporter of Reb Levik's appointment, sent his son Nachum (1905-1976) to study in the *cheder* with the Schneerson boys. "Reb Levik was extremely dedicated to his sons' education," Nachum recalled, "but, as it turned out, he didn't have to toil too much with the three boys. Reb Levik's boys were studious by nature, not with an ordinary studiousness but an exceptional one. It was to such an extent that their mother had to tear them away from the pages of the Talmud to feed them.... They had phenomenal memories. They would look at something just once and recall it permanently."

Nachum recalled how Menachem Mendel and Leibel were both unusually talented, but Leibel's more extroverted personality made him the more superficially impressive character. Menachem Mendel was serious by nature and always had a preoccupied look on his face. Leibel, on the other hand, was "mischievous." He would talk effusively and joke around. "That's why his father and mother would say about the younger brother, Leibel, that he had the better talents," Nachum remembered, "because they were more on display. He would exhibit his talents to others."[55]

When Menachem Mendel reached the age of eleven, Reb Levik decided that his son needed some more advanced, personalized tutelage, and he enlisted the services of another *melamed* from Lithuania, who taught the boy privately. This arrangement, however, did not last too long, and within a year or so Menachem Mendel was sufficiently equipped to study on his own, a path he followed for the rest of his life.[56] "I studied without a *chavruta* (study partner)," he later told Rabbi Mordechai Ashkenazi (b. 1943), the Rav of Kfar Chabad, Israel.[57]

Over the next decade, Menachem Mendel would spend tens of thousands of hours in private study, poring over the Talmud, Midrash and a diverse selection of Jewish texts. His only teacher was his father, with whom he would often spend nights in study. Reb Levik introduced his son, in time, to his own specialized field of interests: the world of the Kabbalah and the teachings of Arizal (Rabbi Isaac Luria) in particular.

Of the thousands of pages of Torah thoughts which Reb Levik penned in his lifetime, only a fraction have reached us, from the very end of his life when he was exiled to Asia,[58] but from what remains, we get a picture of an extremely fertile mind, an exceptional memory, and somewhat eclectic interests. His writings are extremely dense and rich in sources, displaying more than a stroke of genius.[59]

All this was absorbed by Menachem Mendel from his father and we see its influence on the Seventh Rebbe's style of Torah discourse. In the Schneerson home there was a substantial library of Torah books, well beyond the basic texts of the Talmud and commentaries, and it was in this oasis that Menachem Mendel developed his love for research and bibliography. This was something also encouraged by Reb Levik, who, after sharing an original Torah discourse with listeners would often turn to his oldest son, inviting him to suggest the exact sources on which the lecture was based. Menachem Mendel would promptly rattle off a list of references. On one occasion, a listener was perplexed as to the point of this unusual exercise, and questioned why the Rabbi bothered with it. "It's helpful not only for him but for me, too," Reb Levik explained. "Sometimes my son comes up with a source which had not occurred to me."[60]

Menachem Mendel's fascination with sources continued throughout his entire life. As we shall see, during the 1930s he conducted a prolonged study of the sources for Rabbi Shneur Zalman's *Tanya;* in the 1940s he annotated the Sixth Lubavitcher Rebbe's discourses with references, and penned a new edition of the Passover Haggadah tracing the sources line by line;[61] and throughout all the tens of volumes of his edited *Likutei Sichot* (Collected Sermons)[62] and *Ma'amarim* (Chasidic Discourses),[63] the Seventh Rebbe's teachings are copiously footnoted and cross-referenced.

As the world outside was aflame—the pogroms, the First World War, the Bolshevik Revolution—Menachem Mendel spent most of his time secluded at home in his room, standing in private study. Often, when he did not appear for meals, his mother would bring food to him. A brief biographical sketch of the Rebbe found in official Chabad publications (and edited by the Rebbe himself), has nothing to say of his youth except that, "he studied with intense diligence, and he succeeded."[64]

Reb Levik generally did not involve his oldest son with his communal duties, leaving him at home to study. When Nachum Goldshmidt would visit the house, he would often observe Leibel in prolonged discussion with his father, while Menachem Mendel was away in his room.[65]

At the age of fourteen, Menachem Mendel's advanced knowledge made a deep impression on Rabbi Moshe Betzalel Alter (1868-1943), the third son of the Gerer Rebbe (Rabbi Yehudah Aryeh Leib Alter, the *Sefat Emet*), who was a refugee in Yekatrinoslav during the First World War. Nachum Goldshmidt recalled how Rabbi Alter was brought by Reb Levik to test the boys in Talmud. Menachem Mendel was tested on a passage in Tractate *Arachin*, one of the more obscure volumes of the Talmud which discusses complex laws of vows to the Temple. Rabbi Alter pointed to one of the comments of *Tosafot*, the critical glosses printed in the Talmud's margin, and asked the boy to read and explain the text. The particular comment of *Tosafot*, Nachum recalled, consisted of a single question followed by four suggested answers.

Menachem Mendel not only translated and explained the *Tosafot*, he also suggested a deficiency in *Tosafot's* first solution, which necessitated offering the second; a problem with the second solution which necessitated a third answer, and so on.[66] Rabbi Alter proceeded to test Menachem Mendel on other passages in the Talmud, until he could no longer contain himself, exclaiming out loud (in Yiddish): *A bochur'el fun fertzin yohr! Vu me'chapt im on in shas, zohgt er vayter oif oisveynik dem loshon fun gemora mit Rashi, vort ba vort!* ("A young lad of fourteen years! Whatever place you mention to him in the Talmud, he continues to rattle off the text of the Talmud with *Rashi* by heart, word by word!")[67]

IV.

What happened during Menachem Mendel's childhood and youth, when he was *not* studying? We know that at the end of each summer Rebbetzin Chana would take the boys to her parents, the Yanovskys, in Nikolayev. Her father, Meir Shlomo, was the city's Rabbi,[68] and over the course of several visits, he made a deep impression on Menachem Mendel.

In a 1989 sermon, the Rebbe recalled that his grandfather, Meir Shlomo, had been a *yoshev* ("resident") at the court of the Fourth Lubavitcher Rebbe, Rabbi Shmuel Schneersohn (1834-1882). These were the days before Lubavitch had its own *Yeshivot* (academies), and to absorb Chasidic vibes, dedicated young men would take a six months to one-year "residency" at the Rebbe's court shortly after marriage. Obviously this involved a great sacrifice on the part of Meir Shlomo's wife, Rachel, but she consented willingly.

Meir Shlomo's subsequent position as Rav of Nikolayev was quite different to the spiritual oasis of Lubavitch. Nikolayev was a major business center, and much of Meir Shlomo's professional energies were spent settling financial disputes. He was also drawn into political issues as a contact between the government and the Jewish community.

His grandson, the future Rebbe, found the contrast striking: Meir Shlomo was obviously a spiritual man who had enjoyed an extended period of detachment from mundane life in Lubavitch, devoted to matters of transcendence; and yet he also had the business and political acumen to lead a large, diverse community. More importantly, the Rebbe noted how one experience had cross-fertilized the other: amid his often mundane work, Meir Shlomo could always conjure to mind his spiritual home in the "paradise" of Lubavitch, and those vivid memories would energize him and inspire him to carry out his allotted task with dedication.[69] It was this straddling of worlds, the ability to perfume even the spiritually dullest parts of life with "peak moments" from a different time and place, that became a hallmark of the Seventh Rebbe's outlook and teaching. We will see this later on, but it is significant that the Rebbe attributed this quality to his own grandfather, who was a memorable role model in his childhood.

We know very little about Menachem Mendel's grandmother, Rachel Pushnitz of Dubrinka.[70] In 1990, near the end of his life, the Rebbe published a sermon in her memory, writing an unusual, touching note how she "cared for me for a number of weeks at the end of the summer, for several years."[71]

Despite his inclination to stay with his head in the books, away from action, there are a few isolated incidents from Menachem Mendel's youth where we see a willingness to help others in need, even at personal risk. At aged nine, on vacation in Balaklava, Menachem Mendel swam out into the Black Sea to save a boy who was drowning after his boat capsized.[72] At fourteen, as Yekatrinoslav filled with Polish and Lithuanian refugees from the First World War, Menachem Mendel was inspired by his mother's herculean efforts to provide aid, and joined her cause.[73] At twenty, when a typhus epidemic erupted in Yekatrinoslav, Menachem Mendel worked around the clock to provide support for the victims, exposing himself to a high risk of infection. He eventually contracted the disease—which had killed his uncle, and almost claimed the life of his grandfather—and burned with high fever for several days. In his delirium, he mumbled Chasidic jargon.[74]

Besides these few exceptional cases, the only time in the year when Menachem Mendel would "make an exception" and involve himself in something else besides Torah study was to raise money and prepare a festive meal for the annual *farbrengen* (gathering) for *Yud Tet Kislev* (the Chasidic "new year"), in Yekatrinoslav. The *farbrengen* was indeed a sight: Reb Levik would say a few *lechaims*, and expound upon the Kabbalistic significance of the day, as his three sons stood at his side, until the wee hours of the morning.[75]

In the years following the Bolshevik revolution, from the age of fifteen onwards, another communal position was forced upon Menachem Mendel: to communicate with the *Yevsektzia*, the Jewish section of the Communist party. "I grew up in the times of the *Yevsektzia*," he later recalled in a sermon, "and I was educated not to be intimidated by them. This is despite the fact that they could threaten to send a person to Siberia—and actually carry out their threat."[76]

In an emotionally charged 1979 sermon, the Rebbe reflected on how these experiences with the *Yevsektzia* toughened him for later communal work—for those occasions when it would be necessary to take an unpopular position.

> G-d helped me that, not through my own choice or will, I was the firstborn of a father who later became the Chief Rabbi of Yekatrinoslav. In those days, in that country, there was sometimes the need for debates [with the authorities], or to respond to a question or an intimidation, and for this you had to speak Russian. Since I was the oldest son of the city's Chief Rabbi, the task fell on me. From that time on, sixty or sixty-five years ago, I was trained not to wait to be addressed with titles of honor.[77]

When Menachem Mendel was around sixteen, his parents hired him a private tutor in secular studies, so that he would be able to complete public examinations in the local secondary school as an external student—a task which he completed successfully.[78] The tutor, Yisrael Eidelson (1895-1965), was a teacher in the local secondary school as well as leader of the Zionist youth movement in Yekatrinoslav—for which he was eventually arrested by the Soviet authorities, in 1922, and sent to Siberia. Eidelson later became a prominent Israeli politician, known as Bar-Yehudah, acting as Minister of Internal Affairs and Minister of Transportation during the 1950s and 60s.[79]

Menachem Mendel's primary secular interests seem to have been astronomy and mathematics. He knew how to estimate the hour from looking at the skies,[80] and, on one occasion, predicted a solar eclipse. At the age of sixteen, he impressed a local high school teacher by solving a complicated mathematical problem with unusual speed, and, in general, all the Schneerson boys, as well as Reb Levik himself, had a great love of mathematics and problem solving.[81] Israeli politician Yonah Kesse (1907-1985), who was a regular at the Schneerson home, recalled in a 1973 television interview that even though Menachem Mendel was self taught, students and even professors would visit him to discuss issues in physics and mathematics. Kesse also "witnessed his intense diligence in Torah study. I always found him learning in a standing position, never sitting down.... I remember him as an extremely private person, an introvert; his entire being, as I recall it, was Torah."[82]

Another firsthand account we have from the Schneerson home from the early 1920s is the memoir of Yekatrinoslav resident Yeshayahu Sher (b. 1907), a close friend of Leibel.[83] Sher was a student in the Yeshivah established by the town's non-Chasidic Rabbi, Pinchas Gelman, and also took classes in mathematics and physics. The Schneerson family became something of a legend in Sher's home, as his father, who deeply respected Torah scholarship, "was astounded by the talents of the Rabbi's three sons. In our house, he praised them all the time, saying that the Rabbi's three sons were geniuses, gems."

Menachem Mendel, Sher remembered, was known as the "young Rabbi." He was of medium height, and slender build. His complexion was white and fine, with a black beard all around. "I never saw him with friends," Sher recalled. "He was always alone, thinking."

"Berel's features were fuller, and his beard blonde. He was also talented and brilliant. The youngest, Leibel, was taller than his brothers, with a velvety beard which had not yet filled his entire face."

Leibel, had broader interests in secular literature than his brothers. While all the Schneerson boys each had his own set of Talmud and bookcase of *sefarim* (sacred texts) in their shared bedroom, Sher remembered that Leibel had an additional bookcase for his secular reading matter, which was covered with highlights and notes. Leibel was particularly interested in economics and wrote a number of essays on the topic in Russian. He was prone to show off his genius and would say, "Give me twenty-five days and I will learn a language."

Among Sher's other interests, he studied engineering in a local school under the tutelage of a Jewish teacher named Mr. Ostrovsky. On one occasion, Sher spoke enthusiastically about the Rabbi's three brilliant sons to Ostrovsky and how they had acquired considerable mathematical skills without attending high school. Intrigued, Ostrovsky wrote down a complex problem, and suggested that Sher present it to the Schneerson boys. Energized by the challenge, Menachem Mendel, Berel and Leibel sat down that night and, working independently, each devoted the evening to penning a solution. Ostrovksy was more than impressed that all three boys had managed to come to the correct answer.

Sher's relationship with the Schneerson boys ended after three years when Berel was arrested by the Soviets. "His parents suspected that I caused Berel to be arrested due to my activities with Zionism," Sher recalled. Arriving at the house one day, Chana opened the door looking extremely perturbed and said to him, "I am sorry, but it's better you don't come in. Berel has been arrested. Levik is crying."

A further blow came to the Schneersons when Leibel became captivated by Zionism, stepping away from the traditions of his family. Sher himself had carried out an unsuccessful mission, assigned to him by Mordechai Gruber of the Zionist Youth, to draw his friend Leibel to Zionism. Over the course of a few weeks, Sher casually left works by Hayim Nahman Bialik (1873-1934), Shaul Tchernichovsky (1875-1943) and Ahad Haam (1856-1927) in the boys' bedroom, as well as a volume entitled *The Destiny of the Jewish Nation,* by Zionist thinker, Dr. Daniel Pasmanik (1869-1930). Leibel, who devoured the material, was impressed by the idealism and the language, but remained unconvinced by the ideology. Sher soon despaired and gave up his mission. (Menachem Mendel, Sher recalled, took a brief look at the books but was disinterested).

The seeds, however, bore fruit later on when Leibel *did* join the Zionist cause through the influence of Menachem Emanuel Brustein, the *Rav Mitaam* (government-sanctioned Rabbi) of Yekatrinoslav. Chana and Levik were deeply disturbed, fearing that this might be a point of departure for Leibel from traditional Judaism. Levik instructed that all books of Modern Hebrew literature be removed from the house. Chana, who would often converse to members of the community in an eloquent modern *Ivrit,* decided from now onwards to speak only in Yiddish or Russian. Eventually, Zionism lost its appeal for Leibel and he was drawn to Marxism and Communism.[84]

With these developments, and Berel's troubling illness, Levik and Chana may have looked at Menachem Mendel as their future pride and joy—but they could not have imagined that he was to become one of the most celebrated Rabbis of the Twentieth Century. Reb Levik, tragically, would not live to see his oldest son's rise to acclaim, but he remained the Seventh Lubavitcher Rebbe's role model and mentor, indirectly influencing the following generations. The Schneerson's open home in Yekatrinoslav, at the heart of a cosmopolitan, very secularized Jewish community, was probably not altogether different from a contemporary Chabad House. Menachem Mendel Schneerson had not grown up in a gated, insular community, and the image of his parents, dedicated to a very traditional, Chasidic Judaism, yet surrounded by Jews who did not share their outlook, eventually served as a model for the future growth of Chabad in thousands of locations around the world.

CHAPTER TWO

ENTERING THE COURT

1923

Kislovodsk, Russia

While the Jews are known as the "People of the Book," Judaism has always been a living tradition, transmitted from generation to generation through a chain of teachers and disciples. In many cases the transmission process is simplified by the presence of one primary influence, a single teacher who hones and rears his student in his own image. In the Rebbe's formative years, which we might extend all the way until his leadership of the movement began in 1951, his mentorship was dominated by not one, but two primary figures: his father, Reb Levik, and the man who eventually became his father-in-law, Rabbi Yosef Yitzchak Schneersohn (Rayatz), the sixth leader of Chabad-Lubavitch. Both of these luminaries shared much in common: both were uncompromisingly Orthodox, supporting the observance of Judaism in Russia at great personal risk; both were proponents of Chabad teachings; both were "aristocrats" of the Schneersohn "Royal Family." But Rayatz possessed different qualities to those of Reb Levik, and these clearly influenced the future Seventh Rebbe in a number of ways.

Rabbi Yosef Yitzchak was not a "pulpit" Rabbi. His main adherents were his Chasidim, loyal, fervently Orthodox Jews who eschewed modern cultural and intellectual influences, opting for an enclavist existence of study and worship. The Chasidim also tended to opt for sources of income which would minimize the interaction of the "mind and the heart" with the outside world.[1] When Rabbi Yosef Yitzchak did interact with other non-Chasidic and non-orthodox Jews from outside his mold, he often made a powerful impression, making them feel at ease, and establishing meaningful dialogue—but that was not his world, and certainly not his constituency.

Unlike Reb Levik, Rayatz devoted a huge amount of his time and energy to administrative and organizational work on a national scale. In an attempt to save the rapidly eroding underpinnings of Russian Jewish life, he actively supported *melamdim* (teachers), *shochatim* (ritual slaughterers to provide kosher meat), Rabbis, their synagogues and *mikvaot* across the entire Soviet Union. In 1922, he formed the "Committee of Rabbis" to implement this support and succeeded in raising large sums of money from overseas, making its extensive activities viable. By 1925, his executive offices were in direct contact with over seven-hundred communities, on which they kept detailed files. In 1925 he set up a vocational school to train Rabbis and *shochatim* at a faster pace to fill congregational vacancies. This was in addition to the administrative work he carried out for his own Chabad community, establishing and running a network of Yeshivot (Talmudic academies) and other social and communal structures. Rayatz was deeply involved in this work, and was known to spend much time writing personal, detailed accounts of funds that passed through his hands.[2]

First and foremost, Rabbi Yosef Yitzchak was revered for his close communion with G-d, his insightful advice and fruitful blessings. Many of Rabbi Yosef Yitzchak's personal writings were historical and nostalgic in nature—he was the last generation to have grown up in the town of Lubavitch, where the movement's particular brand of contemplation and worship had been practiced for a century. As a child and young adult he had absorbed the cultural history of his community from his father Rabbi Shalom Dov Ber Schneersohn, the Rebbe before him, and from countless hours of conversation with older Chasidim. After the community was uprooted from its home in Lubavitch in

1915, as a result of the First World War, and the subsequent death of his father three years later, Rabbi Yosef Yitzchak became the last living remnant of the Chabad-Lubavitch dynasty, which had yet to successfully replant itself on new turf. Gifted with an exceptional attention to detail and a rich, expressive pen, he spent much time recording his extensive memories of Chasidic life for posterity. He devoted his life and scholarship to ensuring the survival of Lubavitch through its various exiles and incarnations.

1923 was therefore a very important year for the youthful Menachem Mendel, as it was the first time he was to meet Rabbi Yosef Yitzchak Schneersohn and see the court of Lubavitch with his own eyes. Until this point, for twenty formative years, he had been entirely molded in the shadow of his father. For the next twenty-seven years, until the death of Rabbi Yosef Yitzchak, he was to be deeply influenced by the Sixth Lubavitcher Rebbe, marry his daughter, and eventually succeed in fulfilling the dream which history would not allow Rabbi Yosef Yitzchak to fully accomplish: the permanent replanting of the Chabad-Lubavitch court on fresh soil.

As we have seen, Menachem Mendel did not visit the Fifth Lubavitcher Rebbe, Rabbi Shalom Dov Ber (Rashab), and paid his first visit to the court of "Lubavitch" in the winter of 1923, three years after Rabbi Yosef Yitzchak had ascended to the movement's leadership. By this time, the Sixth Rebbe had already been "exiled" from his home town in Lubavitch for some eight years, and had established a temporary court seven hundred miles south, in Rostov-on-Don.

The departure of Rashab from Lubavitch in 1915, represented a potentially lethal blow to the Chabad movement which was suffering, like many Chasidic courts, from the winds of modernity that began to blow through eastern European towns and villages from the end of the Nineteenth Century. Chasidism had gradually lost many of its adherents to radical Haskalah, socialism, nationalism and Zionism, at the same time that Chasidic leadership was fragmenting and crumbling. The death of Rashab, was a further blow to the movement, which by that time was also homeless. While Rashab's only son, Rayatz, did provide an opportunity for a dynastic continuum, the shift of loyalties which is necessary for the acceptance of a new Rebbe has always been fraught with difficulty, even in the best of conditions.

Contrary to the cynics,[3] Rayatz proved to be a powerful and effective leader; but as we shall see, history was to impose upon him some almost impossible challenges.

II.

We do not know with historical certainty the precise date in 1923 of Menachem Mendel's first visit to Rabbi Yosef Yitzchak's court,[4] but it appears that the future Rebbe had a far more positive experience on his second visit. Rayatz pointed to this fact in a letter to his daughter Moussia (b. 1901) after Mendel's second visit, the following summer: "He feels completely different than the first time he was here. He has been left with a very good and pleasant impression."[5]

In order to facilitate the second visit, Rabbi Yosef Yitzchak enlisted the assistance of his close confidant and Chasid, Rabbi Eliyahu Chaim Althaus, who assisted his Rebbe with the running of underground Jewish schools and accompanied him on various trips and missions.

Althaus recalls his involvement in Menachem Mendel's second visit to Rayatz in a memoir from 1930. This meeting would begin at the more private, serene setting of Kislovodsk, a spa-city some three hundred miles to the south of Rostov, close to the Georgian border and Caucasian mountains. Althaus writes:

> I was the first who was granted the undeserved merit that the Rebbe [Rayatz] revealed to me in a private meeting in his room during the summer of 1923, the hidden thoughts of his pure heart: he wanted to give his dear and precious daughter to the man who I will speak about now....
>
> I was the first *shliach mitzvah* [emissary to perform a good deed] and it was I who was chosen to make the introduction to bring him [Menachem Mendel] from Yekaterinoslav to Kislovodsk. I was a simple servant who did as I was told.[6]

In his letter to Moussia, penned after his return to Rostov, Rayatz offers a delightful sketch of his first substantial encounter with the twenty-one year old Menachem Mendel, which he refers to playfully as "studying *Hilchot Mendel*" (the "laws" of Mendel). Rayatz writes that the two men had spent together

> several hours a day, virtually every day, until yesterday evening. On Sunday, the three of us [Rayatz, his son-in-law Shmaryahu Gourary and Menachem Mendel] spoke together all day, and it was extremely pleasant. He remained here for the Sabbath, and presumably he will leave for home, G-d willing, on Sunday.... I can say that I already know him a little, and he was extremely pleased with the hospitality.[7]

Why had Moussia, Rayatz's second daughter, been selected for a possible match with the young Menachem Mendel?

Apparently, the match had already been suggested by Rayatz's father, the Fifth Rebbe of Lubavitch, Rabbi Shalom Dov Ber, in his lifetime. "We should consider the son of Reb Levik," he had said to his wife Shterna Sara.[8] Marriage within the close circle of family was common in Chasidic circles, both in the southern, older Chasidic dynasties, as well as the courts of Lithuania, Byelorussia, and later, in Poland. A perusal of the family trees of the great Chasidic lines reveals countless ties between grandchildren, uncles and aunts, and cousins within the same family, over several generations.[9] As we have seen, Menachem Mendel was a distant cousin of Rayatz, descending directly from his namesake the Third Lubavitcher Rebbe, Menachem Mendel of Lubavitch (Rayatz's great-grandfather), and he bore the Schneerson name.

Due to complexities of which we are not fully aware, this union which would prove so influential to world Jewry was delayed for a number of years (see p. 46). The match would not be formally "negotiated" until Menachem Mendel's mother would meet Rayatz in 1926, and the wedding would take place more than two years later.

From 1923 to 1926, the interim period between Menachem Mendel's first visit to Rayatz's court and Rebbetzin Chana's visit to "negotiate" the match, our young prodigy would have taken time on his regular visits to "Lubavitch" to absorb this new world of Rebbe and Chasidim, the vast libraries of books and writings of the previous Rebbes which were in Rayatz's hands, and the underground work at Chabad's central office to support hundreds of struggling Jewish communities throughout Russia.

III.

To what types of activity would Menachem Mendel have been exposed in Rayatz's court during this period? Since the rise of Communism in 1917-20, Russia had come under the control of a militantly atheistic state which sponsored a campaign against Christianity, Islam and Judaism. This was accompanied by the legal and social emancipation of Russian Jews, enabling them to attend universities and play a part in the Communist movement, the sciences and the arts. These two combined forces of emancipation, on the one hand, and governmental persecution of Judaism, on the other, had a devastating effect on Jewish life—it became easy to leave and very hard to stay. The result was a rapid secularization of the Jewish community, especially the youth, as well as the emigration of virtually every eminent Rabbi,[10] leaving a vacuum filled almost single-handedly by the new Lubavitcher Rebbe, Rabbi Yosef Yitzchak Schneersohn. Due to the success of his work, and the virtual absence of other Rabbinic leadership, Rayatz soon became the uncontested head of the Russian Jewish community.

Years later the Seventh Rebbe would recall the inspirational and heroic qualities of his father-in-law in those days:

> I trust you know of his total dedication to the preservation and, indeed, dissemination of the Torah way even under the most ruthless anti-religious totalitarian regime. Logically there was not the slightest chance that he could possibly succeed, especially after all other religious leaders (not only Jewish) had been silenced or eliminated....[11]
>
> His work was not confined to the Chasidic community, as you know, but to all sections of Jewry, including what you call "the other camp," supporting, materially and spiritually, rabbis, Yeshivot, and religious institutions, also of "the other camp," and with the same selflessness and peril to his personal safety, as he worked for the Chasidic community. This he did from the profound conviction that there are no two camps in the Jewish people; that the Jewish people is one people, united by one Torah, under one G-d.[12]

Working for Rayatz in the 1920s posed a grave personal risk to all those involved. In a secret ceremony in Moscow in 1924, the Rebbe chose eight of the most talented graduates of the Lubavitcher Yeshivah, "and we took a solemn oath that whatever would transpire, we are willing to pursue this mission down to our very last drop of blood."[13] These devoted students were dispatched to different regions to set up underground schools and Yeshivot, replacing those which the Soviets were gradually closing down. Roving emissaries travelled from one community to another, offering words of inspiration to maintain religious observance, putting the Rebbe in direct contact with a huge cross-section of Russian Jewry.

Rayatz's approach of centralized leadership, major funding from abroad, and free legal assistance[14] proved a powerful force in ensuring the continued viability of Jewish communities until the Rebbe's arrest in 1927, after which he was forced to leave the country.

It was against this backdrop that the young Menachem Mendel entered the court of the Sixth Lubavitcher Rebbe. We do not find, though, that the future Rebbe was significantly involved in the day-to-day running of underground activities, political lobbying or fundraising. Rather, Rayatz appreciated his future son-in-law's presence as a kind of scholar-in-residence. Menachem Mendel's mother recalled: "The Rebbe, of sainted memory, who later became our son's father-in-law, immediately recognized his special qualities. He almost never let him out of his sight, always calling on him to come to him for some important purpose or another. The Rebbe said he was appointing him as his 'Minister of Education' and he delegated to him many issues that called for Torah scholarship and secular knowledge to bring to fruition."[15]

While Rashab and Rayatz discouraged the study of secular wisdom among their followers, they did have an appreciation of its value in those instances where its "contaminating" effects on the Jewish experience were marginalized or neutralized completely. Rashab, for example, was extremely impressed at a meeting with the young Rabbi Yitzchak Herzog (1889-1959), whom he felt had delved into secular study without any compromise in his faith or piety. Rashab referred to him as a "fine Torah scholar" and "expert also in secular subjects and languages."[16] Rashab then explained:

> Secular wisdom is at odds with the Torah and has the tendency to "contaminate" it; but for a person who values "fear of sin" more than wisdom, his Torah will deflect that contaminating effect. On the contrary, that person will do a great service to the public as his secular wisdom will enhance his Torah, as we find in the case of Rabbi Sa'adia Gaon and Nachmanides, in their times.[17]

The fact that Rayatz was so strongly drawn to Menachem Mendel, designating him affectionately as his "Minister of Education" and assigning him tasks that required secular knowledge, suggests that the Sixth Rebbe viewed this young man as "a person who values 'fear of sin' more than wisdom," such that "his secular wisdom will enhance his Torah." Rayatz jumped at the opportunity to have such a rare individual as part of his court and, in the course of time, his own family.

What seems like a possible, although oblique, public endorsement of Menachem Mendel's secular prowess can be found in Rayatz's discourse of Purim 1925. During that period Menachem Mendel had intensified his interest in astronomy and paid a number of visits to the Pulkovo Observatory in Leningrad. In the winter of 1925, Menachem Mendel disclosed to Yeshayahu Sher (a close friend of his brother Leibel and regular at the Schneerson home in Yekatrinoslav), that he had predicted a complete solar eclipse on 24th January. This caused much commotion among Menachem Mendel's close circle of friends—including Sher, Yona Kesse, and Mitya Gourary—who were excited to see what would transpire.

Mitya, Sher recalls, expressed total confidence in Menachem Mendel's abilities. But after the eclipse failed to be seen on the twenty-fourth, Mendel appeared dejected. When Sher offered his sympathies at the apparently failed attempt, Mendel responded "unequivocally and with great confidence that his calculations were correct, and that he was prepared to demonstrate them to an expert in this field."

Some time later, Sher read in the weekly Russian magazine, *Oginiok*, that there *had* been a solar eclipse on the 24th, but it had been visible only from Brazil, South Africa and Siberia. When Sher informed Mendel of the news, "his face lit up" with joy.[18]

What is interesting is that just six weeks later, possibly the next occasion that Menachem Mendel was present in Rayatz's court,[19] the Sixth Rebbe devoted part of his public discourse to the idea of elevating secular wisdom *such as astronomy* (!) to holiness:

> Holy wisdom has the power to elevate impure wisdom. This is achieved when a person learns a secular idea according to Torah, *i.e.*, with the intention that he will use it to clarify his understanding of Torah wisdom. Like, for example, when a person uses astronomy to

> comprehend the laws of sanctification of the new moon... this results in the knowledge of astronomy becoming absorbed into the wisdom of the Torah... transforming darkness into light.[20]

Rayatz was probably more than aware of Menachem Mendel's interest in astronomy, and may have been subtly offering some admiration here. If not, then, at the very least, Menachem Mendel would have been encouraged to hear these words!

IV.

Let us retrace our steps back to the summer of 1923, when Menachem Mendel enjoyed a few, very positive days with Rayatz in Kislovodsk and Rostov. Mendel subsequently made the three hundred-mile trip home to Yekatrinoslav on Sunday 24th *Tammuz*, but he returned no more than two months later to spend the festive month of *Tishrei* in Rayatz's court.

On this occasion, Menachem Mendel was struck, probably for the first time, by the particular nuances of how Jewish rituals were practiced in "Lubavitch." For example, according to normative Jewish custom, before each note of the *shofar* (ram's horn) is blown on *Rosh Hashanah* (Jewish New Year), another individual announces verbally which type of note is to be blown.[21] In Rayatz's court, Menachem Mendel noticed that, oddly, this custom was not followed and that the *shofar* was blown without any verbal announcements.[22] Menachem Mendel recorded this in his diary, as he would continue to do with many precise nuances of Rayatz's ritual practice.

Rashab and Rayatz both followed very precise customs (*minhagim*) regarding the *mitzvot* and other laws associated with the Jewish Sabbath and festivals, daily worship and life cycle events. These *minhagim* are powerful, because they heighten the worshipper's consciousness of a *mitzvah's* power, and offer a way to express devotion to a particular affiliation—Chabad. Mendel's personal notes, the *Reshimot Ha-Yoman,*[23] which he began to pen in 1929, are literally filled with references to the minutiae of Rayatz's *minhagim,* and it is striking how much the young man was fascinated by these details.[24]

A few months later, Menachem Mendel returned once again to the court of Rayatz, in Rostov, to participate in what would be his first *farbrengen* (Chasidic gathering) in the presence of a Lubavitch Rebbe.[25] The *farbrengen* is an important feature of Chasidic life which is aimed at strengthening feelings of brotherhood, as well as imparting Chasidic teaching from a senior Chasid or from the Rebbe himself. Spiritually, the gathering of close friends saying toasts of *lechaim* (to life!) and earnestly caring for each other is thought to elicit bountiful blessings from on high to all the participants.[26]

Farbrengens in the presence of Rayatz were warm and intimate. There was often a dialogue, with Chasidim posing questions to their Rebbe—a feature absent in the "Seventh Generation"—and the Rebbe in turn would often turn to individual Chasidim and offer them a personalized message. Rayatz also exuded a kind of fatherly love and often expressed words of affection towards one or more of the participants. He devoted much time to story-telling and general guidance in Chasidic ways of life, often based on vignettes from his youth and his memories of Lubavitch village life which had now ceased to be.

Menachem Mendel's first *farbrengen* in Rayatz's presence was on 27th November (19th *Kislev*) 1923, an important date on the Chasidic calendar, when some one hundred and twenty-five years earlier, the founder of Chabad, Rabbi Shneur Zalman of Liadi, had been released from imprisonment, enabling him to properly establish the movement. Menachem Mendel had already been present on a number of occasions when Rayatz had delivered a Chasidic discourse (*ma'amar*) in public, but those were more formal recitals of highly esoteric material. He had not witnessed the warmth and emotive highs of a *farbrengen* in "Lubavitch."

These were difficult times for Russian Jewry, with Soviet persecution escalating by the month. The departure of virtually every significant Jewish leader from the country had sent worrying signals that perhaps now was an opportune time to leave. Rayatz was adamant that his followers stay in Russia to support existing communal structures and expand Jewish underground activities, but this was fraught with great personal danger to everyone involved. Tensions were extremely high and Chasidim were in need of inspiration and encouragement.

According to recollections of the event penned by one of the participants, the *farbrengen* was "extremely good," with "many revelations."[27] In one, highly charged moment, Rayatz made a plea for volunteers to go "to every city and arrange that there should be regular study, that there should be *mikvaot*, to gather children and hire teachers." A number of Chasidim willingly offered themselves to the task and to each of them the Rebbe said, "I am making a sacred covenant with you!", pouring out a cup of *mashke* (strong liquor) and blessing them with success in their activities.[28]

There is no record of the unassuming Menachem Mendel's making any contribution to the discussion. But what he was witnessing here, probably for the first time, was something to which he would later devote much of his energies: the sending of *shluchim* (emissaries). We can only imagine what an impression it made on Menachem Mendel to watch a Rebbe pleading for his Chasidim to go and spread Judaism, at great personal risk to themselves, and watch one Chasid after another rise to the challenge out of love and devotion.

To explain the importance of the task at hand, Rayatz offered the following insight.

> The main purpose of a Jew is to "make" another Jew, even if it is just one more Jew. That is why the first commandment in the Torah is to *'be fruitful and multiply.'*[29]
>
> Why should such a thing be written first? Isn't the Torah all about holiness? Isn't it the sublime wisdom and will of G-d? Because this needs to be the fundamental orientation of a Jew! A Jew needs to "make" another Jew.[30]

Here was Menachem Mendel Schneerson, the man who would later render Jewish outreach a global phenomenon, hearing that the "foundation" of Judaism—its very first commandment, according to Chasidic interpretation—is to "make" another Jew, to bring one's fellow closer to Jewish observance.[31] To what extent Menachem Mendel was inspired on that occasion we do not know, but in hindsight at least it was an extremely poignant moment.[32]

CHAPTER THREE

SCHOLAR-IN-RESIDENCE

1924–1926

Entrance to Rayatz's residence, 22 Mokhovaya, Leningrad

Leningrad, or St. Petersburg, as it was previously—and later—known, is a city which has featured prominently in Chabad history.[1] It is, to our knowledge, the only city which was visited by all of the Chabad Rebbes (with the possible exception of Rabbi Dov Ber, the Second Rebbe). The founder of Chabad, Rabbi Shneur Zalman of Liadi, was detained there during his arrest in 1798, after he had been denounced to Russian authorities as a threat to the State. The First Rebbe managed to refute all the accusations levelled against him, and the Hebrew date of his release, 19th *Kislev*, is celebrated annually to this day.

Rabbi Shneur Zalman interpreted the imprisonment as a Heavenly resistance to his then-radical departure from the norms of Chasidic teaching. The incarceration, he thought, was a form of Heavenly censorship. His colleagues, the other primary disseminators of Chasidic teachings, had agreed not to cross a "red line" of expounding too much esoteric wisdom in public, keeping their inspirational teachings brief and relatively simple. Rabbi Shneur Zalman had pioneered a more advanced form of Chasidic discourse—Chabad—well beyond anything that his colleagues had advanced. When he was released from jail, the First Rebbe understood that if there had been heavenly resistance to his approach, it had now abated, and he intensified his efforts by greatly increasing the complexity and scope of his discourses.[2] It subsequently became common in Chabad to refer to two periods in the development of its key ideas: "before Petersburg"—when Rabbi Shneur Zalman still delivered relatively brief discourses; and "after Petersburg," when the gates were fully opened to present the most intellectually sophisticated renditions of Chasidic/Kabbalistic doctrine to the masses.[3]

The relocation of Chabad-Lubavitch to Petersburg in 1924, after near arrest and subsequent expulsion of Rayatz from Rostov-on-Don, was also a watershed moment for the movement. "Before Petersburg" 1924, the Chabad Rebbes had always held their courts in small, remote towns: Liozna, Liadi and Lubavitch. "After Petersburg" 1924, the Chabad courts would always be found in significant cities: Riga, Otwock (near Warsaw) and, finally, New York. In a 1952 talk, the Seventh Rebbe compared the innovation of Rayatz's metropolis-centered Chabad to the example set by his Biblical namesake, Yosef (Joseph). In contrast to the Patriarchs who were all shepherds, Yosef was the first protagonist of Judaism to be deeply involved with the higher echelons of society and politics, in his role as the viceroy of Egypt. Chabad thought posits that Yosef's different career belied a certain strength which the Patriarchs lacked: He was able to be immersed in densely secular or mundane activities without losing his attachment to G-d. The reason why the Patriarchs had been shepherds, Chabad Chasidut suggests, is because "worldly matters"—finances, diplomacy, carnal temptation, non-Jewish culture and wisdom—would have proven a fatal distraction from their thoughts about G-d and their union with the Divine. Yosef represented a different caliber of Jew, the "metropolis-mystic" as it were, whose interaction with the culture did not compromise his beliefs and spiritual intensity.

This, argued the Seventh Rebbe, represented the distinction between Rayatz and the Chabad Rebbes that preceded him. The earlier Rebbes shepherded a flock that lived a culturally isolated existence in the small villages of Russia. Rabbi Yosef Yitzchak, as the first "metropolis-Rebbe," was required to offer a greater intensity of inspiration, guidance and spiritual leadership that would be necessary for the city-Chasid. "Rayatz bequeathed us this power," concluded the Seventh Rebbe in a 1952 sermon, "that wherever we will find ourselves, even in a powerful contemporary 'Egypt,' it will not intimidate us at all. To the contrary, we will use it as a platform to spread Torah."[4]

While the young Menachem Mendel had visited Rostov on a handful of occasions, he had only begun to drink from the Rebbe's waters in the court of "Lubavitch." Rostov's geographical isolation had prevented it from becoming a major center, but now in Leningrad, Rayatz was much closer to numerous Chabad communities, and the court became very busy. For the next three years, Menachem Mendel would be present, on numerous occasions, at the court of Rayatz, and receive much personal attention as the Rebbe's "Minister of Education," assigned to "many issues that called for Torah scholarship and secular knowledge."[5]

The first such visit that we know of was about six weeks after the Schneersohn family had relocated to 22 Mokhovaya, around the annual fast of the destruction of the two Holy Temples in Jerusalem, *Tisha B'Av*. At the meal following the fast, Rayatz, his family and Menachem Mendel were joined by an individual who would become a close colleague of the Seventh Rebbe for over half a century, Rabbi Shlomo Yosef Zevin (1886-1978).

Rabbi Zevin had been a disciple of Rayatz's cousin, Rabbi Shmaryahu Noach Schneersohn (1842-1923), the Rebbe of Bobroisk, and for a period of time, Kapust.[6] Rabbi Shmaryahu Noach held one of the parallel Chabad courts that had been established by Schneersohn cousins, with Rebbes in the towns of Liadi, Nezhin and Bobroisk.[7] He was a grandson of *Tzemach Tzedek*, and built one of the most prominent courts in Russia, with thousands of Chasidim; but there was no succession after his passing in 1923,[8] and it appears that Rabbi Zevin now shifted his loyalties to Rayatz, the only remaining Chabad Rebbe.

Rabbi Zevin was a Torah scholar *par excellence*,[9] and during these difficult years he was extremely active in Rayatz's underground work to promote Judaism under Soviet oppression. Decades later, the Seventh Rebbe would testify, "I knew him during the oppressive regime of Russia. Circumstances were such that being involved with spreading Judaism involved real danger. Despite this, nothing deterred him.

He was utterly devoted to the work of my father-in-law, the Rebbe, in spreading Judaism."[10]

Later Rabbi Zevin recalled his first impressions of the young Menachem Mendel, from *Tisha B'Av* 1924:

> I sat in the late Rebbe's room from the time when morning *kinot* (dirges) were completed, until the afternoon prayer (it was one of the long summer days), and we discussed the state of Jewish observance throughout the Soviet Union—in detail—and the activities in this area. After the fast, I dined at the late Rebbe's table, and the Rebbe *shlita* [Menachem Mendel] was one of those present. The next morning, before I went on my way, the late Rebbe said to me that the son of the Rav of Yekatrinoslav (i.e. the present Rebbe), has been suggested as a groom for his daughter, and since it appears that I will be travelling with him for an extended period today—he was also returning home by train—the Rebbe asked me if I would note my impressions of him.
>
> When I reached home, I wrote to the late Rebbe that I was not especially surprised by his [Menachem Mendel's] greatness in Torah, or by the fact that he was astoundingly knowledgeable in every area of Torah which I discussed with him—because the reputation of this future son-in-law as a great Torah scholar had previously reached my ears. What amazed me was his piety. One example was how he constantly refrained from joining me in a meal, with food that had been given to both of us from the late Rebbe's house as sustenance for our long journey. Obviously, there was no question whether the food was kosher, but I gathered that the young man had issues whether the vessel for ritual washing of the hands was *halachically* ideal for this purpose. There was certainly nothing that would disqualify it according to the letter of the law—only a stringency—but in an exceptionally discreet manner, the present Rebbe refrained from ritually washing his hands for a meal."[11]

II.

Shortly after returning from Leningrad, the young Menachem Mendel became *Rabbi* Menachem Mendel Schneerson, after receiving Rabbinic ordination (*semicha*) from his paternal uncle, Rabbi Shmuel Schneerson, the government-sanctioned Rav of Nikolayev. It is unclear why Menachem Mendel sought *semicha* at this point—perhaps it was in accordance with a tradition in the Lubavitcher Rebbe's household that a young man should receive ordination before marriage.[12] Whatever the case, the *semicha* document has survived, dated 19th August 1924, stating: "Menachem Mendel, son of Levi Yitzchak Schneerson is full and overflowing with Talmud and the earlier and later *poskim* (*halachic* works), and the works of the early and later jurists, like one of the great sages. He knows how to reach *halachic* conclusions correctly, and he offers rulings with trepidation." In the remainder of the document, Rabbi Shmuel authorizes his nephew to rule in a number of *halachic* areas: *Yoreh Yoreh* (ritual laws), *Yodin Yodin* (monetary law) and also to arrange divorces.[13]

Who was this man who formally brought the future Seventh Lubavitcher Rebbe into the Rabbinate? Rabbi Shmuel Schneerson was the younger brother of the Rebbe's father, Reb Levik, and a decade his junior. In 1901, Rabbi Shmuel married into the same family as his older brother, wedding Rebbetzin Chana's younger sister, Miriam Gittel. In 1906 Miriam Gittel gave birth to her only son, who was also given the name Menachem Mendel. In 1907, Shmuel was appointed the official, government-sanctioned rabbi of Nikolayev, where he assisted his father-in-law, Rabbi Meir Shlomo Yanovsky (who was, in reality, the leading Rabbi of the town).

In a similar fashion to his brother and nephew, Rabbi Shmuel was fond of drawing parallels between *nigleh* (Talmudic law) and *nistar* (Kabbalah and Chasidut). He once proposed to an audience of Yeshivah students that they should mention any one of the 4191 laws found in the *Mishnah* and he would explain it according to *nigleh* and *nistar*. One of the students picked a text in tractate *Yevamot*—one of the more complex and obscure areas of Jewish Law—but Shmuel adeptly lived up to his promise.

After spending the remaining weeks of the summer at home, Menachem Mendel returned to spend the festive month of *Tishrei* with Rayatz in Leningrad. Things were still highly unsettled at the Rebbe's court. With some assistance from "our friends in America" over the summer, Rayatz had at least begun to repay some of the crippling debts.[14] The financial situation, however, was still dire. Three hundred guests arrived from various *Yeshivot* to celebrate the festivals, but the large hall in the Rebbe's residence that served as their synagogue was not even equipped with benches to sit on. Around eighty percent of the guests did not have enough money to pay for their trip back home, and efforts had to be made to raise funds from the local Chabad community.[15] While the premises at 22 Mokhovaya were substantial, this city residence was obviously more restricted in space than Rayatz had been accustomed. The largest room was only as big as the "small synagogue" back in Lubavitch, and even with twelve additional "substantial" rooms, space was tight.[16]

The moment was an extremely challenging one for Rayatz: the upheaval of relocation, close surveillance by the G.P.O and financial woes inevitably taking their toll. This was also the first Rosh Hashanah that Rayatz experienced away from Rostov, where he still had memories of spending the festivals with his father. It was in this moment of isolation and trepidation about the future that Rayatz recalls: "During the prayers of the first night of Rosh Hashanah I saw a vision of my father the Rebbe [Rashab], just as he looked when he was in Lubavitch. He was dressed in his Sabbath attire and his holy face was aglow." In the vision, Rashab shared with his son a number of inspirational Torah insights, and showered him with blessings for "revealed goodness" and the "transformation of judgment to light and revelation."[17]

Did Rayatz share details of this soul visitation with his future son-in-law? Later, when Menachem Mendel would begin keeping a diary of observations at the court, we know that Rayatz would share with him many such experiences, so it is distinctly possible that he related it on this occasion, too. If he did, it would certainly have opened the young Menachem Mendel's eyes to the strikingly mystical character of the Sixth Rebbe.

During the festive month of *Tishrei*, Menachem Mendel resided with his brother Leibel (who had begun studies at the University of Leningrad around this time), in rented accommodation not far from the Rebbe's court. On one occasion, Leibel spotted Nachum Goldshmidt, the Schneerson brothers' childhood classmate, who was spending some time at Rayatz's court, and suggested, "Come, let's *farbreng* a little." After taking a few shots of vodka, Nachum and Leibel decided to have a bit of fun. They found a *mitnaged* (one opposed to Chasidut) in the street and asked him to join their "Torah discussion." Leibel invited the *mitnaged* to share some of his own original Torah thoughts, which the *mitnaged* did gladly. After allowing him to finish, Leibel took the *mitnaged's* arguments one by one, and proceeded to systematically refute them. Menachem Mendel, who shared the quarters with Leibel, was standing in a corner the entire time, adorned in *talit* and *tefilin.* At some point, as Leibel was joyously attacking the *mitnaged,* Menachem Mendel turned to him and motioned with his hands, expressing his dissatisfaction.[18] Apparently, this type of scene had repeated itself many times in the past, with Leibel's mischievous tendencies contrasting sharply with his older brother's more serious demeanor.

While Leibel was already parting in many ways from Chabad, he still remained a regular presence at the court of Rayatz during his years in Leningrad, up until the Rebbe's departure in 1927. In a brief biographical sketch edited by the Seventh Rebbe himself (in 1990), Leibel is described as having been "extremely adored by the Rebbe Rayatz, who gave him close personal attention. He was also adored by the Chasidim who surrounded him and argued with him about different issues in Jewish law and Chasidut. Many questions were posed to him in both *nigleh* and Chasidut."[19] Leibel would often enter into private audience (*yechidut*) with Rayatz to discuss Chasidic philosophy. In one episode that has reached us, Rayatz refused to answer one of Leibel's questions, claiming he was not a fitting recipient for the answer. Disturbed by this response, Leibel left the *yechidut* and broke into tears. In their following meeting, Rayatz himself raised the issue again and, surprisingly, offered the solution which he had previously held back from Leibel. What, then, was the point of the initial rejection? Leibel offered the Chasidim his own interpretation: To be a fitting vessel for the answer, he had to first break his ego with bitterness and tears.[20]

III.

It is not clear when Menachem Mendel left Leningrad, but we know he was home during the winter[21] as an important letter has survived from this period that was penned in Dnipropetrovsk on 11th of January 1925.[22] The letter—the earliest such document from the Seventh Rebbe to have reached us—was written to an individual who was probably Menachem Mendel's third greatest influence, after his father and Rayatz: the *gaon* ("genius") of Rogatchov, Rabbi Yosef Rosen (1858-1936).[23]

The "Rogatchover," as he was known after the Latvian town of his birth, stood out as a genius even in a generation of Torah giants. Today it is rare to find an individual who has an encyclopedic knowledge of the entire Talmud, but in pre-war Europe many of the major Rabbis had reached that kind of mastery. What made the Rogatchover unique was not just his vast memory of texts or instant recall, but the development of highly original conceptual models to explain the "under the hood" functioning of Jewish Law.

There are over six thousand pages in the Talmud, discussing every imaginable area of life: agricultural law, the rituals of Jewish festivals, the intricacies of marriage, divorce, damages, court procedure, ritual services in the holy Temple, *etc.* Each area of law functions in its own orbit with its own specialized terms and principles. Commentaries on the Talmud will often draw legal parallels and precedents from one area of the law to another, but what we find almost uniquely in the writings of the Rogatchover is the suggestion of sweeping conceptual models[24] behind a vast array of diverse Talmudic laws.[25]

In his published talks, the Rebbe cites works of the Rogatchover many hundreds of times, and they stand out as his most significant influence from any post-medieval scholar. "The world marvels at his phenomenal memory," the Rebbe commented in a 1975 talk, "which was unprecedented in several hundred years before him—but that does not really bring his true greatness to light. His unique brilliance was the ability to take any detail that he learned and find connections with the entire Torah by developing over-arching principles."[26]

The Rogatchover was not the only Twentieth Century scholar to work with a conceptual system. Other notable figures include Rabbi Chaim Soloveitchik of Brisk (1853-1918), and Rabbi Yosef Engel (1859-1920). Rabbi Soloveitchik's system, in particular, has enjoyed exceptional popularity, and is the dominant school taught in advanced Yeshivot around the world today. But in the Rebbe's eyes, the Rogatchover's works were more fascinating. The Brisker method, he once noted, delves into tremendous localized depth in one particular *sugya* (discussion), but the Rogatchover could see the entire universe of Torah in the tiniest detail, deciphering multiple, seemingly unrelated texts with the most abstract and daring conceptual models.[27] "From the mind of the Rogatchover," said Hebrew poet Hayim Nahman Bialik after a meeting with the *gaon*, "you could carve out two Einsteins."[28]

Menachem Mendel began to correspond with the Rogatchover at the age of seventeen,[29] and later, he visited the *gaon* regularly, building a personal relationship.[30] Bearing in mind that the Rogatchover responded to virtually every letter he received—penning an estimated forty-thousand responses in his lifetime—it is not remarkable that the young Menachem Mendel managed to engage him. What is outstanding in the 1925 letter is how, at the age of twenty-two, the future Rebbe already mirrored the Rogatchover's intensity, stringing together numerous, very diverse cross references along a specific theme. Over some three pages, Menachem Mendel offers some forty references to Talmudic and rabbinic texts respectfully attempting to refute a legal position of the Rogatchover (that if a sick animal were to be operated upon it would shed its disqualification as *treife* (non-kosher), and become kosher again). In the letter we also see evidence of Menachem Mendel's individuality and confidence at a relatively tender age: He begins by writing to the *gaon*, some forty years his senior, "Even though who am I to argue with you? But 'Torah it is, and learn it I must.'"[31]

In the spring of 1925, Menachem Mendel was back in Leningrad and probably spent the festival of Purim in the Rebbe's court. By this time, Rayatz had become a little more settled in his new location and had found the peace of mind to deliver a Chasidic discourse virtually every Sabbath, subsequently writing them down for posterity.[32] The Purim festive meal in 22 Mokhovaya was a major event, with tables filling the largest three rooms on the premises. The *farbrengen* accompanying such meals would typically continue for some eight hours, sometimes stretching through the entire night.[33]

We know with certainty, at least, that Menachem Mendel was present a week later, as he was spotted by Rabbi Yisrael Jacobson (1896-1975), a fourth generation *shochet* (ritual slaughterer of kosher meat) from Zuravitz, who was visiting Rayatz with a view to discuss emigration to the United States.[34] This meeting would later carry huge historical significance as, fifteen years later, Rabbi Jacobson spearheaded the campaign to rescue the Sixth Rebbe and his son-in-law from war-torn Europe, saving their lives and the future of the Chabad movement.

Rabbi Jacobson had been present in Leningrad during Rosh Hashanah and was disturbed to see the pitiful state of affairs, how Rayatz could not even afford benches for the synagogue. After the festival, Jacobson met with some other Chasidim, and they decided that it was time to leave the country and establish Chabad communities elsewhere. Rabbi Yisrael was the only Chasid who was "elected" to relocate to America, presumably because he had relatives in the United States.[35]

Despite his reluctance to ask, due to the Rebbe's vehement opposition to Chasidim leaving Russia, Jacobson did eventually see Rayatz after Purim 1925 to discuss leaving for America—and, remarkably, the Rebbe agreed! This was one of the very few exceptions to the anti-emigration policy that Rayatz had adopted during that period.[36] Apparently, he was convinced that Rabbi Yisroel, an extremely committed Chasid, would stay loyal to his faith even in the *treife medinah* (the "unkosher country"). Or was it, perhaps, a higher form of inspiration, guiding the Rebbe to his future salvation?

IV.

Little is known about Menachem Mendel's footsteps during the fall of 1925.[37] By Passover he had left Petersburg,[38] and was presumably at home with his parents. In early October, he was officially appointed as Rabbi of the Old Pobritzna Synagogue in his home town of Yekatrinoslav,[39] but no recollections have survived if he actually served there. (Sometimes documents such as these were acquired for legal purposes.)[40]

In late October, a certain non-Jewish scholar, Alexander Vasilyevich Barchenko (1881-1938), arrived at Rayatz's court from Moscow, requesting a meeting with the Rebbe. When the two men finally sat down a few days later—the guest had initially arrived on *Shemini Atzeret*, when the Rebbe was detained with festival duties—Barchenko told Rayatz his story. According to the recollection of Rabbi Althaus:[41]

> We later learned that he [Barchenko] deals with the wisdom of the unknown, founded on mathematics, aiming to reveal mysteries and predict the future. It also has some connection to Kabbalah... He had already organized a group in Moscow which is researching this field, for which they have received government authorization. Many outstanding scholars had joined the research group.[42]

The "professor," was, in fact, an erstwhile medical school dropout and popular mystery writer who later became a self-proclaimed scientist, carrying out research on the human brain, telepathy, shamanism and collective hysteria. He did not possess a degree but was often referred to as "Doctor" at public addresses.[43]

After witnessing the carnage of World War I, the revolutions and civil war, Barchenko became obsessed with the idea of using lost occult wisdom to heal humanity from the failings of communism. By 1925 he had sparked the interest of Gleb Bokii, Chief Cryptographer of the Soviet Union, and on the top floor of the cryptography office a secret laboratory was opened, directed by Barchenko, to research parapsychology and occult phenomena for the Soviets.

Barchenko, on a mission to acquire esoteric knowledge, sought out—among others—the renowned Rabbi Yosef Yitzchak Schneersohn, who was reputed to be an expert in the wisdom of Kabbalah.[44]

Since Rayatz was under close surveillance from the GPU, and Barchenko was clearly a very eccentric man, the Rebbe's initial reaction to the "professor" was one of suspicion—as the Althaus memoir recalls:

> The Rebbe was unsure and suspicious of this professor's real intent. He treated the professor with courtesy and suspicion at the same time. During the first few minutes... the Rebbe wondered about the professor's sanity. Barchenko, however, sensed this, and pulled out a certificate signed by several of the most respected professors in Moscow, testifying that he had a lucid mind and that he was not insane in the slightest. Barchenko was also concerned that the Rebbe would think he was a spy, so he showed many certificates from the government agency, where he held a respected position.

Rayatz told Barchenko that he considered himself a lover of any science which could bring psychological/spiritual benefits, but he could not be of assistance into matters of predicting the future, an activity prohibited by Jewish Law. Rayatz offered to assign "the learned Mr. M. Schneerson, who has been elected as the secretary of our scientific team," to carry out any research desired by the professor and translate texts for him into Russian.[45]

Menachem Mendel was immediately summoned to Leningrad by Rayatz, and over the next three months wrote a treatise on the meaning of the *Magen David* (Star of David) according to the Talmud, Kabbalah, and Astronomy.[46] During this time Rayatz personally introduced Menachem Mendel to Barchenko, and the young Chasidic scholar subsequently corresponded with the professor for close to a year. (On one occasion at least, Menachem Mendel visited Barchenko's home). During the months of his research, Menachem Mendel shuttled back and forth to his home in Yekatrinoslav. "I remember the large textbook of mathematical formulae on his desk," his mother recalled.

Several months later, the relationship with Barchenko fizzled out and in an apparently final communication, Rayatz penned an interesting memo of what he felt were universal "foundational ideas" of Chasidic wisdom for non-Jews.[47]

Barchenko's research laboratory was relatively short-lived. From 1929 onwards, Stalin's regime began to seriously curtail such "liberal" communists, and eventually, in 1938, he had Bokii and Barchenko executed.[48] While nothing ultimately came from the meetings between Menachem Mendel and Barchenko, the future Rebbe had learned many things. He had learned that Rayatz valued him as a tremendous asset to the Chabad movement, as an in-house Torah scholar. He had learned that Rayatz valued his secular knowledge and perceived how it would be of value to Chabad. And, perhaps most significantly, he had learned that Chasidic Judaism, despite its particular emphasis on the centrality of the Jewish People, had a spiritual message for all humanity. Over sixty years later, in 1988, at a time when the Seventh Rebbe spearheaded a controversial campaign to reach out to non-Jews, he would publicly recall the assignment to Barchenko, citing it as a precedent.[49]

> "My father-in-law, the Rebbe, initiated an unprecedented expansion of the project to 'disseminate the wellsprings [of Chasidic wisdom] outwards'... particularly through translation and citation of Chasidic ideas, even the deepest ones, into the languages of the nations of the world... Through this the nations of the world are able to understand Chasidic wisdom... While still in 'that country' [Russia], my father-in-law the Rebbe once instructed me to explain ideas in Chasidic thought to a non-Jewish professor who had inquired about and was researching extremely deep matters."[50]

V.

Some time during February and March of 1926, Rebbetzin Chana Schneerson made an extended trip to Leningrad to discuss the most significant event in Menachem Mendel's life: his wedding with Rayatz's second daughter, Moussia.[51]

Chana stayed with Rabbi Eliyahu Chaim Althaus, the principal *shadchan* (matchmaker) for this union, who resided in a suburb of Leningrad, an hour's tram ride from Rayatz's residence. "It seemed to us," Althaus' daughter Bat-Sheva later recalled, "that in the beginning there were certain problems regarding the *shidduch*... My father was heavily involved."[52]

We have no record of these negotiations, which took place behind closed doors, but Reb Levik and Chana were certainly in a position to make some considerable demands. Their son not only possessed a Schneerson pedigree, he was an outstanding Torah scholar and observed even the minutiae of Jewish law with exceptional devotion. Rayatz would later praise him to Chasidim as someone who "engages in *tikun chatzot* (midnight prayers) every night. He has mastered the Babylonian Talmud with commentaries of *Ran* (Rabbi Nissim Gerondi, 1320-76), *Rosh* (Rabbenu Asher, 1259–1327) and *Rif* (Rabbi Yitzchak Alfasi, 1013-1103); the Jerusalem Talmud with its main commentaries, the works of Maimonides, and *Likutei Torah* (discourses of Rabbi Shneur Zalman of Liadi), with all the cross references."[53] In writing, Rayatz would later refer to his son-in-law with the appellation, *gaon* ("genius")[54]—even *ha-gaon ha-amiti* ("the true genius")[55]—a term which he did not use liberally.

We know that Rayatz supported Menachem Mendel and Moussia financially for several years after their marriage,[56] and it is possible that this was a major point in the *shidduch* negotiations. Reb Levik had been supported by his father-in-law for ten years after his own marriage, an extended period which had enabled him to fully develop into a world-class scholar. He would have naturally sought such an opportunity for his own son.

There has been some speculation that Menachem Mendel's parents might have demanded as part of the *shidduch* "deal" that their son would be promised as successor to Rayatz[57]—but if such a promise was made, it was not written down, nor do we have any record of such a statement emanating from Rayatz, even orally. In fact, in 1950, when Menachem Mendel would resist being appointed as Rebbe for an entire year, he would repeatedly say that "we did not hear anything from my father-in-law" about succession.[58]

The long delays in bringing the *shidduch* to fruition represent something highly unusual in Chasidic circles, where short engagements are encouraged. The Seventh Rebbe himself would later make a point of discouraging long engagements among his followers, and insisting that engaged couples maintain only nominal contact before their wedding.[59] In this case, many of the delays can be attributed to geographical displacement, arrests (threatened and actual), and dire financial conditions. As we have seen, shortly after Menachem Mendel's first substantial meeting with Rayatz in the summer of 1923, the Sixth Rebbe was nearly arrested the following spring, and was forced to relocate from Rostov to Leningrad that summer. By the end 1924, he was still drowning in debts, and only began to get back on his feet a year later. So Rebbetzin Chana's spring 1926 visit to negotiate the *shidduch* possibly represented the first viable opportunity to do so. As we shall soon see, Menachem Mendel was forced to go into hiding for the remainder of 1926, and in 1927 Rayatz was arrested, imprisoned, and forced to leave Russia. After relocation to Riga, besides continuing financial difficulties for Rayatz and failing health,[60] the question arose as to whether Menachem Mendel's parents would be able to leave Russia to participate in the wedding. This delayed matters for several months,[61] until the great event finally took place in November 1928.

Although the precise dates remain unclear, some time after the *shidduch* was negotiated, Menachem Mendel's personal safety became in jeopardy. (He had definitely come "under the radar" of the GPO through his dealings with Barchenko, who was, in reality, a secret police employee. There is also no doubt that Rayatz's court was under close surveillance). For seven months, Menachem Mendel relocated to the small town of Luga, some ninety miles south of Leningrad, residing with the local Rabbi, Chanoch Henich Hetkin. Rabbi Hetkin was of little interest to the Soviets, since he was known to be a man of very humble means.

Menachem Mendel spent most of the time in solitude, as his host was occupied during the day with bookbinding, from which he earned a living; but the two men found time to study Talmud together. The Rebbe-to-be even introduced his non-Chasidic host, who had been educated in the Mussar school of Novardok, to the study of *Tanya*, the "Bible" of Chabad Chasidic thought.[62]

During this time Menachem Mendel continued working for Rayatz and the Sixth Rebbe even joined him in Luga for a few weeks during the summer to get some rest.[63] But the two men were hardly relaxing: "It seems that this vacation is all about sitting and writing letters," Rayatz wrote from Luga to his eldest daughter Chana and her husband Rashag. "We sit here until three in the morning writing letters."[64] To Moussia, Rayatz wrote veiled references to Menachem Mendel's safety and wellbeing, "We are all well, thank G-d."[65] "We are all well and send you hearty greetings."[66]

By the winter, Menachem Mendel was back in Leningrad, but his stay there was to be short-lived. The year 1927 was to be momentous for the Schneersohn family: Rayatz was to closely escape death, and the court of Lubavitch was to be evicted from its homeland in Russia, never to return again.

CHAPTER FOUR

LEAVING HOME

1927

Menachem Mendel's
Soviet Passport photo, 1927

At the beginning of 1927, Menachem Mendel relocated to Leningrad,[1] taking up residence in the home of the Nimoytin family.[2] As usual, he kept a low profile, even among his fellow Chasidim, and there are few records of his activities. His room mate, Raphael Nimoytin, later recalled:

> It was very difficult to talk to the [future] Rebbe while we were in the room together. He was always a very introverted person, very reserved, and he spoke little. His grace and his seriousness are impossible to describe. He was always busy. He never wasted even a second. Most of the time he was studying or writing. He would almost always come to the room last, and leave first.[3]

The 1927 Purim *farbrengen* in Leningrad a few months later, was to remain with Menachem Mendel for the rest of his life.[4] It was an experience at the Rebbe's court which was described as "totally without precedent. What we saw and heard during the Purim feast was unlike anything we had ever seen or heard in our entire lives; nothing comparable to this had been witnessed by our fathers or our fathers' fathers."[5]

In his detailed memoir of the event, Rabbi Eliyahu Chaim Althaus recalled:

> The Rebbe spoke openly, sharply, and intensely. He wept, his face flushed with emotion, and in his voice was an anger we had never heard before... In the midst of the Purim feast, the Rebbe suddenly stood up.... calling out, 'Elye Chaim, Elye Chaim! I told you to write harshly last year, but you didn't listen, and this is why there has been so much suffering all year. After the Sabbath you will write a letter to all the cities and villages with these words: "We possessed a Rebbe, and he left us his son to guide us, and the son has instructed us to write in his name that anyone handing his child over to the school of the *Yevsektzia* will be severely punished by Heaven, G-d forbid." Will you write this? Remember well what I say to you!' He repeated these words again and again, pounding on his chest....
>
> The Chasidim were greatly alarmed by the Rebbe's open defiance of the *Yevsektzia*. One of the senior Chasidim cried out, "Rebbe, we cannot stand to hear such words. We need a Rebbe of flesh and blood!"....
>
> We were acutely aware of the spies in our midst, as they had been at every Chasidic gathering since our arrival in Leningrad... We begged the Rebbe to stop, but he faced them directly and cried out: "May their names be blotted out (*yemach shemam*)! I know that they are here; I am not afraid of them." We gazed at the agents, and their faces, flushed with anger, deepened our concern for the Rebbe's welfare.[6]

Rayatz's mother, Rebbetzin Shterna Sara, was called to intervene, to prevent the Rebbe from publicly incriminating himself any further. As Rayatz begged her respectfully to go back to her room, he started to cry. Seeing this, she began to sob; the scene prompted the crowd to erupt in tears. Regaining his composure, Rayatz tried to console his mother. "I do nothing on my own," he said. "I consulted with Father," (referring to Rashab, who had departed seven years earlier). It was not long, though, before the Rebbe fainted and was carried out for fresh air.[7]

We have no record of Menachem Mendel's reaction to the Purim *farbrengen*, but there is another episode from the same period[8] which the Seventh Rebbe related at a 1970 public gathering,[9] regarding Rayatz's exceptional self-composure under trying conditions.

Rayatz was about to travel to Moscow for a meeting with one of his supporters who had arrived from abroad. At this time he was under close scrutiny from the authorities, and a trip out of town to the country's capital was extremely risky. Rayatz's undercover activities were already known to the authorities and a meeting of this nature was virtually playing evidence into their hands.

Shortly before Rayatz was scheduled to leave his apartment for Leningrad station, Menachem Mendel entered the Sixth Rebbe's chamber, finding him alone. To the young Rabbi's great surprise, Rayatz did not seem the least bit agitated about the task ahead. "I saw my father-in-law sitting totally at peace, as if it were an ordinary afternoon," he recalled.

Menachem Mendel, who was far from prone to emotional outbursts, was stunned. Here was a man about to carry out a mission that would put his own life, and the future of the Jewish community, at tremendous risk, and his outward composure projected a calm and collected demeanor! Menachem Mendel had studied the Chasidic doctrine of *moach shalit al ha-lev,*[10] that the mind has the power to calm the emotions, but in such circumstances he expected there to be at least some sign of nerves.

"To such an extreme?" Menachem Mendel asked, unable to hold himself back. He wanted to know: How had Rayatz achieved such a degree of self-mastery?

Rayatz explained that he had learned from his grandfather, Rabbi Shmuel of Lubavitch (Maharash), an art called "success in time." Essentially, this is the ability to be fully immersed in the here and now, focusing sharply on the task at hand to the exclusion of other concerns. Rayatz cited the example of the famous Talmudist Rashba (Rabbi Shlomo ben Aderet, 1235-1310), who gave three Torah classes a day and answered complex questions in Jewish law—yet he still managed to take a leisurely stroll every day. The secret of Rashba's "success in time" was a learned ability to hyper-focus on whatever he was doing at the time, even if the current activity was relaxation. Rayatz had apparently mastered this art, and a short while before his dangerous trip, he seemed totally at peace, submerged in the present and oblivious to the anticipated jeopardy of the near future—something which made a deep impression on the young Rebbe-to-be.

II.

Surprisingly, Rayatz was not arrested during the spring and continued to work for another three months after publicly defying the *Yevsektzia* on Purim, before he was finally detained. (Presumably, the Soviets were still searching for hard evidence about his activities).

The arrest occurred on a Tuesday night after midnight 15th June (15th *Sivan*).[11] Rayatz had just spent nearly five hours receiving guests in *yechidut* (private audience), and, quite exhausted, he sat down to eat his evening meal. Twenty minutes later there was a loud banging on the door. Two GPU officers burst into the room, accompanied by armed guards, shouting, "Who is Schneersohn?"

Rayatz replied calmly, "I don't know which Schneersohn you are looking for. If you come into someone's home surely you know in advance who lives there? This drama is pointless." After a few further exchanges, with Rayatz deflecting the officers' abuse and retaining his cool, the Soviets began a full search of the apartment.

Rayatz always feared that his premises might be searched at any time and was careful not to keep at home any documentation concerning his schools or Yeshivot. All this was kept at the home of his secretary, Rabbi Chaim Lieberman (1892-1991).[12] It was crucial that Lieberman be informed of the arrest before the Soviets would reach him, so that he could dispose of any incriminating files.

Moussia was not at home when the GPU arrived, and she was consequently able to act as an important messenger. As she later recalled, "My [future] husband was escorting me home. When we came close, we noticed the house was lit up. I went inside while my [future] husband stayed standing outside. After a few minutes I went to the window and told him discreetly, 'We have guests.'"[13]

Menachem Mendel dashed to the home of Eliyahu Chaim Althaus and banged at his door. At well beyond midnight, Althaus was in bed, but not yet asleep. The knock alarmed him and he ran to the door, calling out, "Who is it?"

"Mendel Schneerson," came the reply.

Even before he opened the door, Althaus feared something terrible. Hearing what had transpired, he told Mendel to run with his own son to Chaim Lieberman's house and instruct the secretary to destroy all evidence of the Chabad schools and Yeshivot in Russia and all financial records.[14]

Arriving at Lieberman's address, Menachem Mendel found the front courtyard's entrance gate locked. Even though it would inevitably arouse suspicion, he had no alternative other than to ask the guard to unlock the gate. (The guard would later inform the GPU of what had happened.) He located the window to Lieberman's bedroom and quickly told him what to do. Lieberman promptly lit a fire and started to burn piles of documents.

Lieberman was alerted just in time, and nothing of importance was left when the GPU arrived at his house a short while later—all they saw was the remains of the fire.[15] Lieberman's Soviet interrogation files state that no incriminatory documents were found. The only material of interest which the search revealed was some correspondence with Barchenko(!)[16]

Both Rayatz and Lieberman were arrested that night and taken separately to Spalerno prison. Apparently, Moussia managed to inform her father, before he was taken away, of Menachem Mendel's mission to Chaim Lieberman's house, as the Sixth Rebbe later worried in prison, "I thought about my future son-in-law, Rabbi Menachem, who had gone to the home of my secretary, Mr. Lieberman. I hoped to G-d that he was not also ensnared in this net of intrigue."[17] Rayatz was also deeply concerned about the precious Chabad Chasidic manuscripts, penned by his father and the previous Rebbes. Even if he would not survive the ordeal, it was crucial that the movement continue, and for this the manuscripts were indispensable. "My eyes flowed with hot tears. I was deeply agitated and my entire body trembled: G-d forbid, was it possible that the sacred Chasidic manuscripts and writings were also taken?" Rayatz wondered to himself. "And if, G-d forbid, this had actually occurred, how calamitous was this situation! How incredible the catastrophe that these sacred manuscripts would also be swept into custody and imprisoned!"[18]

Unbeknown to Rayatz, Menachem Mendel was busy ensuring the safety of the manuscripts. Dividing them into separate bundles so as to ensure they would not all be captured at once, Menachem Mendel sought out various local Chasidim who could be trusted to hide a package of manuscripts, until the Rebbe was brought back to safety, (at which point they were returned).[19]

That night, Rayatz's life was in grave danger. On 7th June, Pyotr Voykov, the Soviet representative in Warsaw, had been assassinated by Boris Koverda, the eighteen year-old son of a White Russian monarchist. When Koverda was subsequently sentenced to just fifteen years imprisonment by the Poles, there was an outrage in Moscow. Voykov had been a hero of the Russian revolution, and was honored with burial in Red Square; a mere fifteen-year sentence was seen as an insult. As a backlash, special clearance had been given from Moscow that night to execute political prisoners. In a 1970 sermon, the Seventh Rebbe noted that Rayatz would have been one of those victims had he not taken a wrong turn inside the prison, resulting in his case being processed several hours later after the special clearance had been withdrawn.[20]

Steering committees in Leningrad and Moscow were established, which, despite his young age, included Menachem Mendel. The committees had initially decided that, so as not to provoke the GPU, political pressure would be applied discreetly and no help would be sought from abroad. But when news arrived on the Sabbath of a death sentence looming over the Rebbe, there seemed nothing to lose in garnering as much attention as possible to the case. Telegrams were dispatched to President Kalinin and Prime Minister Rykov. Large Jewish communities across Russia were enlisted for support. Human rights activist Yekaterina Peshkova, Chairwoman of the *Committee for Assistance to Political Prisoners*, took on the case. News of Rayatz's imprisonment reached Germany where Chief Orthodox Rabbi Israel Hildersheimer, and Reform Rabbi Leo Baeck, lobbied the government. Political pressure was also applied from England, France, Scandinavia and from Rabbi Abraham Isaac Kook, Chief Rabbi of Mandatory Palestine. In the U.S.A., synagogues from across the country pressured the *Joint Distribution Committee* to intervene. Supreme Court Justice Louis Brandeis approached several government officials to join the campaign, including Senators Robert Wagner of New York and William Borah of Idaho, Chairman of the *Senate Foreign Relations Committee*, who was held in high esteem by Kremlin officials. (Borah later explained his motive: "I like to do things that get me votes in the next election in Idaho, but every so often I do something that assures me of votes in that 'final election' which we will all have to stand for someday."[21]) A petition even came from President Calvin Coolidge.[22]

The death sentence was abated—Rayatz himself later saw his file with the command for execution crossed out[23]—but the Rebbe was subject to a further interrogation on 21st June. Despite tremendous pressure and intimidation, Rayatz revealed no information that could lead to his sentencing. The Rebbe was nevertheless found guilty, based on "prior evidence" of infractions no. 14 and 58 ("Acts of Sabotage against the Revolution") and no. 122 ("Teaching Religion to Minors"),[24] and sentenced to ten years of labor in Siberia, in the Solovaki Islands.[25]

Ultimately, on the afternoon of 3rd July (3rd *Tammuz*), Rayatz was informed that his sentence had been reduced to three years exile in the more civil location of Kostroma, a small city on the Volga river, five hundred miles to the east of Leningrad. He would be permitted to return home for six hours, and was required to be on the train out of Leningrad at 8 p.m., otherwise he would be arrested again.

From the step of the departing train that evening, where a large crowd of Chasidim gathered to see off their Rebbe, Rayatz gave a moving speech—words which the Seventh Rebbe would quote countless times, scrutinizing their every nuance:

> We did not depart from the Land of Israel of our own free will, nor shall we return to the Land of Israel through our own capabilities... The nations of the world must know the following: Only our bodies were sent into exile and subjugated to alien rule; our souls were not given over to captivity![26]

The Rebbe was accompanied on the train to Kostroma by his daughter Moussia, his son-in-law, Rashag, and Rabbi Althaus. Moussia remained with her father at their destination, while Rashag traveled to Moscow to begin diplomatic attempts for the Rebbe's full release.

Remarkably, just eight days after his arrival in Kostroma, on 12th July (12th *Tammuz*)—his forty-seventh birthday—Rayatz was informed that he was "totally freed from the need of any further appearances. The order has been received to grant you full freedom."[27]

Overwhelmed, Moussia started to sing to her father the Chasidic melody *Nyet Nyet Nikavo* ("There is nothing besides G-d").[28] She telephoned the Schneersohn home in Leningrad and her sister picked up the phone. "We are coming home for *Shabbat*," she said elatedly.[29]

In a 1961 letter, the Seventh Rebbe recalled the events of Rayatz's arrest and liberation. "I myself was there at the time in 'that country.' And, understandably, all the details of the entire episode are engraved well in my mind, as if they were current events. What one man can achieve, and what formidable obstacles he can overcome, if he makes a firm resolution and devotes himself to it fearlessly—that is the lesson we can all learn."[30]

III.

The following Sabbath, Rayatz celebrated his return home, reciting the blessing *ha-gomel*, a Jewish ritual performed after escape from life-threatening conditions. But his freedom was limited: the *Yevsektzia* newspaper, *Der Emes*, launched a campaign for Rayatz to be re-imprisoned and sent to Siberia. Evidently his life was still at great risk, and there was no possibility of continuing his underground work away from the eyes of the authorities. Chabad's political activists began to seek exit visas for Rayatz and his family to emigrate.

It was Rabbi Mordechai Dubin, a Chabad Chasid and representative of the Latvian parliament, who prevailed on the Soviet Foreign Office to allow Rayatz to leave. Initially, it was only the Rebbe who was granted permission to emigrate; he was told that he must leave his family and library behind. Rayatz refused. Dubin continued diplomatic pressure, using the trade pact between Russia and Latvia as leverage, and eventually, on 28th September, a special meeting was convened in the Foreign Office to discuss Rayatz's release, and full permission was granted.[31]

Rayatz's request for an exit visa for Menachem Mendel had initially been questioned. The young man was, after all, not yet married to Moussia. "Can't you find another son-in-law in Latvia?" the authorities asked.

"I won't find another son-in-law like this!" was Rayatz's adamant response.[32]

Menachem Mendel's Soviet passport was issued on 1st October, a few days after Rosh Hashanah.[33] Realizing that this was a final opportunity to spend time with his parents, he returned home for the Festival of Sukkot.

On *Simchat Torah*, the happiest day on the Jewish calendar, Menachem Mendel's mother, recalled, "It was as if his intention was to wipe from everyone's heart that this might be his final *Simchat Torah* dance at home, under the same roof as his family. He was exceptionally joyful... Nobody besides my husband and I knew that our son was about to embark on his way to a distant place... Every time I saw my son's face I saw how painful it was for him that he was leaving us. His face, though, was also telling me, 'Mother, don't worry!'"[34]

On Thursday October 20th, the day after *Simchat Torah*, Rayatz left Russia with his family, his possessions and his library[35]—filling four full railway carriages[36]—without waiting for Menachem Mendel's return. The family arrived safely in Riga the next day, in time for the Sabbath.[37]

Meanwhile Menachem Mendel was on his way to Leningrad with his mother. During the journey—the last period of time he would spend with her for the next twenty years—something happened that remained engraved in her memory still at the end of her life.

> When it was time for the morning prayer, my son stood up, took out his *tefilin*, and prepared to pray. The coach in which we were riding was full of low-class gentile workers and farmers; that year had witnessed the peak of violent anti-Semitic propaganda campaigns in Russia.

Chana was terrified that her son had rendered himself an obvious target for attack. And then,

> to my astonishment, something incredible took place. Several passengers rose and positioned themselves around my son, forming a human wall, screening him from hostile eyes. They remained there until he had donned two pairs of *tefilin* and completed his prayers calmly. To this day the episode has never ceased to amaze me."[38]

While the road ahead looked dangerous for the young Rabbi, at least Chana had some sign that Providence was taking good care of her son.

Menachem Mendel and his mother spent the Sabbath *en route* in Kursk, before arriving in Leningrad on Sunday. After bidding farewell to senior Chasidim, the future Rebbe left the country of his birth on Tuesday 25th October (29th *Tishrei*) 1927.[39]

As he prepared to depart, he received a final telegram of blessing from his father, wishing him, "May you have success your entire life, as my soulful blessing from the depths of the heart. Your father, who loves you with an eternal love."[40]

Menachem Mendel would never see his father again—nor his brother Berel, nor his grandparents Meir Shlomo and Rachel, nor his uncle Shmuel and aunt Miriam Gittel. For twenty years he would not see his mother either. The decision to leave home would lay heavily on his conscience for years to come: "I shall never forgive myself for emigrating from the Soviet Union and leaving you behind," he later wrote.[41]

But he was joining the "Royal Family" of the Lubavitcher Rebbe, a union which was to have unimaginable consequences.

CHAPTER FIVE

NEW BEGINNINGS

1928

Rayatz (left) and Menachem Mendel (right), shortly before his wedding.

Leaving Russia near the end of 1927 left both Rayatz and his future son-in-law completely uprooted. Rayatz was now geographically isolated and gradually losing touch with the vast majority of his Chasidim back in Russia.[1] Menachem Mendel was displaced from his family, in a foreign land, and not yet married. Rayatz's main occupation over the next few years would be administering support for the Chasidim stuck in Russia and fundraising for that purpose, as well as building outreach institutions in Latvia; but Menachem Mendel does not appear to have been especially involved in these activities. In all likelihood, this was not the kind of work which appealed to him. Throughout his life, he was not fond of fundraising or acting as a travelling diplomat—activities which appealed much more to Rayatz's oldest son-in-law, Rashag, who spent much of this period traveling on behalf of Chabad, when he was not busy with his own business interests. Menachem Mendel, on the other hand, shied away from the limelight. In 1949 he wrote to Rabbi Yaakov Landau, Chief Rabbi of Bnei Brak, with whom he had been acquainted in Moscow back in 1926, "Now, just as when we first met, I do not take pleasure in communal work."[2]

At this time of his life, Menachem Mendel was still consumed with a thirst for knowledge. He had spent most of his life poring over Jewish texts, which from his early teenage years he had done in isolation. He had also accumulated much knowledge of mathematics, astronomy and other fields of secular wisdom. While remaining in close contact with Rayatz, and visiting his court regularly, Menachem Mendel was to spend the better part of the next decade in the halls of academia, studying engineering and other sciences, at the same time furthering his study of Torah at an advanced level. He had already spent some time in college in Russia, though it is not clear exactly when,[3] and from now until 1932 he would be enrolled at courses in the famous Friedrich-Wilhelm University of Berlin (now Humbolt University).

Why did Menachem Mendel choose to spend a prolonged period in university, away from close proximity to Rayatz's court? Why did he choose Berlin? And what were Rayatz's feelings about this plan?[4]

A key motivation was undoubtedly the need for a vocation. At that time, virtually all Chasidim had independent sources of income—even Rashag, the Rebbe's oldest son-in-law, who worked with him closely in communal affairs had many personal business interests. Unlike Rashag, Menachem Mendel did not come from a family of businessmen and, apparently, had little personal interest in this area. While he was trained as a Rabbi, the profession of his father, Rabbinic work was probably unappealing for someone who was generally introverted and, by his own confession, did not "take pleasure in communal work."[5] (We know that a few years later, Menachem Mendel declined a Rabbinic position in Paris, despite encouragement from Rayatz—see p. 116). Menachem Mendel's vocational choice, engineering, seems to fit his talents and natural dispositions: he loved the world of ideas and strategic planning. We know from decades of the Seventh Rebbe's "problem solving" that he was interested not only in *understanding* a concept, but also *applying* it in a useful way. He valued systems and organization, and engineering provided an opportunity to express his insightfulness in that context. His respect for intelligence, knowledge, and competence lent itself towards a highly skilled profession, and we know that from a young age he had a love of mathematics and science. (Interestingly, Menachem Mendel's great-great-grandfather and namesake, the Third Chabad Rebbe, was also known to have an interest in *handasah,* one of the components of modern engineering.[6])

For a Chasidic Jew, one's career is never one's first love[7]: Prayer, Torah study, and happenings at the Rebbe's court are the center of the universe. From his *Reshimot* (notes), we know that Menachem Mendel continued to study Torah at an advanced level during his university years and that he was frequently in correspondence with Rayatz, regularly engaged with activities on his behalf. He was also fascinated by the Sixth Rebbe's customs and practices, noting them carefully in his diary. It is unlikely, then, that his pursuit of an engineering degree represented his all-embracing preoccupation during this period;[8] in the context of his life, it seems that the university setting gave him the opportunity to establish a permanent source of income, while at the same time continuing his independent scholarly pursuits away from the limelight for an extended period after marriage.

Menachem Mendel's father, Reb Levik, was supported by his parents-in-law for the first ten years of marriage to enable him to advance in his studies. Menachem Mendel probably sought a similar period where he could devote himself to study, unencumbered by the pressures of earning a living, and we know that Rayatz supported his second daughter and her husband throughout their decade in Berlin and Paris. The choice of a university setting, rather than a Yeshivah or study hall, seems unusual at first glance, but when we bear in mind that Menachem Mendel enjoyed isolation, was inclined to autodidactic study and wanted to walk out at the end with an engineering degree, the setting does make a lot of sense. If he had spent the time in a Chabad Yeshivah or community, there is no doubt that he would have attracted much undesired attention. In Berlin, Menachem Mendel could keep a low profile, while still benefitting from the facilities of the local orthodox community, such as synagogues and easily available kosher food. In fact, on Menachem Mendel's street of residence in Berlin there were as many as fifteen *shtieblach* (small synagogues).[9]

Berlin did offer the exposure to higher culture and competing ideologies to Torah and Chasidism, but Menachem Mendel had not grown up in a ghetto and was exposed to secular Jews and their ideas his entire life. He was also extremely strong in his own convictions, with a deep attachment to Chasidism and East European Orthodoxy. From a public letter of wedding congratulations issued by his home community of Yekatrinoslav later that year, we get a sense of how the young scholar was known to be at ease in multiple worlds.

> We know and recognize the splendid value of your son, who has filled himself with Torah and, at the same time, has acquired [secular] wisdom and sciences in large measure. But religion and knowledge, faith and intelligence, are not rival wives to him. He is whole with his G-d, and fear of heaven is his fortune.[10]

This, of course, was not the norm in Chasidic circles, but Menachem Mendel was not your typical young man; and, as we have seen, even Rashab and Rayatz had an appreciation for rabbis who had retained their piety and "fear of Heaven" while succeeding in secular studies. Rayatz himself possessed a large library of secular books, and while they were purchased largely for the use of potential researchers, the very fact that he invested in such a library shows a certain respect for broader forms of wisdom.

Besides offering the qualifications necessary for a vocation, and the opportunity to study Torah in isolation, Menachem Mendel's university days in Berlin and later in Paris also offered him the chance to informally expand his base of general knowledge and culture. Throughout the decades of his leadership, the Seventh Rebbe maintained dialogue with academics and intellectuals from a broad range of disciplines, in both the sciences and the arts as well as medicine—significantly beyond his own field of expertise—and there are many accounts of visitors' being impressed with his command of diverse schools of thought. Presumably, much of this wisdom was acquired during the university years. (The Rebbe did write that he "tried to follow scientific developments in certain areas" after leaving higher education in 1938; but, obviously, once he entered the workplace, his time for such pursuits would have been limited, and we can safely presume that the core of this general knowledge was acquired between 1928 and 1938[11]). In one recollection which has reached us from this period, Menachem Mendel was remembered as sitting backwards in a swivel chair speaking for hours to his wife about Russian literature.[12] In another, he was spotted in the afternoon, still adorned in *tefilin*, studying the Jerusalem Talmud.[13] So, from the limited information available, we get a picture of an exceptional mind, immersed day and night in the pursuit of wisdom. In fact, that very year, 1928, at Menachem Mendel's wedding, Rayatz would publicly laud his new son-in-law as always being awake at four in the morning. "Either he has not yet gone to sleep," Rayatz told his guests, "or he is already awake for the day."[14]

On what basis did Menachem Mendel conduct these investigations into the greater wisdom and culture of Western Civilization? Jewish Law, which according to all accounts the future Rebbe observed punctiliously, is generally discouraging of such pursuits.[15] Chabad Chasidic thought makes an even stronger case against secular study, which is seen as having a contaminating effect on the soul.

> With the wisdom of the nations, a person defiles the intellectual faculties of inquiry (*chochmah*), cognition (*binah*) and discernment (*da'at*) in his Divine Soul with the contamination of the negative energy (*kelipat nogah*) contained in this wisdom (Rabbi Shneur Zalman of Liadi, *Likutei Amarim, Tanya,* end of chap. 8).

The *Talmud* does offer numerous sanctions to study secular wisdom, but they all have a common thread: there must be an obvious, pressing need for the study—either to earn a living, or to clarify a point of law, or to defend Judaism from its critics, *etc.*[16] Nowhere do we find that normative *halacha* condones secular study out of plain curiosity, or to understand the culture, or to become generally more knowledgeable. The study must somehow be in the direct service of Torah.

In a 1949 letter,[17] the future Seventh Rebbe offers the bold suggestion that, in exceptional cases, the study of secular wisdom without any immediately foreseeable Torah application *is* permitted. The proof, he argues, is from the above mentioned passage of *Tanya,* where the author cites Maimonides and Nachmanides as a Rabbinic precedent of scholars who immersed themselves in secular wisdom in a permissible manner.

> Unless he employs [this wisdom] as a useful instrument, i.e., as a means of a more affluent livelihood to be able to serve G-d, or he

> knows how to apply them in the service of G-d and His Torah. This is the reason why Maimonides and Nachmanides, of blessed memory, and their adherents, engaged in them (*Tanya* ibid.).

What is curious, the Rebbe asks, is why the *Tanya* cites the comparatively late cases of Maimonides and Nachmanides, when there are many earlier, more authoritative proofs from the Talmud itself? Apparently, the *Tanya's* author deemed these later cases to convey an allowance for secular studies that goes beyond that which the Talmud and earlier codes explicitly condone.

In what way did these two medieval scholars, Maimonides and Nachmanides, absorb secular wisdom which their forebears did not? By Maimonides' own testimony, he studied medicine when there was no immediate need for it, since his brother supported him financially.[18] Only when his brother later died in a tragic accident was Maimonides forced to use his knowledge to earn a living. Nachmanides' life is also replete with examples of secular study which had no immediately pressing justification.

So, concluded the Rebbe, while Judaism does not condone the pursuit of secular wisdom for the sake of curiosity alone, there is room for secular study that has no pressing need—provided that the individual is realistically confident that he will "apply them in the service of G-d and His Torah" *at some later point in time*. This was the *Tanya's* point in citing the practical cases of Maimonides and Nachmanides rather than merely referring to the *Talmud* and the Codes: these two Rabbis both immersed themselves in secular study when there was no pressing need for it, and only discovered what the application might be "in the service of G-d and His Torah" later in life. If these guidelines are adhered to, the *Tanya* assures us, the contaminating effects of secular wisdom will be avoided.[19]

The argument here is subtle, but the ramifications are huge. If the need for secular study can be retroactively unraveled at a later point, then Menachem Mendel's years of general secular engagement can be understood, according to his own insight, as consistent with the views of Rabbi Shneur Zalman of Liadi, author of *Tanya* and founder of Chabad. There is no doubt that, in his later life, Menachem Mendel Schneerson made outstanding use of secular wisdom "in the service of G-d and His Torah." Countless individuals have cited their encounters with the Seventh Rebbe as personally transformative because the notion of a Chasidic Rebbe knowledgeable of the culture and Western thought shattered their preconceptions about the relevance of "old-school" values in the new world. The Rebbe spoke to the most secularly educated people about Judaism in terms that would be meaningful to them, often drawing analogies and precedents from their particular field of interest and expertise. In hundreds of talks and letters, the Rebbe also suggested Torah lessons we might learn from current events, scientific developments and other secular themes. Regardless of whether, in 1928, Menachem Mendel was aware how exactly he would use his broader secular wisdom in the future for the sake of "Torah and worship," his general commitment to do so was in itself sufficient to render it a sacred enterprise.[20]

Besides seeking a vocation and acquiring general wisdom that would be of value in the future, if we consider the times in which Menachem Mendel lived, there might have been a third element to his decision. From around 1880 onwards, Chasidic courts had been in decline and, especially in Russia, there had been a huge disenfranchisement of Chasidic youth. Communism, Zionism and rapid scientific developments had captivated the minds of the younger generation. A significant percentage of the Seventh Rebbe's huge correspondence over forty years falls under the category of "guiding the perplexed," responding to philosophical and otherwise critical questions about Judaism and its contemporary relevance in a modern age. Obviously, his responses to these issues did not dawn on him overnight and they were the result of prolonged personal inquiry. It is likely that, at the very outset of his academic pursuits, Menachem Mendel saw an extended period in university as an opportunity to reflect on the issues that were troubling young Jews and to come up with coherent, unapologetic solutions. Menachem Mendel wanted to purvey a Judaism that, while motivated by *mesiras nefesh* (utter devotion) and faith, was nevertheless intelligent and stood up to critical scrutiny. Even if this was not his own primary motivation,[21] it was definitely something which his generation needed, both in Russia and later in the United States.

Why Berlin? Now in possession of a passport and the ability to travel relatively freely in Europe, he found many opportunities available to him. Of the major centers, Paris, London and Berlin, the third was by far the nearest, only a one- or two day's train journey away through Latvia and Poland, and posed the least language barrier, due to the similarities between Yiddish and German. Rayatz had ties with leading Rabbis in Germany which would prove to be useful connections to gain admission to the university. Berlin was also an extremely strong center for physics, which formed the core of Menachem Mendel's interests.

Rayatz's reaction to Mendel's enrollment in Berlin University is difficult to completely fathom in the absence of any clear documentation. We know that, like his father, Rashab, Rayatz publicly opposed secular study for his followers; but we also know that he was impressed by Menachem Mendel's general knowledge and that he paid for his son-in-law's years of university study out of his personal funds.[22] While this indicates that Rayatz was generally supportive, it is not clear whether attendance in university at this point was Rayatz's own idea, or something to which he merely consented. Menachem Mendel was already versed in secular wisdom before he met Rayatz, and this does not appear to be a facet of his personality that the Sixth Rebbe personally nurtured. On an emotional level, there may also have been some fear associated with sending his young, newly married daughter off to a European metropolis—fears that definitely mounted with the rise of Nazism. Ultimately though, when Menachem Mendel finally graduated, Rayatz penned a very positive letter celebrating his son-in-law's achievements,[23] and the Sixth Rebbe certainly made good use of his young scholar for numerous assignments in Europe, and later, to build Chabad in America.

II.

Upon his arrival in Riga near the end of 1927, Rayatz enlisted the assistance of his future son-in-law as a temporary secretary, and we have a number of letters surviving from this period written in the Seventh Rebbe's handwriting and signed by the Sixth. During his first month in Riga, Rayatz managed to pen almost seventy letters.[24]

Just three weeks later, Rayatz convened a high-profile Rabbinic meeting to discuss the urgent situation of Jews in Russia. Menachem Mendel was present at the meeting, as were the Chief Rabbi of Riga, Menachem Mendel Zak; Rabbi Dr. Hildesheimer from Berlin; and Parliament Member Mordechai Dubin. The meeting was also graced by Rabbi Yosef Rosen, the Rogatchover Gaon who, having left Leningrad several years earlier, now presided over the city of Dvinsk in Latvia.[25]

As a full-time scholar, Rabbi Rosen was not particularly inclined to communal work. Half a century later, in a 1975 Purim sermon, the Seventh Rebbe recalled how the Rogatchover had excused himself from attendance at further meetings.

> We had to confirm who would be involved in the future, and who would participate in future meetings. We wanted to include the Rogatchover among those who would be invited to future sessions.
>
> He said that he would be unable to take that upon himself.
>
> We asked him: Why not? He had recently relocated from Leningrad, where he had lived for a number of years, so he was well aware of the sorry state of affairs there. We were speaking of saving lives.
>
> He said: "It's a dispute between the Babylonian Talmud and the Jerusalem Talmud, and Jewish Law follows the Babylonian Talmud."
>
> "What Babylonian Talmud? What Jerusalem Talmud?" we asked him.
>
> And he explained that he was referring to the famous Talmudic passage in tractate *Brachot*, which describes how the early pietists would spend three hours a day preparing for prayer, three hours in prayer, and three hours meditating afterwards. The Talmud asks: When did they study Torah? and we get two slightly different answers. The Jerusalem Talmud replies, "Since they were pious their Torah *was blessed*,"[26] whereas the Babylonian Talmud explains, "Since they were pious their Torah *was preserved*."[27]
>
> The difference is: *Blessed* implies growth and fresh insight,[28] whereas *preserved* suggests that they merely did not forget what they had already learned.[29]
>
> When there is a dispute between the two Talmuds we follow the Babylonian text, and since the Rogatchover desired his Torah to be "blessed," he said he could not participate in communal work![30]

Rabbi Rosen, concluded the Seventh Rebbe, was one of those rare scholars who could legitimately exempt himself from communal work; but for the rest of us, even Rabbis and scholars, the tone was set by Rayatz, who dedicated much of his personal time that could have been spent in study to communal work.[31] We see, however, from this snippet, the Seventh Rebbe's affection and admiration for the Rogatchover, recalling so many years later how he had exempted himself from communal work with finesse and Talmudic sophistication.

In the winter, on 26th December (2nd *Tevet*), Menachem Mendel departed from Riga for the first of many extended trips to Berlin.[32] His first stop was the annual *Agudat Yisrael* conference[33] which took place in the Atlas Hotel over two days. Menachem Mendel was sent to represent Rayatz, and recorded a detailed report of the proceedings in a letter to his future father-in-law, on 4th *Tevet*.[34] "The speeches," he wrote, "were clearly planned in advance and proceeded in an orderly fashion." Other notable points: "A list of blessings that had been received was read out, and they began with the blessing from the Lubavitcher Rebbe." Menachem Mendel's personal reaction to his first international conference in Western Europe was, "It is joyous to see how they have gathered from the four corners of the earth to discuss Judaism."

"'The representative from London, Rottenberg,[35]" he reported, "is very pleased with Rabbi Gutnick"[36]—Rayatz's emissary to London, England—"and praises him in the strongest terms."

Menachem Mendel also related some calculated diplomacy on his part, intuiting Rayatz's desire not to become too enmeshed with the *Agudah*, "I am afraid to come any closer to the organizers of the convention, so that they do not use the opportunity to get his holiness [the Rebbe] involved. I just made myself known to them. For the same reason, I avoided the evening meal which was arranged for all the attendants."

It is, of course, not uncharacteristic that the future Rebbe chose to maintain a low profile.[37]

III.

Menachem Mendel got straight to work on his university admission. The winter semester was already in progress, so that was ruled out; but the summer semester, beginning on 8th May, was a reasonable goal. The main problem was that, as a life-long Rabbinical student, he lacked documentation of sufficient secular education. As evidence of a high school education in Russia, he had his uncle, Rabbi Shmuel Schneerson (the government-sanctioned Rabbi of Nikolayev), write a note that "R. Menachem Mendel, son of Rabbi Levi Yitzchak Schneerson, graduated from middle school in the City of Yekatrinoslav in the year 1919, receiving very good grades for all courses. The certificate that was handed to him for passing the exam has been lost."[38]

This alone, however, was not enough. So, as a stepping stone to university admission, Menachem Mendel sought quick admission to the highly respected local Rabbinic-academic school, the Hildesheimer *Rabbiner-Seminar*. The *Seminar* was a bastion of German neo-Orthodoxy, combining advanced Talmudic studies with higher academic pursuits. Its graduates would seek to attain both *semicha* (Rabbinic ordination) and a doctorate. While this was not the approach of Lubavitch, Rayatz nevertheless had close ties with the eminent Seminar's rector, Rabbi Yechiel Ya'akov Weinberg (1878–1966)—a then emerging *halachic* authority[39]—spending time together at the healing spa at Marienbad, Czechoslovakia. They developed a warm relationship, and Rabbi Weinberg later commented that Rayatz "loved him."

Introducing himself as the Rebbe's future son-in-law, Menachem Mendel asked Rabbi Weinberg if he could be granted with *semicha* from the *Seminar,* as he was in need of official documentation from an institution recognized by the university. (As we have learned, Menachem Mendel already had received a private *semicha* from his uncle in 1924).

Rabbi Weinberg wanted to help but said it would be unfair to the other students to grant a *semicha* without completing the requisite courses of study. That would take months, if not years, and Menachem Mendel wanted to be enrolled for the summer semester. He had not come to Berlin to be trained in neo-Orthodoxy.

What happened next was something very rare, if not unparalleled in Menachem Mendel's early life, which was characterized by an extreme reticence to "show off" his brilliance. He proposed to Rabbi Weinberg, "Why don't you pick any volume from your library and lend it to me overnight. Tomorrow you can assess me on its contents, and that will be the *semicha* test."

While adamant not to break the rules—this was Germany, after all—Weinberg couldn't resist the temptation. This twenty-six year old scholar had promised to dazzle him and he was curious to see what goods were being purveyed.

"Here, take this, and we will discuss it tomorrow," Weinberg said, handing Menachem Mendel one of his own compositions. It was an extremely complex, fifty-seven page responsum, entitled *Exhumation of the Bones of the Dead,* which had been written by Weinberg in 1926 to clarify *halachic* issues relating to the obscure topic of transferring a buried corpse.

Menachem Mendel went home and pored over the text. His four-page evaluation of Rabbi Weinberg's responsum, written in his personal notebook, has survived.[40] The young Rebbe-to-be is sharply critical, questioning the document's logic in a number of places, invalidating some of its assumptions and suggesting preferable answers to a few of the author's solutions. From even a cursory review of the notes, it is not difficult to understand why Rabbi Weinberg awarded Menachem Mendel with official *semicha* from the *Rabbiner-Seminar* the following day.[41]

Menachem Mendel clearly managed to get all his paperwork in place as on 8th May 1928, after a trip back to Riga for the Passover holidays,[42] he returned to Berlin to attend lectures during the summer semester at the university.[43]

He was, however, registered not as a full, matriculating student but as an "occasional student" (Gasthörer). The "occasional student" does not require a secondary school leaving certificate but is not recognized for entering a full-time course of study nor is he eligible for taking examinations. A tuition fee is paid on a per lecture basis.[44] Presumably, Menachem Mendel saw this as a stepping stone to full university admission at a later point, though, as we shall see, this did not materialize in Berlin, but in Paris.[45]

Interestingly, Menachem Mendel attended Berlin University at the same a time as two of his Rabbinic contemporaries, Joseph B. Soloveitchik and Abraham Joshua Heschel. Rabbi Soloveitchik was in the process of researching a dissertation on the philosophy of Hermann Cohen,[46] and Heschel, too, was in the process of writing his famous doctorate on prophecy.[47]

While he probably studied natural sciences, many of the details of Menachem Mendel's studies in the university have yet to emerge. From a discussion with Professor Yaakov Hanoka many years later, we do know that one of the Future Rebbe's professors was Walther Nernst (1864-1941). A towering figure in academia, in 1897 Nernst had invented one of the first electric lamps, and shortly afterwards, in 1905, he established what would later be known as the Third Law of Thermodynamics, receiving the Nobel Prize in chemistry in 1920. Menachem Mendel was initially surprised that such an esteemed scholar was teaching an introductory course for first year students, but later discovered that it was purely out of financial concerns: teachers were paid according to the number of enrolled students, and, of course, the introductory courses had the largest attendance.[48] Schrödinger was also a legendary scientist, having just proposed what is now known as the Schrödinger equation in 1926, which would win him the Nobel Prize for Physics in 1933.

Menachem Mendel found himself mixing among the intellectual elite of Europe during a honeymoon period in the development of theoretical physics, but his religious devotion still remained intense. Chasidic practice encourages regular immersion in a *mikvah* (ritual bath), and the more pious are careful to do this every day. Among neo-orthodox German Jews this was something of an anomaly—in Berlin, immersion was carried out by ladies only. The *mikvah* attendant was thus rather surprised to find a bearded young man requesting to use the facilities every day, and special permission had to be granted for Menachem Mendel from the supervising Rabbi. Since he was the only man who wanted to access the premises during the day, the Rebbe-to-be was given his own key, and used to surreptitiously pass by the *mikvah* in the early afternoon, when lectures were completed.[49]

Another glimpse that has reached us regarding Menachem Mendel's personal conduct from this period, is a recollection of Rabbi Ezriel Zelig Slonim (1897-1971),[50] a Chasid of Rashab, Rayatz, and later, the Seventh Rebbe, who found himself in Berlin shortly before the festival of *Shavuot,* 1928. Rabbi Slonim had traveled from his home in Israel to spend the festival with the Rebbe Rayatz in Riga, but was denied entry to the country. Discovering that the Rebbe's future son-in-law was in Berlin, he sought him out for help.

Late in the afternoon, Slonim arrived at the address of the Jewish host family's home where Menachem Mendel domiciled, and was informed that "the young man is fasting today." He knocked on the future Rebbe's door and entered. Menachem Mendel was sitting, adorned in *tefilin,* studying the Jerusalem Talmud. Rabbi Slonim had been a guest in the Schneerson home in Yekatrinoslav in 1920, and Menachem Mendel recognized him immediately. Removing his *tefilin* he wished Rabbi Slonim a warm welcome and, after hearing his visitor's predicament, both men rushed to the post office to send Rayatz a telegram. The problem was promptly solved.[51]

During 1928, Menachem Mendel also maintained his scholarly correspondence with the Rogatchover Gaon.[52] (He even took one train ride, that we know of, together with the Gaon).[53] While the letters overflow with Talmudic references, we can also detect an interest of the young university student in finding bridges between Jewish and secular wisdom. In one letter, Menachem Mendel asks his mentor to "please clarify the Talmudic view of astronomy."[54] Unsatisfied with the Gaon's reply, Menachem Mendel clarifies his request in a subsequent letter. "Concerning astronomy... Maimonides relied to some extent on non-Jewish wisdom... Greek wisdom and particularly the works of Aristotle, his students and interpreters... But what I asked and requested from you is to clarify the *Talmudic* sources on astronomy." In the absence of a clear Jewish tradition on this topic, Maimonides had built his systematic treatment of astronomy on non-Jewish sources—but Menachem Mendel wondered whether, drawing on the Rogatchover's genius, it would be possible to reconstruct the authentic Jewish view based on fragmentary insights found in the Talmud.

The year 1928 also represented the beginning of an interesting correspondence between Menachem Mendel and his father, which continued until Reb Levik's arrest by the Soviets in 1939. Most of Menachem Mendel's letters have not survived, but we have a huge number of responses from Reb Levik, filling over two hundred printed pages.[55]

In the letters, we see a father's fervent desire to impart wisdom to his son. Reb Levik writes pages of his own Kabbalistic novellae and if there is any discussion of personal events, it is usually in the context of a mystical explanation. For example, in the first letter, written just before the festival of Passover, Reb Levik adopts the traditional motif of *matzah* (unleavened bread) as a symbol of faith, and applies it to his son's upcoming lifecycle event, marriage. The faith of *matzah*, suggests Reb Levik, is necessary to overcome the irrationality of marriage; and that is why when one combines the words *matzah* and *ishah* (woman), the result is *emet* (truth), a quality that transcends logic.[56] In the following letters prior to his son's wedding, Reb Levik connects themes from each of the festivals to marriage: a *Shavuot* letter draws parallels between the Sinaitic event and the union of man and woman;[57] and a

Sukkot letter compares the *sukkah* booth to the *chupah* (canopy) at a Jewish wedding.[58]

Interestingly enough, while in Berlin, Menachem Mendel also maintained a correspondence with his future mother-in-law, Rebbetzin Nechama Dina. One letter, written in the summer, is unusually descriptive for a young man who lived in the world of ideas and did not enjoy writing about personal events. In it he speaks of the rainy Berlin weather, the peculiarities of how Germans conduct themselves in the street ("with their jacket in one hand, and a handkerchief in the other, to wipe off perspiration"); his fears of crossing the border with valuable objects; a visit he made to a small synagogue of the Chortkov Chasidim ("who barely had a *minyan* [prayer quorum of ten]") during the visit of their Rebbe; and how he randomly discovered the contents of Rayatz's *farbrengen* from a Jew at a bus stop.[59]

During the fall, Menachem Mendel returned to Riga to spend the festival month of *Tishrei* in the court of Rayatz, but he was back in Berlin at the end of October, in time for the winter semester, beginning 1st November. His only new professor was Wolfgang Köhler (1887-1967), a pioneer in the field of Gestalt psychology who taught Menachem Mendel a course in Natural Philosophy.

But his studies that winter were to suffer a major interruption. After seemingly endless upheavals, the date of Menachem Mendel's wedding to Moussia Schneersohn was finally confirmed for 14th *Kislev* (27th November). Menachem Mendel barely attended the introductory lectures to courses on Higher Mathematics and Natural Philosophy, on Monday and Tuesday (5th/6th November), before he was forced to depart back to Latvia on Wednesday, to prepare for the great day ahead.

IV.

It had been just over a year since Rayatz's life had been saved, and neither his family nor the Chasidim had really celebrated (straight after his release Rayatz had gone into self-imposed exile in Malakhovka). The festive month of *Tishrei*, which had just passed, was particularly joyous in the newfound freedom of democratic Latvia—even Menachem Mendel, who was usually not prone to displays of fervor, danced elatedly for hours.[60] But the "royal wedding," six weeks later really represented the peak moment following the abyss of Spalerno.

Rabbi Eliyahu Chaim Althaus, in a letter to his family, who were unable to attend the wedding, painted the contrast with poignancy: "Why on earth was it your lot to watch and experience that *tzadik's* pain so much, but not to merit to take part in his double comfort, this great celebration, his consolation and joyous rebuilding?"[61]

Rayatz himself clearly saw the wedding as a significant moment of "rebuilding," since he donned a *streimel*, for the first time since fleeing from Lubavitch in 1915. The *streimel*, a type of fur hat, carried particular significance in Chabad, since, in contrast to other Chasidic movements, it was worn only by the Rebbe himself and not by his followers. In thirteen years of "exile," neither Rashab nor Rayatz had donned the fur "crown," and its appearance here at the wedding was a clear sign of the "consolation and joyous rebuilding" of the Rebbe's court. From this moment onwards Rayatz wore his grandfather's *streimel* regularly on Sabbaths, festivals and special occasions.[62] (It was, however, a feature discontinued by the Seventh Rebbe, as we shall see).

A wedding is always an experience of joy tinged with sorrow. Under the *chupah*, Jews traditionally break a glass as a reminder, at the peak of joy, of the tragic destruction of the Temple. With tens of thousands of his followers stuck in Stalinist Russia, Rayatz did not need much reminding of things tragic. On the Sabbath before the wedding, when Menachem Mendel was called to the Torah for his *aufruf*, Rayatz devoted part of his speech to the painful topic. Altahaus recalls: "His holy face went white then red and his eyes filled with tears, as he looked heavenwards and said, 'Now I would like to drink a *lechaim* for my brethren who are exiled in our country [Russia].' With a very loud voice, he gave them a great and long blessing, to the extent that all those gathered were overcome by fear. Most of those with an empathetic heart shed tears."[63]

Rayatz's choice of Warsaw as the location for the wedding initially surprised his Chasidim. Althaus refers to "the great question, the unsolved riddle that everyone has been asking, openly or covertly: Why on earth is the wedding in Warsaw?" Besides the difficulties of travel, the need to cross the border meant that a number of senior Chasidim would be unable to attend, including Rayatz's own secretary, Rabbi Yechezkel Feigin, as well as the man who had saved Rayatz's life—and would save it again a decade later—Mordechai Dubin, who could not be excused from an important session in the Latvian parliament.[64]

The Rebbe had actually indicated his reasoning in a private letter penned a few weeks before the wedding, expressing his desire that the ceremony be "in the premises of *Yeshivat Tomchei Temimim*, in the courtyard, so we will at least have a small taste of the atmosphere back in Lubavitch."[65] The main branch of the Yeshivah in Warsaw, which had been established in 1921,[66] was the best possible substitute for the Lubavitch home town, where the Schneersohn "royal" weddings had taken place for the last century.[67]

Rayatz had also been contemplating where to rebuild his court and Poland was home to the most vibrant Chasidic community in the world. Numerous Rebbes had their courts there, spreading their wings over the vast majority of the Polish Jewish population. The Chabad presence was small, but Polish soil seemed to grow Chasidim and Rebbes at an astounding pace. Having the wedding in Warsaw would help to put Lubavitch on the map in this densely Chasidic territory, and it would make it easy for the many local Chasidic Rebbes and Torah scholars to attend. (As we shall see, Rayatz did eventually relocate his court to Warsaw in 1933).

Rayatz probably had another motivation for making the wedding as prominent and well attended as possible: he wanted the Jewish world to get a glimpse of the towering stature of his new son-in-law. From Menachem Mendel's letters to the Rogatchover and notes on Rabbi Weinberg's responsum we see that reports of his encyclopedic knowledge and penetrating mind even at this young age were not exaggerated. Rayatz wanted the Rabbinic elite of Poland to meet this young man and discuss Torah with him, so they could see for themselves what a rare prize Lubavitch had won.

This, of course, represented a huge clash between son-in-law and father-in-law. Menachem Mendel hated attention and "showing off" of any sorts. He was even uncomfortable at being sat prominently at his own wedding, later writing in his diary, "At the head of the table sits the groom on the direction of the Rebbe Rayatz, *and against the will of the groom*."[68]

Huge crowds already assembled en route from Riga to Warsaw, two days before the wedding. As the train stopped in Dvinsk, Chasidim had turned out in huge numbers, hoping to see the Rebbe Rayatz and receive his blessings. After crossing the border, the train stopped in Vilna, and Althaus recalls, "I was astonished and stunned—a joy and trembling seized me—to suddenly see such a massive crowd standing at the station, all of them proud Jews, with beards. With a great commotion they pushed each other forward, each one running with one intention toward the Rebbe *shlita's* car. They all wanted to see him, to wish him *mazel tov,* and to receive a blessing from his holy mouth. After a short while, we heard their thousands of voices singing a beautiful melody in unison in his honor, and in honor of the celebration. We Lubavitchers accompanying the Rebbe, who were standing at that moment on the platform near our car, were inspired to join their joyous melody. How wonderful was this special moment for us!"[69]

The train arrived in Warsaw the following morning, Monday 13th *Kislev* (26th November), where the Schneersohns were welcomed by thousands of men, women, and children, as well as all the students of *Yeshivat Tomchei Temimim.* Menachem Mendel asked Rabbi Althaus to rescue him from the mayhem and accompany him to his hotel. One advantage that the groom possessed was that nobody recognized him, so it was easier to make a quick exit. Althaus recalls:

> The groom appeared in my car and suggested that I travel with him to the hotel, saying that the Rebbe *shlita* requested this. Obviously, I didn't wait a moment and the two of us set off immediately from the wagon to our challenging task. Our arms locked together, with great difficulty we pushed through the many people that surrounded us. When people who knew me came up to bless and welcome me, I didn't answer.
>
> We hurried, pushed around through the mayhem, not speaking a word. We looked at them the same way they looked at us. I was very concerned that no one should learn that this was the groom, whom they were all searching for and hoping to greet. A tactic that worked for me was: to everyone I hurriedly responded by pointing toward the Rebbe *shlita's* car. In this way, I saved the groom from the thousands who stood with their arms outstretched to shake his hand...
>
> Unfortunately, amid the confusion and hurry... we didn't have enough time to ask the name of the hotel that had been arranged for the groom. We didn't know which hotel to go to and drove around for an hour and a half in the taxi until we found a hotel with a vacancy for us.

Althaus thus had the privilege of being Menachem Mendel's personal *shomer* (guardian) for the twenty-four hours before the wedding. Characteristically, the young Rebbe-to-be was a man of few words. "We spoke very little," Althaus recalled.

The following day, as thousands of telegrams poured into Rayatz's quarters, Althaus escorted Menachem Mendel to the *mikvah* and to prayers. In the following hours, this senior Chasid and close confidant of the Sixth Rebbe, watched the young groom study and pray, later penning these impressions.

> While he prepares himself for his long journey, to find life, to build a home with the companion he has found, he does not know where the future will take him. Many pathways are before him, all potentially treacherous: some spiritually, others physically. He cries bitterly, pouring tears before He Who knows the future.

Of course, Althaus was acutely aware that Menachem Mendel had studied secular wisdom extensively and was now a student in the University of Berlin. He therefore scrutinized the young groom carefully to see if he could discern any weakening of Chasidic attachments from these "non-Jewish" interests.

> I have examined his deeds inside and out, and thank G-d, I have not found in him a stain nor a breach. His soul is whole....
>
> I see with my own eyes a precious young man, an astounding Torah scholar—truly G-d fearing, garbed in a silk *gartel*, fasting, studying *Reishit Chochma*[70] the entire day; his immersions in the *mikvah* and his prayers with sincere concentration for the sake of Heaven. You are surely aware of his nature, both from his own natural and inherited tenacity, and he is quite distant from doing something for appearances alone. And although he knows what is outside in the secular world, he also knows well to discern between the holy and the mundane, and his holiness was never tarnished, even the slightest bit.

While special tickets had been issued to avoid overcrowding at the wedding ceremony at Mławska 7, the Lubavitcher Yeshivah, nevertheless, there was a huge amount of pushing. The police, who were easily bribed, were also unsuccessful in stopping the entry of a number of pickpockets, and a number of guests later discovered that they had been relieved of their valuables.

Althaus recalled, "The immense crush, the rushing and trampling, the noise and yelling that was going on in the courtyard, cannot be described. Men, women and children filled the large courtyard from end to end, measuring around 6,000 square feet." The *chupah* was illuminated by "many electric lights," which was apparently something of a novelty in those days.

Rayatz arrived at 6 p.m., followed by the groom a quarter of an hour later. In attendance were the Rabbinic elite of Poland: the Radziner Rebbe, Rabbi Mordechai Yosef Elazar Leiner; the Lubliner Rav, Rabbi Meir Shapiro; the Zlotopoler Rebbe, Rabbi Mordechai Yosef Twersky; Rabbi Menachem Ziemba, a major Torah scholar of international repute; the Novominsker Rebbe, Rabbi Alter Yisroel Shimon Perlow; Rabbi Tzvi Yechezkel Michelsohn of the Warsaw *Beit Din* (Rabbinic Court), and many others.[71] Reporters from all the major Jewish newspapers were present, including *Hatsefirah, Moment, Haynt,* and the *Express.* Important lay leaders included the Chairmen of the Rabbinical Councils of Poland and Warsaw, and representatives of the *Joint Distribution Committee*, which had funded much of Rayatz's work.

Althaus recalls Rayatz's demeanor as the guests were welcomed:

> Suddenly, the Rebbe *shlita's* face turned from red to white. He was literally like an angel of G-d, his eyes shining with a clear, radiant light, like the morning stars. G-d... fear and trembling gripped each person... It is indescribable...
>
> He said, "There is a principle that at a wedding celebration the souls of the parents come from the World of Truth. With all Jews they come from up to three previous generations, sometimes more. There are different levels. As an invitation to the souls of the *tzadikim,* our Rebbes, to come to the *chupah* and bless the couple, I will now say some Chasidut—a piece from the Alter Rebbe, a piece from the Mitteler Rebbe, a piece from my great-grandfather, a piece from my grandfather, the bride's great-grandfather; a piece from the great-great-grandfather of the groom; and a piece from my father, the bride's grandfather...."
>
> His words were uttered with fire. Everyone heard his voice and saw the fire burning within him... Immediately following his awe-

> inspiring introduction, the Rebbe *shlita* began the discourse *Lecha Dodi.*[72] It lasted about half an hour.

Rayatz took the groom into an adjoining room and personally garbed him in sacred garments for the *chupah.* Menachem Mendel was dressed with a *kittel* (shroud) made from a shirt of the Rebbe Rashab, and the Sixth Rebbe tied a silk *gartel* around the future Seventh Rebbe's waist. Rayatz blessed Menachem Mendel, and invited his father-in-law, Rabbi Avraham Schneersohn to do the same. All the Chasidic Rebbes in attendance were also asked to each give their blessings to the groom. (When one Rebbe declined to offer his blessings, professing that he was unworthy, Rayatz insisted, saying, "But your followers think you are great!")

Following Jewish custom, the bride's face was then covered by the groom at the *bedeken.* Immediately afterwards, chaos erupted as the crowd dashed outside to the Yeshivah courtyard where the *chupah* was to be held. Rayatz conducted the entire ceremony, reciting also the traditional *sheva brachot* (seven blessings).

The wedding feast[73] was held "in the American style," in a different location, a banqueting hall at 35 Paska Street. The reception did not begin until 10 p.m., when Rayatz began to distribute drinks to the guests while the groom sat at the head table—something which Menachem Mendel found extremely uncomfortable, as he later recalled in a 1954 sermon.[74] Rayatz took advantage of the opportunity to strengthen the devotion of the Yeshivah students, "When all the students had cups in their hands, the Rebbe himself took a cup as well and said, *lechaim, lechaim,* and began to bless them. Then he began to say, 'In Torah study, one must exert himself. Even the sharpest and most receptive of minds will do better when he toils.'"

At 11 p.m. Rayatz delivered a second Chasidic discourse for about an hour, after which the meal was served to the accompaniment of live music. Then, "everyone stood up and the Rebbes all danced in a circle, as is customary in Poland. When the Polish Rebbes sat down to rest a bit, the Rebbe took his son-in-law and danced with him as they do in Russia—one hand on the other's shoulder. The Rebbe danced quickly."

By around 3:30 a.m. virtually all the Polish Rebbes had departed, and the remaining crowd stood in a half-circle, with Rayatz in the middle, and sang for around half an hour. The Rebbe then continued his Chasidic discourse, during which the Amshinover Rebbe, Rabbi Shimon Sholom Kalish, arrived. The celebrations did not conclude until 6 a.m.

At one point during the proceedings, one of the senior Chasidim asked Rayatz, "Tell me about the groom." The Rebbe's response sums up his utter joy that such an outstanding scholar had joined the family.

> *"I have given my daughter to this man."* (Deut. 22:16) He is wholly fluent in the Babylonian and Jerusalem Talmuds; he knows the Torah writings of the *rishonim* (early authorities) and *acharonim* (later authorities), and much, much more. At four o'clock in the morning, he has either not yet gone to sleep, or has already awoken![75]

But as much as Rayatz wanted to showcase his new son-in-law's brilliance, Menachem Mendel tried to avoid it. He later recalled, in a 1971 sermon, a discussion at his wedding with the Lubliner Rav, Rabbi Meir Shapiro (1887-1933), founder of the elitist Yeshivah *Chachmei Lublin,* and the *Daf Yomi* daily study cycle of Talmud.

> The Lubliner Rav... was at my wedding and later at the *sheva brachot.* My father-in-law wanted me to speak with him in learning, but I evaded it, as is my way. However, since my father-in-law adored him—he had done many things [for the Rebbe]—and he had given me the book he authored, I took a look inside."[76]

Despite Menachem Mendel's reluctance to make his greatness known, Rayatz had achieved his goal of bringing the young genius from Yekatrinoslav into his immediate family, something that would prove of great significance to future generations of Jews. On his return to Riga, the Sixth Rebbe dictated a telegram to his secretary Rabbi Yechezkel Fegin, to be placed on the grave of his father, the Rebbe Rashab, who had originally proposed the *shidduch* (match) in his lifetime. "Father, your will has been carried out."[77]

V.

Lubavitcher Chasidim around the world who were unable to make the trip to Warsaw marked the celebration of the "royal wedding" in their hometowns. But nowhere was the joy—and pain of absence—

more acute than in Menachem Mendel's hometown. Due to the heavy restrictions placed on international travel from Communist Russia, Reb Levik and Rebbetzin Chana had not been permitted to leave the country for their own son's wedding.

As a result, we have a detailed correspondence between the parents and son both before and after the wedding. A week before the celebrations Reb Levik wrote:

> Our Patriarch Jacob... did not have his father and mother with him physically as he went to his mate. Nevertheless, the match went very well, and Scripture says of him, *"And the man became exceedingly wealthy"*(Gen. 30:43).... Don't worry that we, your father and mother, will not be with you at the physical place of your wedding. We are together with you in our hearts and souls, which no physical space can possibly divide at all.[78]

Reb Levik also gave detailed instructions to his son for the wedding day: careful immersion in the *mikvah,* study of *Tanya,* prayer of the Afternoon Service with confessions, the donning of a silk *kapote* (Prince Albert Frock Coat), and how to focus the mind under the *chupah.* Following each of these ritual practices, then, Menachem Mendel would have felt a palpable sense of his father's presence, despite their geographical distance.

The most memorable communication from Reb Levik was received on the day of the wedding. "The tablecloth was wet from my husband's tears as he wrote that telegram," Rebbetzin Chana later recalled.[79] Reb Levik's brother, Rabbi Shmuel Schneerson, similarly noted, "All the love of this father and great man, his deepest emotions, were poured into this telegram from the core of his soul."

> May you walk on the path of Torah and *mitzvah,* and live lives of *nachat* (pleasure), peace and tranquility, amidst all good, forever. May you both be a source of pride and renown amongst Israel. May you engender "*a generation of upright offspring*" (Psalms 112:2), children and grandchildren occupied in Torah and *mitzvot,* literally.
>
> Your father, who is literally together with you.
>
> Levi Yitzchak.[80]

Reb Levik himself later made reference to his heightened emotions when writing the telegram,

> Of all the countless telegrams that you received, I truly desire that my own telegram to you... should remain with you, because it was written from the depths of my heart and soul... Protect it for many long, pleasant years.[81]

On the day of the wedding, a simultaneous celebration was held in Reb Levik and Chana's apartment in Yekaterinoslav. In her diary, Rebbetzin Chana recalled the event in detail.

> The authorities had already confiscated half of our apartment, leaving us only three rooms.... To rent a hall was no longer possible at that time. Our neighbor, an engineer, couldn't bear the Orthodox Jewish practices in our home... so he isolated himself from us, keeping his apartment totally separate from ours. Somehow, however, he heard in town that we wanted to hold a celebration to mark the wedding. For our benefit, he broke through a wall, opening our apartment to his.
>
> Guests came from neighboring towns—and of course, family members did as well, and we received several hundred telegrams. The event at home was attended by representatives of the central Jewish community of our region. Every synagogue, even those with relatively few members, sent representatives, many of them accompanied by their wives. Keep in mind that this took place at a time when any contact with clergymen was forbidden, and such a crime could cost a person his job... Nevertheless, no one held back, and a large number of prominent people came... For two days, special permission was given to receive telegrams in Hebrew, a language already strictly banned.
>
> Besides our pain at being absent from our eldest son's wedding, the atmosphere gave us the sense that we wouldn't be seeing him any time soon. Our longing for him was indescribable, and our anguish was felt by the community.[82]

A huge cake with the names of the community members was presented to the parents of the groom. As a gift for the groom himself, the community had picked something very special, indicative of the young man's penchant for study: a marble antique desk that had belonged to Russian statesman Count Nikolay Pavlovich Ignatyev (1832-1908), inlaid with bronze and gold, along with its original writing tools.[83] The attached commemorative plaque read: "A token of esteem and eternal love, to the exceptional young man... for the day of his marriage to his intended... from the local Jewish religious communities," with the date.

The vigorous dancing continued until dawn. Menachem Mendel's childhood teacher Zalman Vilenkin was particularly joyous, mounting a table and crying out, "I had the merit!" The local non-Chasidic Rabbis were in good spirits; one of them took off his jacket and wore it inside out to increase the joy.

There were seven or eight speeches, but Rabbi Shmuel Schneerson could not recall anything that he thought would be of interest to Menachem Mendel. He simply wrote that Reb Levik's "words this time were very simple. With tears in his eyes, he stated that he was very pained that he was not together with you, but that it was G-d's will."

In a final word of blessing to his son and new daughter-in-law, Reb Levik wrote—switching from Hebrew to a more affectionate and personal Yiddish—"May you always be of one mind, as one person in all things."

The 14th of *Kislev* was a pivotal day in Menachem Mendel Schneerson's life as, without marrying into Rayatz's family, he would not have become the Seventh Lubavitcher Rebbe. As he put it succinctly but powerfully in a 1954 sermon, on his 25th wedding anniversary, "this is the day which bound you"—the Chasidim—"with me."[84]

CHAPTER SIX

STRADDLING WORLDS

1929–1932

Humboldt University, Berlin

Less than two months after their wedding, the young Menachem Mendel and Moussia Schneerson relocated to Berlin, departing from Latvia on Monday 21st January (10th *Shevat*), 1929. For the next three and a quarter years they would spend the university winter and summer semesters in Berlin, boarding with various Orthodox Jewish families;[1] and would shuttle back to Riga to spend extended periods with Rayatz and his family during the High Holidays, *Sukkot* and Passover.

Reflecting on the young couple's decision to live away from the court of Lubavitch, Professor Nehemia Polen has conjectured:

> Rather than seeing Schneerson's relative isolation as indifference to Chasidic culture, it was more likely a decision to develop away from the distractions and conformity of the Chasidic community itself. The Schneersons saw themselves as nobility, indeed, the spiritual aristocracy of the Jewish world. As with most aristocracies, there is not only noblesse oblige and communal concern but also patrician

> reserve and a carefully calibrated distance. At a point in their lives when they were not ready to take on a more public role, the young couple may have chosen to live away from the main Jewish area precisely to ensure that they would not be pestered by overly enthusiastic, curious Chasidim.
>
> The rules are indeed different for royalty, and most commoners have no problem with that fact.[2]

Menachem Mendel's life during this period was multifaceted. He was registered for courses at the University of Berlin for about fifteen hours per week. He was sometimes seen at the *Rabbiner-Seminar* attending the lectures of Rabbi Yechiel Ya'akov Weinberg. While generally introverted, we know that he had various friends and acquaintances, one of whom became a leading figure in Twentieth Century Jewry, as we shall see.

Much of his time was also spent in researching and writing on Torah topics. There are about twenty scholarly treatises in Menachem Mendel's personal notebook (*Reshimot*), from this period[3], demonstrating a sustained interest in creative Rabbinic thinking. Besides his informal, personal study of Talmud,[4] our young scholar also undertook some ambitious research projects, penning detailed indices to a number of Chasidic works,[5] cataloging unpublished Chasidic manuscripts,[6] and it was probably during this period that he penned an extensive line-by-line study of the sources on which Rabbi Shneur Zalman's classic, the *Tanya,* is based.[7] In a regular flow of several letters a year, Reb Levik continued to mold his son's thinking with detailed Kabbalistic readings of Talmudic texts, often touching on theological issues;[8] and Menachem Mendel's scholarly correspondence with the Rogatchover Gaon continued.[9] We also find a number of lengthy public Torah discourses delivered by the young Rebbe-to-be during his times at the court of Lubavitch during the festive month of *Tishrei,* each year from 1929 to 1932.[10]

Let us first turn to Menachem Mendel's academic studies which were, after all, a focal point of the young couple's relocation to Berlin. As with so much of the Seventh Rebbe's life, it is difficult to get a clear picture of what exactly was going on.

The only time he appears to have made a reference to the precise dates of his studies was in a 1962 letter[11]: "I studied science on the university level from 1928 to 1932 in Berlin."[12] Menachem Mendel[13] makes no other substantive[14] reference to his experiences[15] at the university[16] either in his correspondence or his personal notes (*Reshimot*) from the period.[17]

However, from later correspondence with scientists, during the 1960s and 1970s, something can be discerned from the Seventh Rebbe's academic encounters in Berlin. The following passage is one of the most illuminating.

> For many years I studied in the University of Berlin and afterwards in Paris.
>
> My primary fields were the exact sciences such as mathematics, physics, *etc.* I had regular opportunities to meet with experts in these scientific fields (among them Nobel Prize winners). What was bizarre was that, despite the fact that these professors were extremely well versed in the scientific approach, scientific thinking and methodology, nevertheless, when an issue arose in their personal lives, particularly when the solution required a change in what they were accustomed to, or their lifestyle, or a moderation of their natural inclinations *etc.*,—many of them were totally unable to solve the problem scientifically.
>
> More significant was the fact that they were simply unable to see how subjective and unscientific they were in this area, since they genuinely saw themselves as having a rigidly scientific approach.[18]

It is interesting to see how closely Menachem Mendel interacted with his teachers, to the extent that he was aware of issues in their own personal lives. (German professors from that period were characteristically inaccessible and aloof). It is also telling how this very religious young man reacted to the moral dilemmas of his professors. Far from being enamored of the mental detachment and unbiased thinking of these unquestionably great scientists, Menachem Mendel was profoundly unimpressed by the intellectual elite's inability to solve personal problems objectively.

In a 1990 Chasidic discourse, the Seventh Rebbe crystallized his view succinctly. Commenting on the *Midrashic* teaching, *"If someone says,*

'The nations possess wisdom'—believe them; 'The nations have Torah'—do not believe them'" (*Eichah Rabah* 2:13), the Rebbe suggested,

> The reason why Torah is given its name, which means *hora'ah* (direction)—even though in many types of wisdom we seem to find direction—is because the directives implicit in these forms of wisdom are essentially *theoretical* (that, *in principle*, a person should behave in a certain way), but they are not *personalized* directives, since they have no impact on the person. Only Torah, which exerts an actual influence on the person (enabling him to choose something which is at odds with his nature), offers genuine direction.[19]

Without the guiding light of the Torah, he argued, we are prisoners of our own ego. A human being is intrinsically unable, even with elevated forms of wisdom, to choose something which is against his nature or self-interest. The Seventh Rebbe felt that the professors at Berlin University (and later in Paris) were a case in point. They represented the peak of human intellectual achievement, and yet when an issue arose in their personal lives that required "a moderation of their natural inclinations" they were profoundly "subjective and unscientific."

Another instance where the Rebbe made direct reference to German academics whom he knew personally was in regard to the early pioneers of Biblical criticism, in a 1964 letter.

> I trust you know where and by whom Bible criticism originated, and that their criticism was not motivated by pure scholarship. Of course, I am certain that your professors do not share the motivations of the originators of Bible criticism, but, after all, it is not a question of the personality of the teacher, but rather of the approach of the system and ideology. The fact is that in all fields of art and creativity, it is inevitable that the artist's character and sentiments should be expressed in some way in his artistic work, whether it be painting, sculpture or philosophy. It is well known that, insofar as Bible criticism is concerned, it expressed the character and prejudices of those who gave birth to this school, and who have expanded it, and it was their disciples and followers who brought about the terrible Holocaust against the People of the Book only a few years ago.
>
> You need not be taken aback by this harsh expression, which, as already mentioned does not intend, G-d forbid, to cast any personal

> reflection upon those who are your teachers at present, especially as I do not even know them, and we are duty-bound to judge everyone in the scale of merit. However, I happened to have lived in Germany for a number of years, and I have had occasion to meet with and talk to the disciples of the disciples of the founders of the Bible criticism, including Jewish followers of this school, and I have seen the spiritual devastation which it has caused.[20]

Here again we see a certain disillusionment with academic claims to objectivity. All humans—professors included—have motives, and personal bias may significantly influence what is ostensibly presented as an objective study.

From these few glimpses, we get a sense that the young Menachem Mendel was hungry for truth and engaged personally with a wide range of scholars; but he was suspicious of claims to objective detachment, especially in areas relating to moral choice or issues that touched upon the received wisdom of the Jewish religion. Of course, areas where Judaism clashed overtly with science would have easily caught the future Rebbe's attention. When studying astronomy in 1929, if not before, he would have been troubled by the Copernican depiction of the sun at the center of the solar system, with all the planets orbiting around it, *vis-a-vis* the Torah's assertion (later echoed by Ptolemy) that *"the earth stands forever."*[21]

A pathway to solve to such issues, which have perplexed many in the religious world, was reached by Menachem Mendel through an insight penned by his philosophy professor, Hans Reichenbach. Reichenbach had majored in philosophy, but as a practicing engineer and physicist, he was well suited to examining the philosophical implication of theoretical physics.[22]

Menachem Mendel was clearly impressed by Reichenbach's argument on this subject, as he repeated it in numerous letters to scientists and other intellectuals who were perplexed by the notion of a solar orbit and found it a point of departure from observant Judaism.[23] In one striking example from the summer of 1975, a secular Jew who was disturbed by geocentrism argued with Chabad Rabbi Feivel Rimmler that the Rebbe himself, a college-educated man, must surely have rejected this outdated belief. When Rimmler insisted that the Rebbe embraced it, the individual was incredulous. "I did say to you, and am submitting the same in writing by means of this letter," he wrote, "that if the Rebbe would make a public statement to the effect that... since the Talmud states that the sun revolves around the earth, it is therefore his firm belief that the sun does indeed revolve around the earth, that I will: (a) personally observe the laws of *taharat hamishpachah* (family purity), *tefilin* and *Shabbat*; and (b) influence my friends and colleagues to do the same. It is, however, more than obvious to me that the Rebbe will not, in any way, make such a ridiculous statement, because: (a) he does not wish to be labeled as a fool; (b) he himself is not as foolish as some of his ardent but hypnotized followers. I predict, with no hesitation, that I will not hear any more about this matter from you or from the Rebbe or through the press."[24]

In a letter penned on 5th November 1975, the Rebbe stated, for the record, "It is my firm belief that the sun revolves around the earth, as I have also declared *publicly* on various occasions and in discussion with professors specializing in this field of science. In view of the above, I have no objection, of course, if you wish to make this view known to whomever you choose."[25] He then continued (in a separate document) with a brief restatement of Reichenbach's position.

> One of the conclusions of the Theory of Relativity is that when there are two systems, or planets, in motion relative to each other—such as the sun and earth in our case—either view, namely, the sun rotating around the earth, or the earth rotating around the sun, has equal validity....
>
> Every person, including modern scientists, actually has three options to choose from in this matter: (a) that A revolves around B, (b) that B revolves around A, (c) that A and B revolve around each other. But such a choice cannot be dictated by science; it would be one's personal choice and belief.[26]

What frustrated the Rebbe in later years was that the Einstein/Reichenbach view never became the basic position articulated in school textbooks. "This new orientation in science is *ignored*," the Rebbe wrote to Professor Velvel Green in a 1964 letter, "not only on the high school level, but even in specialized studies of astronomy and physics in colleges... Science in many domains is still taught in terms of a scientific orientation which prevailed at the close of the Nineteenth Century."[27]

In a 1971 letter to the *Association of Orthodox Jewish Scientists,* the Rebbe also highlighted the theories of Werner Heisenberg (1901-1976) as contributing to the "new orientation" in science:

> Contemporary science no longer lays claim to absolutes; the principle of probability now reigns supreme... Heisenberg's "principle of indeterminacy" has finally done away with the traditional scientific notion that cause and effect are mechanically linked.... The Nineteenth Century dogmatic, mechanistic, and deterministic attitude of science is gone... The current and universally accepted view of science itself is that science must reconcile itself to the idea that whatever progress it makes, it will always deal with probabilities; not with certainties or absolutes.[28]

The Rebbe felt that contemporary science had shed its arrogant, dogmatic posture, and was open to the notion of multiple ways of looking at things. While this did not mean that science *agreed* with the Torah, it certainly muted the conflict.

Historically, the Torah/science conflict had pushed religious leaders into uncomfortable, defensive positions, often resulting in their tampering with hallowed traditions in order to defend themselves rationally. In its "new orientation," science no longer clashed so fundamentally with Judaism, so this was now unnecessary. As the 1971 letter continues:

> Attempts at reinterpreting the Torah are, of course, the outmoded legacy of the Nineteenth Century and before, when in the face of the dogmatic and deterministic view of science prevailing at that time, a whole apologetic literature was created by well-meaning religious advocates and certain Rabbis, who saw no other way of preserving the Torah heritage in their "enlightened" communities except through tenuous and spurious reinterpretations of certain passages of the Torah in order to accommodate them to the prevailing world outlook. No doubt they knew inwardly that they were suggesting interpretations in Torah which were at variance with *Torat Emet* [true Torah]. But, at least, they "felt" they had no alternative. But surely there is no longer any justification whatever to perpetuate this "inferiority complex!"[29]

It is difficult to gauge to what extent the Seventh Rebbe's refusal to embrace apologetics might have acted as an obstacle to intellectually minded people from coming close to Judaism and Chabad. In the Rebbe's own eyes, though, he was not adopting a fundamentalist position. As he understood it, Einstein, Reichenbach and Heisenberg had made a literalist reading of scripture and Talmud *compatible* with a deep respect for, and acceptance of, science. It was this convergence of worlds in an intellectually rigorous manner that characterized the Seventh Rebbe's outlook.[30]

II.

What acquaintances did Menachem Mendel make in Berlin, outside the walls of the university? Most notably, he began a lifelong friendship with Rabbi Joseph Ber Soloveitchik (1903-1993), who later became a highly influential figure in American Orthodoxy as *Rosh Yeshiva* of Rabbi Isaac Elchanan Theological Seminary at Yeshiva University in New York City. Rabbi Soloveitchik, known to his students simply as "the Rav," stemmed from an important dynasty of scholarly Lithuanian (non-Chasidic) Rabbis. The Rav's illustrious grandfather, Rabbi Chaim Soloveitchik (1853–1918), father of the "conceptual approach" which dominates higher Talmudic learning to this day, worked closely with the Fifth and Sixth Lubavitcher Rebbes,[31] and he had given *semicha* (Rabbinic ordination) to Menachem Mendel's own father, Reb Levik.[32]

In addition to their family ties, the two young men had much in common. They both had mastered the Talmud at a young age and were known for their encyclopedic recall and penetrating analysis; and they were both the first in their respective dynasties to venture beyond the *Beit Midrash* and study in the cultural epicenter of Berlin University.[33]

Surprisingly, despite his decidedly Lithuanian background, Rabbi Soloveitchik had a strong Chabad influence in his early years that molded his theological and philosophical leanings for his entire life.[34] During his childhood, his father had served in Khaslavichy, a town in White Russia which was home to a predominantly Chabad community, and, as a result, Chabad Chasid Baruch Reisberg was hired to be Joseph Ber's teacher. Reisberg took the opportunity to teach the Rabbi's son *Tanya*, the core text of Chabad Chasidut, which continued for the better part of a year until this "underground activity" was discovered and the teacher promptly fired. But the spirituality and depth of Chasidut touched the boy and remained with him.[35] Rabbi Soloveitchik's biographer, Aaron Rakeffet, has argued, "All that we know that the Rav is unique for, the *hashkafah* [worldview], the *drush* [homiletics], the philosophy, everything that makes the Rav, the Rav; everything that placed him in the Y.U. world, if I can put it that way, is a result of that Chabad Rebbi." [36]

Rabbi Soloveitchik had arrived in Berlin in 1926, after completing three semesters of political science in his hometown at the University of Warsaw, and began studies in philosophy, political economy and Semitics,[37] later graduating with a doctorate in 1932 on the philosophy of Hermann Cohen.[38] At some point, probably soon after Menachem Mendel arrived in Berlin, he heard that the young Joseph Ber was residing in the same town, and sought him out. Arriving at Rabbi Soloveitchik's apartment, the future Rebbe said, "My name is Mendel Schneerson. I am here to study in the university. I hardly know anybody in the city. I heard you are here. I know of your name. I came to introduce myself."[39]

The two men soon became acquainted. Menachem Mendel informed his father-in-law, Rabbi Yosef Yitzchak Schneersohn, how much he was impressed with the Rav, as we see from a 1941 letter: "Regarding *Ha-Rav Ha-Gaon* Rabbi Yosef Dov... while he was in Berlin, my son-in-law... told me about his tremendous greatness in learning."[40]

Rabbi Soloveitchik similarly recalled to a number of his students years later, how much he was impressed by the Seventh Rebbe's phenomenal memory, as well as his exemplary piety as a student, attending the *mikvah* every day and conducting regular, personal fasts.[41] He was also struck by how Menachem Mendel managed to retain the garb of an East European Jew in Berlin—beard, beret and all, in contrast to other students stemming from Russian and Polish Rabbinic homes, who made more efforts to blend in. According to some accounts, the future Rav and Rebbe did not see each other that often, though they would sometimes meet in one of the coffee houses and discuss politics;[42] but in a 1983 response to the editors of *Beit Yitzchak* (a Torah publication of RIETS and Yeshiva University), the Rebbe wrote that "the ties of friendship, appreciation and mutual admiration" between Rabbi Soloveitchik and himself were "far greater than you know."[43]

A couple of anecdotes have reached us from this period. In one, Rabbi Soloveitchik recalled how the future Rebbe would often bring a volume of *gemara* (Talmud) to the university. From time to time he would look into the *gemara* during lectures, presumably when the material was not of particular interest to him. (Recall that the Rebbe was a non-matriculating "occasional student" who was not required to take any examinations.) On one occasion, the future Rebbe's *gemara* study caught the eye of the professor, who was somewhat insulted. "Perhaps Schneerson could repeat for us what I have just explained," the professor challenged him. Almost forty years later Rabbi Soloveitchik recalled how, to the professor's surprise, the Rebbe proceeded to review the content of the class adeptly. "And what's more," the Rav concluded, "he could have repeated over to you the *gemara* as well." [44]

On another occasion the Rav recalled how the future Rebbe had, one Purim, imbibed himself with liquor, as is customary on the festival, and shedding his usual, introverted shell, began to do a little "outreach." As the hour approached midnight, Menachem Mendel stood on a chair in the street, and began to preach a Purim sermon to the students—an activity which, in fact, required a police permit. He was soon apprehended by the authorities and temporarily detained. Joseph Ber was called for assistance and soon secured Menachem Mendel's release. Jokingly, he teased, "You have been to jail. Now you can become a Rebbe."[45]

In fact, however, the young Joseph Ber thought it unlikely that Mendel Schneerson would ever assume a leadership role, being extremely introverted and "hidden"—people did not know who he was.[46] Years later, Rabbi Soloveitchik related to his disciple Rabbi Zevulun Charlop (b. 1930), that of the numerous great young minds that were drawn to Berlin from Rabbinic families, "If you asked me who I thought was going to be successful, who was going to be a leader, the last one I would have picked would be Rabbi Schneerson."[47]

Another context where the two young rabbis interacted was in the circles of Rabbi Chaim Heller (1879-1960), who resided in Berlin at the time. Rabbi Heller was a one-of-a-kind scholar, to the extent that his genius rendered him inaccessible to all but the greatest minds. Having mastered the Talmud at a young age—he was almost totally self-taught—Rabbi Heller sought secular knowledge and completed a doctorate at the University of Wurzburg. After a number of unsuccessful Rabbinic positions from 1912 to 1922, he moved back to Germany to establish an elitist academy, the *Bet ha-Midrash ha-Elyon* (Higher

Study Hall). In the Germanic fashion, the *Bet ha-Midrash* stressed a scientific approach to Bible and Rabbinic literature, which focused on the critical examination of texts to produce "corrected versions," based on extensive research of all extant handwritten manuscripts.[48] Rabbi Heller also had a particular interest in Biblical Criticism, which he spent much time refuting on academic grounds.[49]

The *Bet ha-Midrash ha-Elyon* was not a particularly successful enterprise, since its abnormally high standards in both Torah and academic studies precluded most students from attending; but we know that both the young Rabbis Soloveitchik and Schneerson were a regular presence. Rabbi Heller would refer to them as his two "lion cubs."[50]

In later life, after Rabbi Heller emigrated to America to escape Nazi Germany, Rabbi Soloveitchik was extremely close to him, personally raising funds so that his Rabbi could be supported financially, through employment at Rabbi Isaac Elchanan Theological Seminary.[51] Rabbi Heller was very much a "father figure" to Rabbi Soloveitchik while in Berlin, but his impact on the Rebbe is unclear.[52] The phenomenon of a fervently Orthodox, bearded Jew who had total recall in the Talmuds, but was also fluent in Greek, Arabic and Assyrian, and heavily immersed in academic study, must surely have made a striking impression on the young Menachem Mendel.

Ironically, while the Seventh Rebbe did not, as a whole, embrace *Wissenschaft des Judentums,* the scientific-critical approach to Jewish texts and sources, he did appreciate and even utilize some of its methods, particularly the so called lower textual criticism practiced by Rabbi Heller, to a far greater extent than the Rav. In his scholarly lectures and writings, the Rav followed his ancestral "Brisker" approach to Talmudic study, which showed virtually no interest in scientific methods. The Rebbe's discourses, on the other hand, are highly attentive to what one might call "modern" concerns. In his eight hundred lectures on *Rashi's* commentary to the Torah, there is a sustained interest in textual variants of *Rashi,* critical editions, and a proposed system of how to establish the correct text.[53] In fact, the whole thrust of the *Rashi sichot*—which seek to uncover an underlying methodology in the commentary and establish a "literal reading" of scripture, outside the orbit of the traditional commentaries—is a characteristically scientific endeavor.[54] The Rebbe also encouraged the publication of new editions of *Rashi* with multiple textual variants, as well as a "first edition" of *Tanya* from multiple manuscripts with all variants listed.[55] He loved the Frankel edition of Maimonides' *Mishneh Torah,* which contained an extensive list of textual variants and line-by-line indices to hundreds of commentaries,[56] and in his discourses on Maimonides' works, for example, he showed a keen eye for minor textual nuances and their possible sources, parallel readings and new translations of the original Arabic texts.[57] In general, he had a strong penchant for sourcing texts, extensive footnotes, and indices, all of which reflect a partial acceptance of the scientific approach to study. It seems likely, then, that many of these interests were nourished from the Rebbe's contact with Rabbi Chaim Heller, as well as his informal attendance at the Hildesheimer Seminary, where *Wissenschaft des Judentums* was strongly emphasized.

As with so many aspects of the Seventh Rebbe's life and thought, his approach to the scientific study of Jewish texts represented an interesting hybrid between traditional and modern values. For example, contrary to modern scholars, the Rebbe did not favor the "correction" of an existing, widely used classical text (*girsa ha-nefutzah*). Even when elements of these texts can be traced back to copyist errors *etc.*, the fact remains that generations of Jews pored over the *girsa ha-nefutzah* and that sometimes *halachic* authorities had hallowed it as sacred, so it ought to be preserved as the main text, he sometimes argued, with variants recorded in footnotes.[58] Correcting a text also displays a misplaced measure of self-confidence, that one is certain one is right, and that cannot be categorically assured.[59] Similarly, when modern scholars uncovered handwritten documents from Maimonides' *Mishneh Torah,* which proved that the common text of his legal rulings was faulty, the Rebbe did not accept the notion that Jewish law should be amended in accordance with these findings.[60]

While he appreciated certain usages of *Wissenschaft des Judentums,* Menachem Mendel was generally unenamored of the synthesis of *Torah im Derech Eretz* (Torah and secular wisdom), which typified German Jewry. With an already acculturated population, the emphasis on secular studies appeared to him as more of a concession than something desirable. Later in the United States, the Rebbe strongly discouraged the Hirschian model, as we see from a 1962 letter.[61]

> I must say emphatically that to apply his [Hirsch's] approach to the American scene will not serve the interests of Orthodoxy in America.

With all due respect to his philosophy and approach which were very forceful and effective in his time and in his milieu, Rabbi Hirsch wrote for an audience and youth which was brought up on philosophical studies, and which was permeated with all sorts of doctrines and schools of thought and disciplined in the art of intellectual research, *etc.* Thus it was necessary to enter into long philosophical discussions to point out the fallacy of each and every thought and theory which is incompatible with the Torah and *mitzvot.* There was no harm in using this approach, inasmuch as the harm had already been there, and if it could strengthen Jewish thought and practice, it was useful, and to that extent, effective.

However, here in the United States we have a different audience and a youth which radically differs from the type whom Rabbi Hirsch had addressed originally. American youth is not of a philosophic turn of mind. They have neither the patience nor the training to delve into long philosophical discussions, and to evaluate different systems and theories when they are introduced to all sorts of ideas, including those that are diametrically opposed to the Torah and *mitzvot,* and there are many of them, since there are many falsehoods but only one truth, this approach can only bring them to a greater measure of confusion. Whether or not the final analysis and conclusions will be accepted by them, one thing is certain, that the seeds of doubt will have multiplied in their minds, since each theory has its prominent proponent bearing impressive titles of professors, PhD's, etc.

Besides the essential point and approach is *"Thou shalt be wholehearted with G-d, thy G-d"* (*Deut.*18:13). The surest way of remaining a faithful Jew is not through philosophy but through the actual experience of the Jewish way of life in the daily life, fully and wholeheartedly. As for the principle *"know what to answer the heretic"* (*Avot* 2:16), this is surely only one particular aspect, and certainly does not apply to everyone. Why introduce every Jewish boy and girl to the various heretics that ever lived?[62]

III.

Where else was the young Menachem Mendel to be found in Berlin? While he was not formally enrolled in the Hildesheimer Seminary, he was noticed there daily attending the lectures of Rabbi Yechiel Ya'akov Weinberg, who would give an in-depth Talmud class four times a week for two and a half hours. While he refrained from speaking in class, standing at the back by a *shtender* (lecturn), Menachem Mendel often approached Rabbi Weinberg to discuss some Torah after the class, sometimes for a few hours.[63]

For a number of years he was seen regularly each Sabbath at the synagogue of Rabbi Yissachar Berish Rubin, the Dombrova Rebbe (1893-1952), a descendant of the Ropshitz Chasidic Dynasty, who had fled to Berlin after the First World War. One Sabbath, Menachem Mendel had appeared in the synagogue and characteristically tried to maintain a low profile. He simply took a *siddur* (prayer book) and prayed inconspicuously, without introducing himself to anyone. The custom in the synagogue was to invite new worshippers to be called with an *aliyah* to the Torah. When Menachem Mendel was asked if he would like to make a donation to the synagogue in honor of the *aliyah*, he pledged two marks, apparently a generous sum. Later in the week he stopped off to give the donation (handling money being forbidden on the Sabbath), and his name and donation was recorded in the synagogue ledger. Perusing the ledger a few days later, Rabbi Rubin was excited to see the name Schneerson, and rebuked his *gabbai* (sexton), Moshe Rand, for not introducing the young man to him. "Didn't you realize that Schneerson is a relative of the *Baal Ha-Tanya?"* he said. The next Sabbath Menachem Mendel was introduced to the Rabbi, and a warm relationship blossomed. "You cannot imagine what a man your father was," the Seventh Rebbe told Rabbi Rubin's son, Naftali, at a meeting some fifty years later.[64]

Another friend of Menachem Mendel from this period[65] was businessman Itche Meir Furstenberg, a descendant of Gerer Chasidim, who later moved to New York. Rabbi Chazkel Besser (1923-2010),[66] an acquaintance of Furstenberg, remembered him as a sharp, critical man, knowledgeable in Torah who liked to "shmooze" and smoke cigars. In 1929, when Rabbi Aharon Rokeach (1880-1957), the fourth Belzer Rebbe, visited Berlin for eye treatment, Menachem Mendel suggested to Furstenberg that they go together and join the many visitors who had come to welcome the Rebbe—on condition, of course, that not a word be mentioned about Menachem Mendel's identity. Having just undergone optical treatment, the Belzer Rebbe's eyes remained closed and he looked down as he greeted a long line of assembled guests, shaking each person's hand through a towel. When Menachem Mendel approached, dressed in an ordinary suit jacket, the Belzer Rebbe looked up, removed the towel and shook him directly by the hand.

"Who is this young man?" the Belzer Rebbe inquired.

"*A giveinlicher yungerman* (an ordinary person)," Menachem Mendel replied, trying to remain inconspicuous.

Refusing to ignore his intuition, the Belzer Rebbe persisted, "It is a warm hand, young man. From us, you cannot hide."

At this point, with Menachem Mendel's cover blown, the Rabbi Rokeach was informed, "This is the Lubavitcher Rebbe's son-in-law."

"Yes, Yes. I see. I see," the Belzer Rebbe said, pleased that his suspicions had been confirmed. "I felt that this was a refined hand." The Belzer Rebbe and future Lubavitcher Rebbe continued to talk for a few minutes, and Menachem Mendel even participated in the custom of receiving *shirayim* (leftover food) from the Rebbe.[67]

Years later the Seventh Rebbe recalled his impressions of Rabbi Aharon Rokeach's spiritual intensity. "He was form-without-matter, a man totally unencumbered by the physical body," the Rebbe told Rabbi Aharon's successor, Rabbi Yissachar Dov Rokeach (b. 1948), in a 1973 meeting.[68]

While in Berlin, Menachem Mendel also spent much time with his family. Rayatz would make the effort to stop off in Berlin during his extensive travels and spend time with his new son-in-law.[69] From the summer of 1929 until the summer of 1930 when Rayatz was away in Israel and the United States,[70] Moussia's mother, sisters and nephew, Shalom Ber, who did not join the Sixth Rebbe on his trip, relocated to Berlin so that the family could be close together. Even years later, when Shalom Ber's relationship with his uncle soured (over the issue of succession and, later on, over the ownership of the Chabad Library), Shalom Ber fondly remembered his days in Berlin and how Mendel and Moussia had cared for him like parents, taking him regularly to the zoo.

Another family member who joined the young couple in Berlin was Menachem Mendel's youngest brother, Leibel. After Rayatz and his family left Russia with Menachem Mendel in 1927, Leibel had stayed in Leningrad to continue his studies at the university. Leibel had lost his passion for Communism that captivated him earlier in his youth, but this rendered him a target when the Soviets began to eliminate dissident communists in the late 1920s. In the spring of 1930 he managed to leave Russia[71] with a fake passport, bearing the name Mark Gurari—a name he used on formal documents for the rest of his life—and he arrived at Mendel and Moussia's home afflicted with the deadly disease, typhus. At great personal risk of infection, his brother and sister-in-law nursed him back to health, and they spent the following two years together in Berlin. Even though Leibel had wandered far from traditional paths,[72] he remained extremely close to his brother, and it must have been a great joy for Menachem Mendel to be reunited with at least part of his family. It may have also given him some hope that his parents, too, would be able to leave. Leibel did not formally register with the university (in the Department of Specialist Mathematics) until shortly before his brother left in April 1933, so it is unclear exactly what he was doing at the time, though presumably he continued his mathematical studies and research. One year after Menachem Mendel and Moussia left Berlin, Leibel emigrated to Israel along with Regina Milgram (1910-1997), a Russian-Jewish laboratory technician from Berlin, whom he married in 1939.

IV.

Some truly fascinating insights into Menachem Mendel's inner life have surfaced recently in his correspondence with Rayatz, first published in 2010.[73] The Sixth and future Seventh Rebbes were in very close contact during this period; between 1929 until 1932 alone, Rayatz penned some seventy-two letters to his son-in-law and daughter. In contrast to Reb Levik's letters, which were almost exclusively devoted to Torah thoughts, Rayatz's communications were extremely personal. We get a strong sense of what a thoughtful and caring man he was, and how much his relationship with his new son-in-law meant to him. The few letters of reply from Menachem Mendel that have been published are also extremely revelatory—a glimpse of the future Rebbe's self-perception, his concerns, and his spiritual leanings. Material like this is extremely rare. In his fifty years of public work the Seventh Rebbe seldom spoke or wrote about himself.

From the correspondence, we see how important it was for Rayatz to be intimately connected with the personal lives of his family. The Sixth Rebbe chronicles his travels and experiences in detail, along with their emotional ups and downs. He expects Menachem Mendel to reciprocate and is disappointed when requests to his son-in-law to share his life experiences are not forthcoming. Menachem Mendel, by his own confession, lived in the world of thought, and the little details of everyday life were not important to him. "The reason I have not written," he writes in the winter of 1930, "which I am sure without my letter you could fathom for yourself, is that it is difficult for me to find interesting events in my life to tell you. Just to fill a piece of paper with incidental details, to write a letter for the sake of writing a letter—why should I steal your time for that?"[74]

Rayatz is persistent. "I want to clarify," he writes back, "that when you will contemplate the truth as it is, what a deeply personal relationship ought to exist between us, you will always find something interesting that will extend beyond one page."[75]

But Menachem Mendel's world is the world of ideas, not of events and feelings. In his next letter, which represents a fascinating insight into the Seventh Rebbe's self-image, he attempts to clarify the matter.

> The reason why I have not written is due to the lack of interesting events to report. There are people for whom the central, overwhelming focus of their lives is in the world of thought, the world of ideas, and their main activities—activity being the sign of life—are focused inwards, to the "*world set in their hearts*" (*Ecc.* 3:11), and not to the outside world surrounding them.
>
> After this introduction, I must say that, while I do not consider it to be a particular virtue, it seems that—whether as a result of my natural disposition or outside influences—I am such a person. For as long as I can remember, there has been a paucity of interesting *events* in my life, things that I found personally engaging.[76]

This, however, does not stop Rayatz from showering forth his emotions on paper: love and affection, repeated blessings for children and happy marriage, as well as his frustrations. In a letter penned after the festival of *Shavuot*, 1930, Rayatz wishes his son-in-law that "you and your wife, my precious daughter, should have a pleasurable life, with love and affection."[77] In a letter to Moussia on her twenty-ninth birthday, Rayatz writes, "My precious daughter! For everything in this world there is a limit and end, but the deep love of parents has no limit," and he blesses her to have "fine, healthy, bright children."[78] In a letter to Menachem Mendel the following year, Rayatz's affections continue to gush forth, "If my thoughts about you went straight onto paper, I mean if thoughts themselves could write, without the need of an actual hand,

I would already have heaps of letters."[79] In another letter Rayatz signs off, "I am your father-in-law... who loves you at every moment."[80]

Sometimes we find Rayatz expressing his distress. In the spring of 1930, Rayatz writes of his "deep, great pain... that you did not merit to see the face of the 'Holy of Holies' [Rashab], his face literally shining with G-dly light, the Divine presence resting on him... nor to see the Chasidim in Lubavitch, their prayer and worship.... What an awful shame (*chaval chaval*) that you did not see all this."[81] To Moussia he shares mixed emotions of visiting the Western Wall in Jerusalem, "I cried earnestly over the fall of our Lubavitch. I kissed the stones of the Western Wall with a bittersweet pleasure."[82] More than once, Rayatz expresses his concerns at the thought of his religious son-in-law walking the streets in what was becoming an increasingly dangerous city for Jews, "I am always thinking about how you walk in the city, whether you are taking the necessary precautions."[83]

Rayatz also showed, on one occasion, a fondness for allegory and riddle which did not seem to engage Menachem Mendel. In a letter from the summer of 1929, Rayatz concludes, in a postscript, "Contemplate well the fine pearl which G-d has given you for many long, good years, physically and spiritually."[84] Receiving no response, he repeats the following winter, "Regarding the fine gift, the precious pearl, do you still not understand what I mean? Or did you already fathom my riddle?"[85]

Menachem Mendel's reply is brief: "Regarding the 'fine pearl,' I still do not understand to what this refers."[86]

Rayatz has no choice other than to decipher his own riddle: "The fine pearl which G-d has given you, *is my daughter, your honorable wife.* (That was what I implied in my letter, but you did not discern what I intimated)."[87]

Rayatz also takes much interest in his new son-in-law's daily routine. "Write to me in detail your daily schedule," he requests.[88] On another occasion, "I would like to know what you are learning, which tractate? What are you learning in Chasidut? How much time per day, i.e., in each twenty-four hours? Do you have any fixed study times? What are they?"[89] In a 1932 letter Menachem Mendel reports that he is currently learning tractate *Bava Batra,* but that "regarding a fixed daily schedule, since coming from Russia, I still have not managed this." He also confesses to having challenges in his learning, "because of mental exhaustion, or from feeling distracted."[90]

Of particular interest are the future Rebbe's spiritual leanings. In a typically unassuming fashion, Menachem Mendel expresses his yearnings for an arousal to *teshuvah* (return to G-d).

> The month of *Elul* is coming imminently, which is the month of preparation [for the High Holidays] and *teshuvah*. What, then, is the way, and what is the advisable method, that will affect me, so that I can ultimately have a heartfelt sense of *yirat Shamayim* [fear of Heaven]—tangibly in the here and now, so that I actually feel the change?[91]

In response to a request from Menachem Mendel for a blessing to understand Chasidut, Rayatz conveys his wishes, "You should be blessed with a genuine grasp of Chasidut, to become one with it, to study it, to understand it, and to observe it."[92]

Menachem Mendel is extremely grateful, and explains how much Rayatz's blessing means to him.

> The reason why I asked you for a blessing to understand Chasidut... is simply because I pine for it. I wrote a request to Your Holiness for this blessing because I believe that if you desire something from the depths of your heart and being, then, whether it be through a blessing or through prayer, you will influence on High that all these things should take effect down here in this world, in me.[93]

At the end of 1931, Menachem Mendel posed a question to his father-in-law about the very essence of Chabad identity. In Berlin, Menachem Mendel had been exposed to the courts of non-Chabad Rebbes.[94] These strands of Chasidut, stemming mainly from Poland and Galicia, seemed to Menachem Mendel to better capture the spirit of the movement's founder Rabbi Israel Ba'al Shem Tov. They did not focus to such a great extent on the in-depth study of Chasidic wisdom; and just as the Ba'al Shem Tov had been known as a miracle worker, the Chasidim of these movements made much emphasis on their own Rebbes' miraculous powers—something which was more muted in Chabad.

Menachem Mendel's penchant for intellectual honesty could not help him wonder and inquire of his father-in-law, "At first glance, the path and teachings of Chasidut taught by the Rebbes of Vohlynia-Poland-Galicia seem closer to the path and teachings of the Baal Shem Tov's Chasidut than the teachings of Chabad, especially in the emphasis on miracle-working."[95]

The question prompted a fifteen-page reply from Rayatz, rich in anecdotal history of the movement, with many accounts of why miracle-working became unimportant in the Chabad system.[96] Menachem Mendel was ecstatic. His preference for a dialogue of ideas rather than feelings had finally been met, and he found the material gripping.

> From the depths of the heart I thank you for this precious gift. May I be so bold as to make an earnest suggestion from Your Holiness—if a request is necessary and if it will help. I am strengthened by the hope that from time to time you will honor and delight me with letters like this.
>
> I lack a lot of knowledge about the background of Chasidut and its history.... and so with every fact that I gain in this area, I rejoice "*as if finding a great prize*" (Ps. 119:162).[97]

Still, the issue of miracles bothered him. In the current day and age, wouldn't stories that conveyed a sense of the supernatural be helpful to bring Jews closer to Judaism? Intellectual arguments alone did not seem to be sufficient—especially in Germany.

> I cannot restrain myself from requesting additional explanation about a subject that has puzzled me for a long time. Again and again, I hear people say that "In Chabad, we have no interest in miracles," *etc.* I found a similar sentiment expressed in your letter....
>
> This might have been appropriate for the early Chasidim; they certainly had no need of such stories, for their hearts and minds were pure. But nowadays, the pressures of the times *etc.*, have diminished people's spiritual sensitivities, and they are engulfed by material concerns. They perceive everything in a very materialistic way, and their souls are desensitized to the sublime and the lofty.
>
> It seems difficult to fix this through ideas alone... On the other hand, miracles, and stories of the wonders performed by *tzadikim* inspire people to rid themselves from the focus on material mat-

> ters. They will jar even a lowly soul, or someone who has spiritually fallen.[98]

No response from Rayatz to this request is printed, but in these lines we can already discern the Seventh Rebbe's creativity and sensitivity to the needs of a spiritually numbed generation. If the old approach no longer works, Menachem Mendel argued, then we need to re-examine it. It was this bold willingness to introduce new pedagogic methods suitable for the contemporary milieu that would make the Seventh generation of Chabad under his leadership so hugely influential.

V.

During these years, Menachem Mendel's relationship with Rayatz blossomed in different ways. The Sixth Rebbe appointed his son-in-law to numerous missions and tasks, such as to investigate Jewish youth groups in Germany,[99] to arrange the sale of Rayatz's *chametz* before Passover,[100] to evaluate the character and level of scholarship of a candidate for *Rosh Yeshivah*,[101] to arrange transfer of funds for the printing of *Tanya*,[102] to attend meetings on Rayatz's behalf,[103] to make diplomatic efforts for the remainder of Rayatz's library to be released from Moscow, to make copies of manuscripts and library catalogues in Berlin,[104] and to safeguard precious Chabad manuscripts during Rayatz's travels.

Regarding this last point, the Seventh Rebbe made an interesting reference in a 1976 sermon. When Rayatz traveled to the Holy Land and America in 1929, he left a precious collection of his father's manuscripts (*ketavim*) with Menachem Mendel for safekeeping. Without receiving permission from Rayatz, Menachem Mendel immediately made his own copy of the manuscripts, at great personal expense. Later, after the Schneersons escaped Nazi Europe to America, Menachem Mendel's unauthorized copy remained the only source for many of these texts— especially the most precious series of Rashab's works, known as *Hemshech Ayin Beit*. This collection of one hundred and forty-four sequential discourses was penned by the Fifth Rebbe from 1912 to 1917 and is considered to be the most articulate and "wondrous" of all Chabad Chasidic discourses.

> When my father-in-law, the Rebbe, traveled from his home [in 1929] he sought someone whom he could rely upon to look after the

> *ketavim* and return them intact. It seems that he had no choice other than to give them to me!
>
> When I saw that among the *ketavim* was the *Hemshech Ayin Beit*, I immediately made a photostat of the entire series....
>
> For many years previously I had already been suspected—not a baseless suspicion, but a substantiated one, with actual evidence—that if any *ketavim* would reach my hand, especially ones which the public were not aware of, I would copy them. So when my father-in-law left the *ketavim* with me, he presumably realized that I would copy them.[105]

Of course, this was a justification after the fact. Menachem Mendel was actually so concerned that his copy had come through dubious means, that he hesitated to publish *Hemshech Ayin Beit* for almost fifty years. Even in 1976, when he finally sanctioned its publication, he requested that every Chasid participate with a small donation so that the entire community should bear this huge responsibility together.

In addition to correspondence and various missions for Rayatz, Menachem Mendel spent the festival months of Tishrei, and Nissan each year by the side of his Rebbe, leaving Berlin for an extended period.[106] From 1929 onwards, Menachem Mendel penned a diary of these experiences, with detailed observations of Rayatz's personal customs and the stories he related, both publicly and privately. The diary, published posthumously in 2006 (as *Reshimot Ha-Yoman*),[107] is a remarkable document, clearly written by someone who had been thrust into the very heart of the Lubavitch court and was privy to its most hallowed secrets. In its first page, Rayatz shares with Menachem Mendel a Chasidic discourse he heard in his dreams, as well as a conversation with his departed father, who had appeared to him in a vision.[108] The future Rebbe records secrets of how Rashab and Rayatz conducted themselves in private, and stories of the previous Chabad Rebbes which were not public knowledge[109] (such as Rashab's visits to Dr. Sigmund Freud for the treatment of depression).[110] Throughout the fifty or so pages of diary entries from the years 1929 to 1932, one gets the very strong sense that Menachem Mendel, who was not brought up in the house of a Rebbe, is gradually being "installed" into the prevailing "royal family" of Chabad.

Polen reflects astutely on the broader significance of the *Reshimot*:

> Signaling his induction into the Chabad leadership circle... he received transmission of practices that were not well known or deliber-

> ately kept from public view, making him a true member of Chabad's spiritual elite. And his faithful and lovingly meticulous recording of the practices, vignettes, and stories, reflects his desire to internalize that elite status, to inhabit it from within.[111]

In the diary we also find occasional records of intimate conversations between Rayatz and Menachem Mendel. In one entry, from the end of 1932, the Sixth Rebbe encourages his son-in-law to begin the extremely rare pietistic practice of donning four different pairs of *tefilin* each day. The donning of one or at most two pairs, following the opinions of *Rashi* and *Rabenu Tam*, is normative Jewish practice,[112] but the two additional, non-obligatory types of *tefilin*, which follow the opinions of *Ra'avad*[113] and *Shimusha Rabah*,[114] are strongly discouraged unless the worshipper has reached an exceptional degree of self-mastery.[115]

"Do you have *tefilin* of *Shimusha Rabah*," Rayatz inquired of Menachem Mendel, less than a year after the future Rebbe's thirtieth birthday.

"Is this something appropriate for me?" Menachem Mendel asked, fully cognizant of the high spiritual refinement required for this practice.

"For you," Rayatz replied, "everything is appropriate."[116]

"I was apprehensive," the Seventh Rebbe recalled some two decades later, "but when the Rebbe told me to do it, I began. The responsibility was on the Rebbe's shoulders."[117]

Another fascinating exchange from that period, recorded in the diary, concerns the interpretation of a dream which Rayatz shared with his son-in-law.

"For the dream I had today, we need to say a *le'chaim*," Rayatz said one Sunday morning, early in 1932. "Give me a kiss, make a *le'chaim* and learn Chasidut!"

"I wanted to kiss him on the hand," Menachem Mendel writes in his diary, "but he pointed to his forehead. I also kissed him on the cheek."

Rayatz began to relate the dream. "My father, the Rebbe [Rashab], said to me: 'Why are you miserable? In your house it is bright at night!'"

"I woke up," Rayatz continued, "and the moonlight was shining in the room. But I thought, 'That can't be what he's talking about.' So I went to the library and saw you immersed in studying."

"Then I realized what he meant."[118]

VI.

Another interesting development during this period, which became an annual occurrence during the festival month of *Tishrei*, was the emergence of Menachem Mendel as a public speaker in the Chabad community. This began during *Tishrei* of 1929 (5690) when his presence at the court of Lubavitch in Riga in Rayatz's absence (he was in America), drew significant attention. Naturally, the Rebbe's new son-in-law was closely scrutinized by the Chasidim, especially as he was known to be studying at the university.

Of particular interest is Rabbi Eliyahu Chaim Althaus' detailed memoir to Rayatz of these events, which represent Menachem Mendel Schneerson's first exposure as a man of spiritual stature in the public eye. On the morning before *Rosh Hashanah*, when the congregation assembled at 5 a.m. to recite *Selichot* (penitential prayers), the absence of Rayatz pained everyone deeply. Althaus noted, "while reciting Psalms quietly, the first who was unable to hold himself back from bursting into tears—which broke our spirits to the core—was the Rebbe's son-in-law *shlita*."[119]

Regarding *Rosh Hashanah* itself, where around one-hundred people gathered to pray in Rayatz's synagogue, Althaus recalled:

> We had tremendous pleasure and satisfaction from the prayers of the Rebbe's son-in-law, Rabbi Menachem Mendel *shlita*, who, during the first evening service, extended his personal prayers for more than two and a half hours,[120] shedding many tears and cries that emerged from the innermost recesses of his heart. In general, his conduct on *Rosh Hashanah* was wondrous. I closely observed his [*mikvah*] immersions, the prayers, the way he spoke and ate, drank and slept, and I thank G-d for the great kindness He has done to our community....
>
> He categorically refused all the honors usually given to the Rebbe *shlita*. The Rebbetzins encouraged him, not once or twice, and I also tried, speaking with him earnestly at length, urging him to be honored with *maftir* or to recite the verses before the *shofar* is blown—until I realized that he genuinely didn't desire any of this.

In a letter written to Rayatz after *Sukkot*, Althaus again praised Menachem Mendel.

> One night, the community gathered in the Rebbe *shlita's sukkah*, and Rabbi Menachem Mendel *shlita*, sat with us. We heard many beautiful things from his mouth, and it brought great pleasure to us all...
>
> On the night of *Shemini Atzeret*, there was a large *kiddush* in the Rebbe *shlita's sukkah* in which the whole community participated until late into the night.... Rabbi Menachem Mendel *shlita* took a lot to drink, but in his great humility, he acted very discreetly. He spoke for hours on end, without interruption, saying words of Chasidut, spiced with teachings of the sages, *Kabbalah* and *Gematriot*, in his father's style. To the ears of all the listeners, it was sweet and beautiful. There was tremendous excitement among everyone.
>
> The following day, news spread in town of how he had spoken, and of his incredible talents—replete with the inevitable but harmless exaggerations. Now all the critics and cynics had been silenced! People were saying to each other, "The Rebbe has taken a son-in-law that is befitting for him."
>
> As a result of all the talk, a huge crowd gathered for *hakafot* the following night. Before *hakafot* there was a large *kiddush* hosted by the old Rebbetzin... Rabbi Menachem Mendel *shlita* sat at the head and he spoke for four hours straight!... All the Chasidim remained until two in the morning, and as they left people were saying, "In my life I have never seen or heard anything like this..."
>
> I have no words to describe the great name he has acquired for himself this last visit to our town. It pains me greatly that the Rebbe *shlita* did not see any of this, and that you will never see it. Because so long as he [Menachem Mendel] is alongside the Rebbe *shlita*, he is humbled like a single flame in the presence of a torch of fire.
>
> Believe me, precious Rebbe, I am not exaggerating when I say that I cannot fathom him. His piety grows and strengthens from hour to hour, but it is all so hidden and unassuming. It is something extremely special.

Menachem Mendel had made a fantastic debut. The Althaus account represents the first historical account of the future Rebbe inspiring Chasidim at the court of Lubavitch.

In the *Reshimot*, the Seventh Rebbe's notebook, there is no record of what he said on this occasion, but we do have detailed content of his public speeches in subsequent years: A lecture in the hall of *Agudat*

Yisrael during *Sukkot* of 1930 (22 pages),[121] a *farbrengen* in the Yeshivah in Otwock, Poland during *Sukkot* of 1931 (73 pages),[122] and a *farbrengen* in the Yeshivah in Riga, during *Sukkot* of 1932 (67 pages).[123]

While the surrounding circumstances are unclear, Menachem Mendel and Moussia left Berlin permanently in the spring of 1932. In all likelihood, Menachem Mendel's academic progress in Germany was halted by the rise of the Nazi party, which had been making political inroads since 1930 and won huge gains shortly after Menachem Mendel left the country, in July 1932. When Hitler was sworn in as chancellor in January of the following year, Menachem Mendel's former professors of Jewish descent were dismissed, and some of his other non-Jewish professors joined the Nazi party. Besides a brief visit for a couple of weeks in the summer of 1932, presumably to collect their belongings and complete any unfinished business, Menachem Mendel and Moussia did not return to Berlin.

The future Rebbe spent the remainder of 1932 in close proximity to Rayatz. During the summer, Moussia's younger sister Sheina (b. 1904) was married in Warsaw to Menachem Mendel ("Menik") Horenstein,[124] a first-cousin of Rayatz, but it was a much smaller affair than the previous "royal wedding."[125] Meanwhile, the future Rebbe spent the remaining months of the year recording his Torah thoughts in his notebook, journaling Rayatz's every move, and speaking Torah with legendary scholars who came to meet with Rayatz, such as Rabbi Chaim Ozer Grodzinski (1863–1940)[126] and Rabbi Baruch Ber Leibowitz (1864–1939).[127]

A chapter in Menachem Mendel's life had ended. He had learned much in Berlin and was gaining a fine reputation in the court of Rayatz, but he still had not earned the degree or professional qualification that he sought. The quiet backwaters of Riga offered little future for Menachem Mendel, or for Rayatz. The Sixth and future Seventh Rebbes were now embarking on new beginnings—in Warsaw, for Rayatz, and in Paris, for Menachem Mendel and Moussia.

CHAPTER SEVEN

THE QUIET YEARS

1933–1939

Rayatz (left) and Menachem Mendel (right), Purkersdorf Sanitorium, Austria 1935

From the spring of 1933 until the outbreak of World War Two, in 1939, Menachem Mendel and Moussia spent six relatively uneventful years in Paris. Mendel was enrolled in engineering school and eventually graduated with a degree. Moussia was able to spend long periods of time with her sister Sheina, who resided close by in Paris (Sheina's husband was also studying to be an engineer, like Mendel). After a lifetime of pogroms, wars, and watching the rise of Nazism firsthand in Germany, the Schneersons could now enjoy a relatively peaceful life. For the first time, they rented their own apartment, unlike in Germany where they had lodged with different host families, and they no longer shuttled backwards and forwards as regularly to Rayatz's home for festivals. No doubt, their ongoing childlessness was a dark cloud, but they had each other and they were happy, out of the limelight.

A constant source of distress during this period was Rayatz's ongoing, chronic illness which became increasingly debilitating. After returning from his trip to Israel and the U.S.A. in 1929-30, the Rebbe had felt utterly exhausted and was forced to spend the summer months in convalescence at the healing spas of Marienbad, Czechoslovakia.[1] When Rosh Hashanah came, Rayatz noticed that his speech had slowed somewhat, but he paid little attention to it. After two years, unable to ignore the problem any longer, he sought professional help.[2] During January and February of 1933, accompanied by Menachem Mendel, he received medical treatment at a clinic in Berlin. It was probably at this time that Rayatz was diagnosed with Multiple Sclerosis,[3] a disease that would plague him for the rest of his life. The doctor's prognosis was bleak, as the Seventh Rebbe recalled in a 1977 sermon: "We know what the doctors said back then.... but he still lived another eighteen years."[4]

While it was Rayatz's oldest son-in-law, Rashag, who had often been at his side in matters of fundraising and administration, it was Menachem Mendel who primarily rose to the task of caring for Rayatz's health and medical treatment, a role that would take much of his time over the next five years. In a 1933 letter from Berlin back to Moussia (who had stayed in Riga), Rayatz conveyed his delight at how Menachem Mendel had "developed tremendous organizational talents. He is concerned about everything for me... not just like a dedicated son-in-law but like a good daughter. I am extremely happy with the personal relationships he has developed with the professors and doctors."[5]

Rayatz's forced convalescence placed tremendous pressure on his office, both in terms of the mounting workload and the costs of treatment. In Rayatz's absence, his secretary, Rabbi Yechezkel Fegin, was unable to respond to "the huge number of letters we receive daily of Jewish misfortune, particularly from our brothers in Russia.... We do not even have the funds required to keep him [Rayatz] in convalescence."[6] In another letter, after the Rebbe's return to Riga, Fegin attributed the cause of Rayatz's illness to being "extremely broken from inner pain.... Jewish suffering, which increases every day, has a strong effect on his health." The Rebbe was cautioned by the doctors not to work at all, or to deliver public sermons.[7]

The Berlin doctors failed to understand Rayatz's condition and over the next two years, despite close medical supervision, his health gradually declined.[8] The decision to finally relocate his court from Riga to Warsaw at the end of 1933 was a source of additional strain, as he commented in a letter to Mendel and Moussia on 1st November, "the move—may G-d make it successful spiritually and physically—was an extremely demanding task."[9] Perhaps he had hoped that being in close vicinity to the Central Lubavitch Yeshiva would lift his spirits and aid recovery. But towards the end of 1934, the situation was so dire that Menachem Mendel was forced to exempt himself from the 1934-35 academic year to be at Rayatz's side. The summer was spent together at the spas of Marienbad, followed by the High Holidays and *Sukkot* at Rayatz's new court in Warsaw. By the winter, at a mere fifty-four years of age, Rayatz was having extreme difficulty with both walking and speaking. While Moussia remained in Warsaw with the family, Menachem Mendel accompanied his father-in-law to Vienna to seek medical assistance. After meeting with "many professors," they were left with a confusing mess of conflicting opinions, none of which inspired much confidence. It was then that Rayatz met Dr. Max Gerson (1881–1959), a tall, slender and handsome Jewish refugee from Germany, who had intense blue eyes and a gentle demeanor. Gerson claimed to have success in curing a variety of terminal diseases simply through a regimen of diet and injections.[10] Gerson's holistic approach, which viewed the patient's body as an organism whose various parts, including the mind, were interconnected and integrated, probably resonated well with Rayatz's Chasidic spirituality. He told the Rebbe that he knew what the disease was and that it had been caused by prolonged distress and inner suffering. He suggested a five-month course of treatment and Rayatz decided to attend Dr. Gerson's clinic, appointing him as his "chief doctor."[11]

Gerson worked out of the famous Westend Sanitorium in Purkersdorf, a resort hotel and clinic in the outskirts of Vienna. Built in 1904 by architect Josef Hoffmann (1870-1956), the Sanitorium was an upper-class social and artistic venue which boasted reading rooms, a playroom for card games, table tennis, billiard and music-rooms. Rayatz and Menachem Mendel remained there from December 1934, until a few days before Passover, the following April—almost five months.[12]

Rayatz apparently made a deep impression on the Gersons since nearly eighty years later Max's daughter Charlotte, who was twelve years old at the time, still remembered him. At aged 91, Charlotte recalled Rayatz as "a distinguished figure... He was referred to us as the 'Wunder Rabbi' (the Miracle Rabbi) and we children, my two older sisters and I, just admired him from afar."[13]

That summer, after Mendel and Moussia had returned to Paris, Rayatz chose to relocate his court again, this time to Otwock, a resort town fifteen miles south-east of Warsaw. This would provide him with a more peaceful environment and better air, while still remaining within the Jewish orbit, since Otwock was frequented by a number of Chasidic Rebbes for healing. The main Lubavitcher Yeshivah in Warsaw also relocated to Otwock to be in close proximity to Rayatz.[14] Despite his failing health, this was probably the most peaceful period of his thirty-year tenure as Rebbe. The Yeshivah was successful. His influence among the huge non-Chabad Chasidic community grew, and his dream of replanting the court of Lubavitch on new, fertile soil began to materialize.[15]

During July and August 1936, Rayatz made an extended visit to Ville-D'Avray, outside Paris, for treatment by Doctor Gerson,[16] and Menachem Mendel had the convenience of being able to help the Sixth Rebbe in his own hometown. During the trip, Rayatz would spend the Sabbath, when he needed to be near a synagogue, in the home of Yankel and Baila Lax, at 55 Boulevard de Strasbourg (10th Arrondissement). Since Rayatz had considerable difficulty walking, his two sons-in-law, Menachem Mendel Schneerson and Menik Horenstein, would arrive on Saturday morning at around 8 a.m. for assistance, each taking one arm of the Rebbe to assist him downstairs, and to walk to the synagogue. For a healthy person, the walk would take about five to six minutes, but it took the Rebbe a half hour. He would pray until after 2 p.m., drenching his *talit* with tears.[17]

After the Paris visit, Menachem Mendel accompanied his father-in-law to Vienna for further medical consultation. He then joined him back to Otwock, staying for the festive month of *Tishrei*, before returning home to Paris.[18]

In the beginning of 1937, Menachem Mendel was again called upon to help Rayatz find medical assistance. He accompanied the Sixth Rebbe to the Purkersdorf Sanitorium for about a week,[19] and then for further consultations in Paris with "famous professors."[20] During the spring, Moussia accompanied her father to the Perchtoldsdorf Sanatorium in Austria, while Menachem Mendel remained in Paris to continue his studies.[21]

Rayatz made a final four-week visit to Paris for further treatment in the spring of 1938[22] and spent the festival of Purim with his daughter and son-in-law. Menachem Mendel read the Megillah for his father-in-law during what would be their last meeting before the outbreak of World War Two.[23] They would eventually see each other again on the other side of the Atlantic, in 1941.[24]

Besides these health-related visits, Mendel and Moussia spent the entire peacetime period from 1933 until 1939, quietly and uneventfully together in Paris, away from their parents and parents-in-law. Both introverted by nature, they lived very private lives with a small circle of friends. As we shall see, Menachem Mendel was quite busy with his academic studies, continued scholarship, and missions from his father-in-law, but everything was low-key. One gets the sense that Providence granted the young couple a little time for themselves before Menachem Mendel would be catapulted from his unassuming studio apartment in Paris to the international stage, eventually becoming the Lubavitcher Rebbe.

II.

When Mendel and Moussia arrived in Paris in the spring of 1933,[25] there were very few Chabad Chasidim in the city, but Rayatz used his connections to have his daughter and son-in-law welcomed by Rabbi Meir Shochetman (1914-1988),[26] who secured an apartment for the young couple. According to Shochetman's recollection, Menachem Mendel was despondent about continuing his academic studies. While he had a basic knowledge of French, it was inadequate for study at university level, and he had already been forced to abandon his studies twice before, in Leningrad and then in Berlin. Schochetman recalled that it was Rayatz, who was in Paris at the time, who encouraged his son-in-law to seek admission to a French university. While it was the middle of the academic year, through Schochetman's assistance Menachem Mendel managed to get admitted a month later on a trial basis to the specialist Engineering school, *Ecole Spéciale des Travaux Publics du Bâtiment et de l'Industrie*—ESTP ("Special School for Public Works in Building and Industry"). Founded in 1891 as a private institution of higher education and officially recognized by the State in 1921, ESTP is a Grande École ("higher school"), outside the main framework of the French university system, distinguished by a highly selective admission process, a limited number of students and quality programs.

The Grandes Écoles, which are generally elitist schools, have produced many of France's high-ranking civil servants, politicians, scientists, and philosophers.

The ESTP school records have survived which allow us to trace Menachem Mendel's precise academic progress and attendance during this period. His class consisted of around thirty men who were enlisted for a gruelling forty-hour week: in the morning, theoretical courses at 57 Boulevard St. Germain, in the Latin Quarter; and in the afternoons, practical work in the school's larger campus of workshops and laboratories in Cachan, a suburb to the south of Paris. The twenty or so courses each year included: analytical geometry, vectoral geometry, industrial electricity, electronics, electrical testing, thermodynamics, industrial design, labor law and hydraulics.

During 1933, Menachem Mendel was an unregistered student admitted on a trial basis, and, as we have seen, during the academic year of 1934-35 he was forced to exempt himself to assist with Rayatz's medical needs. But he was registered during the academic years of 1933-34, 1935-36, and 1936-37, and we have detailed records of his achievements. In Berlin, Menachem Mendel had studied abstract sciences—philosophy, theoretical physics and mathematics—so he was probably quite unprepared for the more practical courses offered at ESTP. If we add to that the language barrier and the fact that it was an elitist school, he was probably pleased to pass all his first year's courses in 1933-4. After a year of absence, he initially struggled on his return in 1935, but he bounced back and successfully completed the remainder of the degree courses.

There were considerable challenges in maintaining a strictly Orthodox life in pre-war Paris. ESTP was open on Saturday, the Jewish Sabbath, and attendance was strictly enforced. In the winter, Menachem Mendel was forced to leave the laboratory early on Friday to be home in time for sunset, when the Sabbath begins. Initially, he just walked off inconspicuously, but within time the pattern was detected and he was suspended for two days from school as a punishment. When the reason for his absence was explained, special permission was granted for him on 16th November 1935 from the "Conseil de Direction" to leave at 3:30 p.m. during the winter months, so long as he would make up the missed work at another time. While Menachem Mendel had a large number of absences, both excused and unexcused, over the three years at ESTP,[27] it never resulted in his having to retake any examinations, and he graduated each academic year successfully. Finally, during the session held on 24th July 1937, the Board of Examiners decided to propose to the National Minister for Education that "Mr. Mendel Schneerson should be awarded the degree of Mechanical and Electrical Engineer, after he has completed the statutory three-month internship."[28] He eventually received his diploma on 24th March 1938.

A few months later, in a pastoral letter to the Chabad Women's Organization (*Achot Temimim*) of Riga, the Sixth Lubavitcher Rebbe made a proud reference to his son-in-law's achievements. Speaking of how inherited talents may skip several generations, he wrote,

> My great-grandfather, the famous Rebbe who was known as *Tzemach Tzedek* was a genius in *nigleh* (traditional Jewish texts), in Kabbalah and Chasidut, and he was also very great in *handasah* (geometry; engineering). His children and grandchildren were great geniuses in *nigleh,* Kabbalah and Chasidut, but none of them were experts in *handasah.* Only one of his later descendants has inherited the special talent of our holy, great Rebbe, *Tzemach Tzedek* in the science of *handasah.*[29]

Throughout the years at ESTP, Mendel and Moussia had lived in a tiny studio apartment at Hotel Max, 9 Rue Boulard, in the 14th Arrondissement. [30] In March 1938, hoping that Mendel would soon find work, the couple rented a bigger home with two rooms, a kitchen and bathroom, in the 15th Arrondissement at 7 Villa Robert Lindet. In what is possibly the only letter from Moussia to her parents-in-law to have survived from this period, she describes the couple's dilemma in upgrading their accommodation. "It was extremely difficult to decide, because, meanwhile, there are no jobs, and it does not seem that any are coming soon. In such a situation it makes no sense to increase expenses. Mendel insisted that we had to decide, yes or no, as there was no point thinking about it again and again."[31]

In the absence of work, Menachem Mendel chose to advance his academic studies. While his precise motivation is unclear, Menachem Mendel enrolled at the Sorbonne for the academic years of 1937-38 and 1938-39;[32] but whatever he was trying to achieve was abruptly halted when the Nazis invaded Paris in May 1940.

III.

A huge problem facing Menachem Mendel and Moussia from the beginning of their time in Paris was citizenship. Their Soviet passports, which expired in April 1933, could not be extended; so in December 1932, before departing from Riga to Paris, the Schneersons successfully applied for what was known as a Nansen passport. Issued by the League of Nations, the Nansen passport was an internationally recognized identity card made available to refugees during the interwar period.

To receive their Nansen passports they were forced to surrender their Soviet passports to the Soviet embassy in Riga. As result, from 1933, until they eventually received American citizenship in 1946, Mendel and Moussia were stateless (by Russian law, the citizenship of all expatriates was automatically revoked). Their two attempts at citizenship during this period both failed. The first was an application, made with the assistance of Mordechai Dubin, to be granted Latvian citizenship (something successfully obtained by Rayatz and his immediate family). Despite sustained efforts by Dubin during 1933-34, the application was denied.[33] In October 1937, after Mendel had qualified as an engineer, the Schneersons made an application for French citizenship, but this too was eventually denied on 10th June 1939.

The couple suffered greatly from their lack of grounding. In a 1938 letter, while waiting to hear the results of their French naturalization application, Moussia wrote to her parents-in-law, "We are doing all we can to be granted permanent residency... and hope it will be granted to us. Without it, life is extremely difficult."[34]

How did Mendel and Moussia spend their time during the "quiet years" in Paris? Mendel definitely showed no interest in Rabbinic leadership, and when he was offered a position by the ultra-Orthodox community in Paris, he declined it.[35] "At that time, I was very self absorbed," he recalled, years later.[36] On one occasion when he visited Rabbi Yoel Hertzog (1865-1934), head of the Union of Orthodox Synagogues in Paris, he asked to be announced as "a refugee who had recently arrived from Poland" and begged that his identity not be revealed.[37] His low public profile, and physical residence well away from the close-knit Orthodox community centered in the Third Arrondissement,[38] enabled him to spend much time in study and on walks.[39] He was fond of visiting museums and libraries, and no-doubt frequented the Ste. Geneviève Library, home to one of the best Judaic collections in Europe, which was a stone's throw from the ESTP city campus.[40] But he spent most of his spare time at home, with Moussia, poring over books which were kept in crates on the floor. Menachem Mendel was said to mix in "intellectual circles" and was a member of "Club du Faubourg," a club for scientists which he attended with David Bezborodko (1901-1998), a glass specialist and inventor. On one occasion, when challenged by members of the club to defend his stated belief that the world was around 5000 years old, the future Rebbe delivered a two-hour presentation at the club which was met with a round of applause.[41] We also know that he spent some time researching the topic of spontaneous generation, an area of conflict between Talmudic wisdom and modern science, later noting in a 1964 letter, "I carefully studied this matter in France, where most of the scientific research in this area was done."[42]

While Menachem Mendel shied away from communal involvement, recollections have survived of his giving a Talmud class in local synagogues, at least from 1937 onwards,[43] and he certainly studied with friends on an individual basis.[44] He would pray regularly at the Chabad synagogue at 17 Rue de Rosiers,[45] although he frequently attended the non-Chabad *shtiebl* a few doors away, at number 25, where he would receive less attention.[46]

He would sit inconspicuously in the corner. When offered a seat of honor at the front of the synagogue, he declined, saying, "Don't you think G-d is found back here, too?"[47] He was sometimes seen at *farbrengens,* though again, always quietly at the side;[48] but he did deliver an occasional public address in local synagogues, and notes from his 1935 Sukkot and Chanukah lectures were recorded in his diary.[49] There is also some evidence that he was involved with arranging *cheder* classes for Jewish children in Paris.[50]

All in all, Menachem Mendel's tendency towards introversion frustrated his father-in-law. "Hiding from people doesn't lead to anything," Rayatz wrote in a 1933 letter to Moussia, in reference to her husband. "It causes me tremendous aggravation."[51]

Most important to Moussia was close proximity to her sister Sheina,[52] who had moved to Paris in 1932. Sheina's husband, Menik Horenstein, also chose a career path in engineering, and even attended the same school as his brother-in-law, the ESTP (though he failed to qualify for a degree). As soon as the Schneersons arrived in Paris, Rayatz wrote to Menachem Mendel, making "a great request," namely that he should have a positive influence on his brother-in-law "to speak Torah matters with him and to make regular times to study together."[53] The Horensteins would also correspond regularly with Rayatz, and he would send them copies of recent sermons and Chasidic discourses. For a period, Moussia and Sheina started a seamstress business together, and there is even a letter from their father congratulating Moussia on the purchase of a sewing machine.[54] The Horensteins, like the Schneersons, were not blessed with biological children, but they did adopt: in 1937, after Menik Horenstein's sister Sarah passed away, Menik and Sheina took one of her children, Ya'akov Lis, as their own.[55]

IV.

Besides the pleasure of solitude, life had its formidable challenges. Menachem Mendel and Moussia's childlessness, as they both approached their late thirties, must have been extremely worrying. Their parents did not give up hope. On Moussia's thirty-fourth birthday, her father sent blessings "to cheer your beloved hearts with the birth of a fine, healthy child." A few weeks later, on Mendel's thirty-third birthday, Reb Levik blessed his son with "life, children and sustenance... and we should merit to see from you a *'blessed, righteous generation'* (*Psalms* 112:2)." Offering his personal blessings, Levik wrote, "The number thirty-three alludes to the complete sweetening of harsh judgments (*mituk ha-gevurot ve-ha-dinim le-gamray*), so may it be G-d's will that all the harsh judgments should be sweetened."[56]

Keeping a high standard of Orthodox observance in Paris in those days was also a challenge. After some doubt arose over the *kashrut* of the local bakery, Menachem Mendel refused to patronize it, and Moussia was forced to prepare everything herself from scratch.[57] She even traveled several miles on a regular basis to watch cows being milked so that the couple could have *chalav yisrael*.[58] Commenting years later on how she and her husband had paved the way for the future Chabad community in Paris, she said, "We plowed and sowed and planted seeds, and you need to reap the harvest."[59]

Menachem Mendel was also kept busy by Rayatz, who maintained a very close correspondence, penning some 180 letters to his daughter and son-in-law during their six-and-a-half peace-time years in Paris.[60] Among the tasks to which Menachem Mendel was assigned were: to edit the new Chabad journal *Hatamim* (from 1935),[61] to receive funds from the U.S.A., Europe and Israel and channel them to Rayatz in Poland (from 1936),[62] to edit the *sichot* (published sermons) of Rayatz (from 1937)[63], to prepare anthologies of letters penned by Rayatz on various topics and index the material (from 1937),[64] to publish foreign language translations of Chabad thought (1937),[65] to write a scholarly treatise on the kindling of the *Menorah* in the Holy Temple,[66] and to act as Rayatz's secretary during his health trips. As a sign of deepening respect, from 1937 onwards, Rayatz began to consistently address his son-in-law with the honorific "*shlita*" in all correspondence.[67]

Of course, Menachem Mendel and Moussia could never satisfy Rayatz's desire for constant contact, and they often received requests to write more often. "I would very much like to know," the Sixth Rebbe wrote to Moussia during Chanukah of 1933, "how your health is and how life is with you? I can't stop thinking about it."[68] In a letter from the summer of 1937, he writes more sharply, "What can I tell you? When you do not write, I inevitably think about you more; but it has a great price—it costs too much of my health."[69]

In addition to his tasks for Rayatz, Menachem Mendel continued to note personal insights and customs he heard from the Sixth Rebbe in his *Reshimat Hayoman* (diary),[70] as well as pen a number of scholarly letters and *Reshimot.* Reb Levik also continued to pen reams of Kabbalisitic thoughts to his son, and the letters from this period fill 125 printed pages.[71] While the vast majority of Menachem Mendel's letters to his father have not surfaced, we can gain some insight into the advanced scope of the correspondence from one of the 1937 *Reshimot*, which was apparently the draft of Torah thoughts to his father.[72]

In one interesting exchange, from January 1936, Reb Levik tries to correct Menachem Mendel's self-deprecating view of his *chidushei Torah* (innovative Torah thoughts).

> Concerning your *chidushei Torah,* my opinion differs from yours. You belittle yourself and write that you have no novel ideas—but it

is not so, my son. "*Although you are small in your own eyes, did you not become the head [of the tribes of Israel]?*" (I Sam 15:17). They are extremely good!"[73]

In the last surviving correspondence from Menachem Mendel to his parents, from March 1939, we see the "comforter" at work, once again.

> Believe me, I really feel without the slightest doubt, that you and Mother will have *nachas* (satisfaction) and good fortune, well beyond what you have now, even more than you wished yourselves in your last letter... Since things need to be good, surely they're going to be. It's difficult for me to write a lot about this (and for sure, you know better than me), particularly as I know you so well. In truth, I shouldn't have written this either.... I'll conclude with best wishes for you forever.[74]

V.

While the six and a half peacetime years in Paris were relatively uneventful, especially when viewed in contrast with the turmoil which preceded and followed, Menachem Mendel later reflected upon them as a significant period in his life. In a 1991 sermon, he noted why Napoleon had been framed as a profound spiritual enemy by the first Rebbe of Chabad, Rabbi Shneur Zalman of Liadi.[75]

> The French Revolution of 1789, which led to Napoleon's becoming the leader of France a number of years later, was also an ideological war, so fundamental that it brought a major change to the entire world. It was one of the primary events on which was built the founding principles of the "modern world" and its culture, to this day.
>
> Until the Revolution, the rulership of France (and most countries) was totally in the hand of the monarch, who conducted it as he or she wished. The Revolution was based on the conviction that people should be free do as they please, and therefore the monarchy was removed to free the country from their rule and give over the control of the people into the hands of the entire population.
>
> Even though this system has the advantage of free choice, as well as justice and morality, etc., and this would bring freedom and wealth for Jews—nevertheless, since it was not based on a foundation of faith and trust in G-d, it brought with it (particularly through Na-

> poleon) a spirit of freedom from religion, discharging one's sense of responsibility and encouraging people to follow their fleeting desires, *etc.* This attitude also spread to many other countries both in that period of history and the ensuing periods.
>
> In its time, the country... opposed a G-d-fearing lifestyle, particularly a Chassidic lifestyle, *etc.*,—which was the reason for the Alter Rebbe's staunch opposition to their victory.[76]

While Chabad made few inroads into France during the next five generations of Chabad, a shift occurred in Rayatz's times, when,

> In addition to the fact that he was in France on several occasions and delivered both formal Chasidic discourses and other talks there, *he also sent representatives from his own household to France, who lived there for many years* [emphasis added], carrying out their work of learning the revealed parts of Torah and the mystical parts of Torah. He also sent many of his Chassidic essays and holy letters there, and, *in France itself, many of these writings were prepared for publication* [emphasis added]...
>
> Through fear of Heaven and exemplary religiosity, an inner transformation was achieved which led the way, and made it possible to totally crush the spiritual hostility.[77]

The Seventh Rebbe's intuition allowed him to see his presence in France, a country which embodied the spiritually corrupting forces of modernity, as a precursor that, on a metaphysical level, helped prepare the stage for the emergence of a thriving pious, Chasidic life in the country. This came to full expression with the establishment of the Chabad Yeshiva and community in France after the war. At least in retrospect he came to appreciate the "quiet years" to have really been something of a "mystical" revolution.

All this, of course, was to be violently interrupted by the outbreak of World War Two, when all thoughts would shift towards survival. Both Menachem Mendel and Rayatz were to each have a close escape from the hands of the Nazis. Others, as we shall see, would not be so fortunate.

CHAPTER EIGHT

SURVIVAL

1939–1941

The Serpa Pinto

On Thursday, 19th September (eve of 17th *Elul*) 1939, the students of Yeshivat Tomchei Temimim in Otwock gathered through the night in a *farbrengen* to celebrate the founding of the first Lubavitch Yeshivah, forty-two years earlier. When morning broke, as they went off to immerse themselves in the *mivkah*, they heard the unmistakable sound of bombs dropping. Germany had invaded Poland.[1]

One bomb struck the Rebbe's own residence, but no one was injured. A few days later, the Rebbe's secretary Chaim Lieberman, who had managed to escape from Warsaw to Riga, wrote to Menachem Mendel and Moussia in Paris to inform them that Rayatz was alive and well. From Paris, Menachem Mendel spread the news to Yisrael Jacobson in New York, in a letter dated 11th October: "Mr. Lieberman has informed us that they have not been able to leave Warsaw. We are extremely worried about their safety."[2]

A few days later, Menachem Mendel was able to report more news to Jacobson: "I received today a letter from Mr. Lieberman and I hurry to inform you what he wrote to us. The Shmotkin residence in Warsaw, where my father [-in-law] was residing with the family, has been completely destroyed by a fire. Thank G-d, they are all well and safe.... I am certain, my dear Rabbi, that you are doing everything in your means to come to their assistance, especially to bring them out as soon as possible, considering their situation."[3]

Jacobson was already on the case. In recent years, extensive details of these efforts have come to light, and the chronicle of events is a book-length story in itself. Through hundreds of letters and cables, Chabad managed to win support in the higher echelons of the U.S. government.[4]

This was quite an astonishing feat when one considers the limited resources at Jacobson's disposal: He had no staff or supportive infrastructure; his English skills were limited, and he would often have his daughter assist him in deciphering correspondence. But he had the three essential ingredients of a successful Chabad activist: boundless love for the Rebbe, a good measure of tenacity and fine *ba'alei batim,* lay leaders to assist him.[5]

A key player from the German side was a distinguished officer in the German army named Ernst Bloch (1898-1945). Bloch was a *mischling,* a man of mixed Aryan and Jewish descent (his father was Jewish), and while Hitler had personally signed a document "removing" his Jewish blood, rendering him of pure *Deutschblütig,* there is no doubt that Bloch retained a deep sympathy for the plight of Jews. After intense diplomatic intervention, Bloch was assigned with the secret task of finding the Rebbe and leading him to Riga in safety—which is precisely what transpired.[6]

By mid December all the arrangements for the escape of the Rebbe and his family were agreed upon and funds had been received to cover all expenses of the rescue.[7] A Nazi wagon arrived, and Rayatz was ushered with his family, staff and possessions into the vehicle. As a ruse, Bloch screamed out, "OK, you pigs. Get in the truck and wagon," so as to quell the suspicions of SS officers that looked on.

The trip was relatively uneventful, and the main challenge was to pass a series of SS checkpoints. One checkpoint outside Warsaw proved particularly challenging. The SS surrounded the wagon at gunpoint and demanded to know the "real reason" why these Jews were being transported to Berlin. With a gush of adrenaline, Bloch mouthed off a list of high-ranking officials with whom he was personally connected and threatened to have the SS officer arrested if he did not allow the group through. As the wagon passed through the checkpoint,

Bloch assured the Rebbe that they were going to be alright. "The SS is not Germany," Bloch said.

By 15th December, the group reached Berlin, where they were forced to stay over Shabbat. But a sense of relief only came when on Sunday 17th December (5th *Tevet*) 1939, Rayatz finally crossed the Latvian border and reached Riga in safety with his family. He immediately penned a letter to Chabad followers worldwide, petitioning assistance for those still trapped in Poland.[8] On Wednesday, Rayatz wrote to Mendel and Moussia in Paris, informing them of his safe arrival in Riga. He mentioned that he would be traveling with his wife straight to a sanitorium for medical treatment, while Rashag and his family remained in a local hotel. The letter makes no reference to the terrible ordeals they had been suffering for the past few months and the miracle of being saved by a Nazi officer; all that mattered was that they were safe and "thank G-d, the *ketavim* are intact, and so is the library."[9]

II.

Already at the beginning of 1939, Rayatz had begun preparations for relocating his court to the United States, and his secretariat had requested that supporters in America begin to prepare visas for his family (his three daughters and sons-in-law), his close confidantes as well as ten to fifteen Yeshivah students.[10] In January 1939, Rabbi Yisrael Jacobson succeeded in winning the support of Senator William Borah (Idaho) who had been influential in securing Rayatz's release from Soviet imprisonment in 1927. Borah's office contacted the visa department on 12th January 1939, beginning the appeal for Rayatz's family,[11] but the efforts soon came to a halt when the senator died in his sleep from a brain hemorrhage, seven days later.[12]

In the summer of 1939, shortly before the war had erupted, Rabbi Yisrael Jacobson had visited Otwock and discussed the move with Rayatz, who was concerned if his health was good enough for the huge upheaval of relocation. Jacobson encouraged the Rebbe to move, promising to raise the necessary funds, and Rayatz agreed that "in about half a year, please G-d, we will come to America."[13]

Menachem Mendel, it seems, had been reluctant to join Rayatz in America, and preferred to stay in France. In a fascinating letter penned by Yechezkel Feigin to Yisrael Jacobson about the matter, we get a rare, firsthand glimpse into the future Rebbe's character and talents as they were perceived by senior Chabad Chasidim at the time.

> There is another issue about which I wish to alert you, but it must remain a secret... so I ask you to please destroy this letter immediately in order that no one else should see it—but, in my opinion, it would be a good idea to do what is written here. I refer to the fact that the Rebbe [Rayatz] is suffering terribly [due to the fact] that Ramash [Menachem Mendel] is resisting coming to America. I saw that for Ramash, the matter is already decided, and you know his nature, how strong-willed he is. Therefore, I think, that besides the issue of the Rebbe's distress, which is extremely important, in my opinion, all the activities would be vastly improved if he were by the Rebbe's side. He also has a great talent for bringing the youth closer....
>
> Perhaps, then, you could write to him the content of my letter, about his decision not to come to America, and write him a motivational message that his coming is so important for the Rebbe's honor, and it will, as a matter of course, be helpful in *hafatzat ha-mayanot* (the dissemination of Chasidut). But do not overstep the mark in your letter and imply that we are relying on him, because I already know his temperament—this itself will be a reason for him to decline. He doesn't feel capable of responsibilities like these. The main thing is that you should explain to him that his coming is important for the Rebbe's honor and to be a help in the activities. And stress that, with G-d's help, he will also have private time here to study Torah, for he has now already finished his academic studies and is involved only with holy matters.[14]

Many aspects of "Ramash's" character, which we have so far understood only by implication from his life decisions, are stated explicitly in this letter. First, we see how much he valued his independence and did not appreciate being pressured into any decisions. Second, we see that the Chabad establishment was aware of his great organizational talents, and appreciated his potential to inspire young Jews. Third, we see how he shied away from communal work, both due to the inevitable distraction from Torah study, and because he questioned whether it was something to which he was suited. Fourth, we see that his interest in secular studies was not an ongoing aspiration but it had been with a specific purpose, and now that this had been accomplished, Ramash shifted his interests exclusively to "holy matters." Fifth, despite his reservations about involvement in communal work, his love and respect for Rayatz trumped all other concerns; if Ramash would only appreciate how much his presence meant to Rayatz then he would be convinced to relocate.

With the escalating war, the dilemma of resettling in the "unkosher country" was speedily resolved. Staying in Riga was not an option for Rayatz, as it was clear that a Russian occupation was imminent and the Rebbe's return to Soviet territory would be disastrous.[15] A network of Chabad activists in America set to work even before Rayatz arrived in Riga to secure visas for the Rebbe, his family and his staff.[16] In Riga, matters were delayed when on the Sabbath, 27th January (17th *Shevat*), Rayatz fell and broke his right hand and was in a cast for three weeks. His mother, who had just turned eighty, also had a bout of serious ill health, requiring an emergency operation to relieve an abdominal hernia.[17] Even when their visas for entry to the United States were finally received in early February,[18] the Rebbe's party were not able to leave for another month. They eventually crossed the Baltic Sea in a small, eighteen-seat aeroplane to Stockholm on Tuesday, 4th March (25th *Adar* I), just three months before the Russian invasion of Latvia.[19]

From Stockholm, Rayatz and his party took the train at 10 p.m. that evening to Gothenberg, arriving at 8 a.m. the next morning. Thursday, 6th March (27th *Adar* I). They joined 523 passengers on the *SS Drottningholm*, which departed on a direct voyage to New York at 1 p.m. Rayatz occupied Stateroom 13 for the entire journey. [20]

Disembarking in New York, on 19th March (9th *Adar* II) 1940, to a large crowd of assembled Chasidim and well-wishers,[21] were: Rayatz, his wife, his mother, his nurse Mania Lotz;[22] Rashag, Chana and their son Shalom Ber; and members of Rayatz's staff: secretary Rabbi Chaim Lieberman, as well as two administrators with whom Rayatz had worked closely in Latvia—Rabbi Chaim Mordechai Aizik Chodakov (1902–1993, and his wife Etel Tzerna, 1909-2006), and Rabbi Nissan Mindel (1912-1999).[23]

III.

The notable absentees, of course, were the Rebbe's younger two daughters, Moussia and Sheina, and their husbands. At the outbreak of war Menik and Sheina Horenstein had been in Otwock, caring for the health of Menik's ailing father, Moshe (who eventually died in 1941), and, not being Latvian citizens, they were unable to journey with Rayatz from Poland. As citizens of a country conquered by the Germans, they were initially denied visas as part of Rayatz's group.[24]

Menachem Mendel and Moussia, on the other hand, had in principle been approved for immigration into the United States along with the Sixth Rebbe, since Chabad lawyers had successfully appealed to the U.S. government that the entire "Chabad hierarchy" needed to be welcomed to its shores.[25] While few fully-fledged Lubavitcher Chasidim resided in America, there were a purported 150,000 loose affiliates, immigrants or children of Lubavitcher immigrants who had become Americanized, but retained a connection with the movement. Many of them still made a point of following *Nusach Ari* (Chabad prayer rites), and convened at some 200 affiliated congregations across the country.[26] During the 1920s and 30s, through the work of Rabbi Yisrael Jacobson and the Kramer family, these scattered congregations and affiliates were unified under the umbrella of *Agudat Chasidei Chabad* (Union of Chabad Chasidim), an organization which became the instrumental force in the rescue of Rayatz and his family.[27] Chabad immigration lawyers argued that the Rebbe was no ordinary congregational Rabbi: his entire extended family and staff represented a "hierarchy" which was necessary to the survival of this significant segment of American Orthodox Jewry.[28]

Menachem Mendel and Moussia's problems arose from an earlier visa application which they filed with the consulate in Paris in November 1939,[29] which clashed with the "hierarchy" proposal filed by lawyers in New York the following month. Menachem Mendel and Moussia's initial application was for an ordinary quota visa entitled to Russian immigrants, citing Menachem Mendel's profession as an engineer. The "hierarchy" application, which included Menachem Mendel and Moussia with all of Rayatz's family, took advantage of a special exemption in section 4(d) of the 1924 Immigration Act which did not limit active members of clergy to the strict annual quota of 154,000 immigrants.[30] In effect, Menachem Mendel had concurrently applied for two different visas, each claiming different occupations.

The clash was so significant, that the New York lawyers were concerned that it could jeopardize Rayatz's entire application. Since the

Sixth Rebbe was initially in greater jeopardy, Chabad decided not to petition for Menachem Mendel and Moussia until Rayatz had arrived safely from Europe, in March.

Soon afterwards, things took a turn for the worse for all potential Jewish immigrants to the U.S.A. On 27th May 1940, the House approved President Roosevelt's proposed transfer of the Bureau of Immigration from the Department of Labor to the Department of Justice, a move aimed at tightening immigration policy. On the same day, the Senate Judiciary Committee encouraged the enforced fingerprinting and registration of aliens. The president's message was clear: immigrants pose a threat to national security due to the feared increase in "spies, saboteurs and traitors."[31]

The government clamp-down on immigration was apparently a cause of great concern for Rayatz, since on 29th May, the day after news of Roosevelt's reshuffle hit the press, Rayatz penned a *pidyon nefesh* (soul petition) to his father, asking him to intercede on High for the visa application of Menachem Mendel and Moussia.

> Please arouse great mercy from the Source of mercy and genuine benevolence... for your granddaughter Chaya Mushka [Moussia] and her husband Menachem Mendel son of Chana, who are currently found in the city of Paris, France. Menachem Mendel is Nansenist—not a French citizen.... May God place good counsel in the hearts of the American Consul to grant them an American visa."[32]

The new legislation was of particular concern, as it represented the growing influence of Assistant Secretary of State, Breckinridge Long (1881–1958), a wealthy elitist and friend of the President who had been a major contributor to the Roosevelt campaigns. Long was a strong nativist and fervent believer in a restrictive immigration, especially for Jewish refugees, some of whom he imagined might be covert Nazi agents. With fourteen percent unemployment, he also felt that newcomers would take jobs away from Americans.

Long has been dubbed by some critics as the "American Eichmann" for actively preventing the immigration of as many as ninety percent of eligible candidates, which resulted in the death of 190,000 refugees. In a now famous memo to State Department officials, penned on 26th June 1940, Long recommended, "We can delay and effectively stop for a temporary period of indefinite length the number of immigrants into the United States. We could do this by simply advising our consuls, to put every obstacle in the way and to require additional evidence and to resort to various administrative devices which would postpone and postpone and postpone the granting of the visas."[33]

This is precisely what happened to Menachem Mendel and Moussia. While they had initially been pronounced eligible for U.S. immigration as part of Rayatz's successful application for the Chabad hierarchy, on 5th June the American consul in Paris telegraphed Washington that the couple's visas had been denied. The clash between the two different applications was provided as the obvious disqualification.[34]

The decision almost cost the couple their lives. From 10th May, the Germans had already begun their advance into Belgium and Holland. The "second act" of the Battle of France began on 5th June—the day the Schneersons were denied their visa—with the Germans striking southwards from the River Somme, towards Paris. As stateless refugees, Menachem Mendel and Moussia had nowhere to flee.

One option available to them was an offer from a sympathetic neighbor, to go into hiding in his chateau, located outside Paris;[35] but Menachem Mendel deemed it safer to flee southwards, away from the approaching Nazis. He packed a trunk with his most precious possessions: the books which he had received as wedding presents; the hundreds of letters of Rayatz which he had catalogued and prepared for publication; his folder of *Reshimot,* containing his Torah thoughts and customs of Rayatz that he had meticulously documented; the "unauthorized" photostated copies of Rashab's discourses which he had made ten years earlier, and the notes on *Tanya* and indices of Chasidic thought which he had composed. Utilizing a personal connection to obtain a much coveted ticket, the couple boarded one of the last trains to leave Paris, on or before 11th June, joining the mass exodus of some 100,000 Jews who fled Paris before the German conquest of 13th June.[36]

It was the eve of the festival of *Shavuot,* and as sunset approached, the Schneersons had not yet reached their destination in Vichy. Years later, Moussia recalled how Menachem Mendel rented a horse and wagon, mounted on it the heavy trunk filled with his books, *ketavim* and their few possessions and, as the sun set, they continued to walk to their destination. When Moussia could walk no further, she, too, mounted the wagon; but Menachem Mendel continued by foot, so as not to violate the festival laws in any way (even when it would have, no doubt, been permissible to do so).[37]

Many Paris Rabbis, including its Chief Rabbi, had also fled to Vichy, and make-shift synagogues popped up all over the town's two square miles.[38] There was even a tiny kosher restaurant owned by a Monsieur Mehler, which was well patronized by refugees, most of whom resided in hotel rooms where food preparation was difficult. The area was also flooded with some 40,000 Jews who had fled Belgium from the invading Nazis.[39]

We know that for the two months he was in Vichy, Menachem Mendel immersed himself in Torah, since he composed six long *Reshimot* during this short period, which fill some forty-three printed pages.[40] For the most part, the Vichy *Reshimot* follow themes in the weekly Torah portions and in all likelihood represent notes of lectures he delivered in the synagogue. What is immediately striking in the text is a complete lack of any reference to the troubles of the times; there is no hint that the ideas were penned by a man who was fleeing for his life from the Nazis. Instead, Menachem Mendel takes one or two ideas in the Torah portion and suggests an innovative twist, based on Chasidic thought. As ever, the discourses are extremely rich in sources, and, clearly lacking access to a library of Jewish books, the author leaves a number of references blank with a view to filling in the exact page numbers at a later date. Considering the circumstances under which they were written, the depth and complexity of the material is quite remarkable. As in the turbulent years of his youth, one gets the sense that Menachem Mendel found some comfort from the dire and hazardous situation by retreating into abstract thought.

IV.

Back in New York, by the summer of 1940, Rayatz was finally managing to become settled. Since his arrival in March, he had been living in temporary accommodation: the Greystone Hotel, in Manhattan's Upper West Side, room 539, on the fifth floor. After spending Passover in the quiet pastures of Lakewood, New Jersey, he declined an offer to relocate his court there, desiring instead to be at the heart of the Jewish community.[41] He set his eyes on Brooklyn, which was at the time home to one million Jews, constituting what was dubbed as "the largest Jewish community of any city in the history of the world."

The *Building Committee for the Residence of the Lubavitcher Rabbi* struggled to find a well located property that would meet the needs of the Rebbe and his family. An urgent meeting was convened to review the various options, a few blocks from the Greystone Hotel in the home of Hyman Kramer's friend David Tannenbaum on 100th Street. As the meeting reached full swing, Tannenbaum's son-in-law, Hyman Brainson, who had just been out to see a movie with his wife, happened to drop by, and was surprised to encounter a "sea of beards." Brainson, who worked as an assistant principal in a local school, was born and bred in Brooklyn and had lived there until his marriage in 1939, so he knew the district well. Dismissing all the committee's property options as impractical, Brainson suggested that Chabad look into a large home in Crown Heights, which had recently been repossessed by the bank.[42]

While a handful of Lubavitcher Chasidim resided in Brooklyn, mainly in the Brownsville area populated by lower class immigrants, Rayatz had desired a location where his presence would make a greater impact. The upper-middle class district of Crown Heights, a coveted address for wealthy Jewish professionals, seemed perfect. In 1940, there was very little Orthodox presence in the neighborhood, and the community was dominated by the Conservative *Brooklyn Jewish Center*, which was considered the model American synagogue.[43]

One block away from this center, on the other side of the street, was Brainson's proposal: an exquisite, 14,500 square-foot, three-floor, gothic-style mansion, lavishly decorated with imported Italian tile, heavy oak doors and copper doorknobs. The property served as the private home and medical clinic[44] of Dr. S. Robert Kahn (1899-1957), a graduate of the Long Island College of Medicine. Among his activities, Kahn conducted clandestine abortions, and in 1938 he was arrested on charges of manslaughter after one of his patients, a Bronx housewife, died as a result of an "illegal operation." While he was released on bail (after bribing the judge) and eventually cleared of charges, Kahn's woes did not end when, in 1939, he was found guilty of defaulting on income taxes, having declared only $23,000 of his $390,000 earnings during

1930-34. While he was sentenced to two-and-a-half years in jail, his clinic/home at 770 Eastern Parkway was soon repossessed by the bank.[45] The building was ideal for Rayatz as, besides having ample space for a synagogue, library, Yeshivah, administrative offices and accommodations for his family, it had wheelchair access and was equipped with an elevator. The *Building Committee for the Residence of the Lubavitcher Rabbi* managed to raise a down payment of $5,000 towards the $30,000 cost of the property, the rest being funded by a twenty-year mortgage. Rayatz agreed to provide $200 per month in rent, and Rashag $70 per month, for their private apartments on the second and third floors, so as to cover the mortgage payments.[46] A group of locals initially gathered to block the purchase, fearing that property values would drop if there would be an influx of Chasidim, and they even managed to garner support from Boro Hall, City Hall and local congressmen, but Rayatz took no notice of the general public's displeasure.

"Seven-Seventy," which would become an iconic address in the Seventh Generation of Chabad, was purchased by *Agudat Chasidei Chabad* on 16th August (12th *Menachem Av*) 1940, and the Rebbe moved in with his family around a month later, on 22nd September (19th *Elul*), shortly before the High Holidays. But the joy of re-establishing the court of Lubavitch was overshadowed by the chilling thought of Jews trapped in Europe. On the first night of Rosh Hashanah, Rayatz spent four hours reciting the evening prayer, drenching the covering of his *shtender* (lecturn) with tears.[47]

V.

Shortly after "770" was purchased, in the second half of August, notification was received in New York that Menachem Mendel and Moussia had fled from Vichy and had now settled in Nice, on the southern coast of France.[48] This was no doubt prompted by growing evidence that the French government of the so-called "Free Zone," which had relocated to Vichy, was collaborating with the Nazis.[49]

The couple found modest accommodations in Hôtel Rochambeau, 27 Rue Thiers, on the third floor. There they would remain for over nine months, until the end of May 1941, when all their immigration woes would finally come to an end. The hotel was run by an Algerian Jew and his non-Jewish wife, who gave the Schneersons special treatment, saving sugar for the couple from the hotel supplies. But life in wartime was difficult: their accommodation was tight and, among other hardships, electricity was only available for a few hours a day.[50]

In a 1945 letter to one of his former acquaintances in France, the future Rebbe gave a positive spin to the struggles of the time:

> Your letter awakened within me memories of the time we spent together in Vichy and Nice, each one of us in conditions to which we were not accustomed.
>
> When a person is uprooted from his familiar setting, until he becomes accustomed to his new demands and conditions, you can detect in him patterns of behavior that reflect his inner nature—without the external protocol that society demands.
>
> Frequently, these patterns of behavior reveal the hidden good within this person, of which he himself may have not been aware, it having been obscured by a "layer" of societal norms. He will be fortunate if he does not allow these patterns of behavior to become hidden again when he reaches a tranquil situation.[51]

One floor below the Schneersons resided Rabbi Yechiel Gertner (d. 1970), the fourth Rebbe in a dynasty of Polish Chasidut which originated in the small town of Lentshin, near Warsaw.[52] Menachem Mendel found there both a makeshift synagogue and scholarly friendship; he would engage the Lentshiner Rebbe in mammoth sessions of Torah discussion, lasting as long as four hours.[53]

While in Nice, we also know that Menachem Mendel gave at least one series of Talmud classes in a local synagogue, in tractate *Pesachim*. Notes of these classes have survived in his *Reshimot*, and it is likely that other *Reshimot* from this period also represent drafts of public classes, though we lack any personal testimony of attendees.[54]

Generally, Menachem Mendel and Moussia kept a characteristically low profile. When the future Rebbe was seen in the synagogue, few paid much interest to his presence.[55] Unable to communicate closely with Rayatz due to the war, Menachem Mendel and Moussia must surely have felt isolated. Though they did manage to receive some telegrams from New York via a neighbor, they must have been deeply concerned about the fate of Reb Levik and Chana, from whom they had received no communication in over a year, and about Menik and Sheina, who were still trapped in Nazi-occupied Poland.

The Schneersons sat, waited and prayed. Before the Jewish festivals of 5701 (1940-1) which the couple spent in Nice, Menachem Mendel went to great lengths to procure an exemplary Italian *etrog* for *Sukkot*, and hand-baked *shmurah matzah* for Passover, which presented an enormous challenge during the war years.[56]

Distressing news kept flooding in.[57] On 13th November 1940, the State Department informed Chabad Attorney Henry Butler that the earlier decision to grant the couple non-quota visas had been overturned in the absence of sufficient evidence that Menachem Mendel had "been carrying on the vocation of a minister of religion." Rather, evidence suggested that "he has been variously engaged as an engineer, a newspaper correspondent"—his work for the *Hatamim* periodical—"and a mechanic." On 15th January 1941, Menachem Mendel was informed of the decision, which had been confirmed by the Nice consulate.

The young couple had their application transferred to the consulate in Marseille. While the precise reasoning is unclear, we know that the Hebrew Immigrant Aid Society (HICEM), whom Menachem Mendel had petitioned for assistance, had an office in Marseille, and presumably had closer ties with the local consulate. During the final year that the Schneersons' application was in process, HICEM facilitated the emigration of 2167 Jews from France, and the organization, together with its American branch HIAS, proved instrumental in the rescue of the future Rebbe and Rebbetzin.[58]

On 29th January, HICEM notified the young couple that "at our request" the consulate in Marseille had reassessed the file, and requested their presence for an interview to clarify "the complexity of the matter."[59] Meanwhile, Chabad lawyer Arthur Rabinowitz again petitioned the State Department for visas to be granted to the Schneersons and Horensteins, this time appealing directly to the office of the "American Eichmann" himself, Breckenridge Long.

Astoundingly, on 7th February 1941—10th *Shevat*, the very same day on the Hebrew calendar when Menachem Mendel would assume the leadership of Chabad a decade later—Long wrote a personal memo authorizing the issue of visas to both the Schneersons and the Horensteins! The historic document, which is preserved among the

Breckinridge Long Papers in the Library of Congress, Manuscript Division,[60] reads:

> Mr. Arthur Rabinovitz advises me that Rabbi Mendel Schneersohn's visa application was transferred from Nice district to Marseilles district, and he is now refused non-quota visa by Marseilles. We authorized issue of visa. Consul at Marseilles suggests immigrant visa. I see no reason why he should not be granted immigrant visa even though we authorized non-quota. As we have communicated several times about Schneersohn and there seems to be no objection, I see no reason why we should not communicate further to Marseilles on his account.
>
> Also be advised that Rabbi Mendel Hornstein is still at Otwack, Poland, and has not received his visa. I see no reason why he should not receive either an immigrant or a non-quota visa, probably an immigrant. As long as we have telegraphed about him before, you might check the reports and if necessary check again.
>
> Please advise Mr. Rabinovitz about these matters.
>
> B. L.

With written authorization from the highest U.S. official assigned to immigration, it was only a question of time before the Schneersons would receive their visas. The notification finally arrived a month later, on 13th March—the festival of Purim—via telegram to New York, and the couple had the visas in their hands by 17th April (20th *Nissan*).

Nevertheless, two obstacles remained. Menachem Mendel and Moussia needed to secure entry visas into Portugal, since Lisbon was one of the only remaining neutral routes of passage to the United States; and they needed to obtain tickets for the trans-Atlantic voyage.

On 3rd May, the couple received the worrying news that, due to a huge bottleneck of refugees seeking to depart from Lisbon, all Portuguese visas had been suspended until further notice. At every moment the situation in France was worsening for the Jews. As the Schneersons awaited their Portuguese visas, the first wave of arrests took place in Paris, as 5,000 Jewish men were swept from their sleep at 6 a.m. into Nazi custody.

Fortunately, the couple did not have to wait too long. On 24th May (27th *Iyar*), a telegram was received that the Portuguese visas had been granted. By the beginning of June, they were already on their way to

Lisbon,[61] but securing tickets for the trans-Atlantic passage would prove challenging.[62]

As he struggled to find tickets in Lisbon, on 11th June, Rabbi Menachem Mendel penned what would be his final *reshimah* in Europe, a five-page treatise on the obscure Talmudic teaching, "The Son of David will not come until a fish is sought for an invalid and cannot be found."[63] That night, Mordechai Bistritzky—a Boyaner Chasid who had married a Lubavitcher girl, Shifra Lagovier, at a ceremony officiated by the Rebbe Rashab himself—entered into private audience with Rayatz in New York. Bistritzky's parents-in-law, Levi and Ruchma Lagovier, had purchased tickets for the *Serpa Pinto's* voyage the following day, 12th June. Unfortunately, the Lagoviers were stuck in Spain, unable to obtain visas to enter Portugal, and, having heard of Menachem Mendel and Moussia's plight, Bistritzky offered to transfer the tickets to their name. Tragically, the Lagoviers never managed to make the trip and perished in Auschwitz the following year, but through this noble gesture, the future Rebbe and Rebbetzin were saved, arriving in New York on 23rd June (28th *Sivan*), 1941[64]

VI.

Others were not so fortunate. Rayatz managed to send U.S. entry visas for a number of his followers, but in many cases, to no avail.[65]

A year later, in July 1941, the Nazis occupied Latvia and set about exterminating Jews, often by grabbing them off the street, placing them in a synagogue and setting the building aflame. On 30th November (10th *Kislev*) 1941, Rabbis Yechezkel Fegin, Eliyahu Chaim Althaus, and Yitzchak *Der Masmid* Horowitz, three of Rayatz's finest Chasidim, were burned to death by the Nazis in a Riga synagogue. According to one witness, they spent their last moments together dancing with a Torah Scroll, singing the tunes of *Simchat Torah*, the most joyous day of the Jewish year. News of the tragedy did not reach Rayatz until 1945; when he heard what had transpired, he collapsed on the floor, unconscious.[66]

The greatest personal tragedy for Rayatz was the failed rescue of his own daughter Sheina and her husband Menik Horenstein. At the outbreak of war, the couple had been in Otwock caring for Menik's father, Moshe Horenstein, who was severely ill. They remained at Moshe's side until he eventually passed away on 27th March (28th *Adar*) 1941, at which point it was impossible to secure exit visas from Poland, even though entry visas into the United States had by then been successfully obtained.[67] It was only in 1949 that Ramash managed to verify that Menik and Sheina had perished in Treblinka in 1942, along with Menik's mother Chaya Mushka (who was also Rayatz's paternal aunt). Due to Rayatz's extremely weak health, he was not informed that the couple's death had been confirmed, though by that time he had surely given up hope that his daughter had survived the war.[68] The news hit Moussia hard, as she had been extremely close with her younger sister during the years spent together in France. "When my sister passed away, my whole world darkened," she said.

Back in Russia, Menachem Mendel's immediate family also suffered tremendous misfortune. On 29th March (9th *Nissan*) 1939, the Soviets arrested Reb Levik and took him away for imprisonment and trial for conducting "illegal" activities, such as building a *mikvah* and raising funds to support Jewish families. Chana was not permitted to visit her husband in prison for nine months, and seeing him for the first time she was shocked by how emaciated he had become through near-starvation. Found guilty of the charges leveled against him, Reb Levik was sentenced to five years of exile in the remote village of Chi'ili in Kazhakhstan. "You will have to forgive me," he said to his wife before departing on a one-month journey. "I am not sure I have the strength to survive the trip."

While he did arrive alive, Reb Levik was forced to spend the next years in abysmal conditions, most of the time isolated in a mosquito-ridden mud hut, which he shared with an unsympathetic non-Jewish couple. Chana paid extended visits and she too was plagued by starvation and a near-fatal bout of malaria. While he had no congregation to teach, Reb Levik's peace of mind was partially restored when Chana was able to prepare ink from some grasses with which her husband could pen his Torah thoughts. Having no paper, he wrote notes in tiny script in the empty margins of the few books that Chana had managed to bring with her. While the thousands of pages which Reb Levik penned in Yekatrinoslav did not survive, his exile notes did make it out of Russia and were published in four volumes in 1970.[69] For years, he had no contact with his children.

Most of Dnipropetrovsk's 90,000 Jews succeeded in leaving before the Germans occupied the city on 24th August 1941, and the total death toll after liberation by the Red Army two years later was about 20,000. In her memoirs, Chana recalled, "Thank G-d, none of our close friends had remained there."[70] However, during this time, when Reb Levik and Chana were in exile, they were forced to leave their son Berel behind.

In 1941, *Einsatzkommando* (subgroup) 6 of *Einsatzgruppe* (killing squad) C ordered the liquidation of Igren Psychiatric Hospital, a facility in the environs of Dnipropetrovsk (now part of the city), where Berel was residing.[71] Jewish patients were murdered first, led in groups into a large room where they were given lethal injections. According to Soviet documents, 1,000 patients from Igren were murdered in 1941-1942.[72]

There were further tragedies. In Nikolayev, on 20th December (20th *Kislev*) 1939, Chana's younger sister Miriam Gittel, still in her early fifties, died from an illness. Her husband, Rabbi Shmuel Schneerson (Reb Levik's brother and the Rabbi who had given *semicha* to Menachem Mendel), was heartbroken, but this was just the beginning of his woes. Half a year later, on 29th June (4th *Tammuz*) 1941, Shmuel was arrested by the Soviets and sentenced to three years exile in Tomsk, Siberia. Shmuel and Miriam Gittel's only child, Menachem Mendel, remained with his wife Genia in Nikolayev until the German's approach, and then fled to Türkmenabat, Turkmenistan in Central Asia.

While Meir Shlomo Yanovsky had already passed away in 1933, his wife, the maternal grandmother of both Menachem Mendel Schneersons, was still alive. Menachem Mendel and Genia, unwilling to leave their grandmother, planned to take her along with them; but already in her eighties,[73] Rachel was hardly in a fit state for a two-thousand mile journey. Some neighbors who were not Jewish kindly offered to take care of her, and she remained in Nikolayev. When the Nazis occupied the city, the neighbors faithfully hid Rachel away in their home, but, perhaps fearing Nazi intimidation, another neighbor informed the Germans of her presence, and she was taken away to be killed.

Shmuel Schneerson's heart was too weak to survive three years in Siberia, and he was released after a year and a half. He subsequently joined his son in Türkmenabat, but the ordeal had depleted him and he passed away shortly afterward on 8th December (11th *Kislev*) 1943, at the age of fifty-five.[74]

While the Seventh Rebbe never publicly bemoaned the loss of his family members during the war, there is one 1984 letter where he makes a brief reference to the passing of Rachel, Berel and others. In response to an individual who questioned G-d's reason for the Holocaust, the Rebbe wrote,

> The only answer we can give is: only G-d knows.
>
> However, the very fact that there is no answer to this question is, in itself, proof that one is not required to know the answer, or understand it, in order to fulfill one's purpose in life.
>
> Despite the lack of satisfactory answer to the awesome and tremendous "Why?"—one can, and must, carry on a meaningful and productive life, promote justice and kindness in one's surroundings, and indeed, help create a world where there should be no room for any holocaust, or for any kind of man's inhumanity to man.
>
> As a matter of fact, in the above there is an answer to an unspoken question: "What should my reaction be?" The answer to this question is certain: It must be seen as a challenge to every Jew—because Jews were the principal victims of the Holocaust—a challenge that should be met head on, with all resolve and determination, namely, that regardless how long it will take the world to repent for the Holocaust and make the world a fitting place to live in for all human beings—I, for one, will not slacken in my determination to carry out my purpose in life, which is to serve G-d, wholeheartedly and with joy, and make this world a fitting abode—not only for humans, but also for the *Shechina*, the Divine Presence itself.
>
> Of course, much more could be said on the subject, but why dwell on such a painful matter, when there is so much good to be done?

While he was generally averse to mentioning personal misfortunes, in order that the questioner should not get the sense that the answer was too emotionally detached, the Rebbe added in a postscript.

> Needless to say, the above may be accepted intellectually, and it may ease the mind, but it cannot assuage the pain and upheaval, especially of one who has been directly victimized by the Holocaust.
>
> Thus, in this day and age of rampant suspicion, *etc.*, especially when one is not known personally, one may perhaps say —"Well, it is easy for one who is not emotionally involved to give an intellectual explanation..."

> So, I ought perhaps, to add that I, too, lost in the Holocaust very close and dear relatives such as a grandmother, brother, cousins and others (G-d should avenge their blood). But, life according to G-d's commands, must go on, and the sign of life is in growth and creativity.[75]

Menachem Mendel Schneerson demonstrated a remarkable ability to put the past behind him and dedicate himself to constructive activity. His arrival in America in 1941 began what would be over a half-century of public work on behalf of the Lubavitch movement, building from a handful of survivors and salvaged manuscripts what would become the largest Jewish organization in the world. It is a story of remarkable vision, resilience and determination to which we now will turn.

CHAPTER NINE

LIFE IN AMERICA

1941–1949

Ramash (left) with Rayatz (right) in the Sixth Rebbe's study at 770 (1949).

On 22nd June 1941, the eve of Menachem Mendel and Moussia's arrival from Europe, Rayatz called four senior Chasidim into his office: Rabbi Shmuel Levitin, Rabbi Yisrael Jacobson, Rabbi Eliyahu Simpson and Rabbi Shlomo Aharon Kazarnovsky. The Rebbe announced that his daughter and son-in-law were due to arrive by boat the following day and, unable to be at the pier himself due to ill health, he requested the four elders to personally welcome the couple, along with the Yeshivah students.

Perhaps concerned that Menachem Mendel's unassuming demeanor and modern dress might confuse Chasidim, Rayatz briefed the four rabbis about the spiritual caliber of his son-in-law with the following introduction: "He carries out *tikkun chatzot* (midnight penitential rites) every night. He is fluent in the Babylonian Talmud with the commentaries of *Rif, Ran,* and *Rosh*;[1] in the Jerusalem Talmud with its major commentaries; in Maimonides and in *Likutei Torah* with all the cross references.[2] Despite this, he walks with a hat that has its brim turned down."[3] (In formal Rabbinic garb, an upturned brim is usually a sign of esteem.)

The welcoming committee would see a man dressed in a light suit, grey hat and neatly tucked beard, but Rayatz wanted his Chasidim to have some sense of what lay beneath the "turned-down brim."

Chasidim flocked to "770" the entire day to see the Rebbe's daughter and son-in-law, and welcome them to the safe shores of America.[4] Menachem Mendel and Moussia spent most of the night reconnecting with family—Nechama Dina, Chana, Rashag and Shalom Ber—it was no small feat to be saved from the Nazis. Strangely, Rayatz did not participate, nor did he go out to meet his daughter or son-in-law until three days after their arrival, at which point he asked them to come into his office separately.

Menachem Mendel later attributed this to the Sixth Rebbe's intense emotionality[5]—Rayatz had no doubt been utterly devastated by news of the Nazi invasion of Russia, which hit the press in New York the very morning of his daughter and son-in-law's arrival. As the Sixth Rebbe sat in safety, about to be reunited with his immediate family, he was painfully aware that his extended "family" of Lubavitch devotees in Russia were on the verge of extinction.

Chasidim caught another glimpse of Menachem Mendel's thickly veiled piety when, on *Rosh Chodesh* (beginning of the Jewish month) a few days later, he was seen in the synagogue donning four pairs of *tefilin*.[6] Uncomfortable with the undue attention, the future Rebbe decided that he would not perform this ritual in public again.[7]

Rabbi Menachem Mendel (known to the community of Chasidim by the acronym of his initials, "Ramash") was approached and asked if he would *farbreng*, sharing words of Torah at an informal gathering. That Thursday night, American Chasidim tasted from the wisdom of Rabbi Menachem Mendel Schneerson for the first time. There were about twenty people present, a few senior Chasidim and Yeshivah students. Ramash recognized a few of the American students whom he had met in 1939 at the Paris train station, as they made their way to Otwock to visit the Rebbe Rayatz.[8] Ramash asked other Chasidim, most of whom were older than him, to speak first, but they all declined.

"Does anybody have a question in Chasidut?" he asked. A few members of the crowd were forthcoming with questions. Ramash listened intently to each, without responding, asking only "what is your name and your mother's name?" to each questioner.

That morning in synagogue, Ramash had made the blessing of *hagomel,* a short prayer of gratitude for salvation from a life-threatening situation, and he devoted a good part of the *farbrengen* to explaining the significance of the blessing according to Talmudic, Kabbalistic and Chasidic sources.[9] As he weaved together numerous citations, Ramash creatively expounded upon the significance of the names of all the questioners and offered solutions to their queries. It was an intellectual *tour de force* to which the crowd was not ordinarily accustomed. Even the brighter students were unable to completely follow what was being said.

While the joy of being reunited with Rayatz must have been unbounded, Ramash was no doubt still in some shock at having seen his father-in-law for the first time in a wheelchair, the Rebbe's health having deteriorated considerably from his tribulations.[10] At the *farbrengen,* when Ramash mentioned his father-in-law, the Rebbe, his voice choked up and he began to cry.

A few hours into the night, Ramash turned to the American students whom he recognized and said, "Now let's carry on the discussion that we started at the train station." As though time, space and a formenting World War had not intervened, Ramash continued the Torah discourse, as if they had just started the previous day. Later in the evening, Ramash tested the American students on their knowledge of the Sixth Rebbe's published talks, and the *farbrengen* finally concluded at around 3 a.m.[11]

Ramash had made his "debut," and, no doubt, the American Lubavitchers were not exactly sure what to make of him. He had a distinct presence and an astoundingly broad knowledge. He demonstrated an unusual intellectual creativity, vastly transcending the plain storytelling and regurgitating of ideas which was often to be heard from less independent thinkers. His no-nonsense demeanor commanded respect, even a certain degree of awe. While naturally reserved, he seemed resolute, confident and determined; and yet he was refreshingly approachable and down-to-earth. The Lubavitchers must have been intrigued by a man wearing distinctly Western garb who was a qualified engineer, and yet who possessed a profoundly Chasidic demeanor and encyclopedic knowledge of Jewish texts. Seven-Seventy was going to be different with the Rebbe's younger son-in-law around.

For the first time in his life, Ramash was to live at the Lubavitcher Rebbe's court on a permanent basis, surrounded by Chasidim. Initially the couple resided at "770," but due to lack of space they soon moved to an apartment a couple of blocks away, at 346 New York Avenue, Apartment 4D.

At least until around 1944, he worked as an electrical engineer at the Brooklyn Navy Yard, returning to his office in 770 at 3:30 p.m. To compensate for his absence at the Navy Yard on the Sabbath, Ramash was required to attend on Sundays, where he would sit working alone in a vast, rat-infested hall in the Electrical Building. During the week, Ramash worked with three-hundred other white-shirted electrical engineers, who sat at drafting tables, working on wiring diagrams for the *USS Missouri* and *Idaho*.

Milton Fechter, who worked in an adjacent section, remembered how the bearded Ramash was not afraid to stand out. "Boy, I've got to give this guy credit," Fechter recalled thinking to himself. "He sat there so serene as if he is sitting among his *chevre* (buddies)." Over a half-century later, Fechter still remembered that "Schneerson" excelled in Mathematics more than most of the other engineers, and had been able to decipher the advanced, three-volume French textbook *Cours d'Analyse Mathématique*, by Édouard Goursat (1858-1936).[12] Generally, though, Ramash kept a low profile and did not socialize with the other workers. He certainly did not disclose that he was the Lubavitcher Rebbe's son-in-law.[13]

Alongside his work at the Navy Yard, Ramash soon became deeply engaged with Rayatz's activism. As we shall see, within three years, Ramash headed four organizations which had been created by the Sixth Rebbe to serve the needs of American Jewry, and this represented the beginning of half a century of his full-time devoted work to the Chabad movement.

What changed? The Menachem Mendel Schneerson we have known until now, by his own admission, did not enjoy communal work and shied away from positions of honor.[14] He had sought a quiet existence, earning a modest livelihood from professional work that still allowed for many hours of Torah study. Yet, within three years of arriving in America, he would be working full-time for Chabad, leading a number of institutions; and in a decade he would be appointed as Rebbe of the international Chabad movement. All this seems a radical departure from the life Ramash had lived until now.

Since he maintained no diaries or private correspondence that would reveal his inner world, and probably confided these matters only to Moussia, we lack a clear indication as to why Ramash now stepped up to positions of considerable communal responsibility. His temperament certainly had not changed. We never get the sense that he *enjoyed* communal work or that he sought high office, but he seems to have become gradually convinced that this was his duty and life mission.

A number of factors may have been involved in this shift. First, Ramash surely owed a huge debt of gratitude to *Agudat Chasidei Chabad* which, through herculean diplomatic efforts, had saved him from war-torn Europe, perhaps saving his life.[15]

Second, while we are not privy to all the details of Rayatz's health, it had evidently regressed from the last time Ramash had seen him in 1938. In the photos of Rayatz's arrival in the U.S.A. he can be seen confined to a wheelchair, something the Sixth Rebbe had resisted before the German bombing of Warsaw. It was clear that Rayatz needed both his sons-in-law's support more than ever.

Thirdly, knowing that Ramash greatly valued his independence and privacy, Rayatz wisely created a new role for his younger son-in-law that would provide him with absolute autonomy—Ramash would be answerable only to the Rebbe himself. These new organizations were also tailor-made for Ramash's specific talents, interests and familiarity with Western culture: writing and publishing Jewish texts for popular and scholarly consumption, and providing visionary leadership of "outreach" work aimed at engaging secularized, American Jews.

Fourthly, Ramash was undoubtedly inspired by the Sixth Rebbe's exceptional resolve to revive Orthodox life in America, despite enormous pressure to resign to the prevailing sentiment that "America is different." Disregarding advice to retreat to a rural town where his "extreme" views would be less noticeable, Rayatz settled in Crown Heights, right "in the face" of wealthy, Conservative Jews, openly challenging their conviction that East-European traditionalism was a relic of the past.

While he was extremely grateful to the United States for saving his life, writing personal letters of thanks to Secretary of State Cordell Hull, Justice Louis Brandeis and even to President Roosevelt,[16] Rayatz did not perceive his salvation as a mere personal matter. The Sixth Rebbe felt he had been saved to act as a voice for deeply traditional, Chasidic Judaism in a country which had, by and large, rejected it. Today, after the huge renaissance of Yeshivah-style and Chasidic Judaism which has blossomed in America since the war, it is difficult to imagine how outlandish Rayatz's position must have sounded at the time. It was, however, sufficient to anger the Sixth Rebbe's own supporters. "Please respect the honor of your ancestors and do not allow yourself to be ridiculed," Rayatz was warned after his very first public address on the day of his arrival.

"I cried bitterly that night when saying the bed time prayers," he later confided.[17] The Rebbe was deeply saddened, but not dissuaded.[18]

Rayatz's resolute determination, despite his own poor health and the dissolution of his empire back in Russia and Poland, was no doubt a source of great inspiration to Ramash. In a 1983 sermon, he reflected:

> When the previous Rebbe came to America, he announced that the purpose of his coming was not to ensure his own personal safety, but to demonstrate that "America is no different," and consequently, he would continue the same activities, the spreading of Torah and *mitzvot*, in which he was involved in Europe.
>
> On the surface, the very opposite seemed to have been true. The previous Rebbe fled Europe on the last ship to leave before the Nazi conquest. It appeared outwardly that he came to America for his own sake, because America *was* different—the danger which threatened him in Europe did not exist here. So how could he have described the purpose of his coming otherwise?
>
> But when we contemplate the character of the previous Rebbe and his life in depth, it becomes clear that he lived for—and felt constantly the urgency—to spread Judaism in every place, through every means, and to raise consciousness of Jewish unity. Wherever he lived, he worked for these goals. It was impossible for him to do otherwise, because that was his mission in this world.
>
> Just as in Europe, his life mission here was to spread Judaism. The means of accomplishing the mission changed, but the goal remained the same.[19]

II.

These four factors which would have made a deep impression on Ramash—Rayatz's gratitude for personal salvation, positive vision for America, declining health, and the opportunity to direct personalized organizations—no doubt resonated strongly, but they had been present, in one form or another, in the past. Rayatz had, after all, saved his son-in-law from the perils of Communist Russia; the Rebbe's health had been in serious decline for over a decade, and there had been plenty of opportunity for a positive vision and to work on outreach at Rayatz's side in Latvia and Poland. (In fact, Latvia, like America, was a democratic country in the 1930s and Chabad conducted some considerable outreach work there which was, in many ways, a precursor to Chabad activities in America.[20])

There was, however, a totally unprecedented fifth element which came to the fore in 1941, something that was arguably Ramash's strongest motivator: the acute Messianism of Rayatz.

While the Messianic idea is as old as the Bible itself, with apocalyptic yearning filling the books of the Prophets and capturing the imagination of the Talmudic Rabbis, Chasidism had initially muted the Messianic impulse. Hopes for a global redemption were, of course, never abandoned, but the thrust of Chasidism shifted focus from the global to the individual, to acquiring an awareness of the Divine in every moment, event and thing. Reaching a state of awakened consciousness, the Chasidic worshipper achieves a level of *personal* redemption, perceiving G-d in even the most mundane strata of the universe; but this has the concurrent effect of rendering the urge for global redemption less urgent. If G-d is tangibly present in the here and now, then why worry about anything else?[21]

The Kabbalah, which was a precursor to Chasidut, *did* place much emphasis on a global, apocalyptic event to be precipitated by a critical mass of good deeds and Jewish rituals throughout history; and while this general model was upheld in Chabad,[22] the main emphasis shifted to personal growth through prayer, contemplation and the study of Chasidut.

Around the turn of the Twentieth Century, Rabbi Shalom Dov Ber (Rashab) began to invoke some strong Messianic rhetoric for the first time, particularly in his critique of secular Zionism. His vision, however, remained at its core, local and parochial: Chabad Chasidim should be proactive in restoring traditional observance in the Jewish communities of Russia.

Now that Rayatz had relocated to America, his constituency had expanded to include virtually the entire Jewish world. He still cared deeply for the four and a half million Jews trapped in his native Russia, who were being mercilessly persecuted by Stalin; for the three and a half million Jews in his former home of Poland, who stood on the verge of annihilation; and for the close to five million Jews who resided peacefully—but quite irreligiously—in his new home, the United States.

What was the common thread binding these three domains which Providence had placed in Rayatz's direct sphere of influence? And what could be done to help the terrible plight of the millions of Jews in Europe whose lives were in danger? To answer these questions, the Sixth Rebbe drew on the Messianic idea.[23]

Rayatz encapsulated the Messianic ideal in a catchy slogan for his American audience: *le-alter le-teshuvah, le-alter le-geulah,* ("Immediately to *teshuvah,* immediately to redemption"). In a series of "urgent appeals" published in newspapers during the early 1940s,[24] the Sixth Lubavitcher Rebbe made his case: The Jewish people are one organic entity and Judaism classically affirms mass *teshuvah* as a tool of redemption from global catastrophe. Jews in America could possibly avert an imminent catastrophe in Europe if they would recommit themselves, in some serious measure, to observant Judaism, which was their precious inheritance.

Chabad outreach now took on a far greater scope and urgency than ever before. *Teshuvah* in America was seen as crucial for the entire world—and it needed to be invoked immediately, as millions of Jews faced their deaths.

Even if Rayatz's message failed to inspire the majority of American Jews, it did succeed in utterly captivating his younger son-in-law. By Ramash's own admission, thoughts of global redemption had fascinated him since childhood, and this historically unprecedented, acute Messianic call emanating from such an elevated soul as Rayatz resonated with him deeply. Ramash would even sign off his correspondence, "with blessings for *le-alter le-teshuvah, le-alter le-geulah.*"

Even after a few years, when the urgency of the message had passed and the Jewish people had suffered the tragic losses of the Holocaust,

Ramash did not perceive Rayatz's Messianic awakening of the early 1940s as an unsuccessful campaign of the past. In the Seventh Rebbe's view, Rayatz had *permanently* redefined Chabad from a parochial movement into a global-universal force. There had been an irreversible shift in Chabad's sense of mission: From now onwards, the scope and intensity of Chabad outreach would be energized by the heightened Messianic consciousness that Rayatz had kindled.

In a 1987 sermon, the Seventh Rebbe reflected on the ongoing significance of Rayatz's wartime campaign.

> The Rebbe Rayatz initiated a vociferous campaign of *le-alter le-teshuvah, le-alter le-geulah.* He was outspoken, instructing that the message should be printed and aggressively disseminated, which led to various difficulties being imposed by others. (I don't wish to employ a stronger expression, but it was actually something far greater than "difficulties.") Nevertheless, he continued to instruct that the message be printed, so that it would be there for future generations....
>
> When the late Rebbe Rashab had spoken at a *farbrengen* in 5766 [1906] with an acute Messianic urgency, the message only remained with those who had been present at the *farbrengen*, or those who had notes from the talk.... But when the Rebbe Rayatz began his vociferous campaign of *le-alter le-teshuvah, le-alter le-geulah,* he instructed specifically that it should be printed and publicized. On another occasion he himself had taught (citing *Tzemach Tzedek*) that when something is printed it becomes relevant to future generations. He was hinting that even after his life on the earthly plane would end, the message would remain in full force.[25]

In the Seventh Rebbe's understanding, Rayatz's call to *teshuvah* and redemption, while initially articulated in the context of the horrors of World War Two, permanently redefined the mission of Chabad. The task at hand, to which Ramash devoted the next half-century of his life, was to inspire Jews worldwide towards *teshuvah*—in the hope that G-d would then reciprocate with the second part of the formula and bring the people "immediately to redemption."

III.

Prior to 1940, Chabad's main work for decades had been the building of its Yeshivah network, and, arriving in America, it was Rayatz's immediate priority to establish Yeshivot and schools. On his very first day in the country, the Sixth Rebbe refused to retire to bed until he received a promise from devotees that a Chabad Yeshivah would open straight away. The next morning, a handful of young men gathered together to form a makeshift Yeshivah in the basement of *Oneg Shabbat,* a Brooklyn synagogue. The students were mainly American boys whom Yisrael Jacobson had drawn close to Chabad. [26]

Rayatz entrusted the development of the Chabad Yeshivah system in America to his older son-in-law, Rabbi Samarius (Shmaryahu) Gourary (1897-1989), known to the Chasidim by the acronym of his Hebrew names, Rashag. Rabbi Gourary had been deeply involved in the administration of *Yeshivat Tomchei Temimim* network in Europe since his 1921 marriage to Rayatz's oldest daughter Chana Schneersohn (1899-1991), but it was on the safe and free shores of America that Rashag's administrative and fundraising talents began to shine in full force. The son of a wealthy Chabad family which had owned a cigarette factory and lumber mill back in Russia, Rashag was a remarkably talented individual who was considered by the Fifth Lubavitcher Rebbe, Rabbi Shalom Dov Ber, as one of the finest students of his Yeshivah. While Rashag did not share the rare genius of his younger brother-in-law, he was still extremely fluent in Chabad Chasidic thought and was reputed to have committed some six-hundred *ma'amarim* (discourses) to memory.[27]

Interestingly, Ramash played no formal role in building the Yeshivot. Sensing his need for autonomy, and realizing that his talents might be put to better use elsewhere, Rayatz carved a totally independent role for his younger son-in-law, creating three new organizations for him to direct and build: *Machne Israel* ("Camp of Israel"), *Merkos L'Inyanei Chinuch* ("Center for Jewish Education"), and *Karnei Hod Torah* ("Rays of the Torah's Glory").

Machne Israel was a society aimed at practically implementing Rayatz's call of *le-alter le-teshuvah, le-alter le-geulah,* a slogan which was incorporated into the organization's logo. *Machne* sought to enlist Jews who were Torah observant, but not necessarily Chabad, and impart them with an outreach orientation. The name "Camp of Israel" was chosen specifically to convey a message of inclusiveness and the lack of any particular denominational bias. The "dues" of membership payable were: to encourage four good deeds per month among other, less observant adult Jews, such as increased observance in the laws of *Kashrut, Shabbat, Tefilin* and Family Purity (*Mikvah*). Membership was kept utterly confidential so as to keep motivation pure and ensure that participants would not be made uncomfortable by their peers. The goal of all members, according to a 1943 mission statement, was "through their exemplary conduct in the spirit of the Torah and its *mitzvot,* to influence their families, their business acquaintances and the members of their synagogues."[28]

Ramash encouraged the spread of *Machne Israel* to other locations, seeking activists who would carry out the necessary work in Montreal and Israel.[29] Together with Rayatz, he also expanded the activities to include: a special branch to encourage Sabbath observance, a youth division, groups dedicated to the recital of *Tehillim* (Psalms), a branch devoted to visiting the sick, a campaign to establish Torah classes for working men, a special division for Jewish farmers, and a campaign to study texts of *Mishnah* by heart. For at least three consecutive years, from 1942 to 1945, Ramash arranged an annual *siyum* (celebration of completing a study cycle) at 770, where he would deliver an advanced lecture about the importance of *Mishnah* study, and deliver a *pilpul* (Talmudic analysis) of the last *Mishnah* studied.[30] At the first event, which was attended by a few hundred Jews from a variety of denominations, Rayatz himself was well enough to attend. In following years, the Sixth Rebbe listened by live hook-up upstairs, in his room.[31]

The relatively high public profile of *Machne Israel* also placed Ramash in a position where he could correspond directly with a broad spectrum of inquirers about different aspects of Judaism. In one letter, he indicated that this had been one of Rayatz's intentions in founding the organization: "My father-in-law, the Lubavitcher Rebbe, Rabbi Yosef Yitzchak Schneersohn, *shlita,* founded *Machne Yisrael* with the intent—among others—of making known and publicizing to Jews in all different circles the correct meaning and lofty message of Judaism, and to answer any questions that might possibly arise with regard to Yiddishkeit, the Torah, and its *mitzvot....* By writing to you, I would like to clarify that we would be happy to remain in contact and, to the best of our knowledge, elucidate particular concepts involving the above issues."[32]

In the published correspondence of Ramash spanning these years, there are literally hundreds of letters devoted to a scholarly clarification of points of Jewish interest, and the preparation of this material must have taken some considerable time. Ramash also wrote a regular "Ask the Rabbi" column in the Lubavitch journal, *Kovetz Lubavitch* from 1944-46, addressing issues such as: the difference between personal and communal *teshuvah,* the letter permutations of the Divine name *Elokim,* the Talmudic promise that all Jews will merit the World-to-Come, a detailed analysis of sources pertaining to the Resurrection of the Dead, and differences between *Ashkenazim* and *Sefardim* with regards to the blessing on *tefilin.*[33]

From the dearth of publicity and correspondence from the late 1940s onwards, it appears that within a few years of the war's end *Machne Israel* had become inactive. It still existed as an organization on paper, and Ramash would sometimes sign off as its director on formal communications, but its work of inspiring Jews to *teshuvah* seems to have been linked directly to Rayatz's acute Messianic call during the war.[34]

Still, its activities remain significant as some of the future Rebbe's initial outreach efforts on American soil. The man who turned Judaism outwards did not do so overnight, and his directorship of *Machne Israel* was a bold first attempt to bring secular Jews towards increased observance. Many of the features of the Seventh Rebbe's future activities can already be discerned in the work of *Machne Israel:* a highly ambitious national and international vision; an unambiguous and practical method of implementation; a sense of accountability through regular reports to head office; attention to branding, slogans and public relations; a sensitivity to the need for secrecy and confidentiality, where necessary; scholarly support for the ideology through carefully-researched, Torah discourse—and all this, of course, energized by an underlying sense of Messianic urgency.

IV.

A second institution which was directed by Ramash since its founding in 1941 was *Merkos L'Inyanei Chinuch,* originally formed to promote authentic Jewish education among children. Its initial activities were humble: Shabbat gatherings devoted to storytelling and Jewish ideas, and evening classes for children. "The Rebbe [Rayatz] has begun with Shabbat parties," Ramash told listeners at a *farbrengen* in 1942, "and this will eventually lead to us reaching the entire world!"[35] Nobody at the time could have imagined how literally these words would materialize. Seventy years later, *Merkos* would have a physical presence in virtually every Jewish community in the world, manned by thousands of Chabad men and women.

Due to the strict separation of Church and State in America, it was impossible to conduct any activities in public schools, but *Merkos* took advantage of new "Released Time" legislation, sanctioning religious instruction during school hours if conducted off school premises. The *Shiurei Limud Hadat* ("Classes for the Study of Religion") program, founded in 1942, encouraged Yeshivah students to teach "Released Time" classes for an hour every Wednesday to public school students who were transferred to local synagogues.

The program was hugely successful. Rabbi Jacob J. Hecht (1923-1990), who directed operations from 1946, reported in his first year that as many as 8,000 children attended "released time" activities each week, from all over New York City. Ramash was thrilled, Hecht recalled, and deeply moved by the large number of participants. "He loved the fact that thousands of children all gathered on the same day and said *Shema Yisrael* together."[36]

Another innovative program of *Merkos*, which has also enjoyed decades of consistent activity, is the summer placement of Yeshivah students in distant Jewish communities around the world, "to promote Judaism, Jewish education, and give out Jewish books."[37] While some placements were facilitated as early as 1943, the program only gathered momentum in the summer of 1948, when Rayatz openly encouraged it, and that year some twenty students visited one hundred locations in America.

The power of these visitations to reach Jews who had been geographically isolated from a Jewish community for years, was something the Seventh Rebbe appreciated immensely. In an unusual 1977 letter, he personally recounted an inspiring incident he had heard about the ripple effect of the summer placements.

> In the course of this program it so happened that one of the students visited a small, Jewishly isolated town where he found only a few Jewish families, and, as he later reported, he was disappointed to have accomplished nothing there. But several months later, our *Merkos L'Inyanei Chinuch,* which sponsors this program, received a letter from one of the families in that town. The writer, a woman, related that one summer day she happened to stand by her front window when she saw a bearded young man, wearing a dark hat, his *tzitzit* showing, approaching her door. She confessed that when she admitted the young man and learned of the purpose of his visit, she was not responsive, for she and her family were not prepared at that moment to change their lifestyle; yet for a long time after that encounter, the appearance of the young man haunted her. He reminded her of her grandfather and had refreshed her memories of the beautiful Jewish life she had seen in her grandparents' home, though the material circumstances were incomparably more modest than she had come to know in her married life. Finally—the letter went on—she decided to make the change. She made her home kosher, and the family began to observe *Shabbat* and *Yom Tov* [Festivals], and she is raising the children in the Torah way. Since then her home was filled with such contentment and serenity that she decided to write to the M. L. Ch. and express her profound gratitude.[38]

Another major area of the early work of *Merkos* was to initiate Jewish girls schools in New York and the surrounding states, at a time when Jewish education for girls was in its infancy.[39] Ramash, it seems, did not participate in any major fundraising, and the establishments were started through volunteers, assisted by loans made from Rayatz's limited funds to provide seed money. Each school, it was hoped, would soon run autonomously. By 1946, twenty-six girls schools had been started—named either *Beth Rivkah,* after the Fourth Lubavitcher Rebbetzin, or *Beth Sara,* after Rayatz's mother, who passed away in 1942.[40]

With all the organizations that Ramash headed, we find an attentiveness to branding and presentation, each institution having its own elaborate logo and headed notepaper. The *Merkos* insignia is particularly interesting as it visually conveys, even at this early stage, many elements of the future Rebbe's approach and vision. The typeface, Ramash insisted, should be modern, and the presentation avant-garde, a sharp deviation from the ornate French and Old English thematics which were popular among traditional institutions of the day. The two Tablets of the Ten Commandments, which appeared prominently in the top right-hand corner of the logo, were an instantly recognizable Jewish motif but depicted in a way that most American Jews would find unfamiliar. Rather than the near ubiquitous image of two-dimensional Tablets drawn with half-round cupolas at the top, the *Merkos* logo presented the Tablets as perfectly rectangular, three-dimensional cubes. The idea was to restore this ancient symbol to its square, cubic image as depicted in the Talmud,[41] rejecting the rounded-top tablets which have no authentic Jewish source and presumably entered Hebrew literature through the censorship of Christian-owned printing houses.[42] The *Merkos* logo, then, was a subtle form of protest, conveying the organization's intention to be proactive in restoring American Jews to core Biblical and Talmudic values, untainted by cultural influences. Yet, paradoxically, these Old World values were conveyed with state-of-the-art design and modern typography, visually encapsulating the Seventh Rebbe's "signature approach" of employing New World methods to Old World values. The image of the planet Earth in the center of the logo made the ambitious, global scope of *Merkos'* vision quite clear.[43]

As we have seen, Ramash continued to work in the Brooklyn Navy Yard until around 1944 and much of the administrative work of *Merkos* was carried out by his two colleagues in the ground floor office at 770: Rabbi Chaim Mordechai Aizik Chodakov and Rabbi Nissan Mindel. Ramash established a close working relationship with these two men, both of whom continued to work with him for the next half-century, forming the backbone of his staff.

Chodakov was born in 1902 in Beshonkowitz, Russia, but his family relocated to Riga, Latvia two years later. While he had some Chabad ancestors, Chodakov was raised in a devout but non-Chasidic tradition. By the age of eighteen his natural talent for administration had already come to light and he was appointed the principal of the *Torah ve-Derech Eretz School* in Latvia, running a curriculum that incorporated both Torah and secular studies in the Hirschian model. The school grew rapidly and soon became recognized by the board of education to receive government funding. By 1934, Rabbi Chodakov was appointed by the Latvian Ministry of Education as Head of Jewish Education, and he used his influence to steer the schools towards more traditional modes of study, often replacing a non-observant teacher with an observant one. During the time Rayatz was in Riga, Rabbi Chodakov worked with the Sixth Rebbe closely, and, as we have seen, with the outbreak of war, Rayatz managed to convince Chodakov to join his party to America. These young talents would be needed to build Chabad in the New World, which was similar in many ways to democratic Latvia.

Ramash, who had first met Chodakov in Riga back in 1927,[44] appreciated his Latvian colleague's strong work ethic, effective administration skills, frugality, modesty and high level of confidentiality. "If you knew Rabbi Chodakov," Ramash wrote in a 1949 letter, "there would be no doubt in your mind that he is not capable of lies or exaggeration."[45] When he would ascend to the role of Rebbe, Ramash would later appoint Chodakov as his chief of staff, to lead the administration of all of Chabad's educational and outreach activities, under the umbrella of *Merkos L'Inyanei Chinuch.*

The third desk in the *Merkos* office—later to become the Seventh Rebbe's private study—was occupied by another Latvian Jew, Rabbi Nissan Mindel. Born in 1912, Mindel attended Chodakov's *Torah ve-Derech Eretz School.* He studied law and economics at the University of Manchester in England, where he graduated with a B.A. and M.A., while also obtaining *semicha* and serving as assistant Rabbi in the *Holy Law Congregation.* In 1937 he married the daughter of Rabbi Avrahom Sender Nemtzov, a Lubavitcher Chasid who had settled in Manchester.

While visiting his parents in Riga in 1938, Mindel was pressured by Rabbi Chodakov to begin working as a secretary for Rayatz in Otwock. Not desiring to move to Poland, Mindel requested a large salary to make Chodakov lose interest. When the offer was surprisingly accepted, Mindel's wife, who was back in England, advised him to take the position on a temporary basis so that they would at least have a good income. The two-month trial turned into six months and then a year. Two weeks before the outbreak of war, Mindel's visa was about to expire and he was given Rayatz's blessing to return to Riga; but he remained stuck in Riga, unable to obtain the necessary visas to return to England. When Rayatz arrived from Poland a few months later, Mindel actively worked with the Latvian consulate to secure the Rebbe's release, and traveled with the Rebbe's entourage to Sweden and the U.S.A.

Tragically, most of Mindel's family was killed after the Nazi occupation of Latvia, save for three of his siblings.

Though he had never formally studied in a Chabad Yeshivah, Nissan Mindel's excellent knowledge of Torah sources, English and Western thought was a great asset to Chabad. While he was clean-shaven and did not present himself as a Chasid, Rayatz valued him greatly and, soon after their arrival in America, asked him to begin the monumental task of translating the *Tanya* into English, the primary text of Chabad Chasidic thought. The task would take him two decades and eventually earn him a doctorate in Semitic Languages from Columbia University.

Initially, Mindel split his time between working for Rashag in the Yeshivah administration, and for Ramash in *Merkos* and *Machne,* but in 1944 he left the Yeshivah position and dedicated himself completely to Ramash's organizations. Mindel assisted with translation work, correspondence in English and Hebrew, and he also prepared his own original works for Chabad. Most notably, he single-handedly authored *Merkos'* children's magazine, *Talks and Tales,* which ran for forty-eight years, filling almost 7,000 printed pages.[46]

Ramash was also closely involved with the magazine and, among other tasks, he personally guided and approved all the hand-drawn illustrations. In 1944, Ramash employed Michel Schwartz (1929-2011) for this purpose, a student at the Lubavitcher Yeshivah who was also enrolled at the *New York School of Art and Design.* Years later, Schwartz recalled how the future Rebbe had placed a strong emphasis on the power of artwork in influencing American children, requesting a different style of presentation for the Yiddish and English sections of the magazine. Ramash was attentive to modes of expression used in mainstream American comics, requesting—to Schwartz's considerable surprise—that one of the characters in an adventure story be drawn *ess zul oys'zehn vee Dick Tracy* ("He should look like Dick Tracy.") Following Ramash's guideline, Schwartz created a Tracy-like caricature of Brooklyn Dodgers star "Pee Wee Rease," named "Pee Wee Myers."

On another occasion, the future Rebbe told Schwartz to draw a feature, *es zol oys'zehn vee Ripley* ("It should look like Ripley"), referring to the popular "Believe It Or Not" cartoon by Robert Ripley in the *New*

York Mirror. In general, Schwartz was taken aback by Ramash's interest in every stage of the cartoon preparation. "Each segment was first discussed with the [Future] Rebbe," Schwartz later recalled, "he had definite input, after which I would write the script, box by box, and prepare pencil sketches of the scenes with balloons for the text. The [Future] Rebbe would review each scene or representation, and only after I had his corrections and approval did I do the finished art, which then went to print."[47]

Ramash's attentiveness during this period to cultural influences on Jewish children comes to light in a charming letter from Natalie (Nechama) Cohen (b. 1940), who, from the age of five, used to converse regularly with the future Rebbe on the street. "I knew the Rebbe first as Mister," Cohen recalled in a letter some fifty years later, "and then when I learned that Mister was not his name (as I thought it was when I was five) I asked him his name. But I just couldn't get the name that he told me—he must have been saying Schneerson—so he told me that we had similar names, and could I say Menachem. That I got immediately, and so he told me to call him Mr. Menachem. Which I did."

Cohen recalled another exchange on the sidewalks of Crown Heights a few years later, when she excitedly told "Mr. Menachem" how she had been reading science fiction, particularly enjoying works by Robert Heinlein and Isaac Asimov. Ramash seemed intrigued, but told Cohen that he preferred to read Jewish books. The young girl persistently encouraged her "friend" to read the books and within a year Ramash reported that he had enjoyed Asimov's *Foundation*, and that he was far more impressed with Asimov than Heinlin. Cohen was also "thrilled" to hear that Ramash had written to Asimov and even received a reply.[48]

V.

Rabbis Mindel and Chodakov were also closely involved with the third key organization which Ramash directed during this period, *Karnei Hod Torah*—known by its acronym, Kehot—a society dedicated to publishing the teachings of the Chabad Rebbes.[49] Until Kehot was founded in 1941, only a handful of books of Chabad Chasidut had been printed in the movement's one hundred and fifty year history, and huge archives remained in handwritten manuscripts. Lacking significant financial and human resources, the society took many decades to achieve its goals, but within the Seventh Rebbe's lifetime most of the teachings of the Chabad Rebbes had been printed in several hundred volumes. Ramash himself was heavily involved in the early work, especially during Kehot's first decade, when he personally prepared several books and hundreds of pamphlets for print.

Ramash was insistent that Kehot publications meet high standards of accuracy and scholarship, and all published works were carefully checked against manuscripts, with textual variants duly noted, and, in many cases, extensive footnotes were added. Ramash was of the opinion that Chasidut did not benefit from functioning in an intellectual vacuum, and when publishing Rayatz's Chasidic discourses he spent much time adding scholarly notes to help contextualize the ideas in the broader range of Torah literature. His efforts were not appreciated by all the Chasidim, some of whom perceived Ramash's notes as an unnecessary, even offensive appendage to the Rebbe's sublime wisdom. "I used to tear your notes off the bottom of the page so I would not have to look at them," one senior Chasid purportedly told Ramash, "but now you write so much that if I tear off the notes, I will lose part of the Rebbe's discourse on the other side of the page!"

Following the Rebbe Rayatz's directive, Ramash also wrote some of his own compositions, some of which have enjoyed huge, ongoing popularity. His 1943 calendar, *Hayom Yom,* which presents a short thought for the day culled from the writings of Rayatz as well as clarifying many details of Chabad custom, was reprinted thirty-four times in the seventy years since its initial publication, and has been translated into Hebrew, English, Spanish, French, Russian and Braille. Back in Russia, Rashab had been opposed to the notion of rendering Chasidic wisdom into "sound bites,"[50] but Rayatz and Ramash realized that in America, there was a need for information that was more accessible. *Hayom Yom* also disclosed many teachings for the first time which Ramash had gathered during his years of editing *Rayatz's* letters in France and from his *Reshimot.*

Another extremely popular publication penned by Ramash in 1946 was his *Haggadah im Likutei Ta'amim u'Minhagim* (Haggadah with an anthology of explanations and customs). The Passover Haggadah represents the first scholarly, book-length composition which was published by Rabbi Menachem Mendel Schneerson, bringing to light for the first time in writing some of his brilliance.[51] Rabbi Shlomo Yosef Zevin, editor of the *Encyclopedia Talmudit*, praised the Haggadah as "a remarkable work, which is quite unique. It is suited for Jews of all backgrounds, Chasid and non-Chasid alike. If I were not concerned for the aversion of Chasidim to define a Torah text in secular terms, I would say that it is a scientific work of the finest caliber."[52]

A final, fourth task which the Rebbe Rayatz assigned to his younger son-in-law during these years was to head the Chabad *Chevra Kadisha* (burial society).[53] In a charming letter penned in 1944, Ramash drew a parallel between the four institutions he had been appointed to lead and the four levels of a human being, described in Chasidic thought: the G-dly Soul, the Intellectual Soul, the Animal Soul, and the body. His management of Kehot, Ramash explained, which was devoted to publishing the sublime wisdom of Chasidut, corresponded to the G-dly Soul. *Merkos*, which was aimed at Jewish education, corresponded to the Intellectual Soul. *Machneh Israel*, which was aimed at inspiring Jews to *teshuvah*, was associated with freedom from the confines of the Animal Soul, which holds a person back from repentance. And leadership of the Burial Society corresponded to the body itself.[54]

VI.

In 1943, Ramash was finally able to locate the whereabouts of his parents. A telegram to the Jewish community of Tashkent, Uzbekistan bore fruit, and Ramash received a reply with his parents' mailing address. Shortly afterwards Reb Levik and Chana received the first communication from their son after almost five years of harsh exile. "Seeing the signature 'Mendel, Moussia' restored a lot of sparkle to our eyes," Chana recalled. "We could read only the signatures, however, and didn't understand the English to know what was written in the telegram... It took a week and trekking four kilometers before I located a schoolteacher who, with great effort, barely managed to read through the cable. We finally felt a close family voice speaking to us, which we had sorely missed." Ramash was now able, in a small measure, to fulfil the *mitzvah* of honoring his parents once again, and promptly sent them two food parcels.[55]

Drained from living in social isolation in abysmal, swampy conditions for five years, Reb Levik's physical condition deteriorated rapidly. "He tried to improve his mood but was not successful. Our frame of mind was... infused with anxiety," Chana remembered. When the five-year exile sentence was finally complete, the couple had nowhere to go—all the Jews of Dnepropetrovsk had either fled or been killed by Hitler.[56] After Passover, they were finally able to relocate to the city of Alma Ata (Almaty), Kazakhstan. "Seeing a city with tramcars made a deep impression after we had lived for several years in such a primitive place," Chana wrote.[57]

After the festival of Shavuot, a medical professor was brought from Leningrad to attend to Reb Levik's medical condition, but it soon became clear that the Rabbi did not have long to live. Realizing the prognosis, Levik burst into tears, crying out, "What did they have against me? What have they made of me...?"[58] It was especially sad that, after over a decade of Soviet persecution followed by five years of exile, Levik had finally found a Jewish community that he could lead, but his health did not allow it. Within a few weeks, he was bedridden and barely able to eat. Iron bars were installed in his home so that he could keep the windows open at night, enabling him to breath, but it was not long before, on 9th August (20th *Menachem Av*) 1944, at the age of sixty-six, his soul departed.

It took four days for the news to reach New York. When the notice arrived in the morning at 770, Rabbi Shmuel Levitin and Rabbi Yisrael Jacobson immediately called Ramash's home, but Moussia said that her husband was not home. (They didn't tell her the purpose of the call.) Ramash worked during the day in the Navy Yard and was not reachable, so the Chasidim went to his office in 770 and waited outside for him to arrive. Usually he arrived back promptly by 3:30, and when the hour grew late they became increasingly concerned.

Eventually, the door unlocked from the inside and opened—Ramash had been there all along. He was sitting in the dark. The light in the room was off and the shutters closed. When he was told the tragic news, Ramash asked if anyone had a knife. Rabbi Jacobson took a penknife from Leibel Bistritzky and cut into Ramash's garments, who then fulfilled the practice of *keriah*, rending of the garments.

"Were you here all the time?" they asked Ramash.

"Yes," he said. "I sensed that my father was gone."

As he recited the first *kaddish* (mourner's prayer), Ramash wept. His father had suffered terribly for years and he had been unable to offer any support. The Soviets had not only brought about Levik's premature death, they prevented Ramash from seeing his father for the last seventeen years of his life.

It was not long, though, before Ramash regained his composure. During the *shiva*, he did not show any outward feelings at all.[59]

Concerns now shifted to Chana's welfare. Was she alive and well? Could she possibly be brought to the safe shores of the United States? Ramash sent his mother regular packages containing stockings which could be sold locally for a high price, while he sought a method of getting her out of the country.

With no family left back home, Chana made contact with her nephew Menachem Mendel (Shmuel and Miriam Gittel's son), who had relocated to Türkmenabat, Turkmenistan, in Central Asia, and made plans to relocate there. The plan, however, was aborted in the fall of 1945, when Chana managed to obtain tickets to Moscow where she awaited plans to leave the country. Since her son was now a U.S. citizen, Chana wanted to obtain a visa thorough legal means, but friends warned her that with the name "Schneerson," she was liable to be sent right back to the swamps.

After sustained efforts, she managed to obtain a false passport through the assistance of Mrs. Sarah Katzenelenbogen, "Mumeh Sarah" (1891-1952), a Lubavitcher lady who was very active in helping Chasidim to leave the country. Mumeh Sarah accompanied Chana on a risk-laden train journey from Moscow to Lemberg, near the Polish border, more than once deflecting questions from the authorities.[60] Chana crossed the border successfully in a roofless train carriage, and reached Polish soil. (Mumeh Sarah's activities were eventually discovered and she died in jail).

With assistance from Ramash's cousin, Rabbi Zalman Schneerson, in Paris, by 1946 Chana had managed to leave Poland and arrived at the Displaced Persons camp in Poking, Germany, where many Orthodox Jews had found refuge after the war.[61] In Poking, Chana met two Chabad boys, Leibel and Berel Zisman, who had miraculously survived Auschwitz and were on their way to the United States. She asked if they would be so kind as to take a letter for her son.

"Who is your son?" the boys asked.

"His name is Menachem Mendel. You'll ask at the Chabad headquarters. Over there they'll point out who he is."

When they arrived in New York, Ramash was not too difficult to locate. "I remember that he wore a double-breasted gray suit and a grey hat with a black band," Leibel recalled in his memoir. They gave Ramash the letter and he opened it and started to read, spending what seemed to be an exceptionally long time to review a relatively short letter. The boys did not realize how precious the letter was to the future Rebbe—he had received no communication from his mother in years.

Eventually, he turned to Leibel and asked, "How does my mother look?"

"She's an old lady," Leibel replied.

Ramash smiled and said, "Could you describe her?"

"She seemed very thin and pale," Leibel began to recount. "She spoke softly. She wore a long blue dress with flowers which stretched all the way to the ground, and a brown wig, but no makeup or lipstick."

Ramash couldn't hear enough and kept firing questions at the boys for a half-hour. When no more information was forthcoming, he went to the shelf, pulled off two copies of the Chasidic text *Likutei Torah* and gave one as a gift to each of the boys.

As they were leaving, he called them back and said, "Whenever you need something, come to me."[62]

In 1947 Chana finally managed to leave the D.P. camp and she reached the home of Rabbi Zalman Schneerson in France. Ramash boarded a plane for a three-month visit to his former hometown to see his mother and assist her in recovering from her ordeals, while he arranged papers for her entry into the United States.

The meeting was highly emotional as Ramash had not seen his mother in two decades and she had lost almost her entire family: her husband was dead, her son Berel had been murdered, her sister Miriam Gittel and brother-in-law Shmuel were dead, and her mother Rachel had also been killed by the Nazis.

As Ramash *farbrenged* for the many Jewish refugees who had found their way to Paris, he could not restrain his tears as he spoke of how

Biblical Joseph had been kept from his father for twenty-two years and was unable to fulfil the *mitzvah* of honoring parents. But it was a happy time. With all the losses and hardships the family had suffered, at least Chana was alive and generally well, if severely malnourished.

After delivering a number of memorable public addresses to the refugees in Paris, and spending Passover and Shavuot there, Ramash finally accompanied his mother by boat to the shores of the United States, where she would spend the last seventeen years of her life. While pained by all her tragic losses, she did live to see her son become the Seventh Lubavitcher Rebbe and enjoy many honorable years in the Lubavitch community of New York. Ramash would, of course, make a point of visiting her every day.[63]

V.

Ramash addressed the community on a monthly basis, at a *farbrengen* after morning prayers on the Sabbath in 770. With a *talit* still draped on his shoulders, Ramash would speak for approximately forty minutes. Since Chasidim were encouraged to spend many hours in private prayer, Ramash's *farbrengens* were not always well attended, and unfortunately most of them were not recorded in writing.[64] If businessmen or professionals were present, Ramash would sometimes explain the lessons that can be learned from their trade in the worship of G-d. For example, when a wealthy owner of a clothing business was present, Ramash expounded upon the messages implicit in the details of the dry cleaning process.[65] When chess champion Shmuel Reshevsky (1911-1992) was present at the *kiddush*, Ramash offered some fascinating insights into the spiritual lessons of the chess pieces.[66]

During the intermediate days of *Sukkot* and *Pesach*, Ramash also delivered a special lecture pitched at non-Chabad Yeshiva students from the New York area. Speaking without notes, Ramash would mix complex Talmudic and *halachic* analysis with *drush* (Rabbinic homiletics). Ben Zion Shenker (b. 1925) recalled attending these lectures along with Rabbi Moshe Wolfson, today a senior figure in the Yeshiva world, and remembered the terrific impression they made.[67] At the end of each gathering, Ramash would dance round the table with all the boys.[68]

In the 1940s, Ramash was also a popular guest of honor at events in the Chabad community—such as bar mitzvahs, *aufrufs*, weddings (at which he would often officiate), and other communal gatherings—and many of his preparatory notes from these talks have survived.[69] With Rayatz less visible due to failing health, Ramash also provided an important link between the Chasidim and their Rebbe. On more than one occasion, he would rush straight down to the main study hall in 770 and share some interesting revelation he had just heard upstairs from the Rebbe.

On one occasion in 1945, Ramash entered the study hall, banged on the table to get silence and said, "I am coming from my father-in-law. His father has just visited him and asked him: How is it that in your synagogue people are talking during the Torah reading?" Rabbi Yisrael Gordon, who was present at the time, remembered what an impression this report of a mystical visitation had on the congregants. "It made us feel like our synagogue was special," he recalled.

Rabbi Mendel Feldman (1919-2008) recalled Ramash sharing his personal impressions after a meeting with his father-in-law. "There is a rumor in the Yeshivot that the Rebbe [Rayatz] is not a great Torah scholar," Ramash bemoaned. "Believe me, the Rebbe is a *gaon* [Torah genius]." Ramash then shared with Feldman an incident from Poland when Rayatz had presented a fascinating *halachic* discussion in one of his discourses, but chose to leave it out from the transcript he later prepared for publication. Noticing the omission, Ramash asked the Rebbe for an explanation. "I'm not here for that," Rayatz replied, "It's not my mission in life."[70]

On another occasion, Rabbi David Edelman (b. 1924) recalled encountering Ramash exiting the elevator in the foyer of 770. "I was just with my father-in-law," Ramash shared with Edelman. "I told him that I often meet secular Jews in my office and do not always find the opportunity to encourage them to be more religiously observant." Ramash was concerned that this reticence to discuss religious matters might be misinterpreted as a tacit approval. Rayatz responded that a parent loves all his or her children, but that if a child is disabled, missing a hand or a foot, the parent will find extra love. "In a similar way," the Sixth Rebbe explained, "if a Jew comes 'missing' a hand that puts on *tefilin*, or 'missing' a foot that takes him to synagogue, you need to show him a deeper love."[71]

Through these and numerous other incidents which have not reached us,[72] Rabbi Menachem Mendel Schneerson became a highly central figure in the happenings at the court of Lubavitch in the 1940s. By the time Rayatz passed away in 1950, both of the Rebbe's sons-in-law had made an undeniably impressive contribution to the Chabad movement; but as long as the Sixth Rebbe was alive, nobody dared to broach the issue of succession. For a Chasid, the passing of his Rebbe is something utterly unthinkable.

CHAPTER TEN

LUBAVITCH CHOOSES A NEW REBBE

1950–1951

Ramash at the grave of Rayatz, 1950

During the last decade of his life, Rayatz suffered greatly from chronic ill health, requiring a full-time nurse on the premises. 1940 was the only year that the Sixth Rebbe was able to make it downstairs to pray in the main synagogue on the ground floor of 770 for the High Holidays, and in subsequent years special services were carried out in his study on the second floor. His medical condition made it difficult for him to speak, especially for the sustained period needed to deliver a Chasidic discourse (*ma'amar*). From 1942[1] onwards he stopped saying formal discourses altogether,[2] presenting them instead in writing to be copied and distributed before the Sabbath and festivals.[3]

Ramash remained mystified as to why G-d had taken the power of speech from his Rebbe. Even Rayatz's physician expressed his bewilderment, as a 1992 sermon recalled.

> Even his doctor (who was also a professor, more qualified than an ordinary doctor) once protested: Why on earth have his physical hardships affected his power of speech, of all things, preventing him from carrying out his mission in the world as he would have liked? He is so enthusiastically committed to spreading Torah and Judaism, and spreading the wellsprings of Chasidut outwards. G-d should have given him the utmost ability to do so in the best possible manner; He should have been given the power of speech![4]

On 12th November 1944, Rayatz suffered a major heart attack, and was confined to strict bed rest for three months. From the fall of 1945 onwards, he ceased even to write Chasidic discourses.[5] In order to provide the community with material to study—and to camouflage the non-appearance of fresh *ma'amarim*—Ramash collected some of the Sixth Rebbe's early discourses from archivist Rabbi Eliyahu Nachum Sklar,[6] with which Chasidim in America were unfamiliar. With the help of Rabbi Avraham Paris, the *ma'amarim* were published periodically, appearing as if they had just been written by Rayatz. The Sixth Rebbe also rewrote the first few lines and conclusion of each discourse. All those involved in the publication worked under the condition of absolute confidentiality, so that the broader community would not come to realize what was happening. (Only in 1969, when an index of Rayatz's discourses was being prepared for publication, did the Seventh Rebbe allow the ruse to be exposed.)

Early in 1950, Ramash prepared a *ma'amar* for publication in honor of 10th *Shevat*, the anniversary of the passing (*yahrtzeit*) of Rebbetzin Rivka (1833-1914), wife of Rabbi Shmuel of Lubavitch, the Fourth Lubavitcher Rebbe. In the Jewish calendar, a *yahrtzeit* will fall each year on different days of the week, and that year Rebbetzin Rivka's *yahrtzeit* was to fall out on 28th January, on the Sabbath. In Sklar's archive, Ramash found a *ma'amar* which had been delivered by Rayatz in 1923, when the *yahrtzeit* had similarly fallen out on the Sabbath,[7] and he took it into the Sixth Rebbe for the first few lines to be rewritten. Rayatz simply crossed out the first paragraph, so that instead of beginning with the verse *"It was on that very day that all the legions of G-d went out of the land of Egypt"* (Exodus 12:41), the *ma'amar* opened with a citation from King Solomon's Song of Songs, *"I have come into my garden, my sister, my bride"* (Song 5:1).[8] Ramash managed to add his own annotations and had the discourse printed and brought to 770 in time for the Sabbath. On Friday afternoon he took a copy into Rayatz, who was sitting at his desk reading from a prayer-book. The Sixth Rebbe glanced up at his son-in-law and nodded in appreciation.[9]

That Friday night was ordinary and uneventful. Chasidim pored over the freshly published text. Ramash conducted his weekly study session with Rabbi Yitzchak Hutner (1906–1980), who, years earlier, had asked Rayatz to provide him with a teacher in Chabad Chasidut.[10]

Early the following morning, Rayatz asked his nurse to move him from his bedroom to his study, where he would usually spend the day. Curiously, he spent a few minutes gazing around the room, and then asked to be transferred back to his bedroom. Shortly afterwards the Rebbe was seen to be in intense pain and was having difficulty breathing. The nurse panicked and called Rayatz's oldest daughter Chana, who was deeply involved with her father's care. When Chana arrived, Rayatz attempted to say something to her, but he was unable to speak. Immediately, Rayatz's local physician, Dr. Seligson, was called and he rushed to 770. Arriving five minutes later, at 7:55 a.m., Seligson saw that the Rebbe had suffered a major heart attack and was in critical condition. Around two months earlier, Rayatz had experienced a smaller cardiac incident and Seligson had successfully revived him with emergency intravenous medication. Now, Seligson administered the same two injections, but they proved ineffective. By this point Chana was hysterical, screaming, "Father! Father! Save my father!" Calls were made for emergency assistance and for breathing equipment to be brought immediately, but by 8:07 a.m. the Sixth Rebbe of Lubavitch had returned his soul to the Creator. For a half hour attempts were made to resuscitate him, but to no avail.[11]

By this time many Chasidim had arrived in 770 and sat tearfully reciting *Tehillim* (Psalms). When Ramash arrived, the Rebbe Rayatz had already passed away. Holding back any expression of emotion, he instructed that all Chasidim should immerse themselves in the *mikvah* before reciting *Tehillim* and that there should be at least ten men reciting *Tehillim* in proximity to Rayatz's body at all times.

Mordechai Dubinsky, a student in the Yeshivah, spotted Ramash a short while later as he came to immerse. "In the *mikvah* I met the Rebbe's son-in-law, and it was unclear whether or not he knew. The doubt was soon resolved when the Ramash said that the *mikvah* should remain open all day—this was a clear sign that he knew. But from his face you couldn't tell at all. It seems that he has a lot of self control."[12]

Ramash returned and continued to say *Tehillim* along with other Chasidim in the small corridor between Rayatz's bedroom and study. The door of the study was closed, but the bedroom remained open and the Rebbe's body, covered by a sheet, could be seen lying on the bed. When one Chasid, Rabbi Zalman Gurary (1911-2003), looked inside, he burst into hysterical tears. "Control yourself," Ramash said to him—but Gurary could not, and he fainted, falling to the floor.

Rashag said *Tehillim* inside the Rebbe's room, while Ramash remained in the corridor, occasionally gazing through the door at the departed Rebbe. At 10:45 a.m. nobody had yet started the Sabbath prayer services, and Rashag went downstairs to the synagogue to gather a *minyan* (prayer quorum). As he recited the first *kaddish* which precedes the morning service, Rashag choked up, reducing the congregation to tears. The prayers proceeded uneventfully, if a little faster than usual, with the participation of both Rashag and Ramash, who were accorded their usual honors.

The following day at 12:30 p.m. Rayatz's coffin, covered by his black *kapote*, was seen emerging from the front door of 770 to a crowd of three thousand which filled Eastern Parkway. Amid much pushing, which even the police had difficulty containing, the coffin was eventually placed into a vehicle waiting at the corner of Brooklyn Avenue. Immediately behind followed a limousine containing the Rebbe's two sons-in-law, his grandson Shalom Ber (Barry), and secretary Chaim Lieberman. Behind them in another car were: Rayatz's wife, the Rebbetzin Nechama Dina; her two daughters, Chana and Moussia, and Rayatz's nurse Manya. Following were tens of cars and buses filled with Chasidim.

The entourage took a right turn at Bedford Avenue, towards the Yeshivah building, moving slowly as the huge crowd accompanied the vehicles on foot. After stopping briefly at the Yeshivah, the entourage speeded up and made its way to the Montefiore Cemetery in Queens, twelve miles away.

At 2:45 p.m., the Sixth Lubavitcher Rebbe was lowered into his resting place, which had been lined with earth from the Land of Israel. By this time, the Chasidim had no tears left, and the crowd looked on, stony faced but quiet.

"We are doing this on condition," Ramash announced, breaking the silence, "that if we will go to the Land of Israel or to another place, we will not go without you!"

Then Chana started to scream, "Look where they are putting Father!" Nechama Dina could hold herself no longer and started to bawl hysterically. Her daughters held her by the hand and she calmed a little. She was escorted to a nearby vehicle, but by this time everybody was in tears again.

Before the grave was covered with earth, Ramash recited the burial prayers aloud, as the crowd's tears began to subside. The two sons-in-law recited *kaddish*, and Chasidim tore their clothes in mourning.

Returning to 770, it was time to recite the afternoon prayers (*mincha*). Both sons-in-law took upon themselves to lead their own prayer services and recite *kaddish* for Rayatz for the following year, and Rashag first led *mincha* prayers, followed by Ramash.

"The question which everyone had," recalled Yeshiva student Eli Gross in his diary, was, "who will fill the Rebbe's place?"

Rayatz's quarters were searched and no will was found.

II

Despite his very poor health for almost two decades, Rayatz's death at the beginning of 1950 was a huge shock to Chabad Chasidim all over the world. The Sixth Rebbe had shown such an indomitable spirit in the face of some of history's greatest challenges that it may have seemed to some of the faithful that even death might escape him. The Messianic energy which he had emanated during the war also experienced a resurgence before his passing, after he instructed, in 1948, that the writing of a special Torah scroll "to receive Mashiach (the Messiah)" be completed.[13] His physical frailty, while ruling out many public appearances, did not hold the Sixth Rebbe back from maintaining a staggering correspondence, penning thousands of letters in the last sixteen months of his life, and conducting many *yechidut* meetings.[14] Despite a severe speech impediment, he would still manage to speak publicly, usually at festival gatherings, and his talks from the same period (5709-10) fill some 130 printed pages.[15]

In the history of the Chasidic movement it has never been easy, in the best of circumstances, for devotees to shift their loyalties to a new Rebbe. Emotional ties cannot be severed and reestablished at will, and the relatively low stature of a Rebbe-incumbent presents a formidable adjustment after the elevated authority of the prior Rebbe at the end of his life. Even in Nineteenth Century Europe, many Chasidic lines simply fizzled out due to the failure of the community to unite behind an appropriate successor. In America, where a mood of pessimism about the future of Chasidism prevailed, the challenge was all the greater.

The difficulties of dynastic transmission are eased by the presence of male progeny, but Rayatz was the first Chabad Rebbe not to produce any sons. He had one male descendant, Rashag's son, Shalom Ber (Barry), who was twenty-six years old when the Sixth Rebbe passed on. While Rayatz may have originally had some hopes for his grandson,[16] Barry was probably not seen as a viable candidate for succession due to weakening Chasidic attachments after his arrival in America. Barry had not studied in Rayatz's Yeshivah in New York, but in *Yeshivah Torah Vodaath*, which combined secular studies with Jewish studies. From 1943 onwards, he attended Brooklyn College part-time, and after earning *semicha* in 1945, he continued his secular studies on a full time basis, majoring in physics. Admitted to Columbia University graduate school, he was in the process of looking for a sponsor for his PhD when Rayatz passed away. While Barry still lived in 770 with his parents, and was a familiar face to Chasidim, he was in all likelihood too young and too disinterested in Chasidic life to be considered a candidate for Rebbe. By his own admission, he had been disinterested in the job from his early youth.

At Rayatz's passing, there were only two potential candidates for the Sixth Rebbe's replacement: his sons-in-law Rashag and Ramash. Both men evidenced deep Chasidic attachments and had worked closely with their father-in-law in America during the last decade of his life; and both sons-in-law were intelligent, articulate and of fine character. But Rayatz left no explicit directions, neither in writing nor orally, to whom Chasidim should turn for leadership after his passing.[17]

In a sense, at least "on paper," it was Rashag who had the upper hand: He was the older son-in-law and the organizations he led were more prestigious. While it may seem odd today, in 1950, the Chabad movement's pride did not lie in its outreach activities. The organizational focus for several decades had been on its Yeshivot, where Chabad Chasidut was studied alongside a traditional Talmudic curriculum. It was the Yeshivah, more than any other institution, that had really been instrumental in preserving the movement, and hopes for the future rested on its success. As we have seen, in America it was Rashag who directed a network of Chabad Yeshivot single-handedly, and this crowning achievement had been responsible, in a large measure, for the continuation of Chabad-Lubavitch in the New World. Ramash's outreach organizations, on the other hand, were not perceived then as they are today, as the innovative precursor of hundreds of Chabad Houses worldwide. In all likelihood, most Chasidim, while appreciating what was being done by Ramash, probably did not see it as crucial to the movement's future.

Rashag's position was enhanced by his role as Chabad's principal fundraiser, placing him in close contact with major supporters and political sympathizers. He also headed the executive committee of *Agudat Chasidei Chabad*, the movement's organizational umbrella in the United States, which united the broader community of more loosely affiliated Chabad adherents.

Rashag's "education and employment history," if we may use such terms, also seemed preferable. He had studied in Lubavitch, in Rashab's Yeshivah, and received the Fifth Rebbe's personal blessing. Even though Rashag had devoted considerable time to diamond trading in Belgium and real estate interests in Israel, he still managed to work closely with his father-in-law, the Sixth Rebbe, throughout the twenties and thirties, often appearing by his side at official activities. Since his marriage to Chana in 1921, Rashag had always lived at Rayatz's court and was well known to generations of Chasidim.

Ramash, by contrast, had never visited the town of Lubavitch or met Rashab; nor did he study in a Chabad Yeshivah. He spent his married years before arriving in America, living away from the court of Lubavitch and attending university. (His considerable involvement in Rayatz's activities and medical treatment was generally not public knowledge.) He was a known figure, paying regular visits to the court of Rayatz, but far less so than Rashag.

If we add to this the fact that Rashag, by all indications, *wanted* to lead the movement, and that Ramash repeatedly expressed his *disinter-*

est in the position, we are left with the question: What happened? How did Menachem Mendel Schneerson become the Seventh Lubavitcher Rebbe?

As we shall see, immediately after Rayatz's passing, senior Chasidim already turned to Ramash, pleading with him to rise to the movement's leadership. As the weeks passed, with Ramash sharply resisting all of these attempts, Chasidim became increasingly convinced that the future rested with the younger son-in-law, and he garnered the movement's overwhelming support. After around six to nine months, the incessant pleas of so many Chasidim finally moved him and Ramash's resistance to leading the movement gradually eroded. While Rashag was patently aware that his own support had dwindled, when Ramash formally accepted the leadership after one year of ambivalence, it was a huge blow for Rashag and it took him some time to fully come to terms with it.

During the entire year of 1950, when the future of the leadership of Chabad was being decided, not a bad word was voiced in public between Rashag and Ramash. They both prayed together in the same synagogue on the Sabbath[18] and appeared together in public at a number of formal events. Neither "candidate" openly campaigned for himself or criticized his "opponent." In fact the two sons-in-law simply continued their prior organizational and communal activities without any significant change; but they were being constantly scrutinized by the Chasidim to see which man, if any, was worthy of their devotion.

What virtues did the Chabad community discern in Ramash during this period which led them to crown him as their Rebbe?

First, we cannot ignore the significance of Ramash's pedigree. Unlike Rashag, Ramash bore the Schneerson name and was a direct male descendant of his namesake, the Third Lubavitcher Rebbe. In Chasidic communities, which greatly value dynastic continuum, this must have been of supreme importance.

A second strong asset for leadership was Ramash's extreme decisiveness. Both in organizational and personal matters, he was able to quickly offer solutions that were practical, logical and backed by Torah sources. His quiet confidence was alluring and inspired listeners to place their trust in him. Rashag, by contrast, was known to vacillate, and would often change his mind even on major issues.[19]

Ramash also possessed a remarkable command of the entire textual corpus of Rabbinic Judaism and a mastery of Kabbalistic and Chasidic thought. He was someone clearly steeped in Torah and must have studied ever so diligently and fervently, privately and quietly, for many years. His scholarship also displayed a deeply mystical orientation which stood out as a sign of religious transcendence.

This proved instrumental in enhancing his other gifts of leadership, most notably his ability to inspire audiences with thoughtful, relevant messages. At this early stage, Ramash had already developed his own form of very original exegesis which generally sought to buttress Chasidic ideas by creatively reading them into Rabbinic texts. He spiced this discourse with anecdotes, interesting observations about Chasidic practice, hints and *gematriot*, stirring the listener with a veritable torrent of wisdom. While he was sometimes difficult to follow, Ramash never allowed his *farbrengens* to become lost in abstraction, and his thoughts were always coupled with guidelines for practical implementation. Chabad philosophy can sometimes appear abtruse and enigmatic, especially for down-to-earth Americans, but Ramash managed to deploy much of the material to produce what you might call a "scholarly sermon." As listeners were inspired by the message, they were simultaneously dazzled by the breadth of sources and the synergy of their presentation. Ramash was also not afraid to share his broader reflections on the issues of the day: the Sixth Rebbe's passing, the reason why Chabad had come to America, the meaning of the Rebbe-Chasid relationship and the destiny of the Jewish people.

While all this was, no doubt, wonderfully refreshing and unusual, the main question on the minds of Chasidim was: Is this man a Rebbe? The community decided in the affirmative with Ramash, not only due to his Schneerson pedigree and effective sermonizing, but arguably because they sensed that his unusual spiritual intensity and penetrating insight were signs of an exalted soul. The term "charisma," which is often applied in this context, misses the mark. Ramash was not a flamboyant or an especially demonstrative speaker, nor did he gush with warmth or glib charm; but one sensed he was bound to something higher than himself, in a very solid way. In his discourse, Torah, *mitzvot* and the work of Chabad were rendered contagiously urgent. So long as Rayatz was alive, the Sixth Rebbe's presence had eclipsed all other personalities, but with his passing, Lubavitch soon realized that behind Ramash's worldly facade, the "man in the gray suit" inhabited an other-worldly space.[20]

Most of all, the Chasidim were moved by his consuming devotion to his late father-in-law. Ramash's sermons were filled with words of encouragement for Chasidim to rededicate themselves to the Rebbe Rayatz after his passing, and the many anecdotes which Ramash recalled about the late Rebbe's life and teachings displayed veneration and a deep love. (The love had clearly been mutual, and many Chasidim recalled the special esteem which Rayatz had shown his son-in-law, often sending questioners to him for advice.) While Ramash was generally known to be "cool" and not prone to emotional displays, he would often break down in tears when speaking of Rayatz—as a young Rabbi Yoel Kahn (b. 1930)[21] recalled in his diary. "In general, Ramash is a man of great integrity (*ish pnimi me'od*). He appears a cold person. He sits calmly and speaks softly, and then suddenly bursts into tears. Then he carries on speaking again, all the time softly.[22] His utter devotion (*bitul*) to our Rebbe is impossible to describe.[23]"

III

The first official statement from the Schneersohn-Gurary families came eight days after Rayatz's passing. The letter was issued on the letterhead of "N. Dinah Schneersohn of Lubavitch," signed by the old Rebbetzin, along with her two sons-in-law. It was addressed to "our dear friends and all those who cherish the memory of our beloved and revered teacher and leader, the Lubavitcher Rebbe, of saintly memory." The document made no reference to succession and sent the message that business would continue as usual with each of the Rebbe's sons-in-law maintaining their pre-existing roles, at least for the time being. Chasidim were called upon to rededicate themselves to their work for the sake of the late Rebbe's memory, "to safeguard, with G-d's help, the gigantic spiritual heritage which our late Rebbe left us all: the world renowned institutions for the spreading of the Torah and the light of true Judaism."[24]

From a letter penned in this period by a senior Chasid in Israel, Rabbi Eliezer Karasik, we see further indication that a "collectivist" model had been contemplated where each of the Rebbe's two sons-in-law would continue to manage their respective institutions, without a nominated successor. This would have the obvious advantage of avoiding a rift in the Schneersohn household; but, Karasik argued, it would not be beneficial to the Chasidic community which was in need of definitive leadership.

> While I hear that, thank G-d, relations between the late Rebbe's sons-in-law are peaceful, nevertheless, in my opinion, this approach will not bring the appropriate results, since the broader community will not recognize such a collective authority....
>
> In order to strengthen the Chabad community and the young students under our influence, there is no other option than to crown one of the sons-in-law as Rebbe. The hour is pressing and with each day that passes we see the urgency of the matter. I shudder when I contemplate the consequences that might follow from a failure to act in this way. Understandably, this course requires sacrifices to be made....
>
> The only thing I wish to stress to you is that here in Jerusalem we are considering only this arrangement that I have written to you. As to whom is the more appropriate candidate, it should be self-evident.[25]

The letter was the outcome of a meeting held in the Nachalat Binyamin Synagogue in Tel Aviv, immediately after the news of Rayatz's passing had reached Israel. Present, among others, were senior Chasidim, Rabbis Eliezer Karasik (1898-1960), Shmeryl Gurary (1905-1984), Moshe Gurary (1899-1973), Alexander Sender Yudasin (1909-1983), Shaul Dovber Zislin (1881-1964), Pinchas Althaus (1898-1963) and Avraham Paris (1889-1968).

Despite the anguish at Rayatz's passing, Paris took this early opportunity to launch Ramash's candidacy. Many Chasidim from Israel were not well acquainted with the Rebbe's younger son-in-law, but Paris had lived in the United States for an extended period (1938-49) and knew Ramash well from their editorial work together.

"I worked with him," Paris told the gathered crowd, "in the same room for ten years, my desk next to his. I barely did any work, as I was watching him the whole time to see what he was doing. I am telling you that he is concealing himself. He has fooled us all! I am telling you—he is a Rebbe."[26]

We lack a complete picture of how the candidacies of Rashag and Ramash were perceived at this time around the world.[27] Rashag was generally more known, having made an official trip to Europe in 1947 on behalf of the Rebbe Rayatz to aid Chabad refugees, visiting Germany, France, Holland and England,[28] and a similar trip to Israel in 1949.[29] He had made a good impression on various audiences, reciting Chasidic discourses from memory with fluency, so it is likely that he had some sympathizers there.[30] Ramash, on the other hand had not traveled extensively, never visiting Israel,[31] but he had maintained a voluminous, international correspondence, answering questions posed to him by scholars in the movement. One thing is clear, that a number of important Chasidim from Chabad communities abroad, such as Paris and Karasik, supported Ramash's candidacy from the very beginning.

Another early example of support for Ramash came from Rabbi Yitzchak Dubov (1886-1977), who had studied in *Yeshivat Tomchei Temimim* in Lubavitch and lived in Riga from 1921-1928, before settling in Manchester, England, where he served as a lecturer in a local non-Chabad Yeshivah for several decades. Dubov had come to know Ramash in Riga, and was extremely impressed.[32] At Rayatz's passing he happened to be in New York for his son's wedding, and later recalled: "I saw the attachment of the young married Chasidim and the Yeshivah students to the [future] Rebbe, as my dear friend Rabbi Moshe Leib Rothstein said, 'They're sticking to him like bees around honey'—and they virtually elected me to speak with the [future] Rebbe about the appointment."[33]

On 31st January (13th *Shevat*), just three days after Rayatz's passing, Dubov approached Ramash and pleaded that he should formally accept the leadership of Chabad. Ramash appeared incredulous. "What are you thinking? That Mendel Schneerson is a Rebbe?" he retorted, as if the notion was laughable.[34]

The response was typical of a number of sharply dismissive comments about the possibility of his future Rebbehood that Ramash made, both orally and in writing, during these months. In a letter to Rabbi Yeshaya Horowitz (1883-1978), a Chabad scholar from Tzefat who served as communal leader in Winnipeg, Ramash deflected a request to accept the Chabad leadership in unequivocal terms: "I was shocked... that you demanded from me something which I do not possess and with which I have not been empowered, not in the very slightest. I have no complaint against you, since you do not know me personally, but you should have done a little research first."[35]

Perhaps the most striking dismissal from Ramash that he would consider replacing his father-in-law, came in a letter to Rabbi Yisrael Noach Belinitzky (1883-1982).[36] Belinitzky was a revered spiritual mentor (*mashpia*) for generations of Chasidim at the Lubavitcher Yeshivah in Kremenchug, Russia, and later in Brunoy, France. On 16th May (*Erev Rosh Chodesh Sivan*), Ramash responded to Belinitzky's requests that he should accept the leadership.

> As for what you write about me... I don't know what to tell you. This matter is not my responsibility. What I know with certainty is that I lack Chasidut, I lack guidance, and much, much more. I make no attempt to conceal this from others.... I have said this in the past and I say it again now. (I do not write that I lack a Rebbe, as I trust that the Rebbe [Rayatz] will continue to lead me...)
>
> As for what will be with the Chasidim—that is for the Rebbe [Rayatz] to worry about. It is *his* responsibility.[37]

Besides rejecting personal requests to assume the leadership, Ramash publicly preached a mystical conception of the Rebbe Rayatz's passing that precluded any need for succession. He drew extensively on the *Tanya's* teaching that "the life of a *tzadik* (saintly person) is not a life of flesh, but a spiritual life... and after his passing... anyone who is close to him may receive from his spirit."[38] This meant, Ramash argued, that Rayatz could continue to lead Chabad even after his passing. If a blessing or direction was required, one simply needed to send petitions to his grave site and wait for the results.[39]

Rabbi Yoel Kahn discerned Ramash's unstated intent in these sermons, noting in his diary: "On the last day of Passover, the Ramash *shlita* spoke for more than four hours. He spoke very well. The message was that the late Rebbe is still with us just as he was before, even more powerfully so. This is the general content of all his talks. He speaks about this at length—despite the fact that the Chabad community are requesting him to be a replacement—as a kind of indirect response to them."[40]

It is difficult to fathom why Rabbi Menachem Mendel Schneerson, who did such a spectacular job as the Seventh Lubavitcher Rebbe, initially deemed himself so unworthy of the position. However, the phenomenon of a man of deep introversion resisting what would later become a historic position of leadership is not without precedent. Author Susan Horowitz Cain has noted, "Some of our transformative leaders in history have been introverts.... They all took the spotlight, even though every bone in their bodies was telling them not to. And this turns out to have a special power of its own, because people could feel that these leaders were at the helm, not because they enjoyed directing others and not out of the pleasure of being looked at; they were there because they had no choice, because they were driven to do what they thought was right."[41]

As letters of request poured in from around the world,[42] and an increasing number of local Chasidim[43] pleaded with him to become Rebbe, Ramash gradually came to the realization that this was his destiny. Moussia is also said to have played her part, reputedly telling her husband, "You cannot allow my father's thirty years of dedicated work to go to waste."[44]

One of the most moving letters of recommendation for Ramash was actually penned from outside the Chabad community, by Rabbi Ephraim Yolles (1891-1988), a brilliant Torah scholar of Galician Chasidic descent, and later the Chief Rabbi of Philadelphia.

> I recall the holy and pure words which emanated from the holy mouth of the late Rebbe [Rayatz], especially on the night of *Hoshanah Rabah* 5706 [27th September 1945], when he told me that he had given the Ramash *shlita* willow branches for me, saying, "his hand is like mine." Obviously, then, his mouth too, is like [Rayatz's] holy and pure mouth.
>
> I am astounded at you young followers: Why do you delay in attaching yourselves to that pure and holy *tzadik*?[45]

An early sign that Ramash might accept the leadership was his willingness to accept *pidyonot*, personal letters of "soul redemption" given from Chasid to Rebbe. When one individual asked why *pidyonot* were being accepted by someone who had not been appointed as Rebbe, Ramash wrote, "This is really a question for those who present the *pidyonot*, and not for me." Ramash also noted that, even in Rayatz's lifetime, he would accept *pidyonot* and pass them on to the Rebbe, which is exactly what he was continuing to do now.[46]

Chasidim did not share the same perception. They understood Ramash's willingness to accept *pidyonot* and advise Chasidim on a personal basis as clear signs of Rebbehood. In a letter to Rabbi Chaim Shaul Brook (1894-1965), a *mashpia* (mentor) of *Yeshivat Tomchei Temimim* in Tel Aviv, Rabbi Yisrael Jacobson reported, "The Ramash *shlita* carries out all the activities [of a Rebbe]: he answer questions, letters are sent to him, and *pidyonot* are passed to him."[47] Similarly, Rabbi Shmuel Zalmanov informed his uncle in Israel, "As of now, the Ramash *shlita* refuses to accept the leadership... although in many areas he responds to our requests: He answers questions posed by the Chabad community concerning physical and spiritual matters, and he accepts *pidyonot* to be read at the grave of the late Rebbe. There are other things, too. But openly, he says that he refuses to accept the position."[48]

Even the elder of 770, Rabbi Shmuel Levitin, stated publicly that he had discerned signs of Rebbehood in Ramash. "The fact that he answers people's spiritual questions," Levitin observed at a Chasidic gathering on 27th February (10th *Adar*), "is no proof that he will accept the leadership, since you could always argue that the answers to these questions are found somewhere in the sacred books. But the fact that he answers questions about physical matters, such as medical issues—this is proof that he will become the Rebbe."[49] By the summer, this sort of advice had become a daily occurrence, as Yoel Kahn noted: "Every day people come to him, until the late hours of the night, and he answers them all with absolute conviction, even on matters of life and death."[50]

Another thinly veiled indication of Ramash's willingness to lead was evident at a meeting he called on 11th June (26th *Sivan*). "The Rebbe [Rayatz] headed and administered the many projects of *Merkos L'Inyanei Chinuch* until his passing," Ramash told the assembled group of elders and activists. "He appointed me to implement them, which involves endeavoring to cover the considerable expenses."

Ramash reported that, as of late, *Merkos* had regrettably become less active due to lack of funds. Then he came to the main point: "It goes without saying that there can be no thought of this organization weakening, G-d forbid, which would be the opposite of what the Rebbe intended and wanted. So, if the current situation continues, I will have no choice other than to be personally involved in all aspects of the work, and I will have to push away other tasks."[51]

The message was clear: If you want me to accept new "tasks"—such as becoming the next Lubavitcher Rebbe—I need to be relieved from the fund-raising burden of *Merkos.*

The amount required, Ramash promptly clarified, was a formidable fifty-thousand dollars per year.[52]

IV

During the summer, Ramash conducted himself increasingly like a Rebbe. Besides accepting *pidyonot* and receiving Chasidim for private counseling (*yechidut*), his regular sermons were faithfully transcribed by Chasidim, edited by Ramash himself, and dispatched to Chabad communities around the world.[53] On 31st August (18th *Elul*), Ramash penned a pastoral letter, rendered into Yiddish, Hebrew and English, addressed to "Our brothers and sisters, sons and daughters of Israel, wherever you may be," offering blessings and an inspirational message for the upcoming Jewish New Year. On the eve of *Rosh Hashanah*, when all Chasidim customarily present a *pidyon* to their Rebbe asking him to pray for a bountiful year, the vast majority handed their notes to Ramash. Many audaciously addressed their *pidyonot* to Ramash personally, referring to him as the "Rebbe *shlita*," rather than merely appointing him as an agent to beseech Rayatz. Regardless as to whom the *pidyonot* were addressed, Ramash accepted them all, and it took him three and a half hours to read them at Rayatz's grave.[54]

Ramash's residual resistance to accepting the leadership manifested itself in his clothing—he still wore a short jacket[55]—and his refusal to deliver a *ma'amar* (formal Chasidic discourse), the symbolic ritual of "crowning" a new Rebbe. By this point, it seems that Ramash would have already been willing to accept the position had it not been for the rift that would inevitably erupt in the Schneersohn-Gurary household. On 22nd September (11th *Tishrei*), Rabbi Yoel Kahn noted in his diary that Ramash "has still not accepted the leadership, as they say, 'officially.' Much depends on the Rashag, since [Ramash] wants to avoid resentment, *etc.*"

Ramash himself wrote during this period, apparently referring to his own leadership of the movement, "It is not possible at the moment without entering into conflict. Obviously, I am not running after this."[56]

As we have seen, Ramash's father, Reb Levik, had only won his Rabbinic position after much communal friction, but in that case Reb Levik had received direct instructions from the Rebbe Rashab to pursue the post. Ramash, however, repeatedly reminded Chasidim, "I did not hear anything from my father-in-law."[57] With the exception of Moussia, Ramash's appointment as Rebbe was unsupported by any of Rayatz's surviving family: his widow, Rebbetzin Nechama Dina; her older daughter, Chana; son-in-law Rashag, and her grandson, Barry.[58] How these relationships panned out behind closed doors, we do not know; but Ramash's eventual appointment did create fault-lines which eventually cracked, several decades later, resulting in a very public court case about the ownership of the Chabad library (see p. 359).

Nechama Dina did have tremendous respect for her younger son-in-law and was known to be impressed by his politeness and fine manners. She had even said of Ramash, "If he had lived in the generation of the Alter Rebbe, they would have been impressed by him."[59] What appeared to concern her most was that in a Ramash administration, Rashag might cease to be respected by Chasidim and would lose his central role in the Lubavitcher court. "She is extremely angry at the Chabad community," wrote Yoel Kahn in his diary, "for not acting respectably towards Rashag."[60]

Chasidic courts, when they are unstable, can easily foment zealous conflicts, and it is likely that as Ramash's popularity swelled, Rashag suffered from more than democratic protest. In one incident that has reached us, some mischievous Ramash supporters leaked copies of a segment from Rayatz's diary from the summer of 1929, in which the late Rebbe had penned disparaging remarks about his older son-in-law. When Ramash discovered what had happened, he was outraged and banned anyone from owning a copy of the document, describing it as akin to possessing a bomb. Still, incidents such as these only served to inflame existing familial tensions.

Nechama Dina, Chana, and Barry were never able to forgive Ramash for acceding to the Chasidim's requests to become the Seventh Lubavitcher Rebbe.[61] Ironically, the only member of the late Rebbe's family that *did* accept Ramash's leadership was Rashag himself, who became a loyal Chasid of the Seventh Lubavitcher Rebbe (although this took some time, as we shall see.)

During the entire period of 1950, when the leadership issue had not been decided, both Rashag and Ramash were accorded their usual respective honors in the synagogue and at public functions, and no attempts were made to give special treatment to Ramash in the older brother-in-law's presence. It was only on the festival of *Simchat Torah,* when Rashag was absent,[62] that one of the Chasidim—Rabbi Dovber Chaskind (1897-1958)—took the audacious move of calling Ramash to the Torah with the honorific *Adonenu Morenu ve-Rabenu* ("Our Master, Teacher and Rabbi"), a title reserved exclusively for a Rebbe. Ramash made no protest; in fact, he did not react at all. He simply walked up to the Torah as if he had been called in an ordinary fashion. Only when he took hold of the Torah and began to recite the customary blessings, could he be seen shedding a tear.[63]

Kahn's description of *Yud Tet Kislev*, the Chasidic "New Year," (28th November, 1950) gives us a sense of how Rashag's dignity was still maintained even when faced with overwhelming support for Ramash. On the eve of the festival, Rashag spoke for about two and a half hours, after which Rabbi Shmuel Levitin continued the *farbrengen.* There were about fifteen students present and a handful of other Chasidim. The next day, a formal gathering was held in Rayatz's study, where the *Yud Tet Kislev Farbrengen* had taken place in his lifetime, with Rashag and Ramash both present. Rashag spoke a little, but Ramash said nothing, except for *le-chaim* over a toast. After the singing of some Chasidic melodies, the gathering came to an end. Then, the Chasidim made their way downstairs to the main synagogue where Ramash *farbrenged* for the rest of the evening. "The synagogue was packed from wall to wall," Kahn recalled. "I have never seen it so packed."[64]

While requests for Ramash's leadership had arrived from all over the world, the Chabad Chasidim of the United States had not yet made a formal, unified letter of *hitkashrut* (attachment), largely due to the delicate issue of Rashag's opposition. But this changed when, on the evening of 1st January (24th *Tevet*) 1951, one hundred and thirty-nine years after the first Rebbe of Chabad's passing, around thirty Chasidim assembled outside Ramash's office. The group included representatives from communities around America, as well as senior Chasidim who had studied in Rashab's Yeshiva. As they entered, Ramash must have had some inkling of what was going to transpire.

"What do you want?" Ramash asked.

"We want to give you a letter," replied the chief of the group, handing over a letter of *hitkashrut.*

Ramash read only the first line, "We, the undersigned, truly and wholeheartedly accept upon ourselves the leadership and authority of the son-in-law...," before closing it and placing it to the side. Then he burst into tears.

"Please leave," he said, regaining composure. "This has no relevance to me."[65]

The Chasidim, unrelenting, decided to give the matter a necessary push. They informed the major Yiddish newspapers of the day, *Der Morgen Journal, Der Tag* and *The Forward,* that a committee of Chasidim led by Rabbis Meir Ashkenazi, Shlomo Aharon Kazarnovsky and Zalman Gurary had chosen Rabbi Menachem Mendel Schneerson as the next Rebbe of Lubavitch and presented him with a letter of *hitkashrut.* On Thursday, 4th January the headlines ran: "Rabbi Menachem Schneerson will be the Successor of the Lubavitcher Rebbe o.b.m."[66]

The Gourary family was incensed and Barry was seen screaming lividly at his uncle in 770. Ramash, of course, had not given his permission that this public announcement be made and he went straight to Shmuel Levitin's quarters, on the ground floor of 770, in search of the guilty parties. There he found, besides Rabbi Levitin, the other "instigators," Shlomo Aharon Kazarnovsky, Shmuel Zalmanov and Zalman Gurary.

Ramash wasted no time. "If you do not publish a clear retraction," he stated, "I will contact the newspapers and inform them personally of my retraction."

"What are you going to retract?" Levitin replied. "The article merely states that we handed you a letter of *hitkashrut,* which, in fact, we did."

Ramash offered no response, and walked off.

A short while later, Barry entered the room, fuming. "If you do not cease from this activity immediately," he threatened, "I will have no choice other than to go into the Rebbe's study and recite those chapters of *Tehillim* (Psalms) which grandfather taught me to say against enemies!"

Despite pressure from all sides, the Chasidim remained determined and no retractions were published.[67]

V.

The long awaited acceptance of the Chabad leadership by Ramash finally came a year on the Jewish calendar after the passing of the Rebbe Rayatz, on 17th January (10th *Shevat*), 1951. After the morning prayers, a group of Chasidim led by Rabbi Meir Ashkenazi entered Ramash's room and presented him with a letter of *hitkashrut*, imploring him to accept it. For the first time, Ramash was not dismissive. "You all have to help me," he said.[68]

After spending most of the day at Rayatz's grave site, Ramash went to visit his mother, before the "big event."

At 9:45 p.m., adorned in a black silk *kapote*, Rabbi Menachem Mendel Schneerson entered the main synagogue in 770, finding it overstuffed with an expectant crowd. Ramash took the main seat at the head table, flanked by Rabbi Ephraim Yolles to his right, and Rabbi Yitzchak Meir Rapoport (1898-1982), the erstwhile Rav of Prague, to his left.

The *farbrengen* began uneventfully, with Ramash sermonizing about Rayatz's passing and the importance of spreading Chasidic teachings. Then, in the second section of his talks, Ramash began to lead up to the evening's main event. "Here in America, people like to hear a 'statement,'" he said, quaintly employing the English word in his Yiddish discourse, "something different, preferably alarming."

Ramash's opening "statement" of his leadership of Chabad was a message which really underpinned all his later initiatives: *"The love of G-d, the love of the Torah and love toward a fellow Jew are all one."*[69] A wholesome Judaism integrates a deep attachment to Jewish text and ritual, a profound faith, along with a sense of humanism and social responsibility. Often, Ramash explained, you will find Jews who excel in one area but neglect another. It is time to nurture a Judaism which harmonizes all of these sentiments.

As Ramash concluded his second talk, about an hour into the gathering, senior Chasid Rabbi Avraham Sender Nemtzov—who had been one of the earliest supporters of Ramash, a year back—stood up and pleaded: "The sermons are beautiful but we want to hear Chasidut! Will the Rebbe please say Chasidut!" Nemtzov was referring to the recitation of a *ma'amar* (discourse), which was considered the formal, ritual acceptance of Rebbehood.

There was a quiet pause. As Ramash started to speak he shifted into the special tune with which a formal Chasidic discourse is delivered. *"I have come into my garden, my sister, my bride* (*Songs* 5:1)," he began, opening his first discourse with the title of Rayatz's last published *ma'amar.*

Referring to what was now the "Seventh Generation" of Chabad, Ramash creatively deployed the *Midrashic* teaching, *"all those that are seventh are cherished."*[70] In Jewish thought, there is generally considered to be a spiritual decline from one generation to the next, which would, in theory, render the Seventh Generation the lowest of all. But, Ramash argued, this last generation is "special" in that it has the privilege of completing the task begun by the first.

> It is this that is demanded of each and every one of us of the Seventh Generation— and "all those that are seventh are cherished." Although the fact that we are in the Seventh Generation is not the result of our own choosing and our own service, and in certain ways it is perhaps contrary to our will, nevertheless, *"all those who are seventh are cherished."* We are now very near the coming of Mashiach. Our spiritual task is to complete the process of drawing down the *Shechinah* (Divine Presence) to our lowly world.

Embracing a Messianic theme, Ramash intimated that what could be achieved in the current era was the globalization of Chasidic spirituality in a way that was tangible, widespread and universal. With its epicenter now in America, Chabad Chasidism needed to reexamine its own purpose and unique assets.

About halfway through the *ma'amar* Ramash made a pause to offer a toast of *le'chaim.* Nemtzov, who was already in his eighties, jumped on the table and shouted joyously, "Chasidim! We need to make the blessing *shehecheyanu.* G-d has helped us and we have a Rebbe!" He then proceeded to recite the special blessing which is offered as thanks to the Almighty on reaching special times in life, and the crowd responded with a resounding "Amen!"

Ramash could not help but smile. "Please get down off the table," he asked Nemtzov.

After the crowd chanted a few melodies, the newly crowned Rebbe continued with the second section of his discourse. The Rebbe shifted to storytelling, something unusual for a Chasidic discourse, and related an incident from the lives of each of the previous six Chabad Rebbes which brought their deep humanism to light. It was as if he were calling on his predecessors to support his "mission statement" of *ahavat Yisrael* (Jewish inclusiveness).

As the *ma'amar* drew to an end, Nemtzov stood up again and, on behalf of the community, offered the new Rebbe his blessings on accepting the leadership. Once again, there was a roaring "Amen" from the crowd.

"Now listen," Ramash said, "the Rebbes always demanded from Chasidim that they act autonomously, and not rely on their master to do everything for them." Ramash's immediate concern, which he reiterated countless times during the decades of his leadership, was that the Rebbe-Chasid relationship should not be plagued by an unhealthy codependency. Ramash warned the Chasidim that he intended to *empower* them to achieve greater heights, not to spoon feed them or relieve them from personal responsibility.

As the hour passed midnight, the *farbrengen* drew to a close. The final point was a call for communal harmony. "There needs to be peace in all matters pertaining to the Rebbe, my father-in-law," he said.[71]

At 12:25 a.m., as the crowd sang rapturously, the newly crowned Rebbe stood up and began to walk off. "*Mazal tov*," said Shlomo Aharon Kazarnovsky, who had campaigned heavily for the appointment. Ramash smiled, and went on his way.

But the celebrations had only just started. Even the older Chasidim danced elatedly, before the crowd finally sat down to review the sermons and the *ma'amar*. After the first review was completed at 3 a.m., the students stayed on until 6:30 a.m. repeating the discourse lovingly again and again. Amid all the excitement, bodily needs such as sleep and food simply seemed irrelevant.

VI.

While he had overwhelming support, not all Chasidim shifted to the new Rebbe immediately. Rabbi Shmuel Levitin, for example, who had been a supporter of Ramash, and had even participated in the efforts to crown him, still wanted to remain on good terms with Rashag and the old Rebbetzin. Initially he told his children to follow the new Rebbe, while refraining himself from attending Ramash's *farbrengens*—something which irked the young Yoel Kahn. "He is being very stupid," Kahn wrote, breaking from his diary's characteristically cerebral tone, "even though generally he is a very wise Jew."[72]

27th January (20th *Shevat*) was the first Sabbath after Ramash's appointment that the two sons-in-law prayed together in the main synagogue at 770. Rabbi Yochanan Gordon's face turned pale when he called Ramash to the Torah as *Adonenu Morenu ve-Rabenu*. Rashag just gazed blankly at the wall. Ramash appeared somewhat tense, and he recited the *haftarah* quickly.

"Obviously, for the first few weeks it is going to be difficult," Kahn wrote.[73] But it took more than a few weeks for Rashag to come to terms with the new order in Lubavitch. A month later, Kahn noted that Rashag was still "disorientated by the fact that the Rebbe *shlita* accepted the leadership. There are those in the community that say he is opposed to the Rebbe *shlita*, but I don't think you could call him an opponent. It's something emotional, not rational. He just can't take it."[74]

Initially, Rashag resisted accepting the Seventh Rebbe's symbolic presidency over the Yeshivot,[75] but by the end of 1951 the wounds had considerably healed and he already referred in correspondence to "my brother-in-law, his holiness, *Adonenu Morenu ve-Rabenu*, Rabbi M. M. Schneerson, *shlita*, President of the *Yeshivot Tomchei Temimim* Lubavitch."[76] A week later, Rashag called a meeting to introduce the new Rebbe to his major donors that funded the Yeshivah system.[77] By the end of 1952, Rashag also began to attend the *farbrengens*, and the Rebbe requested that a place of honor be prepared for his older brother-in-law at the head table.[78]

A few months later, after imbibing a considerable amount of wine, Rashag's high spirits drove him to publicly pledge allegiance to the Seventh Rebbe. "The only heir of the Ba'al Shem Tov is *my* brother-in-law. I hereby give you all the powers that I have as an older brother-in-law.

I said it at the [Rebbe's] grave site and I will say it now in public!"

Uncomfortable with the outburst, the new Rebbe said nothing. At one point he even tried to stop Rashag. "Do you have to do this in public?" he asked.

But Rashag was adamant, "This is the truth. Everyone may hear it!"[79]

By the summer, Kahn noted, "the relationship between the Rashag *shlita* and the Rebbe *shlita* has changed completely for the good. He comes to every *farbrengen*, and even in matters relating to the Yeshivah—some say in his personal life too, but I don't know for sure—he consults with the Rebbe *shlita* virtually every week... for several hours."[80]

In a peaceful conclusion to the drama over succession, Rashag became, by all indications, a devoted Chasid of his younger brother-in-law. Some say, in fact, he was even more devoted to the Seventh Rebbe than he had been to the Sixth.[81]

Perhaps the best encapsulation of the entire ordeal was a summary heard firsthand from Rayatz's two sons-in-law themselves, in a 1957 interview with Reform Rabbi Herbert Weiner. When Rashag was asked how a new Rebbe is chosen, he looked at Weiner sharply for a moment, and replied, "If the Rebbe leaves a will, his instructions are followed. Otherwise, the 'Elders' of the movement decide."

The Seventh Rebbe's response to the same question was especially candid. "It is always pleasant to run away from responsibility," he said. "But what if one's running might destroy the congregation, and suppose they put the key into your pocket and walk away. What can you do then—permit the books to be stolen?"[82]

Menachem Mendel Schneerson had accepted the position as Lubavitcher Rebbe, not because he had desired it, but out of a sense of duty to the Chabad community, and to the Jewish people.

Now he had some work to do.

1. Rabbi Menachem Mendel Schneerson (*Tzemach Tzedek*), the Third Lubavitcher Rebbe.

2. Rabbi Meir Shlomo Yanovksy, maternal grandfather of the Rebbe.

3. Rabbi Levi Yitzchak ("Levik") Schneerson, father of the Rebbe (1939).

4. Rabbi Zalman Vilenkin, the Rebbe's childhood teacher.

5. Rebbetzin Chana Schneerson (née Yanovsky), mother of the Rebbe.

6. Rabbi Shmuel Schneerson (left), younger brother of Reb Levik; his wife, Miriam Gittel, younger sister of Chana (middle); and their son, Menachem Mendel, "double" cousin of the Rebbe (right).

7. Chana's first cousin Tziporah and her husband Tuvia Shlonsky, the Schneersons' neighbors.

8. The Rebbe's childhood home at 20 Marinova Street, Yekatrinoslav (Dnepropetrovsk).

9. The Shlonsky children, cousins of the Schneersons, who lived next door. Standing from right to left: Avraham (the Rebbe's classmate), Miriam, Dov, Feiga. Seated: Yehudit, Verdina.

10. Childhood acquaintances of the Rebbe: Nachum Goldshmidt (left), Yonah Kesseh (middle), and Yeshayahu Sher (right).

11. Rabbi Shalom Dov Ber Schneersohn (Rashab), the Fifth Lubavitcher Rebbe (left), and his wife Shterna Sara (right).

12. Rabbi Yosef Yitzchak Schneersohn (Rayatz), the Sixth Lubavitcher Rebbe (left), and his wife Nechama Dina (right).

13. The Court of "Lubavitch" in Rostov, home to Rashab and Rayatz (1915-1924).

14. Moussia Schneersohn in 1918 (left); and on her wedding day in 1928 (right).

15. Moussia's older sister Chana (left), her husband Shmaryahu Gourary (right) and son Barry (behind).

16. Moussia's younger sister Sheina (left), and her husband Menik Horenstein (right).

17. Rabbi Menachem Mendel Schneerson, aged 28, shortly before his wedding.

18. Rabbi Eliyahu Chaim Althaus, devotee of Rayatz and chronicler of significant events in the Rebbe's early life.

19. Alexander Vasilyevich Barchenko, eccentric Russian scientist for whom the Rebbe carried out research in Kabbalah.

20. Significant Rabbinic figures in the Rebbe's early life: Rabbi Yosef Rosen, the Rogatchover Gaon (left), Rabbi Chaim Heller (bottom-left), and Rabbi Yechiel Ya'akov Weinberg (bottom-right).

21. One of the Rebbe's professors in Berlin University, Walther Nernst.

22. The Court of Lubavitch in Riga, Latvia (1927-1933).

23. Rabbi Mordechai Dubin (right), Latvian Parliament member who arranged Rayatz's rescue from Russia in 1927 and again from Latvia in 1939; and Rabbi Mordechai Isaac Chodakov (left), head of the Jewish school system in Latvia and later the Seventh Rebbe's Chief-of-Staff—at a *farbrengen* in Riga, 1930s.

24. Rabbi Menachem Mendel Schneerson, in *Jardin du Luxembourg*, Paris, 1930s.

25. Max Gerson, Rayatz's doctor (left), Vienna 1935; Westend Sanitorium in Purkersdorf, outside Vienna (right), where Dr. Gerson treated Rayatz, who was accompanied by Menachem Mendel, from December 1934-April 1935.

26. The Lubavitcher Yeshivah in Otwock, Poland, 1935 to 1939.

Auditeur Libre N° d'inscription 151.032

T S3
ME

Ecole Spéciale des Travaux-Publics
du Bâtiment et de l'Industrie

Ecole de Plein Exercice 1932-1933.

Cours Techniques Secondaires 3e année
Section de Mécanique et d'Electricité

Nom et Prénoms Schneerson, Mendel

Entré au Cours le: 24 Avril 1933

Parti le:

Entré à la Maison de Famille le:

Parti le:

Né le 1er Mars 1895 à:

Adresse des Parents:

Adresse particulière de l'Elève: 11, Rue Blomet 11 Paris XV

Nom et adresse du Correspondant:

Assiduité

A. Absent sans excuse — E. Absences excusées — M. Absences pour maladie.

Octobre			Novembre			Décembre			Janvier			Février			Mars			Avril			Mai			Juin			Juillet			Totaux		
A	E	M	A	E	M	A	E	M	A	E	M	A	E	M	A	E	M	A	E	M	A	E	M	A	E	M	A	E	M	A	E	M
																		7	—	—	18	—	—	25	—	—				60	—	—

Conduite.

Punitions encourues avec l'indication des motifs. C: consigne. R: réprimande. Rp: renvoi provisoire. Rd: renvoi définitif.

Dates	Motifs	Dates	Motifs

Année antérieu[re]

MM. SCHNEERSON Mendel [struck out] sont autorisés à quitter la séance d'application le Vendredi, pendant les mois d'hiver à 15h,30 mais ils devront avoir remis avant leur départ les travaux qui doivent être remis normalement en fin de séance. ... ne pourront se prévaloir de la présente autorisation pour ... faire des travaux en retard.

Conseil de Direction du 16 Novembre 193[illegible]

... d'hiver ... départ les travaux qui doivent ... normalement en fin de séance. Il ne pourra se prévaloir de l'autorisation ci-dessus pour demander à exécuter des travaux en retard.

27. Page from the Rebbe's academic records at *Ecole Spéciale des Travaux Publics du Bâtiment et de l'Industrie*—ESTP. Inset shows special permission he obtained to leave early for the Sabbath on Friday afternoons in the winter.

28. Rayatz and Rashag (second to right and right), at the White House after being received by President Hoover, in 1929. To the left are chief officers of *Agudat Chasidei Chabad* which would be instrumental in saving the Sixth Rebbe's life a decade later (left to right): Arthur Rabinovitz, attorney for Chabad, Elchanan Fogelman, (vice-president), and Hyman Kramer (president).

29. Ernst Bloch, a German officer whose father was Jewish who saved Rayatz and his family from Nazi-occupied Warsaw in 1939.

30. Rabbi Yisrael Jacobson, who spearheaded the political campaign to save Rayatz and the Rebbe from Nazi-occupied Europe.

A-L

February 7, 1941.

VD

Mr. Arthur Rabinovitz advises me that Rabbi Mendel Schneersohn's visa application was transferred from Nice district to Marseilles district, and he is now refused non quota visa by Marseilles. We authorized issue of visa. Consul at Marseilles suggests immigrant visa. I see no reason why he should not be granted immigrant visa even though we authorized non quota. As we have communicated several times about Schneersohn and there appears no objection, I see no reason why we should not communicate further to Marseilles on his account.

Also advised that Rabbi Mendel Hornstein is still at Otwack, Poland, and has not received his visa. I see no reason why he should not receive either an immigrant or a non quota visa, probably an immigrant. As long as we have telegraphed about him before you might check on the reports and if necessary check again.

Please advise Mr. Rabinovitz about these matters.

B. L.

A-L:BL:WA

Rabbi Mendel Schneersohn - Rabbi Mendel Hornstein

31. Memo issued by Breckenridge Long, the "American Eichmann," authorizing U.S. visas for the Rebbe and his wife, who were trapped in Nazi-occupied France.

32. Rabbi Yosef Yitzchak Schneersohn, in his state room on the *SS Drottningholm,* shortly before disembarking in New York, 1940.

33. 770 Eastern Parkway, the home and synagogue purchased for Rayatz in Brooklyn, New York that became Chabad's iconic headquarters.

34. Rabbi Joseph Ber Soloveitchik (left) is guest speaker at the Lubavitcher Yeshivah Dinner in New York, 1942. To his left: Rashag, Rayatz and the future Rebbe.

35. The Rebbe (center right) is reunited with his mother (center left) in Paris, 1947, after not seeing her for twenty years. Standing between them is Rabbi Bentzion Shemtov.

36. Moussia Schneerson, the Rebbe's wife (left); her mother, Nechama Dina Schneersohn (middle) at the wedding of Manya Lotz (right), Rayatz's nurse, at the Lou G. Siegal Restaurant in New York, 1949.

שמות 32 דרך אמת

37. Notes penned by the Rebbe's father, Reb Levik, in the margin of a copy of the Zohar while he was in exile in central Asia (early 1940s). The ink was prepared by his wife Chana, from grasses.

38. Rayatz accepts U.S. citizenship, 1949 (Ramash stands to the right; behind: Shlomo Aharon Kazarnovsky).

39. Funeral of Rayatz, Eastern Parkway, 1950.

CHAPTER ELEVEN

AT THE COURT OF THE SEVENTH LUBAVITCHER REBBE

1951–1964

The Rebbe, early 1950s

Throughout his four decades of leadership, the Rebbe barely ever left the two blocks that separated his home and office at 770. He would arrive every morning to work, around nine or ten a.m., and stay in his office until around midnight or later, usually taking home a large pile of papers to read and edit. The next morning he would arrive with his "homework" done.

It was in his wood-paneled study, some twelve by fifteen feet, that he spent most of his life: writing letters, preparing his discourses and sermons, and immersing himself in private study and prayer. A Chasidic discourse, he once said, took him many hours to prepare,[1] and from 1952 to 1964 alone he delivered over four hundred of them.[2] On most of these occasions he would deliver several sermons too,[3] all of which required research and thought.

He visited his mother every day, in her apartment on President Street, and always took a tea break with Moussia, a time which he said was as precious to him as putting on *tefilin*.[4] During the 1950s, he would visit the grave site of his father-in-law in Queens once a month, but that was the extent of his travel, besides rare visits to comfort a mourner. From 1954 onwards he ceased to attend weddings in other areas of New York, and required that they be conducted outside 770 if he was to officiate. He left New York City just a handful of times in 1956, 1957 and 1960 to visit the children's summer camps he had founded in the Catskill mountains.[5] His sheer stamina and dedication to his work was spectacular, never taking even a day's vacation. "If you find me someone to take over while I'm on vacation," he once told his secretariat, "I'll be able to go."[6]

He did not attend even major Chabad events and refrained from being a guest at the annual dinner in honor of the Chabad Yeshivot—an event that Rayatz had attended in his lifetime. In 1951, one of the Chabad supporters put considerable pressure on him to attend the dinner, pledging $5,000 to the Yeshivah if the Rebbe would not attend, and $10,000 if he would participate. "It's ten years since Pearl Harbor," the Rebbe responded, "which gave us the phenomenon of an unconditional surrender. Why do you have to attach conditions? Give the ten thousand unconditionally!"[7]

The Rebbe maintained a staggering correspondence with his own followers and institutions, as well as with non-Chabad Rabbis and a growing number of Jews who turned to him for advice and blessing. His published correspondence in Hebrew and Yiddish[8] from 1952 to 1964, which represents around two-thirds of the material actually penned during this time,[9] and contains more than seven and a half thousand letters.[10] There is also a large correspondence in English, most of which has not been published,[11] as well as thousands more routine letters for life cycle events and holiday greetings, all of which received the Rebbe's personal attention. Through the medium of the letter, the Seventh Rebbe's court spread its wings over all seven continents, engaging both Chasidim and non-Chasidim, Jews and non-Jews.

When one of his secretaries suggested that routine letters could be signed by use of a rubber stamp, he found the idea distasteful. "How can I send prayerful wishes to a person in such an artificial manner," he said, "and how would anyone feel receiving from his Rebbe good wishes in a letter that is signed with a rubber stamp?"[12] The Rebbe also inconvenienced himself to open all his mail personally, so as to retain complete confidentiality.[13] He even refused an electric letter-opener, reputedly saying that it de-humanized the correspondence which had sometimes been sealed with tears.[14]

Rabbi Nissan Mindel, who dealt with the English correspondence, recalled spending approximately three hours a week in dictation, during two sessions on a Monday and Thursday. The Rebbe, he said, would work at an alarming pace, and would even be reading the next letter in the pile as he was dictating a response to the previous one. As a result, the dictation was almost uninterrupted: as soon as one response had been dictated, the Rebbe was poised to begin the next.[15]

"In general, my custom," the Seventh Rebbe once explained, "following a directive of my father-in-law the Rebbe, is to answer every query."[16] While the volume of mail no doubt changed with time, one internal estimate placed the volume of correspondence at 250-300 letters per day.[17] There was a priority system for important mail, and many letters were forced to begin with an apology for the lengthy delay in response. Interestingly, the Rebbe would usually give precedence to a letter from a non-Lubavitcher over a devoted follower, and to a gentile over a Jew. "My Chasidim will understand the delay; others might feel slighted," he explained.[18]

While all correspondence was confidential, some particularly sensitive issues were dealt with an extra measure of prudence. If a letter was marked with the Hebrew letter *chet,* it was classified as *chashai* (secret), indicating that the secretariat should be especially careful about its confidentiality. If the letter was marked with a *samech* it was classified as *sodi* (top secret), to the extent that, on occasion, even the recipient was not permitted to keep the letter and was required to send it back to head office after it had been read.[19]

Besides the huge volume of mail, the telephones in the main office at 770 rang day and night with questions pouring in from all over the world, as well as reports of activities. The secretaries would write down the questions received and hand them into the Rebbe, who would pen his responses, enabling the secretaries to call back the questioners. Sometimes the Rebbe would prefer to respond with a letter.[20] But he rarely conversed on the phone, although there are many reports of the Rebbe listening in on the line during calls to Rabbi Chodakov and occasionally interjecting with a remark.

Besides a significant chunk of his correspondence which was devoted to the building and management of Chabad institutions, the Rebbe received, and answered, questions spanning an extremely wide range of topics: anything to do with Jewish faith[21] and practice,[22] Chasidism, health and medical issues,[23] business questions,[24] science,[25] relationships, current affairs, education,[26] as well as life decisions such as marriage[27] (and divorce), employment and relocation. People shared their frustrations, pain, joy and dreams with him. Many Rabbinic authors sent him their latest works, and he would often reply with detailed comments on an insight or two that he had found in the text.

Letters came in a host of languages, and the Rebbe was able to understand English, Yiddish, Hebrew, Russian, Italian, German, French and Latin,[28] (though the secretaries were only able to send out letters in English, Yiddish, Hebrew and Russian). Replies were penned by the Rebbe to Jews and non-Jews, Chasidim and Mitnagdim, Rabbis and secular Jews, Sefardim and Ashkenazim, Kabbalists and poets, academics and businessmen, politicians and members of the military, friends of Chabad and its critics—there were no real defining limits.

One area where, surprisingly, the Rebbe generally preferred *not* to give an original response were questions in matters of Jewish law.[29] While he was extremely well versed in *halachic* literature, he probably steered away from questions of this nature—usually referring an inquirer to seek another expert in the field—so as to maximize time for his work of building institutions and "turning Judaism outwards." He also described himself as being "fearful of giving *halachic* rulings."[30]

The Rebbe was assisted on a day to day basis by a small, dedicated and talented staff of secretaries. Besides Rabbi Chodakov, who was the chief of staff, and Nissan Mindel, the Rebbe "inherited" two important secretaries who had been office members in Rayatz's lifetime. Rabbi Avraham Eliyahu Quint (1900-1974), was a considerable Torah scholar in his own right, originally hired by Chodakov in the 1940s to assist with the work of *Merkos*. After Rayatz's passing, Quint continued in the Rebbe's secretariat, assisting with the huge correspondence. Like Chodakov and Mindel, Quint did not grow up as a Chabad Chasid, and had studied in the illustrious Slabodka *Yeshivah* in Lithuania, receiving ordination from its *Rosh Yeshivah,* Rabbi Moshe Mordechai Epstein (1866-1933) as well as from Rabbi Avraham Yitzchak Kook (1865–1935). Quint never became a Chasid and, like Mindel, did not wear a beard, but he came to admire the Rebbe's court immensely. "I encountered the world of Chabad," Quint wrots in his 1965 volume of Torah novellae *Menuchat Eliyahu,* "a world of Torah and fear of G-d, a noble world, a world where its leaders do everything to spread Torah... Being with them, I have learned a lot."[31] The Rebbe deeply valued Quint's participation in his work, and they would converse at length. "He knows the whole Talmud," the Rebbe once told a junior member of his staff. "If you need to clarify something ask him." Eliyahu Quint's son, Emmanuel, recalled how his father would spend hours studying Torah at night and would frequently pick up the phone and call the Rebbe to discuss questions in Talmud, Maimonides and even books of *Mussar*.[32]

The only member of the older tier of the Rebbe's secretariat who *was* a Lubavitcher Chasid from his youth was Rabbi Moshe Leib Rothstein. Rothstein was born in Russia as Zusha Shurpin at the turn of the century and studied at *Tomchei Temimim* in Lubavitch. After the First World War he fled to Poland on a false passport under the alias of Moshe Leib Rothstein, a name he retained for the rest of his life. From 1928 he assisted with the administration of *Yeshivat Tomchei Temimim* in Warsaw and Rayatz appointed him as a personal secretary in 1932. At the outbreak of World War Two he fled Poland to Riga, and through the efforts of Rayatz was evacuated to Japan, from where he reached the United States. After initially settling in Chicago, Rothstein relocated to New York in 1946 to resume work as Rayatz's secretary, a task he continued until the Sixth Rebbe's passing. After the Seventh Rebbe assumed the leadership of Chabad, he asked Rothstein to continue to work in his secretariat, assisting with the preparation of Hebrew and Yiddish correspondence. Rabbi Rothstein would enter the Rebbe's office for dictation nearly every day, and spent many subsequent hours fleshing out his shorthand notes into more substantial, eloquent letters, which the Rebbe would then edit and sign. After his passing in

1967, Rothstein was not replaced, and as a result there is a notable curtailment of lengthy, scholarly correspondence from this date onwards. Instead the Rebbe shifted more into writing brief but extremely precise responses in his own handwriting which were communicated by the secretaries.[33]

There were four young men—all of them Lubavitchers—who were asked to join the secretariat during the early period of the Rebbe's leadership, and along with Rabbis Chodakov and Mindel, they worked closely at the Rebbe's side all the way through to the 1990s.

Rabbi Yehudah Leib ("Leibel") Groner (b. 1931), moved to America with his parents at the age of eight, and his father, a Karliner Chasid by birth, became an integral part of Rayatz's court. Leibel's mother, Menucha Rachel, was a descendent of the first Chabad Rebbe, Rabbi Shneur Zalman. Leibel studied in the Lubavitch school and Yeshivah system in New York from its earliest days, and in 1949 was asked by the Rebbe—then the Ramash—to assist with some of the work of preparing Kehot publications for print. When the Rebbe assumed the leadership of Chabad, he asked Groner to assist him at *farbrengens.* Groner gradually assumed the role, not only of a secretary, but also an assistant who cared for many of the Rebbe's personal needs. He was often seen at the Rebbe's side and for many years had the unenviable task during the nights of *yechidut* (private audiences) of ensuring that each appointment ended on time, often dealing with some difficult and vociferous personalities. As the years progressed, Leibel also acted as one of the main points of contact through whom questioners could obtain a response from the Rebbe. He was admired for being well read, extremely hard working and a good speaker.[34]

Rabbi Shalom Mendel Simpson (b. 1928), the son of Rayatz's secretary Eliyahu Simpson (1889-1976),[35] joined the secretariat in 1952 at the Seventh Rebbe's request. "Your father is always confidential (a *baal sod*)," the Rebbe said to him, "and I trust that you will be, too." Like Quint and Rothstein, Simpson's main work involved the preparation of Hebrew and Yiddish correspondence. Initially, the Rebbe did not want any letters to leave his office, and Simpson worked for two to three hours daily in the same room as the Rebbe, on a small desk by the window, opposite the door. Generally, Simpson tried to keep his eyes to himself, but occasionally could not resist watching the Rebbe at work. "He would take a letter in one hand," Simpson recalled, "and with his other hand he held a pencil and moved it very fast down the page. He then placed the letter in a pile of letters that he had read and went on to the next letter. I was shocked how quickly the Rebbe read."

All the secretaries that worked on correspondence—Quint, Rothstein, Mindel and Simpson—each typed the letters which they had prepared, but it was Simpson who was assigned by the Rebbe to make an orderly archive of *all* correspondence. "Over the years, I put a lot of work into arranging the archive," he recalled, "and whenever I saw how pleased the Rebbe was by how quickly I was able to find a letter that he wanted, it encouraged me to continue maintaining the archives in meticulous order." Simpson also helped the Rebbe acknowledge receipt of the thousands of *pidyonot* (prayerful notes) which were received from Chasidim around the world on special occasions throughout the year. Later on, he moved to an office adjacent to 770 and, as a result, was not as familiar a face to the public as the other secretaries who worked in the general office across the hallway from the Rebbe's room.[36]

Rabbi Chodakov also hired two other young men in this period who worked closely both with himself and with the Rebbe, gradually becoming notable figures in the secretariat. Rabbi Yehudah ("Yudel") Krinsky (b. 1934), grew up in Boston, Massachusetts, and was educated in the prestigious *Boston Latin School*, and later in the Lubavitch educational system. In the summer of 1957 he was hired by Chodakov to work in the secretariat and, among other tasks, was responsible for media relations, establishing the *Lubavitch News Service* to prepare press releases.[37] Krinsky was involved with legal matters, such as the purchase of the two apartment buildings adjacent to 770 (784-788 Eastern Parkway), to enable expansion of the offices and synagogue;[38] and he arranged the copyright registration of Kehot books.[39] He also functioned (alongside Klein) as the Rebbe's main driver for the many hundreds of trips to Rayatz's grave that were made over the decades of leadership. Always well-groomed and soft spoken, Krinsky stood out as the only member of the secretariat who was not an immigrant, having a deeper appreciation of American culture and values.[40]

Rabbi Binyamin Klein, was the last individual to join the secretariat. Klein was born in Israel in 1935 to a non-Chabad, Yerushalmi family, and his mother died tragically at childbirth. He studied in Chabad Yeshivot in Israel before arriving in New York in 1956 to study in 770. He spent a period in Australia, helping to establish the Chabad Yeshivah there, and following his return to America and marriage in 1966, he was enlisted to work as an assistant to Rabbi Chodakov. Rabbi Klein became one of the most familiar faces in the secretariat, acting as an accessible point of contact for many who sought the Rebbe's advice and blessing on many confidential issues, especially for those living in Israel.[41]

All the Rebbe's secretaries worked with complete confidentiality, and even years after his passing, they remain reluctant to disclose "behind-the-scenes" details of their work. Since they represented the exclusive channel of access to the Rebbe, who could not be contacted directly, they must often have been under tremendous pressure. One document which has come to light from which we can glean some of the difficulties of working in the secretariat, concerns those delicate situations where a Chabad organization wished to fire a staff member and had requested approval from the Rebbe. In such cases, the Rebbe often chose not to mix in with local institutional "politics" and simply gave no reply, leaving the organization to decide the matter for themselves. This placed the secretariat in a difficult position, prompting them to issue the following official guidelines in an internal memo.

> 1. Rumors spread in the name of the Rebbe or the secretariat are not to be relied upon. If the secretariat sees it fit to give an instruction, it will be done only in writing.
>
> 2. In the event that a question concerning the dismissal of an employee is sent to the Rebbe *shlita* and no answer is received, the lack of response is not to be interpreted as a positive or negative reply. Rather, it is as if the question has not been asked. Therefore it is unnecessary for further clarification by telephone with the secretariat.[42]

One can only imagine the difficulties of having to work under conditions of absolute secrecy, while being subjected to a barrage of inquiries from eager Chasidim on crucial issues, many of them heart-wrenching. Working in the Rebbe's office cannot have been an easy task.

The secretaries relate that the Rebbe was always polite and respectful. To call a secretary into his office, he would ring the internal telephone and ask respectfully, "If it is not difficult for you, please come in."

He expressed his thanks for any assistance offered, even if it was just opening a door, repeatedly offering a polite "*ah-dank*" ("thank you"), even to his junior assistants. He was kindly, often inquiring about the welfare of his staff's family, but retained a certain professional distance. "At work, the Rebbe always called me by my surname," Binyamin Klein recalled, "never my first name." He expected his staff to be punctual and that everything be organized and efficient.[43]

The Rebbe's physical needs were extremely meager. He ate little, avoiding chicken and meat during the week, and is reputed to have slept only a few hours per night.[44] While his clothes were always clean and presentable, his *kapotes* were sometimes shabby on the inside, and he only bothered to replace his hat every few years. Even at the office he was frugal, often writing notes on a scrap of paper or torn envelope, rather than wasting a fresh sheet. His humble allowance of $420 per month was passed to Moussia for housekeeping.[45]

Moussia lived an extremely private life, and she did not attend communal events or her husband's farbrengens. She never referred to herself as the "Lubavitcher Rebbetzin," but as "Mrs. Schneerson from President Street," the address of the home she shared with her husband from 1955 onwards. While the Rebbe would spend time with her every day, she was left with many, many hours to herself, but she is not known to have complained about what must have been a generally lonely existence. She had a small circle of close friends and family with whom she was close: her sister Chana and mother, her childhood friend Necha Rivkin; Mania Lotz, who had been her father's nurse; Schneerson cousins such as Leah Kahn and Hadassah Carlebach, and others. She enjoyed reading, especially Russian literature, and would sometimes go out shopping, away from Crown Heights.[46] The Rebbe and his wife did not host guests for weekday or Shabbat meals in their home, and, until Moussia's mother passed away at the end of 1970, they would eat the festival meals with her in 770, along with various guests.[47]

While we know little about the couple's relationship, Rebbetzin Moussia was an extremely close support to her husband and greatly admired his work. She made great sacrifices for the Rebbe, and she was no doubt cognizant that if not for her, the huge success of the Seventh Generation of Chabad would never have transpired. She was happy to have been instrumental behind the scenes.

II.

The transition from the Sixth to Seventh generations of Chabad required a considerable adjustment on the part of the Chasidim. The new Rebbe was far more frugal with praise than his predecessor and, while often pleased with the good efforts of Chasidim, never appeared satisfied. The point is illustrated well by an experience of Rabbi Yochanan Gordon, who, among other roles, was responsible for a local *gemach* (free loan fund) in Brooklyn. Previously, he had met with Rayatz each year to report on the successes of the fund, how many loans had been granted and how many had been repaid. The year following the Sixth Rebbe's passing was a particularly good one for the fund, and Gordon imagined how thrilled the late Rebbe would have been to see such a marked improvement and the warm encouragement he would have received. "How will the new Rebbe react?" he wondered.

The Seventh Rebbe quickly perused a report of the year's activities and turned to Gordon: "Reb Yochanan, *mehr hot ihr nit gekent tohn?"* ("Couldn't you have managed more?") Noticing dejection pass over Gordon's face, the Rebbe shared a little of his own struggle. "Reb Yochanan, why don't you learn from me?" the Rebbe said. "At night, before I go to bed, I always say to myself: Is this all I have done? Could I have done more?"[48]

The Rebbe soon earned a similar reputation from his Chasidim overseas, as Rabbi Moshe Ashkenazi (b. 1920) recalls: "When the Rebbe assumed the leadership, there was a complete revolution. Straight away, he began to campaign in a way that Chasidim found difficult to swallow. He wanted the educational institutions in the Holy Land to cater not just to the Chasidic population, which was not huge, but for thousands of others.... Communal activists in Israel tried to accomplish this, but it was difficult for them to work according to the terms which the Rebbe demanded, again and again."

Ashkenazi's father-in-law, Rabbi Eliezer Karasik, bore the brunt of the Rebbe's demands for increased activity in Israel, which would sometimes drive him to exasperation. "In each letter that arrived for my father-in-law," Ashkenazi recalled, "the Rebbe would reprove him for not doing enough, and he would take it to heart." Devorah Ashkenazi remembered her father once crying out, as he typed a response to the Rebbe, "I have to tell him that I'm not cut out for this. I'm not used to this." Karasik penned a note of resignation, that he was unable to keep up the pace which was being demanded of him, but before the letter was mailed he had a change of heart and tore it up.[49]

Although the new Lubavitcher Rebbe offered less praise than his predecessor and was more expectant of results, Chasidim embraced the new leadership as they saw the Rebbe pushing himself even harder than he pushed others. The Seventh Rebbe manifested a spiritual intensity and boundless energy that was contagious. His dedication to the Chasidim and to the Jewish people was so consuming that it inspired adherents to shed a bit of their own selfishness and dedicate themselves to the service of others.

The Rebbe was less inclined than his father-in-law to single out a particular Chasid and appoint him with a mission. He preferred that the Chasidim themselves be forthcoming. "The Rebbe was concerned that not enough was being done about the activities he promoted," recalled Rabbi Zvi Hirsh Gansbourg (1928-2006) in his 1958 diary of the happenings at 770. When the Rebbe was told that Rayatz "would himself urge people to be active in his projects," he replied, "My way of doing things is different."[50]

Even his few emissaries (*shluchim*), who had relocated to different parts of the world to carry out the work of Chabad on a full-time basis, were often not given specific orders. When Rabbi Nachman and Fradel Sudak asked the Rebbe for directions when departing as emissaries to England in 1959, the Rebbe simply replied, "There are thousands of things you could do. You decide."[51] While he was willing to share his vision, and lend guidance where necessary, the Rebbe preferred a bottom-up style of leadership, which he felt was more conducive to long-term growth. He would often cite the Talmudic dictum, "*A person desires one measure that is his own, rather than nine measures of his fellow*"[52]—when you own something, you are motivated to do more.

Unlike his predecessors, the new Rebbe did not spend hours in contemplative prayer, and his mannerisms in general were unassuming and non-demonstrative; but many found his public appearances spiritually exhilarating, and the crowds grew incrementally. When Chasid Rabbi Moshe Gurary (1899-1973), acclaimed as an outstanding scholar of Chabad Chasidut, visited the Seventh Rebbe's court from Israel for the first time, early in 1952, he wrote back home: "It is impossible to describe in writing what I have both seen and felt here, his enormous dedication to communal work in general and to matters pertaining to Israel, and how earnestly he answers every question.... On Shabbat there was a *farbrengen* and he delivered a Chasidic discourse.... The intense bouts of tears from the Rebbe literally tore even the coldest of hearts. He tried to hold himself back as best he could, but he was unable, and tears streamed down the table. Every word was uttered from the depths of his soul."[53]

Interestingly, it was *not* through the medium of the Chasidic discourse (*ma'amar*) that the Seventh Rebbe was most influential, even upon his own flock. This was partially due to the fact that, unlike his predecessors,[54] he did not personally write each discourse after it had been delivered (nor did he edit or approve students' renditions until much later);[55] and partially because the popularity of his discourses was overshadowed by those of the Fifth Rebbe, Rashab. In the 1950s and 1960s, many of the *mashpi'im* (spiritual mentors) that taught Chasidut in Chabad had studied in Lubavitch and still felt a particular loyalty to the discourses of Rashab. This was more than a sentimentalism. Rashab had been acclaimed as the "Maimonides" of the Chasidic movement[56] due to the outstanding discourses which he delivered and penned that invigorated Chabad ideas with an intensity that had not been experienced in generations.[57] In particular, Rashab developed the genre of a *hemshech* (series), where the elaborations of one discourse would dovetail into the next, providing the student with a meditative "stroll" through the intricate and labyrinthine terrain of Chasidic/Kabbalistic theosophy.[58] A *hemshech* of Rashab would progress at a slow pace, taking months, sometimes years, to deliver, as each idea was reflected upon exhaustively from various angles with multiple analogies, as the student gradually became lost in another world. Sometimes pages of reflection would pass with little citation from Rabbinic or Kabbalistic sources, the emphasis being on ruminating over a nugget of mystical wisdom as its contours were gracefully drawn.

The Seventh Rebbe barely touched the genre of *hemshech*, instead offering a faster pace of highly varied discourse, rich with citations, resembling more the intellectual heritage of the Third Lubavitcher Rebbe, *Tzemach Tzedek*. In *Tzemach Tzedek's* discourse, one encounters the entire corpus of Biblical, Talmudic, Midrashic and Kabbalisitic literature, which is drawn upon to buttress and contextualize the teachings of Chabad Chasidut. Besides the biological connection between the Third and Seventh Rebbes, their minds seemed to have operated on a similar wavelength, being drawn more to the parallel development of traditional and Chasidic thinking than the isolation of Chabad as an independent system. In general, though, the Seventh Rebbe showed no consuming favoritism to any of his predecessors, and his discourses might be based on ideas drawn from any one of the first Six Rebbes. After citing an earlier discourse, he would offer his own elaborations, focusing particularly on nuances in the text and the juxtaposition of ideas. While the Seventh Rebbe's discourses often display an innovative streak, they are relatively conventional when compared with his *sichot* (sermons), which he developed into a highly original genre.[59] With regard to the discourses, the Rebbe is best viewed, as Elliot Wolfson has written, as "a repository, a vessel overflowing with the gnosis he received from the six masters who preceded him."[60]

While a *sichah* would be spoken without any special fanfare or protocol, the *ma'amar* had a special mode of delivery. During the course of the evening the Rebbe would signal that he was about to present a *ma'amar*. As the crowd would begin to chant a special song of "preparation," the Rebbe's demeanor would change noticeably, becoming more serious, and the sense of holiness would intensify. The Rebbe would discretely tie a handkerchief on his fingers to ground him during moments of transcendence, to keep his soul contained. As the preparation song would end, everyone in the congregation would stand, and they would continue to stand during the twenty to sixty minutes that the Rebbe would speak. The Rebbe himself would stay seated, and his eyes would remain closed as he spoke.[61] The *ma'amar* would be recited in a different tone of voice than the *sichah*, with a different verbal melody. When the Rebbe concluded, more songs would follow.[62]

A rare personal insight into the Rebbe's own experience of delivering a *ma'amar* came to light in the early 1950s. After each *farbrengen* a group of students with excellent memories—the Rebbe's human "tape recorders" (*chozrim*)—would gather together and review the *ma'amar* and *sichot* word by word. With the departure of the Sabbath or festival, when transcription became permitted, the text would be carefully written down, copied and shared with the community. While the *chozrim* did a stellar job of committing hours of very profound material to memory, including hundreds of citations, there were inevitable patches which remained unclear to them, and they would later send in questions to the Rebbe for clarification.

At the beginning of his leadership, the Rebbe had requested that recordings not be made, even of a weekday *farbrengen*, imposing a particular burden on the human tape-recorders at a time when an actual tape recorder could have been used. In the summer of 1953, Rabbi Yoel Kahn, who headed the group of *chozrim* throughout the Rebbe's leadership, obtained a special dispensation from the Rebbe to make a recording for his exclusive purposes. After the first recording was made, on 25th June (12th *Tammuz*), and duly transcribed, Kahn inquired of Rabbi Chodakov, "Perhaps the Rebbe would like to listen to the tape?"

The Rebbe agreed to the suggestion. Chodakov later reported to Kahn that the Rebbe had been particularly interested to hear the *ma'amar*, more than the *sichot*. "It's good that I listened to this," the Rebbe commented after hearing his own *ma'amar*, "because I had wondered why the *chozrim* had questions. Now I see that I had left room for questions." Then he shared what the experience of delivering a *ma'amar* was like from the other side of the table. "When there is a strong flow of consciousness (*neviat ha-mochin*)," he said, "it is difficult to be contained in words."[63]

As with so many of his activities, the Rebbe did not generally appoint the *chozrim*, and various individuals would simply rise to the task. As Rabbi Simon Jacobson, who was a *chozer* from the late 1970s recalls: "They weren't necessarily picked by the Rebbe. They emerged. After a *farbrengen*, people would gather and discuss it, and some people just excelled at remembering it. Maybe some were appointed, but even Reb Yoel wasn't."[64]

The *farbrengen*, an intimate gathering of master and disciples, which the Seventh Rebbe used as the platform to deliver most of his teachings,[65] has been eloquently depicted by a number of non-Chasidic visitors. In a 1964 memoir, American social critic and author Harvey Swados (1920-1972) describes his attendance at a "ceremonial of oratory, toasts, and singing," noting in particular the contrast between "two aspects of Rabbi Schneerson, the coolly analytical and the gaily earthy."

I had been prepared for a crowd, but not for this crushing mob of bearded males, many of them like myself in winter overcoats which they could not possibly raise their arms to remove; nor for the little seven- and eight-year olds, their heads uniformly covered with leather helmets (the kind that we called 'Lindy hats' when I was that age), squeezed and swaying so that I feared for their safety.

Someone recognized me as an invited guest, and I was passed along through a side entrance, and so found myself wedged on a corner of the platform not six feet from the Rebbe, who was addressing the throng from a chair in which he was seated behind a long table covered with a white cloth, and flanked by two rows of the dignified, black-frocked elders of the Chasidic movement.

Looking out at the congregants, I saw what the Rebbe must have seen: a most remarkable assemblage, and one which for my part I shall never forget.

Seated facing each other at three long tables, also covered with linen cloths on which stood an occasional bottle of Tokay kosher wine, a dish of cookies, a paper sack filled with cakes, were several hundred men, ranging in age from their twenties to their seventies. Some were in business suits, others in the elegant black dressing gown that a pious Chasid wears for festive occasions, tied in the middle with a *gartel*, the sash that symbolizes the separation of man's higher mental and spiritual qualities from the inferior ones. Perhaps nine out of ten were bearded—not for convenience, or perhaps vanity, as I was myself, but in accordance with religious prescriptions—and for some moments I was lost in contemplation of the immense variety of thickets, red, brown, black, gray, some sparse, others extravagantly luxuriant, in which many of their wearers allowed their fingers to stray, thoughtfully and proudly.

But as I freed myself from contemplation of the panorama of beards over the white tables, I became aware of the younger men closely packed against either wall, standing on raised planks like bleachers, of the many hundreds wedged tightly together at the rear of the hall, among whom I too had been squashed, and of those in the balcony, which was concealed from the rest of us by tinted green glass—because, I realized, it was reserved for female congregants, some carrying little ones, their noses pressed to the glass. I became aware, too, of how these hundreds thronged together were attending, with a kind of passionate patience, to the speech of the Rebbe, who was addressing them calmly and steadily in a fluent Yiddish, without rising or raising his voice.

Since I could not follow the complex line of his discourse, with its parables taken from traditional Chasidic tales and homely incidents, interwoven with abstruse philosophical theory, I was free to stare at all those around me—rabbis, merchants, scholars, small businessmen, students, workmen—who were listening with an intensity I had never encountered, whether in a classroom, at the public lectern, or at a religious or political rally.

Several teenage boys, their beards just starting to sprout, their eyes half-closed, trancelike, unseeing, swayed back and forth rapidly from the waist up, almost as if their torsos were propelled by some independent internal motor, in the contained ecstasy of their participation in the Rebbe's peroration.

Behind me, his hands clasped in his lap as he listened, quite motionless, sat a well-known mathematician from a midwestern university. Just below me, a sturdy rough-hewn man hunched over the table in profound thought as if carved of wood, his shaggy brows and greying beard shaded by the peak of a Russian workman's cap of the kind that one sees in old photographs of Russian revolutionaries and litterateurs. Who could he be? I discovered later that he had been released only two weeks before from twenty years of captivity in Soviet prison camps (where he had gained extraordinary renown for selfless generosity), and that he had flown from London relatives directly to this *farbrengen* in order that he might listen to the Rebbe.

Meanwhile the Rebbe, having concluded his first address of the evening, moistened his lips with the wine glass, and accepted, with a smiling inclination of the head, toasts eagerly offered him by those about him. It was then that the singing began.

At first spontaneous, soon encouraged and "conducted" by the Rebbe, who swung his forearms gaily, rhythmically to the beat of the music from his seated position, the simple song rose to a pitch of unrestrained enthusiasm, with the chorus repeated ten, fifteen times, each time wilder and faster. A man would have had to be made of stone not to respond to this great release of joyous energy. I did not know the words, but I found myself singing along with all those who showed their teeth through their beards bobbing from side to side in time to the music, often hopping up and down as well.

Suddenly, at the slightest of signals from the Rebbe, everyone fell silent. Refreshed and restored, they reverted to their posture of rapt

> attentiveness while the Rebbe resumed speaking for another three quarters of an hour. Fascinated by this alternation of intense intellectual virtuosity and physical release through song (the Rebbe continued speaking, I was told later, until about three o'clock in the morning), I stayed until perhaps midnight.[66]

The "crushing mob" rapidly outgrew the small synagogue on the first floor of 770, and from 1954 it became necessary to hold larger *farbrengens*[67] in ballrooms around the Crown Heights area: the Franklin Manor Ballroom (Union Street/Franklin Avenue), the Biltmore Hotel (Church Ave/Bedford Ave), the Gayheart Ballroom (Eastern Parkway/Nostrand Avenue) and the Albany Manor Ballroom (Rutland Road/Albany Avenue). Other gatherings and even prayer services were held in the courtyard between 770 and the adjacent apartment building at 784 Eastern Parkway, a space no more than twenty-five feet square which was completely exposed to the elements, save for the flimsy canvas sheet spread over the top as a makeshift roof. This far from ideal situation was finally remedied in 1960, when proper walls and a roof were built for the courtyard, with heating and air-conditioning systems installed. In time, the walls were paneled and five chandeliers were added—donated personally by Rebbetzin Moussia—completing the first phase of the now-familiar "downstairs" synagogue at 770.[68]

In the early years, *farbrengens* were still small enough to engender close, personal interaction between the Rebbe and participants. He would sometimes even call out individuals by name, encouraging them to make a toast of *le'chaim*—sometimes two or three toasts, to "loosen up" a new visitor. At peak moments, especially on joyous occasions such as the festivals of *Simchat Torah* and *Purim,* the Rebbe would very occasionally single out an individual and urge him to change or improve himself, usually with a touch of humor. For example, to an Italian businessman, Avraham Hertzman, who would attend *farbrengens* regularly while at the same time keeping his store open on *Shabbat,* the Rebbe would occasionally make a comment—in Italian—encouraging him to embrace Sabbath observance. Eventually his resistance melted and, on one memorable occasion, he walked up to the Rebbe's dais and publicly handed over the keys to his store.[69]

Holocaust survivor and humanitarian Elie Wiesel was another individual moved by a personal exchange with the Rebbe amid the heightened spirits of a *Simchat Torah farbrengen* in the early 1960s. The Rebbe immediately recognized Wiesel, who was wearing a damp trench coat—"I looked like James Bond," he later quipped—and the Chasidim all but carried their guest to the Rebbe's side.

"I am not your Chasid," Wiesel opened, alluding to his childhood roots from a different Chasidic dynasty, the Vizhnitz Chasidim.

"The important thing is to be a Chasid," came the reply. "It matters little whose."

The Rebbe handed his guest a cup of vodka, inviting him to a toast. "In Vizhnitz a Chasid does not drink alone," Wiesel said.

"Nor in Lubavitch," the Rebbe replied, emptying his glass. Wiesel followed suit. After the Rebbe joined his guest in a second toast, Wiesel's head began to spin. "I was not sure where or who I was, nor why I had come to this place, why I had been drawn into this strange scene. My brain was on fire," he later recalled.

Wiesel had been invited to visit 770 by a Lubavitcher colleague in the Yiddish Press, Gershon Jacobson (1934-2005). Wiesel initially resisted, until Jacobson suggested that he simply "come as a journalist." By the third toast, however, Wiesel's professional guard had been lowered.

"You deserve a blessing," the Rebbe said, "Name it."

His head spinning, Wiesel did not know what to respond.

"Would you like me to bless you so you can begin again?" the Rebbe offered. (The offer was particularly poignant as it was, in fact, Wiesel's birthday).

"Yes, Rebbe," he said. "Give me your blessing," as he downed the third toast, promptly passing out.

Years later, Wiesel reflected on why he had found the encounter so compelling, "When a Chasid came to the *farbrengen*, it wasn't only about the bond with the Rebbe. *Emunat tzadikim* (faith in the *tzaddik*) is one thing, but *dibbuk chaverim* (bonds between friends) is something else. And the Rebbe achieved that."[70]

Wiesel developed a close relationship with the Rebbe and later described their discussions about the Holocaust as a turning point in his writing.[71] "Wiesel did not become a Lubavitcher," observed scholar Nehemia Polen, "but that is just the point: Schneerson's ability to touch souls was not limited to movement insiders, to those in thrall to his image and mystique. Encounters similar to the ones with Wiesel took place all the time, day after day, for decades. It is their incrementally cumulative effect that endowed the man with the stature he came to have."[72]

As a result of the Rebbe's broader appeal, his *farbrengens* were attended by a diverse crowd. As early as 1953, attendees could be seen from all types of background—non-Chasidim, Chasidim, Litvish, old and young, non-religious and Orthodox. The same was true for the women.[73] At a 1955 gathering, Herbert Weiner was surprised to see a Conservative Rabbi who confessed to having been raised as a Lubavitcher and, even after straying from Orthodoxy, still attended *farbrengens* regularly. When Weiner questioned if this renegade Chasid was perturbed by "the powers which the Chasidim attributed to the Rebbe," he answered: "I know only this: nobody is more concerned with the fate of Jews—every Jew—than the Rebbe, and that is what attracts me to him."[74]

At *farbrengens*, the Rebbe transgressed most of the rules of public speaking but still managed to attract growing crowds. He did not routinely tell jokes and stories, nor expound consistently on current events. "He began speaking in the manner of a teacher picking up the threads of a discussion with his students," author Lis Harris observed. "No audience-grabbing anecdotes, no pink lights, no uplifting chorale."[75] He would sit almost motionlessly, with his hands under the table, avoiding animated gesticulation. He would speak with a slightly melodious intonation, raising his pitch at the end of a sentence, but the rhythm soon became quite repetitive. "As soon as he began speaking," Weiner observed, "it was apparent that the Rebbe's discourse was in the realm of *sod* [esotericism], and it was also obvious that very few of the Chasidim present could follow his words—after fifteen minutes or so had passed, I noticed that eyes were closing all around me, and not in mystical ecstasy."[76]

The Rebbe would rarely raise his voice or change intonation to add emphasis; and he would speak endlessly, with interruptions for song, sometimes for five hours straight or more. As he spouted hundreds of citations from the entire corpus of Rabbinic literature, the Rebbe never looked down at any text. "*Beim Rebben iz nisht geven kayn zachen*" ("In front of the Rebbe there was nothing at all"), Rabbi Joseph Ber Soloveitchik said incredulously after attending a *farbrengen* and seeing the Rebbe speak for hours without notes.[77]

The songs (*nigunim*) chanted at the *farbrengen* often had no words. Wordless *nigunim* are perceived by Chasidim as more spiritual than those with lyrics and are better able to connect with the divine realm—pure music is the language of the heart, the First Chabad Rebbe taught. Ellen Koskoff describes how the Rebbe would "indicate by moving his fists that the men should continue repeating this section or increase its dynamic level. Tonight, the Rebbe is standing to encourage the men, and their intensity causes a slight rise in pitch with each repetition, so that by the end of the performance, the singers are at least a minor third higher than where they began.... Again, the men repeat the song over and over; again, there is a rise in pitch; again, the stamping of feet resounds. Many of the men sway back and forth, the vodka and persistent singing have begun to take effect.... The Rebbe's talk and the singing continue in alternation throughout the night. By midnight, the men have become more and more raucous in their singing and swaying. Some have reached a state of extreme excitement, even ecstasy (*devekut*), brought on by the commingling of the music, vodka, heat of the room, and nearness of the Rebbe."[78]

Koskoff also describes the experience from the women's section. "I sit in the gallery above with the women who have remained through the night. Although present all along, we have experienced a somewhat different *farbrengen*—no less exciting but far more modest in its expression. Many of us have been deeply affected by the Rebbe's talk. Although not all of the women... understand Yiddish, simply being in the Rebbe's presence creates an intensity that will carry them through the next few days of more worldly concerns."

"Some of the women have also participated in the singing portions of tonight's gathering. Singing quietly, or under their breath, the women sing the familiar tunes more or less individually rather than as a chorus; but their intensity, even without the vodka, matches that of the men below them."[79]

III.

With what messages did the Rebbe inspire and motivate his audiences during the early period? In a survey of *sichot* delivered between 1950 and 1964, three overarching themes have been identified: a) positive view of the individual, b) personal and global transformation, and

c) the Torah's sacredness and contemporary relevance.[80]

The Rebbe did not see people as being instinctively good, but he did believe in a latent inner good that lurked just below the surface and could come to light relatively easily through good deeds. A person is always in a state of essential preparedness for full realization of the gifts bestowed to him or her by G-d; only the external factors need to be removed which obscure the latent good.

It is this inner good that really defines the person; morally and religiously deviant behavior are, in fact, alien to the essential identity. Regressions, even if they span many years, are seen as temporary losses. "A person does not sin unless he is caught by an irrational impulse," the Talmud says,[81] implying that only positive behavior is true to a person's real self, and any departure from that norm is the result of delusional thinking.[82] Tangible evidence of spiritual failings proves nothing; the incorruptible Divine essence of the individual renders any negative self-perception erroneous. Consequently, despair is never justified, and very often one small step will redeem a person from their prior state of confusion.

From this positive vantage point, all difficulties are essentially surmountable. With G-d's help, the Torah's inspiration, and powers latent within the soul, life's challenges are a preordained victory, if only we would not exaggerate the potency of obstacles. The command to remember the Egyptian Exodus (*Yetziat Mitzrayim*) daily is, spiritually speaking, a call to defy all constraints (*metzarim*) and limiting beliefs.[83]

This conviction was conveyed powerfully by the Rebbe to his followers on *Rosh Hashanah* 1956, when the entire community trekked a mile down Eastern Parkway in heavy rain to perform the ritual of *tashlich*, symbolically casting sins into water, at the Brooklyn Botanic Garden. When they arrived at the garden, already soaked to the bone, the Chasidim were terribly disappointed to find it closed, the gates locked. What was there to do except to return back home? The Rebbe, who was fifty-three years old at the time, handed his prayerbook to one of the Chasidim, and proceeded to scale the huge fence. As he swung over the top and began to descend the other side, the Rebbe motioned to the crowd, as if to say: What are you all waiting for? Rashag, who had been standing next to the Rebbe, tried to climb up, and with the help of some Chasidim, he managed to get over. Rabbi Chodakov, who had just donned a long black *kapote* for the first time, ripped it as he topped the fence. One by one, everybody cleared the fence; some needed help while others managed on their own. But the experience had been more than sentimental; it embodied the Rebbe's persistent message that all difficulties are essentially surmountable.[84]

A particularly empowering idea, reiterated hundreds of times in the *sichot*, is the notion that "every 'descent' (setback) is for the sake of subsequent 'ascent' (progress)."[85] A setback represents the preparatory groundwork for further progress because it requires a person to draw on previously untapped potential, leading to growth.[86]

A second major theme in the *sichot* is *transformation*—of the self, of others, and of the universe. Complacency, the Rebbe argued, was utterly antithetical to the Torah's spirit, and much of his thought can be viewed as an argument against self-satisfaction and *halachic* mediocrity. With the Rebbe there is a heightened sense of urgency to constantly surpass achievements and replenish aspirations. Chasidic thought, he would often point out, refers to the human as a *mehalech*, a "mover" who is always changing and progressing, in contrast to the angels, who are depicted as *omdim*, stationary, and lacking the potential for real growth.[87]

The key to avoiding complacency is *mesirat nefesh* (selfless devotion) and *bitul* (emptying of the ego), fostered through a rejection of cynicism alongside the passionate embrace of Jewish teachings. This transformational energy must not be kept for oneself—as in the case of Biblical Noah, who was willing to save himself while the world around him was destroyed—and ought to be directed at outreach efforts.[88] The Jewish people are an organic whole, and their fundamental interconnectedness needs to be reflected in an attitude of *Ahavat Yisrael* (inclusiveness), which is the "foundation of the entire Torah."[89] To work with others necessitates a profound empathy, on the one hand, and an uncompromising presentation of religious ideals on the other.[90] It also requires a person to see little acts in the context of a broader vision: even the smallest *mitzvah* brings a positive energy into the universe, contributing to its ultimate transformation.

It is in the third of the major themes of the *sichot*, Torah, that the Rebbe's esoterical leanings are most detectable. Esotericism is, generally speaking, the awareness of something concealed whose knowledge or experience is of decisive or even redemptive import. Jewish esotericism teaches that the Torah text has a hidden interpretation which endows all religious activity with new meaning. It also renders the text dynamic, a medium of ongoing revelation that continues to gush forth through mystically enlightened teachers.[91]

That the Rebbe embraced esotericism is no wonder, considering his background steeped in Chasidut and Kabbalah. What stands out, however, is the vigor with which he encouraged the *dissemination* of Jewish esoteric teachings. There is always a tension between concealment and disclosure when dealing with the esoteric, because a secret, by its very nature, is one whose existence remains unknown. By maintaining the secret, the masses are protected from its potentially destabilizing and antinomian effects. To disseminate a secret is to rupture a hallowed boundary, and is always fraught with conflict.

The history of the Chasidic movement, which aimed at bringing more than just a taste of Jewish esoteric teachings to the mainstream, is the story of the tension between concealment and disclosure. There is an anarchic and antinomian potential in mystical teachings which the Rabbinic establishment deemed was best kept out of the public's hands, especially after the debacle of Shabbatai Zvi and his offshoots. Here is not the place to recount the struggles of Chasidism against its opponents, but the history was a long and bitter one. The founder of the Chabad movement, Rabbi Shneur Zalman, deepened the tension when he differed with his colleagues as to where to draw the line between concealment and disclosure, favoring a greater disclosure of mysticism to the masses. This resulted in a backlash even from other Chasidic groups, dislocating Chabad from the Chasidic mainstream.[92] While Chabad was eventually accepted by the broader Jewish community as an acceptable approach already in the times of the Third Rebbe, that did not mean to say that the mainstream fully embraced its esoteric thrust; they simply tolerated it.[93]

The Seventh Rebbe's plan to turn Judaism outwards was not just to share *mitzvot* with the non-observant. He also desired to turn the Torah *itself* outwards, and share the deepest esoteric teachings with the world. He would often cite the famous "soul ascent" described in a letter of Rabbi Yisrael Ba'al Shem Tov, who was informed on High that the world would be redeemed of its ills only when "your wellsprings will spread outside," *i.e.,* when Jewish esotericism will become mainstream.[94]

The call to disseminate esoteric teachings lay at the core of much, if not most, of the antagonism from other religious Jews toward the Seventh Rebbe's leadership. Some observant Jews perceived it as insulting that something could be lacking in their centuries-old commitment to tradition if they did not avail themselves of esoteric teachings; this was coupled with the age-old fear of the anarchic, subversive potential of the wisdom itself to the uninitiated. The Rebbe's detractors were always eager to point to any traces of *halachic* deviance or other imbalances they perceived in Chabad, which "proved" that the esoteric initiative was misplaced. The Rebbe was one of a long line of mystics who paid the personal and public price for breaking normative conventions about keeping hidden wisdom hidden.[95]

The Rebbe, however, felt that the wisdom of Chasidut and Kabbalah, presented in a well balanced manner and appropriate vernacular, would be highly beneficial, even indispensable, for the broader public. In many *sichot*, he elaborated on the arguments posed against esoteric exposure, and why he deemed them to be unfounded. Special times called for special measures. The lure of the secular, the sciences and societal conventions, not to mention the myriad challenges confronted by a post-Holocaust Judaism, convinced the Rebbe that the vitalizing and unifying power of Chasidut was now crucial. If, in past generations, Jews had managed without it, that was because their challenges cannot be compared to ours. For the contemporary Jew to remain passionate, for many lost souls to find their way back home and for the Jewish spirit to be revived, dry legalism and even exhilarating Talmudic dialectics are important but not enough. Jews need the transcendent, holistic vision and spiritual vitality that only an esoteric teaching such as Chasidut brings. But arguing about the matter was pointless; one simply had to share the wisdom through oratory and in writing, and its value would become self-evident.[96]

Suffused with mystical energy and enlightenment, the early *sichot* proved to be extremely influential, perhaps even more than the later sermons, which shifted towards elaborate textual analysis. While there is a remarkable consistency of message spanning the four decades of the Rebbe's public sermons, it is the early talks, the highlights of which were edited and published in the first four volumes of *Likutei Sichot* (anthologized sermons), which have probably enjoyed the greatest popularity.

At the time they were delivered, many of the messages were probably lost on his audience, but for thousands of Chasidim and *shluchim* today, the ideas we have briefly touched upon constitute the bread and butter of daily guidance. In what might be termed a succinct *motivational theology* articulated in the early *sichot,* the Seventh Lubavitcher Rebbe empowered subsequent generations of students with tools to live an inspired, passionate and selfless Judaism and to share it with the world.

IV.

The court at 770 offered a variety of other experiences besides the *farbrengens.* The Rebbe could be seen at prayer, and at the Torah reading, where he would chant the *haftarah* (portion from the Prophets) each Sabbath. He would perform the rituals of the Jewish time cycle: blowing the *shofar* on *Rosh Hashanah,* dancing with the Torah on *Simchat Torah,* carrying out the precise customs of the Passover Seder,[97] and many other such activities. He would spend hours personally handing out *matzah* (unleavened bread), before Passover, and at the conclusion of a festival, he would pour wine from his cup (*kos shel bracha*) into the cup of every attendee, a ritual which would extend well into the night as the crowd sang along. Another mode of bonding which took place annually from 1955 to 1964, on the festival of *Simchat Torah,* was the teaching of a new *niggun* (Chasidic melody) by the Rebbe. These were not songs which the Rebbe himself composed; they were usually Chabad tunes from earlier generations which had been all but forgotten. But the direct connection between Rebbe and Chasid through the imparting of a devotional melody enriched the relationship with yet another type of numinous experience.

Unlike Rayatz, who would often mention soul visitations from his departed father, the Seventh Rebbe preferred not to speak of the paranormal. Occasionally, after visiting Rayatz's graveside, he would intimate in private that he had "received" a certain directive from his father-in-law, but references such as these were highly irregular.

A rare occasion where the Rebbe did make a public reference to a mystical visitation was in a *farbrengen* at the close of the festival of *Shavuot* in 1955, in the presence of around four hundred people. Scholar Naftali Loewenthal describes the event, based on an eyewitness account.

> The gathering began before sunset. The Rebbe would normally recite Grace after Meals, signifying the end of the gathering, before midnight. On this occasion he made the assembled gathering sing Chasidic melodies for more than two hours. During this time he sank deep into himself, his eyes becoming glazed. At certain moments, however, he would suddenly lift himself from his seat, as if greeting someone. Around 2:45 a.m. the Rebbe delivered a brief speech about the way Rabbi Shneur Zalman would say "Greeting!" (*baruch ha-ba*) to the soul of the *Ba'al Shem Tov* at the Chasidic gathering on *Shavu'ot* (the *yahrzeit* of the *Ba'al Shem Tov*). The Rebbe then in effect greeted each of the Chabad leaders in turn, from the Previous Rebbe back to Rabbi Shneur Zalman, and then the Maggid and the *Ba'al Shem Tov.* He also mentioned Elijah and Achiyah the Shilonite (the heavenly teacher of the *Baal Shem Tov*). He stated openly that all were present and said, "Anyone who can see them should say *baruch ha-ba!"* The Rebbe then began the *Shir ha-Ma'alot* Psalm which introduces Grace. Then, in an extraordinary way, the Rebbe invited everyone present to say *le'chaim* to the Previous Rebbe, Rabbi Yosef Yitzchak, who had passed away five years earlier. Everyone said *le'chaim.*[98]

While the Rebbe made contact with his adherents in many ways, the closest was *yechidut,* the private meetings in his study, an activity to which he devoted a huge amount of time and energy.[99] *Yechidut* took place three times a week, on Sunday, Tuesday and Thursday evenings, with appointments beginning at 8 p.m. and continuing through to the early hours of the morning, in extreme cases for twelve or fourteen hours straight. A meeting could last one minute or several hours, but the average was probably around ten to fifteen minutes. By 1965, the Rebbe was conducting, according to one estimate, some three thousand such meetings per year, a large percentage of which were not with born Lubavitchers.[100]

Jonathan Sacks has observed that visitors at *yechidut* tended to "emerge somewhat unnerved, taken by surprise. They expect, perhaps, the conventional type of a charismatic leader, imposing his presence by the force of his personality. What they find is the reverse: a man who, whatever the complexity of his current concerns, is totally engaged with the person he is speaking to. It is almost like coming face to face with oneself for the first time. Not in the simple sense of, as it were, seeing oneself in a mirror, but rather seeing oneself revealed as a person of unique significance in the scheme of things, discovering one's purpose. So much so, that it is difficult to talk of the Rebbe's personality at all, so identified is he with the individuals he guides."[101]

Elie Wiesel has painted a similar image, garnered from his own experience of *yechidut* in the 1960s: "When the Rebbe was alone with anyone, it was an opening. He opened doors for his visitor, or his student or Chasid—secret doors that we all have. It wasn't a break-in. It was just an invitation. And that was really the greatness of the Rebbe. I think the Rebbe had a great talent for that—one of the greatest and the best that Judaism has ever seen."[102]

The protocol for a Chasid at a *yechidut* would be to enter the Rebbe's room, men wearing a *gartel* (prayer sash), and to silently place a note with questions or requests for blessings on the Rebbe's desk. The Rebbe, seated behind the desk, would not extend his hand in greeting and would read the note as the Chasid remained standing. Responses were offered orally.

Never dictatorial in tone, and usually phrasing his directives as "suggestions," the Rebbe was extremely decisive and rarely hesitated to offer a clear, practical response. The Rebbe's court was not led by consensus, and he had no substantive advisors, so there was no "red tape" to cut through to receive a formal response. But despite his authority and high office, visitors reported that the Rebbe was less formal in private than at *farbrengens*, more personable, and that the mood was usually one of ease, not intimidation.

In his multi-volume memoir of some seventy visits to the Rebbe's court, spanning three decades, British businessman Zalmon Jaffe (1913-2000) captures the more relaxed tone of *yechidut* from his first taste in 1959. "Until this meeting," Jaffe writes, "we had only seen the Rebbe at the services and at the *farbrengen;* it was amazing for us to behold such a transformation in a human being. Instead of the serious expression and faraway look which the Rebbe habitually seemed to wear, we found ourselves conversing with a very cheerful, happy and friendly—albeit holy—person. He had a gorgeous smile, and the dazzling twinkle in his eyes lightened the seriousness of the occasional criticism or rebuke."[103]

While Chasidim were careful to follow the custom of remaining standing in *yechidut*, and not shaking the Rebbe's hand, the Rebbe obviously did not expect these formalities from his non-Chasidic guests. Confusion, however, would sometimes arise when more zealous Chasidim would try to impress in advance upon their non-Chasidic friends the importance of following *yechidut* protocol. For example, Jaffe recalls:

> Rabbi Shemtov gave me the full rundown. I took particular note of his instructions such as, "Don't shake hands with the Rebbe," "Don't sit down," and so forth....
>
> Upon entering the Rebbe's sanctum, we were startled and amazed to see the Rebbe actually stand up and come forward to greet us, with his hand outstretched.
>
> "Oh," said I. "I am sorry, but Rabbi Shemtov said that I must not shake hands with the Rebbe."
>
> "Never mind," answered the Rebbe, smiling, and with a lovely twinkle in his eye. "We won't tell Rabbi Shemtov." He shook hands with me. He then invited us to sit down.
>
> "Oh, dear, no," said I, horrified. "Rabbi Shemtov told me that on no account must I sit down."
>
> The Rebbe laughed it off and said, "After the third time, I will see about you standing during *yechidut*." So I sat down.[104]

Both men and women were welcome in *yechidut* and couples would often enter together. The Rebbe was gifted with an exceptional memory for details and facts, and it was not unusual for him to recall, for example, the names of a couple's children many years after an initial meeting. He would also show a surprising preparedness when meeting scientists, professionals, politicians and artists, often startling a visitor with concrete knowledge of their own field, even of the visitor's own work. The Rebbe would use these common ties as an opening to press upon his more secular visitors the importance of re-evaluating the role of Judaism in their personal lives.

At a *yechidut* with Harvey Swados and his wife, for example, after responding to Swados' questions about Hannah Arendt's book on the Eichmann trials and the works of Martin Buber, the Rebbe began to prod gently into Swados' inner world. "Now that you have interviewed me, I'd like to interview you. Unless you have any objections?" the Rebbe asked. "But I am afraid that I won't be as diplomatic with you as you have been with me."

The Rebbe turned the conversation, seemingly innocuously, to a discussion of Swados's 1957 book *On the Line,* a series of fictional portraits of auto assembly workers. "What relation would you say that your book bears to the early work of Upton Sinclair?" the Rebbe asked.

"I was flabbergasted," Swados recalled. "Here I was, sitting in the study of a scholar of mystic lore late on a wintry night, and discussing not Chabad Chasidism, Aristotelianism or scholasticism but proletarian literature! 'Why,' I said, 'I would hope that it is less narrowly propagandistic than Sinclair's. I was trying to capture a mood of frustration rather than one of revolution.'"

Swados immediately realized that the Rebbe had led him to answer his own earlier question. When discussing the Arendt book, the Rebbe had argued the Holocaust was not a unique visitation upon the Jewish people, but had arisen from a cultural-historical phenomenon of obedience to authority. Swados found the argument hard to swallow, but now the Rebbe had managed to tease out from him the same sentiments in the context of his own writings.

"Suddenly I realized," Swados recalled, "that he had led me to the answer that he was seeking—and what was more, with his next query I realized how many steps ahead he was of my faltering mind."

"You could not conscientiously recommend revolution for your unhappy workers in a free country," mused the Rebbe, "or see it as a practical perspective for their leaders. Then how could one demand it from those who were being crushed and destroyed by the Nazis?"

As the Rebbe continued his "interview," he steered the conversation towards his own concern: a Jew's responsibility to his people. The Rebbe spoke of Swados's responsibility both as a writer and as a Jew, and how those concerns might intersect, to the point where Swados was "hypnotized by the elegance with which he was leading me to meet him on his own grounds."

As Swados recalls in his memoir of the *yechidut,* the Rebbe now began to probe a little more deeply:

> "You have a certain talent, a gift for expressing yourself so that thousands are swayed by what you write. Where does that talent come from?"
>
> I was beginning to sweat. "Partly from hard work. From practice, from study."
>
> "Naturally. But is it unscientific to suggest that you might owe some of it to your forebears? You are not self-created, you did not spring from nothing."
>
> "I recognize," I said desperately, "that in the genes, the chromosomes..."
>
> "If you wish. The point is, isn't it, that something has been transmitted to you by your father, your grandfather, your great-grandfather, down through the ages? And that you owe them a debt, a debt which you have the responsibility to try to repay?"
>
> Now I was sweating heavily. In the silence that enveloped the room I could hear my watch ticking; my wife's hands, I noticed, were clenched as tightly as my own. But the Rebbe sat relaxed, seemingly with all the time in the world for me to fumble for responses. I had the feeling, like a student faking, that if I didn't say something, no matter what, I would be stuck here forever.
>
> "Are you suggesting, Rebbe," I asked, "that I should re-examine my writing, or my personal code and my private life?"
>
> "Doesn't one relate to the other? Doesn't one imply the other?"
>
> "That's a complicated question."
>
> "Yes," he smiled amiably, "it certainly is." He paused. "I warned you that I wouldn't be diplomatic, didn't I?"[105]

From this colorful account, we get a sense of the courtesy and nobility with which the Rebbe treated his interlocutors, and how he employed his broad general and cultural knowledge to establish personal ties which could then be "leveraged" in the service of Judaism and the Jewish people.

Unfortunately, the meetings at *yechidut* were almost never recorded, and we lack any record of the vast majority of these thousands of encounters. But over the years, many individuals did share their recollections of meeting the Rebbe, with varying degrees of clarity, so we can at least get some picture of the broad scope of visitors and the results of their encounters.

For example, Israeli politician Menachem Porush (1916-2010) would meet with the Rebbe every six months from the early 1950s onwards for around one and a half hours to discuss recent developments in Israel. Porush recalled, "We spoke about complicated, practical matters which with most people, the biggest minds in Torah included, took a lot of explaining. He understood them right away. I didn't have to finish my sentences. He knew everyone, religious people, secular people, all of the leaders." Porush mentioned that he had personally known many influential Jewish leaders.[106] "However, the Lubavitcher Rebbe was totally unique... With respect to intuition there is no comparison to him. With the feeling of responsibility for all Jews and every Jew, every individual, no comparison."[107]

Israeli Talmud scholar Haim Zalman Dimitrovsky (1920-2011) consulted the Rebbe at a 1951 *yechidut* about whether to remain in an academic position at the *Jewish Theological Seminary.* While the Seminary was Conservative and Dimitrovsky Orthodox, the presence of Professor Saul Lieberman (1898-1983), an Orthodox Jew, as the school's dean, provided a clear precedent for possible employment. When Dimitrovsky, an Israeli, had initially accepted the position, he was not fully aware of the conflicts inherent between Conservative Judaism and Orthodoxy. Now he was deeply concerned about whether or not to stay. "As long as Professor Lieberman is in the Seminary you can stay there," the Rebbe told him. "If you resign it won't make a good impression. If he decides to leave, then you leave as well."

When Dimitrovsky was asked why he, a Lithuanian Jew and descendant of the Vilna Gaon (1720-1797)—a fierce opponent of the early Chasidic movement—had sought advice from a Chasidic Rebbe, he explained: "If I had gone to Reb Moshe Feinstein, aside from his tremendous learning, he was a very considerate person, and he would not say something without thinking. But still, I knew he was not familiar with the activities of the Seminary.... However I knew the Rebbe's judgment would be more comprehensive, *le-tovat ha-inyan,* for the cause."

Embracing the Rebbe's advice, Dimitrovsky jested to the Rebbe, "Look, a descendant of the Gaon came now to Lubavitch!"

"No, he didn't come to me," the Rebbe replied. "We are going together, hand in hand."[108]

Newspaper editor and poet Herb Brin (1915-2003), who published the *Los Angeles Jewish Heritage* from 1954 until 2001, recalled how he had felt empowered by the Rebbe in a *yechidut* shortly after starting the newspaper. When prompted to share his concerns, Brin asked the Rebbe bluntly: "Do I have the right to act as an editor for a Jewish newspaper when I know so little of *Yiddishkeit* (Judaism), when I can't even *daven* (pray traditionally)?"

Attempting to convey how even Brin's humble prayer offering was meaningful, the Rebbe launched into a Chasidic tale of a boy who was unable to pray formally and simply whistled before G-d from the synagogue balcony.[109]

"Rabbi," Brin interjected, unsatisfied, "I don't whistle in balconies. I've got to know I am doing the right thing."

"Then the Rebbe did a startling thing," Brin recalled. "He got up from his chair at the desk. I was sitting there, so I got up too. Was this the end of the interview? The Rebbe got up and reached into his wallet and said, 'How much is a subscription to your newspaper?'"

"Three dollars and fifty cents," Brin replied.

"I want a subscription," the Rebbe said, handing him the full amount in cash.

In a 1995 interview Brin reflected upon how the Rebbe's gesture had moved him. "I am in tears now, as I'm telling this. He had a subscription for the rest of his life to *Heritage*.... He looked at me right square in the eye and said, 'Do you have a right to withhold that which you know?' I took the money and I remained editor of a Jewish newspaper."[110]

Another unusual element of the Rebbe's personal guidance at *yechidut* was his encouragement of artists from a variety of backgrounds. Hendel Lieberman (1900-1976) was born into a Chabad Chasidic family in Russia, and suffered much internal conflict between his attraction to the world of art and his Chasidic attachments that seemed to preclude such interests. His artistic career blossomed in 1927 after winning a scholarship to the Moscow Academy of Art, and he managed to straddle two worlds. When his wife and two daughters were killed by the Nazis, he slumped into a deep depression and, in 1951, turned to the new Rebbe for advice. In a fascinating letter, the Rebbe offered an insight into how Lieberman might find consolation through both his faith and his art.[111] When Lieberman finally relocated to New York, a short while later, the Rebbe was personally supportive of his artistic work. "Each person on this earth is allotted a task," the Rebbe told him. "You have a talent. Use it. Use it to encourage Jews to return to their Judaism. True, in the old days, painting was not considered an acceptable way to achieve this aim. Today it is. It is your way."[112]

As a result of the broad range of visitors at *yechidut* the Rebbe developed a following of what has been referred to as "non-Orthodox Chasidim,"[113] individuals whom the Rebbe influenced deeply and with whom he maintained a lifelong connection, but were not fully observant in their day-to-day lifestyle. An interesting example is that of cubist sculptor Jacques Lipchitz (1891-1973), who first visited the Rebbe in 1959, after a near-fatal bout of stomach cancer. While he was hospitalized, Lipchitz's wife Yulla had visited the Rebbe and asked for his blessing. "Your husband will live," the Rebbe told Yulla. "When he gets out of the hospital, ask him to come and see me."[114]

At his first *yechidut,* Lipchitz was fully transparent about his religious life. "I'm not kosher," he confessed, "I do not pray; I do not go to synagogue. I sculpted a Virgin for the Catholic Church." The Rebbe offered no harsh critique, and simply encouraged Lipchitz to put on *tefilin* daily and to say some prayers. A few days later the Rebbe had a pair of *tefilin* delivered to Lipchitz who began, at the age of sixty-seven, to don them regularly, resuming a practice he had discontinued at the age of eighteen. "It is of great help to me," Lipchitz later commented about his rediscovered religiosity. "He really did something for me by advising me to do that."[115] Lipchitz became both a friend of Lubavitch, paying visits to a number of Chabad institutions, and a devotee of the Rebbe, sometimes spotted at farbrengens. "I wish it was possible for everyone to attend a *farbrengen* of the Rebbe," he wrote.[116]

Besides the direct influence on his guests, the *yechidut* experience also offered the Rebbe an opportunity to absorb firsthand information from a huge cross-spectrum of sources, placing him at the forefront of developments in politics, science, and Jewish communal activities. For example, when Yaakov Hardoff, an electrical engineer, entered *yechidut* in 1957, the Rebbe asked him to describe the latest developments in the field of solid-state transistors. As his guest launched into a full-scale scientific lecture, the Rebbe jotted down notes on a yellow pad for close to two hours. "The man was eager to know as much as possible in detail," Hardoff recalled, "about the developments in solid state versus vacuum tubes in controls, motors, and amplifications."[117] When we consider the huge volume of visitors that the Rebbe received, *yechidut* must have placed him in a virtually unique position with regard to access to contemporary developments, in addition to what he had already absorbed from his correspondence and from newspaper clippings which the secretariat prepared for him.[118]

The Rebbe would also ask his visitors, on occasion, to convey an important personal message on his behalf at some great geographical distance. For example, when Marguerite Kozenn-Chajes (1908-2000), an Austrian soprano and Holocaust survivor, told the Rebbe in a 1959 *yechidut* that she was planning to visit her hometown of Vienna, the Rebbe asked if she would do him a favor. The mission, to which she readily agreed, was to track down a certain Dr. Victor Frankl, who headed the Policlinic of Neurology, and convey a personal message from the Rebbe—in German—to be strong and continue his work, with complete resolve. Chajes was shocked when, arriving at Frankl's home, she saw a crucifix on the wall—Frankl's second wife was a devout Catholic. This was shortly before Frankl's work reached international acclaim with *Man's Search For Meaning* and, apparently, he was undergoing some serious deliberations at the time, with active plans to relocate to Australia. Chajes recalled that when she delivered the Rebbe's personal message, Frankl was visibly moved. "The Rabbi came to my aid during a very difficult time in my life," Frankl reminisced in a 1995 phone conversation with Chabad Rabbi Yaakov Biderman. "I owe him a tremendous debt of gratitude."[119]

While the Rebbe was fiercely independent, and chose not to attend public meetings of the American Rabbinic leadership, such as the *Moetzet Gedolei Hatorah* ("Council of Torah Sages") of *Agudath Israel*,[120] he did receive Rabbinic figures at *yechidut* and made the occasional visit to a figure of importance to comfort the bereaved.[121] The Rebbe's broad vision and exceptional knowledge would, on occasion, overwhelm even seasoned Torah scholars who had been exposed to giants of pre-war Jewry. For example, after British Rabbi Kopul Rosen (1913-1961), a graduate of the Mirrer Yeshiva in Poland, first met the Rebbe in

1959, he shared with a colleague in private correspondence: "I am not a starry-eyed hero worshipper and I do not easily become any man's disciple, but my meeting with the Rebbe brought me into contact with a person who seemed to be on a plane quite different from what I had experienced hitherto. I spent hours on two occasions talking to him. I was not only amazed by his breadth of knowledge of all that was going on in Jewish life throughout the world, even in areas where I should have had a far more detailed knowledge than he, but there was such an outpouring of love and concern in every opinion which he expressed... I am guilty of no exaggeration when I say that in the course of my life I have never met a man who impressed me more profoundly and in whose presence I sensed a greater feeling of wisdom, insight, and utter selflessness."[122]

The Rebbe also exerted influence over some Modern Orthodox Rabbis who sought his advice, such as Shlomo Riskin (b. 1940),[123] David Hollander (1913–2009),[124] and Herbert Bomzer (1927-2013);[125] and he particularly impressed Rabbi Efraim Sturm, who headed the *Young Israel* movement. Sturm went to see the Rebbe in the early 1960s after consulting with a number of leading Rabbinic figures about how to approach the huge rates of assimilation among Jewish youth in American colleges. The answers he had received seemed impractical: to increase the number of Orthodox college professors, to improve the quality of Jewish high school education, or to ban the attendance of Jewish youth from out-of-town colleges. The Rebbe suggested to Sturm that, in contrast to college students in Berlin who were deeply philosophical, Americans were concerned more with religious consistency. Once they stumbled in one area, often in matters of *kashrut* (kosher food), it usually led to a huge disenfranchisement. "How long is a student going to put on his yarmulke and eat cottage cheese every single day?" the Rebbe asked Sturm, "And what is he going to do when a girl says to him, 'Take a taste of my lunch, it's delicious!' How can he deny her?" Highlighting the non-classroom area as the point of greatest vulnerability, the Rebbe suggested that kosher-dining clubs be started on campus.

"Of all the advice that we were given, the only one that we found practical was the Rebbe's suggestion," Sturm recalled.[126] He put the plan into action starting with the first kosher dining club at Cornell University in 1964, followed by a further fifteen clubs on different campuses, including Yale and Princeton. According to a 1987 survey, the clubs became "a haven for traditional students seeking an Orthodox environment."[127]

In addition to general dialogue with intellectuals, by the early sixties the Rebbe began to develop a small following of academics who, in the course of time, became full-fledged Lubavitcher Chasidim—such as microbiologist Prof. Velvel Green (1928-2011),[128] solar physicist Dr. Yaakov Hanoka (1935-2011),[129] and Aristotelian philosopher Prof. Yitzchok (Irving) Block (b. 1930).[130] The Rebbe was also visited from time to time by politicians, whom he would never endorse personally,[131] but would usually encourage to carry out the duties of public office diligently and courageously. Some of the more prominent visitors included New York Mayor Robert F. Wagner, in 1963,[132] and Robert Kennedy, in 1964.[133] The Rebbe was also visited by Israeli politicians, such as Menachem Begin (1913-1992), whose first *yechidut* was in 1960, and Geulah Cohen (b. 1925), who shared her impressions of the meeting in the Israeli national, *Ma'ariv*. "I have been in the company of wise men," Cohen reflected, "men of great learning and intelligence, men who were superior artists. But sitting opposite a true believer is quite a different matter. After having met a wise man you remain the same as before—you have become neither less of a fool nor more of a sage. The education of the man of learning hardly rubs off on you, nor does the artist endow you with any of his talents or inspiration. Not so with a believer. After having met him you are no longer the same. Though you may not have accepted his faith, you have nevertheless been embraced by it. For the true believer believes in you as well."

Cohen, like many others, was surprised by the Rebbe's familiarity with her life and work: "He knows more about me than I might be able to tell him. He knows not only what I have done but what I ought to have done, not only what I am doing now but what I am not doing and should do. His disciples had told me that he reads the papers every day and took a lively interest in Israel, but it was a little unnerving nonetheless."[134]

The Rebbe's most intimate and celebrated political relationship with an Israeli official was with Zalman Shazar (1889–1974), who was a Knesset member from 1949 to 1956, Minister of Education in Ben-Gurion's first government, and President of Israel from 1963-1973.

Shazar, who stemmed from Chabad ancestors, had a working relationship with the Sixth Rebbe, assisting with the founding of the Kfar Chabad settlement in 1948 (see p. 273); but it is with the Seventh Rebbe whom he bonded particularly, visiting 770 thirteen times for *yechidut,* in addition to an exhaustive correspondence. Upon his appointment as president, the *New York Times* noted, "In recent years, Mr. Shazar has resumed observance of some of the Sabbath restrictions he had followed in his father's house, but he has not been strictly observant. He has a warm feeling for Jewish traditions and has puzzled his Socialist friends by becoming a devotee of a Chasidic sect headed by the Lubavitcher Rabbi."[135]

V

Throughout the 1950s and early 1960 the Rebbe devoted numerous sermons to curbing the tides of materialism among his own followers. These exhortations were always delivered lovingly, and with sarcastic wit, but the middle-class aspirations of his community clearly bothered the Rebbe since they detracted from Torah study and worship. In a 1962 sermon, he noted that the Fifth Lubavitcher Rebbe had lived in a two-room apartment for several years after his marriage and was content. "Certainly, then, if you happen to enjoy much more luxury than two rooms," the Rebbe said, "even if you don't yet have every *imaginable* luxury, then you can be 'happy with your lot' physically, and devote yourself to further spiritual growth.... But in this country, who would dare even suggest living in a two-room apartment? Such a thing would demean our status as human beings, G-d forbid!" he jibed. "For peace of mind, you need, of course, several rooms, and even that is insufficient without spreading out onto the roof or into the basement."

While the point was clearly a painful one for the Rebbe, it was driven home with a touch of humor.

> For this we dedicate ourselves completely, with the very essence of our souls... all in order to add more luxuries that will snatch a person away for another brief moment from studying Torah and observing *mitzvot,* G-d forbid.

> We delude ourselves that this is a real accomplishment. We imagine that it's truly impressive for a human being to show that you can earn a few more dollars. And you take those few dollars, for which you toiled with your very soul, and you buy some inanimate matter to cover your floor and walk all over it with your feet. That's where your soul ended up!
>
> And what's the whole point? That your neighbor should be jealous of your beautiful floor.[136]

Even the Lubavitcher community did not manage to shield itself from the lures of materialism. In another sermon from this period the Rebbe bemoaned the fads of the day, an obsession with wall-to-wall carpet and "Hollywood kitchens."

> In America—a land of crazy ideas—not only does the *furniture* have to be extravagant, but even the *floor* needs to be covered in carpet so that you shouldn't see any bare wood, G-d forbid. Not only that, but the carpet has to extend from wall to wall. And G-d forbid it should be made from two pieces! No, it must be one single piece of carpet, which, of course, costs a lot more.
>
> At the end of the day we're talking about the floor that you are trampling with your feet. It's not for the benefit of your mind, or your heart, but just for your feet—and, in truth, even the feet don't really benefit. Actually, no one benefits, neither the husband nor the wife. It's just a matter of pride: the wife can now show off to her neighbors and friends that in her house the carpet is made from one single piece!
>
> For the sake of this pride, they spend large amounts of money that they could have given to charity, and the husband is forced to devote many more hours to his work, when he could have been studying Torah.
>
> Unfortunately, this epidemic has also crept into Lubavitcher homes.[137]

What was particularly baffling to the Rebbe was that these were the same immigrants who had demonstrated great personal sacrifices for Judaism back in Europe, even under the harshest of conditions. Yet, after a few years in America, their devotion to Judaism had quickly been supplanted by the materialistic impulse.

> Funnily enough, some of the culprits actually lived in Russia, where it was a *basic instinct* for them to have self-sacrifice for Judaism. They were not perturbed in any way by being in a minority of observant Jews. And yet, after coming here... *now it's a basic instinct for them that they must have a Hollywood kitchen.* This is, of course, in addition to a television, so that they can see things which are not to be found in the *Code of Jewish Law,* or other Jewish books.
>
> Not only that, but if their house has a basement, then obviously there must be another television in the basement too, so that wherever the children choose to play they will be able to be corrupted by television.[138]

Despite barely leaving the two blocks that separated his home from 770, the Rebbe's most radical message in these early years, which ultimately proved to be his most celebrated achievement, was that of Jewish outreach. Judaism can no longer afford to remain insular and must turn outwards, he argued. It is time to "go to the youth instead of waiting for them to arrive," he told *Forward* journalist Asher Penn. "In the *shtetl* [village], when Judaism was passed on from generation to generation, the Rabbis could relax and sit at home with the knowledge that Jews of all ages would approach them whenever necessary. But America is very different. Here we must find the youth, awaken them and strengthen them. We need to speak in their language."

Inspiring youth to influence youth was the method through which the Seventh Rebbe built his own movement. Virtually all the centers and schools that he established were built by young men and women in their twenties and thirties who had been inspired by Chabad during their youth. Even among his own followers, the Rebbe had limited success in motivating those who were already steeped into adulthood in the early years of his leadership. "It seems," he bemoaned privately as late as 1965, "that my leadership has influenced mainly the Yeshivah students."[139] On another occasion he lamented that he had merely "inherited" many of the older Chasidim but they did not really care to listen to his guidance.[140]

One of the Rebbe's first priorities upon assuming leadership of the movement was to galvanize the Chabad youth, forming *Tzeirei Agudat Chabad* (Lubavitch Youth Organization), first in Israel in 1952, and in America, in 1955.

In the summer of 1951, after just four months as Rebbe, he proposed the idea formally to activists in Israel: "In my opinion, the time has come to establish a special organization for the Chabad youth and those close to the spirit of Chabad... a task which requires its own special approach."[141]

These were the days before Chabad had many *shluchim* (emissaries) who would be dedicated to outreach full-time, and the Rebbe perceived young Chasidim as a potential army that could be galvanized in the service of Judaism. *Tzeirei Agudat Chabad* (*Tzach*) was aimed at young Chabad people who had left the educational system and, by and large, were already in the workplace. The goal was to make them feel part of an organizational framework through which they would be inspired to dedicate much of their available time to outreach efforts. In this way, the urgency of spreading Judaism would become deeply ingrained and would shape their identity as young Chabad Chasidim.

The Rebbe's approach to leadership, which we will see in numerous instances, was a careful balance between empowering others with a sense of autonomy, while retaining accountability. He would usually put forward an idea, by means of a letter or a sermon, and leave "space" for volunteers to come forward and formulate their own approach to running the organization. In the initial proposal for *Tzach* in Israel, the Rebbe made clear that he wanted Chasidim to formulate the approach and not to simply follow orders from headquarters: "I will not enter here into details, since much depends on local conditions. I trust you will suggest a detailed plan of activities which are appropriate for the demands of the locality and time. I await your proposal and thank you in advance."[142]

To retain accountability, the Rebbe would request regular, detailed reports of all activities, offering him the opportunity to guide and critique. The need to report also offered a source of motivation, since Chasidim would maximize activities in an attempt to please the Rebbe; but he was an extremely hard man to satisfy, and most efforts met with at least some expression of disappointment that more could have been done. Even in his first response to the newly formed committee of *Tzach,* the Rebbe expressed his "joy on the one hand and sadness on the other"—joy that actual work was commencing, but disappointment that "several names were missing from the list of participants."[143]

Sensitive to the tensions that would arise when senior Chasidim would see the youth taking the lead, he advised the new committee: "It would be highly appropriate for you to consult with the directors of *Agudat Chasidei Chabad*. Even though a great deal of this work, which requires extensive travel and high levels of enthusiasm, rests on the shoulders of the youth—nevertheless, on the other hand, our Sages have taught, 'Even the destruction of the elders is constructive,'[144] so certainly their constructive efforts would be helpful." On the same day, the Rebbe also wrote to the "elders" who directed *Agudat Chasidei Chabad* and advised them to encourage the youth, offer them some direction, but also to leave them space to do their work.[145]

On a spring Sabbath in 1955, the Rebbe suggested to his followers in America that they too open a branch of *Tzach*. "My intention is not merely to add another organization with its own stationery and honorary officers," he quipped, "but that there should be activities.... In Israel there is already such an organization, and, like everything in the world, it has its strengths and weaknesses. You need to learn from its strengths and emulate them, and learn from its weaknesses, how to avoid them."[146]

In a fascinating sermon the following year, the Rebbe offered perhaps his clearest articulation of why he felt Judaism needed to turn outwards and take a proactive approach. Drawing on the military analogy of an offensive versus a defensive war, he argued that taking the offensive has two advantages: 1) the attacker always has the upper hand; and 2) losses are minimized by planning in advance.

> Unfortunately, the norm has been up until now that observant Jews settled in their own localities and busied themselves with their own affairs. When opponents would pose a threat to them, they would call an "emergency meeting," and each individual would offer their suggestions, one contradicting the next. Meanwhile, souls were lost. One generation, then another, then another....
>
> When we take a defensive approach, responding only when a new threat is upon us, it is never possible to eliminate the negative influence completely; there is always some level of concession. Sometimes we do not win at all. What is more, thousands of Jews remain to the "left" because we did not carry out an offensive war, but a de-

> fensive one, and even that was only at the last moment when the "enemy" was upon us.[147]

Drawing on the Chasidic principle that all negative phenomena are a blessing in disguise,[148] the Rebbe suggested that the cultural rebellion of the youth be perceived positively: their tremendous energy ought to be harnessed for the good in the service of outreach. Rather than despair at the gradual decline of Jewish observance over decades, the revolutionary spirit of the youth should be seen as a unique opportunity to reverse the trend.

> A Jew may ask: Since in previous generations there were lofty Jews and yet we still managed to reach the place where we are today, how then can we be expected not only to halt further regression, but to reverse and fix the problem, inspiring others to *teshuvah?*
>
> The answer is found in the tried and tested words of the Talmud: "The youth will embarrass the old."[149] The youth need to influence their elders to be more observant! We need to rid ourselves of the approach we have taken until now, secluding ourselves away on our own turf and protecting it. We need to switch to an offensive war. Then, not only will our own troops stay intact, but ultimately we will win over the opposition too....
>
> This is the task facing our youth in general, and *Tzeirei Agudat Chabad* in particular. Let us not be concerned by how many troops we have, and how many the other side possess—"One youth will be like a thousand."[150] And what is more, in the enemy ranks themselves, inwardly they are already on our side. We simply need to go out in an offensive war, with energy and dedication, and certainly we will succeed.[151]

Through his campaign to mobilize the youth, the Seventh Lubavitcher Rebbe managed to flip a seemingly insurmountable problem—the doubtful future of Chabad—into a solution: phenomenal expansion and growth. "Every Chabad leader made their own contribution, founding an organization that was especially his own," the Rebbe shared privately on one occasion. "Mine is *Tzeirei Agudat Chabad.*"[152]

If young people would be busy spreading Judaism they would not be allured by their surroundings and the Rebbe felt confident that he could dispatch them anywhere. Even today, most religious Jews cannot quite fathom how Lubavitchers are able to operate in places geographically distant from any Orthodox community. But the Rebbe understood offense to be the best form of defense: If you are proactively spreading Judaism, you will not be tempted by other cultural alternatives. "Our Chasidim can be sent into any environment, no matter how strange or hostile, and they maintain themselves within it," the Rebbe said, with a hint of pride, in a 1955 interview.[153]

In 1958, outreach efforts were invigorated by the introduction of a slogan, *Ufaratzta,* a Hebrew term borrowed from the Biblical passage, "Your descendants shall be as the dust of the earth; *you shall spread* out to the West and to the East, to the North and to the South."[154] This message of limitless expansion became the movement's institutional motto, appearing in song, literature, and graphic design, eventually rendering Chabad and outreach as synonymous.

Still, it took some time to turn the Jewish world outward. In a 1965 survey, Charles Liebman pointed to Chabad outreach as an utterly unique phenomenon within Orthodoxy. Isolationism was the accepted view, and Liebman predicted that it would continue that way.[155]

Jonathan Sacks, former Chief Rabbi of England, described the Rebbe's initial efforts at outreach in the 1950s as, "an extraordinary move, nothing less than the reinvention of the early days of the Chasidic movement when, in the 18th Century, followers of the Baal Shem Tov had traveled from village to village taking with them the message of piety and faith.... Nothing was less likely than that a strategy from the old world could succeed in the new. But it did. Drawn by its warmth, intrigued by its depth, hitherto assimilated Jews were attracted to Lubavitch and, on meeting the Rebbe, became his disciples... If today we are familiar with the phenomena of *ba'alei teshuvah* (religious returnees) and Jewish outreach, it is almost entirely due to the pioneering work by Lubavitch."[156]

Even as early as 1951, an editorial in the Rabbinic journal *Ha-Pardes* observed, "The new Lubavitch Rebbe has marvelous organizational talent. In a short time he succeeded in organizing American youths... If today one finds young men openly going about with beard and sidelocks, proud and not intimidated ... if hundreds of emissaries circulate all over America, arousing the public to return to Judaism, to observe the laws of family purity, to found schools and *Yeshivot*—if the standing of the religion has acquired new sanctity, has been strengthened and extended to remote corners of the United States, it is all thanks to the devoted efforts and spiritual dedication of the new Lubavitch Rebbe, who served his Rabbi and father-in-law, the late Lubavitch Rebbe, with all his heart and soul. It is he who has actually realized the command of the late Lubavitch Rebbe and who is to credit for the success of the spiritual revolution that has been taking place in the United States in recent years."[157]

While the success was spectacular, there were the inevitable cases where outside influences did draw young men away from Chabad. Most famous is the story of two young Rabbinical students, Shlomo Carlebach (1925-1994) and Zalman Shachter (b. 1924), who did not stem from Chabad families but were drawn to the movement in the 1940s. Both men had been raised with considerable secular education and were more culturally aware than the Chabad boys from Russian and Polish families. Carlebach was the son of a German Orthodox Rabbi who, like many of his peers, had earned a PhD and taught in a gymnasium in Leipzig. Shachter stemmed from a family of Belzer Chasidim with "liberal tendencies" and, growing up in Vienna, he had attended both a Yeshivah and secular school. After fleeing the Nazis, both ended up in New York, where they were drawn to the Sixth Rebbe's court. In 1949, two months before his passing, Rayatz called in the two men and suggested that they begin outreach work on campuses, beginning on Chanukah in Brandeis University.

"I'll never forget that day," Reb Zalman recalled decades later. "We walked up an icy stairway to the campus cafeteria where a 'Chanukah Dance' was in progress. When Shlomo and I walked in, laden with packages, the music came to a halt and everyone just stared at us, two Lubavitcher Chasidim with yarmulkes, beards, and *tzitzit*. We divided up the cafeteria like two generals: 'you take the right side, I'll take the left!' and we started doing our thing. Shlomo began telling Chasidic stories, and I started speaking about Jewish mysticism." At 3 a.m., Zalman offered a free pair of *tefilin* to anyone who could put them on three times, giving out all the thirteen pairs that he had brought along. "The Brandeis adventure marked the beginning of our outreach careers," he later acknowledged.[158]

During the early 1950s Shlomo formed a close relationship with the Seventh Rebbe, describing him as "a great and awesome genius... deep and well versed until the high heaven. Each and every word of the Torah shines before his eyes."[159] At the time, Shlomo was studying in a Lithuanian style Yeshivah in Lakewood, which was not sympathetic to outreach, but the Rebbe succeeded in drawing Shlomo to work for Chabad. Initially, "nothing in the world would move me out of the Yeshivah," he recalled. "Every time I came from Lakewood, I entered the Lubavitch Headquarters and would talk with the Rebbe about learning. The Rebbe wanted to know what they are studying there, how are the *shiurim* [classes], what *Rambam* do they discuss."

"Once I went in, after he had become Rebbe. He told me: 'Listen, I must make a deal with you, I want you to be my *shliach*.'"

"I told him: 'I learn everyday.' The Rebbe then told me: 'Forget about yourself a little.' He really infused me with a new energy, and suddenly I felt responsible for every Jew."[160]

Shlomo rose to the challenge, and in the absence of any structural framework or comparable peers in outreach work, he conducted activities on an ad-hoc basis. One incident from 1952 captures the flavor of these nascent efforts.

> I used to walk in the street and when I met a Jew I started talking with him. When I started, Lubavitch was not like it is now—that all its energy is focused on outreach. When I used to take the subway, I did not leave until I found at least one Jew.
>
> Once, 2 a.m. on the eve of *Shavuot*, I was in Lubavitch and returned to Manhattan. I sat there and saw a young man full of joy. He looked Jewish. I walked over and asked him, "Why are you so happy?"
>
> He said, "I'm Jewish and thank G-d, I'm getting married on Saturday to a non-Jew in a church."
>
> I told him: "That's very nice that a Jew is marrying a gentile, to bring peace to the world." Obviously if I would tell him that it's not right, I would not be able to speak to him at all. So I told him, "It's so wonderful. You should get a blessing from the Rebbe."
>
> When he asked where is the Rebbe, I told him, "I'm sure you know tomorrow night is *Shavuot*. But tonight it is possible." I had access to the Rebbe in those days.

> We arrived at Lubavitch Headquarters at 3:30 a.m. I knocked on the Rebbe's door and told him: "Holy Rebbe, I brought you a present for *Shavuot*. A Jew that needs repair."
>
> They spoke in the room until 7 a.m. I have no idea about what, but I know one thing: the young man left the room with swollen eyes. He never saw her again.[161]

Shlomo continued to work closely with the Rebbe, describing himself as "*mamash* [literally] the Rebbe's right-hand man," until their now-famous split in 1955. The disagreement centered around whether concessions should be made in Jewish Law for the sake of outreach. "I said to the Rebbe that we are talking about youth that are marrying non-Jews tomorrow, so therefore we must do everything in order not to lose them," Shlomo recalled.

Trimming off some of the stringencies of the law might superficially appear to aid outreach work in the present, but it could also introduce an element of instability, opening a "slippery slope" to endless concessions. As in many instances, the Rebbe stayed committed to his long term vision of Judaism's sustainable growth, something which Shlomo was unwilling to accept, and he parted on his own way.[162]

Two years later, the Rebbe addressed the issue of *halachic* compromise for the sake of outreach in a public sermon, noting a response made by the Fifth Lubavitcher Rebbe, Rashab, at a 1910 conference.

> One eloquent speaker after the other had made the same appeal: It is now a time of emergency. Many Jewish people are being lost to the tides of assimilation. We must do everything within our power to bring our lost brethren back, so it is crucial that Rabbis do not "restrict" communal activists with the confines of Jewish law. If a fire is burning, they argued, we must use any water available to extinguish it. Does it really matter if that water is pure or contaminated?

Rashab cleverly turned the parable around, highlighting the dangers of propagating anything less than pure Judaism.

> If a person brings kerosene or petroleum instead of water to extinguish a fire, then I don't know what title he deserves.[163]

Zalman Schachter's departure from Chabad was less sudden but more radical. While Shlomo essentially remained committed to Orthodox observance, Reb Zalman departed completely from the traditional mold—a journey which began with the study of other religions in Boston University in 1955 and culminated with the establishment of the "Jewish Renewal" movement.

We do not know how the experiences with Carlebach and Shachter impacted the Rebbe directly, but most of the *shluchim* which he subsequently sent out in the late 1950s and early 1960s were far less culturally savvy and secularly attuned. Many were Russian born men who could barely converse in any language other than Yiddish: Berel Shem Tov to Detroit in 1958, Gershon Mendel Garelik to Milan, Nachman Sudak to London and Leibel Raskin to Casablanca in 1959,[164] Avraham Korf to Miami in 1961, and Shmuel Azimov to Paris in 1963. These young men shared a solid commitment to Jewish Law, Chasidic values, and, of course, to the Rebbe, lending the movement the sustainability that it needed. They remained at their posts for decades, overcoming huge hurdles, and eventually built institutional empires for Chabad.

The Rebbe disagreed with the ideal held in most Yeshivah circles of a secluded life devoted exclusively to Torah study. His response to the "*kollel* philosophy" in a 1957 letter is typical: "Regarding what you wrote about an overall arrangement for Yeshivah study, continuing to sit and study [indefinitely] even after marrying... the ruling of our sacred law is well-known: that fulfilling a commandment which cannot be performed by others takes precedence over all else (BT *Moed Katan* 9b).[165] In recent generations working in the field of the Rabbinate and education in sacred matters, etc., has actually become a matter of saving lives."[166]

In a 1964 letter to a resident of New York city, he articulated the argument more forcefully: "The House of Israel is on fire, and the younger generation, as things now stand, are largely trapped. You are surely not unaware of the "dry" statistics of intermarriage and assimilation in this country, and of the fact that the situation is similar in other countries.... The existing emergency demands immediate action—to save Jewish souls, of the old, the middle-aged and the young. This is the primary obligation of each and every one of us who desires to counteract the Hitlerian objective."[167]

Paradoxically, at the same time the Rebbe was turning Judaism outwards, he directed his local educational program inwards. In a passionate 1954 *Simchat Torah* sermon, he bemoaned the fact that even in Chasidic institutions children were taught secular wisdom at a very young age, and he set forth his vision of a school on American soil which would be devoted exclusively to Torah study. Rabbi Michoel Teitelbaum (1912-2005), who had studied at *Tomchei Temimim* in Russia, was captivated by the idea and shortly after the sermon, informed the Rebbe he was ready to begin work. The result, *Educational Institute Oholei Torah,* started with just three students, but it eventually overtook Rashag's "Lubavitcher Yeshivah" as the movement's largest school. The curriculum helped its graduates develop a single-minded devotion to Chabad, inspiring many to join the *shlichut* movement. The lack of outside influences during their formative years helped to sharpen their devotion to Judaism and outreach.

Besides his message for junior and high school education, the Rebbe was also outspoken against young Jewish men and women attending college, at an age where he felt they would be too impressionable. "Studies in college take place at an age when a man's character is not yet crystallized," he said in a 1956 interview, "usually before the age of thirty. Exposure then is dangerous."[168]

Rabbi Aharon Lichtenstein (b. 1933), a leading Modern Orthodox Rabbi and *Rosh Yeshivah* at *Yeshivat Har Etzion,* lived in Crown Heights during the 1950s and recalled an interesting exchange he had with the Rebbe about college attendance. At that time the Rebbe would walk daily from his home to 770, unaccompanied. "I saw him walking alone," Rav Lichtenstein recalled, "I approached him and said hello. He asked me, 'Where do you study?'"

Lichtenstein told the Rebbe that he was studying at *Yeshivat Yitzchak Elchanan* under the auspices of Yeshiva University, where both Torah and secular studies are vigorously encouraged.

"That's good," the Rebbe replied, "but remember, fear of Heaven comes before wisdom."[169] The Torah sees secular wisdom as a potential asset, but only in such cases where it does not compromise religious attachments.

"That certainly was his motto," Rav Lichtenstein reflected in a 1994 eulogy. "The Rebbe had significant intellectual prowess and a great, broad knowledge of Torah, but this motto, 'Fear of Heaven comes before wisdom,' guided him throughout the years."[170]

A significant problem confronting this outreach enterprise, especially in the 1950s, were the sharp lines which divided the three major Jewish denominations, Orthodox, Conservative and Reform. Unlike today, when most Jews find the notion of "labels" unappealing, in the postwar era it was natural and expected to identify strongly with a particular denomination. The majority of Jews could probably not explain the precise nuances of their movement's theology and how it differed from that of other groups, nor were they particularly interested in doing so; it was more a question of where one felt comfortable. Since Chasidim clearly fell into the Orthodox camp, this was an obvious reason for instant dismissal by their Conservative and Reform brethren. Long before non-denominationalism and post-denominationalism came into vogue, Lubavitch articulated an explanation of why the categories of Orthodox, Conservative and Reform were unhelpful. In one letter, the Rebbe sums up an argument which can often be heard today from Chabad activists.

> The classification of Jews into so-called Orthodox, Reform and Conservative denominations is a purely superficial one which has no basis in the essence of a Jew which is bound up with his Divine soul. For, all Jewish souls were present at Sinai, including those to be born on this earth, and to each one of them G–d addressed Himself in the second person singular, "I am the L-rd *thy* G–d" [Exodus 20:2], when He gave the Torah and *mitzvot* to our people. To be sure, there are fully observant Jews and less observant Jews, but all this has to do only with external manifestations and influences, whereas essentially all Jews are fully committed to Torah and *mitzvot.* It is, therefore, necessary only to shed the external "garments" or "layers" to reveal the inner Jewish essence, and this is something which every Jew has the capacity to do, where there is a firm will and determination.[171]

In the eyes of Chasidut, deep identification with the soul leads us to a kind of supra-denominational egalitarianism. By virtue of the Divine energy in the Jewish soul, all Jews are, in essence, fully bound to G-d. The extent to which they are religiously observant is merely the manifestation of that connection. We define the Jew, however, not by the degree of manifestation, but by the equally shared essence. [172]

There is a warm sense of validation here, as we rid ourselves of the unpleasant judgments which often plague religious circles about "good Jews" and "bad Jews." The Rebbe's outreach message was: You are, at your core, already a perfect Jew. If you will begin to manifest that essence just a little more, you will probably begin to feel more true to yourself and more comfortable in your own skin. Or, as the Rebbe put it to Gershon Kranzler, "Many of those who may think they are lost... are really not, and need only some stimulation, some bridge to find the way back." He then recounted how the Sixth Rebbe had suggested to an avowed non-believer to put on *tefilin*. When the man protested, Rayatz told him, "First put on *tefilin*, and you will discover that you needed only such a bridge to find yourself."

In a 1957 interview, the Rebbe proposed, "The great fault of Conservative and Reform Judaism is not that they compromise, but that they sanctify the compromise."[173] A Chabad Rabbi will never send the message that Judaism *permits* driving a vehicle on the Sabbath, but he will demonstrate a patient understanding that many congregants are not yet ready to make such a commitment. The subtle distinction as to whether a compromise is formally legitimized ("sanctified") or informally tolerated makes all the difference. "Sometimes, a person cannot undertake to perform all of Judaism," the Rebbe told journalist Asher Penn, "so in the meantime he takes on fifty percent or even less. But he knows that he's on the correct path and he knows he's dealing with the right merchandise."

On occasion we find that the Rebbe would even encourage an individual to join a Conservative Temple when it might lead to a growth in Torah observance. In a 1972 meeting with Frank Lautenberg (1924-2013), who later became Senator of New Jersey, the Rebbe suggested that he shift affiliation from Reform to Conservative. "If you try to go in this direction, you will have a great influence upon your children," the Rebbe said. "If they see that you have changed in the coming days from Reform to Conservative, it will hasten them towards a new reckoning of the future of their lives."

Of course, the Rebbe added the necessary caveat: "Afterwards, a year from today, you'll make from a Conservative home, Orthodox... I won't be satisfied if you'll be Conservative."[174] But the very notion of a Chasidic Rabbi advising somebody to embrace Conservative affiliation, if only as an interim measure, underscores the Rebbe's nuanced approach to the issue. The compromise is not "sanctified" so long as one makes clear that it is part of a journey towards traditional observance. (The subtlety of this message, however, required it to be articulated only in private.)

The Rebbe deemed compromise as being especially toxic and unnecessary for the youth. "They do not want the easy way out," he told Penn. "They want a sincere and true Judaism, just like everything else in life. Children and teenagers dislike insincerity. The American youth does not want a Judaism that is fifty-fifty. When you give a young man the complete picture of Judaism, he sees and feels that it's one hundred percent the real thing."

VI

Other positions which the Rebbe took in his early leadership which were radical at the time for an Orthodox Rabbi were his approach to women's issues and to the use of technology. He also became increasingly involved with issues facing the broader community, by voicing opinions in relation to the operation of Israeli ocean liners on the Sabbath, school vouchers and public prayer.

One of his first initiatives, suggested at a public gathering in 1952, was to found *Agudat Neshei u'Benot Chabad* (Organization for Chabad Women and Girls). The organization's initial goal was to provide a platform to discuss "Jewish Law as it relates to women, Jewish education, to study sermons of the Rebbes, and Chasidic stories." This organization hoped to maximize publicity and stimulate participation.[175]

While the Rebbe did not claim credit for the idea, and pointed to the fact that Rayatz had previously established Chabad groups for women,[176] the name of the organization itself implied a subtle but important shift of emphasis. Rayatz had referred to *Neshei u-Benot ha-Chasidim* (Wives and Daughters of the Chasidim), suggesting that a woman's affiliation to Chabad was only through her husband or father. The Seventh Rebbe's chosen title for the group reflected an elevation of women to full status as Chabad affiliates, *Organization for Chabad Women and Girls.* In the Seventh Rebbe's eyes, women were not merely wives of Chasidim, they were full-fledged Chasidim themselves.

Over the years, the Rebbe molded the Chabad women's movement to a semi-autonomous group with their own sense of Chasidic identity and mission. While he careful not to tamper with time-honored practices, in the Seventh Generation of Chabad, women would be accorded full equal status in the most sacred of activities: outreach. Already in June 1953, at a meeting with the female leadership of Chabad of Worcester, Massachusetts, the Rebbe encouraged the group to be active in reaching out: "A woman's first responsibility is to the spiritual care of her family," he initially noted. "However, as the founder of Chasidism, Rabbi Israel Baal Shem Tov, would say, all Jews are brothers and sisters. Thus, her efforts of bringing people closer to Judaism should extend beyond the confines of her immediate family to encompass any and all of her fellow Jews."[177]

In 1956, *Agudot Neshei u-Benot Chabad* began to hold annual conventions, to which the Rebbe would sometimes dedicate a special address and always a formal letter.[178] In the same year, he spoke publicly about the necessity for women to study Chabad Chasidut, "just like the men."[179] This was a daring position, since Chabad teachings contain extensive discussions of Kabbalistic doctrines which had long been perceived as an area taboo for women.

Most remarkable, though, was the Rebbe's sustained attention to a feminine-positive exegesis, and discussion of the virtues of women consistently in his letters and sermons.[180] While the Kabbalistic sources from which the first Six Chabad Rebbes drew their discourses are replete with references to the superior qualities of spiritual feminine "powers," these discussions always remained abstract and were not applied to the actual, physical community of women on earth. This changed sharply in the Seventh Rebbe's exegesis, and he made the subtle but highly significant move of referring to these theosophical abstractions as real, this-world energies accessible to Jewish women.[181]

A second significant innovation of the Seventh Generation of Chabad was an eagerness to use modern technology for the goal of Jewish outreach. While it may seem odd today that it had even been a question whether or not to make use of technology, in the 1950s and 60s this was still a sensitive issue for religious Jews. The demise of religion and the secularization that characterized modern culture were generally seen as triumphs of science and rationalism. To make use of science was equated, at least emotionally, to allying with the enemy. As a scientist himself, the Rebbe immediately sensed the fallaciousness of this argument. "Is the knife good or bad?" he asked a young girl who had questioned whether technology is something positive. "It depends what it is used for," the little girl replied. "If it is used to cut food, then it is good. If it is used to hurt someone, then it is bad." The Rebbe praised the girl for answering her own question. "The same could be said for atomic energy or any other technology that man has developed," he said.[182]

Still, like many innovations of Chabad, the use of technology for spreading Chasidic wisdom was not something initially proposed by the Rebbe himself, but an initiative which came from one of his followers. In a 1958 meeting, Rabbi Yosef Weinberg (1934-2012) first proposed the idea of broadcasting classes of the Chabad classic *Tanya* over the radio, but the Rebbe was reluctant. "It's not yet the time for it," he said.

When Weinberg next met with the Rebbe a year later, he pushed the idea again, noting that in Israel, Rabbi Nachum Goldshmidt had launched a similar initiative. The Rebbe remained reluctant, claiming that Israel was different, but Weinberg did not give up. A few weeks later he penned a draft script of a *Tanya* class for the radio, and submitted it to the Rebbe, noting that it was based on the *Tanya* classes he had heard in the Lubavitcher Yeshivah in Otwock. This time the response was positive: the Rebbe personally edited the class, adding his own annotations, and returned it to Weinberg with his blessing and a hundred-dollar donation towards the venture. Following the first broadcast on 27th February 1960, the Rebbe continued to edit the weekly classes for several years, which were broadcast each Saturday night over the WEVD radio network. After twenty-two years, when the entire *Tanya* had been completed, the Rebbe encouraged Weinberg to start the cycle again, and it became one of his lifetime preoccupations, when he was not busy with his "day job" of fundraising for the Lubavitcher Yeshivot.[183] Over the decades of his leadership, the Rebbe would often make public reference to the value of *Tanya* classes on the radio.[184]

The radio classes set an important precedent for Chabad's use of technology, which would later extend to numerous other media: video, television, fax machines, satellite broadcasts and, in our day, internet and smartphones. It represented another case of the Seventh Rebbe's willingness to embrace paradox, utilizing New-World methods to promote Old-World values.

A further area of controversy in which the Rebbe was uniquely placed to add his voice was the operation of Israeli ocean liners on the Sabbath. The shipping line company Zim was established in 1945 by the Jewish Agency, to bring refugees and settlers to Israel. Through ocean liners *SS Israel* and *SS Zion*, Zim offered a highly popular trans-Atlantic service for passengers, sailing from Haifa, Piraeus, Naples, Gibraltar, and Funchal to New York. By the 1960s Zim's boats accounted for 81 percent of the total seaborne passenger traffic on the New York-Israel route.[185]

The long voyage necessitated the boat to be operated on the Sabbath, and since the crew were Jewish, it represented a huge public desecration of *halachah*. Surprisingly, there was no clear consensus from Orthodox Rabbis in Israel or America on the matter, either because it had not been brought to their attention, or because they had been misled into believing that the boat operated automatically on Shabbat.

As early as 1952 we find the Rebbe advising questioners, in the strongest of terms, not to make use of these boats. This letter, written the following year, is typical.

> You write that you plan to make a trip to the Holy Land in June, and that you have reserved a place on the *SS Israel*.
>
> I am answering your letter immediately because of the seriousness of the matter. No doubt you know that the captain and the crew of the said ship are Jews, and that it will be en route at least two *Shabbosim* [Sabbaths]. The voyage is therefore prohibited, involving open and public *Shabbos* desecration...
>
> The question may be asked, "If this is so, how come so many Jews, unfortunately, use these boats to make their trips to the Holy Land?" I cannot go into this very painful question as to why this matter has not been brought to public attention and how these passengers have been misguided or misled into believing that there is nothing wrong in making a voyage, or that it should even be given preferences above other means of transportation. I can tell you, however, most emphatically, being myself an engineer and knowing intimately the mechanical intricacies involved in navigating a modern ship, that there is no question whatever that such a voyage involves a multiple desecration of the *Shabbos*, which is aggravated by the fact that it is open and publicized, and that such a voyage is definitely forbidden

> by the Torah. If you want to go the Holy Land very much, you could go by *El Al*, or by a non-Jewish boat.[186]

Over the next few years, the Rebbe communicated—with varying degrees of success—the impossibility of an ocean liner operating automatically for twenty-four hours to leading Orthodox Rabbis, including: Chief Rabbis of Israel Isaac Herzog and Yitzchak Nissim,[187] Chief Rabbi of Jerusalem Tzvi Pesach Frank,[188] and Rabbi Moshe Feinstein.[189] "There has never been such a case," the Rebbe wrote to Rabbi Moshe Yair Weinstock, "that observant Jews have stumbled in such a widespread fashion, in such an important *mitzvah*, in public."[190]

In 1957 the Rebbe's view reached public attention in Israel in the Israeli newspaper *Ma'ariv*,[191] and in July 1958 the American journal *Ha-Pardes* published a responsum from the Rebbe on the matter.[192] In the February 1959 issue of *Ha-Pardes*, its editor Rabbi Simcha Elberg (1915–1995) informed readers that the Rebbe's responsum had garnered "a great response" and made a significant impression "in all circles." Rabbi Elberg called on all his readers to bring knowledge of this prohibition to wider circles, and he encouraged Rabbinic colleagues to issue formal rulings to this effect.[193]

As the awareness of the ruling gained momentum, an engineer from Zim wrote a detailed explanation to the Rebbe of how the boats "are equipped with fully operational features and the duties of the engine room crew are supervisory rather than functional." The Rebbe immediately responded with a series of questions.

> I still am not clear... Does this mean, for instance, also that the rudder of the ship operates automatically when the ship is in motion? ...And if the steering has to be adjusted, occasionally, at least by hand, is it not true that the rudder is connected with the engine room, and that a change in the position of the rudder influences the engines, increasing or decreasing the operations of the *boilers, etc.*?
>
> Another point I would like you to clear up: Is it not necessary for a ship on the high seas to send out periodic radio messages about its position?...
>
> I understand that certain parts of the oil burners, especially the atomizers and oil strainers, have to be taken out frequently during the course of the day...

> Do the fuel oil pumps never have to be adjusted?...
>
> What about the functioning of the evaporators, the water supply, lighting, heating, ventilation *etc.* Can all these too be operated automatically, without any adjustment, for a period of 24 hours?[194]

In a detailed letter from this period to a Jewish student named Marilyn Bell, who had inquired about the permissibility of traveling on the boats, the Rebbe presented a detailed analysis elaborating on many of these points. In conclusion, he lamented,

> The claim that everything is done automatically during the 24 hours of the Sabbath is absurd, and I state it with the fullest authority, being an engineer myself and having studied marine mechanics...
>
> Unfortunately, there have been Rabbis who have been misled, and have misled others, on this subject. In their ignorance of the technical aspects involved, and under the influence of misleading statements by technicians who, for reasons of their own, did not choose to disclose all the facts, these Rabbis have regretfully been misled into thinking, or even declaring openly, that no Sabbath desecration was here involved...
>
> I would like to enclose a copy of a questionnaire which I sent a year ago to an executive of the shipping company, who had claimed that the ships are navigated automatically during the Sabbath. This communication remains unanswered to this day, for obvious reasons, for I am sure there will not be found anyone who will state that any of the enumerated items can be worked automatically, if he has any regard for truth and does not wish to be caught in making false statements.[195]

The Rebbe continued to campaign vigorously, but within a few years the affair became a non-issue, as the reduced cost of air travel led to a vast reduction in the patronage of Zim. In 1964, the passenger boats became a financial failure and ceased to operate.

Throughout the decades of his leadership, the Rebbe rarely involved himself in the *halachic* issues of the day, and exceptions such as this one were usually areas in which he felt that an area of law had been seriously neglected or misunderstood. Politics, too, was not an area where he was particularly active, but in the early 1960s he did involve himself in two related issues which would become an ongoing concern: school vouchers and public prayer.

The last third of the Nineteenth Century had witnessed a major shift in American Jewish attitudes to issues of religion and state. Previously, there had been a pro-religion stance which allowed for impartial government aid to all religions, including Judaism, but sentiments changed to favor a government free of any religious influence. Half a century later, with the rise of Catholic and Jewish religious schools in the 1940s, voices emerged for a re-evaluation of the strict separatist position. When some gradual inroads were made, with 1947 legislation permitting government funding for transport costs to religious schools, there was a huge backlash from the Jewish community. Jews feared that the "wall of separation," which protected their religious rights and shielded them from Christian influences, had been breached.[196]

Even though it was contrary to their self-interests, even Orthodox Jews who had to bear the huge costs of Jewish day school and Yeshivah education initially opposed tampering in any way with the "wall of separation" to allow for government support. For Modern Orthodox groups the position was less surprising, being a community that was strongly influenced by American values of civil religion. What made less sense was that, throughout the 1950s, even right-wing Orthodox groups, who were less acculturated, still resisted lobbying for government aid for schools and Yeshivot. Their position was largely a result of the European culture from which they stemmed which had a long history of government intervention with matters of religion. The "wall of separation" provided European Jews with a safe refuge from the menacing governments they had known back home, and they were highly fearful of what might occur if the wall was breached. Another emotional obstacle for European Jews to supporting school vouchers was the fact that it represented a political alignment with, and indirect support for, Catholics. After centuries of persecution and forced proselytizing, European Jews had long perceived all Christians as their enemy, and the American climate of religious pluralism was foreign to them. Even if it meant losing millions of dollars in support, these Jews were loath to ally with the Catholic lobby.

One of the first voices from right-wing Orthodoxy favoring government support for religious schools came from the Rebbe, in 1961.[197] It followed the election of John F. Kennedy in January, who promptly fulfilled his campaign pledge the next month, asking Congress to appropriate $5.6 billion for education. The Catholic lobby declared that it would vehemently oppose the legislation unless religious education would be included. Breaking into the political sphere for the first time, the Rebbe devoted a major sermon to the topic, on June 10th, 1961.

Most of the sermon was dedicated to the issue of allying with the Christian lobby, but the Rebbe first made some brief reference to other concerns. Regarding the issue of the Constitution, he simply argued that it was for the Supreme Court to decide and that it should not stop the Jewish community lobbying for their own interests. The fear that a breach in the "wall of separation" may lead to government intervention in matters of religion, he dismissed as "a concern which has no foundation in reality," noting that government aid was already provided in some areas, and this had not resulted in any negative results. "If they have not intervened until now," he asked, "why should they start now?"

He then turned to the objection which had been frequently aired: to support aid for religious schools indirectly assisted Christians to practice their faith, thereby putting "a stumbling block in front of the blind"[198] and promoting "idol-worship."

"Never have I heard such a warped argument," the Rebbe protested. First of all, the issue under consideration was government support for the *secular program* in religious schools, not for the study of the Christian religion. Secondly, while Maimonides did see Christianity as a form of idol worship,[199] other leading authorities did not, including the pre-eminent Ashkenazi authority Rabbi Moses Isserles (1520–1572), who had deemed Christian faith as monotheistic at its core and totally acceptable for a non-Jew.[200] In any case, the Rebbe argued, Christianity was surely preferable to the atheism prevalent in public schools. "It is easier to 'fix' an idol-worshipper than a non-believer," the *Ba'al Shem Tov* had once said.[201]

The Rebbe's position received wider attention after he penned an article on the topic, restating the contents of the sermon, which was published in the *Jewish Forum* the following summer and was later mentioned in the *New York Times*.[202] The Catholic community was delighted at the Rebbe's support for religious aid, and they reprinted his article in their journal, the *Commonweal*. "An Orthodox Rabbi's Plea for Parochial School Aid, by Menachem M. Schneerson," which appeared in the 28th September 1962 issue,[203] probably represented the first (and the last) instance of a Chasidic Rebbe writing in a Catholic journal. "I am of the firm opinion that it is both in the national interest as well as in the Jewish interest that such aid should be given," the article declares at the outset, before echoing the contents of the 1961 sermon. At the end of the essay, one fresh argument is offered: "Federal aid to parochial schools is certainly not conceived in terms of *compulsion.* Any school will have the right to accept such aid, or to refuse it, for whatever reason it chooses to refuse it. Consequently, those schools that fear government interference need not accept the aid, but they certainly have *no right whatever* to deny other schools the benefit of federal aid."[204]

The issue of prayer in public schools was a further example from the same period where the Rebbe was outspoken against the majority Jewish opinion, adopting a position that was also favored by Christians. The conflict erupted in 1962 as a result of the ban on non-denominational prayer from a landmark case in the U.S. Supreme Court, *Engel v. Vitale.*

Since early American colonization, most schools had begun their day with a prayer or Bible reading. In 1951, in an attempt to uphold the tradition while remaining sensitive to the plurality of American religions, the State of New York Board of Regents prepared an optional non-denominational prayer for use in public schools. Commonly referred to as the "Regents Prayer," the text was extremely simple and acceptable to both Christians and Jews: "Almighty G-d, we acknowledge our dependence upon Thee, and we beg Thy blessings upon us, our parents, our teachers and our country. Amen."

When Stephen Engel observed his son reciting the prayer one morning in Searingtown Elementary school, the boy's hands folded and head bowed, he was outraged at the imposition of a religious ceremony which he felt was contrary to the family's Jewish faith. Convincing nine other parents to join him in legal action, the notion that *any* prayer in a public school represented a violation of the First Amendment, was finally accepted by a six to one majority in the Supreme Court.

Jews across the political and religious spectrum were overwhelmingly positive about the decision. An official brief of support was issued by the *Synagogue Council of America* and *National Relations Ad-*

visory Council, which claimed to represent the view of "thousands of Rabbis and organizations" including Orthodox, Conservative and Reform congregations. The document made clear that Jews feared the prayer would render Jews open to Christian influences: "Experience has shown that sooner or later so-called non-denominational religious exercises acquire certain sectarian additions or deviations." This, the brief argued, would eventually result in children's participating in religious activities, "in violation of their religious convictions and upbringing, rather than subject themselves to the pain of not belonging."

What is fascinating about the Rebbe's response to the issue is that, unlike the question of government funds for religious schools, it was clearly devoid of any self-interest. He was deeply concerned that both Jews and non-Jews who were educated in public schools should not grow up in a godless environment, which would have later repercussions for the moral fabric of American culture.

In a 1964 letter, he made his case:

> Children have to be "trained" from their earliest youth to be constantly aware of *"the Eye that seeth and the Ear that heareth."*[205] We cannot leave it to the *law-enforcing* agencies to be the keepers of the ethics and morals of our young generation. The boy or girl who has embarked upon a course of truancy will not be intimidated by the policeman, teacher or parent, whom he or she thinks fair game to "outsmart." Furthermore, the crux of the problem lies in the success or failure of bringing up the children to an awareness of a Supreme Authority, Who is not only to be feared, but also loved. Under existing conditions in this country, a daily prayer in the public schools is for a vast number of boys and girls the *only* opportunity of cultivating such an awareness....
>
> Some argue further that the principle of separation of State and Church must be maintained at all costs, in order to prevent a resurgence of religious persecution so prevalent in the Middle Ages, when an established state-religion denied equal, or any, rights to other religions, etc.
>
> The fallacy of this argument should be quite obvious. By way of illustration: Suppose a person was ill at one time and doctors prescribed certain medication and treatment. Suppose that years later the same person became ill again, but with an entirely different, in

fact quite contrary, malady. Would it be reasonable to recommend the same medication and treatment as formerly?

In medieval times the world suffered from an "excess" of religious zeal and intolerance. In our day the world is suffering from an excessive indifference to religion, or even from a growing materialism and atheism. Even where religion is practiced, it often lacks depth and inspiration. (The subject is too painful to discuss in detail). Thus, if separation of Church and State was necessary, it is not at all the answer to the problems of our contemporary youth. Besides, the preservation of the principle is not at stake here, and the introduction of a non-denominational prayer in the public school will not endanger it in the least. Moreover, a special clause to this effect can be included in the amendment.[206]

What is refreshingly unusual about the Rebbe's approach is his acute concern for the welfare of the general population, and his ability to envision huge, long-term repercussions of small acts of religious observance in even a secular setting. Political scientist Jan Feldman has characterized the Rebbe as a "friendly critic of American democracy.... He continually expressed his appreciation for the religious freedom that American life afforded.... But he did not believe that the secularization of American culture had been a boon to the Jews or any other Americans... He did not believe that a commitment to justice could be sustained in the absence of religion."[207]

In his 1994 eulogy, Rabbi Aharon Lichtenstein was particularly moved that the Rebbe "fought for religion and prayer in public school classrooms out of concern, not for the Jewish children but for the gentiles, to encourage Christians to embrace their Christianity....This illustrates his long-sightedness, his willingness to fight, and more than anything, his concern."

VII.

How did the Rebbe perceive his own identity and mission in those pioneering years?

While he spoke very little about himself, from a number of interviews during the period and other brief exchanges a lot can be gleaned. In a 1952 interview, when asked to clarify the difference between a "Rabbi" and "Rebbe," he answered, "A Rabbi is one who teaches his pupils when they come to him and will answer a question when brought to him. A Rebbe does not wait for you to come to him. He reaches forth among the people and tries to awaken them and inspire them, and tries to find ways and methods to bring them their religion."[208]

When asked if anyone can become a Rebbe, he replied, "Not everyone can become a Rebbe. One needs something from Above to fill this mission. It is easier when a Rebbe has inherited his position, just as it is easier for one who has inherited a talent to perform and develop his talents than one who has to develop them without immediate inherited talent."[209]

On another occasion, in 1959, he restated the conviction that Rebbehood was a meritocracy, despite the near ubiquitous phenomenon of inherited positions in Chasidic dynasties, "The reason for the leadership is not because he was his son, but because he has maximum piety, education, and enthusiasm; he received it from his father and his environment and thus has a bigger chance."[210]

To illustrate the special, soul connection that a Rebbe shares with his followers, in a 1960 meeting he suggested a physical analogy of "the relationship of an electric powerhouse with a lamp that is connected to it by a wire. In order to light his lamp, one must find the right switch, or push the correct button. The soul of every Jew is a part of and is connected with G-d Almighty, but in order that one can enjoy the great benefits of it, the correct switch must be found or the proper button pushed."

This, he argued, was the role of a Rebbe, whose mission is "to explain and proclaim that every Jew without exception is connected with 'the powerhouse,' and every one of them has a switch in his innermost, that will be found if searched for.... One can never know what will make the connection, perhaps one word. But by this, you open up the well or inner fountain of his soul."[211]

A Rebbe will often empower others with his *brachah* (blessing), which in the 1952 meeting he framed as a kind of aid to spiritual awakening.

> A *brachah* is like rain. If the soil is plowed and ready to be sown, and one throws seeds into the soil, the seeds will grow and blossom when rain falls upon them. If however, the soil is unprepared the seed

> finds difficulty in sprouting forth even when there is an abundance of rain.
>
> When an individual comes for a *brachah* and he is emotionally and spiritually equipped, the *brachah* will help him to grow and blossom into a meaningful individual.
>
> If, however, one is in a deep coma, a good doctor would not abandon his task of trying to awaken him. He would do his utmost to help this individual,

One of the ways a Rebbe touches a soul is through avoiding any hint of self-interest and dedicating himself entirely to the recipient. "When a psychiatrist speaks to his patients," the Rebbe suggested in the 1952 meeting, "he regards them as objects of study. Though he is interested in curing his patient and in helping him adjust to life, his approach is to derive not only a healthy being but an accumulation of information about human beings for his further knowledge. A Rebbe gives himself over completely to the person. When one is seeking a solution, the Rebbe does not study him but is more emotionally involved with the person who comes to see him."

A Rebbe's dedication to the people is so overarching that it totally eclipses his personal life and aspirations. In a very personal correspondence, Reform Rabbi Herbert Weiner once asked the Rebbe to disclose what personal feelings lurked behind the veil. "I'm afraid I have the impertinence to think of you as a human being who, while accepting his task as a very important leader in Israel, also has a private world with private 'accounts,'" Weiner wrote to the Rebbe. "I even think of you as one who also asks himself from time to time, 'Where am I?' and receives answers that make him wonder."

The Rebbe's response suggested that, in fact, his devotion to public work left him with almost no private life. "When the question *Ayeka* ['Where am I'] is raised," he replied in a letter, "it is likely to refer to the individual and his immediate family, while the same question put to a person of influence and communal responsibility... the question calls for an assessment as to where he stands and what he has accomplished in the public domain." The Rebbe's self-assessment, his "where am I" was nearly always focused on the tangible results of his work: "I wonder what were the 'practical' results of our meeting and discussion with you and your wife, when I was not only a listener but a speaker.

My *Ayeka* makes me wonder to what extent were my words effective—not in terms of pleasant recollections, but in terms of practical implementation."[212]

In the 1952 meeting, the Rebbe made a similar evaluation. "A Rebbe does not consider himself as superior to his Chasidim. He merely contains those parts of the souls of his Chasidim that are connected with him. When a Chasid comes to the Rebbe with a problem, he tries to find in the Rebbe the part of his own soul which is included in the Rebbe's and connect it with his soul—and thus be connected with the Rebbe's soul."

When asked if he possessed supernatural powers, the Rebbe would occasionally admit to having been granted special gifts, but always desisted from being painted as a miracle worker. "We are, of course, all of us only flesh and blood, and I'm not responsible for all the stories you may hear," the Rebbe told Rabbi Weiner in a 1955 interview. "But you must approach the facts of the case without preconceived theories. Science, after all, means the willingness to observe facts and follow them to whatever conclusions they will lead, not to try to push the facts into a desired pattern."

Weiner pressed the Rebbe further, "Do you believe, then, that the Rebbe has special insight and can see things and know things beyond the comprehension of ordinary people?"

"Yes," came the reply, a rare admission on the Rebbe's part to extraordinary gifts.[213]

On one occasion, when asked if he could perform miracles, the Rebbe used the opportunity to flip the tables back on his audience. "If each of us, beginning tomorrow, should add in his own personal life more Torah and *mitzvot* and influence the environment in the same direction, if we all will do this, myself included, this indeed will be our miracle."[214] To Israeli diplomat Yehudah Avner (b. 1928) he was extremely dismissive of those "who ascribe to the Rebbe powers which the Rebbe does not ascribe to himself," saying, "Evidently, there are people who need crutches." Rabbi Nissan Mindel, who worked closely with the Rebbe for five decades, stated: "I do not know of a single instance where the Rebbe took credit for any 'miracle' or even alluded to it, though he receives many letters from people who inform the Rebbe that his prayer had helped them 'miraculously.'" [215]

Perhaps more than any other Chabad Rebbe, the Seventh leader saw himself very much a mere representative of his predecessors, especially his father-in-law the Rebbe Rayatz. "I am nothing but a funnel," he wrote in 1956, "I try, according to my abilities, to help the institutions and work of my father-in-law, the Rebbe."[216] Sentiments such as these were commonplace in the Rebbe's writings and sermons.

Along with this humility, he also displayed tremendous confidence. He felt capable of discerning the Torah's opinion with an unbiased detachment: "In reply to your inquiry as to whether or not there has been a change in my views... Let me assure you at once that my views... are firmly anchored in the Torah, *Torat Chayim*. Their validity could therefore not have been affected by the passing of time."[217]

The Rebbe's approach in general when advising questioners was to take himself out of the picture. He offered what he felt was the Torah's opinion and left it up to the other person whether or not to follow. "I am not a dictator who issues decrees," he wrote in a 1963 letter, "rather, when I am asked a question, I offer my opinion."[218] In another letter from the same period, the tone is sharper: "As for what you write about transgressing my will. Who am I to speak in such terms? All I did was to *quote clear rulings* of our sacred Torah which was given to every single Jew at Mount Sinai."[219]

Despite his unapologetic and demanding mode of presentation, the Rebbe viewed himself as having an extremely positive energy. "I don't want you to convey the impression that I am merely giving *mussar*—moral exhortations," the Rebbe told Gershon Kranzler in 1951. "It has never been the way of Lubavitch to give *mussar* only. *Mussar* serves us only as a means towards actions. Whatever we say or preach must be geared to some active goal." In a 1952 letter, the message is more pronounced: "Obviously there was no intention to distance you, G-d forbid. I am here to do nothing other than draw people close. Distancing people, even when it is necessary, G-d forbid, can be done by others."[220]

VIII.

During this early period, the Rebbe experienced a number of personal tragedies, notably the premature passing of his brother Leibel in 1952, and the death of his mother in 1964.

While there is very little documented about Leibel's life and the extent to which he was in contact with his older brother, oral reports indicate that he worked as a librarian and later owned a store in Tel Aviv, which eventually failed. In 1944 the couple had a baby daughter, Dalia, who, as of this writing, represents the only surviving strand of the Rebbe's immediate family.[221] In 1950 Leibel managed to relocate to England, subsequently enrolling in a PhD program at Liverpool University in theoretical physics, which he did not complete, before his sudden death on 8th May (13th *Iyar*) 1952, following a heart attack, at the age of forty-six.[222]

Moussia, who was the first to hear the news, was immediately concerned as to how her mother-in-law would react. "I fear for the *shvigger* (mother-in-law), how she will cope with this," she said. Chana Schneerson had suffered over a decade of Stalinist oppression, the untimely death of her younger sister Miriam Gittel, the prolonged suffering and premature death of her husband, and the loss of both her mother and son in the Holocaust.[223] Was she able to withstand yet another huge loss? The Rebbe felt that she could not, and chose to conceal the tragedy from his mother. At a time where Leibel's only means of communication had been an occasional letter, this was not too difficult. For the following twelve years, at the end of correspondence from Genia, Leibel's widow, the Rebbe forged a brief line of good wishes and his brother's signature, to maintain the impression that he was still alive.[224] The few Chasidim that knew what had transpired were sworn to secrecy.

With so little family remaining, it must have been a great joy for the Rebbe to live in close proximity to his mother for the last seventeen years of her life. However busy his schedule, the Rebbe made a point of paying a visit to his mother's apartment every day, to uplift her spirits. "He visits me daily," Chana recorded in a 1951 diary entry. "He makes my life much better.... My apartment where I am now is not very large. It so happens that during the time he sits here with me, the room seems to be much bigger! During his visits, I don't at all feel many things that I find unpleasant, and under the inspiration of his noble devotion... I manage to live with them until his next visit twenty-four hours later."[225]

Like any mother, Chana was perpetually concerned for her son's health. "It pains me," she wrote, "to notice when he doesn't feel well and is very fatigued, although he tries very hard to conceal it from me. First of all, he works very hard. Besides that, he often experiences issues on which his pure sincerity of character is incapable and unwilling to compromise, troubling him greatly and disturbing his calm disposition. Only his commanding intellect enables him to overcome these feelings."[226]

Despite the Rebbe's efforts, Chana was often unhappy, as a 1952 diary entry reveals, "My son, may he be well, does whatever he can, perhaps even more than he can, to improve all aspects of my life and to make me feel good. Nevertheless—and I make every effort to ensure he doesn't sense this—all is not right."[227] On another occasion she wrote, "other than him, I have nothing."[228] In a 1957 entry she is more graphic, "Sometimes my mood gets dark, the clouds becoming dense enough to slice with a knife. But after I see my son, the clouds become much sparser and hopefully less glum."[229]

While her existence was lonely,[230] Chana did participate in communal events, and very much enjoyed attending her son's *farbrengens*. "I was delighted to see such a large number of young people attending," she wrote in 1953, "and how great was their interest in all the activities of my son, *shlita*. I observed how they look upon him with such a love that is indescribable. It was apparent from the way they were hurrying, by subway, by car, in groups, each trying to get ahead of the other in order to get a better place so that they should be able to see and hear as much as possible."[231] In 1957 she wrote, "My greatest pleasure is to listen and watch as my son leads a *farbrengen*. It's a joy for me to hear his voice, and I find the content, as much as I understand it, to be very interesting."[232]

Rebbetzin Chana would also receive brides before their wedding and offer them her blessing, as well as other guests, as Jaffe recalls in his 1963 memoir. "The Rebbetzin held court like a queen. Although she exuded grace, charm, majesty and regality, she was very much down to earth. She sat at the head of a large table surrounded by her admirers and courtiers and insisted upon hearing all the latest news and events, especially relating to births and marriages. She had a lively and energetic mind. She was fond of discussing the 'old days' in Russia... Best of all, she loved to talk about her son, the Rebbe (so did we all)."[233]

A further tragedy struck the Rebbe on 12th April 1956 when Arab *fedayeen* terrorists opened fire on students in a school in Kfar Chabad, as they recited their evening prayers, killing five boys and one teacher, and wounding ten others. The school, which had recently been founded with the Rebbe's encouragement, provided Chasidic education alongside vocational courses in agriculture, carpentry and other fields and was mainly attended by young Jewish men from African countries. The horrific scene of blood spattered over the whitewashed walls and drenching the *siddurim* (prayer books) sent shockwaves through the immigrant community of Kfar Chabad, many of whom contemplated abandoning the settlement in Israel.[234] In a series of communications, the Rebbe's response was resolute: We will find comfort in rebuilding; let the tragedy spur us to redoubled activity. In one letter he wrote, "The terrible event that occurred, ought to arouse in them the hidden powers through which we are so profoundly connected with the holy Rebbes. This will lead to each individual adding, in whichever way possible, to the expansion of Chabad institutions in the Holy Land."[235]

In a moving letter to the mother of Simcha Zilberstram, the schoolteacher who was killed by the terrorists, the Rebbe praised her for attending the ground-breaking of the new wing of the school to be constructed in memory of the victims, *Yad Ha-Chamishah,* adding that when a departed soul inspires increased activity on earth it represents "a victory over death."[236] The Rebbe also dispatched an envoy of ten personal *shluchim* (emissaries) for an extended visit to the Holy Land, offering personal comfort on behalf of the Rebbe.[237]

The attack inevitably shook the faith of many. Senior Chasid Rabbi Avraham Drizen Mayorer was seen in the center of the village crying out, "Master of the Universe, why? How have the children sinned?"[238]

In a number of private letters and a public sermon, the Rebbe addressed the issue, responding to those who had compared the victims to the sons of Aaron who died prematurely, of whom G-d said, *"I will be sanctified through those whom I have chosen, and I will be glorified before all the people"* (Lev. 10:3). In a *Shavuot* sermon, the Rebbe said:

> There are those who wish to explain what happened by invoking the idea of *"I will be sanctified through those whom I have chosen."* But really, this explains nothing.... We have no idea why G-d is *"sanctified through those whom I have chosen,"* and to explain something which is not understood with something else which is also not understood is an empty consolation...
>
> As of now, I have found no explanation for what happened, but what is certain is that we must redouble our efforts. Eventually we

> *will* have some understanding, and will say *"thank You G-d for afflicting me"* (*Isaiah* 12:1).[239]

The Rebbe's response to tragedy was: Don't question G-d, or try to understand Him. Allow the event to stir you to increased positive activity, and you will eventually perceive the tragedy in the context of the tremendous good that it inspired.

Was it this very sentiment that drove the Rebbe to work eighteen hour days and stretch himself to the limits of human dedication? Was it the pain he had absorbed throughout his life—the pogroms, the Russian revolution, the terrors of Stalin and Hitler, separation from his parents, his childlessness, the death of his family members, and the prolonged suffering of his father-in-law? Was it all this that propelled him to find some consolation in the global rebuilding of Jewish life? Since he did not share his feelings with us, we can only speculate.

A source of joy for the Rebbe during this early period was a reunion with his childhood teacher, Zalman Vilenkin, who escaped Russia in 1947 and made it to the shores of the United States in 1953. On seeing Reb Zalman at his first *yechidut*, the Rebbe rose from his chair and walked forwards to greet his teacher, whom he had not seen in over a quarter-century, and invited him to sit down. Reb Zalman, sensing that it was disrespectful, even at his advanced age, to sit in front of the Lubavitcher Rebbe, chose to remain standing. The Rebbe, not wishing to insult his teacher, also continued to stand throughout the half-hour *yechidut*.

After settling in Philadelphia for several years, Vilenkin relocated back to New York in 1960, to spend his final years in proximity to the Rebbe's court. At his second *yechidut*, Reb Zalman was still reluctant to sit down, but, now in his eighties, he apologized to the Rebbe that he could not remain standing. "It doesn't matter," the Rebbe consoled him. "Fifty years ago we both sat together by the Gemara. Let's sit together again now, too."

While it was difficult for him to attended the Rebbe's *farbrengens* on the Sabbath, he did often attend weekday gatherings. If Reb Zalman arrived after the Rebbe had already begun speaking, the Rebbe would rise from his chair on seeing his teacher until Reb Zalman was sitting in his place. After a period he was unable to attend even weekday gatherings and, on 23rd *Iyar* 1963, Zalman Vilenkin passed on. The Rebbe attended his funeral, accompanying the coffin to the cemetery, and contributed to the costs of his tombstone.[240]

On the first day of Rosh Hashanah 1964, the Rebbe's mother, then eighty-four years old, was feeling poorly, but she pushed herself to attend services at 770 and greatly enjoyed hearing her son blow the *shofar.* The next day, however, she was too weak to attend. Very early the next Saturday morning, 12th September (6th *Tishrei*), Chana's caregiver found her on the floor. The Rebbe rushed to her apartment, and spent a few hours with his mother until it was time to begin the prayers at 10 a.m. During the afternoon *farbrengen,* Dr. Seligson was seen giving regular updates to the Rebbe, and after the gathering ended at around 4 p.m., the Rebbe returned to see his mother. By that time, she was having difficulty breathing and appeared to be in pain. Three doctors were summoned, all of whom agreed that she needed to be hospitalized. The Rebbe accompanied his mother in the ambulance, while it was still Shabbat, to the Brooklyn Jewish Hospital at 545 Prospect Place—a celebrated institution where Einstein had once received surgery—and at around 6 p.m., Chana returned her soul to her Maker, as her son stood by. After she passed, the Rebbe gazed out of the window, crying intermittently.

At the funeral the following day, around twenty bus-loads of people flooded in as well as some one thousand private vehicles. As the grave was covered and the Rebbe recited *kaddish,* he choked on the words, before bursting into a prolonged bout of tears.[241]

The Rebbe sat *shiva* (seven days of mourning) in his mother's apartment, and was comforted by visits from Rabbinic figures such as: Rabbi Yoel Teitelbaum, the Satmar Rebbe; Rabbi Joseph Ber Soloveitchik; Rabbi Yitzchak Hutner; Rabbi Yehudah Perlow, the Novominsker Rebbe; Rabbi Moshe Yehuda Leib Rabinowitz, the Munkatcher Rebbe; and Rabbi David Hollander.[242] "The Rebbe continues to be accorded a certain universal deference within Orthodoxy that no other leader enjoys," noted political scientist Charles Liebman in the *American Jewish Yearbook.* "When his mother died in 1964, both the Satmar Rebbe and Rabbi Soloveitchik were among those who came to 'comfort the mourner.' Few Orthodox Jews would expect the Lubavitcher Rebbe to do likewise in similar circumstances."[243]

After the crowds had subsided, it is hard to imagine that the Rebbe was not, at some point, struck by a profound sense of loneliness. While Moussia was still at his side, he had now lost both his parents, his two brothers, and he had no children. At sixty-two, he was nearing retirement age. His achievements were impressive: he had energized and cultivated a tiny remnant of Chasidic life over which he established a virtually unquestioned authority; he had inspired the building of a number of Yeshivot, schools and summer camps; he continued to publish Chasidic texts and deliver voluminous sermons and discourses; and he had touched tens of thousands with letters, *yechidut* and *farbrengens.* But where was it all heading? The movement of *shluchim*, full-time emissaries of Chabad who today dedicate themselves to communal work in every corner of the globe, had barely started. The phenomenon of "Chabad Houses" which now grace thousands of communities, had not yet come to be. Chabad outreach was something that even Chabad had not fully embraced, and other strands of Orthodoxy still opposed.

Not many people can point to their greatest achievements in the last decades of their life, but in the case of the Rebbe we find something quite remarkable—it was during his next quarter-century that he would rise to become one of the most influential Rabbis in modern history.

CHAPTER TWELVE

RIDING THE COUNTERCULTURE

1965–1977

The Rebbe encourages a "*Mitzvah* Tank," 1974

From the early 1960s, hippies were seen, from time to time, walking the streets of Crown Heights and wandering into 770. In search of enlightenment and countercultural alternatives, Chasidism was being considered as a possible path. Many Lubavitchers steered clear of these strange young men, concerned that they would introduce their children to illegal substances and lead them astray, but a handful of Chasidim chose to take the Rebbe's persistent sermons about Jewish inclusiveness to heart. By 1962, Rabbi Avraham Lipskier, the son of Russian Lubavitcher immigrants, was spending part of his day teaching a group of long-haired young men texts of Bible, Jewish Law, Talmud and Chasidut in a corner of 770. Lipskier then approached Yisrael Jacobson, who was part of the faculty, and asked if he could develop these ad-hoc sessions into a formal program. After consulting the Rebbe, who was encouraging of the idea, Jacobson and Lipskier founded the first yeshivah for *ba'alei teshuvah* ("returnees," sing. *ba'al teshuvah*). Named *Hadar Hatorah* ("The Glory of the Torah"), its attendance soon swelled, requiring the use of dedicated premises, half a block away at 824 Eastern Parkway.[1]

While there had been sporadic cases of previously secular Jews embracing an Orthodox or even Chasidic lifestyle, by the late 1960s the phenomenon became sufficiently commonplace that it could be termed a movement. In Chabad, more institutions were established to service the growing population of returnees: *Yeshivat Ohr Temimim* in Kfar Chabad, Israel in 1967; *Yeshivat Tiferet Bachurim* in Morristown New Jersey in 1972; and for women, *Beit Chana* in Minnesota in 1971,[2] *Machon Chana* in New York in 1972, and *Machon Alte* in Tzefat, Israel in 1979. While there has been some ebb and flow over the years, the *ba'al teshuvah* movement has been wildly successful, maintaining its momentum to this day.[3] According to one estimate, by 1994 the number of graduates from Chabad schools in Crown Heights coming from *ba'al teshuvah* families began to exceed those with uninterrupted Orthodox lineage, and by 2000, children of *ba'alei teshuvah* had a seventy percent dominance.[4]

What was it that moved throngs of college-educated, secular young men and women from middle-class homes, to embrace the very lifestyle which their parents and grandparents had abandoned? In one richly drawn letter, the Rebbe shares his thoughts on the social and religious conditions that inspired the *ba'al teshuvah* movement.

> Has the present young generation been prepared to cope with the real aspects of life?
>
> Unfortunately, in America at any rate, most parents, however well-intentioned, have been more concerned about their children's material, rather than spiritual, well-being. The reason for this is not hard to find. Having themselves had to face economic hardships, as immigrants or the children of immigrants, and having found that religious conviction and principles not infrequently proved "restrictive" in a materialistic society, they decided to do their utmost to shelter their children from the economic hardships which they had experienced. They were thus primarily interested in providing their children with careers and professions and other means of economic security, leaving it to their children to find their own way, eventually, in regard to such things as religion and a world outlook. However well-meaning

> the parents may have been, the result is the same: It fostered a way of life where principles have been sacrificed to expediency, and time-honored traditions have been relinquished for material gains, actual or imaginary.
>
> Under these circumstances, it is small wonder that the tremendous upheavals which shook the world in general, and the Jewish world in particular, in our generation, have found young men and women almost totally unprepared. World wars on an unprecedented scale, followed by economic booms and busts, have made a shambles of hopes and aspirations even in the material sphere.
>
> As for the world of the spirit, the bankruptcy of ideas and ideologies have left many young people terribly disillusioned morally and spiritually. A void has been created in their hearts and minds which they did not know how to fill. The widespread disillusionment and frustration among the young generation, and even among the not so young, with the resultant ethical, moral and social ills, are too well known, and too painful, to be elaborated here.
>
> Fortunately, one has been able to clearly discern a new trend among our young Jewish men and women, especially academic youth, who come closer to the world of ideas and thought. Being children of the People of the Book, of essentially spiritual and holy people, they are by nature and heredity inclined, subconsciously at least, towards the spiritual. Their disillusionment and dissatisfaction have prompted them to search for a new way of life which would give them a slice of *terra firma* under their feet, make their life meaningful and put their mind at peace with themselves.
>
> Some of them have been fortunate in making fateful encounters, by design or "accident" (everything is, of course, by Divine Providence), which have put them on the right track. Others, unfortunately, are still groping in the dark. It is the momentous duty and challenge of our day to help these young Jewish men and women to find their way back to the "fountains of living waters" to quench their thirst for life. We of Lubavitch have made it our "business" to do all we can to help them. But this, of course, is the duty and privilege of every Jew, since the commandment *"Love your fellow as yourself"* (Lev. 19:18) applies to every one of us.[5]

Upon embracing observant life, returnees are often thrilled to discover that, far from being "tainted goods" that have been sullied by the indulgences of a secular life, they are seen by the Torah as a kind of spiritual elite. "At the level where *ba'alei teshuvah* stand," says the Talmud, "even the completely righteous cannot stand."[6] Maimonides explains: "The reward of the *ba'al teshuvah* is great—for he has tasted sin, pushed it aside and overcome his evil inclination. His level is greater than that of the righteous, as the latter has never sinned, while the former has succeeded in overcoming his evil inclination."[7]

Chabad Chasidic thought, especially as taught by the Rebbe, further highlights the merits of *ba'alei teshuvah*. Their *teshuvah,* it is taught, brings to light the intense bond between a soul and G-d, which is so powerful that a multitude of sins could not separate the soul from her Creator. This same bond exists, too, with the soul of a person who is observant since birth, but it does not have the opportunity to be revealed.[8]

Curiously, while the Rebbe is often looked upon as the father of the returnee movement, he discouraged use of the term *ba'al teshuvah* as a descriptive appellation for individuals. In a *yechidut* with Rabbi Shneur Zalman Gafni, who led *Yeshivat Ohr Temimim* in Kfar Chabad, the Rebbe said, "Why use a term which implies something negative in the past? Call them your 'students'."[9]

The Rebbe also was unhappy with the term used commonly among outreach professionals, *kiruv ha-rechokim* ("bringing close the distant ones.") "There is no such thing as a Jew who is genuinely distant from Judaism," he argued, following the Chasidic teaching that Jews have an inner predilection to observe the Torah by virtue of their souls.[10] When one individual wrote to the Rebbe in 1977, describing himself as *chiloni* (a term used in Israel for non-religious Jews derived from the Hebrew word *chulin*, meaning secular or profane), the Rebbe similarly objected to its use. The "secular" part of the Jew, he argued, was an "external layer concealing the essence present in every individual of your family, each a descendent of Abraham, Isaac and Jacob (or a daughter of Sarah, Rivkah, Rachel and Leah), as well as *tens* of generations of Jews observant in Torah and *mitzvot.* G-d only gave a person free choice with regards to his *actions*, but he is in *no way* empowered to alter his essence, his true inner identity."[11]

These were not mere semantics. The notion of a mystical core uniting all the Jewish people was a central driving force behind the Rebbe's worldview and all his outreach efforts—as Jonathan Sacks has noted eloquently: "The very existence of the Jewish people for the last 2,000 years depended on a belief that even outside Israel, even without power, even dispersed across the world, the Jewish people remains one nation linked to one another, responsible for one another—a single nation bound by a covenant of mutual responsibility. That is a mystical belief, but it was that belief that kept us as a people since the destruction of the Second Temple to today. It was, of course, that self-same belief that lay behind every single act the Lubavitcher Rebbe took. If one Jew suffers, we all feel pain. Many of us can understand that sentence as a metaphor, but only a true mystic can experience that sentence as a reality—can actually feel the pain. And that is why the Rebbe sent messages and messengers to every corner of the Jewish world. Because if one Jew is suffering, if one Jew is not yet written into the Torah scroll—the book which is our book of life—he felt pain."

Noting that most models of Jewish unity are built on negative ideas, such as fears of anti-Semitism or memories of the Holocaust, Sacks observed: "The Rebbe taught the opposite message. What unites us, he taught, is not that other people don't like us, but that G-d loves us; that every one of us is a fragment of the Divine presence and together we are the physical presence of G-d on earth."[12]

II.

The Rebbe's response to the Six Day War in June 1967 was a watershed moment in his leadership that altered the way he was perceived both internationally and within his own movement. The weeks preceding the war were a particularly bleak period for the Jewish people. Egypt and Syria had taken a number of steps which led Israel to believe that an Arab attack was imminent, as they amassed troops on the borders of the tiny Jewish state, while the U.N. withdrew all forces from Sinai. Fears escalated as the media, both in the Middle East and throughout the Western world, repeated Arab threats that Israel and all its citizens were going to be wiped off the face of the earth. After signing a defense pact with Jordan's King Hussein, President Nasser of Egypt declared, "The armies of Egypt, Jordan, Syria and Lebanon are poised on the borders of Israel... standing behind us are the armies of Iraq, Algeria, Kuwait, Sudan and the whole Arab nation. This act will astound the world. Today they will know that the Arabs are arranged for battle, the critical hour has arrived. We have reached the stage of serious action and not declarations."[13] President Abdur Rahman Aref of Iraq added his own sentiments, "The existence of Israel is an error which must be rectified. This is our opportunity to wipe out the ignominy which has been with us since 1948. Our goal is clear—to wipe Israel off the map."[14]

Fears escalated quickly in the absence of a clear decision from the Israeli government on how to react. Yitzchak Rabin, who was then the Chief of Staff of the Israel Defense Forces, became temporarily incapacitated by a nervous collapse.[15] The military indecisiveness which emanated from Prime Minister Levi Eshkol became patently clear to the public a few days later, on 28th May, in a stuttered radio speech conveying hesitancy and doubt in a time of crisis. While the Israeli army was far more developed than it had been during the wars of 1948 and 1956, panic spread about a possible impending genocide, which was persistently threatened by Arab neighbors. Many of those who were able to leave Israel did so, further exacerbating the concerns of the majority that remained.

The Rebbe, however, was adamant that foreign students who were in Chabad Yeshivot in Israel should not leave. To four students in the Chabad *Yeshivat Torat Emet* in Jerusalem, who asked whether to follow the advice of their local embassies and leave immediately, the Rebbe replied: "Continue to study with diligence. It is an absolute certainty that, '*The Guardian of Israel neither slumbers nor sleeps*' (Psalms 121:4). I await good news."[16] To Rabbi Ya'akov Yehudah Hecht, who expressed concern over his son Shalom Ber, who was studying in Israel, the Rebbe wrote: "There is absolutely no cause for concern... The verse, '*I will grant peace in the Land*' (Lev. 26:6) will be fulfilled."[17] To a Chabad Chasid who had recently arrived in Israel and asked if now was an appropriate time to visit 770, the Rebbe replied: "Now is not the time to travel from the Holy Land. We will see each other, G-d willing, next *Tishrei*."[18] In a number of other communications, the Rebbe warned against unwarranted fear, and encouraged trust in G-d. "I am not at all happy," he wrote to one individual, "with all the panic and the exaggerations. G-d will protect.... especially in a place where, '*the eyes of G-d are upon it always*' (Deut. 11:12)."[19] The sheer confidence of these responses, at a time of national emergency, soon received public attention and they were reported extensively in the Israeli press.[20]

On 25th May 1967, the Rebbe dispatched Rabbis Chodakov and Kazarnovsky to Montreal to convey personal greetings to President Zalman Shazar, who was attending Expo '67 as part of a three week tour of Canada, Iceland and Scotland.[21] After they had departed, the Rebbe's office received a call from Rabbi Leibel Kramer (1917-1999), who led Chabad institutions in Montreal, with the news that Shazar had been forced to cut his visit short after less than a week, and was returning to Israel that evening. All appointments had been canceled. "They won't be able to meet with him," Kramer apologized.

Kramer heard another voice speak up on the line, "He will accept the appointment."

"Who is this?" Kramer asked, somewhat confused.

"Schneerson," came the response.

When Shazar met with Chodakov and Kazarnovsky he shared that the Rebbe had telephoned him with words of encouragement about the impending crisis in Israel. The Rebbe had reminded him how Chasidim always follow the weekly Torah portion as if it were current events, and in that week's portion of *Bechukotai*, Jews are promised by G-d, *"You will live safely in your Land. I will grant peace in the Land, and you will go to sleep with nothing frightening you."* (Lev. 26:5-6). Shazar said that he had been greatly encouraged by the call and that he would publicize the Rebbe's words on his return to Israel.[22]

On 28th May, in the presence of 20,000 children gathered on Eastern Parkway for the annual celebration of *Lag B'Omer*, the Rebbe delivered a highly charged sermon, assuring listeners that "our brothers and sisters in the Holy Land, the Land of Israel, are being protected by G-d who sends them His blessings and salvation to be relieved from the current situation with success." In a move reminiscent of the Biblical Mordechai, who "gathered twenty-two thousand Jewish children, prayed with them and taught them Torah"[23] to avert the decree of Haman, the Rebbe encouraged the children to help their brethren in Israel by "studying one more verse in Torah, one more *mitzvah* before the opportunity passes, in the spirit of love, and to influence friends and family to do the same."[24] Before leaving the podium, the Rebbe asked Rabbi Chodakov if his talk had yet been transcribed, saying that he would like to edit it for publication immediately. (As the Rebbe departed, Rabbi Ya'akov Yehudah Hecht, who arranged the parade, asked the

Rebbe if he was happy with the turnout. "Very," the Rebbe replied, adding, "but next year it should be bigger.")[25]

A transcript of the edited sermon was sent by the secretariat to Rabbi Tuvia Blau in Israel, who was asked "to publicize it to the greatest extent possible, as is, and to translate it into Hebrew."[26] A tape of the sermon was also sent to Israel the same night, and was broadcast on the radio.[27]

How was the Rebbe able to assure his followers in Israel from other countries, with the utmost confidence, that they would be safe, and need not leave? At the festival meal of *Shavuot*, in the presence of several guests, Rashag posed this very question to the Rebbe. "It was based on a Biblical prohibition," the Rebbe replied, "*'You should not be afraid of them!'* (Deut. 20:1)."[28] Other unconfirmed oral reports indicate that the Rebbe may have offered more personal responses in private. Scholar and author Rabbi Avraham Sofer-Schreiber (1897-1982) reputedly said to the Rebbe, "Rabbi Zevin can accept this because he is a Chasid, but I am Ashkenazic. So I am asking the Rebbe: How could you bear such a huge responsibility?" The Rebbe is said to have responded, "I felt in my heart that nothing would happen to the residents of Israel."[29] Rabbi Avraham Gerlitzky (b. 1947), at the time a student, recalled in his diary a story circulating in 770 that the Rebbe had said privately, "I was at the grave site and my father-in-law took responsibility."[30]

While it is impossible to know what was passing through the Rebbe's mind, it seems plausible that each of the three accounts might convey different facets of his decision-making process: profound faith in the Torah compounded by a deep intuition which was further honed at the sacred space of Rayatz's grave.

Whatever the case, after Israel's war of anticipatory self-defense ended spectacularly in just six days, it was difficult for the Rebbe's followers not to perceive him as having near-prophetic status. The Rebbe had, of course, been responding decisively to life and death issues since the beginning of his leadership, but nearly always in private and to particular individuals. With the Six Day War, his promises of absolute safety for an entire country had been made publicly and reported in the media in advance, amid widespread fears that the war might result in genocide and the obliteration of Israel. For Chasidim, belief in the Rebbe's higher intuition seemed to have been demonstrably confirmed. At the very least, he had shown himself to be a fearless and decisive leader at a time of crisis.

One of the most successful initiatives of the Rebbe's four decades of leadership arose from a sermon on 3rd June 1967, two days before the outbreak of war. While all the Torah's commandments, he noted, ought to be observed out of submission to the Divine will, we do find that certain precepts are identified with certain this-worldly benefits. When speaking of war, it is the commandment of *tefilin* (phylacteries)—the black leather boxes containing sacred parchments bound daily by Jewish men upon their heads and close to their hearts[31]—which has the potency to avert undesirable effects. First, the Talmud promises "long life" to those who don *tefilin,*[32] which ought to minimize the casualties of war. Secondly, the Talmud teaches that *tefilin* has the propensity to scare off an enemy.[33] "I am not speaking theory," the Rebbe concluded. "People should be influenced to put on *tefilin.*"[34]

The response was nothing less than spectacular. Israeli soldiers and citizens showed an incredible willingness to don *tefilin,* and the campaign reached some 100,000 men during the war. Even after the exhilarating victory, many Israelis chose to express their reawakened faith and gratitude to G-d by donning *tefilin* at the newly liberated Western Wall (*Kotel*). Upon the Rebbe's suggestion, a booth was erected at the *Kotel,* and as Jews flooded to the Wall *en masse, tefilin* were donned a staggering 400,000 times in the next few months.[35] "Almost no one refused to put on *tefilin,*" recalled Rabbi Ben Zion Grossman, who was one of the first to man the booth.

The *tefilin* campaign received a special boost when General Ariel Sharon was photographed adorned with the small black boxes when visiting the liberated Kotel in July, an event reported widely in the press.[36] In a personal letter to Sharon, the Rebbe expressed his gratitude for "the great inspiration that you brought to the hearts of a great many of our Jewish brethren when you put on *tefilin* at the Western Wall, an act which garnered much publicity and echoed powerfully and positively across a broad cross-spectrum of our people, in places near and far."[37]

Not everyone, however, was delighted with the notion of secular Jews' putting on *tefilin.* The most vociferous opponent was Rabbi Yoel Teitelbaum, the Satmar Rebbe (1887-1979), who offered a harsh critique of the Chabad campaign in his polemic *Al Ha-Geulah ve-al Ha-*

Temurah, penned shortly after the war. Rabbi Teitelbaum argued, that "This whole thing is nothing other than the Satan.... who has the power to make illusory *ba'alei teshuvah*.... We have not heard that people stopped eating non-kosher food, or refrained from publicly violating the Sabbath, or that they have corrected their children's education, which until this point was heretical. The only evidence of their *teshuvah* of which we have heard is that they donned *tefilin*... but it is really the wicked tricking us."

Citing the prohibition of having lustful thoughts while wearing *tefilin*,[38] Rabbi Teitelbaum argued, "Those wicked, utterly impure people whose thoughts and affairs are entirely devoted to forbidden relations, who strive to increase lewdness by enlisting women in the army, and who are as unprincipled as the worst of the nations—are forbidden by the law to don *tefilin*. That is why the Satan has given them the idea of fooling others with the *mitzvah* of *tefilin*, because through its performance a sin is actually carried out, strengthening the forces of *sitra achra* (evil)."[39]

Shortly afterwards, the Rebbe addressed these points, as well as others that he had received, in a sermon on 28th October 1967 (*Shabbat Bereishit*).

> If we had merited, there would have been the recognition that this was not from the "left side" [i.e. Satanic]—because the "left side" doesn't do such things and can't do such things—and we would have seen that this is, in fact, the "Great Shofar" [Isaiah 27:13, arousing Jews to genuine repentance].
>
> Why didn't they immediately become Torah observant? Well we saw at least that they were deeply stirred. As for becoming observant, G-d desires that this should follow later from their own initiative.[40]

Responding to the complaint that secular Jews would have inappropriate thoughts when donning *tefilin*, the Rebbe argued,

> When a person sees something new, especially when it is a new experience for him, his thoughts are entirely focused on that new thing. For those who are not accustomed to the *mitzvah* of *tefilin*, obviously their thoughts will be focused at that moment on the *tefilin*.[41]

The Satmar Rebbe was not the only outspoken critic of the *tefilin* campaign. At the *Agudath Israel* convention in November, one speaker launched a further attack, precipitating more controversy.[42] In response, a "declaration" supporting the Rebbe's campaign was subsequently signed by thirty-six leading Roshei Yeshivah, Rabbis and Chasidic Rebbes.[43]

Since Israel's founding in 1948, the Rebbe had been extremely devoted to the country's welfare. He was concerned with the agricultural,[44] industrial and economic[45] welfare of the country, personally encouraging the establishment of Israel's first automobile assembly plant, Kaiser-Frazer, in 1950.[46] He instructed his followers in Israel to be loyal, taxpaying citizens of the State,[47] to be scrupulously honest with regard to army service,[48] to vote in elections[49] and to fly *El Al* whenever possible.[50] He was particularly concerned with the welfare of Israeli defense forces, persistently encouraging his followers to offer soldiers both physical and spiritual support. He spoke in glowing terms of the bravery and unparalleled merit of Israeli soldiers,[51] and established a fund to assist the wives of soldiers killed at war and to provide bar-mitzvahs for their orphaned children.[52] Countless sermons and letters were dedicated by the Rebbe to the sanctity of the Land, its special relationship with the Jewish people, the special Divine providence it enjoys, the preciousness of its sacred sites and the value of visiting it.[53] He invested huge personal energies to the building and expansion of educational institutions in Israel—his published correspondence with Rabbi Efraim Wolf (1920-2003), who coordinated many Chabad activities in Israel, fills over 3,000 pages.[54]

While he did not usually encourage Diaspora Jews to make *aliyah* when there was still work to do in their own communities,[55] he did consider it sacred to live in Israel and advised many of his followers to settle there, especially refugees from Russia. He vigorously encouraged the building of Kfar Chabad II, personally raising funds for the project, and established new Chabad settlements in Jerusalem, Kiryat Malachi and Tzefat. "I, too, am not complete in the *mitzvot*," the Rebbe told Ariel Sharon in a private audience. "The fact that I do not live in the Land of Israel does not allow me to be complete."[56]

The Rebbe insisted that Chabad have no formal representation in the Israeli government, which could result in some Jews' alienation from the movement—and the study of Chasidut— due to political affiliation.[57] He did, however, maintain high-profile ties with Israeli leaders from across the political spectrum, secular and religious, sharing a warm, personal relationship with all of Israel's prime ministers from Rabin onwards. Regular delegations were sent by the Rebbe throughout the year to greet Israeli officials and bring them his blessing.[58]

Before the establishment of the State, the Fifth and Sixth Chabad Rebbes had opposed any form of fraternity with the Zionists and their enterprise, fearing that Jewish nationalism, if given exaggerated importance, could lead Jews away from traditional observance.[59] In 1947, however, when the State of Israel was becoming a reality, the Sixth Lubavitcher Rebbe was among the very first to encourage many of his followers to settle there.

It was on the eve of the historic vote for the U.N. Partition Plan on 29th November 1947 in Lake Success, New York, that Zalman Shazar received a call in his hotel from Rashag. "The Rebbe wants to know how things are proceeding," Rashag inquired. Shazar was moved that Rayatz, with whom he barely had any contact, was showing concern. and it aroused in Shazar warm memories of the Chasidic attachments of his childhood.[60] "Please tell the Rebbe that we are in need of great mercy," Shazar responded.

While still on the line, Rashag conveyed the message to Rayatz and returned to the phone. "The Rebbe requested that I convey that 'G-d will help.' The Rebbe also asks that, after the vote, would you come to visit him?"

"That is how my connection with Chabad began," Shazar recalled.

The day following the U.N. approval, which was passed 33 votes against 13, Shazar had a long discussion with Rayatz, who proposed a Chabad settlement in the new state, later to be known as Kfar Chabad. Shazar, who was fully aware of Rashab and Rayatz's historic anti-Zionist posture, initially expressed his surprise. "Don't think I regret the past," Rayatz responded. "Then, the answer was 'no.' Now, it is 'yes.'" The Sixth Rebbe immediately sent a telegram to Paris, informing Chabad refugees from Russia that plans had changed and they were no longer going to settle in Canada, but in Israel."[61]

This, of course, did not mean that Chabad embraced the idea of secular Zionism. The Seventh Rebbe, as we have seen, was extremely concerned—often consumed—with the welfare of Israel, but he did take certain measures to distance himself from the secular ideals and nature of the State. For example, he made a point of using the term *Eretz Yisrael* (Land of Israel), rather than *Medinat Yisrael* (State of Israel), arguing that the former conveys the Jewish people's Biblical right to the land, which is not at the mercy of other nations to decide.[62] Similarly, he chose not to refer to the President of Israel with his official title, *Nasi,* claiming that the term had been employed by traditional Judaism with a different intention.[63] But this formal distancing from the State and its secular ideals did not compromise in any way his vigorous involvement in supporting Israel's wellbeing and security, which was real and tangible.

There is no doubt, however, that he was personally saddened by the fact that Israel had not been founded with a more positive embrace of Torah values. "In 1948," the Rebbe lamented in a meeting with Rabbi Chaim Gutnick after the Six Day War, "it was a time of opportunity. But Jewish leaders stood by and debated whether or not to make mention of G-d's name in the 'Declaration of Establishment.'"[64] In a 1957 interview, the Rebbe was particularly sharp, noting that when Israel was founded, "gentile codes of living and a gentile form of government were adopted by Jews... bringing *Galut* [Exile] to Tel-Aviv and Jerusalem... This is not the Zion we have yearned for."[65]

But, as in so many areas, the Rebbe was willing to embrace paradox in his positions on Israel. "I have broad shoulders," he once said in relation to this issue, "because my father-in-law, the Rebbe, has paved my path."[66] While the State was lamentably secular[67] and historic opportunities had been missed for more Torah influence, the Rebbe appreciated Israel for the great blessing that it was and endeavored to support it as best he could. In fact, helping Israel and its people became one of his greatest concerns.

(What he did reject strongly, however, was the belief held by many religious Zionists, that the return of Israel to Jewish rule was something Messianic, the *Atchalta De-Geulah* (Beginning of Redemption), a position which gained significant momentum after the recapture of Jerusalem after the Six Day War.[68] Only by fully realizing the unfortunate gravity of the current reality, the Rebbe felt, the lamentable distance of many Jews from Torah and *mitzvot,* can we gather sufficient focus to reverse it. "If we call darkness, darkness," he surmised on one occasion, "then we will merit to call light, light.")[69]

Perhaps inspired by the strong reaction of the Israeli people to the *tefilin* campaign following the Six Day War, and his growing influence among Israeli politicians and military leaders, the Rebbe began to speak publicly at *farbrengens* on a regular basis about issues facing Israel. One matter, in particular, consumed him: the question of territorial concessions for the sake of peace.

From 1967 until as late as 1991, some of the most emotionally charged sermons delivered by the Rebbe on a consistent basis were devoted to what he referred to as *sheleimut ha-Aretz* (the integrity of the Land), a sustained polemic against any territorial concessions on the part of Israel. Over one hundred and twenty five sermons were devoted to the topic, and the central argument remained consistent throughout. In matters of national security, the Rebbe argued, it is imperative to listen to military experts rather than the opinions of politicians who are inevitably swayed by an array of conflicting diplomatic concerns. "All military experts, Jewish and non-Jewish, agree," the Rebbe wrote to British Chief Rabbi Immanuel Jakobovits (1921-1999), "that in the present situation, giving up any part of them would create serious security dangers. No one says that giving up any part of them would enhance the *defensibility* of the borders. But some military experts are prepared to take a chance in order not to antagonize Washington and/or to improve the 'international image,' etc."[70]

While he campaigned vigorously with the message, both in sermons and in correspondence, this was not an area where the Rebbe succeeded in winning instrumental Rabbinic or political support. There is no doubt that his voice made some impact, but the course of the peace process in Israel has often proceeded in a way which the Rebbe warned would threaten national security and result in the unnecessary loss of life. When asked why he continued to speak about the issue amid the tepid response, he replied, "When you are really in pain, G-d forbid, you scream." A 2002 anthology of the Rebbe's talks on the topic, published as part of a campaign against the Gush Katif disengagement plan, was sorrowfully entitled, *"I called and nobody responded."*[71]

III

On 3rd October, 1967, Ariel Sharon's eleven-year-old son Gur was killed in a tragic accident while playing with an old rifle. Among those who visited Sharon to pay their condolences was a Chabad Chasid, Rabbi Yitzchak Gansburg (1927-2006). Gansburg recalled the Rebbe's disappointment that nobody had visited Sharon the day after he had donned *tefilin* at the Kotel to help him perform the *mitzvah* again,[72] and this now seemed like an opportunity to correct the previous error and re-establish ties.

Upon seeing an obviously religious Jew, Sharon called Gansburg into a side room and asked if he could provide any explanation for the tragedy. Gansburg suggested that Sharon write to the Rebbe, which he subsequently did, receiving a lengthy letter of condolence delivered personally by Gansburg and a delegation of Chasidim.[73] "Sharon read the letter very carefully and we discussed it for an hour and a half," Gansburg reported back to the Rebbe. The following summer, when Sharon had planned an official to visit to the United States, upon Gansburg's suggestion he agreed to meet the Rebbe at 770.

The 19th June *yechidut* began at 12:10 a.m. and lasted until 1:30 a.m.[74] Sharon, expecting a conversation with a Chasidic Rabbi to be devoted to religion, was taken aback when the Rebbe entered into a detailed discussion about the military tactics employed in the Six Day War. "Why did eight soldiers fall during the battle for Qalqilyah?" the Rebbe asked him. When Sharon explained that the troops had to cross a wadi in which an ambush of Jordanian soldiers had been lying in wait, the Rebbe questioned the necessity of crossing the wadi at all, penning a diagram of the area to indicate how Israeli troops might have approached the city from another direction. The discussion also turned to the different weapons and military vehicles used by the Israeli army, and the Rebbe asked Sharon why certain particular models of gun were used in preference to others.[75]

The meeting was particularly fateful for Sharon, as a suggestion given to him by the Rebbe appears to have saved his life. On 23rd July 1968, *El Al* Flight 426 from Rome to Tel Aviv was hijacked by the *Popular Front for the Liberation of Palestine*—the terrorists had expected Sharon to be on the plane. Later, rumors began to circulate that Sharon had changed his travel plans upon the advice of the Rebbe. When Zev Segal (1917–2008), Rabbi of Congregation Young Israel in Newark, was in *Yechidut* shortly afterwards, he took the opportunity to clarify whether the rumors had any substance. "Is it true that you stopped Sharon from going on that plane that was hijacked?" Segal asked the Rebbe.

The Rebbe confirmed that he had. Segal could not help but inquire: "So why didn't you stop the plane altogether?"

"I didn't know that they would hijack the plane," the Rebbe replied. "Sharon came to say goodbye to me. I told him not to go."[76]

Rabbi Jean Kling (1928-2003), then the Chief Rabbi of Lyons, posed the same question to the Rebbe at a *yechidut* and was given a similar answer, with a few more details. Sharon had looked at his watch several times, Kling was told, and it had caught the Rebbe's attention. When Sharon explained that he was in a hurry to get to the airport, the Rebbe said, "Is there only one plane? Why don't you stay with me a little longer and take another flight?"

While he denied having prophetic insight, the Rebbe was humbled at having been chosen as G-d's instrument to save Sharon's life. "I was the emissary of the Holy One, Blessed be He," he told Kling.[77]

At the *yechidut*, Sharon asked the Rebbe to encourage his followers to settle in the newly acquired Hebron, a move which would help to permanently secure the territories in Israeli hands. While the Rebbe was adamant that the territories not be returned, he was also reluctant to direct settlers there in the absence of full support from the Israeli government. In a letter following the *yechidut*, the Rebbe made his point clear. "What if, for example—may it never happen—a fight breaks out between an Israeli lad and an Arab lad," the Rebbe conjectured, "and the Jew, who would presumably be outnumbered, is injured? On whose side, in your opinion, would the Israeli military police stand?"[78]

In 1969 Sharon visited the Rebbe again, with his wife, and spoke of the experience publicly in Kfar Chabad several months later. "The Rebbe is perhaps the greatest believer I have ever met in the G-d-given strength of the Jewish people," he told the assembled crowd of Chasidim. "He believes in the strength of the Jewish nation, and his feeling is that we don't believe enough in our own strength."[79]

Sadly, an insight which the Rebbe shared with Sharon could have saved many lives, but was not taken seriously enough. In the early 1970s Israel constructed an elaborate anti-tank ditch consisting of a 60 ft. sand wall supported by concrete, spanning 100 miles along Suez

Canal. The fortification chain, known as the Bar-Lev line after Israeli Chief of Staff Haim Bar-Lev, cost around $300 million and was expected to delay any oncoming army by 48 hours.

"It was a bitter conflict in the Israeli army," Sharon recalled in an interview near the end of his life. "The Rebbe knew about it and he sent me a letter three or four years before the Yom Kippur War, describing the disaster that will happen to the Jewish people, what terrible damage and tragedy this Bar-Lev line will bring—totally, I would say, dealing with the military problem; analyzing as a military expert what would happen."

When the Yom Kippur War erupted in October 1973, the Egyptian army overran the Bar Lev Line in less than two hours and with some 70,000 Egyptian troops attacking five hundred Israeli soldiers, it quickly became a slaughter. Lamenting the accuracy of the Rebbe's analysis, and the failure of Israel to take it seriously, Sharon recalled, "As a matter of fact, that happened. It was a tragedy, but that happened."[80]

On another occasion after the war, the Rebbe bemoaned in a letter to Jakobovits what he felt had been tragic losses as the result of Israel's unwillingness to carry out an attack of anticipatory self-defense in 1973, as it had done in 1967.

> Days and hours before the attack, there were urgent sessions of the government discussing the situation with the military. Military intelligence pointed to unmistakable evidence that an Egyptian attack was imminent, and the military experts advised a preemptive strike that would save many lives and prevent an invasion. However, the politicians, with the acquiescence of some military experts, rejected this action on the grounds that such a step, or even a general mobilization, before the Egyptians actually crossed the border, would mean being branded as the aggressor and would jeopardize relations with the U.S.A.... Many lives were needlessly sacrificed, and the situation came close to total disaster, but for G-d's mercies. Suffice it to mention that the then Prime Minister later admitted that all her life she would be haunted by that tragic decision.[81]

In a 1973 letter, the Rebbe put it more succinctly, "The essential point of this whole tragic war is that it could have been prevented and, as in the case of medicine, prevention is more desirable than cure."

To some extent, the Rebbe felt that a dose of "preventative medicine" had been delivered before the war, in the form of a directive he had given the previous summer for children's Torah rallies to be conducted. "Now it is quite evident," he wrote two weeks after the war had ended, "how important and urgent was the appeal made last summer, centered on the verse, *'Out of the mouths of babes and infants You have ordained strength (oz)...to still the enemy and avenger'* (Psalms 8:3)."[82]

With a spiritual "offensive," the Rebbe had hoped to bring merit to the Jewish people at a time of need by invoking the special power of children. In a public letter to "Boys and Girls, of pre-bar (bat)-mitzvah age, in all summer camps, everywhere preceding the summer vacation," the Rebbe wrote:

> I want you to consider carefully the special merit which Jewish children have, a privilege which affects our entire Jewish people, to which King David refers in the following words: *"Out of the mouths of babes and infants You have ordained strength—oz...to still the enemy and avenger"*—including also the enemy that... still seeks vengeance to this day. In other words, the way to vanquish and silence the enemy is through the study of the Torah, called "strength" (*oz*), by the mouths of young children. Indeed, so great is their power, that our Sages of blessed memory declare: *"The whole world exists only by virtue of the breath of little Jewish children, whose breath is pure and free of sin,"*[83] referring to children who have not yet reached the age of responsibility for wrongdoing, that is, boys and girls of pre-Bar/Bat Mitzvah age.[84]

In a sermon during the war itself, the Rebbe actually pointed to the summer children's campaign as a sort of premonition on his own part. Citing *Rashi's* commentary on the Torah, that a person can "prophesy without knowing what he is prophesying,"[85] the Rebbe made an unusual reference to his own prescience: "Sometimes one does something, unaware at the time what the reason is, and only afterwards one appreciates that it was timely."

"The entire summer," he noted, "I spoke about the topic of *'Out of the mouths of babes and infants You have ordained strength, to still the enemy and avenger.'* What pushed me to speak about it? Why all of a sudden? Now it has been made clear how much we needed 'to still the enemy and avenger.'"[86]

While the casualties were ultimately far greater in the Yom Kippur

War than they had been in the Six Day War, the Rebbe noted that one could still detect the miraculous hand of G-d.

> You wrote about the difference between the Six Day War and the so-called Yom Kippur War, in that G-d's miracles were more obvious in the Six Day War, etc.
>
> As a matter of fact, there were ample miracles, and quite obvious ones, in the last war. The overall miracle, which has now been revealed, although not overly publicized, is the survival after the first few days of the war, when even Washington was seriously concerned whether the Israeli army could halt the tremendous onslaught of the first attack...
>
> The greatest miracle was that the Egyptians stopped their invasion for no good reason only a few miles east of the Canal. The obvious military strategy would have been to leave a few fortified positions in the rear and with the huge army of 100,000 men armed to the teeth, to march forward in Sinai, where at that point in time there was no organized defense of any military consequence. This is something that cannot be explained in the natural order of things, except as it is written, *"The dread of the Jews fell upon them"* (Esther 8:17), in the face of their intelligence reports about the complete unpreparedness of the Jews in *Eretz Yisrael* at that time.
>
> There are also scores of reported miracles in various sectors of both fronts.[87]

While it had been Sharon who ultimately secured a victory for Israel, by thwarting the commands of his superiors and crossing the Suez, the Rebbe was upset that Sharon had subsequently been ordered to halt his division. "Why did Prime Minister Meir stop Arik Sharon from taking his troops all the way to Cairo?" the Rebbe asked IAF commander Ran Pekar (b. 1936), in a 1975 *yechidut.* "He should not have been stopped."

In the same *yechidut,* the Rebbe criticized Sharon, too, for not continuing the offensive on his own initiative. "There are times that superiors cannot say yes, but if officers take it upon themselves to act without asking, they would be glad that the mission is getting done. If Sharon had continued to Cairo without asking, the government would have been glad; but when he asked for permission, none of them had the courage to give it."

After Israel began to speak again about concessions, the Rebbe commented on what he saw as an emerging trend. "Israel won a great military victory in 1973," the Rebbe reminded Pekar, "but the political leadership did not know how to capitalize on it and wasted it. This is a recurrent theme in Israel's wars. Ben Gurion was a strong and dignified leader, but he too made the same mistake and returned the Sinai in 1956. How is it possible that we win and then beg the enemy to take the territory back?"[88]

A few years later, following the Camp David Accords in 1978, the Rebbe would offer a similar analysis.

> Of late, our title to *Eretz Yisrael* has been challenged by the very nations who, by force of arms, repeatedly sought to rob us of our everlasting possession.
>
> Sadder still, there appeared some Jewish leaders who, for the sake of peace, or rather the illusion of peace—and frightened by threats of further violence in the midst of a hostile and callous world—were prepared to, and actually did, surrender portions of our land, in the ill-conceived belief that our enemies would thereby be appeased. Moreover, contrary to all experience and common sense, which have demonstrated again and again that every act of appeasement and concession only invites stronger pressures to yield to even more avaricious demands, there are still those among our own people who persist in following this dismal course. The so-called Camp David Accords are only the culmination of the first phase of this ill-fated and self-defeating policy.
>
> As you may have heard, when the Camp David negotiations were initiated, I considered it my sacred duty to call attention to the true nature of this disastrous expediency. There was no basis in law, nor in justice, nor in reality, to give in to pressure to sign an accord and treaty by which one party gives all and the other party takes all; namely, first giving away tangible and vital resources in terms of territory, fortifications, air fields, oil wells, and the dismantling of settlements, etc., all vital to its security, while the other gives in return no more than promises, such as the establishment of communications, exchange of ambassadors, and "normalization" of relations, all of which could be revoked at any moment under one pretext or another. I warned that far from bringing real and lasting peace, this "accord" would only whet our enemies' appetite for more "grabs," encouraged by the weakened security position of their adversary. I also warned that it was folly to put one's trust in the USA's part of this agreement,

for it was obvious that the U.S.A. was leaning heavily towards the Arab position....

The question is: Now that we have a Camp David agreement signed, sealed and delivered, don't we have to live with it? Would it be legally and morally right to abrogate it unilaterally?

There are two major answers to this question. First of all, an agreement is binding on either party only as long as the other is carrying out its part. As noted above, and as a matter of record, the Egyptians have not acted in good faith, and have broken, and are breaking, many of their pledges under the agreement. (To cite one more glaring example, which should have created a much greater public shock than the tiny ripples it started: By their own admission, once the fact was discovered, the Egyptians had been reporting to other Arab nations, as well as the PLO, on the negotiations conducted with the representatives of Eretz Yisrael under the Camp David Accords.) In view of the systematic violations of the agreement by the Egyptians, the other party need not feel either legally or morally obligated to abide by it.

The second answer, which is equally valid, is that the Camp David Accords were based on a presumption that invalidated them in the first place. Clearly, no government official has the right to sign away the very security of the people and country he represents, nor the security of the next generation and subsequent generations, for no person can possibly have such a mandate, actual or implied. Certainly, in the present case, no such mandate was given—on the contrary; there is an explicit and expressed unanimity that the security of the Land of Israel and its three and a half million Jews is not negotiable. Since the Camp David agreement does indeed jeopardize the security of the people and land of Israel, no signature, or even ratification, can be binding....

Hence, Jews everywhere must stop bickering and must demand in one voice: No more concessions! No more giveaways! No more pressures!....

Eretz Yisrael is ours by Divine covenant, as indeed is recognized by all who believe in the sanctity of the Bible; and the "facts of life" and "truth" are that Jews are not "occupiers" or "aggressors" in their homeland, but that which has passed into our hands is only a restitution of what is rightfully ours by Divine will and grace, not by the "false grace" of the United Nations.

> And we cannot afford to be magnanimous and give away any part of our tiny land in response to the threat of force, since the retention of every last inch of it is a matter of vital security for its three and a half million Jews—men, women and children—as well as for our Jewish people as a whole.[89]

Ironically, Menachem Begin had made the first—and only—visit of a sitting Israeli prime minister to the Rebbe in 1977, on his way to the White House to discuss the peace accords with President Jimmy Carter. The Rebbe's hopes for a change of heart in the Israeli government had risen in 1977, when Begin's right-wing Likud Party defeated Mapai for the first time in Israel's history. The Rebbe had enjoyed a close relationship with Begin for many years, who had visited 770 for *yechidut*. Now it seemed that some Jewish pride might be restored to the government and that the Rebbe's campaign against concessions would have a receptive and very powerful listener.

The prime minister's visit to 770 was high profile, and covered extensively in the media. "I have come this evening to our esteemed teacher and Rabbi, to ask for his blessing for my upcoming visit to Washington and my talks with President Carter," Begin told reporters who had gathered outside Lubavitch Headquarters. "We will be having important talks about the future of our region. The people of Israel pray for the success of these talks. I will not call them fateful, because the destiny of our people, an eternal people, is not dependent on any political meeting. Nevertheless we all know this meeting holds great importance for our future, and therefore I have asked for the blessings of the Rebbe, our great teacher."

"Rabbi Schneerson is a great man of Israel. All of us respect him; all of us accept his judgment. He is a great lover of the House of Israel. He has shown his deep sentiment and love for our children. Now, this evening I come to receive his blessing which will undoubtedly strengthen and embolden me, and I hope that with G-d's help, our meeting with the American president will prove successful, through which we will strengthen our security and advance our nation and our land towards the peace we all long for."

After a two-hour *yechidut,* Begin told reporters on his departure, "I have met with the Rebbe before, many times, when I served my people in the opposition. As always, what I say to the Rebbe, and what the Rebbe says to me, is private and not to be shared publicly. I do leave with a feeling of confidence, and am greatly encouraged as I move toward my meeting with the President."

It would not be long, however, before Begin would capitulate from his earlier position, signing an agreement which the Rebbe described as a "great hardship" for the Jewish people.[90] The matter was even more painful for the Rebbe in that it was perpetrated by a man who was an avowed believer in G-d. "You certainly know Mr. Menachem Begin," the Rebbe told Moshe Katzav at a 1992 meeting, "who at the outset did not agree with the Camp David ideas, and was strongly opposed to them. But eventually he began to make compromises, and from what we hear today, he has great remorse over having given up a part of the Land of Israel. Had people who do not believe in G-d been responsible for this, we could understand this. But that the signature for abandoning parts of the Land of Israel should be from Jews who believe in G-d—this is a desecration of His Name."[91]

Another issue which brought the Rebbe much aggravation from 1970 onwards, leading him to become deeply enmeshed in a politically charged debate, was Israel's Law of Return. Originally introduced by the Knesset in 1950, the law declares the right of every Jew to immigrate to the country. At the law's inception, two ministers of the religious parties—Yehuda Leib Maimon (Fishman) of Mizrachi and Yitzhak Meir Levine of Agudat Israel—wanted formal clarification of the term "Jew," but Ben-Gurion opposed discussing the question because of its potentially divisive nature. Israel could not afford a government crisis at a time when the state's existence was still seriously threatened by the Arab countries. But in 1956-7 there was a new wave of immigrants from Eastern Europe, many of whom were mixed-marriage couples, forcing Israel to formulate an official policy. On 10th March 1958, the incumbent Minister of the Interior, Israel Bar-Yehuda—who, by a strange twist of fate, had been the Rebbe's childhood tutor back in Yekatrinoslav (see p. 18)—issued a directive: "Any person who could honestly declare himself a Jew must be registered as such without having to provide any further proof." In the case of children, "both parents must declare that their children are Jews and that they regard this declaration as the children's own legal declaration."

Ministers of the Mafdal (religious party), Hayim Moshe Shapira and Yoseph Burg, protested bitterly and, when Ben Gurion refused to capitulate from Bar-Yehuda's policy, Mafdal submitted their resignation from the government. "In our opinion," they stated in a letter, "the decision as passed by the government contravenes Torah Law and is likely to create a split in the nation—in Israel as well as the Diaspora; it also constitutes a blow to the status quo on matters of religion as per the coalition agreement when the government was formed."

With the coalition now destabilized, the issue became a political impasse. A refusal to overrule Bar-Yehuda's policy would leave the government significantly weakened by the departure of Mafdal; agreeing to Mafdal's demands would result in the resignation of the Mapam and Ahdut HaAvodah parties. To bypass the problem, Ben Gurion proposed a highly novel solution. This fundamental issue of Jewish identity, he argued, was beyond the scope of the government to decide and needed a broader consensus from a cross-section of Jewish intellectuals and leaders. The government would present the question to fifty "Savants of Israel" around the world, both Orthodox and liberal, and be swayed by their consensus. The proposal was aired in the Knesset on 15th July 1958, and the following October, letters were dispatched to a broad range of undisclosed rabbis, heads of religious courts, Yeshivah principals, academic scholars, and other intellectuals in Israel, Europe, and the United States.

One of those chosen was the Rebbe, who responded in a detailed letter on 16th February (8th *Adar* I) 1959, stating, "My opinion is absolutely clear, in conformity with the Torah and the tradition accepted for generations, that in these matters there can be no validity whatsoever to a verbal declaration expressing the desire to register as a Jew. Such a declaration has no power to change the reality."[92]

Ultimately, forty-five of the fifty "Savants of Israel" approached by the government offered a response,[93] of whom thirty-seven argued that *halachah* must be the basis for defining who is a Jew. A formal response to this consensus, however, was delayed when Ben Gurion's government fell apart, in July 1959, over a debate about the sale of arms to West Germany, and was not reconvened until November. To win the support of Mafdal in forming the Fourth Knesset, Ben Gurion promised that revised rules would be established for registering religion. In the new government, Hayim Moshe Shapira, the head of Mafdal, was given the Internal Affairs portfolio, and in 1960 he published new directives to the registry clerks, ordering them to accept as Jews only those who were born to a Jewish mother or those who had undergone conversion to Judaism according to *halachah*. Shapira issued the directives on his own authority as Interior Minister, without bringing the matter to the Knesset; but Ben Gurion was able to point to the consensus of the "Savants of Israel" to show that he had not been religiously coerced. The concession had been necessary to maintain national unity.[94]

Shapira's directive remained in force for a decade, until it was overthrown as a result of the high-profile "Shalit" case, in the Israeli Supreme court. Benjamin Shalit had married a non-Jewish Englishwoman who became a naturalized citizen of Israel (not under the Law of Return). She chose not to convert to Judaism and, like her husband, was agnostic. Shalit had wanted the identity cards of their two children to read "nationality Jewish, religion none," and when the proposal was rejected by the government, Shalit successfully petitioned the Supreme Court in 1969, who decided in his favor with a five-to-four majority. The ruling, which effectively annulled Shapira's earlier directives, provoked a public storm and political crisis. Prime Minister Golda Meir soon backed down, and in 1970, after fierce debate, the Knesset passed an amendment to the Law of Return that re-introduced the 1960 directive, stating that a Jew is one "born to a Jewish mother, or who has converted to Judaism, and who is not a member of another religion." There was, however, one very significant omission from the new amendment. The 1960 directive had required that a conversion be "according to *halachah*," but the 1970 amendment did not include this clause, meaning that a non-Orthodox conversion would now be acceptable.[95]

The Rebbe perceived long-term undesirable ramifications if the State of Israel were to formally legitimize non-*halachic* conversions, and chose to make an exception to his policy of political neutrality, spearheading a hotly contended offensive against the 1970 amendment. "I am breaking from my mold," he announced in a sermon on 22nd March (*Purim*) 1970, three days after the amendment was passed by the Knesset, beginning a bitter campaign that would consume him for the next two decades, always chasing its goal.[96]

The Rebbe, never a knee-jerk reactionary, always gave careful consideration before taking a public position. He was surely aware that the campaign of *Mihu Yehudi* ("Who is a Jew") would be extremely unpopular, altering the image of Chabad and labeling it as a public enemy of the powerful Reform and Conservative movements. "Before the Rebbe flexed his political muscle with the Law of Return issue," one *New York Times* journalist observed, "Israelis usually viewed Chabad as benign: a sort of warm, rustic, 'Fiddler on the Roof' reverie of their absent Eastern European elders."[97]

Apparently, the Rebbe felt that the issue was so severe, threatening the integrity of the Jewish people (*shleimut ha-am*), that it was worth sacrificing much of Chabad's positive image. He soon became a vocal opponent even of the religious parties Mafdal and Agudat Israel, whom he lambasted as being insufficiently active on this crucial issue. Emotionally wrenching sermons on the topic were a regular feature at his *farbrengens* throughout the 1970s and into the 1980s.[98]

Why was the issue of *Mihu Yehudi* so important for the Rebbe? In a 1970 *yechidut* with Israeli journalist Moshe Ishon (b. 1928), the Rebbe highlighted what had stirred him to start the campaign. "If religious education is undermined today, there is hope that tomorrow or the day after we will be able, with G-d's help, to overcome the problems and restore education to what it used to be. If today, many desecrate the Sabbath, there is hope that in the future this will diminish. But if non-Jews integrate into the Jewish People, we will never be able to fix this."

"The question here is not whether one family or another converted or will convert according to *halachah* or not. The problem is more fundamental: A few years down the road, will the Jews remain a Jewish nation or will there be a joining of masses of non-Jews? This, then, is an existential war, for the existence of the nation is in danger if they bring in hundreds of alien families."

Ultimately, the Rebbe felt that the religious parties were at fault for not defending their own values. "The government is avoiding amending the laws only because the religious ministers are not pressuring them enough," he lamented to Ishon.[99]

A huge factor tempering the response of religious parties was the significant government funding for Yeshivot and other institutions which they stood to sacrifice by opposing the 1970 amendment or leaving the government. "It's not that they accept money so as to be silenced," the Rebbe bemoaned to Rabbi Tzvi Weinman, an Orthodox activist in the *Mihu Yehudi* campaign, "it's just that once they have accepted funds they are inevitably biased."

"Don't Chabad institutions also receive government support?" Weinman protested.

"For many years, I have had no direct involvement in this matter," the Rebbe explained. "I purposefully refrain from it so I can express my opinion with neutrality."[100]

While the campaign rendered the Rebbe extremely unpopular in some circles, many in Chabad and beyond could not but admire his courage in adopting a difficult position from which neither he nor his movement directly benefitted. Zalmon Jaffe, for example, recalled in his memoir of 1974: "When I am in Israel, especially in Jerusalem, certain Israeli Cabinet Ministers call me, spitefully, Mr. Lubavitch. They take me to task because the Rebbe is fighting to amend the law of *Mihu Yehudi* so that it should read 'according to the *halachah*.' They also allege that the Rebbe has split the religious party into two. I, however, retort and emphasize, that the Rebbe's fight is for the 'sake of Heaven' and for the 'sake of Israel,' whereas *their fight* was for the 'sake of themselves.'"[101]

The Rebbe's willingness to embrace paradox is evident, once again, in his attitude towards Israel during these years. Alongside his harsh critique of the Israeli government, he vigorously encouraged immigration to the country, personally initiating settlements in Kiryat Malachi[102] and Tzefat.[103]

His international concerns extended not only to Russian immigrants in Israel, but also to his brethren still stuck behind the Iron Curtain. While it was now around fifty years since he had left the country, Russian Jews remained very close to the Rebbe's heart and he spoke about their plight regularly at sermons, often breaking into tears.[104] On a rare occasion, when Russian immigrants were present, he would break from Yiddish, and speak publicly in Russian.[105]

He strongly opposed public demonstrations in support of Russian Jewry, which angered the Soviets and hindered the plight of refuseniks, a fact that was painfully clear to him from inside sources. While throughout the 1950s and 1960s emigration from Russia had been almost impossible, from 1969-1973 there was a considerable shift and some 150,000 Jews managed to leave. In one particularly memorable sermon in 1970, which stretched on for some two hours, the Rebbe bemoaned the counterproductive effects of American demonstrations for Soviet Jewry. "People have been asking," he noted, entering into an unusual public critique of another Jewish organization, "where is the certainty that my opinion is correct? Now I have no choice but to speak negatively about some Jews. I will tell you a story that transpired during the initial period of my efforts to work covertly that the demonstrations should stop."

The Rebbe told his audience that three years previously, it had become possible to speak directly via telephone to Russia and that he had managed to arrange visas for a large number of families to leave the country. Upon discovering a planned demonstration for the plight of Soviet Jewry, the Rebbe contacted the organizers. "I do not expect you to accept my view about demonstrations," he had said, "but instead of making your demonstration on the eve of Passover, could you please delay it [seven weeks] until the eve of *Shavuot.* I have verified reports that a hundred families are about to receive their exit visas and this would be jeopardized now by a public demonstration."

"They considered my request," he noted, "and subsequently I received notification that my view was not being taken into account, since the notifications I had received were 'doubtful.' The demonstration was scheduled to continue as planned on the eve of Passover. What was the result? Those hundred families are still in Russia to this day."[106]

Besides helping Jews leave the country, in 1964 *Lishkat Ezrat Achim* (Bureau to Assist Brethren) was founded to send parcels with items of high resale value to those trapped behind the Iron Curtain; and, beginning in the 1970s, to arrange regular support groups, trips to Russia by American Chasidim posing as tourists. The organization was started through the prompting of Rabbi Mendel Futerfas (1906-1995), one of the first Lubavitchers to leave Russia through the intervention of British Prime Minster Harold Wilson in 1964, after almost twenty years of blocked emigration. Numerous secret missions were conducted by the *Lishka* until the collapse of the Soviet Union. Rabbi Meyer Gutnick recalls one such mission in 1985, when he was sent by the *Lishka* to train Russians how to check *tefilin,* repair Torah scrolls, and carry out *shechitah* (ritual slaughter). In the absence of any available *sofer* (scribe) in Russia, he also prepared *gittin* (ritual divorce documents) for several couples. Previously, missions had been largely to offer moral support and to study, and this was the first time that actual training sessions were offered in practical Rabbinics. Upon seeing the photographs taken by Gutnick, the Rebbe was visibly moved.

All the missions were conducted in absolute secrecy. As an additional precaution, the organizers of the *Lishka* did not communicate with the Rebbe via his secretariat to discuss upcoming missions and would be in contact with him directly, sometimes in "casual" conversations outside his house.

It was not unusual for the foreign visitors to be interrogated by Russian authorities on entering or leaving the country. Gutnick recalls how he managed to smuggle in religious items through packing them creatively. "We were detained overnight by the KGB, and they wanted me to explain some of the items in my case. The black ink used for writing *tefilin*, I told them, was shoe polish. The parchment, I wrapped around a jar of peanut butter and said it was to protect the glass from breaking. The slaughterer's knife I had placed with more food, and the sharpening stone I packed in a shoe and said it was to keep the shoe in shape. The authorities confiscated a few religious books, but I managed to get the other items through."[107]

IV

What were some of the major events at the Rebbe's court during this middle period of his leadership?

In hindsight, the most important development was undoubtedly the growth of the *shlichut* movement. By the mid 1960's a new generation of young adults began to emerge who had spent their formative years in the Rebbe's court and were committed to dedicating their lives to his work. While the numbers were still modest, an increasing body of intelligent and talented young couples would consult with the Rebbe shortly after marriage and express a willingness to relocate to a place currently devoid of a Chasidic presence. In 1969, the outreach movement acquired its first dedicated building when a "Chabad House" was opened on the UCLA campus in California by Rabbi Shlomo Cunin, who had relocated to the West Coast four years earlier to establish activities.

The *shlichut* movement, however, took off slowly. The thousands of Chabad centers around the world today are a phenomenon which mushroomed only in the last few years of the Rebbe's life, and continued exponentially in the decades after his passing; but even as late as 1977 there were probably less than a hundred full-time *shlichut* couples. Chabad was still vigorously dedicated to institution building during this period, but more to its schools and *yeshivot* than to outreach centers.

While it is hard to identify concrete trends, during this middle period of 1965-1977 the focus on outreach began to dominate Chabad to a far greater extent, and was enthusiastically welcomed by more Chasidim as a defining expression of devotion to the Rebbe. This was intensified when, in the wake of the success of the *tefilin* campaign, the Rebbe launched further campaigns in 1974: to promote Torah study, to ensure kosher *mezuzot* were affixed to Jewish homes and business, to encourage Jews to fill their homes with sacred Jewish books, to urge women and girls to light Shabbat candles. In 1975, he added campaigns for eating kosher food, for women's ritual immersion (*taharat ha-mishpacha*);[108] in 1976, campaigns were launched for Jewish education, regular donations to charity (*tzedakah*), and Jewish inclusiveness (*ahavat Yisrael*).[109] While the Rebbe introduced hundreds of initiatives during his four decades of leadership, it is these ten in particular that were referred to as "campaigns" (*mivtzoim*) and, through constant stress in sermons and correspondence, helped to galvanize the movement with an outreach mentality.

The campaigns were successful in part because they helped standardize outreach into a simple, practical application which also rendered the achievement of goals extremely clear. For some Jews, the fresh encounter with a practical *mitzvah* would evoke deep emotions, leading them towards increased observance and Jewish involvement; for others, the experience would merely lurk in the back of their minds. But regardless of the outcome, the Rebbe taught his followers to see any *mitzvah* successfully encouraged as an achievement of cosmic importance, suffusing the universe with Divine light and bringing religious merit to the recipients. As early as 1974, Chasidim began to carry out the *mitzvah* campaigns in specially decorated motor caravans which were described as "*Mitzvah* Tanks," an appellation which immediately garnered the Rebbe's enthusiastic support.[110]

While outreach has since become a ubiquitous phenomenon in the Jewish world, the stress on initiating an encounter with a non-observant Jew through the observance of a practical *mitzvah* has remained almost exclusively a Chabad approach. When a person overcomes the inertia necessary to perform one single ritual, it can be transformative, achieving something which a mere conversation cannot.[111] The practical *mitzvah* also engages the body, rendering it a vessel and "temple" to the Divine, as Rabbi Shneur Zalman teaches in his *Tanya: "When a person studies Torah, his soul... his speech and thought are submerged in G-d's light... but in order to draw the light and radiation of the Divine presence on his body and 'animal instinct,' he needs to observe the practical mitzvot which are performed with the body itself."*[112]

During this middle period of his leadership, the Rebbe also rose to a greater national prominence through more regular coverage in the national media and high-profile recognition from Washington. By the 1970s, the *New York Times* was covering the work of Chabad several times per year, and on the Rebbe's seventieth birthday in 1972, the newspaper printed a full feature interview with him.

Objecting that his Orthodoxy characterized him as a conservative, the Rebbe told *Times* reporter Israel Shenker, "I don't believe that Reform Judaism is liberal and Orthodox is conservative. My explanation of conservative is someone who is so petrified he cannot accept something new. For me, Judaism, or *halachah* [Jewish religious law], or Torah encompasses all the universe, and it encompasses every new invention, every new theory, every new piece of knowledge or thought or action."

Responding to concerns that he was fostering a cult of personality, the Rebbe told Shenker, "I do all in my power to dissuade them from making it that."[113]

Attempts to dissuade his followers from unhealthy veneration can be seen in a number of cases. For example, in 1976, when Rabbi Yekutiel Farkash asked the Rebbe for a blessing in *yechidut* for his daughter who was suffering from cancer, Farkash said, "Rebbe, I have heard that many miracles come from this room. Please give my daughter a blessing that she should be cured!"

The Rebbe immediately censored him, saying, "Only G-d does miracles," adding that he would visit the grave of Rayatz and beseech him to intercede before G-d, but that was all.[114]

An even sharper response was penned to a woman who, after suffering a miscarriage, was subsequently blessed by the Rebbe and advised that she need not fear becoming pregnant, provided that she observed the laws of family purity meticulously. When she followed his instructions only to be beset by another miscarriage, the Rebbe responded with a number of suggestions as to what might have gone wrong. The last of four conjectures he offered was, perhaps, "the couple forgot that G-d is the source of blessing and its provider etc., and they trusted instead in a man of flesh and blood—in me."[115]

From 1975 onwards, recognition of the Rebbe's achievements began to emanate from the nation's capitol. In celebration of twenty-five years of leadership, President Gerald Ford congratulated the Rebbe in a letter on 17th January 1975: "Your efforts on behalf of education and your countless humanitarian endeavors have greatly benefited and strengthened our society. By giving direction to the movement's commitment to preserve Jewish tradition, you have perpetuated a legacy that is a source of comfort and courage to many of our citizens." After receiving a warm letter of thanks from the Rebbe, with prayerful wishes, the President responded, "Having your support and especially your prayers means a great deal to me."[116] The following May, Ford honored the National Conference Dinner of *American Friends of Lubavitch* with his presence, the first address of his presidency to a Jewish organization.[117]

While the Rebbe's court continued to grow, with major expansions to the main synagogue at 770 Eastern Parkway in 1967 and 1973,[118] the face of Crown Heights was altering rapidly as mass migration of middle-class Jews to the suburbs was supplanted with a wave of immigrants from the Caribbean. In 1960, seventy-one percent of Crown Heights' two hundred thousand residents were white, but ten years later the figure had shrunk to twenty-seven percent.[119] Other Chasidic courts and Jewish groups in the neighborhood fled, but the Rebbe was insistent that Chabad stay and save the community from the expense and trauma of transplantation. Abandoning a Jewish neighborhood would be catastrophic, he argued in a keynote 1969 sermon, destroying Jewish institutions and isolating poorer Jews who would be left behind[120]—a position that was encouraged by a letter of support from leading *halachic* authority Rabbi Moshe Feinstein.[121]

As the Lubavitch community in Crown Heights continued to expand, the area became a hotbed of racial tension and violence. In July 1970, two dozen Jewish-owned properties were set on fire and a bomb destroyed the storefront of the Jewish Community Council, in protest over the allocation of funds. In September 1975, Israel Turner was shot and killed while returning home to his family on a Sabbath evening; in 1979, Russian immigrant David Okunov was shot in the head while walking to synagogue. In general, Jews were subject to a slew of verbal and physical attacks, and felt that the police were not doing enough to protect them.[122]

Conflicts, however, were not limited to blacks and Jews. During this period tensions with the Satmar community in Williamsburg escalated, culminating in a violent attack by Satmar Chasidim on a *Mitzvah* Tank that was returning from Manhattan on 14th January 1977.[123] Satmar had become increasingly hostile to Lubavitch due to the outreach enterprise which they felt was deeply misplaced, as well as the Rebbe's support for Israel, and the situation had not been helped by inflammatory rhetoric from the movement's leadership.[124] The Rebbe encouraged his followers not to respond to the violence, even with a written critique. "The Rebbe stipulated that I should not write about their ghastly exploits," Zalmon Jaffe noted in his 1977 memoir. "One should not talk evil about Jewish people, especially about those who daven three times a day and put on *tefilin*," the Rebbe told Jaffe.[125]

It was during this period, that the Chabad community in Crown Heights established its own private ambulance service, *Hatzalah*. The move was prompted in 1976 when a member of the community suffered a heart attack and the city ambulance arrived too late to save his life. Upon the Rebbe's advice, the *Hatzalah* ambulance was not kept in a garage, but parked outside 770. That way, it would remind people to be proactive with their health and take steps to staying healthy, he argued.[126]

Despite all the local setbacks, the Rebbe's following grew steadily. From 1970 onwards, major weekday *farbrengens* were broadcast live around the world, making 770 the first truly international Chasidic court.[127] In a 1975 memoir, Jaffe depicts the scope of operations at the Rebbe's office at the time.

> Letters, in batches of a hundred, are delivered by post, sometimes three times a day; many more are delivered by hand. Urgent messages are being continuously received on the four or five telephones, which are always busy, all for the personal attention of the Rebbe. The Rebbe does not speak directly to the caller on the telephone, but he is constantly at hand to answer everyone's problems.... Obviously, it is humanly impossible to reply to every letter received—about 1,800 a week or 90,000 a year. One can be certain, however, that every single letter has been opened and read by the Rebbe. In these days of easy communications, most people phone through for an urgent reply to their letters.
>
> In addition to the above, the Rebbe has to attend to the regular Lubavitch business. One can visualize the constant stream of queries coming from, in particular, the scores of branches throughout the U.S.A. and Israel, besides those from our five branches in Britain.
>
> The Rebbe's talks are printed and published each week. These are edited by the Rebbe.
>
> During the course of a year, the Rebbe presides over approximately forty *farbrengens*, at which he speaks for about five or six hours, often even longer. All these words of Torah require intensive and concentrated preparation. Obviously, the Rebbe works extremely hard. He has no time to stop or to "take it easy." He spends about twelve hours a day in his office. For the twenty-five years since he became our Rebbe he has never had one day's holiday. He is tied, absolutely, to 770, for seven days a week. [128]

The schedule of *yechidut* also changed during this middle period of leadership. From his mother's passing in 1964, *yechidut* appointments were reduced from three evenings per week to two, on Sunday and Thursday nights.[129] Due to the growing crowds, the Rebbe requested in 1973 that *yechidut* meetings be kept as brief as possible. Longer questions could be presented on a separate paper, and answered at a later time in writing or via a message from the secretariat.[130] The following year the Rebbe discontinued a custom—which he himself had initiated—that Chasidim enter into *yechidut* on their birthday. "The idea was that this should produce significant results," he lamented, "which, apparently, it did not."[131] Visitors from abroad were permitted only one *yechidut* every twelve months, irrespective of the number of journeys and the long distance they had traveled.[132]

Even with the increasing burdens, and his advancing age, the Rebbe still appeared fresh and alert at these private meetings throughout the night, until as late as 5 a.m. "The Rebbe, at a *yechidut*, seems very different from the person we normally see at a *farbrengen* or at a prayer service," Jaffe recalled in 1975. "He is so relaxed and yet so alert. It is impossible to believe that he has been nonstop at work for about fifteen hours. What is more important and significant is that one is given the impression that the Rebbe has all the time in the world, and that he is only interested in just you and your problems."

Jerusalem editor and translator Uri Kaploun similarly recalled that when entering *yechidut* at 2:45 a.m., he was the forty-third person the Rebbe had seen that night, and yet, "the Rebbe looked refreshed, like I was the first person to see him."[133] This was despite the fact that the Rebbe refused to take a break during the night for refreshments. When secretary Leibel Groner once suggested that the Rebbe take a ten-minute break, he protested, "But people have been waiting to see me for hours!" Groner argued that the people would be pleased to wait an extra ten minutes for the Rebbe to refresh himself, but the Rebbe politely declined.[134]

While no formal record of most of the thousands of *yechidut* meetings from this period exists,[135] a few high-profile encounters were recorded, such as a visit from New York City Mayor John Lindsay on 26th November 1968,[136] and a meeting with Frank Lautenberg in 1972.[137] Israeli politicians were regularly welcomed at 770, and there were *yechidut* meetings with President Zalman Shazar (in 1966, 1971 and 1973),[138] Yitzchak Rabin (in 1972),[139] and Shimon Peres (in 1966 and 1970).[140] Secretariat member Binyamin Klein recalled that on one occasion the Rebbe was visited by three Israeli politicians of different persuasions—Menachem Begin of the Herut party, Joseph Burg of the Mafdal, and Menachem Porush of Agudath Israel—all of whom emerged energized by their meetings.[141] Numerous Rabbinic guests were also welcomed: Rabbi Avraham Sofer, Rabbi Yitzchak Hutner, Rabbi Nachum Partzovitz of Mir, Rabbi Shlomo Goren, Rabbi Mordechai Eliyahu, Rabbi Yochanan Twersky of Rachmastrivka, Rabbi Yissachar Rokeach of Belz, Rabbi Ya'akov Alter of Ger, Rabbi Chaim Meir Yechiel Shapira of Narol,[142] and Rabbi Moshe Feinstein.[143] Three years after their 1974 meeting, Rabbi Feinstein sent the Rebbe a letter congratulating him on his 75th birthday, recognizing the Rebbe's "astounding dedication, guarding the walls of faith and spreading Torah.... bringing close many who have regressed from our Father in Heaven."[144]

A particularly striking Rabbinic recollection of a *yechidut* has been preserved from Rabbi Michoel Fisher (c.1908-2004), senior Rabbinic Judge (Dayan) of the Federation of Synagogues in London. In Europe, Fisher had studied under some of the most illustrious rabbinic figures, such as Rabbi Shimon Shkop (1860-1939), Rabbi Boruch Ber Leibowitz (1864-1939), Rabbi Yisrael Meir Kagan, the saintly "Chafetz Chaim" (1838-1933), and Rabbi Chaim Ozer Grodzinski (1863-1940). While not of Chasidic persuasion, he had also met with the great Chasidic Rebbes in Warsaw before the war, such as the Gerer Rebbe, the Bobover Rebbe, the Belzer Rebbe and the Alexander Rebbe. Rabbi Fisher was known for an encyclopedic knowledge of the Talmud, and there are reports that he could recall any one of its thousands of pages by heart.

In a 1976 *yechidut,* Rabbi Fisher posed the Rebbe a Talmudic question that had troubled him, saying that he had searched hard but not found an answer. The Rebbe did not reply, but at the following *farbrengens* he addressed the issue at considerable length.[145] Concluding his response which had spanned several hours, the Rebbe turned to Rabbi Fisher, saying, "I've paid back my debt."[146]

After returning to England, Rabbi Fisher penned his impressions in an article published in the *Ha-Maor* journal of the *Federation of Synagogues.*[147]

> I am not an ignoramus in Torah, and I testify that the Lubavitcher Rebbe is one of the greatest minds of our time in Torah. As far as mysticism is concerned, I did not understand a word of what the Rebbe said.[148] I need a dictionary for the Lubavitch language.
>
> But what I did understand was Jewish law. I heard the Rebbe give a lecture on the conclusion of tractate *Sotah* which lasted more than eight hours[149] and I noted how he tied up the loose ends at the finish. The Rebbe spoke for eight hours without notes, without a Talmud, without a Chumash, and not only did he quote everything perfectly, but if there were two readings in the Talmud, he quoted both—exactly.

> I can testify that I have rarely met in the last thirty years, since the destruction of Eastern Jewry, a man who can "learn" so well and is fluent in the entire Torah, in the Babylonian and Jerusalem Talmuds, *Shulchan Aruch, Tosefta, Mechilta, Rishonim* and *Achronim* and in the literature of Chasidut.
>
> I was personally amazed at the Rebbe's vast knowledge and particularly the way the Rebbe built up a subject, from a single word in a seemingly unnecessary gloss of *Rashi* at the end of Tractate *Sotah* on a remark by Rav Yosef. The Rebbe went through the whole of the Talmud wherever Rav Yosef is mentioned and found the connecting links between all the sayings of Rav Yosef... and everything fell into place like a jigsaw in such a masterly way that I have never experienced in my life.

Rabbi Fisher also expressed his surprise at the Rebbe's detailed knowledge of even small communities in the United Kingdom.

> The Rebbe told me how many Jewish schools there are in England, how many teachers and of what type. And he knows what is going on in Wales and in Scotland, in the *Federation of Synagogues* and in *Jews' College*. It is amazing how a man who is steeped in Torah day and night should have the time and interest to bother himself with Swansea and Cardiff.

The hallmark of Lubavitch in returning "lost" Jews was also not lost on Rabbi Fisher.

> I regard the Rebbe as the greatest lover of the Jewish people I have ever met. With his great love he sees in every Jew... an uncut diamond. I have seen six-, seven-foot tall cowboys from Dallas, Texas, with big cowboy hats, standing in the hall, inspired and electrified just by looking at the Rebbe. All types of professional people, with great learning and secular knowledge, *ba'alei teshuvah*, great scientists, doctors, lawyers, dentists... Such love of Israel I have never seen.

Other individuals who met the Rebbe earlier on in their lives were inspired to devote their careers towards serving the Jewish people. A wonderful example is that of Jonathan Sacks (b. 1948), former Chief Rabbi of Great Britain, who first met the Rebbe in 1968. Sacks was in the middle of a degree in moral philosophy in Cambridge University, for which he would earn first class honours the following year. "I had met dozens, dozens of other leaders," Sacks recalled, "and from every other leader I had asked questions and I had received answers. The Rebbe was the only one who asked me questions."

"And what questions they were! 'What are you doing for Jewish life in Cambridge? I remember beginning my answer. 'Well,' I said, 'in the situation in which I find myself'—what a wonderful English beginning—and the Rebbe interrupted me in the middle of the sentence and he said to me, 'No one ever finds himself in a situation. You put yourself in a situation. And if you put yourself in one situation, you can put yourself in a different situation.'"

"And at that moment I understood," Sacks reflected, "that the Rebbe was not interested in creating followers. He was interested in creating leaders. He was quite the most selfless and self-effacing leader I have ever met."[150]

After completing his degree the following year, Sacks spent some time in the Chabad *ba'al teshuvah* Yeshivah in Kfar Chabad, under the tutelage of Rabbi Shneur Zalman Gafni.[151] Sacks, however, found himself in a state of turmoil. "Could I really embrace this life, which seemed so narrow after the broad expanses of Western culture?" he wondered. "Where in this world was there a place for Mozart and Milton, Beethoven and Shakespeare? Where in this focused existence was there room for the glittering achievements of the European mind?" Sacks wanted to live more fully as a Jew, but at the same time was reluctant to give up his love of art and literature, music and poetry, most of which was outside the orbit of Judaism.

After sharing his frustrations in a letter to the Rebbe, Sacks received what he described as a "marvelous reply," the truth of which, he noted, became more clear to him as years passed. In a 2000 memoir, Sacks recalled and interpreted the Rebbe's reply, which was phrased as a parable.

> Imagine, he said, two people, both of whom have spent their lives carrying stones. One carries rocks, the other diamonds. Now imagine that they are both asked to carry a consignment of emeralds. To the man who has spent his life transporting rocks, emeralds too are

> rocks—a burden, a weight. After a lifetime, that is how he sees what he is asked to carry. But to the man who has spent his life carrying diamonds, emeralds too are precious stones—different, to be sure, but still things of value and beauty. So it is, he said, with different civilizations.... His may be diamonds, the other emeralds, but he sees the beauty in each. So, the Rebbe ended, in most cases, if not all, you will find that your attachment to Judaism will heighten your appreciation of the gifts of other cultures. In other words, the more deeply you value what is yours, the more you will value the achievements of others.[152]

Although he eventually completed Rabbinic ordination, Sacks was not drawn to a career in the Rabbinate, and in a 1978 *yechidut* asked the Rebbe to guide him in the choice of one of three paths: academia, economics, or law. The Rebbe, unenthused by any of the proposals, suggested that Sacks devote his life to the Jewish people, training future Rabbis in *Jews College* as well as seeking a congregational post. A decade later, the Rebbe encouraged him to apply for the job of Chief Rabbi.

In a 2011 lecture, Sacks reflected that by following the Rebbe's advice, all three of his earlier dreams had been indirectly realized: he became an honorary professor in several universities, he had delivered two of Britain's most prestigious economics lectures, and he had been made an honorary barrister, lecturing before the country's legal elite.[153]

Another Rabbinic figure upon whom the Rebbe made a strong impression relatively early in his career was former Chief Rabbi of Israel, Yisrael Meir Lau (b. 1937). Lau, who referred to the Rebbe as his "spiritual mentor," first became intrigued by the Chabad leader after hearing a lecture in 1965 from left-wing Israeli politician Yitzhak Gruenbaum (1879-1970). "Should the day arrive when the Iron Curtain is raised," Gruenbaum told his Tel Aviv audience, "and the Soviet Union opens its doors to citizens of the State of Israel—if we go and find one person who is a Jew, it will be thanks to one man who lives in Brooklyn, the Lubavitcher Rebbe." Lau was surprised to hear such a comment from "a leftist such as Gruenbaum," but was impressed because "he knew what he was talking about."

Lau's first *yechidut*, in 1974, lasted over two hours. The Rebbe "spoke Lithuanian Yiddish with a Russian lilt, peppered with many Hebrew words and a few English ones as well." Much of the discussion centered around education, being that Lau was a high school teacher at the time; but later in the meeting, the Rebbe posed a question which caught Lau by surprise. "Perhaps you can enlighten me on a point about which I am very curious," the Rebbe asked. "In the last century, the world has witnessed many revolutions. Russia, for example, usually a very dogmatic country, experienced a revolution in 1917. Then in the Fifties, Khrushchev initiated a revolution that overturned the previous one of Lenin and Stalin. In America as well, Kennedy was completely different from his predecessor, Eisenhower. Martin Luther King started his own revolution. In England, you cannot compare Attlee to Churchill, and in France, Pompidou is no de Gaulle."

"The only place where nothing has changed is Israel," the Rebbe observed. "For forty years, the same individuals have gripped the helm of government.... Now, two months after the Yom Kippur War, elections are held again, and it's the same old thing: Golda Meir, Pinhas Sapir, Moshe Dayan are elected, while Begin has lost nine times already, and there is no revolution."

"What has to happen so that Israel will experience what is taking place all over the world—change?"

Lau had never contemplated the point before and was caught unprepared. Himself a survivor of Buchenwald, Lau began to tell the Rebbe a long story of an Israeli waitress whose entire family was killed in the camps, and whose husband later perished in the Israeli War of Independence. When her only son was conscripted to fight in the Yom Kippur War, she told Lau that, if he did not return, she would take her life. The Rebbe listened intently.

"Perhaps we are a bit tired of revolutions, Rebbe," Lau suggested. "This waitress is a living example of what my generation went through. All we want now is a bit of peace and quiet."

"I understand," the Rebbe said, tears swelling in his eyes. "I understand very well."

On one of Lau's many visits to 770, he was joined by his father-in-law, Yitzchak Yedidya Frenkel (1913-1986), Chief Rabbi of Tel Aviv, and the two Rabbis attended a *farbrengen* together. After hearing the Rebbe lecture for four hours without notes, quoting classic and esoteric sources, early and late authorities, and citing entire sections by heart, Frenkel was overwhelmed. While the Tel Aviv Chief Rabbi was, by nature, "critical, difficult to impress, and rarely given to superlatives," the *farbrengen* overwhelmed him. "I witnessed the magnificence of Polish Jewry," he reminded his son-in-law, "I had the honor of visiting Rabbi Kook, who gave me a personal letter; and I have known most of the great scholars of recent generations. But I have never seen such command of the material. That is genius."

Lau's relationship with the Rebbe continued until their last encounter in 1991, when the Rebbe pushed him to seek the position of Israel's Chief Rabbi, a post he held from 1993-2003.[154]

While the Rebbe's influence was mainly directed at Jews, we do find interesting accounts of him touching souls from other pastures. Shirley Chisholm (1924–2005), the first African-American woman elected to Congress, first met the Rebbe in 1968 when she sought his endorsement. Chisholm won the election, but in an attempt to marginalize her influence, she was assigned to the House Agricultural Committee which, given her urban district in New York—including Crown Heights—made her irrelevant to her constituents. Responding to a call from the Rebbe's secretariat, she visited 770 for a second meeting.

"I know you're very upset," the Rebbe told her.

"I am upset," she confessed. "I'm insulted. What should I do?"

While her appointment to the Agricultural Committee had been intended to slight her, the Rebbe encouraged Chisholm to see it as a Divinely orchestrated opportunity for further influence. "This country has so much surplus food," the Rebbe observed, "and there are so many hungry people. You can use this gift that G-d gave you to feed hungry people. Find a creative way to do it."

Energized by a new sense of mission, Chisholm spent the following years working to expand the Food Stamp program, which eventually became legislated as a requirement in every state. At her 1983 retirement party, Chisholm recalled the Rebbe's inspiration at her time of need. "A Rabbi who is an optimist taught me that what you may think is a challenge is a gift from G-d," she said. "If poor babies have milk, and poor children have food, it's because this Rabbi in Crown Heights had vision."[155]

Another particularly interesting account of a *yechidut* from this period was penned by Professor Herman Branover (b. 1931), a Russian academic and refusenik, who later led the Center for Magnetohydrodynamics at Ben Gurion University in Beer Sheva. Branover, who had already become a *ba'al teshuvah* in the Soviet Union through the influence of Lubavitcher Chasidim, first met the Rebbe in 1972, a few months after emigrating to Israel. "The Rebbe was interested in knowing all the minute details of the situation in Russia and our first days in Israel," Branover recalled in his 1982 memoir, *Return.* The Rebbe mentioned dozens of names of families throughout Russia and Siberia and inquired if Branover knew any details of their welfare. "He knew everyone's age, occupation, interests, problems and needs. Even though I had heard a great deal about the Rebbe's phenomenal memory, I was astonished. What amazed me more was his ability to listen... with total involvement, cutting off distracting thought... Whatever your topic, your point of view, the Rebbe is totally there with you, feeling your problem or story more than you do, and with a decision or advice coming immediately. He does not have to confer with anyone, and you always feel that his advice or decision is made solely with the good of the Jews in general and of yourself in particular in mind—both in the spiritual and the worldly sense."

Many of the discussions were of a scientific nature, and Branover was surprised that the Rebbe was abreast of recent scientific developments. He recalled discussing many technical issues in *yechidut:* the advantages of direct contact heat transfer in liquids, the suppression of turbulence in a magnetic field, and the difficulties of separating phases while preserving the kinetic energy of a liquid.

In another *yechidut,* a few years later, the Rebbe showed even more attention to the precise details of Branover's research. While in the United States, Branover had lectured at a number of universities about a new magnetohydrodynamic device he had patented for converting solar energy into electricity. At *yechidut,* the topic piqued the Rebbe's interest and he asked to know more. Branover offered a brief summary, but the Rebbe was not satisfied. "I'd like to hear the full report that you delivered at the universities," he said.

"Of course there was no blackboard and chalk," Branover recalled, "so I just had to say the equations. I couldn't write them, but everything else was the same. I tried to shorten it but it still took at least twenty minutes."

As soon the "lecture" was over, the Rebbe promptly made two observations. First, he suggested that the efficiency of the device might be improved dramatically, as much as fifty percent, by utilizing the climactic conditions of a desert with wide temperature shifts between day and night—a point which none of Branover's academic colleagues had raised.

Second, the Rebbe objected that two of the figures relating to the apparatus—the "system efficiency" and the "two-phase velocity"—did not square. "These two numbers do not correlate to one another," the Rebbe argued. "Either one, or both of them must be incorrect." Branover protested that his team had used the most reasonable theory and that the highly complex and time-consuming data had been processed on a mainframe university computer, but the Rebbe would not change his mind. "You are the expert," the Rebbe said with a smile, "but to me, these two numbers do not go together." On returning to Beer Sheva, Branover had his assistants check and re-check all the data, but no mistake was found.

Two years later, a new doctoral student approached Branover one morning with an issue he was having difficulty understanding. In the process of answering the student's question, an error was discovered in how one of the integers had been recorded in the equations. When the calculations were repeated with this detail corrected, the results were drastically different, correlating to the correction which the Rebbe had made two years earlier at *yechidut*. "The most complex calculations using the most advanced computer were of no help," Branover observed, "because computers are helpless when fed with incorrect data." Despite the fact that Branover was by this time already an avowed Chasid, he remained astounded by the incident. "The Rebbe didn't even use a pen and paper," he marvelled.[156]

V

After the passing of his mother in 1964, the Rebbe expanded the scholarly content of his *farbrengens* and began to deliver a long-running series of intellectually rigorous lectures on *Rashi's* commentary to the Torah.[157] Through the next twenty-five years, until the lectures were discontinued around 1989, he would deliver some eight-hundred *Rashi Sichot*—around half of which he would subsequently develop, with the assistance of an editorial team, and publish as densely annotated essays.[158]

The *Rashi Sichot* are striking in their originality. After centuries of Rabbinic scholarship had produced some very fine super-commentaries on *Rashi*, there appeared to be little room for something radically new.[159] While *Rashi* was a self-avowed *pashtan* (literalist), and did not seek merely to anthologize earlier Rabbinic interpretations, it was difficult for most super-commentators not to read *Rashi* through a traditional lens of Talmudic and Midrashic hermeneutics. The super-commentaries often seek to decipher *Rashi* by referring back to the classical texts from which the author had drawn, and to perceive him as simply having selected the most straightforward Rabbinic interpretation.

The Rebbe proposed a hyperliteral reading of *Rashi's* statement, "I have come only to explain the literal meaning of the text."[160] *Rashi* was concerned *exclusively*, he argued, with the most simple and precise rendition of scripture in a way that was detached from traditional Rabbinic hermeneutics. *Rashi* had sought the most straightforward, textually accurate, and contextually consistent interpretation, sourced in simple logic alone, totally disregarding whatever the earlier Rabbis had to say. The "proof" of this, the Rebbe argued, was that *Rashi* wrote his commentary not for scholars, but primarily for children studying the Pentateuch (Chumash) for the first time. In Jewish tradition, this begins from the age of five,[161] so *Rashi* could not have expected his reader to be familiar with Rabbinic hermeneutics. The only skills *Rashi* presumed were the ability to translate basic Hebrew and to follow a simple, logical argument.

The obvious problem with the Rebbe's understanding of *Rashi*, which explains why it had never been suggested before, is that *Rashi* *does* cite Rabbinic teachings from the *Talmud* and *Midrash* extensively. The easiest way of understanding *Rashi's* statement, "I have come only to explain the literal meaning of the text," was that he did not mean it literally! *Rashi's* commentary appears to be a blend of simple, literal interpretation alongside multiple citations from *Talmud* and *Midrash* which gradually introduce the beginner to higher schools of thought. In fact, this is in all likelihood why *Rashi's* commentary gained such popularity over other "literalists" (*pashtanim*) such as *Rashbam*, *Ibn Ezra* and *Sforno*, since in addition to offering simple interpretations, he also initiates the reader with a core knowledge of classic Rabbinic thought.

The eight hundred *Rashi Sichot* could essentially be seen as a sustained attempt to buttress the hyperliteral approach, taking comments of *Rashi* one-by-one and, through a careful reading of the text and its Rabbinic antecedents, demonstrating that Rashi was *always* concerned with a purely literal exegesis. *Rashi*, the Rebbe argued, never simply "cites" the *Talmud* or *Midrash*. He will often accept a Rabbinic interpretation, but only when he deems it to be the most logically (or contextually) straightforward way of explaining a nuance of Scripture. Rashi never expects the reader to be familiar with the source text, and when he quotes *Talmud* or *Midrash* he is, in fact, *borrowing* Rabbinic language for his own exegetical purposes.[162]

What is particularly striking about the *Rashi Sichot* is an unusual blend of intellectual creativity and textual precision. Since the arena of *peshat* is outside the orbit of traditional, received wisdom, there are no bounds to its creative potential; the only proviso is that the conclusions must be borne out by the text. The typical format of a *Sichah* would begin by noting a slew of textual nuances and peculiarities, sometimes as many as twenty detailed observations, before launching into a highly creative theory that aims to resolve them. The success of the theory relies on its ability to satisfactorily explain all of the textual nuances highlighted beforehand.

In contrast to normal Rabbinic dialogue which commonly follows the path of an astute question followed by a source-based answer, the Rebbe's *Sicha* will typically note multiple "microscopic tensions" which are subsequently resolved by elevating the plane of thought to a new paradigm. The combination of a highly intuitive theory which instantly resolves not one, but a host of diverse textual concerns, can be intellectually exhilarating. Once exposed to the unique genre of a *Sichah*, many readers become quickly convinced that others, too, would realize that the Rebbe's teachings are "something different" if only they were exposed to them.

Perhaps the highlight of a *Rashi Sichah* is when, after a complex and rigorous clarification of the literal meaning (*peshat*) in isolation from traditional Rabbinic thought, the *Sichah* then rebounds back into the world of classical sources in a kind of comparative study. How does our newly established *peshat* square, for example, with the view of *halachah* (Jewish Law)? Can any parallels be found between the *peshat* and esoteric interpretations of the verse (*sod*)? And, most crucially to the Rebbe's world, how can our new insight motivate us to be better people and better Jews?

The subtle interplay between different schools of Torah interpretation (*peshat*, Rabbinic, esoteric, *etc.*), was also the subject of a seminal *Sichah* delivered and edited for publication by the Rebbe during this period, and later published as *On the Essence of Chasidut.*[163] Drawing on the traditional four-fold categorization of Rabbinic exegesis into *peshat* (literal), *remez* (allusory), *derash* (homiletic) and *sod* (esoteric), the Rebbe suggests that Chasidut falls neither in the category of *sod*, nor does it represent a new, fifth category. Rather, Chasidut represents the "soul" or "essence" of *all* four layers, and its disclosure has the power to reinvigorate each of the four types of classic interpretation with more pertinent, spiritually relevant meaning.

To illustrate the point, which at first comes across as a little obscure, the Rebbe takes one particular idea and first examines it at each of the four traditional levels of *peshat, remez, derash,* and *sod.* Then he reviews each of the four interpretations, but this time with the "spice" of a Chasidic insight which adds a palpable vitality to each of the ideas. Finally, he demonstrates a fundamental interconnectedness of the four Chasidically enhanced ideas, making the point that Chasidut is the inner "energy" and "glue" that binds the other parts of Torah together.

The essay is powerful because it convincingly argues a point which seems counterintuitive. Historically, Chasidut was a later development in Judaism and was consequently perceived as an "appendage" to the previously received forms of wisdom. The notion that something which has only reached us recently is, in fact, the "essence" of everything that preceded it, represents a striking inversion of the generally accepted view that revelation gradually decreases with time. Traditional Judaism tends to glorify the distant past as a time of closeness between G-d and mankind, and the transmitted texts of earlier received wisdom are the source for all religious authority. The present is seen as a pitiful reflection of days gone by, and the hope of renewed intimacy with G-d is relegated to the distant future. The view of Chabad, which comes to light powerfully in this essay, turns the picture on its head. The past was, of course, a time of great revelation, but time has brought us now to a renewed spiritual ascendance. The disclosure of Chabad Chasidut in recent generations, as the future period of spiritual bliss draws palpably close, has brought us nearer to understanding the nature of the Divine and it has opened a new hermeneutical gateway.

Other important developments in the teachings Torah during this period include a series of lectures elaborating on his father's Kabbalisitic insights, subsequent to their publication in 1970 from marginal notes penned by Reb Levik while in exile;[164] and a series of lectures on Rabbi Shneur Zalman's *Igeret Ha-Teshuvah* (Tract on Repentance), which were initiated after the winds of *teshuvah* began to blow in the wake of the Six Day War.[165] Another text which received much attention at the *farbrengens* was *Pirkei Avot* (Ethics of the Fathers), which, over the years, was subject to a substantial treatment of around a hundred *sichot*.[166]

As the sermons became more scholarly, it seems that the Rebbe desired to rear a serious group of disciples who would examine his ideas critically and challenge him from time to time. While the *Sichot* did stimulate much interest and excitement, the Rebbe would often complain in public about what he felt was a lack of serious attention. In one 1965 sermon, near the introduction of the *Rashi Sichot*, he moaned, "I see that people are falling asleep... But I've been working on this all night!"[167]

Another comment, at the opening of a 1975 *Rashi Sichah*, is typical.

> I'm going to speak about a comment of *Rashi* which was discussed in 1971, in considerable detail, but an obvious question (*klotz kashe*) was left unanswered. Four years have passed and not one person has asked that obvious question. There is already a printed transcript of the talk which was seen by others who were not here, as well as by those that were here but who were dreaming of other things at the time—at least they saw it afterwards. Nevertheless, not one person asked a question. Obviously, there is no point in waiting another four years, because even then, nobody will ask. So I'm going to address the issue myself.[168]

The most important development of the Rebbe's Torah thoughts during this period was the formalization of their publication in weekly pamphlets entitled *Likutei Sichot* ("Collected Sermons"). This began in 1970 and continued each week until 1992.[169]

While every sermon that the Rebbe delivered since 1950 was lovingly transcribed and printed by his disciples, the Rebbe did not encourage the widespread distribution of these "students' notes" (*hanachot*), which were inevitably plagued with inaccuracies and were essentially a typed speech that had not been re-edited as a written document. During two years, 1958 and 1963, the Rebbe had agreed to edit a weekly pamphlet of *Sichot*, but the venture had not solidified into a consistent activity. It was only in 1970, when the *Sichot* were prepared for publication by a more involved editorial board who re-worked the sermons with the written word in mind and sourced the ideas in extensive footnotes, that the Rebbe showed a willingness to participate on a consistent basis.[170] He would spend hours every week editing and re-editing the text, as the editorial board would send various drafts his way, prompting him to respond with extensive modifications.

Besides the Rebbe's great achievements in global outreach, the thirty-nine published volumes of *Likutei Sichot* represent an important intellectual legacy for the Jewish people, breaking much fresh ground in Torah thought in a way that it is hard to find any close parallels.

VI

While by this period the Rebbe had very little time for personal and family life, a few significant events did occur. On 7th January 1971, Rayatz's wife, Rebbetzin Nechama Dina passed on, at the age of eighty-nine.[171] Besides the obvious loss for Moussia, her mother's departure significantly affected the court at 770, since Nechama Dina had always hosted public festival meals where guests had been able to spend these special occasions in the Rebbe's presence. The Passover Seder in particular had been a time when many Chasidim would join the festivities in 770 after completing their own private Seder, and the cessation of these public events represented a great loss. From this point onwards, the Rebbe spent the festival and Sabbath meals alone with his wife. (After her passing, he ate on his own.)

Some time near the end of the 1960s the Rebbe was able to renew a childhood friendship when he was visited by his cousin Avraham Shlonsky—now a famed Israeli poet—in a *yechidut* which is said to have lasted some five hours. "It's fortunate that I got out when I did," Shlonsky later quipped, "because if I had remained there a little while longer I would have emerged a complete believer and ardent Chasid."[172]

Shlonsky related that much of the conversation had been devoted to childhood memories of Yekatrinoslav, and while he and the Rebbe had followed different paths in life, both were directed towards the "world of faith and song." In one particularly moving exchange, Shlonsky recalled the Rebbe saying to him, "You, perhaps, do not observe the *mitzvot* like me, but you are a man of faith. You, perhaps, do not pray in the synagogue like me, but you pray in your own way. We both pray in different ways, but it is the same faith." The conversation inspired a number of poems in Shlonsky's 1968 collection *Me-Shirei Ha-Prozdor Ha-Aruch,* which he subsequently sent to the Rebbe, adding that it would take some time to emotionally process the Rebbe's words.[173]

Still, the thought was not lost on the Rebbe that he might inspire Shlonsky back towards Torah observance. In a 1970 letter congratulating Shlonsky on his seventieth birthday, the Rebbe observed that his cousin had always been "against the grain," and for Shlonsky now, the greatest expression of that trait would be to become more religiously observant. "Obviously," the Rebbe noted, "one doesn't begin to observe the *mitzvot* merely to show that one can go against the grain; but as a motivator, such a trait can be effective." As for the question why such an awakening should come now, of all times, "the answer—if one is necessary—is your seventieth birthday."[174]

In a final letter penned by the Rebbe in 1972,[175] he wrote to his cousin, "Following what we discussed when you visited here: I believe, that you believe, that we both believe—as the saying goes, 'with perfect faith'—in the fundamental connection between the Jewish people, the Torah and G-d." Notwithstanding that Shlonsky may have, in his own life, acted and spoken in a way contrary to such a belief, the Rebbe argued that this was "superficial, and does not indicate at all what is deeply within a person, what Chasidut refers to as his 'essence and being.'"

"Eventually," the Rebbe concluded, "the inner essence will inevitably rebel against the superficial layer that opposes it, and it will find the opportunity to express itself."[176]

Another connection with the past which the Rebbe forged during this period was a move in 1975 to get an academic paper penned by his brother Leibel published posthumously. After Leibel's passing, an incomplete study into an area of advanced mathematics (written in German) was found among his possessions, and through a relationship that the Rebbe developed with mathematician Paul Rosenbloom (1920–2005), it was eventually published in 1978 as *The Location of Eigenvalues and Eigenvectors of Complex Matrices* in the *Journal of Approximation Theory.*[177]

Rosenbloom first met the Rebbe in 1963, after an encounter with Chabad *shluchim* Rabbi Moshe and Mindy Feller, who had just begun to establish Chabad activities in Minneapolis. Before departing, the Rebbe had advised Mindy, who had recently graduated in mathematics from Hunter College, to seek a teaching position in a local university as part of her *shlichut.* That is how Rosenbloom, who was head of the Department of Mathematics in the University of Minnesota at the time, came into contact with Chabad, ending up in *yechidut* a year later.

At their first meeting, the Rebbe impressed upon Rosenbloom the importance of bringing an awareness of G-d into academic teaching. "Children should be taught to appreciate that everything is connected with the Torah," the Rebbe told him. "When they perform an experiment in a science lab, they should know that it is G-d's creative power causing the chemical reactions they observe."

Emphasizing the importance of an integrated approach to Torah and science, the Rebbe made another point. "There are some who have two sets of bookshelves, one for Jewish religious books and another for secular books," he observed. "That is the wrong approach. If a person thinks of secular wisdom as being unrelated to the Torah, he does not understand the Torah, nor does he truly understand the secular subject he is studying."

The relationship blossomed. Gradually becoming an observant Jew, Rosenbloom moved to New York, taking a position at Columbia University. On his regular visits to 770, Rosenbloom would present the Rebbe with his most recently published paper.

One day in 1975, Rosenbloom received a call from secretary Leibel Groner asking if he knew of a mathematician who could read German. Rosenbloom replied that a more pertinent issue was the content of the paper than its language, and he agreed to take a look at it. The next day, when the paper arrived, Rosenbloom was somewhat confused. "It had no introduction, and no conclusion," he recalled. "There were some elements that were well known and there were aspects that appeared to be new."

"I figured that this must be someone who has no access to a library," Rosenbloom explained to himself, "and I thought it might be some Russian refugee that the Rebbe is interested in helping."

At the next *farbrengen* he attended, Rosenbloom presented the Rebbe with a written evaluation of the paper and some suggestions on how to make it publishable. "It needs an introduction. It needs references and the manuscript is not complete," Rosenbloom said.

"The author is deceased," the Rebbe informed him.

The Rebbe asked Rosenbloom if he could find a student to work on the paper to prepare it for publication, offering to provide financial compensation. Rosenbloom was hesitant. The material was too advanced for a graduate student and no professor would be interested on working on another person's paper. Realizing that the matter was important to the Rebbe, he offered to do the work himself.

It was only at this point that the Rebbe made a full disclosure. "I was not willing to tell you who the author is, not to influence you, but it was written by my brother. He was younger than I am and he's dead.... this is the only thing left of him."

When Rosenbloom commented that the author did not appear to have access to a library, as he cites no references, the Rebbe explained, "He was an independent character. He was not willing to look at anything... Only afterwards would he look in a reference to see if someone had explained the same thing."

Working on the manuscript the entire summer, Rosenbloom discovered that Leibel had independently reached the same conclusions as some prominent mathematicians—such as Ferdinand Frobenius (1849–1917) and Oskar Perron (1880–1975)—though he had done so with different proofs. The paper's final publication three years later no doubt brought the Rebbe much satisfaction. The Rebbe instructed Rosenbloom not to make any mention that the author was the Lubavitcher Rebbe's brother. "I want it to stand on its own merits," he said.[178]

While we know few details, the Rebbe maintained close contact with Leibel's daughter, Dalia, who would sometimes stay with the Rebbe and Rebbetzin in their home, on the third floor. "Uncle Menachem was very fond of me," Dalia recalled in a rare 2008 interview, as she reminisced how the Rebbe would come out of the house to help carry her suitcases. Her husband, Avner, who also stayed at the Rebbe's home, recalled discussions they had about his professional field of drug development.[179]

Rebbetzin Moussia continued her "behind the scenes" life during this period. We do find, however, some charming recollections in Zalmon Jaffe's memoirs of his annual visits to the Schneerson home where his family would be received by the Rebbetzin. This account, from 1975, is typical.

> One of the highlights of our *Shavuot* holiday is our visit to see the Rebbetzin at her home on President Street. She is a very charming and friendly person. She makes us feel so much at home, that even when we take our leave after two or three hours, she expresses deep regret that we "have to leave so soon."
>
> The Rebbetzin told us that the Rebbe had divulged to her that we spent over an hour at *yechidut* and he thoroughly enjoyed it. She expressed the hope that I would continue to make the Rebbe happy, "as I am now doing."
>
> We also showed her scores of photographs, which we had brought specially for her to see. We were delighted that the Rebbetzin chose some of these to keep for herself.... Thank G-d, the Rebbetzin was her usual gracious and elegant self. We enjoyed nice refreshments—unlimited supplies of ice-cold pineapple juice and fresh strawberries. She expressed a desire to see our children and grandchildren who were presently in Crown Heights.
>
> I asked the Rebbetzin whether she would be pleased to officially receive the members of the *Tanya* Committee. They wished to present her with a specially autographed leather-bound *Tanya*. She demurred a little—she dislikes ceremony. She would have been quite satisfied to accept this special *Tanya* signed by and presented by me, alone. On reflection, however, she decided that it would be nice for her and for the committee if all the members signed, and came along to present this *Tanya* to her....
>
> The Rebbetzin sat at the table—she is only a small lady, but her personality filled the entire large room. No queen receiving her faithful and loyal subjects, could have looked more regal and gracious than our dear Rebbetzin.[180]

While the Rebbe was never satisfied with his achievements, by 1977, approximately two thirds of the way through his leadership, Chabad had been transformed significantly. It was hard to believe that just thirteen years earlier the Rebbe had bemoaned privately that Lubavitchers had not adopted the "Ufaratzta" mentality.[181] A call from the Rebbe to establish seventy-one new Chabad institutions in honor of his seventieth birthday had produced a fantastic response,[182] and even outside the major centers in America and Israel, Lubavitch now had a significant presence in Australia, England, Scotland, France, Italy, South Africa, Argentina, Venezuela and Canada. In America alone, official figures from this period point to around sixty institutions in twenty-eight states.[183] While many of these were more inwardly focused schools and *yeshivot*, or Chabad Rabbis in employment at non-Chabad synagogues, a modest group of *shluchim* dedicated to full-time outreach had already assumed the proportions of a small movement. The numbers, too, were growing each year.

The Rebbe, however, now in his mid-seventies, had neither a biological heir, nor an obvious second-in-command. Every major decision in the movement, as well as most of the minor ones, hung on his shoulders.

"Who is to be the eighth Lubavitcher rabbi?" Israel Shenker had asked the Rebbe in his seventieth birthday *New York Times* interview.

"The Messiah will come and he will take all these troubles and doubts," was the Rebbe's response. Then he added, "My intention is to live many years more... There's a very great deal to achieve."[184]

The Rebbe's conviction that he would live "many years more" turned out to be correct; but at the end of 1977 his life would hang in uncertainty for several weeks with the court at 770 gripped with concern. It was 3rd October 1977, the night of *Shemini Atzeret*, one of the most joyous festivals on the Jewish calendar; a time when the Rebbe would dance exuberantly with the Torah scroll in the presence of a packed synagogue. Amid the fourth round of dancing, the Rebbe's face paled. He asked for his chair to be brought, sat down, and closed his eyes. He requested from Rabbi Groner that any doctors present be brought near, but he did not allow them to inspect him. Not wanting to cause a scene, he instructed the celebrations to continue and stayed until their conclusion, even participating in the final dance with his brother-in-law, Rashag. He then walked up the steps to his study, refusing offers of physical support.

After consultation with Dr. Mordechai Glazman of Toronto, who was present at 770, it became clear that the Rebbe was suffering major heart problems and needed to be rushed to hospital so that his condition could be properly monitored and stabilized. The Rebbe, however, insisted that he wished to stay in his office and could not be persuaded otherwise. "I cannot even begin to tell you what transpired at this desk," he told Glazman. "The cure will come from here."

After eating a small meal, the Rebbe still suffered from chest pains and had some difficulty breathing. Since he was adamant about not leaving, Glazman had no choice other than to monitor the Rebbe's heart with equipment brought into his office at 770.

At around 5 a.m. the Rebbe's blood pressure dropped and his heart became unstable. Glazman alerted Rebbetzin Moussia that the Rebbe's life would be at serious risk if he were not be taken immediately to hospital. The doctor requested permission to sedate the Rebbe and take him in an ambulance. "At this point it would really be criminal of me to let him stay," he said.

The Rebbetzin went over to a corner to think things over for a few minutes. She returned to Glazman and said: "All the years that I've known the Rebbe, there was never an instance that he was not in total control of himself, so I can't consent."

She took secretary Yudel Krinsky into a side room and asked him, "Rabbi Krinsky, you know so many people. Can't you find a doctor for my husband?"

Krinsky recalled a young cardiologist from Chicago named Ira Weiss, who had recently sent the Rebbe a copy of his book on heart arrhythmias, and was presumably an admirer of the Rebbe.[185] Krinsky made a phone call to Weiss and succeeded in waking him up.

"The initial question I got from Rabbi Krinsky," Weiss recalled, "was, 'Can this kind of care be given outside of the hospital?' Of course I said it can be done because I have witnessed this. My own teacher Dr. Bernard Lown had done these things for people who wanted to be cared for in a private setting."

"His next question was, 'If that's true, can I come and do it?' But I was concerned because the Rebbe was in critical condition and it would have taken me at least four hours to get to New York."

Weiss called Dr. Louis Teichholtz, a colleague at Mount Sinai Hospital who was one of the developers of echocardiography, and asked if he could attend to the Rebbe for the next few hours while Weiss was en route. Teichholtz had an important paid lecture that morning, and though he had no connection with Lubavitch, he canceled the engagement and rushed to 770. He made it possible for the Rebbe to get immediate expert care, and by the time Weiss arrived about six hours or so later, the Rebbe's blood pressure was restored and he was able to communicate.

"When I was introduced to the Rebbe," Weiss remembered, "he already was in a good humor and we had a very thorough conversation. He asked questions with a little twist to them that was humorous. I asked him what he thought had happened to him, and he had very good working knowledge of what might have happened. I said most people have a little bit of warning that they're on the wrong track before they have a heart attack. He said to me that he did not have any signals like that."

A short while later, the Rebbe asked Dr. Weiss if he would be allowed to speak at the *farbrengen*. "It's clear as a bell that you can't go out in this heart attack state to have a *farbrengen*," Weiss insisted.

The Rebbe suggested speaking while still attached to a heart monitor in his room into a microphone (after the Sabbath), which would be broadcast live into the synagogue. "I made a deal with the Rebbe," Weiss recalled. "I told him, 'When twenty minutes come, I'm going to give you a signal and we're off the air.'"

After twenty minutes, Weiss gave his signal, but the Rebbe continued talking. His talk went for about thirty-five, forty minutes, "but he was in very good spirits," Weiss recalled.

While the Rebbe was "hospitalized" at 770, Dr. Weiss kept in contact with the Rebbetzin every day. "She herself was very well read," Weiss remembered, "and she was perceptive. She knew I was an avid Chicago Cubs fan and she knew when I was a little down. She'd say, 'Did the Cubs lose today?' I could tell from the conversations that she would always have liked to have had a son herself, just to talk about small things like that with her boy."

Weiss also noted the tremendous support that the Rebbetzin offered her husband. "She was the Rebbe's intellectual sparring partner, so she could take the Rebbe to task at home, as a good wife would, when she saw him going a little too far afield. And I felt that was a very great support."

While the Rebbe's workload had been greatly reduced by doctors' orders, he did read and respond to some letters during this period. "I could see that he was very, very distressed by some things he would read," Weiss remembered. "I'd see anguish in his face. And it would often be a personal letter from someone. It would be someone's personal misfortune that would grieve him."

After about eighteen days, when Weiss was ready to leave, the Rebbe turned to him and said, "You've done so much for me, Dr. Weiss. Can I do anything to help you?" Weiss mentioned that he would like a blessing for a friend who was suffering from Multiple Sclerosis.

Weiss was quite taken aback when the Rebbe "got up, went to his cabinet and found in his catalog of science articles an article he had saved about multiple sclerosis and its possible connection to the immune reaction to measles. I had not heard about this myself, but the Rebbe had a file on this and he knew exactly where it was. And I then noticed the file cabinets were just full of all kinds of articles. So I think he always kept his eye on the areas of science that he never went into, but he kept abreast of it remarkably."

On 10th November (*Rosh Chodesh Kislev*) at around 7:30 p.m., a little over a month after the heart attack, the Rebbe finally returned home for the first time. His followers rejoiced at this clear sign of recovery, and etched the date as a new "festival" on the Chasidic calendar.

But all was not over yet. In honor of *Yud Tet Kislev* on 29th November 1977, Dr. Weiss reluctantly let the Rebbe *farbreng* in public for the first time, while hooked up to a heart monitor. During the first sermon, a crisis erupted when the Rebbe's heart suddenly became unstable.

"We didn't know how to deal with it," Weiss recalled. "We had monitor proof that he was in danger, and Dr. Resnick[186] and I were frantic. We didn't know if we were doing the right thing or the wrong thing by letting him continue and endanger his life. But going up on the stage and stopping him did not seem like an option. It came with its own risks.... So we let him go through it and he finished the sermon—and the same thing happened in the next sermon."

"And then he finally got to a *ma'amer* [esoteric discourse] where his rhythm was much more stable and we were thankful that we were through the crisis, but we really misjudged that terribly. Had we known that, we never would have had the *farbrengen* in the first place."

For the first time in history a Chasidic Rebbe had been attached to a heart monitor while delivering a *ma'amar,* and medical professionals were able to observe empirically that the higher state of consciousness reached by the Rebbe during *ma'amar* delivery had a tangible, calming effect on his heart.

Through attending to the Rebbe's health, Ira Weiss had the rare opportunity to observe him up close for an extended period and later reflected on his experiences. "I think he was always feeling such pressure, like he was carrying the world on his shoulders. I never saw him really have a moment of absolute, pure, unadulterated joy. He enjoyed being with his Chasidim, he enjoyed being at the *farbrengens*; he really put a lot into it. But it's not like we ever really had a good laugh together."

"His solace was that he always had a time designated to be with Rebbetzin Schneerson, whom he really, truly loved. They were a wonderful couple; they really were a close couple. And having a 'tea session' every day, almost at the same time the British have it at four o'clock or something—I think that was the routine—was very, very valuable to him."

Though he did not become a Chasid, over the fifteen subsequent years that Weiss cared for the Rebbe's health, his admiration swelled. "The more I would get to meet the Rebbe the more I recognized his magnitude, his grandeur, and his stature. This was in distinct contrast to my usual experience in meeting famous personages; from a distance they look great and grand, but as you get closer you are disappointed with the human frailties that we all have."

"My experience with the Rebbe was analogous to my experience of visiting the White Mountains. From a distance they looked magnificent, but as you got closer, they were even more grand, more magnificent, even impassable."[187]

CHAPTER THIRTEEN

THE REBBE'S ARMY

1978–1987

As the Rebbe distributes wine (*kos shel bracha*) after a festival, he engages with a child.

Following the Rebbe's heart attack at the end of 1977, there were significant changes at his court. Even after he returned fully to work, private *yechidut* appointments were vastly reduced, and in 1981, they were discontinued altogether as a regular fixture.[1] While the correspondence from this period has not yet been fully published, there is no doubt that the number of letters sent from the Rebbe's office from 1978 onwards was significantly reduced—though he did continue to respond to thousands of inquiries through brief written notes, verbal communication with the secretariat, and simply by underlining certain words in a letter that he had received, indicating the reply.[2]

What did expand significantly during this period were the sermons, which probably doubled in length, as *farbrengens* stretched on for five, six hours, or more.[3] This afforded the opportunity to expand the time devoted to the analysis of Torah texts, to launch new initiatives, and to comment upon the local and international issues of the day.

By this time the Rebbe had amassed a sizeable following of devotees, most of whom had either grown up in his court or been drawn to it. The period, in general, was characterized by a huge army of followers who hung on to his every word and were poised to spring into action. While the late 1960s and early to mid-1970s had witnessed a number of campaigns launched at *farbrengens*, the late 1970s and 1980s saw this phenomenon expand significantly, and barely a month would go by without the Rebbe's proposing a new venture. By way of illustration, the Chabad inspirational calendar *Hayom Yom*, whose introduction lists many of the Rebbe's notable initiatives over four decades, devotes some five pages to the years 1950-1977 and twelve pages to the years 1978-1992.[4]

In many instances, the Rebbe did not single out a particular individual or group to carry out a new campaign. He simply presented the idea at a *farbrengen*, explaining its underpinning in Jewish sources and perhaps some details of the proposed implementation, then wait to see the response. While some suggestions were wildly successful and continue to this day, others did not proceed to swift implementation or fizzled out after a short period.

In a 1980 sermon, for example, the Rebbe complained about how an earlier suggestion to print pamphlets for children had failed to materialize.

> I did not then appoint anyone to head this project and, apparently because of that, nobody has done anything about it! Five weeks have passed, and not one booklet has been published. Who suffers? The children. For five weeks children have had no booklets....
>
> As in all other matters, I am held responsible. Why did I not appoint one individual to be in charge, instead of leaving it up to everyone? Know, however, that a person's share in the World-to-Come is dependent on this thing—and it is not my business to apportion shares in the World-to-Come. Therefore I did not appoint any particular individual, for it is everyone's business. And yet five and a half, weeks have passed by, and nothing has been done...
>
> I could have chosen an individual, grabbed him by the beard, and instructed him to be the one in charge of the entire operation. But then everyone else would have been frightened off, thinking that only

> that individual is allowed to be involved in printing the booklets and no others.[5]

With the army of devotees expanding, and his own stature growing by the year, the Rebbe was faced with a new set of concerns. In the 1950s and 1960s he had complained that Chasidim were not sufficiently inspired by the idea of *ufaratzta*, of outreach, and were busy with their own personal worship or their material concerns. Now, the tables had turned, and outreach was becoming such a priority that some Chasidim now imagined that stress on worship, such as prolonged contemplative prayer, was unimportant.

In one memorable sermon in 1980, the Rebbe made clear that this had not been his intention.

> There are those who argue that the Previous Rebbe laid a heavy stress on the study of Torah and the spreading of Torah and *mitzvot* to others. They maintain that it is necessary to apply oneself to these areas with self-sacrifice, but that other areas of Judaism—for example, contemplative prayer—are not that important. They will explain that in the era of the Rebbe Rashab, contemplative prayer was important... but times have changed and now those efforts are no longer relevant to us.
>
> The reply to such an argument is clearly expressed in the Torah, in Pharaoh's statement to the Jewish taskmasters: *"Lazy, you are lazy; therefore you say, let us go sacrifice to G-d"* (*Exodus* 5:17). They are too lazy to be involved with prolonged, contemplative prayer. However, rather than admit the truth, they try to rationalize their behavior, arguing that since the Previous Rebbe stressed the service of spreading Torah, it is unnecessary to become involved with prayer.[6]

Another growing concern was the issue of unhealthy veneration toward the Rebbe. While, as we have seen, the Rebbe had been openly concerned with combatting misplaced hero worship for some time, the huge success of the movement intensified these challenges further. To one individual in 1986 who asked if the Rebbe would send him a photo of himself, the Rebbe replied: "This is not my custom at all. You should learn the weekly Torah portion (among your other regular studies) which I am learning too, and this will bring us together in a far superior manner than a photo."

In a 1982 sermon, he protested vehemently that during the synagogue services, instead of reading inside a prayer book as they prayed, Chasidim gazed at the Rebbe.

> What has become the custom? That when coming together to pray, people are enthusiastically gazing at a man of flesh and blood. It has even become an issue of Chasidic "piety"—the whiter the beard, the more devoted he is to staring without interruption at a man of flesh and blood!
>
> Your students are standing around you, and they see that as you say *Ashrei* (Psalm 145), and prepare for the *Shmoneh Esrai* (silent prayer), and as you listen to the repetition of the *Shmoneh Esrai—when you are supposed to be thinking about G-d,* what do they see? What are you doing? You are looking at one, single corner. So they do the same....
>
> I was hoping that when an important Rabbi would come here, he would protest about this obvious concern, but nothing has transpired. On the contrary, he too, acts in the same way![7]

Most devotional energies, however, were channeled in a positive direction. From 1978 onwards an adaptation of the Rebbe's sermons began to appear regularly in English, and from 1981 the full content of each *farbrengen* was published weekly in Hebrew, in addition to the Yiddish transcripts which had appeared for decades.[8] In 1980, *Jewish Educational Media* was founded to arrange live broadcasts of the Rebbe's *farbrengens* over satellite and Cable TV channels,[9] and by 1987 a digest of each sermon was already being distributed internationally via fax. Shortly afterwards modern computers costing five thousand dollars each were purchased to assist with the work of transcription.

The movement of *shluchim* continued to grow, and in 1983 the first *Shluchim* Conference was initiated, attended by some seventy emissaries from around the United States. The following year, the conference was expanded to include *shluchim* from Canada, and by 1987, upon the Rebbe's suggestion, the first fully international conference was held, with some five hundred *shluchim* from around the world.[10] President Reagan sent his best wishes for the conference: "The representation of the Lubavitch movement in so many countries is a testimony to the power and strength of its ideas," the President wrote in a letter dated

20th November 1987. "You combat the anti-religious forces that have caused so much misery in our lifetimes. I applaud your work."[11]

Through the efforts of the Chabad representative to Washington D.C., Rabbi Avraham Shemtov (b. 1937), from 1978 onwards, the Rebbe's birthday has been declared each year, by every U.S. President since Carter, as "Education Day U.S.A." The resolution was passed by the ninety-fifth Congress at the second session, when it was declared:

> Congress recognizes a need for the nation to set aside on the calendar a day devoted to the importance of education to the lives of its citizens and to the general well-being of the nation... and whereas world Jewry marked in 1977 the seventy-fifth birthday of the revered and renowned Jewish leader, the head of the worldwide Lubavitch Movement, Rabbi Menachem Mendel Schneerson... and whereas the seventy-sixth birthday of this celebrated spiritual leader will occur on April 19, 1978... Now, therefore, be it resolved by the Senate and House of Representatives of the United States of America in Congress assembled, that the President is authorized and requested to issue a proclamation designating April 19, 1978, as "Education Day, U.S.A."[12]

Following a lengthy sermon on the first Education Day, pointing to the importance of education in areas of human rights and morality, and the role of America in providing foreign aid, the Rebbe was delighted when, the following year, Carter won "one of the largest legislative victories of his presidency"—a bill to create a new Department of Education.[13] In a personal letter to the President, the Rebbe offered his enthusiastic approval.

> It will come as no surprise to you, Mr. President, that your proposal to establish a Cabinet-level Department of Education has received my fullest endorsement and acclaim....
>
> I am, of course, referring to education in a broader and deeper sense—not merely as a process of imparting knowledge and training for a "better living," but for a "better life," with due emphasis on character building and moral and ethical values.
>
> Indeed, the U.S. government, and you Mr. President personally, are in a unique position of influence among the nations of the world, particularly those benefiting from U.S. economic, cultural and other

forms of aid, to encourage them to follow your example and to share your "conviction that the noblest task of government is education"—to quote your statement (2/28/78)—a conviction which has been translated into bold, comprehensive action. I am confident that the response will be positive, and I venture to say that it would have a favorable feedback impact on those in this country who, for one reason or another, are not, as yet, enthusiastic about Congress legislation on the submitted project.[14]

Shortly afterwards, the Rebbe shared some further reflections on the importance of moral education in a letter to Vice-President Mondale.

Dear Mr. Vice-President:

I read with profound interest your remarks at meeting of Ad Hoc Committee for a Cabinet Department of Education, Jan. 24, 1979. Needless to say, I fully endorse the substance and urgency of your message. Indeed, in light of the saying of our Sages, *"Words coming from the heart penetrate the heart and are eventually effective,"* I am confident, Mr. Vice-President, that your words will find the proper response they deserve.

You will surely recall, Sir, the meeting at the Caucus Room of Congress, which you graciously chaired, in celebration of the H. J. Res. 770, authorizing and requesting the President to issue the Proclamation designating April 19, 1978, as "Education Day, U.S.A." I trust you also read some of my remarks in this connection that appeared in the Congressional Record, the thrust of which, permit me to reiterate, was:

Education, in general, should not be limited to the acquisition of knowledge and preparation for a career, or in common parlance, "to make a better living!" We must think in terms of a "better life," not only for the individual, but also for society as a whole. The educational system must, therefore, pay more attention, indeed, the main attention, to the building of character, with emphasis on moral and ethical values.

The above principle, which is surely indisputable, assumes added significance now that the Administration is making an all-out effort to promulgate the required legislation to implement the President's proposal for a Cabinet-level Department of Education—for the following reason:

> The skepticism on the part of those who, at present, oppose the Administration's educational program (of which you make mention in your remarks) is, I believe, in large measure due to the shortcomings of the educational system in this country, which leaves much to be desired in the way of achieving its most basic objectives for a better society. In a country, such as ours, so richly blessed with democracy, freedom of opportunity, and material resources, one would expect that such anti-moral and anti-social phenomena as juvenile delinquency, vandalism, lack of respect for law and order, etc. would have been radically reduced, to the point of ceasing to be a problem. Hence, it is not surprising that many feel frustrated and apathetic.
>
> I submit, therefore, that the Administration's resolve to restructure the Federal education role—long overdue—would be well served if it were coupled with greater emphasis on the objective of improving the quality of education in terms of moral and ethical values and character building that should be reflected in the actual everyday life of our young and growing generation....
>
> With prayerful wishes and blessings for success in your endeavors to upgrade the educational system, and in all your public and personal affairs,
>
> I remain, Mr. Vice-President,
>
> Cordially yours,
>
> M. Schneerson

Years later, the Department of Education would formally recognize the Rebbe's role in its formation. In a 1997 address, U.S. Secretary of Education Richard Riley said of the Chabad leader, "His voice, so respected and beloved, helped to make it happen, so I owe my job to him and I join with millions around the world who owe so much to the Rebbe. These millions include the children of America. He was a strong champion of excellence in education not only in our religious schools, but in our public schools as well."[15]

In recognition of the thirtieth anniversary of the Rebbe's leadership on 28th January 1980, Carter's Assistant for Domestic Affairs, Stuart Eizenstat (b. 1943) shared at a special tribute dinner in New York how the President appreciated what the Rebbe had accomplished in Crown Heights. "As one of the principal architects of the President's urban policy," Eizenstat told dinner guests, "I am familiar with what the Rebbe has done in stabilizing your community. You did not run. You have served as a shining example for urban America throughout the United States. You have shown that our cities can and will be safe."

Speaking on behalf of the President, who honored the celebrations with a warm letter, Eizenstat congratulated the Rebbe for "fostering the moral and ethical values of education, which transcend the Jewish community. The Rebbe is concerned not only with the Jews of his own community but with all Jews... The whole day school movement would not be what it is today if not for your movement."

After the dinner, Eizenstat was escorted to 770, where he joined the Rebbe's farbrengen, which stretched from 9:15 to 2:30 a.m., and was heard by telephone hookup in 118 cities throughout the world. Eizenstat subsequently commented in a letter to the Rebbe, "I found the whole evening, particularly the *farbrengen*, to be one of the most moving experiences I have ever had."[16]

With the Reagan administration, the Rebbe's relationship with Washington strengthened. In honor of his eightieth birthday in 1982, Reagan wrote to the Rebbe, "You have so much of which to be proud. Since your first moments in the United States in 1941, you have shared your personal gift of universal understanding to the benefit of all. Time and again, your love and spiritual guidance have brought hope and inspiration to those confronted with despair. In bringing solace and comfort to the human spirit, you have helped to strengthen the foundation of faith which is mankind's most vital asset. Your life's work has been a response to that special calling few are privileged to hear."[17]

The Rebbe was particularly moved by the letter, making mention of it during his birthday *farbrengen,* when discussing "Education Day" of that year. "This Proclamation is in honor not of me personally," he noted, with characteristic humility, "but of the movement which, for over two hundred years, has had but one goal: to effect peace and unity among Jews, among other peoples, and between Jews and others, until the whole world will serve G-d together."[18]

In a subsequent letter of gratitude to the President, the Rebbe stressed America's role as "the world's foremost superpower—not merely in the ordinary sense of this term but even more importantly, as a moral and spiritual superpower, whose real strength must ultimately derive from an unalterable commitment to the universal moral code of the Ten Commandments. Indeed, it is this commitment to the same Divine truths and values that, more than anything else, unites all Americans in the true sense of *E Pluribus Unum*."[19]

Perhaps inspired with a fresh optimism that his voice was being heard increasingly in Washington, the Rebbe decided in 1983 to revisit the idea of prayer in public schools. In attempt to bypass the complex issue of the separation of Church and State, the Rebbe proposed a "moment of silence" in public schools, which would provide children with the opportunity to make a morning prayer, while avoiding any overt mention of religion.

> The only effective way of dissuading the "inclination to evil" is by teaching it that there is a Master of the world.... We do not have to look beyond the last generation for a clear proof of these statements. The nation which was most developed in the areas of science, ethics, and philosophy perpetrated brutalities never before conceived by man. The very same people who set themselves up as a paradigm of morality committed barbarities that we find difficult to understand. How was this possible? Because their morality and ethics were based on human intellect without taking into consideration the existence of a Creator....
>
> A moment of silence should be instituted at the beginning of the school day in the public schools. During this time, the child will meditate on the existence of G-d as explained to him by his parents. Everyone should do what is possible to influence the members of the Senate and Congress and similarly, the officials in the local governments of the importance of these steps.[20]

The Rebbe also took the opportunity to re-emphasize the importance of government support for religious schools, noting that "statistics will clearly prove that the percentage of children educated in parochial schools whose behavior has swerved from the proper path is far less than that of those educated in the public schools."[21]

At a sermon later in the year, the Rebbe bemoaned that while the President was pushing to allow mention of G-d in the public arena, the legislation was being opposed by Jews.

> In the past, such an idea was opposed by government leaders. Today, the nations' leaders, including its President, are in favor

> of amending the law and allowing G-d's Name to be mentioned in school.
>
> Unfortunately... Jews, who lack the proper Jewish upbringing falsify the facts and try to prevent the passage of such a law with the claim that it is against the Constitution. Why does the Constitution bother them when it doesn't bother the President?...
>
> We are not suggesting that a prayer be said which would involve problems of what to say, and which would be enmeshed in the issue of separation between state and religion. We are merely proposing that a moment of silence be held at the beginning of the day, and a child will ask his parents or grandparents what to think about in those sixty seconds. This way the teacher or principal will not interfere, and the Establishment Clause of the Constitution will remain inviolate. Similarly, those parents who do not wish their children to think of G-d or pray in the minute of silence, can instruct their children to think of the basics of justice and righteousness.[22]

In his State of the Union Address on 25th January 1984, Reagan challenged the opposition to public prayer. "I must ask," the President said, broaching the topic directly for the first time, "if you can begin your day with a member of the clergy standing right here leading you in prayer, then why can't freedom to acknowledge G-d be enjoyed again by children in every schoolroom across this land? America was founded by people who believed that G-d was their rock of safety. He is ours. I recognize we must be cautious in claiming that G-d is on our side, but I think it's all right to keep asking if we're on His side." Reagan also promised, "I will continue to press for tuition tax credits to expand opportunities for families and to soften the double payment for those paying public school taxes and private school tuition."[23]

Writing the next day in the *Los Angeles Times,* Nick Thimmesch commented that the address had been "another success," noting that "Reagan is a champ, hands down. He was applauded forty-two times and he deserved it."

While the Rebbe rarely offered political commentary in his sermons, he had been concerned for decades about public prayer and aid to religious schools, so such words from a U.S. president, followed by a warm reception in the press, was something he could not allow his followers to overlook.

"The foundation of the President's speech," the Rebbe observed that

Sabbath "was belief and trust in G-d. Since he believes in G-d, he declares in the name of the entire country—notwithstanding what the Supreme Court might say—that we need to help those who send their children to religious schools, where they are taught about G-d."

"He himself stressed that 'G-d is with us, but we have to be with G-d,' which translated into Hebrew means, *'that they may all call upon the name of G-d, to serve Him with one consent'* (Zeph. 3:9)."

The Rebbe also noted how newspapers had picked up on the forty-two rounds of applause that Reagan's speech elicited. "For those of you who do not read the papers," the Rebbe told his Chasidic audience, "may you be blessed. You are busy with loftier things.... But this is something relevant to all Jews."[24]

Hopes for a change in the law, however, were dashed on 5th June 1985, when the Supreme Court ruled, by a vote of 6-3, that the "moment of silence" was unconstitutional. The Court's decision was viewed as a setback for President Reagan, who had campaigned for a return to school prayer, but was hailed as a "major victory" by the *American Jewish Committee, American Jewish Congress, Anti-Defamation League of B'nai B'rith,* and *B'nai B'rith International.*[25]

Despite this prohibitive setback in the campaign, the Rebbe's overall reaction to the issue is important as it provides some insight into his views on Messianism, an issue which would dominate his sermons increasingly in the coming years.

From this response, and others, we see that the Rebbe viewed Messianism as sitting at the intersection between current events and religious belief. Rather than understanding the future utopia promised by the prophets as an outright rupture of history and escape from reality, the Rebbe adopted Maimonides' view that redemption would occur *within* history and be heralded by political regimes and their constituents embracing monotheism and Torah principles.[26]

The point has two important ramifications. First, it means that Jews ought to be involved in the cultural and political landscape of their host cultures and utilize their influence to guide their societies towards monotheism and Biblical morality (as the above example shows). In this way, the redemption is not hoped for as an isolated Divine intervention, but, in whatever way possible, it is initiated within history.

Second, when a major shift occurs and a non-Jewish government radically embraces monotheistic and Torah values, it should be interpreted as a proto-Messianic act of Divine grace. While we must do all we can to influence the world's decision makers, ultimately, *"the heart of kings is in the hand of G-d"* (Prov. 21:1), and a sweeping change of sentiment among human rulers should be seen as reflecting a Divine intention to facilitate redemption in the near future.

For the Rebbe, then, Jewish Messianism was seen as a blend of both *proactive* and *responsive* elements. We ought to influence the culture as best we can toward the goal of universal morality and faith; but since only Providence can bring history to its climax, there needs to be an equal measure of trust in Divine power. When politics, especially of a global Super Power, takes a major turn in the direction of Judaism's utopian vision, it ought to validate our perception that Divine power is at work, and heighten expectation for the next overture. G-d looks to our hearts to see if we react to these gestures, and His further activity may depend on our eager response. If the hand of Providence is going to act *through* history, it is crucial that humans consciously mirror its strokes.

(Interestingly, the Maimonidean position on this issue is at odds with the view generally espoused by Chabad Chasidut, following Nachmanides, that the future era *will* be characterized by a rupture of the natural order.[27] However, in a seminal essay on the topic first published in 1985,[28] the Rebbe argued that miracles, even when they occur, do not *define* the goal of Jewish Messianism or the process by which it is brought about.[29] Our task is to perfect the world order, not to supplant it. Miraculous activity has no integral role in the redemption or the goal of history, representing a sign of additional Divine satisfaction resulting from some exemplary activity.)[30]

These two facets of the Rebbe's Messianism—the requirement to be both socially *proactive*, and emotively *responsive* to Divine Providence—correspond very roughly to two periods in his sermons. From 1983[31] to 1987 he spoke consistently about the need to vigorously disseminate Jewish values to the broader culture, following the framework of the Seven Universal Laws of Noah. From 1987 onwards his rhetoric shifted more to a "responsive" Messianism, as he marveled at the wondrous collapse of Communist Russia and the Gulf War, and encouraged his followers to "open their eyes" to discern the Divine hand in other current events. But, as we have seen, the "proactive" and the "responsive" impulses are two sides of the same coin, both envisioning the Messianic perfection of humanity as having a political axis. We must do our part, and sometimes we will observe G-d doing His, but the goal is the same, "*that they may all call upon the name of G-d, to serve Him with one consent*" (Zeph 3:9). Or, as Reagan had put it, "I recognize we must be cautious in claiming that G-d is on our side, but I think it's all right to keep asking if we're on His side."

II

What are the Seven Universal Laws of Noah and why did the Rebbe deem them to be so important?

One word which sums up the Rebbe's life and thought very well is *inclusivism.* His vision was, of course, always defined by a rigorous commitment to *halachah* and Jewish texts which he understood to convey the Divine will; but unlike many of his co-religionists who shared a similar commitment, his way, generally speaking, was not to reject or to ban. At every turn, we find that when faced with the question of whether or not to include a group of people or a set of ideas in his Judeo-centric world-view, he opted for inclusiveness, often requiring a creative re-evaluation of texts and assumptions. When the Rebbe assumed leadership of Chabad in 1951, Judaism was still exclusively preoccupied with the male, Jewish, observant worshipper. Everybody else, if they mattered at all, existed to support this elite group of the faithful. Thirty years later, the Rebbe had articulated a Jewish vision which gave special attention to women, non-observant Jews, children, the elderly and the disadvantaged. Each of these groups had been offered an elaborate theology and sense of mission which clarified why their allotted task in life was crucial to the universe and why it could not be carried out by anyone else.

With Torah wisdom, too, the Rebbe was a bold inclusivist. In other fervently Orthodox circles, study of Talmud was idealized, scripture and *midrash* were deemed secondary, and mysticism (Kabbalah/Chasidut) was either of marginal importance or totally irrelevant. Throughout his thousands of pages of sermons, the Rebbe persistently deconstructed this hierarchy, devoting much scholarly energy to *midrash,* the literal meaning of Scripture, Jewish esotericism, in addition to intricate Talmudic analyses. The various disciplines were also not treated in isolation, and much effort was made to demonstrate how one area of Torah might cross-fertilize another, with insightful parallels drawn even between the distant worlds of the literal and the esoteric.

In Jewish practice, too, the Rebbe sought to de-emphasize the traditional hierarchy of Biblical commands, Rabbinic Law and Jewish custom, arguing that Rabbinic law and even customs emanate from a sublime spiritual source.[32] And, as we have seen, even from his youth the Rebbe found a place for secular wisdom in his Torah-centered world, and was celebrated for a broad appreciation of the sciences, medicine, and the arts, as well as his efforts to diffuse conflicts between science and religion and to derive religious lessons from scientific discoveries.[33]

By the early 1980s only one piece was left to be included in this vast system—the non-Jew. How did Judaism perceive its relationship with, and obligation to, the non-Jewish world?

To answer this question, the Rebbe drew on a formulation of Maimonides, based on the Talmud,[34] that while G-d does not expect the non-Jew to observe the detailed rituals of Judaism, the Divine will is revealed to all humanity in the form of seven laws of religious and moral behavior. These principles, which Jewish tradition traces back to a revelation to the Biblical figures Adam and Noah, represent *categories* of behavior, each with their own complex set of parameters: to avoid idolatry, murder, theft, sexual immorality, and blasphemy; to practice compassion[35] and to establish courts of law.[36]

While the concept of the "Noahide Code" was well known in Rabbinic circles since the Talmud, there had never been a notable effort to disseminate it or even to clarify its practical implementation. This is despite the fact that Maimonides frames it as a religious obligation incumbent on the Jew which *"Moses our Teacher was commanded by the Almighty to compel all the inhabitants of the world to accept the commandments given to Noah's descendants."*[37] The reason for this omission, the Rebbe argued in an essay published in 1984, was that throughout history any activity that might appear as proselytizing is likely to have offended the religious sentiments of the host culture and endangered its Jewish community. In America and other religiously free countries this no longer represented a concern, he observed, and the Maimonidean injunction to influence the culture remained in full force.[38]

Jewish insularity cannot be undone overnight, and it may come as no surprise that the Rebbe's message—articulated relentlessly during this period[39]—was not only lost on the broader Jewish world, but also on many of his own followers. Various suggestions proposed by Chasidim in response to the "Noahide" campaign were either rejected by the Rebbe, ignored, or elicited a warning that "this bears a tremendous responsibility."[40] What he did clearly appreciate was recognition of the Noahide Code at the governmental level, and as early as 1982 Ronald Reagan signed a declaration that "the Lubavitcher Rebbe's work stands as a reminder that knowledge is an unworthy goal unless it is accompanied by moral and spiritual wisdom and understanding. He has provided a vivid example of the eternal validity of the Seven Noahide Laws, a moral code for all of us regardless of religious faith. May he go from strength to strength."[41]

In a letter written shortly afterwards, the Rebbe expressed his appreciation to the President, noting that by "reaffirming the eternal validity of the G-d-given Seven Noahide Laws (with all their ramifications) for people of all faiths—you have expressed most forcefully the real spirit of the American nation."[42]

After Reagan mentioned the Noahide Code a number of times in subsequent years, the Rebbe thanked him again in a 1987 letter, noting the cumulative impact: "We have reason to believe that your forceful, supportive stance to help upgrade the moral standards of human relationships on the basis of the so-called Seven Noahide Laws (with all their ramifications) as imperatives of a Supreme Being who monitors all human conduct has made a great impact on the consciousness of the contemporary troubled generation of mankind."[43]

The Rebbe, however, was interested in more than recognition from Washington; he wanted to alter the orientation of the contemporary Jew to feel a responsibility to the broader culture. This was not a campaign where he would be satisfied with a special organization devoted to the cause, or particular "outreach" activities to gentiles; he was aiming for the fullest expression of an inclusivist mentality. It was the culmination of his worldview, articulated on his seventieth birthday to the *New York Times*, "For me, Judaism... encompasses all the universe, and it encompasses every new invention, every new theory, every new piece of knowledge or thought or action."

An overstated Jewish insularity was not only theologically misplaced, a neglect of the imperative to be "a light unto the nations," it was also bad for the Jews. "This activity," the Rebbe argued in a 1987 sermon devoted to disseminating the Noahide Code, "will increase the respect that the other nations have for the Jews, when they see that Jewish people do not only care for themselves but for the world's civilization."[44]

On another occasion, he pointed to the importance of Noahide morality from the example of "righteous gentiles" who had abhorred murder and had consequently saved Jews during the Holocaust.[45] As we have seen from Harvey Swados' *yechidut*, the Rebbe understood that the Holocaust was not a unique visitation upon the Jewish people, but had arisen from a cultural-historical phenomenon of obedience to authority and a desensitization to basic belief in G-d and morality. To Swados' great surprise, the Rebbe had argued that the Holocaust could repeat itself "tomorrow morning" if the same cultural mileu which produced it was allowed to reappear. The Rebbe, who had witnessed the rise of Nazism firsthand in 1930s Berlin, was concerned that any society could deteriorate over time to potentially genocidal activity if it lost sight of the basic message of the Noahide Code. In a 1986 letter to Israel Drazin, Assistant Chief of Chaplains in the U.S. Army, he made the point dramatically: "In our day and age, it does not require much imagination to realize that, by way of example, had these Divine Commandments been observed and adhered to by all the 'Children of Noah,' namely, the nations of the world, individually and collectively, there would not have been any possibility, in the natural order of things, for such a thing as a Holocaust."[46]

It is unlikely, however, that the "benefits" of disseminating Noahide Laws for Jews—respect for the community, possible aversion of persecution, *etc.*—represented the Rebbe's overall concern. In a broader context, it was the final piece of the puzzle which completed his lifelong devotion to inclusivism: to appreciate, understand and guide every facet of existence through the lens of Torah.

An interesting question is how the Noahide campaign perceived the dominant faith of America, Christianity. Was Noahidism compatible with being a Christian, or was it being presented as an alternative?

Again, we see here a certain pragmatism in the Rebbe's positions.

While the notion of the Trinity is rejected by the absolute monotheism of Judaism, the Rebbe pointed to numerous *halachic* rulings that the Trinity is not idolatrous for a non-Jew and is an acceptable form of worship for him.[47] According to this view, it would be a positive fulfilment of the Noahide Code when Christians embrace their faith, especially if the alternative is atheism.[48]

The point comes to light in an incident recalled by David Chase (b. 1927), a major supporter of Chabad in New Jersey, after he began to don *tefilin* daily at the Rebbe's suggestion in 1981.[49] Chase spent time on his private yacht and, having started to pray daily, would regularly ask his captain, Dick Winters, what direction the boat was facing so that he could turn towards Jerusalem. After a few days, Winters was perplexed by Chase's repeated questions and asked if his employer had been learning the principles of marine navigation. "Oh no," Chase replied, explaining that he needed to know the information for religious reasons.

The following Sunday, when the yacht docked at Block Island, Winters made an unusual request to leave his post for an hour, together with his wife. "Of course," Chase replied, inquiring why Winters wished to leave his duties.

"When I discovered that you recite daily prayers," Winter explained, "you made me feel guilty that I don't follow my own faith. So I would like to leave for one hour to attend church with my wife."

"I later told the Rebbe what had happened," Chase recalled, "and he got a big 'kick' out of it."[50]

While the Rebbe seemed to appreciate Christians' re-embracing their faith, he perceived the *ideal* for the non-Jew was pure monotheism and an embrace of the Torah as the only authentic source of religion for all people. In fact he even encouraged non-Jews to embrace the non-dual, acosmism taught by Chasidic thought—the idea that "nothing exists outside of G-d" (*ein od milvado*).[51]

The Rebbe felt that Christian clergy, too, would benefit from an awareness of Noahide law. When Brigadier General Israel Drazin informed the Rebbe of five lectures on the subject that he had given to audiences of Christian chaplains,[52] the Rebbe expressed his appreciation that the talks were well received and he encouraged Drazin to continue with more lectures and to publicize them in print.[53]

An interesting development in the Rebbe's sermons during this period was a creative re-examination of universal spirituality in Chabad thought, to accommodate a greater measure of inclusiveness. In many instances, Judaism can appear to be quite "tribal," obsessed with itself and its own people, and relatively unconcerned with the rest of the world. It was Maimonides especially who brought to light elements of Judaism which Jews and non-Jews can both avail themselves of, and de-emphasized those features which are particular to Jews.[54] Among contemporary Orthodox thinkers, there are those which have embraced, to some extent, the Maimonidean/universalist strand of classical Jewish thought, and there are those who have taken a more ethnocentric, particularist position.[55]

In the evolution of Jewish thought, Chasidism, which emerged in the 18th Century, was a direct outgrowth of the Kabbalah, which had gained momentum from the 13th Century onwards. Kabbalah took the "chosen people" idea and sharpened it, arguing for an essential difference in human "hardware"—to borrow a term from computer technology. In the Kabbalistic worldview, the Jew is constructed differently from the non-Jew and blessed with a different type of soul, which makes his uniquely Jewish relationship with G-d possible.[56] Like other strands of Chasidism, Chabad embraced this position, and it did so with vigor. At the beginning of his *Tanya*, the "Bible" of Chabad Chasidic thought, Rabbi Shneur Zalman of Liadi echoes the position of the Zohar and Kabbalistic writings, that Jewish and non-Jewish souls are different. While the *Tanya* says nothing particularly new, it did succeed in taking a somewhat obscure, unknown teaching from a small, elite group of Kabbalists and popularizing it among a very wide audience, since Chasidism was—and remains today—an extremely influential movement.

Awareness of the "special" qualities unique to the Jew, are helpful in energizing outreach activities. Chabad adherents are inspired to carry out the difficult work of painstakingly seeking out Jews who have become "lost" and deeply assimilated in the host culture, in the belief that they are redeeming individuals who possess a unique, Jewish soul. The *Tanya's* position was instrumental in reversing the Orthodox marginalization of the secular Jew as "evil" or "irredeemable," opening the doors for outreach—first in Chabad, and later by others.

But how could these deeply particularistic ideas be reconciled with a more universal spirituality?

In a number of published sermons from the early 1980s, the Rebbe took giant steps towards the idea of a universal spirituality, narrowing the gap separating Jew and non-Jew in traditional Chabad thought, though taking care not to erase it completely. For example, while Chabad had always taught that only the uniquely Jewish soul provides the opportunity of an embodied spirituality,[57] the Rebbe suggested that "nevertheless, the giving of the Torah, as we know, deconstructed the binary distinction between 'upper' and 'lower' (between Divine emanation and created entities), which also affected Noahides, empowering them to be conscious of the Divine power which is embodied in them. And through a consciousness of the Divine power (the power of unity) they can also achieve a certain unity, comparable to the unity of Jews (though not precisely the same)."[58]

Here the Rebbe employs one of the most familiar ideas in Chabad Chasidut to suggest something unprecedented, and we could almost be fooled into thinking that we had been familiar with the concept all along. Every student of Chabad knows that Sinai represented a "deconstruction of the binary distinction between 'upper' and 'lower,'" (*bitul ha-gezeirah bayn Elyonim ve-tachtonim*), namely, the possibility of spirituality becoming embodied in the physical world.[59] So why not apply this to the non-Jew, and say that he or she too can enjoy an embodied spirituality? In prior Chabad thought, such an experience had been considered the exclusive domain of the Jew, but the Rebbe proposes here that a more inclusivist position is actually implied by one of Chabad's own primary teachings. And while the gap between Jew and non-Jew is merely narrowed and not completely closed, the fact that the non-Jew is seen as a vehicle for an embodied spirituality which is "comparable" to that of the Jew represents a notable shift from earlier Chabad sentiments.

In another sermon from 1983, the Rebbe argued more forcefully for a near-complete democratization of spirituality in the Messianic era, following the Maimonidean vision that "the entire world will serve G-d together."[60] In this formulation, the non-Jew's connection to G-d is not mediated by the Jew, nor is it limited to an inferior, veiled emanation;[61] rather the very essence of G-d (*Atzmut Ohr Ayn Sof*) will be disclosed to both Jews and non-Jews.[62]

III

Another facet of the Rebbe's inclusive vision which was developed during the early 1980s was a series of sermons on the importance of Jewish children and the founding of a special organization dedicated to them, *Tzivot Hashem* ("The Army of G-d"). While the Rebbe had frequently mentioned the importance of children, and as far back as the 1940s he had been personally involved in organizing children's rallies and other educational activities, it was during this time that this younger "community" gained particular attention. In 1976 the Rebbe had introduced a highly successful formula of "twelve verses and Rabbinic teachings" that could be memorized by the children, internalized as fundamental life lessons, and recited enthusiastically at gatherings.[63] Now, with the formation of *Tzivot Hashem*, the value of children's worship would be infused with greater meaning.[64]

"Children are freed entirely from all the worries of earning a living and maintaining a household, and can devote themselves entirely to Torah," the Rebbe noted in a 1980 sermon. "Someone who is free of other worries can give all of his effort and strength to Torah and *mitzvot* without reckoning with the evil impulse, but can, on the contrary, wage war against it and be victorious."[65] Rather than painting the child as a hopelessly amateur worshipper, in a sustained exegesis—delivered, on many occasions, to crowds of children—the Rebbe emphasized the purity of children and their potential for a particularly sincere, untainted form of worship.[66]

Just as he had paid attention to the images in children's publications in the 1940s, the Rebbe would review artwork on the cover of *Tzivot Hashem* publications and often point to small details which he felt might make a negative or misleading impression on the children. Dr. David Shalom Pape recalled that in January 1981, "Just before going to print, one of the senior members of the overseeing board, an elderly and respected Chasid, who hadn't seen the magazine earlier, was disturbed by the cover drawing. He argued, that it is neither proper nor acceptable to portray a picture (or drawing) of a girl on a Jewish and Chasidic magazine." Not only did the Rebbe approve the cover, but when a draft of the April issue was presented to him with just a boy on the cover, he wrote back, "There needs to be a girl as well."[67]

Interestingly, the Rebbe also felt that the exaggerated features that are often drawn in comics could be confusing for a child. "It is not advisable," he wrote to the magazine's editors in 1984, "that the drawing of human figures be intentionally unreal (overly fat, an overly enlarged nose, *etc.*), although this is the norm in comics. In my opinion, this is a seriously misplaced pedagogy, because with children, the more straightforward and normal something is, the better."[68]

Responding to one questioner who had expressed concern at the "glorification of the military" implicit in the *Tzivot Hashem* motif, the Rebbe offered some personal insight into why he had founded the organization, only after thinking "long and hard."

> As an educator, you know that children need motivation, but that is only one aspect of the problem. The most important aspect, in my opinion, in this day and age, is the lack of *Kabalat Ol* [obedience], not only of *Ol Malchut Shamayim* [obedience to G-d], but also general insubmission to authority, including the authority of parents at home and of teachers in school, and the authority of law and order in the street. There remains only the fear of punishment as a deterrent, but that fear has been reduced to a minimum because there has in recent years been what amounts to a breakdown of law enforcement, for reasons which need not be discussed here.
>
> On the other hand, American children have been brought up on the spirit of independence and freedom, and on the glorification of personal prowess and smartness. It has cultivated a sense of cockiness and self-assurance to the extent that one who is bent on mischief or anti-social activity feels that one can outsmart a cop on the beat, and even a judge on the bench; and, in any event, there is little to fear in the way of punishment.
>
> As with every health problem, physical, mental or spiritual, the cure lies not in treating the symptoms, but in attacking the cause, although the former may some times be necessary for relief in acute cases.
>
> Since, as mentioned, the root of the problem is the lack of *Kabalat Ol*, I thought long and hard about finding a way of inducing an American child to get used to the idea of subordination to a higher authority, despite all the influence to the contrary—in the school, in the street, and even at home, where parents—not wishing to be bothered by their children—have all too often abdicated their authority and left it to others to deal with truancy, juvenile delinquency, *etc.*
>
> I came to the conclusion that there was no other way than trying to effect a basic change in the child's nature, through a system of

> discipline and obedience to rules which he/she can be induced to get accustomed to. Moreover, for this method to be effective, it would be necessary that it should be freely and readily accepted without coercion.....
>
> This brings us to the point that although the ideal of peace is so prominent in the Torah, as mentioned, the fact is that G-d designed and created the world in such a way that leaves man subject to an almost constant inner strife, having to wage relentless battle with his *yetzer hara* [evil impulse]....
>
> This is the only kind of "battle" the children of *Tzivot Hashem* are called upon to wage. By the same token, the only "secret weapon" they are encouraged to use is strict Shabbat observance and other *mitzvot* which have been the secrets of Jewish strength throughout the ages.[69]

The organization proved to be extremely successful and by 1984 claimed to have 100,000 members in the U.S.A. alone.[70] "Our experience with *Tzivot Hashem*," the Rebbe reported, "wherever the idea has been implemented, in the U.S.A., Canada, *Eretz Yisrael*, and in many parts of the world—has completely convinced us of its most successful positive results, with no negative side-effects whatever."[71] In addition to the varied programs offered by *Tzivot Hashem*, from 1981 particular energies were devoted to a campaign—framed by the Rebbe as "not a new decree, but a suggestion and request"—to have a letter written in a special Torah scroll for each child, symbolically uniting Jewish children through Judaism's most sacred object. In the following three decades, over a million letters were dedicated in five Torah scrolls specially written in Israel and housed in Synagogue *Tzemach Tzedek* in Jerusalem.[72]

The Rebbe's particular appreciation of children comes to light in a few personal incidents from this period that have reached us. During the summer festival of *Shavuot* 1978, as the Rebbe was walking to the Chabad library which adjoins 770, a small child ran up to him and grabbed his hand, mistaking the Rebbe for his father. As the weather was very hot and the child was sweating, the boy took a flap of the Rebbe's *kapote* (Prince Albert) and wiped his forehead with it.

After the festival, the child's mother promptly sent a note into the office apologizing for the incident and for any "distress" caused. In reply, the Rebbe wrote, "On the contrary, it caused me great pleasure. The great warmth, innocence, sincerity and genuineness of a child is beyond measure. If only adults would show a fraction of these qualities."[73]

Another charming incident which has surfaced recently was related by Shulamith Saxon (née Brodsky), concerning a letter she wrote to the Rebbe shortly before her bat mitzvah (twelfth birthday) in 1981. "I thought," Shulamith recalled, "if I'm writing a letter to the Rebbe to ask for a blessing, it probably would be nice if I give the Rebbe a blessing also. I shouldn't just be taking, I should be giving." Not being sure of the correct protocol and feeling somewhat shy about the idea, Shulamith decided to write the message in code. Learning from her younger brother a form of encryption used by Jewish scribes where each Hebrew letter is swapped for the next letter in the alphabet, Shulamith wrote at the end of her letter, in Hebrew code: "My blessing to the Rebbe, is that children should be born to him, even though this has not been decreed for him."

On receiving the Rebbe's letter of blessing, Shulamith paid little attention to a string of eleven Hebrew characters which had been typed at the foot of the page, imagining it to be some sort of office reference system. But when her brother saw the letter, he said, "No, that's the Rebbe's answer to you in code!" Shulamith replaced each letter of the string (שהגד סכ דאקיד) with the following letter in the alphabet, to decipher the reply: *todah al ha-brachah,* "Thank you for the blessing."[74]

In public sermons, too, the Rebbe spoke of the importance of immersing in the mindset of a child.

> We find a wondrous *Midrash* particularly applicable to children. On the verse *"His banner over me was love"* (*Song* 2:4), the *Midrash* states: "Even if a child jumps on the Name of G-d (written in holy books)... G-d declares "his dancing upon Me is [received] with love." Even if children, who, in their natural playfulness before and after learning, climb and spring over holy books which contain G-d's Name, G-d considers such actions with love.
>
> This *Midrash* teaches us how important it is to lower oneself to the level of children—even to the extent where G-d Himself allows them to jump on His Name, regarding such actions with love![75]

The Rebbe's inclusivist vision during this period was also expanded to include the elderly, whom he felt had been unwisely marginalized by American culture. Besides founding an organization in his father's memory to provide Torah classes for elderly men and women, the Rebbe also devoted several sermons to the issue of retirement, which he recommended avoiding wherever possible.[76] The Rebbe was certainly a living embodiment of this message, as he continued to work an exhausting schedule into his ninth decade. When asked in 1982, by Zalmon Jaffe's wife Roselyn, how the Rebbe was faring, the Rebbetzin replied, "I really don't know, I do not see him too often."

"She gave us just two examples," Jaffe recalled. "On Friday he stayed, working at 770, with no respite, from 10:00 a.m. until nearly 8:00 p.m.—time for the Sabbath. The Rebbe was back at 770 at 9:00 p.m. for evening services, and did not return home for some considerable time. On Saturday, the Rebbe arrived at 770 at 8:30 in the morning and left after the evening service at 9:30 p.m. He had just a half hour break for lunch at 6:30 p.m."[77]

Even in his early and mid-eighties, the Rebbe can be seen on video recordings walking with a remarkably fast gait, and displaying an energy that would be impressive from somebody ten or twenty years his junior. At a *farbrengen* celebrating his eightieth birthday in 1982, the Rebbe spoke of the importance of continued work into old age. "People think that their work and mission in life is dictated by their birth-certificate," he noted, with a touch of humor, "and when they reach a certain age, it is time to retire and enjoy the fruits of their labor of previous years. Torah says differently: As long as G-d grants a person life, he cannot do less than before."

Reflecting on the inevitable weakness which comes with aging, he pointed to the power of faith in surmounting even that obstacle. "People ask, a person at sixty feels his powers are less than at fifty, certainly than at thirty. How can he possibly do more? The answer to this is: *When one is connected Above, one does not fall below.* When one connects oneself to the Above, to that which is above the limit of time and space, then, even when he is within time and space (in this world), G-d gives him the opportunity to rise ever higher."[78]

IV

While Chabad Chasidim had always shared the festival of Chanukah with their Jewish brethren, activities were intensified in 1974 when the Rebbe launched a campaign to ensure that as many Jews as possible observed the ritual of kindling a Chanukah Menorah (Candelabra).[79] The response from Chasidim was strong, and just two years later, reports were reaching the media that Chabad had distributed an estimated 900,000 Chanukah Menorahs to Jews on five continents for the holiday that year. Employing its "trademark" approach of applying New-World methods to Old-World values, in New York, twenty vans, each equipped with a 10-foot high Menorah, cruised through business and residential districts, bringing awareness of the festival to the local Jewish population in a striking manner.[80]

In what would become the most influential—and controversial—element of the Chanukah campaign, Chabad began to erect large Menorahs in public places, first at the foot of the Liberty Bell in Philadelphia in 1974, and the following year at Union Square, San Francisco. By 1976 the modest wooden Menorah in Philadelphia had grown to a 22 1/2-foot high and 17 1/2-foot wide structure which was slated as "the world's largest Menorah," kindled in the presence of Mayor Frank Rizzo, Senator Richard Stone, actor Herschel Bernardi and other celebrities.[81] By 1978, public Menorahs graced two major sites in Manhattan, all New York City bridges and tunnel entrances, as well as ten other cities in North America.[82]

Earlier that year, the Rebbe received a letter from leading Reform Rabbi, Joseph Glaser (1925-1994), head of the *Central Conference of American Rabbis,* who objected to the Menorah campaign as a "violation of the Constitutional principle of separation of Church and State." Glaser asked if he could meet with the Rebbe personally "to discuss the matter further, and also to indulge in a desire I have had for a long time to know you personally."[83] Through his secretariat, the Rebbe invited Glaser to pen his views in a letter and send them to 770 for consideration and response.

In a letter written on 31st May 1978, Glaser argued that public displays of Jewish observance threatened "considerable success in recent decades in preventing Christmas displays, creches especially, on public property, and in preventing religious assemblies and prayer-periods in public schools" thereby sparing Jews from supporting "Christianity through our taxes or to be exposed, and have our children exposed, to government-sanctioned proselytizing."[84]

In reply, the Rebbe shared his view in a letter dated 8th June:

> Had I received your letter years ago, when this practice started, I would have had a more difficult task of defending it, for the simple reason that the expected positive results were then a matter of conjecture. But now, after the practice and the results have been observed for a number of years, my task is an easy one, since the general acclaim and beneficial results have far exceeded our expectations. The fact is that countless Jews in all parts of the country have been impressed and inspired by the spirit of Chanukah which had been brought to them, to many for the first time....
>
> This year, too, now that some six months have elapsed since Chanukah and reports have come in from various places where Chanukah Lamps were kindled publicly, the results have been most gratifying in terms of spreading the light of the Torah and *mitzvot*, and reaching out to Jews who could not otherwise have been reached, either because some of them are unaffiliated with any synagogue, or, though loosely affiliated, always thought that religious practices belong within the confines of a synagogue and do not relate to the personal everyday life of the individual. It was precisely through kindling the Chanukah Lamp in public places, during "ordinary" weekdays, with dignity and pride, that it was brought home to them that true Judaism is practiced daily, and that no Jew should feel abashed about it.
>
> With regard to the "Constitutional" question, I can most assuredly allay your apprehensions on this score. I am fully certain that none of all those who participated in, or witnessed, the kindling of a Chanukah Lamp in a public place (and in all cases permission was *readily* granted by the authorities) felt that his or her loyalty to the Constitution of the U.S.A. had been weakened or compromised thereby. Indeed, many expressed surprise that this practice had not been inaugurated many years earlier, seeing that the U.S. Congress opens with a religious invocation by a representative of "one of the major religions" in this country; and, surely, the U.S. Congress, comprising each and every State of the Union, is *the* place where the Constitu-

> tion of the U.S.A. should be most rigidly upheld. There is surely no need to belabor this point.[85]

Glaser expressed his appreciation for the Rebbe's involved response, but was not swayed by his argument. In a letter dated 14th August, he insisted that "to mingle religion and state is to pervert American democracy and to endanger American religion", and urged the Rebbe "to research the matter further and to reconsider your policy."[86]

The Menorah campaign, however, only intensified. By far its most important development was on 17th December 1979, when President Jimmy Carter participated in a public Chanukah Menorah lighting at Lafayette Square, ending a one hundred-day self-imposed seclusion over the Iran hostage crisis. In a brief comment following the ceremony, the President said: "This miracle showed that G-d meets our needs. If we depend on Him, He will meet our needs.... The first candle that I lit, the *shammes* candle, has given its light now in this glass cage to five other candles. It has not itself been diminished. It shows that when we give life and love to others, the life and love in our own hearts is not diminished. As a matter of fact it grows the more we share it."[87]

Carter subsequently received a warm letter of thanks from the Rebbe, expressing "genuine gratification at your personal participation in the ceremony of lighting the Chanukah Candelabra in front of the White House. The symbol of light is universal for all people on earth, Jews and non Jews. The intrinsic power of light, in that even a small light dispels a lot of darkness, is surely a source of inspiration to all men of good will with its eternal message of the eventual triumph of all that is good and bright in human life."[88]

The president's participation in the public Menorah lighting strongly bolstered Chabad's claim that the activity was not unconstitutional, an argument which the Rebbe employed later in 1981, when a giant Menorah outside the District Courthouse in Bergen, New Jersey provoked the ire of the local Jewish community.

> The fact is that there are numerous precedents over the years in various parts of the U.S.A. To mention a most conspicuous one is the public lighting of a Chanukah Menorah on public property in the Nation's capital. It was in 1979 that a huge Menorah was installed

> in Lafayette Park, across the street from the White House, with President Carter personally participating in the ceremony. Like all matters relating to the President of the United States, this event, too, received wide national coverage. Since then, the Menorah in Washington has become an annual event.
>
> Let me emphasize that the Menorah in the nation's capital was introduced without anyone making an issue of it, as a self-evident event in the public interest. That it was also Constitutional, legal and proper goes without saying, since the President of the United States personally participated in it.[89]

In the following years, the presence of public Menorahs erected by Chabad grew considerably, and during Chanukah of 1985, the Rebbe asked his secretariat to ask each *shliach* to send him pictures of their Menorah lighting and the accompanying celebrations. In the broadcast room which was used to transmit the Rebbe's *farbrengens* across the world, there were fifteen active phone lines which were all put to use until the Rebbe's request had reached every Chabad representative around the world. These images of the Menorahs were later published by Kehot in a remarkable album *Let There Be Light,* in 1986,[90] and in a sequel *...And There Was Light,* the following year.[91]

The matter, however, continued to be contentious, and in 1989, a dispute over the Chabad Public Menorah erected in Pittsburgh ended up in the Supreme Court. The landmark decision *County of Allegheny v. American Civil Liberties Union* ruled that the Menorah did not constitute a state endorsement of any religion given its "particular physical setting" next to a Christmas tree. While pleased with the result, the Rebbe instructed his secretariat not to allow Chabad to be drawn into a media debate about the decision, and on 3rd July, authorized a brief press release, expressing "our fervent hope that the Jewish community will now come together to fully utilize the religious freedom guaranteed and protected by this great country."[92]

As time has passed, many non-Orthodox clergy have tempered their opposition to the activity, and Chabad Public Menorahs have become a prominent fixture in the American celebration of Chanukah. For example, Mark Diamond, executive vice president of the Board of Rabbis of Southern California, related in 2006 that while he had initially maintained strong opposition to public Menorah displays, he since witnessed how beautiful many of these ceremonies can be.[93]

Chabad had something significant to say not only about the position of the Menorah, but also about its shape. In a 1982 sermon the Rebbe argued that the familiar figure of a Menorah with curved branches had been copied from the Arch of Titus in Rome and was at odds with the received tradition from the Jewish sages, such as *Rashi*[94] and Maimonides,[95] that the branches were straight and diagonal. Besides being inaccurate, it was also lamentable, the Rebbe said, to perpetuate Titus' image which had been created to celebrate a victory over the Jewish people by their enemies.[96]

Another interesting initiative from the Rebbe during this period, which never reached its desired momentum, was an effort to establish meditation centers. By the 1970s, the number of Jews participating in cults in the U.S.A. stemming from the Far East was as great as twenty to fifty percent, which is strikingly high when one considers that Jews constitute only two to three percent of the American population. Especially popular was Transcendental Meditation (T.M.), many of the mantras and rituals of which were associated with Hindu gods.

From the early 1960s, the Rebbe had shown interest in developing clinically effective forms of meditation that would be compatible with the Jewish religion. Around 1962 the Rebbe had sent a proposal to Rabbi Dr. Abraham Twerski (b. 1930), a Chasidic psychiatrist who later became a popular author, to develop a system of meditation. "He sent me a paper on meditation in English," Twerski recalled, "in which he crossed out parts that he thought were inappropriate and had written his own comments in the margins, and asked me to develop it. The parts which were crossed out as inappropriate had to do with secular and Oriental forms of meditation. His comments had to do with what to substitute for the omissions." Twerski kept pushing off the idea until, when he finally found time to work on it, he could no longer find the paper.[97]

In January of 1978, with the rise of Jews turning to cults, the Rebbe penned a confidential memorandum highlighting the current problem, and a proposed solution, to be shared with select "Rabbis, doctors, and laymen who are in a position to advance the cause." While the approach of Rabbinic authorities had been simply to ban T.M., the Rebbe, always the inclusivist, understood both the therapeutic benefits of meditation and the ineffectiveness of banning something without offering an acceptable alternative.

The memo stated:

> It is well known that certain oriental movements, such as Transcendental Meditation (T.M.), Yoga, Guru, and the like, have attracted many Jewish followers, particularly among the young generation.
>
> Inasmuch as these movements involve certain rites and rituals, they have been rightly regarded by Rabbinic authorities as cults bordering on, and in some respects actual *Avodah Zarah* (idolatry)....
>
> Moreover, the United States Federal Court also ruled recently that such movements, by virtue of embracing such rites and rituals, must be classified as cultic and religious movements. (Of. *Malnak V. Maharishi Mahesh Yogi, U.S.D.C. of N.J.* 76-341, esp. pp. 36-50, 78)
>
> On the other hand, certain aspects of the said movements, which are entirely irrelevant to religious worship or practices, have a therapeutic value, particularly in the area of relieving mental stress.
>
> It follows that if these therapeutic methods—insofar as they are utterly devoid of any ritual implications—would be adopted by doctors specializing in the field of mental illness, it would have a two-pronged salutary effect: Firstly, in the view of the fact that these methods are therapeutically effective, while there are, regretfully, many who could benefit from such treatment, this is a matter of healing of the highest order, since it has to do with mental illness. It would, therefore, be very wrong to deny such treatment to those who need it, when it could be given by a practicing doctor.
>
> Secondly, and this too is no less important, since there are many Jewish sufferers who continue to avail themselves of these methods through the said cults despite the Rabbinic prohibition, it can be assumed with certainty that many of them, if not all, who are drawn to these cults by the promise of mental relief would prefer to receive the same treatment from the medical profession—if they had a choice of getting it the kosher way. It would thus be possible to save many Jews from getting involved with the said cults.
>
> It is also known, though not widely, that there are individual doctors who practice the same or similar methods as T.M. and the like. However, it seems that these methods occupy a secondary or subordinate role in their procedures. More importantly, there is almost a complete lack of publicity regarding the application of these methods by doctors, and since the main practice of these doctors is linked with the conventional neurological and psychiatric approach, it is generally assumed that whatever success they achieve is not con-

> nected with results obtained from methods relating to T.M. and the like; results which the cults acclaim with such fanfare.
>
> In light of the above, it is suggested and strongly urged that:
>
> Appropriate action be undertaken to enlist the cooperation of a group of doctors specializing in neurology and psychiatry who would research the said methods with a view to perfecting them and adopting them in their practice on a wider scale.
>
> All due publicity be given about the availability of such methods from practicing doctors.
>
> This should be done most expeditiously, without waiting for this vital information to be disseminated through medical journals, where research and findings usually take a long time before they come to the attention of practicing physicians. This would all the sooner counteract the untold harm done to so many Jews who are attracted daily to the said cults, as mentioned in the opening paragraph.[98]

Dr. Yehuda Landes, a psychologist practicing in Palo Alto, California, was one of the recipients of the memorandum, and he responded to the Rebbe on 22nd March with a proposal to set up a "kosher" meditation center. A week later, Landes received a reply from the Rebbe, thanking him for his "comprehensive response" which was read "with understandable interest." After noting that he did not wish to micromanage the implementation so long as the goals detailed in the memorandum were met, the Rebbe did offer some comments about Landes' proposed idea.

> The suggestion that an institute employing the said healing techniques might be linked with a strictly Orthodox, even Lubavitch, orientation should be examined in light of its being a possible, or even likely, deterrent for many candidates who might hesitate to turn to such an institute for fear that it may impose upon them religious demands and commitments which they are not yet prepared to accept.
>
> The above is not to say that the idea should be rejected out of hand, since there may be individuals who would not be deterred by it. But I believe that if the project is to attract a wider circle of candidates for therapy, it would have a wider acceptance if it is not overtly tied in with such an orientation, or discipline; at any rate, not in the initial stage.

> Needless to say, the emphasis is on the overt orientation of the projected institute, which should have no religious or other preconditions for anyone seeking its services. But the institute itself should, of course, be run in strict keeping with the Torah, with a kosher, indeed glatt kosher, kitchen, strict Shabbat observance, with *mezuzot* on all doors—just as there are glatt kosher hotels and institutions.

In the memo, the Rebbe had proposed that the meditation services be offered by medical professionals. Landes was concerned that spiritual seekers and members of the general public might be uncomfortable with a formal, clinical setting, and suggested a less formal setup. The Rebbe conceded to the point.

> With regard to the basic point you make in your letter, namely, that most people for whom our plan is envisaged consider themselves "normal" and would not be interested in a program that offers professional (medical) services, but would prefer a more simplistic setup for relaxation, etc.—this should certainly be taken into account, since the ultimate goals of our plan would not be affected. And, if as you suggest, this would be the more practical setup for attracting more people and achieving our two objectives—healing and elimination of *Avoda Zara*—then by all means, this method should be given due consideration.

With regard to the proposed therapies, the Rebbe raised only one objection, regarding the use of hypnosis.

> I would like to make a further point, though entirely not in my domain, namely, in reference to hypnosis as one of the techniques used in psychotherapy, as mentioned in your letter.
>
> I have always been wary of any method that deprives a person of the free exercise of his will, and which puts him in the power of another person, even temporarily—except, of course, in case of *pikuach nefesh* [saving life]. Certainly I would not favor the use of such a method on a wider scale, least of all to encourage psychologists and psychiatrists enrolled in our program to use it.

In a final note, the Rebbe offered to provide seed money, conveying some measure of his enthusiasm for the project's swift execution.[99]

On 9th April, Landes sent the Rebbe a description of the proposed treatments to be offered at the center, which would include breathing exercises, bodily postures, correct nutrition, soul music, social gatherings in the spirit of a *farbrengen,* relaxation in a hot *mikvah,* and contemplative meditation of Chasidic ideas.[100]

At the time Rabbi Aryeh Kaplan (1934-1983) was exploring meditative techniques from Kabbalistic and Chasidic sources with a group of Jewish psychiatrists,[101] but the Rebbe directed Landes not to utilize Kaplan's approach and to avoid mysticism altogether. Obviously, this was not because the Rebbe did not value Jewish mysticism, but due to practical concerns that it would limit the target audience and perhaps send a message that the meditation program would not offer concrete benefits.

> I do not think it advisable to use the term "mystic" for the planned healing center, since the goal is to attract the greatest number of Jews and save them from *Avoda Zara,* and the said term might discourage some. Moreover, generally mysticism connotes something that lies beyond the pale of human comprehension, while the therapeutic benefits of the techniques are quite understandable rationally. Besides, to emphasize the mystical aspect would leave the door open also, *lehavdil,* to non-Jewish cults.
>
> For the same reason it is advisable to be circumspect in regard to the description of the techniques to be used in the healing center. For example, you mention the use of *mikva'ot.* While it is not in my domain to assess the therapeutic effect of relaxation in a hot *mikvah,* I fear that to include a *mikvah* "officially" in the regimen might be suspected—by some people, at least—that it is a gimmick to involve them in *mitzvot.* I think that veiling it in some such term as "immersion"—hot bath and the like—would entirely allay such suspicion.

While noting the general value of a "well planned and systematic approach," considering the urgency of the situation, the Rebbe encouraged Landes to put the plans into action as soon as possible. The Rebbe reiterated his offer to provide seed money, requesting a tentative budget, at the same time expressing his hope that "before long it will not only be self-supporting, but also profitable, considering the popularity of the techniques involved."[102]

In a subsequent letter, the following year, the Rebbe stressed more emphatically that he did not advise a meditative approach based on Jewish mysticism.

> The methods of Rabbi Kaplan and Rabbi Polit and their aim are not at all the aim and purpose I had in mind, of which I spoke with you. The intent is not that you should teach Kabbalah or Chasidut or Torah in general, but only and exclusively teach meditation and mental concentration and the like such as are kosher and permissible according to the *Shulchan Aruch* [Code of Jewish Law]—it is possible to attain peace of mind, *etc.* Especially to attain peace of mind by those in whom this is acutely lacking, due to anxiety in business, *Shalom Bayit* [marital issues], health, and similar stresses. Therefore, you should not teach Kabbalah, mysteries of the Torah, Zohar and similar subjects in your sessions (or workshops). In other words, your function is that of physicians (not Torah teachers) and an essential purpose is preventive therapy[103].

Dr. Landes recruited Dr. Chaim B. Rosen, an anthropologist of religion, and together they led workshops in Palo Alto, Los Angeles, Miami Beach, and New York from 1979 to 1982. Rosen's techniques included: attentive breathing, shaking, self-massage, and individualized dance, all geared toward assisting people to relax and center themselves, prior to engaging in the actual meditations. He also employed visualization of Hebrew letters, candles, "partner sharing," and "spontaneous blessings."[104]

The fact that these efforts eventually lost momentum is especially surprising in light of the fact that the Rebbe not only encouraged the matter personally, but even devoted a public sermon to the issue in 1979. "Those who have implemented kosher meditation therapies have been successful," the Rebbe noted to the crowd at 770, presumably referring to Landes' efforts. Regarding Kaplan's approach, he commented more obliquely, "Meditation on Kabbalah and Torah's inner teachings is certainly worthy and commendable. But here we are talking about fellow Jews who have stumbled into a form of idolatry, so first and foremost, they must be rescued from that predicament." In general, the sermon praised the therapeutic value of meditation, noting that the Patriarchs chose a solitary profession as shepherds so as to follow meditative spiritual life and that in modern society, mental health and peace of mind can be attained by taking oneself out of the noise of urban living through meditation.[105]

Another campaign from this period which *did* meet with an especially enthusiastic response from Chasidim all over the world was a suggestion in 1978 that Rabbi Shneur Zalman's *Tanya,* the primary text of Chabad Chasidut, be printed "in every place that has a Jewish population"[106]—the rationale being, "When a Jew sees that it is an edition that has been printed in his city, in his town, he will be more enthusiastic about studying it."[107] In the subsequent two decades the *Tanya* was printed a staggering five thousand times in different locations, with each new edition containing a list of all the versions printed to date. The Rebbe showed much continued enthusiasm for the idea, and at the conclusion of his eightieth birthday *farbrengen,* he personally distributed a commemorative version of the *Tanya* containing the cover pages of all editions printed up to that point. The gathered crowd of men, women and children lined up for hours to received a *Tanya,* dollar for charity and blessing from the Rebbe, who did not complete his night's "work" until 6:10 a.m. "The point of this," the Rebbe explained before distributing the books, "is that you study from them until they fall apart, and then we will have to print more."[108]

IV

As the Rebbe's reputation and following grew, especially in the last part of his life, the Orthodox world became increasingly polarized in their attitude to Chabad. Many Rabbinic leaders could only marvel at the Rebbe's influence in inspiring *ba'alei teshuvah,* and at his remarkable *Likutei Sichot,* which received wide dissemination from the 1970s onwards. Other right-wing leaders, on the other hand, were angered by his independence and felt that some of his creative initiatives were not in the spirit of Orthodox conservatism.

Rabbi Moshe Feinstein, one of the preeminent *poskim* (halachic decisors) of the late 20th Century, showed increasing admiration for the Rebbe, especially after their meeting in 1974. When the Rebbe suffered a heart attack in 1977, Rabbi Feinstein penned a letter to his Rabbinic colleagues asking them to make a public appeal for congregants to involve themselves in the *mitzvah* campaigns of Chabad, such as *tefilin, mezuzah* and *Shabbat* candles, arguing that "since it is into this that the *tzadik* and genius of Lubavitch *shlita* puts his entire soul... certainly every activity in these campaigns will strengthen his health."[109]

In honor of the Rebbe's eightieth birthday, Rabbi Feinstein penned a glowing letter, stating that "throughout the years I have known the Rebbe *shlita,* our relationship has been an extremely warm one. I have had a number of opportunities to indulge in conversation with him in intricate matters, both in Jewish law and mysticism, and I always considered him to be at the peak of brilliance and genius."[110]

Even in his personal worship, Rabbi Feinstein was open to influence from the Rebbe. In a 1976 sermon, the Rebbe suggested that Jews in general, and Rabbis in particular, fulfill the pietistic practice of donning a second pair of *tefilin* each day (Rabbenu Tam's *tefilin*).[111] Four years later, a Chabad Chasid from Israel named Tzvi Hirsh Spritzer, who had in the past checked the *mezuzot* in Rabbi Moshe Feinstein's home, paid a visit to Rabbi Feinstein and mentioned the Rebbe's suggestion about *tefilin.* Rabbi Feinstein wrote to the Rebbe explaining that in the past he had observed the precept, but in America he had not found a sufficiently adept scribe to prepare the Rabbenu Tam's *tefilin,* and that since they were not obligatory in Jewish law, he had discontinued the practice. "Now that I have been informed in your name," Rabbi Feinstein wrote, "that you have an expert scribe who you are willing to send to me so that I can instruct him to write for me the Rabbenu Tam *tefilin* passages as I wish, this is a tremendous thing. I shall be able to fulfil the *mitzvah* of donning the *tefilin* of Rabbenu Tam as I did in the past."[112]

As usual, the Rebbe wasted no time. Rabbi Feinstein's son-in-law, Rabbi Dr. Moshe Tendler recalled that when arriving at the Feinstein home at 6 a.m., "much to my surprise, I saw a Jew with a beard sleeping in the hallway right next to the door. I woke him and asked him who he was and what was he doing here so early in the morning? He answered that he was a *sofer* (scribe) from Lubavitch in Crown Heights, and the Lubavitcher Rebbe had ordered him to visit Rabbi Moshe Feinstein that morning to discuss with him his requirements and requests for the best possible *tefilin.* Since he didn't know what time my father-in-law began his day, he was waiting outside the door until someone opened it."[113]

Numerous other Rabbinic figures of note enjoyed a warm relationship with the Rebbe, and during this period we have transcripts of his discussions at *yechidut* with the Gerer Rebbe in 1978; the Belzer Rebbe in 1981; the Skulye Rebbe in 1981; Rabbi Pinchas Menachem Alter of Ger in 1979, 1982, 1983, and 1984; Rabbi Menashe Klein in 1983; the Nadvorner Rebbe in 1983; the Alexander Rebbe in 1983; the Sadigurer Rebbe in 1980 and 1983; Chief Rabbis of Israel, Rabbi Avraham Shapira and Rabbi Mordechai Eliyahu in 1984 and 1986; the Oksover Rebbe (of Be'er Sheva) in 1984; Rabbi Yitzchak Yedidya Frenkel in 1984 and Chief Rabbi of France, Rabbi Shmuel Sirot in 1985.

In 1980 Rabbi Joseph Ber Soloveitchik attended a *farbrengen* at 770, where he was warmly welcomed by the Rebbe and remained engrossed by the sermons for several hours, despite his initial intention to leave after a short period.

Other Torah scholars showed their respect for the Rebbe and Chabad by participating at celebrations of the annual *Siyumei Ha-Rambam* (Celebration of Completion of Study of Works of Maimonides) around the globe. Daily *Rambam* study, so as to complete the entire Oral Law in one year, was a highly successful initiative from the Rebbe dating back to 1984, and to strengthen the campaign he suggested that high-profile *Siyumim* be held all over the world. A scholarly journal was also produced to celebrate the *Siyum,* and the first edition included essays from Rabbis Moshe Feinstein, Ya'akov Kamenetzky, Aharon Soloveitchik, Eliyahu Fisher, Efraim Greenblatt, Zalman Nechemia Goldberg, Menashe Klein and Pinchas Hirshprung.[114]

The late 1970s and 1980s was also a period when the Rebbe came under sharp public disapproval from an important voice in the ultra-Orthodox community in Israel, Rabbi Elazar Menachem Man Shach (1898–2001), a Rosh Yeshivah of Ponivezh in Bnei Brak. While the Rebbe was no stranger to criticism, the vitriol emanating from Rabbi Shach was particularly acrimonious and personally offensive, which succeeded in further polarizing an ultra-Orthodox community already divided about the activities of Chabad.[115] While the Rebbe rarely responded to these attacks, he did once comment that since *tefilin* have the effect of refining the mind, he doubted whether Rabbi Shach's *tefilin* were kosher![116]

Even though *yechidut* had all but ceased during this period, there were still fateful encounters, and visitors would sometimes catch a moment to converse with the Rebbe at a *farbrengen* between sermons. A particularly significant visit took place in 1984, on the festival of

Simchat Torah, when 770 welcomed the new Israeli Ambassador to the U.N., a young Benjamin Netanyahu.

Netanyahu had received a visit earlier in the week at his office from a "young man who says he knows you." Allowing his guest in, Natanyahu was surprised to see a bearded Chabad Chasid whom he did not recognize. "It's Shmaya," the Chasid announced enthusiastically. "Don't you remember me? I've become a Lubavitcher." It was only then that Netanyahu realized that Shmaya was one of his former soldiers from the *Shomer Hatzair.*

"The Rebbe wants to see you," Shmaya announced. "I'll pick you up tomorrow at midnight."

As they navigated the sea of Chasidim in the main synagogue at 770, Shmaya directed Netanyahu to stand close to the Rebbe's dais. "Suddenly a door opens and shuts," Netanyahu recalled. "And you can't see anyone—because the Rebbe was of enormous stature, but not of great height. You saw the 'sea' parting, like the Red Sea, there's movement. The Rebbe came up and went to the *Sefer Torah* and he started to read with his back to the crowd."

"Now!" Shmaya shouted. "Go to the Rebbe now."

Netanyahu marveled that it was the soldier who now was giving the commander orders. "When in Lubavitch, you do as the Lubavitchers," he thought to himself, and walked up to the dais. The Rebbe turned around.

"I came to see you," Netanyahu said.

"Just to see? Not to talk?" the Rebbe asked.

Switching to Hebrew, the Rebbe engaged Netanyahu in an extended dialogue lasting some forty minutes, as the crowd of 4,000 assembled Chasidim grew gradually more impatient.

"The Rebbe said many things," Netanyahu later recalled, "but he said one *big* thing: You will go into a House of Lies. Remember that in a hall of total darkness, if you light one small candle, its precious light will be seen from afar, by everyone. Your *shlichut* (task) is to light a candle for truth and for the Jewish people."[117]

The parable resonated with Netanyahu deeply as some twenty-five years later he shared it, now as Prime Minister of Israel, in a public address at the U.N. "Here, majorities can decide that the sun rises in the West," he jibed to the General Assembly in 2009, bemoaning some of the anti-Israel resolutions that had been passed in the chamber. "I don't want any of you to be offended," Netanyahu apologized in advance, "because I know from personal experience of serving here that there are many honorable men and women, many capable and decent people serving their nations here. But here is what the Rebbe said to me..." Then, in a moment of audacious personal disclosure, he recounted the Rebbe's parable, referring to the place where he was standing as, "the house of many lies."[118]

Netanyahu, who grew up in a secular home, also recalled being moved by the atmosphere in 770 that night of *Simchat Torah,* as he watched the Rebbe dance with his brother-in-law, Rashag, both in their eighties by that time. "Something happened that I will never forget to the end of my life. The Rebbe and his brother-in-law... took a *Sefer Torah,* a Torah scroll, and they went to the center of the hall, surrounded by all the Chasidim. There was a light shining from the ceiling that bathed them in a pool of light, and I see these two old bearded Jews dancing in a circle of light with a Torah. I felt the strength of generations, the power of our traditions, our faith and our people."[119]

V

After enjoying a remarkable recovery after his 1977 heart attack, the Rebbe was able to resume a very full work schedule into his late eighties. "This is something that one could not remotely predict as a doctor," cardiologist Ira Weiss reflected, "that you could possibly save someone and bring them into functionality of that nature for that length of time at that point in life. That was unusual."

The Rebbetzin asked Weiss if he would encourage the Rebbe to take a vacation, "Maybe you can tell him, Doctor, that it would be good for him. Maybe you can propose a little travel, that we should go away for a little, away from the community, where he can recover a little bit more." But the Rebbe, with a characteristic devotion that inspired so many of his followers to work without rest, politely declined.

Years later, Weiss reflected that the Rebbe's 1977 heart attack might have been a blessing in disguise. "I think that had he not had restraints put on him from the heart attack, he would have submitted himself to a schedule that would've harmed him, especially as he would get older.

So this heart attack, as badly timed as it was in his career, also shielded him from being overwhelmed."

It was the Rebbetzin, though, who began to suffer increasing ill health as she entered her eighties, and a medical intervention made by Dr. Weiss in 1981 probably saved her life. "I feel that saving the Rebbetzin's life, as we really did in 1981 (I had diagnosed her several years earlier with an aortic valve problem), gave her those additional seven years. It would have taken away a lot from the Rebbe's effectiveness as a Rebbe I think, had that intervention not been made on her health. That's how important she was to him."[120]

In 1981 the Rebbetzin broke her foot, considerably limiting her mobility. A chair-lift was installed in the staircase at her home, but on seeing the new contraption she was initially fearful of riding in it. Noting her apprehension, the Rebbe promptly sat himself in the chair-lift and rode up and down the stairs to demonstrate its safety.[121]

The Rebbetzin, uncomfortable sharing distressing news about her health with the Rebbe, often pleaded with her confidants not to divulge problems to him. On one occasion, for example, when the Rebbetzin's eye doctor posed a dilemma about the best method of treatment, Rabbi Zalman Gurary (who assisted the Rebbetzin with doctors' appointments), suggested that the question be posed to the Rebbe.

"I don't want to bother him," the Rebbetzin responded.

Gurary was incredulous. "The entire world is turning to the Rebbe with their medical dilemmas," he said, "why should you, of all people, not benefit from his advice?"

"Saving the Rebbe from distress," she explained gracefully, "is more important to me than his opinion about my eye treatment."[122]

In the summer of 1983, the Rebbetzin fell on the terrace outside her house, breaking her leg, and was rushed to the *Hospital of Joint Diseases* in Manhattan. Esther Sternberg, who acted as an assistant, recalled how before the Rebbe's visit to the hospital each evening, the Rebbetzin would ask her nurse to make her appear as presentable and pain-free as possible. The nurse later expressed her surprise to Sternberg. "Female patients usually want their husbands to see how poorly they are, and to pity them," she observed, "but this woman goes to great lengths to ensure that her husband doesn't see her in pain."

A broken leg at the age of eighty-two is no small matter, and the Rebbe contemplated how his wife's recovery might be aided by boosting her spirits. "Try to find a refined lady of similar age who has suffered from the same complaint and recovered," the Rebbe told Zalman Gurary, "and bring the lady to my house." Understanding that state of mind is an important element of recovery, this simple suggestion is likely to have brought untold benefits.[123]

With similar insight, the Rebbe on one occasion advised his own doctor, Ira Weiss, how to help Weiss's father, who had suffered a debilitating stroke. "What does he like? What are the things that make him have fun?" the Rebbe asked Weiss.

Apologizing if he was breaking into inappropriate ground, Weiss told the Rebbe that his father "loved playing cards with his friends in the poolroom and hearing about the horseraces."

The Rebbe said, "Well, why don't you take him back to the poolroom and maybe on a Sunday you could bring him there to see his old friends and at least watch the cards being played and hear about the horseraces."

That was not the answer Weiss had been expecting. "I did it with his blessings and it was very successful," he later reflected. "The Rebbe really considered every case individually. He asked a brilliant question: What was his fun?[124]

From 1983 onwards, the Rebbetzin required full-time assistance at home, but the Rebbe certainly did not share any of his personal problems with the public, and "business" continued as usual at 770. The only notable occasion that an internal matter of the Schneerson household did receive public attention was a high-profile court case over the ownership of the Lubavitch library, which lasted from 1985 to 1989.[125]

As we have seen, the Rebbe's leadership of Chabad was originally resisted in 1950 by Rebbetzin Moussia's sister Chana, her husband Rashag, and mother Nechama Dina; but after the Rebbe accepted the leadership in 1951 and Rashag subsequently re-aligned his loyalties as a devoted Chasid, it appeared that the matter had reached closure.

But it had not. One public outburst in 1953, hinted at an unresolved tension. At a *farbrengen,* Rashag, who was by that time already coming to terms with the new leadership, turned to the Rebbe and said, "I would like the Rebbe to treat me the same way that our father-in-law treated me."

Rabbi Zalman Gurary, who was aware of the behind-the-scenes activity at 770, shouted out to Rashag, "Shmerel, give over the books!"

Zalman was referring to a disagreement that had erupted privately over the ownership of Rayatz's huge library of sacred books.[126] Rashag's family had proposed that the valuable library be divided equally among Rayatz's beneficiaries, but the Rebbe had rejected the idea, understanding that the library was a legacy for the community and not mere personal property. With the matter unresolved, the keys to the library had remained in the hands of Chana and Rayatz's librarian Chaim Lieberman, but direct access had been withheld from the Rebbe.[127]

Rashag, who was obviously angered by Zalman's outburst, repeated his request to the Rebbe, "I would like the Rebbe to treat me the same way that our father-in-law treated me."

With typical tenacity, Zalman shouted out again: "Shmerel, give over the books!" After the exchange repeated itself a third time, the Rebbe, who had offered no response to either party, opened his prayer book, recited a short grace, and departed.[128]

Perhaps the only other sign of an ongoing tension in the Schneerson family was the fact that, unlike previous Chabad Rebbes, the Seventh Rebbe never donned the ceremonious garb of a *spodik* (fur hat) on Sabbath and festivals. The circulating rumor was that the Rebbe had requested Rayatz's *spodik* after his passing, but upon encountering some resistance from his mother-in-law, Nechama Dina, he simply dropped the issue.

The issue of the library, however, remained unresolved. The Rebbe remained on good terms with Chaim Lieberman, and they would spend hours in discussion together; but while Lieberman would bring whatever books the Rebbe wanted for study, he never handed over the key. An older bachelor, Lieberman had no immediate family and would often dine with Rashag and Chana, with whom he became extremely close. At one point, he even resided in Rayatz's vacant apartment.

As the years passed, the Rebbe began to amass his own substantial library, largely from authors who sent their books to 770 for review or as donations to Chabad. This collection, known as the library of *Merkos L'Inyanei Chinuch,* swelled to tens of thousands of volumes, and in the absence of storage space in 770 was initially kept in a temporary warehouse. In 1963 the adjacent building at 766 Eastern Parkway was placed on the market, and it was subsequently purchased by Chabad to provide a permanent home for the *Merkos* library.[129]

In 1977 Rabbi Shalom Ber Levin (b. 1948) was hired as a librarian to care of the *Merkos* collection. Levin, like most Lubavitchers, was unaware of any dispute regarding the ownership of Rayatz's library, though he did find it odd that only Chaim Lieberman and Chana Gourary held the keys to Rayatz's books, housed in the basement of 770 and in the Sixth Rebbe's study on the second floor. Levin developed a warm relationship with Lieberman, and the two librarians worked closely together.

In the summer of 1980, Lieberman celebrated his eighty-eighth birthday. Due to the difficulties of his advancing age, he approached Levin and asked if his junior colleague would be willing to assist with managing Rayatz's collection, in addition to existing duties at the *Merkos* library. "This request is coming directly from Rebbetzin Chana Gourary," Lieberman added. "Please visit her upstairs and she will ask you personally."

Having received requests from both parties, Levin thought it a relatively straightforward matter and penned a letter to the Rebbe, asking for his approval. The Rebbe's sharp reply shocked him. "It is totally out of the question to mix the two libraries," the Rebbe wrote in a response marked *urgent and confidential.* "I am extremely surprised that you are involving yourself with 'politics,' and what is more, you wish to drag me into this too."[130]

Levin suggested instead that his assistant, Rabbi Yitzchak Wilhelm, leave the *Merkos* library to work exclusively for Chaim Lieberman in Rayatz's collection, and the issue was speedily resolved. But Levin had become aware, for the first time, that even thirty years after Rayatz's departure, the library remained a sore point of contention.

As we have seen, Chana and Rashag had one son, Barry, who had opposed the Rebbe's appointment in 1951. Following that, Barry, no longer wishing to be part of the court at 770, relocated to Silver Spring, Maryland, to work as a physicist. In 1953, he married Mina Chaskind, a statistician at George Washington University and daughter of Chabad Chasid Dovber Chaskind.[131]

Barry would visit his parents occasionally at 770, often spending the festivals there, and he was not afraid to express his rejection of the

Rebbe's leadership. For example, at the Passover Seder it is customary to lean to the left when eating *matzah* (unleavened bread) and drinking wine, as an expression of the spirit of freedom which characterizes the festival. Jewish Law, however, rules that one must not lean in the presence of one's Rabbi, as it would be considered a sign of disrespect. At the Rebbe's Seder in 770, none of the attendees leaned—except for Barry.[132]

At the end of 1984, apparently in dire need of some funds, Barry began to enter his grandfather's library surreptitiously, gradually removing books of value, which he sold to private collectors. He did this without prior discussion with the Rebbe or Rebbetzin Moussia.[133]

Initially, his efforts went undetected. At the end of 1984, Meir Shlomo Junik, one of the Yeshivah students who assisted in the Gourarys' apartment, mentioned to Levin that, unusually, Barry was now visiting his parents every week, each time bringing with him two suitcases. When Meir Shlomo carried the cases to Barry's car after the Sabbath, he noticed that they were extremely heavy. Levin thought little of it. At the time, Barry was taking volumes only from Rayatz's study, where Wilhelm did not have access, so the matter remained unnoticed.

When the supply of valuable books from the second floor became depleted, Barry began to draw from the larger collection stored in the basement of 770. Even though Chaim Lieberman had not maintained a comprehensive catalog, within a short time Wilhelm noticed that some books were missing. "I think we have a thief," he told Levin, around March 1985.

Neither Levin nor Wilhelm had any inkling as to whom the culprit might be. Through the help of Chaim Baruch Halberstam, who assisted with the maintenance of 770, a buzzer system was attached to the library door that would alert Halberstam to any intruder when Wilhelm was not present.

Shrewdly, Barry chose to enter the library during the Rebbe's *farbrengens* when no Chasidim were around and the buzzer system had been deactivated. By Passover, the library shelves were being carefully monitored and the books taken during the *farbrengen* of the last day of the festival were noticed immediately.

But who was it? Levin and Wilhelm imagined that it was probably an unscrupulous Rabbinical student.

Within the next few weeks, Halberstam installed a twenty-four hour video surveillance system, costing an exorbitant four thousand dollars at the time, in an attempt to identify the intruder. After the festival of Shavuot departed on 27th May, the video produced its desired result. The tape showed Barry entering, leaving the library with books in his hands.

Halberstam informed the Rebbetzin of what had transpired. "We never dreamed of such a thing, even in our darkest dreams," Levin wrote in his memoir of the saga.[134]

Sadly, the development thrust an impenetrable wall between Rayatz's two surviving daughters. Previously, Rebbetzins Moussia and Chana had enjoyed an extremely warm relationship, speaking regularly on the phone and often going out for rides together.[135]

In a particularly distressing call, Rebbetzin Moussia raised the issue with her sister. "People saw Barry going into the library and he took out books," she reported.

"My son is not a thief," Chana retorted.

"He went in secretly," Moussia said.

The discussion became more heated. "If Father wanted to leave anything for the children," Rebbetzin Moussia argued, "he would have written a note or something about the library. Since he didn't write anything, it definitely doesn't belong to me."

At some point, the discussion broke down completely and Rebbetzin Moussia cried in exasperation, "We had a younger sister who went to the concentration camp. Just as she died and she is not here, in this matter, I am not here. It's as if I died. Do whatever you want." Then she hung up the phone.[136]

Through the mediation of Rashag, the Rebbe initiated negotiations with Barry in an attempt to resolve the issue amicably, but a point of no return had passed, since Barry had already sold a good number of books. Some had subsequently been resold at much higher prices and were probably not retrievable by Barry, even if he did have a change of heart.[137] In any case, Barry refused to return the items and insisted that they were his rightful property. The Rebbe notified Barry that he intended to express his views publicly in a forthcoming sermon, which, of course, would be broadcast all over the world (although Barry would not be mentioned by name).[138]

The Rebbe's position was based on statements by Rayatz, both orally and in writing, that his library did not constitute personal property but belonged to *Agudat Chasidei Chabad,* the communal umbrella of Chabad in the U.S.A., founded in the 1920s. While this information was already documented in correspondence, in a sermon on 13th July, the Rebbe encouraged those Chasidim who remembered Rayatz's mentioning the point to write down their recollections.

Though this evidence seemed proof enough that the library was not the personal property of the Schneersohn family, the Rebbe also argued that the *content* of the library demonstrated that it had not been intended exclusively for Rayatz's personal use. A substantial part of the collection consisted of material which, from an Orthodox perspective, would be considered "heretical." What use would a Chasidic Rebbe have for such books? Clearly, it was Rayatz's intention to establish a research library to attract a broad spectrum of Jews and non-Jews to Chabad, providing the opportunity for interaction with a wider audience and the sharing of Chabad ideals.[139]

Many collectors of antique and valuable Judaica consider their purchases a source of blessing for the owner. Conscious that his sermons were heard around the world, the Rebbe shared his view that acquiring a book from Rayatz's library should not be seen as a rare opportunity or special merit. Since these books were the legally documented property of *Agudat Chasidei Chabad,* their sale represented a violation of Jewish Law, and would therefore not bring blessing, only the opposite.[140]

Throughout his years of leadership, while the Rebbe often spoke passionately about certain issues, he almost never seemed wounded personally. On this occasion, however, he made a striking disclosure.

> A good friend of mine, whom I have known for forty or forty-four years, told me: "Why are you getting so angry about this? Don't take it to heart."
>
> I am not angry. I am aware that, "*Any person who gets angry* [*it is as if he worshipped idols*]."[141] I have not dealt with any person angrily, and this is not a war or any sort of revenge, G-d forbid. I am only speaking about the issue.
>
> But regarding not taking it to heart—how can I not take it to heart? Some people are cerebral enough that they can control all

> their emotions, but I do not claim to be one of them. I *absolutely* take it to heart, and it is disorienting me.
>
> I sit before a *farbrengen* and I want to prepare a *Rashi* to speak about, and I am disoriented. My mind wanders.[142]

Why did this issue "disorient" the Rebbe in a way that, apparently, nothing had done so before?

As a man of deep intuition, with a profoundly spiritual worldview, the Rebbe often interpreted communal events in terms of their long-range implications and religious significance. This approach dated back to the first Chabad Rebbe, Rabbi Shneur Zalman of Liadi, who viewed his imprisonment by the Russian government as a sign of Providential disapproval of his work. His subsequent vindication from charges and release, encouraged him to continue his prior activities of teaching Chasidut with more vigor.

In his sermons about the court case the Rebbe framed the affair in comparable terms, as a heavenly tug-of-war over his leadership trajectory. The legal dispute over the ownership of the library belied a much broader uncertainty: Menachem Mendel Schneerson had led Chabad very successfully, hugely expanding its institutions and human resources, but had the Seventh Rebbe done so in a way that was loyal to the spirit of the Sixth? Rayatz's wife, older daughter and grandson did not seem to think so, and that concerned the Rebbe immensely. When they had maintained their views privately it was one thing, but liquidating the Chabad library without even so much as consulting the Chabad leader represented a powerful rejection of his position and achievements. From Chana's later testimony in court it emerged that, in her view, Lubavitch had died with her father and the new Rebbe was simply doing his "own thing." In a similar vein, it came to light that Nechama Dina, Chana's mother, considered herself to be "the last Lubavitcher Rebbetzin."[143]

While the court case itself and the public sermons beforehand were largely centered around the specific issue of the books, the affair took on a much broader connotation of whether the Rebbe had authentically molded Chabad into its "Seventh Generation." Although he did not say so explicitly in public,[144] that is the way Chasidim came to understand why the Rebbe was so "disoriented" by the whole affair.

The subsequent vindication in court resolved the doubts which had plagued the movement and invigorated the Rebbe with renewed energies to continue on his path. While his references in public were vague—he referred to a "negative energy" whose influences had been deflected—the point was clear enough.[145]

After the Rebbe's initial sermon about the misappropriation of books, on 1st July (12th *Tammuz*) 1985, at 3 a.m., Rabbi Zalman Gurary telephoned attorney Nat Lewin, waking him up. "There is a problem in Lubavitch," Gurary told him, as they discussed the details of the case briefly on the phone. Lewin agreed to help. "You had better win this case," Gurary urged, with a tinge of Chasidic chutzpah, "because otherwise you will have nowhere to flee. Lubavitch is everywhere."[146]

A couple of days later, Rabbi Yehuda Krinsky was in Lewin's Washington office. An important initial discussion concerned the necessity of taking action in civil courts. Jewish Law requires that disputes between Jews be settled in a Rabbinic court, and taking action in civil courts is sharply censured. Under certain extenuating circumstances there is Rabbinic sanction to proceed to civil courts, and Krinsky produced some citations from the *Code of Jewish Law* which had been prepared for him by Rabbi Yisrael Yitzchak Piekarsky (1905-1992),[147] demonstrating that this was such a case. Lewin understood that the sources furnished by Krinsky were, "not to prove it to me," but, "to make sure that I understood that the question of going to *Beit Din* (Rabbinic Court) had been thoroughly considered."

Krinsky and Lewin explored the matter further, to see what legal options were available and potentially justifiable in Jewish Law. Lewin suggested that Chabad file for a restraining order to keep Barry from disposing of the books he already had in his possession, and then the actual case could be held in Rabbinic court. "If we went to Rabbinic court," Lewin later explained, "he would go out immediately and try to dispose of all the remaining books. The *Beit Din* would not be able to issue any effective restraining order against him."[148] After returning to New York, Krinsky called Lewin and instructed him to go ahead.

The case fell out under Judge Charles Sifton (1935-2009), who happened to be on summer vacation at the time. Since the need for a restraining order was urgent, Lewin managed to get a court hearing on 29th July with a judge assigned to emergency matters, Leo Glasser (b.

1924). Lewin recalled that Glasser was "Jewish enough" that he had a old manuscript of Maimonides framed on his wall.

"This looks like the kind of case that should go to a Rabbinic court," Glasser proposed at the brief hearing.

"If we get an order that he can't sell the books," Lewin explained, "we are prepared to go to Rabbinic court for the rest of the case."

Al Hellerstein, Barry's lawyer, interjected. "Now that we're in court, we confess that we are going to challenge the ownership of the library, and we are going to do this in court here, so we are not prepared to go to Rabbinic court."

Glasser agreed and signed the restraining order. Barry was required to present the court with a list of all the books in his possession. It turned out that he had taken a total of 550 books and sold 102 of them.[149]

Through the efforts of Rabbi Moshe Bogomilsky, Chabad had in fact already managed to obtain a list of most of the books that Barry had taken and were in the process of tracking them down and repurchasing them. In order to hear from an impartial source, the Rebbe requested a Rabbinic opinion about ownership of the books from an authority outside Chabad. Bogomilsky consulted with the Haleiner Rav, Rabbi Ephraim Fishel Hershkowitz (b. 1922), who opined that, while he obviously could not give a formal ruling without hearing from both sides, Barry's actions did not seem justifiable in *halacha*. As chronicled in Bogomilsky's memoir, through extensive international efforts, 94 of the 102 books sold were tracked down and repurchased, at a cost to Chabad of $433,000.[150]

Around the end of July, Rabbi Krinsky approached librarians Levin and Wilhelm. "You have probably heard that the library case is going to court," he said. "The Rebbe wants you to prepare documents for the case."

Levin and Wilhelm dropped everything they were doing and spent the next four months plowing through tens of thousands of documents on file that might shed light on the issue. Virtually every day they were in contact with Chabad's lawyers.

Five days before the case was scheduled to begin, on 27th November 1985, Levin wrote to the Rebbe, informing him, "according to the evidence I have accrued, all our lawyers say that it is as clear as day that we will have a complete victory in court."[151]

The Rebbe's spirits, however, had been evidently weakened. One Rabbinical student noted in his diary, "the whole story affected the Rebbe's health. On *Shabbat Parshat Devarim* [27th July], the Rebbe was obviously not well." When the Rebbe recited the portion from the prophets (*haftarah*), as was his custom, "even those who were standing very close could hardly hear. The next day, *Tisha B'Av* morning, it was also very hard to hear the *haftarah*, as the Rebbe's voice was very ruffled because of his crying."[152] Near the end of 1985, he also discontinued the formal delivery of *ma'amarim* (Chasidic discourses), which in many ways defined the office of Rebbe. Clearly, the implications of the current events were huge.

Early on in the preparations for the case, the Rebbe requested a meeting with Nat Lewin and a second attorney who had joined the case on behalf of Chabad, Joe Shestack of Philadelphia. A table was placed in the corridor outside the Rebbe's office to form an *ad hoc* meeting room. The Rebbe sat on one side of the table, Lewin and Shestack on the other, while Yehuda Krinsky and Avraham Shemtov—two legally savvy Lubavitchers who had been assigned to the case—stood at the side. Lewin recalled that at the meeting, which lasted around an hour, the Rebbe "had read all the pleadings and was fully familiar with where the case stood."

An initial position about which the Rebbe felt very strongly was that Barry's surreptitious entry at night did not reflect the actions of a rightful owner. Lewin remembered that the point "made very good sense to me, although the judge did not accept it as a means of finishing the case at the outset."[153]

Lewin then recalled that the Rebbe "pointed out what ended up being a key piece of evidence, a 1946 letter written by the Previous Rebbe to Professor Alexander Marx at the Jewish Theological Seminary. The Rebbe very strongly felt that the document showed the Previous Rebbe had intended this to be the property of *Agudat Chasidei Chabad*, or the community, and not the personal property of the family. The Rebbe spent some time discussing that letter and the ramifications of it, and what it meant in terms of proving what the Previous Rebbe's intention was."[154]

Avraham Shemtov later marveled how the Rebbe had singled out that one single letter which proved to be so decisive. "They had already prepared thousands of documents," he recalled, "and it was really amazing that the Rebbe said to build the case on just one letter." According to Shemtov, the lawyers had initially resisted the Rebbe's emphasis on the letter, claiming that they already had enough evidence and that the document added nothing significant.

The letter, however, proved highly instrumental in the case, and Judge Sifton later cited it in full in his ruling, describing it as "one extraordinary letter.... which sets forth clearly and unambiguously the relationship between the books, their owners, and the community."[155]

Another issue discussed at this initial meeting was whether the Rebbe himself ought to testify in court. Initially, the Rebbe indicated that he preferred not to be called as a witness. Lewin thought this was fair enough, as the Rebbe "had a lot to say, but not direct evidence.... He had his opinions, his opinions were stated in *farbrengens,* but that was not evidence."[156]

Barry's lawyers, however, were insistent that the Rebbe be summoned as a witness. "The other side was trying to use that as a means of harassing us," Lewin surmised, "because they knew that it was not seemly."

Seeing that his testimony might be necessary, the Rebbe said he would comply, but Krinsky was adamant that the Rebbe not be deposed. "I told the Rebbe that I wouldn't let it happen," Krinsky remembered. "It was the only time ever that I said something like that to the Rebbe, contradicting him."

"Later a special hearing was held," Krinsky explained. "The Judge appointed a certain magistrate to go through the whole question about the Rebbe, whether it was relevant or not to depose him. And we won. The public was not aware of what was going on, but in my mind, although we eventually got every book back, this was the biggest victory of the whole episode—the Rebbe's honor."[157]

Rebbetzin Moussia's testimony, however, was deemed indispensable. "The Rebbetzin could speak about her father," Lewin explained, "and what her father's intention would have been with respect to his library."

Initially, Krinsky tried to spare the Rebbetzin from this ordeal too. "I suggested to the Rebbe that perhaps we try to avoid it somehow. But the Rebbe said, 'No, leave her be, they can depose her, she'll be all right.'"

On 12th November 1985, a videoed deposition took place in the Rebbetzin's dining room, in the presence of lawyers from both sides, as well as Chana and Barry. Towards the end of the questioning, Rebbetzin Moussia was asked to whom the books in her father's study and in the library belonged. Without hesitation she replied, "I think they belonged to the Chasidim, because my father belonged to the Chasidim."

Marveling at the Rebbetzin's "eloquence and sophistication," Krinsky commented, "I have had opportunities to be deposed and it's easy to lose your cool. But she didn't."

Later, the Rebbe told Krinsky, "I told you that she would come through with flying colors."

When Judge Sifton later watched the videotape, he was similarly impressed. "Remarkable," he said. "That was remarkable."

During the case, which lasted twenty-three court days, the Rebbe spent most of the time at Rayatz's grave. "After returning, he would call me into his room," Krinsky recalled, "I would spend about an hour to an hour and a half reporting to him about all the proceedings that happened that particular day and then he would give me advice and instructions."[158]

The courtroom was an unusual scene, packed to capacity with Chabad men and women who had come to show their solidarity. Testimonies for Chabad were heard from Nobel laureate Elie Wiesel and Louis Jacobs (1920-2006), a scholar and founder of the Masorti (Conservative) movement in the UK, who had penned significant works on Chabad Chasidut. Barry's case was supported by his mother, and, most importantly, by Chaim Lieberman who provided a lengthy deposition on his behalf. Professor Menachem Friedman (b. 1936), a sociologist from Bar Ilan University, served as an expert witness for Barry.[159]

A huge hurdle for Barry's lawyers was how to deal with correspondence from Rayatz which stated unambiguously that the library was the property of *Agudat Chasidei Chabad*. The counterargument, presented by Chaim Lieberman, was that Rayatz had written these words for strategic purposes, since the American authorities would not have been interested in saving a private collection from Europe. It did not represent the Sixth Rebbe's actual view, he said.

The argument was deeply offensive to Chabad as it implied that Rayatz had been duplicitous, penning a mistruth for the sake of personal gain. After the Rebbe was informed of Lieberman's testimony, he wrote to Levin, "The darkness of exile is well known, but to this extent I had not anticipated."[160] In a subsequent note, the Rebbe marveled that while "those who ought to have been defending the honor" of Rayatz were pontificating, "the Christian judge expressed his opinion before the court and before the lawyers" that it was simply unthinkable that the Sixth Rebbe could have been duplicitous.[161]

In his final, published decision, Judge Sifton stated his absolute confidence in Rayatz's integrity. "Not only does the letter, even in translation, ring with feeling and sincerity, it does not make much sense that a man of the character of the Sixth Rebbe would, in the circumstances, mean something different than what he says, that the library was to be delivered to plaintiff for the benefit of the community."[162]

The strongest argument presented by Barry's side was that in Europe, before the need arose to rescue the library from Nazi-occupied Poland, Rayatz's finances had not operated within the framework of formal, communal trust. Monies (known as *ma'amad*) given to him by Chasidim were spent at the Sixth Rebbe's sole discretion. In Chana's testimony she recalled how her father would spend hours visiting book dealers, and that book collecting was something of a personal hobby.

Chabad's counterargument was subtle and depended on conveying to the Judge some sense of the absolute devotion of a Rebbe to public service, to the exclusion of all personal gain. Judge Sifton's first wife Elizabeth was, in fact, the daughter of noted Christian theologian Reinhold Niebuhr, which perhaps gave Chabad's attorneys some confidence that the contours of a deeply religious personality might be appreciated from the bench.

In his testimony, Elie Wiesel made the point eloquently. "The attitude of the Rebbe toward personal wealth was one of disdain. First, because he didn't have it. And even if he had it, he never kept it."

Wiesel also elaborated on the intense mutual devotion of Rebbe and Chasid. "Strangely enough, the choice is made by the Chasid and not the Rebbe. It is not the Rebbe who chooses the Chasid; it is the Chasid who chooses the Rebbe. But once that choice is made, it is boundless. It is total, total loyalty.... I have seen followers of Chabad do for others with self-sacrifice things that I cannot even repeat because they were too dangerous."[163]

Chabad's lawyers initially argued that as a result of his devotion to the community, a Rebbe had no personal property at all. The point, however, was too subtle for the court to appreciate, and Judge Sifton later offered a more legally reasoned argument. "The library was never held by the Rebbe as personal property, for his personal benefit and his private, as opposed to religious, purposes," Sifton concluded in his written 1987 decision. "It was held as personal property for the community's benefit and for charitable uses."

In a landmark decision, which was unanimously upheld by a Federal Appeals Court two years later, Judge Sifton argued that Rayatz's wartime actions effectively created a trust, legally transferring the books into communal hands. "What the letter to Marx and the other manifestations of intent to the Government of the United States both before and after the war supply," the decision clarified, "is what the law requires for the creation of a trust."[164]

"Of course, the Marx letter is not itself a trust instrument, but it is evidence of the strongest sort, taken together with the way the library was treated after its arrival in the United States, that upon its arrival in this country it was delivered into the custody of *Agudat Chabad* with an express declaration that it was to be held by that corporation in trust for the benefit of the Chabad Chasidic community."

Demonstrating, once again, his penchant for flipping a negative experience into something positive and practical, the Rebbe framed the Hebrew date of the court's decision, the 5th of *Tevet*, as an annual "festival of books," when Chasidim were encouraged to expand their own libraries. The notion of the Seventh Rebbe's leadership being vindicated at trial was also not lost on Chasidim, and it has since become the dominant theme of annual gatherings on this date.

The renewed sense of stability in Lubavitch and the retrieval of its sacred assets had sadly come at a huge personal price to Rayatz's family. Rashag had sided with the Rebbe during the dispute, opposing his own wife and son. Shortly after Barry's visits to the library became public knowledge in 1985, Chana was assaulted by a Rabbinical student, injuring her badly. The student, whom community leaders said was deranged, escaped to Israel before he was apprehended by police. While Chana spent her last days at Barry's New Jersey home, Rashag chose to remain in 770, visiting his wife once a week. Rashag, who had already been partially disabled by a stroke in 1980, must have suffered terribly throughout the ordeal, before he finally passed on in 1989.

When Chana passed away on 1st March 1991, Barry rejected a plea made by an official delegation of four Lubavitchers for her to be buried in the Lubavitch cemetery in Queens, and Rayatz's older daughter was laid to rest in the Munkatch burial ground in Floral Park, New Jersey.[165]

Rebbetzin Moussia was, no doubt, traumatized by the entire ordeal, and the Rebbe later intimated that the affair probably shortened her life.

Despite these immeasurable losses, the foresight of persisting with the case has become all the more apparent in recent years, especially after the Rebbe's passing in 1994. Beyond the specific legal issue, a broader question was debated in the courtroom: Who are a Rebbe's true heirs? His physical (biological) descendants? Or his spiritual "children," his disciples and devotees? Barry may have been Rayatz's biological grandson, but it was the Rebbe—a very distant cousin of Rayatz, but an ardent devotee—who upheld his legacy.[166] The obvious corollary was that, after his own passing, the Lubavitcher movement would be bequeathed to all the Rebbe's spiritual heirs, his Chasidim. (Whether this was something the Rebbe had in mind at the time, we can only speculate.)

There was another important point for the future of the movement which was brought sharply into focus by the case. As a result of the Rebbe's remarkably successful, charismatic leadership, the Lubavitch movement had become increasingly synonymous with his own persona. The Rebbe not only *led* Lubavitch, it was almost as if he *was* Lubavitch.

The court case was a powerful repudiation of this misconception. The 1987 ruling made it patently clear that *Agudat Chasidei Chabad*, the Lubavitcher movement, existed as an entity unto itself.

In 1994, when the Rebbe finally passed on, many feared that Lubavitch would die with him. The response of Chasidim, as we now know, was to rededicate themselves to his work of outreach and institution building with even greater commitment, and the movement grew far more after his passing than during his lifetime. While the factors that inspired this expansion are complex, there is no doubt that the 1987 ruling played a role. Seven-seventy, the library, and by extension, all the institutions of Chabad *were* Lubavitch. The kingdom, as well as the king, was vitally important.

In a 1970 *yechidut*, the Rebbe had expressed a very similar sentiment to British businessman Benzion Rader. Rader presented the Rebbe with a proof of the album *Challenge* which he had prepared to showcase the work of Chabad around the world. The Rebbe immediately noticed that an additional picture of him had been added at the last minute to the end of the book. "I know there is a picture of me at the beginning of the book," he noted, "and I assume there are some of me in the middle of the book, now there is one of me at the end of the book. Won't people say, 'there is too much Rebbe'?"

Rader immediately protested, "I thought the Rebbe was the beginning, the middle and the end of Chabad?"

The Rebbe's face became serious, as he rejected Rader's conclusion, noting a glaring error in the analysis. "Well, Chabad is two hundred years old," the Rebbe said, "and I am only sixty-eight."[167]

In 1994, Chabad took time to absorb the fact that the Rebbe was not "the beginning, the middle and the end of Chabad," but the point had already been implied by the 1987 ruling.

In fact, the ruling had been ratified—as he stressed in a later sermon—"in a manner that achieved the total approval and legal assistance from the nations of the world, for all to see in a secular court of law."[168] For the Rebbe, that meant its truth had become self-evident.

40. Some of the influential figures in the appointment of Ramash as Seventh Rebbe (left to right): Rabbis Shmuel Levitin, Shlomo Aharon Kazarnovsky, and Zalman Gurary.

41. An early *farbrengen* in what was then the main synagogue in 770, in 1952. The Rebbe is seated at the center of the table, speaking into a microphone. To his left are Rabbis Shmuel Levitin and Mordechai Chodakov (standing). Sitting to his right in a gray suit and tilted hat is Shlomo Carlebach.

42. The Rebbe's secretariat. Top: Rabbi Chaim Mordechai Aizik Chodakov, Chief of Staff. Middle row (left to right): Rabbis Nissan Mindel, Avraham Eliyahu Quint, Moshe Leib Rothstein. Bottom row: Rabbis Yehudah Leib Groner, Yerachmiel Binyamin Klein, Chaim Yehuda Krinsky, Shalom Mendel Simpson.

43. The Rebbe speaks outside 770 at a *Lag B'Omer* Parade, 1957.

44. The Rebbe *farbrengs* at the Franklin Manor ballroom in 1953 (*Yud Tet Kislev*).

45. The Rebbe always walked with a brisk gait. To his left is Rabbi Chodakov. Mid 1950s.

46. The Rebbe emerging from 770, as Rabbi Chodakov follows. 1960s.

47. A *farbrengen* at 770, 1967.

48. A meeting in the Rebbe's office, 1960s.

49. The Rebbe studying in his office (above and below).

50. The Rebbe with Rebbetzin Moussia in his office.

51. The Rebbe's niece, Dalia Rothman, circa 1970.

52. The Rebbe entering his office at 770.

53. Rebbetzin Moussia (left) and Rebbetzin Chana, the Rebbe's mother (right), at a wedding in the Aperion Manor, Brooklyn, 1949.

54. The Rebbe leaves the Chabad Library, housed adjacent to 770, flanked by secretaries Leibel Groner (right) and Binyamin Klein (left).

55. The Rebbe distributes charity to injured Israeli soldiers.

56. As the Rebbe delivers a *ma'amar,* a formal Chasidic discourse, he closes his eyes and shifts to a higher state of mind. All the assembled stand while he remains seated.

57. By 1971, the crowds at *farbrengens* at 770 have swelled considerably.

58. As the Rebbe leaves 770, he hands children coins for charity.

59. The Rebbe visits art exhibition of Baruch Nachshon.

60. On one of hundreds of trips to Rayatz's grave in Queens.

61. The Rebbe addresses a Chabad women's convention at 770, 1980s.

62. Doctors of the Rebbe's household (left to right): Lawrence Resnick, Louis Teichholtz, Avraham Abba Zeligson, Ira Weiss, and Robert Feldman.

63. Nat Lewin, attorney for Chabad, speaks with Zalman Gurary.

64. Chaim Liberman, Rayatz's librarian, with Leibel Groner and Binyamin Klein.

65. After court victory, the books removed from the Chabad library are returned. Left to right: Leibel Groner, Avraham Shemtov, Yehuda Krinsky.

66. The Rebbe leaves his house on President Street.

67. Rashag in his later years.

68. Funeral of the Rebbe's wife, Rebbetzin Moussia Schneerson, 1988.

69. The Rebbe encourages the crowd at a weekday sermon, delivered in 770. circa 1990.

70. After 28 months of ill health, the Rebbe is finally laid to rest in the *ohel* (mausoleum) next to his father-in-law, Rayatz.

71. The Rebbe's gravestone, next to his father-in-law. Below, a portion of the hundreds of petition notes read daily at the *ohel* by visitors.

72. As late as 1985, after the Rebbe had already been leading Chabad for 35 years, the Annual *Shluchim* Convention was still relatively small (right). In the following years the movement mushroomed, with a staggering 2400 new *shluchim* establishing Chabad centers in the first sixteen years following the Rebbe's passing. In the above image from the 2010 convention, nearly 4000 Chabad Rabbis were in attendance from 76 countries around the world.

CHAPTER FOURTEEN

FUTURE VISIONS

1988–1994

The Rebbe entering his car on a trip to the *ohel.* In his hand is a bag of petitions to be read.

On Monday, 8th February 1988, Dr. Robert Feldman, private physician of Rebbetzin Moussia, was called to the Schneerson home. He diagnosed the Rebbetzin—now approaching her eighty-seventh birthday—with a gastrointestinal problem, and strongly recommended that she be taken to the hospital for tests and surveillance. The Rebbetzin, who apparently did not feel terribly ill, initially resisted the suggestion.

The Rebbe asked Rabbi Zalman Gurary, who supervised the Rebbetzin's medical care, to call a conference of physicians to discuss the question of hospitalization. The following evening, Doctors Feldman, Moscowitz, and Weg gathered with the Rebbe at his private quarters on the second floor of his house for nearly two hours to debate the issue. While the Rebbetzin was not deemed to be in critical condition, the consensus was that she needed to be hospitalized. Gurary suggested that medical equipment might be installed in the house to spare the Rebbetzin the ordeal of hospitalization, but the Rebbe rejected the idea. "Perhaps they will need something suddenly that only a hospital can provide," he argued.

Gurary informed the Rebbetzin of the doctors' decision, stressing that it had met with the Rebbe's approval. She asked to speak with the Rebbe, and he entered her room for around a half hour for what would be the last time they would speak together.

The Rebbetzin was taken to Cornell Hospital by car, walking from her house to the vehicle unaided. Accompanying her were her nurse, Zalman Gurary, Dr. Feldman, and Shalom Ber Gansburg, a Chasid who assisted the Rebbetzin personally at home. The Rebbe asked Gansburg to telephone him every fifteen minutes with developments. "I will pick up the phone myself," he said.

The Rebbetzin was sitting in a wheelchair in a hospital corridor waiting to be admitted to her room, when she turned to Gansburg. "Shalom, I'm really thirsty," she said. "I'd like a bit of water." After reciting *shehakol,* the traditional Hebrew blessing on a drink, and sipping some water, her face paled.

"Are you with us?" the attendant doctor asked, checking her blood pressure, which had dropped.

"Yes," she said.

As her face continued to pale, the doctor asked again, "Are you with us?" This time there was no reply.

After the Rebbetzin was taken into a treatment room, the doctors announced that her heart had failed. A short while after midnight, they emerged again with the unfortunate news that she had passed on.

Gansburg, who had been in constant contact with the Rebbe, did not want to be the one to deliver the shocking news. The Rebbetzin had only been admitted for tests, and nobody had expected her sudden death. Gurary's daughter, Esther Sternberg, who was present at the hospital, called the home of secretary Leibel Groner. "Please go to the Rebbe's house and inform him of the news," she requested.

When Groner reached the Rebbe's house, some four long blocks away, Gansburg and Dr. Feldman had already arrived back and were standing outside. Nobody wanted to inform the Rebbe that his wife of fifty-nine years, and closest friend, had suddenly died. Eventually,

Groner convinced Feldman to make the unpleasant call. "You're the doctor," he said. "It's your job."

Feldman picked up the phone and dialed the Rebbe's home number. The Rebbe was in the middle of editing a transcript of his sermon from *Tu Bishvat* (3rd February), and picked up the phone immediately. As Feldman informed the Rebbe of the news, the line went silent.

"Rabbi Groner is here with me," Feldman told the Rebbe, breaking the silence.

"Let me speak to him," the Rebbe said.

Groner took the receiver. "Please go to my office and fetch my *talit, tefilin* and some books on the laws of mourning," the Rebbe requested. "And please do not let anyone enter my house until the coffin arrives."

At around 5:20 a.m., a vehicle containing the coffin arrived and the Rebbe escorted it into his home. It was laid on the kitchen floor upon some leaves.

The Rebbe turned to Rabbi Shalom Ber Lipskier, who supervised the burial society. "How much will the burial cost?" he asked.

"It's already been paid for," Lipskier replied.

Unsatisfied, the Rebbe opened his wallet, took out one thousand dollars in cash, and handed it to Lipskier. "Please check if this is enough," he asked, "and inform me if more is required."

The Rebbe also handed Lipskier an envelope containing a ring which had belonged to the Rebbetzin's sister Sheina, who perished in the Holocaust. "Please bury this with my wife," he asked.

The Rebbe turned to Zalman Gurary. "Please inform all those who have worked personally for my wife's care that their work has been completed, and make sure they are fully compensated before the funeral." He thanked Gurary profusely for attending closely to the Rebbetzin's care.

A quarter of an hour before the funeral, the Rebbe entered the kitchen, along with Leibel Groner and Tzvi Hirsch Fuchs, of the burial society. As the two men stood back, the Rebbe approached the coffin and could be seen muttering a few words. Then, for the first time since his wife's departure, he burst into tears.

After a while, the Rebbe turned to Fuchs. "What about the *keriah?"* he asked, referring to the Jewish custom that mourners tear their clothes. With a small scissors, Fuchs cut the right lapel of the Rebbe's jacket. Reciting the traditional formula, "*Blessed are You, G-d, Our G-d, King of the Universe, the True Judge,*" the Rebbe continued to tear his jacket.

"Enough, enough," Fuchs said.

At 12 p.m., the Rebbetzin's coffin was carried by a group of Chasidim down President Street to Kingston Avenue, as the Rebbe walked behind. At Kingston Avenue, the entourage turned left and walked two blocks to Eastern Parkway, adjacent to 770. The coffin was then placed into a vehicle and taken to Montefiore Cemetery in Queens, where the Rebbeztin was laid to rest next to her mother and grandmother, amid a huge crowd.[1]

The Rebbe sat *shiva* (seven days of mourning) at his house, while thousands of followers, *shluchim*, admirers and prominent Rabbis poured in to offer words of comfort.[2]

On the afternoon of the day of the funeral, Wednesday 10th February 1988, following prayers and comforting of the mourner, the Rebbe asked secretary Rabbi Yehuda Krinsky to come up to his home office on the second floor.

"I want to speak about three things," the Rebbe said. The first was to establish a fund in memory of the Rebbetzin, *Keren Chamesh*, to assist Jewish women and girls. The second regarded the legal paperwork of Chabad's three central organizations, *Merkos Inyanei Chinuch, Machne Israel* and *Agudat Chasidei Chabad*. The Rebbe asked Krinsky to check the corporate papers of these organizations and to ensure that all the vacancies on these boards were filled and that all documents were up to date.

The third issue was a little more sensitive. "This was not something I had to think about before, but now the time has come for this and we need to act. I would like to prepare a will, preferably before the *shiva* is over."

Krinsky got to work quickly, and the following Sunday, 14th February, the Rebbe signed a legal will prepared by attorney Nahum Gordon and witnessed by secretaries Leibel Groner, Binyamin Klein and Yehuda Krinsky. In a very simple document, the Rebbe instructed that, after payment of his funeral expenses, the balance of his property "real, personal and mixed... including, but not limited to, any books, manuscripts, *objets d'art*" is to be bequeathed to *Agudat Chasidei Chabad*.

Rabbi Yehuda Krinsky was appointed executor of the will, and in his absence, Rabbi Avraham Shemtov and Rabbi Shalom Simpson were listed as alternatives.[3]

The will, which dealt only with the Rebbe's personal effects, was not made public knowledge; but the following Saturday evening, the Rebbe gave a first—and only—public sermon about resolving organizational dilemmas following his eventual passing. After prefacing that the other Rebbes of Chabad had made preparations for after their death, "and this brought them a long, good life," the Rebbe turned to his own situation. Regarding future issues requiring an authoritative resolution, "one should consult with three Chasidic *Rabbanim*," *i.e.* Chasidic rabbis trained as *halachic* authorities, and follow their consensus. Then he repeated, "the answer is clear, in a way that leaves no room for doubt, that this is the jurisdiction of three Chasidic *Rabbanim*."

The Rebbe was not suggesting that a specific body of Rabbis be elected to run Chabad; he had in mind a form of localized autonomy. "This applies to towns and cities, and in every single place there is a committee of Chasidic *Rabbanim* of that place—whether for that city, for that neighborhood, or for the entire country. Wherever there are three Chasidic *Rabbanim*, they are themselves the *Beit Din*. In a location that has less than three, they can combine *Rabbanim* from elsewhere."

Again he repeated, "This is being said in a clear manner, one that leaves no room for any doubt. There is no need to ask about this matter again."

The message, however, was not something Chasidim were willing to hear. Despite the fact that the sermon was said publicly, to a gathered crowd at the Rebbe's home, and recorded on videotape, the usual printed transcripts released after a sermon, failed to appear. The Rebbe asked his editorial board, which usually transcribed the text of sermons for him, to work on a draft, but they were not responsive. When the (unedited) sermon finally appeared as an addendum to the published talks of 1988, the sensitive passage discussing Chabad after the Rebbe's passing was simply omitted.[4]

"Rabbi Schneerson is 86 and childless," an article in *Newsday* on 16th May 1988 noted, "and questions about his likely successor are turned away politely by Lubavitch leaders. They say it is not even discussed privately."

The Rebbe had, in fact, already suggested the model of localized autonomy, at the Sabbath *farbrengen* following his wife's departure. In a sermon encouraging the establishment of new Chabad organizations in memory of the Rebbetzin, the Rebbe noted that, given the huge number of new organizations, there might be some "boundary issues" (*hasagat gevul*), with the activities of one proposed new organization potentially overlapping or competing with another. The solution, he proposed, was for local Rabbinic authorities to decide the issue among themselves. "Questions about the types of organizations and their establishment ought not to be sent here," the Rebbe requested, "but decided locally, as stated, and subsequent notification may be sent here about the institutions and their activities, after a Rav has been consulted."[5]

While this particular directive was associated with the Rebbetzin's passing, the Rebbe had already began to shift much of the decision-making of Chabad out of his hands in the prior weeks. In a sermon of 30th January 1988, the Rebbe had asked that medical dilemmas be posed, not to him, but to a *rofeh yedid,* a doctor who was also a sympathizer and personal acquaintance of the questioner. The model of the *yedid,* the sympathetic advisor, was also suggested for questions of business and law. In matters of worship, each Chasid was encouraged to choose a mentor who would offer personalized advice.[6] (In fact the proposal for personal mentorship had been stressed in unusually strong terms the previous summer. "I am proposing, and I am requesting, with a heartfelt request," the Rebbe had said. "In fact it is greater, but a more appropriate expression does not spring to mind."[7])

How could a Chasid possibly resolve his dilemmas without asking the Rebbe? Now that Chabad had developed immeasurably, and so much had been achieved, "each individual is now invested with the powers to successfully discern correct solutions," the Rebbe suggested. One simply had to study the teachings of the Chabad Rebbes, he said, and live by them, and a solution would be found.

While he had sent the clear message that questions ought to be resolved locally, the Rebbe noted that requests for blessings could still be sent his way—"and I am making it publicly known that, G-d willing, I will read them at the graveside of the Rebbe, my father-in-law, for a blessing from G-d, the source of blessing, in all matters spiritual and physical."[8]

Of course, many Chasidim continued to send their questions to the Rebbe's office for clarification, and replies were still forthcoming. But if an inquirer did not receive a response, he or she knew why.

The Rebbe also instructed his librarian, Rabbi Shalom Ber Levin, in the spring of 1987 to begin publishing *Igrot Kodesh,* a multivolume chronological series of correspondence penned by the Rebbe. Arguably, this was to assist the autonomous resolution of a host of difficulties in light of Chabad teachings. Appropriate materials were selected from the confidential archives by Rabbi Shalom Mendel Simpson and prepared by Rabbi Levin for print.[9] The Rebbe encouraged that the volumes be published at great speed, and in the remaining seven years of his life, an impressive twenty-two volumes were published containing over eight thousand letters, on a breathtakingly diverse host of issues.[10]

Perhaps the first overt public statement of the Rebbe's desire to "decentralize" Chabad decision making away from his direct control, was at a Purim *farbrengen,* on 15th March 1987, just a couple of months after the court victory, when he spoke of a passage "from the leader to the people."[11] At that time, the reference had been more veiled, but by 1988 a pattern had begun to emerge: While continuing to lead and inspire, the Rebbe was attempting to steer his followers away from a dependency on his own decision-making.

The motivation for this shift might be perceived superficially as the practical reality of a growing movement alongside the Rebbe's advancing age; but, it would arguably be more accurate to say that the Rebbe was seeking a *maturation* of the leader-disciple relationship. He had been teaching and guiding for almost forty years now, and he felt that the time was ripe for his followers to grasp the contours of his approach. He had interpreted Torah texts and clarified the positions of Chabad in countless areas, not only to lead, but to *empower* his students with the wisdom to carry out the process on their own.[12] While the Chabad community did not take the Rebbe's eventual passing in 1994 easily, the subsequent growth and stabilization of Chabad shows us that he did provide the necessary tools for thousands of followers to function autonomously.

Even the *Rashi sichot* had shifted towards greater participation on the part of Chasidim. In 1986 the Rebbe announced that he would no longer be delivering his own independent *Rashi sichot,* as in the past. He requested Chasidim to pen their own commentaries on *Rashi* in one of the journals published by Chabad *yeshivot,* to which he would add his own critique and alternative solutions at subsequent *farbrengens.*[13]

Always difficult to please, he later expressed his dissatisfaction with the results. The following winter he spoke of "absolute astonishment that people have just posed questions and not tried to find an answer. We see in the journals, published both here and in Israel, that a multitude of questions are asked without any solutions—sometimes thirty questions, without one solution!"[14]

After more solutions began to appear, he again expressed his disappointment. "After so many lectures on *Rashi* have been delivered, there had been the hope that eventually people would begin to study *Rashi* appropriately. What has actually happened is that they have only learned to ask the simplest of questions... but not to take one step further." The Rebbe then smiled, and said, "I'm not worried about giving rebuke (*musar*), because each person will be convinced that I am not speaking about him."[15]

II

How did his wife's passing affect the Rebbe, and what were some of the changes that took place in his court during this period?

During the *shiva,* Leibel Groner recalled seeing the Rebbetzin's household cleaner in tears. "I'm crying for the Rebbe," she told Groner. "The only time that the Rebbe could sit without pressure was that half an hour he would spend each evening with the Rebbetzin, sitting in the living room, conversing over a cup of tea. You could see the Rebbe was relaxed at that time. Who is going to give the Rebbe that half-an-hour now? It's making me cry."[16]

The Rebbe's cardiologist, Ira Weiss, also noticed first-hand how much the Rebbe sorely missed his wife. "I saw the Rebbe just really kind of fold inward a lot from this loss. He was much more withdrawn. Not having the daily meeting with his wife anymore was a very, very big loss to him."[17]

While the Rebbetzin had not been a familiar figure to the vast majority of the community, her passing sent shockwaves through the movement. Lubavitchers began to name their daughters after her, and the Rebbe was later presented with an album of all the namesakes born during the first year of her passing— 324 Chaya Mushkas from around the world.[18] She had been such a private figure that nobody was even sure how to pronounce her actual name. Was it Chaya Muska (resembling the name by which she had been known, Moussia), or Chaya Mushka? When librarian Rabbi Shalom Ber Levin suggested that it was the former, the Rebbe corrected him.[19]

In a 1992 sermon, the Rebbe would later refer to the date of his wife's passing in 1988 as a "new era" for Chabad, explaining in somewhat esoteric terms that a certain shift had taken place.[20] That fact, though, was immediately apparent after her passing, when several major changes took place in the Rebbe's court. Weekday *farbrengens,* even on special occasions, were discontinued. From the end of 1988, the Rebbe virtually stopped delivering Chasidic discourses.[21] In 1989, the *Rashi sichot* and other analytical discourses were discontinued as a regular fixture.

The energies saved by these activities were devoted to other areas, and during the last years of his active life the Rebbe spent much more time with his followers. The Sabbath *farbrengens*, though significantly shortened, were intensified from a monthly occurrence to a weekly one. While in the past the Rebbe had prayed in the smaller synagogue upstairs in 770 during the week, only joining the larger crowds downstairs on Sabbaths and festivals, from 1989 onwards he participated in the daily prayers downstairs.[22] While there were no weekday *farbrengens,* after the evening prayers the Rebbe would often ask for his lecturn to be brought over and he would deliver a short sermon while standing—for the Rebbe "short" meant thirty to forty minutes! Over time, these mini-sermons would become more frequent and take place every few days.

During these last years the Rebbe also intensified the publication schedule of his edited sermons and discourses. In addition to the weekly *Likutei Sichot,* he also edited and published a weekly annotated transcript of the sermons delivered at the previous week's *farbrengen.* As if that were not enough, from 1987 onwards he began to regularly edit *ma'amarim* that had been delivered in earlier years, which were published to coincide with special occasions throughout the year.[23] If we bear in mind that the *Igrot Kodesh* series was also being vigorously published during this period, the last six years of the Rebbe's active life witnessed a remarkable scholarly output of some forty-seven volumes of Torah thought.[24]

In addition to his regular practice of distributing to all his followers wine ("cup of blessing") after festivals and honey cake before the New Year, during this final period the Rebbe also spent considerable amounts of time personally distributing new Kehot publications by hand. From 1987 to 1992 he stood on his feet for hours on some twenty occasions, handing out a copy of a new pamphlet, or sometimes an entire book, to thousands who stood patiently in line.[25]

But by far the widest exposure of the Rebbe to the public, which had already began in 1986 but dominated this final period, was the distribution of dollars for charity on a Sunday morning. After private *yechidut* was discontinued in 1981, very few individuals were given the opportunity for personal interaction with the Rebbe. Even prior to 1981, *yechidut* appointments would be filled for months in advance. But now anyone could simply turn up on a Sunday, wait in line, and have a personal moment with the Rebbe. While most of the five thousand or so visitors each Sunday would simply receive their dollar and pass by, the event provided the opportunity for several of the visitors to have brief conversations. And unlike the private *yechidut* experiences in the Rebbe's room which, by and large, were not recorded, the distribution of dollars was videotaped, providing a vast archive of fascinating interactions.[26]

The visitors were extremely diverse, including Torah scholars, Rabbis, communal activists, authors, journalists, and politicians from Israel and the United States. But what is most interesting is how the Rebbe interacted with ordinary people, Jews and non-Jews, often giving, in just a brief moment, some penetrating insight into how a life dilemma was to be resolved, and offering hope and consolation in times of need.

The encounters at "dollars" would sometimes offer a continuum to *yechidut* experiences many years earlier, and there are numerous accounts of visitors being surprised at the Rebbe's near-total recall of names and faces. American businessman, author and presidential advisor Gordon Zacks (1933–2014), recalls in his memoir how at dollars in 1987 the Rebbe spontaneously picked up on a conversation that had taken place some seventeen years earlier.

In January 1970, Zacks had spent one and a half hours at *yechidut* when the Rebbe had presented him with a number of reasons why he ought to embrace a more observant life, in what Zacks later described as an "incredibly woven tapestry of the universe."

"His ultimate goal was to bring you to the ways of Jewish life," Zacks wrote, "but his means were not confrontational and demanding. You could literally feel his warmth and love in addition to the power of his vast intellect."

After a series of philosophically oriented arguments failed to penetrate Zacks' resistance, at the 1970 meeting, the Rebbe employed a literary argument.

"He quoted Kazantzakis' book *Zorba the Greek* to me during our conversation," Zacks recalled. "Do you remember the young man talking with Zorba on the beach, when Zorba asks what the purpose of life is? The young fellow admits he doesn't know. And Zorba comments, 'Well, all those damned books you read—what good are they? Why do you read them?' Zorba's friend says he doesn't know. Zorba can see his friend doesn't have an answer to the most fundamental question. That's the trouble with you. 'A man's head is like a grocer,' Zorba says, 'it keeps accounts.... The head's a careful little shopkeeper; it never risks all it has, always keeps something in reserve. It never breaks the string.' Wise men and grocers weigh everything. They can never cut the cord and be free."

"Your problem, Mr. Zacks," the Rebbe told him, "is that you are trying to find G-d's map through your head. You are unlikely to find it that way. You have to *experience* before you can truly feel and then be free to learn."

"Let me send a teacher to live with you for a year," the Rebbe offered, "and teach you how to be Jewish. You will unleash a whole new dimension to your life. If you really want to change the world, change yourself! It's like dropping a stone into a pool of water and watching the concentric circles radiate to the shore. You will influence all the people around you, and they will influence others in turn. That's how you bring about improvement in the world."

Zacks politely declined the Rebbe's offer, and the meeting ended. Over the following years the Rebbe wrote to Zacks five times, asking him to reconsider the offer, and each time Zacks wrote back and declined. Eventually, the letters stopped coming.

In 1987, Zacks' youngest daughter, Kim, had just returned from Israel and asked her father if he would take her to Sunday Dollars. "I neither called nor told anyone who I was when we arrived," Zacks recalled, "I stood in line with her. It had been seventeen years since I had seen the Rebbe and ten years since he wrote me his last letter."

After greeting Zacks and his daughter, and encouraging Zacks to be more Jewishly active, the Rebbe said, "Don't wait so much time since last time, when I spoke with you about 'good news' in spreading *Yiddishkeit* (Judaism), especially in the realm of Jewish education."

Zacks, who had arrived unannounced and unidentified, was taken aback that the Rebbe had recalled their earlier meeting and its content from seventeen years earlier.

"You're amazing," he exclaimed. "You remember that."

Always uncomfortable with adulation, the Rebbe tried to steer Zacks' excitement to a practical goal. "What will be the benefit to the community that I'm amazing?" the Rebbe asked him.

Zacks broke into laughter, eliciting a warm smile from the Rebbe.

"He may not have gotten exactly what he wanted from me," Zacks later reflected in his memoir, "but the Rebbe surely taught me the power of changing yourself to influence others."

After detailing personal encounters with figures such as Ben-Gurion, Wiesel, Sharansky, Reagan and Bush, Zacks surmised of the Rebbe, "He may have been the most charismatic man I ever met. He had an incredible aura to him, partly because he was such a combination of charisma and pragmatism."

"The most amazing thing? The Rebbe saw himself as perfecting G-d's will. He had no power in the sense that a police commissioner, a general, or a tax collector does. He had no one enforcing his decisions. What he did have was the authority of his holiness, which caused others to connect to him. It wasn't his title that gave the Rebbe authority. It was his presence and his profound grasp of bringing the principles of the Torah to life in himself and in others."

"The Rebbe didn't declare himself a leader. His overpowering presence inspired those around him to declare him their leader and to revere him. Through earning respect and trust, people endowed him with leadership."[27]

In virtually every "Dollars" encounter, the Rebbe could be seen trying to utilize the few seconds available to squeeze a little more faith out of a soul and to direct it to a tangible goal. Comedian Jackie Mason, for example, recalled how the Rebbe would encourage him to see his successes as a Divine blessing.

"When I went to see him on the Sunday Dollars/Blessings line," Mason said, "the Rebbe always asked me, 'How's show business?' and I would always tell him that I was a hit and things were going better than ever. The Rebbe then always said, 'Do you attribute it to yourself or to G-d?' Smiling, I'd say, 'Rebbe, if I attribute it to myself you'd throw me out of here. So even if I believed that I'm not going to tell you.' Then I'd get real serious and I'd say, 'Of course, Rebbe. It's because of G-d.' And the Rebbe said, in perfect English, 'That's worth a dollar (and a blessing).' And the Rebbe gave me a dollar."[28]

At a 1989 "Dollars" encounter, Senator Joe Lieberman brought along his family, and was surprised that the Rebbe seemed to intuit the feminist leanings of his daughter, Rebecca.

"To me it was very interesting," Lieberman recalled, "because everyone assumes that if you are Orthodox, or if you are Chasidic, you don't respect women. When my daughter stood before him, the Rebbe said to her, 'Very often a daughter can do more to carry out a parent's ideals than a son can.' I could see Rebecca was very impressed."

"Did the Rebbe correctly size Rebecca up?" Lieberman later pondered. "You know, he had that wonderful ability to do just that. Anyhow, the Rebbe saw into her Jewish soul, and he responded with words that, in my mind, gratified and encouraged her."[29]

Some feminist sensitivities were also in evidence at a 1989 encounter with UJA President Peggy Tishman (1919-2004) and two of her board members. Tishman first asked the Rebbe if he remembered their earlier meeting from 1975. "You told me then that I would be the president," Tishman said. "I don't know if you remember that?"

"Yes," the Rebbe replied, adding quickly, "and I remember also that I told you about your duties that you have to perform in the future."

One of Tishman's colleagues turned to the Rebbe and said, "You know, we're now providing from the UJA-Federation campaign a quarter of a million dollars a year to the Lubavitch school system. This is a new development."

With a warm smile, the Rebbe replied, "And you expect me to be satisfied about a quarter of a million?"

The UJA director chuckled. "If you were satisfied I'd be worried."

"Then you have no reason to be worried at all," the Rebbe quipped, as the whole group began to laugh out loud.

When the delegation bade their farewells, the Rebbe turned to Tishman and said, unprompted, "Don't forget about feminine rights."

As one of the first women to gain national recognition as the chief executive of a major charitable federation, Tishman was surprised at the comment. "You're talking to me?" she said, rhetorically. The Rebbe, of course, knew that Tishman would not forget the plight of women, but he wanted her to know that he cared about the issue, too.[30]

III

The last few years of the Rebbe's life were a period of outstanding creativity. Besides the huge effectiveness of the Sunday Dollars program, conceived when the Rebbe was already eighty-four, after *farbrengens* began to take place on every Sabbath from 1988, barely a week passed by without the Rebbe introducing a new suggestion or initiative.[31] Just a month after his wife's passing, on what would have been her eighty-seventh birthday, the Rebbe launched a campaign for Jews to celebrate their birthdays with good resolutions, additional Torah study (and *aliyah* to the Torah the previous Sabbath), donation to charity (on a weekday) and *farbrengen*.[32] The suggestion was unusual because, in Jewish tradition, there is barely any discussion of the idea; and while the Rebbe had elaborated on it several times before and held a celebratory *farbrengen* on his own birthday for many years, it had never been issued as a formal directive.[33]

On 19th September 1988, shortly after the beginning of the Jewish New Year 5789, the Rebbe launched another major initiative. "At the beginning of a new year we look for a new goal," he told a group of Chabad supporters. Referring to himself as an "old friend" and noting his advanced age, the Rebbe quipped, "I am not as old as it says on my passport.[34] If you'll carry out what I am requesting now, it will be a sign that you do not perceive me as an old Jew, but as a young man with young ideas."

Announcing a "Year of Building," the goal was "to purchase new buildings for Jewish purposes." The size of the buildings ought to be larger than the current need, as this will provide a stimulus to further activity and growth. Those currently renting properties should endeavor to purchase them.

Appealing directly to the supporters, whom the Rebbe described as "partners" in Chabad work, he asked that the burdens not be placed on their *shluchim*, "because the *shliach* has enough trouble in his activities." Fundraising, as well as choosing and purchasing properties, he argued "will be done better by an experienced businessman than by a *shliach*, who studied in *Yeshivah*... This is my proposition."[35] The response was fantastic, and Chabad not only expanded significantly throughout the course of the year, it also intensified the importance of property ownership for the movement in the future.

While from the 1970s, the Rebbe's sermons had been broadcast live via telephone, and during the 1980s by cable television, the years 1989 to 1991 represented a peak in the use of technology to globalize the Rebbe's court when several cities around the world were connected via live satellite hook-up for the celebration of Chanukah. The *Chanukah Live* program, facilitated by a huge mobile studio parked outside 770 that was extremely advanced for its day, provided audio and video feeds from other large Chanukah gatherings around the world. The opportunity for communities to interact live with the Rebbe in 770 was exhilarating. As he waved his arms in encouragement, crowds could be seen erupting joyously in Manhattan, Hong Kong, Melbourne, Moscow, Buenos Aires, London, Sydney, Johannesburg, Cape Town, Paris and Montreal—communities that he had built personally through tireless meetings and correspondence. After barely leaving 770 for forty years, the Rebbe was able to see firsthand some of his achievements. The hook-up with Moscow, which took place shortly after the fall of the Soviet Union, must have been particularly moving. Following sixty years of Communist oppression, which the Rebbe had lived through and experienced, one can only imagine how it must have felt to see Jews lighting a giant Menorah in Red Square and dancing joyously, and for them to see the Rebbe deliver a live sermon.[36]

The annual *Shluchim* Conference continued to grow each year, in honor of which the Rebbe would deliver a special sermon.[37] In 1992, at the Rebbe's suggestion,[38] a conference for *shluchot* (female *shluchim*) was initiated, an event which has continued to take place each year around the time of the Rebbetzin's *yahrtzeit* on 22nd *Shevat.*

As a wonderful celebration of the Rebbe's achievements and the growing army of *shluchim,* a commemorative album containing pictures of the *shluchim* around the world was published in 1991. Upon receiving an early edition of the album—which made "a strong impression" on the Rebbe[39]—he requested that an enhanced version be prepared, with pictures "of all the *shluchim's* family—men, women and children" together. The purpose of including children was so that, "when a child will look in the album and see his picture, he will remember that he is, in essence, a *shliach,* even though, practically speaking, his task now is to study Torah for many years until he will grow up and become a *shliach.*"[40]

IV

The last few years of the Rebbe's active leadership presented its own set of challenges. In 1990, a media storm erupted after it was rumored that a political intervention by the Rebbe had thwarted Shimon Peres' attempt to form a new government. In what was dubbed the "stinking maneuver,"[41] Peres succeeded in dismantling the Shamir government on 15th March with a vote of no confidence after Shamir had refused to capitulate to U.S. pressure for territorial concessions. In order to form a majority, Peres relied on a coalition with the religious *Agudat Yisrael* party, which held five Knesset seats. The new government was due to be sworn in on 15th April, but only after arriving at the Knesset did Peres discover that two members of *Agudat Yisrael* vital for their majority, Eliezer Mizrachi and Avraham Verdiger, would not be attending. The "stinking maneuver" had failed, and Shamir succeeded in reforming a government on 11th June.

It soon became widely reported in the media that Mizrachi and Verdiger had pulled out of the coalition under instruction from the Rebbe. "The last minute failure of the Israeli Labor Party to form a new government," the *New York Times* reported, "has again focused attention on the role of a charismatic Brooklyn rabbi who asserts an unusual amount of influence in Israel."[42] An angry editorial in *Yediot Achronot* lamented that Israel's fate was "in the hands of a Rabbi who lives in

Brooklyn, who has never set foot in Israel." One activist sent a cable to the *United Jewish Appeal,* urging the organization to withhold funds from Lubavitch.[43]

The Rebbe's involvement had been intimated by Mizrachi and Verdiger who, the *Associated Press* reported, "cited loyalty to Schneerson's teachings in explaining why they refused to vote for Labor." But Lubavitch spokesman Yehuda Krinsky denied that the Rebbe had personally contacted the politicians. "They did not speak to the Rebbe," Krinsky told the *Associated Press,* clarifying that Verdiger had called 770 before Passover and asked if there had been any change in the Rebbe's opposition to land-for-peace negotiations. He was told no, and decided on his own to oppose a Labor government. "It was on his own, it was his own initiative," Krinsky emphasized.[44]

There was one element of the "stinking maneuver" in which the Rebbe *did* involve himself personally, responding to a speech delivered at the height of the affair by Rabbi Eliezer Menachem Shach. Initially, Peres had hoped to form a coalition with the religious parties controlled by Rabbi Shach who was known to be in favor of a land-for-peace deal. But at a historic speech in the Yad Eliyahu Stadium in Tel Aviv on 26th March, broadcast live on national Israeli television, Rabbi Shach took the opportunity to deliver a scathing attack on secular Israel, as embodied by Peres' Labor party. "Today one can meet children who don't know what *Shabbat* is," Rabbi Shach bemoaned, placing the blame firmly on Labor's shoulders. "There are kibbutzim that don't know what Yom Kippur is. No idea, and they raise rabbits and pigs there. And this is called the Jewish people?" Shach denounced secular Israelis as an *ever meduldal*—a distended limb no longer receiving life support from the vital organs. "Do they have any links with their forefathers?" he asked.[45]

The shock waves from that remark rocked Israel, as one commentator later observed: "Their assumption had always been that whatever one may eat, do, or say he would remain a fully qualified member of the fold. It had now been authoritatively pronounced that devout secularists had irreversibly crossed the line."[46]

Rabbi Shach's comments touched on one of the Rebbe's most preciously held convictions, that *every* Jew, regardless of religious observance, was a full member of his or her people. While the Rebbe all but ignored over a decade of sharp personal criticism emanating from

Rabbi Shach, now it was the Jewish people's honor he was called upon to defend, not his own. In a sermon the following Sabbath, the Rebbe reiterated a number of sources on the topic of Jewish inclusivity before calling on Rabbi Shach (though not by name) to repent for his error. "Verbal expressions such as these which dishonor the Jewish people (to put it mildly), especially in public, in the presence of countless Jews and non-Jews, requires correction (*tikun*) and repentance."[47]

It was only a few months later that the Rebbe would respond to another public statement of Rabbi Shach, this time at much greater length. In December 1990, the Israeli media was outraged after Rabbi Shach had declared the Holocaust as "definitely a punishment. The Holy One Blessed Be He kept score for hundreds of years until it added up to six million Jews." Convinced that G-d had enacted retribution on sinful Jews for violating the Sabbath and eating pork, Shach suggested, "Because of the sins, the Almighty may bring another Holocaust upon us, and it may already be tomorrow."[48]

Over the years of his leadership, the Rebbe had responded privately to various individuals who had asked his views on theodicy and the Holocaust, but he had rarely spoken about it in public.[49] For the Rebbe, Judaism ought to be motived by positive sentiments: a belief in the sanctity of the people and G-d's love for them, the joy of worship and the achievement of sacred goals. But in a sermon following Rabbi Shach's comments, the Rebbe delivered what was probably his most thorough and passionate treatment of Holocaust theology. After noting that rebuke and threat of punishment was, in our days, an ineffective method of bringing Jews closer to Judaism, the Rebbe rejected Rabbi Shach's notion of a punitive Holocaust as "untrue, disrespectful to G-d, and disrespectful to the Jewish people."

"Those who are not observant in this generation," the Rebbe argued, "have the legal status of children taken into captivity,"[50] victims of circumstance who are not culpable for their transgressions. On the other hand, when such a person fulfills even one commandment it is valued and cherished by G-d, to the utmost." Then he added:

> What kind of a person would consider himself qualified to calculate in his own mind (of flesh and blood) the account of sins? Then, he allows it to pass his lips that, because in our times there are many Jews who are not currently observant, terrible consequences are im-

pending (may G-d protect us that it should never happen). Such an approach is in complete contradiction to what is documented in the Torah, that such Jews are like children taken into captivity and are not culpable.

Rabbi Shach's graphic depiction of a vengeful G-d were "disrespectful towards G-d," since:

A conception of G-d as One who sits counting sins, waiting to exact punishment and who refuses to move until He has settled all His debts, and then, straightaway begins again counting and punishing—is extremely disrespectful to the Almighty. To compare G-d to a merciless dictator who waits expectantly to punish is a complete misrepresentation, since, in truth, He is "the merciful Father," as clearly documented in Scripture and the Oral Law.

The Rebbe argued, that G-d was also concerned with the respect of the Jewish people.

Scripture depicts G-d's relationship with the Jew as being like a father to a son, *"You are children to G-d, your G-d"*,[51] and, in places even as a firstborn son.[52] References of G-d's intense love to the Jewish people are numerous. G-d does not "appreciate" insulting comments about His children, and, furthermore, He takes them personally, as is explicitly documented in Scripture, *"One who touches you is as if he has touched the apple of His eye."*[53]

Then, he launched into a theological discussion:

Our generation lives in the wake of the Holocaust which witnessed the murder of six million innocent Jews, may G-d avenge their blood! May G-d save us from those who pass judgment on the few of us that remain, and say that the present conduct of such Jews will cause another Holocaust, G-d forbid, may it never occur. Such words are a blatant insult to those who gave up their lives.

According to Jewish theology, there are certain negative occurrences which do not come as a punishment for sin but simply because G-d decrees so, without any rationale that it is fathomable according to the logic of Torah. In reference to Rabbi Akiva, who was murdered by scraping his flesh with iron combs, our Sages coined the phrase, *"Silence! That is what arose in His will."*[54] Furthermore, in

> the Bible itself, it is documented (at the Covenant of the Parts) that the Exile in Egypt was not because of sins, but was simply a decree of the Almighty.[55]
>
> The massacre of six million Jews with such horrific brutality, such an awesome Holocaust that has no comparison throughout history (and never should have, may G-d protect us!), could not conceivably be a punishment for sins. Even Satan himself could not concoct an account of sins from the last generation that could justify (G-d forbid) such a heinous punishment!
>
> We have absolutely no explanation whatsoever in Jewish theology for the Holocaust, except, *"that it is what arose in His will."* Certainly it was not commensurate with the inner will of G-d, but rather, in the spirit of Isaiah's comment, *"for a brief moment I abandoned you."*[56] Without any doubt, it was certainly not a punishment for sins.
>
> On the contrary, all the victims of the Holocaust are holy, since they were killed on the basis that they were Jews, may G-d avenge their blood! Certainly, this event was in total discordance with G-d's innermost desire.[57]

Rabbi Shach's comments, and the Rebbe's response, also need to be viewed in the context of the time. The end of 1990 was just a few weeks before the beginning of the Gulf War, when Israel faced a possible attack of chemical weapons. The notion of a "second Holocaust" must have felt palpably real and represented a particularly ominous form of intimidation. The Rebbe's sermon was not merely aimed at clarifying obscure points of theology; he was also seeking to calm and comfort a nation in panic.

The Rebbe's response to the fears preceding the Gulf War mirrored almost precisely his position before the Six Day War. Both at Sunday Dollars encounters and in correspondence, he consistently cited the Biblical reference to the Land of Israel, "*The eyes of G-d are upon it always*" (Deut. 11:12) and assured both those living and visiting the country that they had nothing to fear.[58]

Always mixing faith with pragmatism, the Rebbe encouraged his followers on 14th January 1991, to follow the instructions to wear gas masks, insisting that "this does not contradict my stance on the situation." When the Scud missiles started to land on civilian targets in Israel, the Rebbe asked his secretariat to be informed with news after each missile had landed, regardless of the time.[59]

After the thrity-nine Scuds produced an shockingly miniscule casualty rate, scholars struggled to explain what had happened. Among the different theories—inaccuracy of the missiles at long distance, the strength of Israeli buildings, the failure of some warheads to detonate—even scientists could not ignore the role of an unusual degree of what they could only attribute to "coincidence."

"Luck must have played a crucial role in determining the overall casualty rate," a 1993 article in *Nature* concluded. "Indeed, there is considerable anecdotal evidence that good fortune played an important role in reducing casualties in Israel. Of the warheads that detonated in Israeli cities, one hit the only empty lot in a densely populated neighborhood; two others hit a factory and a partially constructed shopping mall during the night. Several other Scuds landed near unoccupied buildings: an underground bomb shelter, a municipal center, and a school. Even when Scuds severely damaged occupied buildings, casualties were remarkably low."[60]

For the Rebbe, such "luck" was clearly the providential hand of G-d at work, a sentiment he shared in a pastoral letter before Passover.

> These were *revealed miracles*, obvious miracles, not only for Jews but also for all nations, "seen in all the corners of the earth"; everyone saw the great miracles that unfolded at this time.
>
> In view of the existing international conditions it seemed inevitable that not only would there be a declaration of war, etc., but that the war would engulf many nations and trigger a new world war, G-d forbid, yet, in a most extraordinary turn of events, not only was a world war prevented, but the war ended shortly after it had begun.
>
> While all signs pointed to the outbreak of a massive war, requiring a huge army with massive weaponry of the most advanced technology, and after everything was duly assembled and in place for a long war expected to last weeks and months, victory came in a matter of days.
>
> The victory was so wondrous that not only was much bloodshed (as had been feared) avoided, but the enemy was forced to relinquish its spoils, and to free captives and hostages, including some that had been held from before.[61]

Blood, however, would be spilled on the Rebbe's own doorstep that summer with the eruption of the Crown Heights riots. Depicted by historian Edward Shapiro as "the most serious anti-Semitic incident in American history,"[62] the riots were prompted when on Monday 19th August 1991, a car in the motorcade following the Rebbe (from a trip to Rayatz's grave), accidentally collided with another vehicle at the intersection of Utica Avenue and President Street. The vehicle, a 1984 Mercury Grand Marquis station wagon driven by Yosef Lifsh, veered out of control onto the sidewalk on President Street, tragically killing Gavin Cato, a seven-year old son of Guyanese immigrants, and his cousin Angela.

While the accident was devoid of any malicious intent, it brought to the surface long-simmering tensions in the black community about what they felt was preferential treatment by the political authorities for Jews. Numerous false rumors about what had transpired soon reached the mobs, inciting them to a rampage of assault and robbery. Around three hours after the two children had been killed, Yankel Rosenbaum, a non-Lubavitcher Orthodox Jew who was visiting from Australia to research a doctorate in Jewish history, was stabbed to death by a violent black mob as he walked on Brooklyn Avenue. In the three days of rioting that followed, 152 police officers and 38 civilians were injured, 27 vehicles were destroyed, seven stores were looted or burned, and 225 cases of robbery and burglary were committed.[63]

The following Sunday, 25th August, with the wounds still raw and the local community devastated, Mayor David Dinkins met publicly with the Rebbe at around 4 p.m, surrounded by members of the press. Jewish advocates had been, and would continue to be, highly critical about the failure of the police to restore law and order quickly, even referring to the event as a "pogrom"; but at the meeting, the Rebbe appeared calm and was devoid of accusation. Ever the inclusivist, his only point was to articulate a vision of future unity where Jews and blacks would not see themselves as two conflicting communities, but as one single brotherhood.

"I am confident," Dinkins assured the Rebbe, "that with the good people of all of our communities, both sides, we will come together and do those things necessary to protect everyone."

The Rebbe responded, "We need to forget the 'both sides.' There is one side, one people."[64]

The Rebbe had, in fact, shared his views on racism with Dinkins at a previous meeting on 1st September, 1989, shortly before the mayoral elections in November when Dinkins would be victorious. Speaking of "the multitude of nationalities in New York which is a melting pot for many nations," the Rebbe expressed his hopes that "all these nationalities live in good peace and in harmony and each one of them will strengthen all the nationalities around them, especially in matters of charity."

Apparently, the Rebbe saw acts of inter-communal charity as the most powerful antidote to racism. The mind and heart, very often, will follow a person's actions—a principle we see underlying many of the ritual acts of Judaism—and simply helping a person of another race or creed can help to quickly erase prejudices.

The Rebbe then conveyed to Dinkins his hope that belief in G-d would lead humanity to shed the divisive obsession with racial identity and difference. "I hope that in the near future the 'melting point' will be so active that it will not be necessary to underline every time that 'they are Negro,' and 'they are white,' or 'they are Hispanic,' *etc., etc.*, because they are no different. All of them are created by the same G-d, and created for the same purpose, to add all good things around them, especially beginning with themselves and their families."[65]

The Rebbe reiterated a similar argument in a letter to Ardadiusz Rybicki, President of the Council for Polish-Jewish Relations, following an anti-Semitic attack on a Warsaw Synagogue on 14th September 1991.

> I would like to add that last month, in the beginning of *Tishrei*, we ushered in the current Jewish Year, 5752, with the celebration of *Rosh Hashanah*, the anniversary of the creation of the first man, Adam. Our Sages of the *Talmud* explain why the creation of man differed from the creation of other living species and why, among other things, man was created as a single individual, unlike other living creatures created in pairs. One of the reasons—our Sages declare—is that it was G-d's design that the human race, all humans everywhere and at all times, should know that each and all descend from the one and the same single progenitor, a fully developed human being created in the image of G-d, so that no human being could claim supe-

> rior ancestral origin; hence would also find it easier to cultivate a real feeling of kinship in all inter-human relationships.[66]
>
> Indeed, although *Rosh Hashanah* is a Jewish festival, our prayers for a Happy New Year include also all the nations and dwellers on earth. And true happiness includes everyone's peace and prosperity both materially and spiritually.[67]

Further tragedy struck just sixth months after the riots in February 1992, when Pesya Leah (Phyllis) Lapine, a thirty-eight-year old mother of four children, was stabbed to death in her Crown Heights apartment by a local resident, Romane LaFond, who was posing as a handyman. Her children were playing in the next room at the time. While it was not deemed a racially motivated incident, the fact that the perpetrator was black only served to widen the chasm already dividing the community.

Lapine was a *ba'alat teshuvah* (returnee) to Chabad from Texas, who had made sacrifices to move to Crown Heights from her suburban hometown because she wanted her children to be close to the Rebbe. She was known to be unassuming, humble and honest to the core.[68] Due to the huge size of the Chabad community, the Rebbe had long ceased to attend funerals, refusing to give preferential treatment even to the most wealthy and influential Chasidim, so his personal participation at Pesya Leah's funeral made a strong impression. The marked expression of grief on his face, which can be seen in photographs, was poignant and unusual. "For a mother to leave behind her children," the Rebbe said in a sermon delivered in her memory the following week, "is a greater sacrifice than giving up her own life."[69]

V

During the last year of the Rebbe's public sermons he spoke at length about the global redemption (*Geulah*) and the coming of the Messiah (*Mashiach*) almost every week. This represented the climax of increasingly frequent discussions, which had intensified throughout the 1980s.

In 1980, he adopted the phrase "We want Mashiach now!" to promote a sense of urgency and longing for Judaism's time of future promised bliss, and the slogan became a popular song at children's rallies.[70]

In a sermon printed in 1982, he alerted the public that the current Jewish year, 5742, had been identified by one Rabbinic author as an auspicious time for the coming of Mashiach.[71] In the following years, these kinds of associations gradually increased.

Why was Messianism so important to the Rebbe, especially as he neared the end of his life? And how did he perceive his own role?

While Jews have long been divided as to whether Messianic speculation is something beneficial or dangerous,[72] the Rebbe pointed to a surprisingly preeminent string of Rabbinic figures who did dabble in such activities. In the early 1950s, when an erstwhile supporter of Chabad explained that he had "distanced himself from Lubavitch" when Rayatz began to declare that Mashiach's coming was imminent, the Rebbe wrote, "In that case, the person ought to distance himself from all those who predicted a *ketz* (time for Mashiach), namely: Saadia Gaon, *Rashi*,[73] Maimonides,[74] Ibn Ezra,[75] *Baalei Tosafot* on Torah,[76] Nachmandies,[77] Ibn Yichyeh,[78] Rabbi Yitzchak Abarbanel,[79] *Ohr Ha-Chaim*,[80] the Vilna Gaon,[81] Arizal[82]—and many more."[83]

Speculation of a *ketz*, the Rebbe suggested in a 1982 discussion, was not, as it first may seem, a plain attempt to predict the future; rather, the issue touches upon the subtle dialectic of the leader-disciple relationship. The role of the leader is to inspire, but this influence must be carefully calibrated so as not to strip the disciple of autonomy. Too much inspiration delivered the wrong way might bring about an unhealthy co-dependency or compromise the disciple's individuality.

On the other hand, there is a contrary argument that, at least sometimes, there is value in a leader sharing some of his own uniquely elevated insight and experience that the average disciple will never reach. Even if most people will not be able to fully appreciate these revelations, they may at least absorb something by osmosis and be uplifted by the experience. Dazzled by a glimpse of the extraordinary, a disciple may well be inspired to make an unprecedented leap of personal growth.[84]

The Rebbe argued that this was the goal of a Messianic awakening initiated by a Jewish leader. The long list of Rabbis who had intrigued their followers with the hope of imminent, radical transformation, were, in a sense, waving the carrot in front of the donkey. "If you will just push yourself that little bit harder," they were intimating, "there will be something fantastic in store for you." These leaders aimed to inspire their disciples to new heights of worship by painting the Redemption as tantalizingly within reach—noting auspicious dates or pointing to contemporary events that heralded Redemption—if only an extra push would be made by the people to grow in Torah and *mitzvot*.[85]

Messianism preoccupied many a Jewish leader near the end of his life, since, as the Rebbe writes, "close to the time of departure, his worship reaches a peak of personal perfection."[86] Having reached his own peak, it is only natural that the leader will want to share at least a modicum of his experiences with his disciples, hoping to lift them towards him. Thus, the Rebbe suggested, when Jacob desired to reveal "the end of days" to his children, shortly before his passing,[87] "he empowered Jews to attain at least a glimmer of those revelations associated with the 'end'—a worship that is free from societal influence and the evil impulse.... And it could be argued that this is precisely why many Jewish leaders, such as R. Saadia Gaon, Maimonides *etc.*, involved themselves with Messianic speculation."[88]

What frustrated the Rebbe throughout this latter period, when he vigorously stressed the need to pray for the Redemption and pointed at signs of its imminence, was the recurring tendency of his followers to place the ball back in his court.

A striking example took place at Sunday dollars on 14th April 1991. "Rebbe," one lady burst forth, "we have relied on you all the years that you would bring the Mashiach.... The task is too great for us. We want you to bring Mashiach."

"If it's something too difficult for the Jewish people," the Rebbe responded, "how could it be possible for me? I am just one person."

The lady persisted. "But you are our Rebbe! You must bring the Mashiach."

The Rebbe pointed to himself and said, "If I am Rebbe, then I have spoken clearly that this needs to be done by the Jewish people, including you." Pointing to the people standing around, he continued, "and this person, and this person."[89]

The Rebbe did not want to be perceived as a soothsayer who had predicted an event that people were simply waiting to unfold.[90] The point of the Messianic arousal had been to stimulate growth among the people, to radically uplift their standards of worship. Arguably, he was attempting to share some of the exceptional intuition he was privy to in his last years with the broader community, so as to energize, inspire, and uplift them. But it was always in the context of an *empowering* leadership—he wanted to narrow, not widen, the gap separating him from his followers.

While many factors may have contributed to the Rebbe's strong focus on Messianism, the three most outstanding were probably: his deeply intuitive temperament, the Messianism of Rayatz in the 1940s, and the turbulence of the Twentieth Century. The last two of these influences he pointed to explicitly in a 1963 letter: "You ask for an explanation of a statement in one of the general messages, a statement to the effect that we are living in the era of 'the footsteps of the Messiah.'[91] This is based on many statements of my father-in-law (*ztz"l*). See also the signs of this era as indicated by our Sages (see end of *Sotah*[92]). It is not difficult to see these signs in our present generation."[93]

The Rebbe was a man of deep intuition, something which, as we have seen, impressed Rabbi Menachem Porush, who met regularly with leading politicians and the Rabbinic elite. "The Lubavitcher Rebbe was totally unique," Porush said. "With respect to intuition there is no comparison to him."[94]

Intuitive people tend to focus on the big picture and possibilities. They look for what *could* be and are capable of perceiving the unifying thread running through very diverse ideas and phenomena. The concept of Mashiach could be described as— to borrow a term from theoretical physics—Judaism's "unified field theory"which ties all forces in the universe together into one functional system.

Throughout the Rebbe's entire life we see that he was drawn to intuitive activity: from his childhood dreams of the Messianic era (p. 2), to his fascination with the highly abstract theosophy of Chabad Chasidut; to his sustained interest in physics and engineering; to his statement, at the age of twenty-seven, that the "overwhelming focus" of his life was "the world of thought, the world of ideas" (p. 99); to his fascination with the Messianism of Rayatz; and, most especially, his forty years of creative problem-solving in correspondence and personal meetings.

A classic example of the Rebbe's ability to see the "big-picture" in problem-solving can be seen in a 1979 response to a man who complained that he was constantly worrying about being overweight. After advising the individual to "try to stop thinking about it, at least all the time, which will help you to resist excessive eating," the Rebbe suggested, "If you will strengthen your peace of mind, your metabolism will improve and you will burn more fat."[95] Speaking about a field in which he had not been trained, the Rebbe's intuition guided him to suggest a solution based on the "bigger picture." Attitude and state of mind are poorly addressed by western medicine, and must be the focus of health and healing. The Rebbe refused to look at this man's obesity as an isolated problem, and guided him to view the human body as a complex *system* of interconnected parts. If the general health of the system will be improved, the details will fall into place.

The role of intuitive thinking in the Messianic transformation was the topic of a particularly brilliant sermon, delivered on the festival of *Shavuot* in 1991. Why, the Rebbe asked, do Jewish sources predict that there will be a shift in Rabbinic consensus in the Messianic Era, with the historic precedent favoring the School of Hillel overruled by their opponents, the School of Shammai?[96]

> The reason for this change of thinking could be argued upon the lines of the Talmud's statement that, *"The School of Shammai were of sharper mind."*[97] In the past, they were unable to achieve a majority because most of the High Court judges were unable to appreciate their wisdom—like the Talmud's comment that the law does not follow Rabbi Meir, even though *"he was the wisest of the generation,"* because *"his colleagues could not fathom the depth of his wisdom."*[98]
>
> However, in the Messianic age, when as Maimonides states, *"the Jewish people will be great in wisdom,"*[99] the majority of the High Court (or perhaps all of them) will attain the "sharpness of mind" necessary to appreciate the School of Shammai, and consequently, will rule in their favor.
>
> Thus, in the future there will be changes in Jewish law, ruled (as always) according to the understanding of the human mind, due to the fact that there will be a substantial increase in the depth at which Torah is studied.[100]

What will give rise to the "substantial increase in the depth at which Torah is studied" in the future? Earlier in the sermon, the Rebbe indicated that he did not view this as some sort of miracle, but a result of "the revelation of secrets of the Torah," i.e., the influence of Jewish esotericism. In Jewish thought, *halachic* rulings may not be issued based on ideas in Kabbalah and Chasidut, and must follow a strictly Talmudic hermeneutic. But what could (and will) happen, argued the Rebbe, was a general honing and expansion of the mind through esoteric teachings that would indirectly elevate the depth at which the Talmud is studied, leading to different conclusions.

What we have here is arguably a core feature of the Rebbe's Messianism: the application of higher forms of wisdom, to solve problems in a broader context. Here the application is Jewish Law, but in the Rebbe's view there is no limit to the relevance of Torah wisdom, especially as illuminated by Chasidut. "Torah encompasses all the universe," the Rebbe told the *New York Times* on his seventieth birthday, "and it encompasses every new invention, every new theory, every new piece of knowledge or thought or action."[101]

The Messianic Era is essentially the fulfillment of this vision, where every facet of reality is illuminated by Torah and Chasidut, thereby diffusing the conflicts which have historically plagued it. Rabbi Yisrael Ba'al Shem Tov had envisioned the Messiah telling him that when "your wellsprings will spread outside" the world will be perfected, because Chasidut represents a new paradigm of human thought, capable of healing our fractured world through nourishing an advanced ecology of the mind.

All this, the Rebbe felt, was not something to be completely relegated to the future, but must be initiated in the current era, as a "bridge" to the Era of Redemption. As we have seen, the Rebbe viewed the Messianic event as largely in the hands of G-d, but also as something that required human participation (see p. 330). In order that the Redemption should not represent a rupture of history by G-d, it is crucial that man first become receptive and actively prepared for it. In the Rebbe's view, this "preparation" encompassed two key areas: a.) increased *mitzvah* observance, and b.) broadening the study and application of Chasidut.[102]

That was, more or less, the full extent of his practical message. He did not favor any this-worldly efforts to rebuild the Third Temple in Jerusalem.[103] He did not encourage *aliyah* (emigration to Israel) as an activity that would hasten the coming of Mashiach.[104] He did not point to any physical "Wars of G-d" to be fought.[105] He certainly did not encourage any changes in Jewish law, which he consistently encouraged to be observed meticulously. And while he upheld the traditional belief that the Mashiach would be a man of flesh and blood, he did not deem the identification of Mashiach's identity as important.

This last point seems to have been based on Maimonides' ruling[106] that Mashiach's identity cannot be known with certainty until the Third Temple has been built and the exiles gathered in. As the Rebbe stressed in a 1968 letter, that even after Mashiach has

> impelled all the Jewish people to study the Torah and to mend its fences, we are still not sure and require a further sign, namely, *and built the Holy Temple in its place* (clearly in the holy city of Jerusalem, indicating that there would be a large Jewish population in that city, yet we are still not certain of the end of the *Galut* (Exile), so a further factor must be fulfilled, namely), *and he gathers in the dispersed ones of Israel—then he is certainly the Mashiach*."[107]

Unlike Christianity, where belief in a particular individual as the Messiah is seen as a crucial condition of Redemption, the normative view of Judaism, as codified by Maimonides, is that the identity of the Messiah cannot be known with certainty before he completes his work. He will eventually be identified only as the *result* of this activity, from which it follows that, to bring the Redemption, we need to focus on the work and not on the persona. As we have seen, in the Rebbe's view this work consisted primarily of spreading Torah and *mitzvot*, disseminating Chasidut, and encouraging the belief in, and yearning for, the future era.

Ironically, any focus on the persona of Mashiach is liable to *detract* from the work of bringing the Redemption. After Judaism's long history of false and failed Messiahs, especially the huge debacle of Shabbatai Zvi in the 17th Century, Jews have tended to view any Messianic pretender with intense suspicion and distrust. If we do not need to know, and cannot know with certainty, who the Messiah is—as Maimonides implies[108]—then this potentially contentious issue ought to be avoided.

This was the Rebbe's view, articulated in a memorable 1984 sermon. When some of his followers began to sing a song in his presence identifying him as the Messiah, he interrupted them and said:

> I would like to speak about something negative that requires fixing... There are some overzealous Chabadniks (*shpitz Chabad*[109]) who imagine that *they* are the ones who know what needs to be done, and how it should be done. They are unmoved when those around them sometimes attempt to dissuade them from something negative. They think to themselves: Who are these people to tell me what to do? Not one of them is *shpitz Chabad!*
>
> What I am referring to is those who, as a result of their statements, verbal and printed, and their songs, have alienated many Jews from the teachings of the Ba'al Shem Tov, the study and approach of Chasidut. In fact there are Jews who had begun to study Chasidut and as a result of these individuals' activities, they have stopped doing so. Not only are they failing to bring Jews closer, they are alienating those who have already begun to come close....
>
> Let it therefore be known that anyone who continues with such activities, fights a war against Chabad Chasidut, against the Rebbe [Rayatz], against the Ba'al Shem Tov, and against Mashiach himself, who wants to come but is waiting for the further dissemination of Chasidut. These people, on the other hand, are distancing Jews from studying Chasidut, G-d forbid.
>
> May G-d spare me from having to repeat this directive again.[110]

The sermon made a very strong impression and effectively silenced any attempts to publicly identify the Rebbe as a potential Mashiach for several years.

Seven-and-a-half years later, however, the issue resurfaced. Shock waves had been sent through Chabad on a spring Thursday evening, after the Rebbe delivered what was possibly the most eye-opening sermon in forty years, one which he would even refer to himself as the *sicha ha-yadua* ("famous sermon"). Much had happened in the preceding period. Communist Russia had imploded after sixty years of tyranny for the Jews, and Israel had experienced miracles in the Gulf War—both events which the Rebbe had interpreted as signs of exceptional Divine grace and potential Messianic awakening. While the Rebbe's global influence and activities continued to grow, he had just celebrated his eighty-ninth birthday and fears were quietly mounting as to what would become of Chabad if the "unthinkable" were to transpire.

Despite the Rebbe's advanced age, his "ship" appeared to be cruising smoothly towards its goal, with the captain still firmly at it head. That perception, however, was shattered when the Rebbe uttered the following words:

> How is that ten Jews can gather together and, notwithstanding everything that has been done, we have not brought Mashiach? It's utterly incomprehensible.
>
> Then people offer their explanations, and ask yet another question. There is another *farbrengen*, which obviously is written down, and the assiduous students remember everything that is written; but then it just sits there. But the thought is deemed acceptable, G-d forbid, that Mashiach won't come tonight, or tomorrow, or the next day.
>
> You cry out for Mashiach, and you follow my instructions to do so, but if you really meant it sincerely there is no doubt that Mashiach would have come a long time ago, with the true and complete Redemption.
>
> What more I can do, I don't know. Because everything I've done until now has been futile and ineffective. Nothing has come of it. We have remained in exile, and what is worse, our worship suffers from an ingrained exile mentality, as I have stated on a number of occasions.
>
> The only thing I can do is to hand this over to each one of you: *Do everything you can to bring Mashiach!*[111]

The sense of frustration and resignation in the Rebbe's words, even in print, is palpable. From that evening, until the Rebbe's eventual passing three years later, Chabad remained haunted by the sermon. The Rebbe doesn't know what to do? Everything has been futile and ineffective? He has resigned the matter into our hands? Such thoughts were unprecedented and absolutely shocking.[112]

Desperately seeking some unexplored angle, some Chasidim decided to revisit the idea which had provoked the Rebbe's ire seven years earlier. Maybe things were different now? Maybe Mashiach was so close that it was acceptable to now broadcast whom they imagined him to be?

But at a *farbrengen* later in 1991, the scenario from 1984 repeated itself. After some of the participants chanted the same song in the Rebbe's presence intimating him as the Messiah, he reacted critically:

"It's absurd that you should sing this song, with these words, while I sit here by the table. The truth is, I should have walked out."[113]

In written communications from the period, the Rebbe was even more reprimanding. To the editors of *Kfar Chabad* magazine, who proposed to publish an article speculating about the identity of Mashiach, the Rebbe wrote, on 30th April 1991: "If you will, G-d forbid, do anything resembling this, it would be better to close down the magazine completely."[114]

To another author, who wished to publish a treatise on identifying Mashiach, the Rebbe wrote on 17th February 1992: "I have already responded to you that articles such as these alienate many people from the study of Chasidut, reversing efforts to disseminate it to broader audiences."[115]

His position was consistent with the 1968 letter: If we can only be sure of Mashiach's identity after the Temple has been built and the Jewish people are living in Israel, as Maimonides rules, then what would be the point in discussing his identity before then? If one person is alienated from Chasidut, a necessary tool to bring the Redemption, we have thwarted our intentions.

What, then, *did* the Rebbe hope to achieve with his stirring 1991 address? Two weeks later, as the question of what to do next continued to burn, the Rebbe proposed what he deemed to be the most straightforward way to bring the Redemption: to study about it. He simply recommended people to absorb discussions of the topic from the Scriptures, Talmud, Zohar and teachings of the Chabad Rebbes.[116] It was far from radical, but consistent with his message all along: We need to elevate the way we think. We need to hone our intuition.

VI

The story of the Rebbe's final illness and passing is painful for many to recount even today, some twenty years after the events transpired. In hindsight, his followers can be comforted that his life's efforts did not go to waste, and that the movement he worked so hard to build has expanded greatly even in his physical absence. A new generation has grown up that has never met the Rebbe but still seems to be inspired by his memory and his ideas. But Chabad has never been quite the same since that fateful day of Monday 2nd March 1992, when, standing at the graveside of his father-in-law, the Rebbe suffered a debilitating stroke.

Rabbi Yehuda Krinsky, who had accompanied the Rebbe on hundreds of such visits, was the only person present at the time. "At twenty to six in the afternoon," Krinsky remembered, "shortly before the time I expected him to leave the *ohel* (mausoleum), the Rebbe suddenly was not well. I tried to communicate with him, but he was unresponsive. I understood what had happened. I've seen stroke victims before. We were out in the cemetery alone and I knew it was extremely serious. I called the main office at 770 right away and told them to send *hatzalah* (an ambulance)."[117]

"It was a devastating, dominant hemisphere stroke," Dr. Ira Weiss recalled, "and we were all just so troubled by the fact that the Rebbe was in such bad condition."

Just a month before his ninetieth birthday, the Rebbe was now paralyzed on the right side of his body and confined to a wheelchair. He was unable to speak, although he could communicate minimally by nodding his head in response to a questioner. He would spend most of the next two years confined to his office in 770, with intermittent visits to hospital for gallbladder surgery, cataract removal and brain scans.

Dr. Weiss recalled his satisfaction at bringing the Rebbe a little joy under such terribly sad circumstances. "I play the flute, and one day I pulled it out of my pocket and sat and played a little Chasidic melody. It took everyone by surprise, and it was worth everything. I'm a little bit choked up because I'm remembering the Rebbe's expression, but he was brought to a real smile. We had not gotten a single smile out of him. So that was a little moment of happiness for him when he heard the melody. Music is very penetrating. I felt that it was just worth a remote try since nothing else could help him."[118]

Two other things appeared to bring him some happiness during this period. The Rebbe enjoyed watching children at play, and, when he was well enough to do so, he enjoyed having some contact with his followers atop a special balcony built for the purpose in the main synagogue at 770.

In his memoir from the summer of 1993, Zalmon Jaffe expressed his concern that the Rebbe's health did not seem to be improving. "Leibel

[Groner] had requested my views on how the Rebbe looked when I saw him in the Royal Box. I had to admit that, in my opinion, the Rebbe did not look as well today as when I had seen him last during *Sukkot*, over seven months ago. At that time the Rebbe had spent over two hours during *Simchat Torah* in the Royal Box and had even been called up for *Chatan Bereshit*. But today, it was becoming more infrequent and irregular to see the Rebbe even for a few minutes only. It was frustrating for us, but even more frustrating for the Rebbe. Mentally, the Rebbe was extremely alert and he replied to all queries through Leibel. But physically, the Rebbe was very poorly. He needed, very urgently, the blessings and assistance of the Almighty to restore him to good health."[119]

By the fall of 1993, the Rebbe was no longer well enough to make public appearances in the synagogue, and on 10th March 1994—exactly two years to the day (on the Hebrew calendar) after his stroke at the *ohel*—he suffered another major stroke, and slipped into unconsciousness. He spent his last weeks on a respirator in Beth Israel hospital, Manhattan, which became abuzz with a constant flow of hundreds, sometimes thousands of Chasidim who wanted to be close to their Rebbe and pray for his recovery.

On Saturday night, 11th June 1994, after he went into cardiac arrest at 7 p.m., the doctors were able to stabilize his condition. But at 12:55 a.m., after the Hebrew date had switched from 2nd to 3rd *Tammuz* at nightfall, he suffered a second cardiac arrest. At 1:50 am, exactly fifty-three years and five days after he had stepped on American soil for the first time, the hospital announced that all efforts to resuscitate the Rebbe had failed. He was interred the following afternoon in Montefiore Cemetery in Queens, next to his father-in-law, Rayatz, amid huge crowds of an estimated fifty to one hundred thousand mourners. His coffin was made from the wood of two tables that he used throughout his life: at one he would pray with his followers; at the other he would greet visitors who came for advice and blessing. "He symbolically carried his dual concerns—for his own and for the larger world—right to his grave," noted journalist Ari Goldman.[120]

Those who came to show their respects included: Rabbinic leaders from all over the world; New York Mayor, Rudolph Giuliani; Binyamin Netanyahu, then leader of Israel's opposition; Gad Yaacobi, Israel's ambassador to the United Nations; and Malcolm Hoenlein of the Conference of Presidents of Major American Jewish Organizations. Tributes were made to the Rebbe's life from a wide spectrum. President Bill Clinton noted, "He, as much as any other individual, was responsible for advancing the instruction of ethics and morality to our young people." Israeli Prime Minister Yitzchak Rabin wrote of "a loss for all the Jewish people"; and Foreign Minister Shimon Peres described the Rebbe as "a leader of the highest stature." Mayor Rudolph Giuliani declared the Rebbe "a religious leader for all people."[121]

As he had no biological relatives, there was nobody to say *kaddish* for him, but many of his spiritual children, his disciples, took upon themselves to recite *kaddish* during the year of mourning. The tombstone erected shortly after his passing summed up his life's achievements humbly, in just three words: *ve-rabim hashiv me-avon*, "And he caused many to return from sin."[122]

AFTERWORD

There is a tradition in Chabad that the formula "here concludes the Pesach Seder" is not recited after reading the Passover Haggadah. The rationale offered is that the story of the Jewish people does not end. The narrative always continues. In a similar vein, it is difficult to write a concluding thought about the Rebbe, as his story continues to unfold some twenty years after his passing.

As a man who eschewed personal honor, I wonder how much he would have cared to be posthumously awarded the Congressional Gold Medal, the nation's highest award to a civilian. Would he have felt rewarded to hear dignitaries in Washington praising his lifetime of achievements? If it would help the Chabad movement, or the Jewish people, then perhaps the answer would be yes.

The story of Chabad's staggering growth in the two decades after the Rebbe's passing could fill another book. "The Rebbe did not leave a legacy," Israeli scholar Rabbi Adin Steinsaltz observed, "He left marching orders."[1] The Rebbe desired growth and that, his followers understood, would be the greatest tribute to him in his afterlife.

The success has been phenomenal. In the first sixteen years following the Rebbe's passing, a staggering 2400 new *shluchim* established Chabad centers around the world, bringing the total number of full-time Chabad outreach workers to over 4000. In fact, one of the biggest problems now facing the movement, ironically, is that the world has become too small, as even the tiniest, most geographically distant Jewish communities already have their own full-time Chabad *shliach.*

Each *shliach* and *shluchah* has absorbed something of the Rebbe's spirit, most notably his wide-reaching concern and focus on implementing goals. In a 1994 eulogy, Rabbi Aharon Lichtenstein, Rosh Yeshivah of *Yeshivat Har Etzion,* highlighted these two areas as the Rebbe's most notable qualities. "To the best of my knowledge," Rabbi Lichtenstein wrote, "no one in this generation compares to the Rebbe—or even comes close—in terms of applying his vision and implementing it.... The Rebbe's primary quality was *concern.* Not in the narrow sense of the word, i.e., concern for his own home, movement or synagogue, but seeing the big picture. This included the big geographical picture, a movement with emissaries, men and women, on every continent, as well as the big cultural picture. Not only in the yeshiva world but in the university world; not only in the religious world but in the secular world, in places from which he should have ostensibly kept his distance. What did he have to do with the IDF? It was his concern that brought this about. He cared enough to see things on a historic and national scale."[2]

Perhaps even more noteworthy than the huge following he amassed within Chabad, is the Rebbe's significant influence on other segments of Jewry, both to his right and to his left. As right-wing Orthodoxy has increasingly devoted itself to the outreach ideal, departing from its initial resistance to the idea, scholars have begun to speak of the phenomenon of "Chabadization." Adam Ferziger has observed that many in the non-Chasidic Yeshiva world have, "veered away from insularity and have adopted significant aspects of the outreach ideal first championed on American soil by Schneerson," following "a worldview reorientation from a formerly sectarian direction toward a more inclusive, outreach posture.... A transformation has taken place that has touched the broadest spectrum of American *mitnagedic* Orthodoxy."[3]

Today, the combined result of the Chabad and non-Chabad outreach forces represents an enormous presence. One scholar has estimated it to be a total of 5,000–7,000 men and women working full time in the U.S.A. alone, which is more than double the number of active Conservative, Reform, and all other permutations of liberal rabbis combined.[4]

The admiration stemming from Reform circles, which is in many ways Chabad's diametric opposite, points to an exceptionally broad influence of the Rebbe. Chabad, which vigorously preserves the hallowed traditions of Jewish law, might appear to be terribly disadvantaged in terms of appeal to a secular audience over Reform, which does not require the observance of *halacha*. But Chabad's exceptional warmth and non-judgmentalism has impressed even Reform leaders as a model worth emulating. In a keynote sermon in 2003, Reform leader Eric Yoffie, declared: "It is hard for me to say this, but I will say it nonetheless: We must follow the example of Chabad." Noting that he disagreed with Chabad about "practically everything," Yoffie continued, "But I envy the selflessness of their young men and women who fan out across the world to serve Jewish communities in distress. We must foster among our members the same sense of mission and spirit of service to the Jewish people. We, too, in our own way, must provide teachers, Torah, and spiritual sustenance to Jews who require them."[5]

On another occasion, Yoffie praised "Chabad's monumental contribution to Jewish life... its willingness to serve Jewish populations not served by others. In North America, Chabad's representatives minister to Jewish prisoners long neglected by the Jewish establishment and reach out to college students in dozens of isolated communities. Throughout the world, in virtually every city where a Jewish community of even modest size is to be found, Chabad *shluchim*—emissaries—conduct religious services, visit hospitals, teach children, organize Jewish holiday celebrations, and offer Shabbat meals to lonely Jewish students and tourists. The work is done by Chabad couples—usually young couples—who commit themselves to this effort with tremendous devotion and at great personal sacrifice."[6]

Yoffie was also impressed by Chabad's willingness to be proactive in carrying out outreach, even in the absence of significant seed money. "A lot of people in the Jewish world talk about their desire to do outreach—if only they could get a grant. But Chabad does not wait for grants, and no other Jewish movement has been able to produce a corps of similarly devoted young men and women prepared to serve the Jewish people with such personal sacrifice."[7]

Reform Rabbi and historian Dana Evan Kaplan has also written admiringly of Chabad. "Virtually everyone—no matter what their religious views—is positively impressed with the sincerity and enthusiasm of the *shluchim*. They model a selfless idealism that seems almost unbelievable in today's self-centered world.... Chabad seems able to touch souls in ways the established Jewish denominations cannot. Mainstream *machers* still find this fact unbelievable."[8]

How does Chabad appeal in ways that others struggle to emulate? Or, as author Jay Michaelson puts it: How is it that "guys with beards" are "doing a better job reaching the unaffiliated than smart Ivy grads with masters degrees in public relations?" Michaelson argues that the secret of Chabad's appeal lies in its focus, not on community and continuity—what he calls "tribalism"—but on spirit. Chabad, he says, is "about ultimate reality, about asking deep questions and searching for answers. Again, one may disagree entirely with a Chabad *shliach's* view of the universe, but look into his eyes, and anyone can sense the earnestness. Not only does the Chasid believe in G-d; he believes there is nothing but G-d: that this moment is charged, filled and energized by the Divine Presence. And that mystical belief translates into enthusiasm, open-heartedness and devotion. It shows, and it works."[9]

Many have wondered why the Rebbe chose not to appoint a successor, and since he did not address the question directly we can only speculate why this was the case. Arguably, he may have perceived that the movement was too large and too diverse for any single individual to establish themselves effectively as leader, especially as the Schneerson dynasty had come to its end. What we do know is that as he neared the end of his life he spoke on a number of occasions about a more localized system of decision-making and leadership (see pp. 379-381), which is essentially what transpired. As Rabbi Tzvi Hersh Weinreb, Executive Vice President Emeritus of the Orthodox Union has observed, "Every Chabad rabbi has taken upon himself the role of leader, if not over a mass movement, then over his own small circle. And the evidence is that in the years since the Rebbe is gone these leaders are presiding over a fantastic further growth of Chabad and all that it represents."[10]

Chasidim, of course, may always appoint a new leader, but in this case they opted not to, choosing instead to keep the Rebbe's memory sharply in focus, and to make his ongoing spiritual presence palpable through studying his teachings, following his directives, watching recordings of his sermons and visiting his grave site (*ohel*) regularly. The *ohel*, in particular has become a site of regular pilgrimage, with as many as 15,000 visitors attending on special dates, such as the annual anniversary of the Rebbe's passing (*yahrtzeit*). The brightly lit, air-conditioned welcome center which has been constructed at the location, is open 24 hours a day, offering complimentary refreshments to visitors. (The center typically goes through 780 pounds of cookies in a week!)[11] The *ohel* draws a very wide range of visitors: Rabbinic figures, Jews of every description, and a significant number of non-Jews. Senator Cory Booker, for example, visited the *ohel* to pray on the night before his electoral victory in 2013.[12]

Chabad has both gained and suffered from the lack of a single, centralized leader. It has gained from the incredible growth that a grassroots-style autonomy can lead to; but has suffered from the lack of a unifying force that only powerful, charismatic leadership can bring. Still, the fact that it has survived and grown exponentially since the Rebbe's passing is a testimony to the potency and clarity of his message. While as time passes, each subsequent generation struggles to be as inspired by the Rebbe as their parents and grandparents, who knew him personally, success rates still seem to be high. Young couples who were babies when the Rebbe passed on continue to leave Brooklyn almost every week, to carry out Chabad work on distant shores.

But the Rebbe and his teachings are not just for Chabad people. Chasidut is a tremendously uplifting wisdom which has much potential to elevate the way people think and make decisions. Dr. Domenico Lepore, an expert in systems-based management, is not Jewish but makes consistent use of the Rebbe's teachings in his daily work. He is convinced that "Chasidic thinking can inform and guide better choices and create sustainable wealth" and that the Rebbe's teachings contain "unparalleled wisdom for the world at large."[14] While examples such as these are few, they do foster the hope that the Rebbe's wisdom might one day inform widespread decision making in the higher culture. One gets the sense that the Rebbe's sermons and discourses represent a volcano of content waiting to erupt as soon as the correct language, useful application, and appropriate media will be found.

A wonderful anecdote, which brings to light the Rebbe's belief in Jewish esoteric wisdom as a source of enrichment for mankind, is told by Yaakov Brawer, Professor of Anatomy and Cell Biology at McGill University. Brawer was surprised when his weekly class in the Rebbe's Chasidic discourses in the 1990s began to be regularly attended by an Episcopalian of undiluted Christian lineage. The individual, who Brawer refers to as "Winston," later explained his avid interest. As a teenager, some thirty years previously, Winston had been waiting for his aunt to pick him up on the corner of Kingston Avenue and Eastern Parkway, when he heard a commotion and turned around. Though he had no knowledge of anything Jewish, Winston was struck by the sight of the Rebbe emerging from 770, amid an entourage of Chasidim.

The lad moved aside to let the procession pass, but the Rebbe stopped by the step where Winston was sitting.

The Rebbe looked at the young man and asked, "Do you have any questions?"

Winston was taken aback.

"Ask anything you like," the Rebbe added.

"In that case," Winston replied, "I would like to know how you would be able to answer *any* question?"

The Rebbe looked intently at Winston for what seemed to him to be a very long time, and answered "Kabbalah."[14]

The Rebbe's lifelong conviction was that Torah, especially Chasidut and Kabbalah, can enrich the human mind and bring us to a new paradigm. Chabad, after all, stands for *chochmah, binah* and *da'at* (wisdom, understanding and knowledge), the belief that your intelligence is your operating system and that if you change your intelligence a new dimension of reality is available. Chasidut awakens us to the interconnectedness of all life and empowers us with the ability to live an enlightened existence even in lower states of mind and functioning. By studying the Rebbe's life these abstractions become real since they are the values by which he lived and breathed.

May his memory be a blessing for mankind, and an inspiration for personal growth and intelligent living.

PUBLISHED WORKS CITED

BY THE REBBE, MENACHEM MENDEL SCHNEERSON

WORKS PENNED BEFORE 1950

Haggadah Shel Pesach im Likutei Minhagim ve-Ta'amim. New York: Kehot, 1946.

Hayom Yom. New York, Kehot 1943

Hatza'at Tochen Sichah Be-Hitva'adut u-Mesibat Benei Torah, Choveret Rishonah, Shnayim Ochazin be-Tallit. New York: Kehot, 1996.

Teshuvot u'Biurim. New York: Kehot, 1987.

Reshimot. New York: Kehot 1995-2011, 188 installments.

Reshimat Ha-Menorah. New York: Kehot, 1998.

Reshimat Ha-Yoman. New York: Kehot, 2006.

Reshimot al Ha-Tanya. New York: Kehot, 1995-2007, 67 installments.

Sefer Ha-Mafteichot le-kamah mi-sifrei u-ma'amarei Chasidut Chabad. New York: Kehot, 1966.

Sefer Ha-Toldot Admor Maharash. New York: Kehot, 1947.

SERMONS AND DISCOURSES (EDITED FOR PUBLICATION BY THE REBBE)

Likutei Sichot. New York: Kehot, 1966-2001, 39 vols.

Sefer ha-Ma'amarim Melukat,. New York: Kehot, 1987-1992, 6 vols.

Sefer ha-Sichot 5748-5752. New York: Kehot, 1989-1993, 10 vols.

SERMONS (STUDENTS' NOTES—UNEDITED)

Sichot Kodesh 5710-5741 (Yiddish). New York:1985-1987, 50 vols.

Torat Menachem—Hitva'aduyot 5710-5727. New York: Va'ad Hanachot Lahak, 1993-2014, 50 vols.

Torat Menachem—Hitva'aduyot 5742-5752. New York: Va'ad Hanachot Lahak, 1982-1993, 43 vols.

Sichot Kodesh 5752 (Hebrew). New York: Va'ad Kitvei Kodesh, 1992, 2 vols.

Sichot Kodesh Kodem Ha-Nesiut. New York: Va'ad Chayalei Beit David, 2010.

DISCOURSES (STUDENTS' NOTES—UNEDITED)

Sefer Ha-Ma'amarim 5711-5729, New York: Va'ad Hanachot Lahak, 2006-10, 18 vols.

Sefer Ha-Ma'amarim 5730-5737, New York: Va'ad Kitvei Kodesh, 1989-1994, 5 vols.

Sefer Ha-Ma'amarim 5738-5751, New York: Va'ad Hanachot Hatemimim, 2002, 8 vols.

CORRESPONDENCE

Davar Melech: leket teshuvot meyuchadot. Kfar Chabad: Ufaratzta, 1992.

Jaffe, Avrohom (ed.). *Mr. Manchester: Forty Years of Correspondence from the Lubavitcher Rebbe.* private publication, 2003.

Kuntres Tzadik Le-Melech vols. 4-6. New York, 1993.

Laufer, Mordechai Menasheh (ed.). *Heichal Menachem,* Jerusalem: Heichel Menachem, 1994-5, 3 vols.

Lesches, Elchonon (ed.) *Letters from the Rebbe.* New York: 1997-2005, 6 vols.

Letters by the Lubavitcher Rebbe shlita, Rabbi M. M. Schneerson To N'shei u'Bnot Chabad 1956-1980. New York: Kehot, 1981.

Levin, Shalom Ber (ed.), *Igrot Kodesh Admor Menachem Mendel Schneerson.* New York: Kehot, 1987-2009, 30 vols.

Me-Otzar Hamelech. Israel, 2005.

Mindel, Nissan (ed.). *The Letter and the Spirit: Letters by the Lubavitcher Rebbe, Rabbi Menachem M. Schneerson.* (New York: Nissan Mindel Publications 1998-2014), 2 vols.

———. *Moreh Le-dor Navuch: Igrot Kodesh Admor Menachem Mendel Schneerson.* Kfar Chabad: 2004, 3 vols.

Notik, Tzvi Hirsh, Liberov, Mordechai and Zaklikovsky, Eliezer (eds.). *Nalchah B'Orchotav.* New York: Private publication, 1996.

Schapiro, Shalom Ber (ed.), *Sparks of Chasidut for Young and Old.* New York: Nissan Mindel Publications, 1999.

Shaikowitz, Levi Yitzchak, (ed.). *Professor Greene, Greetings and Blessings* (Heb.). Central Beit Chabad, Bet Sheva, 2011.

Teshurah Avtzon-Simpson, 2005.

Teshurah Friedman-Grossbaum, 2009.

Teshurah Groner-Pinson, 2013.

Teshurah Krinsky-Dechter, 2007.

Teshurah Krinsky-Stazakovsky, 2013.

Teshurah Lipskar-Krinsky, 2013.

Teshurah Baruch Shneur and Chaya Krinsky, 2010.

*Teshurah Aron and Dinie Rabin,*1999.

Teshurah Rimler-Schneider, 1995.

Teshurah Simpson-Zajac, 2010.

Torat Menachem—Igrot Melech. Kfar Chabad: Kehot, 1992, 2 vols.

Wolf, Zusya (ed.). *Days of the Temimim: Fifty years of activities in building and expanding Chasidut Chabad in the Holy Land.* Kfar Chabad: Kehot, 2008-2010, 8 vols.

TRANSCRIPTS OF DISCUSSIONS (STUDENTS' NOTES—UNEDITED)

(Mordechai Menasheh Laufer ed.). *Ha-Melech be-Mesiboh.* New York: Kehot, 1993. 2 vols.

Siach Sarfei Kodesh. Jerusalem: Machon Oholei Tzadikim, 1998.

Zorea Tzedakot Matzmiach Yeshuot. New York: Fax a Sicha, 1993.

ANTHOLOGIES OF TEACHINGS

Bistritzky, Shmuel (ed.). *Ha-Mivtza'im Ke-Hilchatam.* Israel: Private publication, 2009, 2 vols.

Blau, Tuvia (ed.). *Klalei Rashi.* Kfar Chabad: Kehot, expanded edition 1991.

Feldman, David (ed.). *Torat Menachem—Tiferet Levi Yitzchak.* New York: Kehot, 1990, 3 vols.

Friedman, Alter Eliyahu (ed.). *Biurim le-Pirkei Avot.* New York: Kehot, 4th edition 1996, 2 vols.

Goldstein, Levi (ed.). *Index to issues of education and guidance.* New York: Private publication, 2001.

Golomb, Michoel (ed.). *Sha'arei Limud Ha-Chasidut.* New York: Kehot, 1994.

Greenglass, Zev Wolf and Groner, Yehudah Leib (eds.). *Sefer ha-Minhagim—Chabad* New York:

Kehot, 1963.

Groner, Levi and Karishovsky, Moshe (eds.). *Karati V'en Oneh.* Jerusalem: M.L. Publications, 2002.

Havlin, Yosef Yitzchak (ed.). *Sha'arei Chinnuch.* Jerusalem: Heichal Menachem, 2007.

———. *Sha'arei Eretz Yisrael.* Jerusalem: Heichal Menachem, 2002.

———. *Sha'arei Halacha u'Minhag.* Jerusalem: Heichal Menachem, 1993-2001, 5 vols.

Laufer, Mordechai Menashe (ed.). *Sefer Ha-Shlichut.* Kfar Chabad: Kehot, 1987.

———. *Klalei ha-Rambam.* Kfar Chabad: Kehot 1991.

———. *Machshevei Rebbi.* Private publication, 2000.

———. *Nitzutei Rebbi* in *Hitkashrut.* Chabad in Israel, 1995-2014 (weekly).

Miller, Chaim (ed.). *Kol Boi Ha-Olam.* New York: Va'ad mi-Golah le-Geulah, 1999.

Mondshine, Yehoshua (ed.). *Otzar Minhagei Chabad.* Jerusalem: Heichal Menachem, 1995-6, 2 vols.

Newhouser, Yehoshua Menachem (ed.). *Ha-tzafnat Pane'ach be-Mishnat ha-Rebbi.* New York: Va'ad Le-Hafatzat Sichot, 2002.

Oirechman, Yechiel Baruch (ed.). *Lema'an Tatzliach: Anthology of directives and advice in earning a living and business.* Kfar Chabad: Eishel, 1998.

Seligson, Michoel (ed.). *Sefer ha-Mafteichot le-Sichot Kodesh* 5695-5752. New York, 2011.

Sinai, Dov, and Ginoser, Zev (eds.). *Ish Emunah.* Tel Aviv: Askilah, 2011.

Wolf, Zusha. *Diedushka: The Lubavitcher Rebbe and Russian Jewry.* Moscow: Committee of Shluchim of the Soviet Union, 2006.

———. *To Jewish Women and Girls: The Jewish mother, wife and daughter in the thought of the Rebbe* (Heb.) Kfar Chabad: Kehot, 1996.

———. *Torat Ha-Shlichut: The Task of our Generation in the Lubavitcher Rebbe's Teachings.* Kfar Chabad: Kehot, 2003.

TRANSLATIONS

Ginsburg, Joseph, and Branover, Herman (eds). Arnie Gotfryd (trans.). *Mind over Matter: Teachings of the Lubavitcher Rebbe on Science, Technology and Medicine.* Jerusalem: Shamir, 2003.

Greenberg, H. and Handelman, S. (trans.). *On the Essence of Chassidut.* New York: Kehot, 1986.

Kaploun, Uri (trans.). *In Good Hands: 100 Letters and Talks of the Lubavitcher Rebbe, Rabbi Menachem M. Schneerson on Bitachon, Trusting in G-d.* New York: Sichos in English, 2005.

———. *Proceeding Together: The Earliest Talks of The Lubavitcher Rebbe* . New York: Sichos in English, 1995-2009, 4 vols.

Miller, Chaim (trans.). *Chumash Kol Menachem.* New York: Kol Menachem, 2006.

———. *Rambam: Thirteen Principles of Faith—Principles 8-9.* New York: Kol Menachem, 2007.

———. *The Kol Menachem Haggadah.* New York: Kol Menachem, 2008.

Sichos in English. New York, 1978-1992, 51 vols.

Sones, Mordechai and Koncepolski, Yankel (trans.). *When Silence is a Sin: The Obligation to Protest and The Obligation to Settle the Entire Land of Israel.* New York: Sichos in Engish, 2005.

Touger, Eliyahu (trans.). *I Will Write it in Their Hearts: A Treasury of Letters from the Lubavitcher Rebbe.* New York: Sichos in English, 1999-2006, 5 vols.

———. *Eyes Upon The Land.* New York: Sichos in English, 1997.

Touger, Eliyahu and Wineberg, Sholom B. (trans.), *Basi LeGani: Chasidic Discourses.* New York: Kehot, 1990.

Wineberg, Shalom B. (trans.). *Eternal Joy: A Guide To Shidduchim and Marriage from the works of the Lubavitcher Rebbe.* New York: Sichos in English, 2000-2001, 3 vols.

———. *Healthy in Body, Mind and Spirit based on the Teachings of the Lubavitcher Rebbe.* New York: Sichos in English, 2005-2007, 3 vols.

WORKS BY THE REBBE'S PARENTS AND GRANDPARENTS

Lavut, Avraham David. *Kav Naki* (Warsaw, 1868).

———. *Sha'ar Ha-Kolel* (Vilna 1896).

Schneerson, Baruch Shneur (Aharon Leib Raskin, ed.). *Reshimat ha-Rabash.* New York: Kehot, 2001.

Schneerson, Chana. *Memoirs.* New York: Kehot, 2001-2, 39 installments.

———.(Alter Friedman ed., Tilles Yerachmiel trans.), *A Mother in Israel.* New York: Kehot 2006.

Schneerson, Levi Yitzchak. *Likutei Levi Yitzchak.* New York: Kehot 1972, 3 vols.

———. *Torat Levi Yitzchak.* New York: Kehot 1985.

———. *Michtavei Hachatuna.* New York, 1999.

———. (Shalom Ber Levin ed.). *Kovetz Chaf Menachem Av, Shishim Shanah.* New York: Kehot, 2004.

WORKS BY THE EARLIER CHABAD REBBES

Shneur Zalman of Liadi, *Likutei Torah.* New York: Kehot, 1992.

———. *Shulchan Aruch Admor ha-Zaken.* New York: Kehot, 2001-2005, 6 vols.

———. *Torah Ohr.* New York: Kehot, 1992.

———. *Tanya.* New York: Kehot 1989.

———. *Likutei Amarim, First Versions, based on earliest manuscripts.* New York: Kehot, 1982.

Schneersohn, Menachem Mendel, *Shu't Tzemach Tzedek ve-Chidushim al ha-Shas*γ New York: Kehot, new edition 1994, and supplement 2009, 6 vols.

———. *Tzemach Tzedek, Chidushim al ha-Shas,* New York: Kehot, fifth edition, 1992γ

———. *Tzemach Tzedek, Piskei Dinim.* New York: Kehot, fifth edition, 1992.

———. *Derech Mitzvotecha—Ta'amei Ha-Mitzvot.* New York: Kehot, 2006.

Schneersohn, Shalom Ber. *Be-sha'ah She-hikdimu 5672,* vol. 3. third Edition: New York, Kehot 1992.

Schneersohn, Yosef Yitzchak. (Shalom Ber Levin, ed.), *Igrot Kodesh Admor Yosef Yitzchak Schneersohn.* New York: Kehot, 1982-2014, 17 vols.

———. (Zalman Posner trans.). *On the Study of Chasidut.* New York: Kehot 1997.

———. (Zalman I. Posner trans.). *The Tzemach Tzedek and the Haskala Movement.* New York: Kehot, 1969.

———. *Sefer Ha-Ma'amarim* 5685. New York: Kehot, 1986.

———. *Sefer ha-Sichot* 5680-5710. New York: Kehot. 1992-2001, 6 vols.

———. *Likutei Dibburim.* New York: Kehot 1992, 2 vols.

———. (Neubort, Shimon trans.). *Branches of the Chassidic Menorah,* vol. 1. New York: Sichos in English, 1998.

———. (Neubort, Shimon trans.). *The Making of Chassidim.* New York: Sichos in English, 1995.

RABBINIC SOURCES

Ba'al Shem Tov, Israel. (Schochet, Immanuel ed.), *Keter Shem Tov.* New York: Kehot, 2004.

Babylonian Talmud.

Bacharach, Naftali Hertz. *Emek HaMelech.* Amsterdam, 1648.

Feinstein, Moshe. *Igrot Moshe,* New York: 1959-2011, 9 vols.

Gourary, Yochanan, *Chikrei Minhagim.* Kfar Chabad: Machon Oholei Shem, 1999-2006, 2 vols.

Jerusalem Talmud.

Kasher, Menachem Mendel, *Mefaneach Tzefunot.* New York, 1960.

———. *Ha-Tekufah Ha-Gedolah.* Machon Torah Shleima, 1968.

Maimonides, Moses (Kapach ed.). *Commentary to the Mishnah* (1967).
———. *Epistle on Resurrection.*
———. *Mishneh Torah Mehadurat Shabatai Frankel,* Hotza'at Shabse Frankel, 1973-2007, 14 vols.
———. Responsa *Pe'er Ha'dor.* Amsterdam, 1765.
Midrash Rabah.
Quint, Eliyahu. *Menuchat Eliyahu* vol. 1. New York, Private publication, 1965.
Rosen, Yosef. *Tzafnat Paneach al ha-Rambam, Laws of Tefilin.* Israel: 1979, 2 vols.
Shach, Elazar. *Michtavim v'Ma'amarim.* Israel: 1986, 2 vols.
Teitelbaum, Yoel. *Al Ha-Geulah ve-al Ha-Temurah.* Brooklyn, 1967
———. *Divrei Yoel,* vol. 7. Brooklyn, 1980.
Weinberg, Yechiel Ya'akov. *Seridei Aish.* Jerusalem: Mosad Harav Kook, 1961-69, 4 vols.
Zacuto, Moshe, *Igrot Ha-Ramaz.* Livorno, 1780.
Zevin, Shlomo Yosef. *Sofrim u'Sefarim.* Tel Aviv: Avraham Zioni, 1959

OTHER SOURCES

Abelow, Samuel P. *History of Brooklyn Jewry.* Brooklyn: Scheba Publishing Company, 1937
Abrahamson, Irving (ed.). *Elie Wiesel, Against Silence: The Voice and Vision of Elie Wiesel,* vol. 3. New York: 1985.
Alpenbaim, Yisrael, *Yirat Shamayim Otzaro, the life of Harav HaChasid Rabbi Yitzchak the Masmid* (Heb.). Kfar Chabad 1996.
———. *Hamashpia Reb Shlomo Chaim Kesselman,* 2 vols. Israel: Private publication, 2013.
Altein, Rachel and Zaklikovsky, Eliezer. *Out of the Inferno: The efforts that led to the rescue of Rabbi Yosef Yitzchak Schneersohn of Lubavitch from war-torn Europe in 1939-40.* New York: Kehot, 2002.
Altein, Ya'akov Leib (ed.), *Heichal Ha-Besht,* issue 32, 2011.
Aronson, Mishael. *And the Living Shall Take it to Heart* (Heb.) Private publication, 2009.
———. (Daniel Goldberg, trans.). *The Rebbetzin: Biography, Reminiscences and Stories about Rebbetzin Chaya Mushka Schneerson.* Private publication, 2012.
Ashkenazi, Yosef, *Otzar Hachasidim—New York.* Israel: Chazak, 2013.
———. *Otzar Hachasidim—Eretz Hakodesh.* Israel: Chazak, 2012.
Ashman, Charles R. *The Finest Judges Money Can Buy, and other forms of Judicial Pollution.* Los Angeles: Nash Publishing, 1973
Assaf, David (trans. David Louvish). *The Regal Way: The Life and Times of Rabbi Israel of Ruzhin.* California: Stanford University Press, 2002.
Avner, Yehuda. *The Prime Ministers: An Intimate Narrative of Israeli Leadership.* New Milford, Conneticut: The Toby Press, 2010.
Avtzon, Sholom Dovber, *Tzemach Tzedek—Rabbi Menachem Mendel of Lubavitch.* New York: Avtzon Books, 2012.
Beizer, Mikail. *The Jews of Leningrad* (Heb). Jerusalem: Zalman Shazar Center for Jewish History, 2005.
———. *The Jews of St. Petersburg: Excursions Through a Noble Past.* Philadelphia: Jewish Publication Society 1989.
Ben-Rafael, Eliezer. *Jewish Identities: Fifty Intellectuals Answer Ben Gurion.* Leiden: Brill, 2002.
Berger, Shneur Zalman, *The History of Chabad in Petersburg* (Heb.). Israel, Kfar Chabad: Kehot 2010
———. *Eved Avraham Anochi: The Life and Activities of Rabbi Chaim Eliezer Karasik.* Israel: Machon Oholei Shem Lubavitch, 2012.
———. *Yisrael Noach Ha-Gadol.* Israel: Private publication, 2006.
Blau, Yosef (ed.). *The Conceptual Approach to Jewish Learning.* New Jersey: Ktav Publishing House Inc., 2006.

Bleich, David. "Survey of Recent Halakhic Periodical Literature: Piscatorial Parasites" in *Tradition, a Journal of Orthodox Jewish Thought* 44:1, Spring 2011 and 44:4, Winter 2011.

Block, Irving. *G-d, Rationality and Mysticism.* Marquette Univ Press, 2008.

Bogomilsky, Moshe. *Hei Teves—Didan Notzach: The Victory of the Sefarim.* Private publication, fourth impression 2012.

Branover, Herman and Naveh, Avraham (Mika Tubinshlak trans.). *The Ultimate Jew.* Jerusalem and New York: Shamir, 2003.

Branover, Herman. *Return: The Spiritual Odyssey of a Soviet Scientist.* Israel: Shamir, third edition, 2002.

Brook, Chaim. *To Still the Enemy and Avenger: Forty Years since the Miracles of the Yom Kippur War* (Heb.). New York, 2014.

Cain, Susan. *Quiet: The Power of Introverts in a World That Can't Stop Talking.* Crown Publishing Group, 2012.

Carmel, Aryeh and Domb, Cyril (eds.). *Challenge: Torah Views on Science and Its Problems.* The Association of Orthodox Jewish Scientists in association with Feldheim Publishers, 1976

Challenge: An encounter with Lubavitch-Chabad. Lubavitch Foundation of Great Britain, 1970.

Dahan, Alon. *Dirah ba-Tachtonim.* PhD dissertation, Hebrew University 2006.

Dalfin, Chaim. *Conversations with the Rebbe, Menachem Mendel Schneerson.* Los Angeles: JEC publishing, 1996.

———. *The Seven Chabad-Lubavitch Rebbes.* New Jersey: Jason Aronson, 1998.

———. *Who's Who in Lubavitch.* New York: Jewish Enrichment Press, 2003.

———. *Who's Who in Lubavitch II.* New York: Jewish Enrichment Press, 2011.

Davidman, Lynn. *Tradition in a Rootless World: Women Turn to Orthodox Judaism.* University of California Press, 1991.

Deutch, Shaul S. *Larger than Life: The Life and Times of the Lubavitcher Rebbe.* New York, 1995-7, 2 vols.

Di Yiddishe Heim. New York: Kehot, 1963-4.

Dov Schwartz, *Chabad Thought: From Beginning to End.* Israel: Bar Ilan University Press, 2011.

Dresner, Samuel H. *The Doctrine of the Zaddik According to the Writings of Rabbi Ya'akov Yosef of Polnoy.* New York: Schocken Books, 1980.

Dubov, Nissan Dovid. *To Love A Fellow Jew: The Mitzvah of Ahavat Yisrael in Chasidic Thought.* New York: Sichos in English, 1999.

Duchman, Zalman. *Le-Sheima Ozen.* New York, 1963

Elior, Rachel (Yudith Nave and Arthur Millman trans.). *Jewish Mysticism: The Infinite Expression of Freedom.* Portland: Littman Library, 2007.

——— (Jeffrey Green trans). *The Paradoxical Ascent to G-d: The Kabbalisitc Theosophy of Habad Hasidism.* Albany: State University of New York, 1993.

Epstein, Joseph (ed.), *Shiurei Harav: A Conspectus of the Public Lectures of Rabbi Joseph B. Soloveitchik.* New Jersey: Ktav, 1994.

Etkes, Immanuel (trans. Jeffrey Green), *The Gaon of Vilna: The Man and His Image.* California: University of California Press, 2002.

———. *The Besht.* Massachusetts: Brandeis University Press, 2005.

Farber, Seth. *An American Orthodox Dreamer: Rabbi Joseph B. Soloveitchik and Boston's Maimonides School.* Brandeis University Press, 2004.

Feldestein, Ariel L. *Ben-Gurion, Zionism and American Jewry 1948-1963.* New York: Routledge, 2006.

Ferziger, Adam S. "From Lubavitch to Lakewood: The Chabadization of American Orthodoxy," *Modern Judaism,* Volume 33, Number 2, May 2013.

Fishkoff, Sue. *The Rebbe's Army: Inside the World of Chabad-Lubavitch.* New York: Shocken, 2003.

Fishman, David E., "Preserving Tradition in the Land of Revolution: The Religious Leadership of Soviet Jewry, 1917-1930," in Jack Wertheimer (ed.), *The Uses of Tradition: Jewish Continuity in the Modern Era.* New York 1992, Jewish Theological Seminary of America.

Friedman, Menachem, and Heilman, Samuel. *The Rebbe: The Life and Afterlife of Menachem Mendel Schneerson.* Princeton University Press, 2010.

Friedman, Yosef B. (ed.). *Let There Be Light: Thirty Days in the Lives of the Chabad Lubavitch Lamplighters.* New York: Kehot, 1986.

Gerson, Charlotte and Walker, Morton. *The Gerson Therapy.* New York: Kensington Books, revised edition, 2006.

Glitzenstein, Avraham Chanoch, Steinsaltz, Adin and Wolf, Berke (eds.). *The Rebbe: Thirty Years of Leadership.* Israel, 1980.

Glitzenstein, Avraham Chanoch (ed.). *Sefer ha-Yechidut.* Kfar Chabad: Kehot, 1989.

———. *Sefer Ha-Toldot Rebbi Yosef Yitzchak Schneersohn of Lubavitch.* Kfar Chabad: Kehot, 1974.

Golan, Avirama. "Messiah of Flesh and Blood, Piecing Together the Rebbe's Secret Years." *Haaretz* 20th April, 1998

Goldberg, Hillel. *Between Berlin and Slobodka.* New Jersey: Ktav, 1989

Goldberg, Shelly. *The Spiritual Voyage of the Soul: The Soul of the 'Tzaddik' and the Eternity of the Spirit in Chabad's doctrine.* Israel: Rubin Mass, 2009.

Goodwin, Doris Kearns. *No Ordinary Time. Franklin and Eleanor Roosevelt: The Home Front in World War II.* New York: Simon and Schuster, 1994

Gotlieb, Jacob. *Rationalism in Hasidic Attire: Habad's Harmonistic Approach to Maimonides* (Heb.). Ramat Gan: Bar Ilan University Press, 2009.

Gotleib, Naftali Tzvi, (Elchonon Lesches trans.). *Rabbi, Mystic, Leader: The Life and Times of Rabbi Levi Yitzchak Schneerson.* New York: Kehot, 2008.

Greenberg, David and Witztum, Eliezer. *Sanity and Sanctity: Mental Health Work Among The Ultra-Orthodox In Jerusalem.* Yale University Press, 2001.

Greenberg, Yosef Yitzchak and Zaklikovsky, Eliezer: *Yemei Bereishit: Historical Biography, 1950-1951.* New York: Kehot 1993.

Gutnick, Yosef Yitzchak. *Shleimut Ha-Aretz.* Private publication, 1996.

Ha-Admor he-Hadash mi-Lubavitch (anonymous editorial), *Ha-Pardes* (25,2) *Iyar* 5711 (1951).

Halbertal, Moshe (Jackie Feldman trans.). *Concealment and Revelation: Esotericism in Jewish Thought and its Philosophical Implications.* Princeton University Press, 2007.

Hallamish, M. "The Attitude of the Kabbalists to Non-Jews" (Heb.), in Hallamish and Kasher, *Filosophia Yisraelit.*

Halperin, Hagit, *The Maestro: The Life and Works of Avraham Shlonsky.* Tel Aviv: Sifriat Poalim, HaKibbutz Hameuchad Publishers, 2011.

Halprin, Shmuel Eliezer, *Sefer ha-Tze'etza'im.* Private publication: Jerusalem 1980.

Hanoka, Yaakov. *A Time For Everything.* Private publication 2012.

Harari, Yehiel. *The Secret of the Rebbe* (Heb.). Tel Aviv: Yeditoth Ahronoth and Chemed Books, 2013.

Harkavi, Zvi and Goldburt, Yaakov. *Dnepropetrovsk Memorial Book.* Jerusalem and Tel Aviv: Yekatrinoslav-Dnepropetrovsk Society, 1973

Harris, Lis. *Holy days: The World of a Hasidic Family.* New York: Touchstone, 1985

Hecht, Avraham B. *My Spiritual Journey: An Autobiography.* New York: Private Publication, 2006.

Heilman, Chaim Meir. *Beit Rebbe.* Berdichev, 1902.

Herberg, Will "The Sectarian Conflict Over Church and State," in *Commentary* 14, November 1952.

Hertzog, Isaac (Ehud Spanier, ed.), *The Royal Purple and the Biblical Blue.* Jerusalem: Keter, 1987.

Heschel, Abraham Joshua, *Moral Grandeur and Spiritual Audacity.* Farrar, Straus and Giroux, 1997.

Hoffman, Edward. *Despite All Odds: The Story of Lubavitch.* New York: Simon and Schuster, 1991

Jacobson, Simon, *Portrait of a Chassid: The Life and Legacy of Rabbi Zvi Hirsh Gansbourg.* New York: GJCF, 2008.

———. *Toward a Meaningful Life, New Edition: The Wisdom of the Rebbe Menachem Mendel Schneerson.* New York: William Morrow, 2004.

Kahn, Yoel. *Sefer Ha-Arachim—Chabad,* 7 vols. New York: Kehot, 1970-2009

———. *Shiurim Be-Torat Chabad.* Israel: Mayanotecha, 2006.

Kalmanson, Mendel. *Seeds of Wisdom.* New York: Jewish Educational Media, 2013.

Kalms, Peter. *A Place of Their Own: The Founding of Shamir.* London, 2005.

———. *Guidance From the Rebbe 1961-1993, Personal Recollections.* London: Lubavitch Foundation, undated.

Kaplan, Aryeh. (Abraham Sutton ed.). *Inner Space: Introduction to Kabbalah, Meditation and Prophecy.* Jerusalem: Moznaim Publishing, 1990.

———. *Jewish Meditation: A Practical Guide.* New York: Schocken Books, 1985.

———. *Meditation and Kabbalah.* York Beach, Maine: Samuel Weiser, Inc., 1982.

———. *Meditation and the Bible.* York Beach, Maine: Samuel Weiser, Inc., 1978

Kaplan, Edward and Dresner Samuel, *Abraham Joshua Heschel: Prophetic Witness.* Yale University Press, 1998.

Kaploun, Uri. *A Partner in the Dynamic of Creation, Womanhood in the Teachings of the Lubavitcher Rebbe, Rabbi Menachem M. Schneerson.* New York: Sichos in Enlgish, 1995.

Katz Steven T., Biderman, Shlomo, and Gershon Greenberg (eds.).*Wrestling with G-d: Jewish Theological Responses during and after the Holocaust.* Oxford University Press, 2007.

Katz, Maya Balakirsky. *The Visual Culture of Chabad.* Cambridge University Press, 2010.

Kaufman, David. *Shul with a Pool: The "Synagogue-Center" in American Jewish History.* Hanover, New England: Brandeis University Press, 1999.

Kelman, Wolfe, "Moshe Feinstein and Postwar American Orthodoxy," in William Frankel (ed.) *Survey of Jewish Affairs 1987.* New Jersey: Associated University Presses, 1988.

Kfar Chabad Magazine. Israel, 1982-2014 (weekly).

Klapholtz, Yisrael. *Admorei Belz,* vol. 4. Bnei Brak, 1977

Koskoff, Ellen. *Music in Lubavitcher Life.* University of Illinois Press, 2001.

Kovetz 28 Sivan, Jubilee Anniversary. New York: Kehot, 1991.

Kovetz Hadrat Melech. New York: Kehot, 1985.

Kovetz Yechidut. New York: Va'ad Talmidei Yeshivat Tomchei Temimim Lubavitch Ha-Merkazit, 2010.

Kovetz Yud Gimmel Iyar. Tzefat: Va'ad Chalei Beit David, 1999.

Kozak, Warren. *The Rabbi of 84th Street: The Extraordinary Life of Haskel Besser.* New York: Harper Collins, 2004.

Kramer, Milton E. *The Kramers: The Next Generation.* Kramer Family Centennial Committee, 1995.

Kraus, Shmuel. *Nasi ve-Chasid.* Kfar Chabad: Agudat Chasidei Chabad, 1999.

Kraus, Yitzchak. *Ha-Shevi'i.* Israel: Yedioth Achronoth Books, 2007.

Krisnky, Yehudah. Interview in *Mishpacha,* 30th September, 2009.

Kurzman, Dan. *Soldier of Peace: The Life of Yitzhak Rabin.* New York: Harper, 1998.

L'Chaim. New York: Lubavitch Youth Organization, 1992-2014 (weekly).

Lamm, Norman. *The Shema: Spirituality and Law in Judaism.* Philadelphia: Jewish Publication Society, 1998.

Lau, Israel Meir (Jessica Setbon and Shira Leibowitz Schmidt trans.). *Out of the Depths: The Story of a Child of Buchenwald Who Returned Home at Last.* New York: Sterling Press, 2010.

Laufer, Mordechai Menasheh. *Yemei Melech.* Kfar Chabad: Kehot, 1991, 3 vols.

Leibler, Isi. *The Case for Israel.* Melbourne: The Executive Council of Australian Jewry, 1972.

Lesches, Elchonon. *The Third Judge and Other stories of the Tzemach Tzedek.* New York: Kehot, 2008.

Letter in a Torah Scroll (Heb,). Kfar Chabad: Va'ad Le-Ketivat Sefer Torah Shel Yaldei Yisrael, 2009.

Levin, Faitel. *Heaven on Earth: Reflections on the Theology of Rabbi Menachem M. Schneerson.* New York: Kehot, 2002.

Levin, Shalom Ber, *A History of Chabad in Czarist Russia.* New York: Kehot, 2010.

———. *A History of Chabad in Poland, Lithuania, and Latvia, 1790-1946.* New York: Kehot 2011.

———. *A History of Chabad in Soviet Russia* (Heb). New York: Kehot, 1989.

———. *A History of Chabad in the U.S.A—1900-1950.* New York: Kehot, 1988.

———. *Avodat Ha-Kodesh.* New York, 1995.

———. *Mishpat Ha-Sefarim—Didan Naztach,* undated.

———. *The Lubavitch Library: a sketch of its history based on letters, documents and recollections* (Heb.). New York: Library of Agudat Chasidei Chabad, 1993

———. *Treasures from the Chabad Library: Rare Volumes, Manuscripts, Letters, Documents, Sacred Objects, Marriage Contracts, Portraits and Photographs selected from the Central Chabad Lubavitch Library and Archive Center.* New York: Kehot, 2009.

———. *Zikaron Livnei Yisrael.* New York: Kehot 1996.

Lichtenstein, Aharon. "Justice shall be the girdle of his loins, and faithfulness the girdle of his waist—eulogy for Rabbi Menachem Mendel Schneerson, the Lubavitch Rebbe," in *Alon Shevut le-Bogrei Yeshivat Har Ezion,* 4, *Tishrei* 5755 (1994).

Lieberman, Mordechai and Zaklikovsky, Eliezer. *Bine'ot Deshe.* New York: Kehot, 1993.

Lieberman, Shmuel. *Hey Teves Story* (undated).

Liebman, Charles S. "Orthodoxy in American Jewish Life," in *American Jewish Year Book,* vol. 66 (1965), pp. 79–92.

Lipchitz, Jacques (with H. Harvard Arnason). *My Life in Sculpture.* Viking Press, 1972.

Lipkin, Binyamin. *Cheshbono Shel Olam.* Israel: Machon Ha-Sefer, 2000.

Lipkin, Binyamin and Elitov, Yosef Yitzchak, *In all my house he is faithful: The life of Rabbi Shneur Zalman Gurary* (Heb.). Kfar Chabad: Machon Razag, 2011.

Litvin, A. (S. Hurwitz). *Yiddisher Neshamos* vol. 2. New York, 1917.

Loewenthal, Naftali. *Communicating the Infinite: The Emergence of the Habad School.* Chicago and London: University of Chicago Press 1990.

———. "Self-sacrifice of the Zaddik in the Teachings of R. Dov Ber, the Mitteler Rebbe" in Ada Rapoprt-Albert and Steven J. Zipperstein (eds.), *Jewish History: Essays in Honour of Chimen Abramsky.* London: Peter Halban, 1988.

Longerich, Peter, *Holocaust: The Nazi Persecution and Murder of the Jews.* Oxford University Press, 2010.

Lundgren, Svante. *Particularism and Universalism in Modern Jewish Thought.* Academic Studies in the History of Judaism, 2000.

Magid, Shaul. *From Metaphysics to Midrash: Myth, History, and the Interpretation of Scripture in Lurianic Kabbala.* Bloomington and Indianapolis: Indiana University Press, 2008.

Maimon, Y. L. *Sefer Ha-Besht.* Jerusalem: Mosad Harav Kook, 1960.

Mandelbaum, Yitta Halberstam. *Holy Brother: Inspiring Stories and Enchanted Tales about Rabbi Shlomo Carlebach.* New Jersey: Jason Aronson, 2002.

Marinovsky, Moshe, *Pegishot im Ha-Rebbi.* Kfar Chabad Publications, undated.

Metzger, Alter B. *The Heroic Struggle.* New York: Kehot 1999.

Michaelson, Jay. *Everything is G-d: The Radical Path of Nondual Judaism.* Boston and London: Trumpeter Books, 2009.

Mishulovin, Mendel and Raitchik, Levi (eds.). *Sefer Ha-Yovel Ha'arot U'Biurim.* New York: Oholei Torah, 2010.

Mondshine, Yehoshua (ed.), *Shivchei Ha-Besht.* Jerusalem 1982

———. *Ha-Masa Ha-Acharon.* Russia: Knizhniki Publishing Houses, 2012.

———. *Derech Ha-Melech: Translation of the Rebbe's Russian Passport 1927-1933* (Heb.). Souvenir distrubuted at the Annual *Shluchim* conference 2000.

Naor, Bezalel and Alpert, Reuven. *G-d's Middlemen: A Habad Retrospective.* Ashland, Oregon: White Cloud Press, 1998.

Naparstek, Yitzchak. *Shiurei Limud Hadat: Historical review of the Released Time program of the National Committee for the Furtherance of Jewish Education* (Heb.). New York: Kehot, 2006.

Navot, Suzi. *Constitutional Law of Israel.* Netherlands: Kluwer Law International, 2007.

Oberlander, Boruch and Shmotkin, Elkanah. *The Rebbe's Early Years—Excerpt.* New York: Jewish Educational Media, 2012.

Ophir, Natan. "The Lubavitcher Rebbe's Call for a Scientific Non-Hasidic Meditation," *B'or Ha'torah*, vol. 22, 2013, pp. 109-123.

Piekarz, Mendel, *Hasidic Leadership: Authority and Faith in Zadikim as Reflected in the Hasidic Literature* (Heb.). Jerusalem: Bialik Institute, 1999.

Polen, Nehemia, review of *The Rebbe* in *Modern Judaism*, volume 34, number 1. February 2014.

Possen, David D. "J. B. Soloveitchik: Between Neokantianism and Kierkegaardian Existentialism" in Jon Stewart (ed.). *Kierkegaard's Influence on Theology, Tome III: Catholic and Jewish Theology*. Ashgate Publishing, 2012.

Poznanski, Renee (Nathan Bracher trans), *Jews in France During World War II*. Tauber Institute for the Study of European History and United States Holocaust Memorial Museum, Brandeis, 2001.

Raichik, Shimon. "From Poland to the United States: The harrowing tale of Rabbi Shmuel Dovid Raichik's journey from war-torn Europe to freedom" in *Memento from the Wedding of Moishy and Rivka Raichik, May 2013*.

Rakeffet-Rothkoff, Aaron. *The Rav: The World of Rabbi Joseph B. Soloveitchik, Volume 1*. New Jersey: Ktav, 1999.

Rapoport, Chaim. *Shitat Rabenu ziya bi-davar harigat kinim be-shabbat bizman ha-zeh* in *Ha'arot u'Biurim Oholei Torah*, 11th *Nissan* 2004.

———. *The Afterlife of Scholarship*. Oporto Press, 2011.

Rapoport-Albert, Ada. "From Woman as Hasid to Woman as Tsadik in the Teachings of the Last Two Lubavitcher Rebbes" in *Jewish History* (2013) 27:435-473.

Ravitzky, Aviezer (Michael Swirsky and Jonathan Chipman trans.). *Messianism, Zionism, and Jewish Religious Radicalism*. University Of Chicago Press, 1996.

Rigg, Bryan Mark. *Rescued from the Reich: How One of Hitler's Soldiers Saved the Lubavitcher Rebbe*. Yale University Press, 2004.

Riskin, Shlomo. *Listening to G-d: Inspirational Stories for my Grandchildren*. Jerusalem: Maggid Books, 2010.

Rolde, Neil. *Breckinridge Long, American Eichman??? An enquiry into the character of the man who denied visas to the Jews*. Solon, Maine: Polar Bear, 2013.

Rosen, Robert. *Saving the Jews: Franklin Roosvelt and the Holocaust*. New York: Harper Collins, 2007

Rosmarin, Aaron. "Reb Chaim Heller—One in Generations," in *The Jewish Criterion* (Pittsburgh), 15th September 1944.

Rottenberg, Dov Zev, *Masa ha-Rebbi be-Eretz ha-Kodesh*. Kfar Chabad: Aishel, 1999

Rubenstein, Joshua, and Altman, Ilya. *The Unknown Black Book: The Holocaust in the German-Occupied Soviet Territories*. Indiana University Press, 2008.

Rubin, Moshe Yosef. *A Father to so Many Chasidim: The Story of Reb Avrohom Drizen Mayorer*. New York: Geder Avos Jewish Heritage Group, 2010.

Ryan, Donna F., *The Holocaust and Jews of Marseille: The Enforcement of Anti-Semitic Policies in Vichy France*. University of Illinois Press, 1996.

Sacks, Jonathan. *A Letter in the Scroll: Understanding Our Jewish Identity and Exploring the Legacy of the World's Oldest Religion*. New York: Free Press, 2000.

———. "In Search of the Soul: Thirty Years of the Lubavitcher Rebbe," *Jewish Chronicle*, 1st February 1980.

———. "The Man Who Turned Judaism Outwards—A Personal Tribute to the Lubavitcher Rebbe," in Chabad Journal. Albany, June 1994.

Sarna, Jonathan and Dalin, David. *Religion and State in the American Jewish Experience*. Indiana: University of Notre Dame Press, 1997.

Schachter-Shalomi, Zalman Meshullam. *Spiritual Intimacy: A Study of Counseling in Hasidism*. New Jersey: Jason Aronson, 1990.

———. *Yishmru Daat: Chassidic Teachings of the Fourth Turning*. Ohalah, 2009.

Schneider, Stanley and Berke Joseph. "Sigmund Freud and the Lubavitcher Rebbe" in *Psychoanalytic Review*, 87(1), 2000.

Schneurson-Mishkovsky, Zelda (Marcia Falk, trans.). *The Spectacular Difference: Selected Poems of Zelda*. Hebrew Union College Press, 2004.

Scholem, Gershon. *The Messianic Idea in Judasim, and other essays on Jewish Spirituality*. New York: Schocken Books, 1971.

Schwartz, Dov. *Habad's Thought: From Beginning to End* (Heb.). Ramat Gan: Bar Ilan University Press, 2011.

Shapiro, Edward S. *Crown Heights: Blacks, Jews and the 1991 Brooklyn Riot*. Massachussets: Brandeis University Press, 2006.

Sharfstein, Chana. *It Was Evening, It Was Morning: Scandinavia in the Aftermath of World War II*. Devora Publishing, 2012.

Sharon, Ariel (with David Chanoff). *Warrior*. New York: Simon and Schuster, 1989.

Shazar, Zalman. *Ohri Dorot*. Jerusalem 1971.

Sherman, Moshe D. *Orthodox Judaism in America: A Biographical Dictionary and Sourcebook*. Connecticut: Greenwood Publishing, 1996

Shevicha Eliyahu, *Toldot HaRav Menachem Mendel Horenstein*, in *Teshurah Misimchat Nisuiun Eliyahu ve-Chaya Shevicha* 2012.

Slonim, M. S. *Toldot Mishpachat ha-Rav mi-Liadi*. Tel Aviv: Hotza'at Zohar, 1946.

Slonim, Rivka (ed.). *Total Immersion: A Mikvah Anthology*. Urim Publications; 2nd revised edition, 2006.

Solomon, Aryeh. *The Educational Teachings of Rabbi Menachem M. Schneerson*. New Jersey: Jason Aronson, 2000.

Staiman, Mordechai. *Diamonds of the Rebbe*. New York: Otsar Sifrei Lubavitch, 1998.

Steinsaltz, Adin. *My Rebbe*. Jerusalem: Maggid Books 2014.

Straus, Howard and Marinacci, Barbara. *Dr. Max Gerson: Healing the Hopeless*. Ontario: Quarry Health Books, 2002.

Swados, Harvey. "I Am Interviewed by the Lubavitcher Rebbe." Harvey Swados Papers, University of Massachusetts Amherst Libraries, Box 20:222.

Szubin, Adam Jacob. "Why Lubavitch Wants The Messiah Now" in Albert Baumgarten (ed.). *Apocalyptic Time*. Leiden, Netherlands: Brill, 2000.

Talks and Tales. Merkos L'Inyanei Chinuch, 2003, 16 volumes.

Teitz-Blau, Rivkah. *Learn Torah, Love Torah, Live Torah: HaRav Mordechai Pinchas Teitz, the Quintessential Rabbi*. New Jersey: Ktav, 2001.

Touger, Eliyahu. *To Know and To Care, volume 2*. New York: Sichos in English, 1996.

Twersky, Isadore. *Rabad of Posquières, A Twelfth-Century Talmudist*. Cambridge, Massachusetts: Harvard University Press, 1961.

Unterman, Yael. *Nehama Leibowitz: Teacher and Bible Scholar*. Jerusalem and New York. Urim Press, 2009, p. 29.

Weil, Eldad. "The Beginning of the Women's Era: Women and Womanhood in the teachings of the Lubavitcher Rebbe" (Heb.), in *Akdamut* 22 (1999).

Weiner, Herbert. "Farewell, My Rebbe: Thoughts On Leadership" in *New Jersey Jewish News*, 2nd June, 1994.

———. *Nine and a Half Mystics*. New York: Touchstone, 1997.

———. *The Lubovitcher Movement II* in *Commentary*, April 1957.

Weiner, Moshe. *Sefer Sheva Mitzvot Hashem*. Pittsburgh: Ask Noah International, 2008-2013, 3 vols.

Wellen Levine, Stephanie. *Mystics, Mavericks, and Merrymakers: An Intimate Journey among Hasidic Girls*. New York University Press, 2003.

Wiesel, Elie. *All Rivers Run to the Sea: Memoirs*. Schocken, 1996.

———. *Souls on Fire: Portraits and Legends of Hasidic Masters*. New York: Random House, 1972.

———. *The Gates of The Forest.* New York: Avon Books, 1966.

Wilensky, Mordechai. *Chasidim and Mitnagedim* (Heb.), 2 vols. Jerusalem: Bialik Institute, 1970.

Wolf, Zusha and Gopin, Shimon. *Beit Chayenu 770.* Jerusalem: Heichal Menachem, 2004.

Wolf, Zusha. *Kehot Publications: The History of the Chabad Publishing House* (Heb.). Israel, Kfar Chabad: Kehot, 2013.

———. *The Founding and Expansion of the Kiryat Chabad in Tzefat.* Kfar Chabad, 2009.

———. *The Founding and Expansion of the Nachlat Har Chabad Community.* Kfar Chabad, 2008.

———. *Admorei Chabad ve-Yahadut Germania.* Kfar Chabad: Kehot, 2007.

Wolfson, Elliot R. *Open Secret: Postmessianic Messianism and the Mystical Revision of Rabbi Menachem Mendel Schneerson.* Columbia University Press, 2009.

———. "Revealing and Re/veiling Menahem Mendel Schneerson's Messianic Secret," in *Kabbalah: Journal for the Study of Jewish Mystical Texts* 26 (2012), pp. 25-96.

Wolpo, Shalom. "Limud Chochmot Chitzoniyot be-Mishnat Admor mi-Lubavitch" in *Techumin* vol. 19. Israel: Machon Zomet, 1999.

———. *Da'at Torah Be'inyanei Ha-Matzav B'Eretz HaKodesh.* Kiryat Gat: Private publication, 1981.

———. *Eved Melech: The Life of Rabbi Ezriel Zelig Slonim* (Heb.). Private publication, 2008.

———. *Shalom Shalom V'Ein Shalom.* Jerusalem, Private Publication, 1982.

———. *Shemen Sason Mechaveirecho.* Private publication 1995-2009, 4 vols.

Yovetzky, Meir Shlomo, *Toldot Meir Shlomo.* New York, Talmidei Yeshivat Tomchei Temimim Hamerkazit, 2009.

Zacks, Gordon. *Defining Moments: Stories of Character, Courage and Leadership.* New York: Beaufort Books, 2006.

Zadoff, Mirjam (William Templer trans.). *Next Year in Marienbad, The Lost Worlds of Jewish Spa Culture.* University of Pennsylvania Press, 2012.

Zaklikovsky, Eliezer. *Mekadesh Yisrael: Talks and Images at Wedding Celebrations 1943-1963.* New York: Kehot, 2000.

Zaklikowski, Dovid. "A Letter to the Rogatchover," *Ami Magazine,* March 28, 2012.

Zalmon Jaffe, *My Encounter with the Rebbe,* New York: PCL publishing, 26 vols.

Zigelboim, Menachem, *Stories from the Rebbe's Room.* Israel: Private publication, 2009.

Zisman Leibel (Leo). *I Believe: The Story of One Jewish Life.* New York: GJCF, 2011.

Znamenski, Andrei. *Red Shambhala: Magic, Prophecy and Geopolitics in the Heart of Asia.* Illinois: Quest Books, 2011.

NOTES

FOREWORD

1. David Assaf (trans. David Louvish), *The Regal Way: The Life and Times of Rabbi Israel of Ruzhin* (California: Stanford University Press, 2002), introduction.
2. Immanuel Etkes (trans. Jeffrey Green), *The Gaon of Vilna: The Man and His Image* (California: University of California Press, 2002), p. 139.
3. Nehemia Polen in *Modern Judaism*, volume 34, number 1 (February 2014).
4. Elliot R. Wolfson, *Open Secret: Postmessianic Messianism and the Mystical Revision of Rabbi Menachem Mendel Schneerson*, (Columbia University Press, 2009), introduction.

CHAPTER 1: LIFE AT HOME

1. From 1881 to 1914, two and a half million Jews, almost half the national population, emigrated from Russia, mostly to the United States.
2. Rabbi Alter Eliyahu Friedman (Yerachmiel Tilles trans.), *A Mother in Israel* (New York: Kehot 2006), pp. 10-11; Chana Schneerson Memoirs (New York: Kehot, 2001-2), installment 33. With all due consideration for a mother's bias, one cannot undermine the significance of Chana Schneerson's first person accounts, recorded (not for publication, but) in a private diary and alongside many details the authenticity of which can be established from other sources.

   Another valuable source for this period is Rabbi Naftali Tzvi Gottleib (Rabbi Elchonon Lesches trans.), *Rabbi, Mystic, Leader: The Life and Times of Rabbi Levi Yitzchak Schneerson* (Brooklyn: Kehot, 2008). Notwithstanding the nature of such "in-house" publications and their lack of objectivity, I have relied on their accounts only in such places where they support the narrative as gleaned from other more reliable sources and they cite clear evidence for their statements.
3. Letter dated 11th *Nisan* 5716 (1956) to Yitzhak Ben-Zvi Shimshelevitz (1884–1963), second President of Israel, printed in Rabbi Shalom Ber Levin (ed), *Igrot Kodesh Admor Menachem Mendel Schneerson*, vol. 12 (New York: Kehot, 1989), p. 414 (henceforth "*Igrot Kodesh*"). Ben-Zvi had actually been active with the local Jewish defense organization in Poltava during the pogroms of 1905.
4. Chana Schneerson Memoirs ibid.; *Kuntres Tzadik le-Melech*, vol. 4 (New York: Private publication, 1993), p. 150.
5. See Friedman, *A Mother*, pp. 9-10.
6. For a detailed catalog of over 1400 Schneerson descendants see: M. S. Slonim, *Toldot Mishpachat ha-Rav mi-Liadi* (Tel Aviv: Hotza'at Zohar, 1946). A more updated work which lists over 3,500 Schneerson descendants is Shmuel Eliezer Halprin, *Sefer ha-Tze'etza'im* (Private Publication: Jerusalem 1980)
7. Elie Wiesel, *Souls on Fire: Portraits and Legends of Hasidic Masters* (New York: Random House, 1972), p. 122
8. For discussions in academic literature of the role of Rebbe see: Zalman Meshullam Schachter-Shalomi, *Spiritual Intimacy: A Study of Counseling in Hasidism* (New Jersey: Jason Aronson, 1990); Samuel H. Dresner, *The Doctrine of the Zaddik According to the Writings of Rabbi Ya'akov Yosef of Polnoy* (New York: Schocken Books, 1980); Mendel Piekarz, *Hasidic Leadership: Authority and Faith in Zadikim as Reflected in the Hasidic Literature* (Heb.), (Jerusalem: Bialik Institute, 1999).
9. For a detailed description of the infrastructure of a Chasidic court by an academic scholar, see Assaf, *Regal Way*, chapters 12-14.

10. Another point worth consideration is that Reb Levik's public discourses had been criticized by some Lubavitchers who felt that his emphasis on Kabbalah was unwarranted (see Chana Schneerson Memoirs, installment 20. See also Lesches, *Rabbi, Mystic, Leader,* p. 74, for an incident where Reb Levik was challenged to legitimize his method of Torah exegesis by a senior Chasid when delivering a lecture to the Chabad community in Leningrad). A prevailing sentiment in the Rebbe's court, which exists to this day, is that a Chasid's task is to loyally teach the words of his Rebbe and not formulate thought systems of his own. If Chasidim were critical of Reb Levik to his face, in his own home town, there might have been an even greater antipathy in some circles back in Lubavitch.

    Rabbi Zalman Duchman suggested (*Le-Sheima Ozen,* New York 1963 p. 151) that Reb Levik kept his son from seeing Rashab, so that the young Chasid would be able to devote himself exclusively to Rayatz, in a similar way to Rabbi Shneur Zalman who was kept from seeing the Ba'al Shem Tov in order to strengthen his connection with the Magid of Mezritch.

    See also theories proposed by Rabbi Shalom Ber Levin in *Kfar Chabad,* issue 663.

11. According to one testimony, it was a conscious decision on the part of Reb Levik. Menachem Mendel's mother Rebbetzin Chana, commented that her son "wants to go, but his father does not allow it" (Rabbi Mordechai Menasheh Laufer, *Yemei Melech,* vol. 2, (Kfar Chabad: Kehot, 1991), p. 891).

12. *Shu't Tzemach Tzedek* and *Chidushim al ha-Shas,* 6 volumes (New York: Kehot, new edition 1994) and supplement (2009). *Tzemach Tzedek, Piskei Dinim* (New York: Kehot, fifth edition, 1992); *Tzemach Tzedek, Chidushim al ha-Shas* (New York: Kehot, fifth edition, 1992); *Mafteichot* (indices), (New York: Kehot, 1998). For a bibliographic sketch of the responsa see introduction by Rabbi Shalom Ber Levin, *Mafteichot,* pp. 5-13.

13. For more on *Tzemach Tzedek* see Rabbi Sholom Dovber Avtzon, *Tzemach Tzedek—Rabbi Menachem Mendel of Lubavitch* (New York: Avtzon Books, 2012); Rabbi Joseph Isaac Schneersohn (Zalman I. Posner, trans.), *The Tzemach Tzedek and the Haskala Movement* (New York: Kehot, 1969); Rabbi Elchonon Lesches, *The Third Judge and Other Stories of the Tzemach Tzedek* (New York: Kehot, 2008); Chaim Dalfin, *The Seven Chabad-Lubavitch Rebbes* (New Jersey: Jason Aronson, 1998), chapter 3; introduction by Bezalel Naor in Reuven Alpert, *G-d's Middlemen: A Habad Retrospective* (Ashland, Oregon: White Cloud Press, 1998), pp. xxvii-xxix

14. Rabbi Yehuda Leib Schneersohn (*Maharil*) (1808–1866) founded the Kopust (Kopys) branch of Chabad; Rabbi Chaim Schneur Zalman (1814–1880) set up court in in Liadi; Rabbi Yisroel Noach (1815–1883) founded the Niezhin (Nizhyn) branch of Chabad; Rabbi Yosef Yitzchak (1822–1876) set up court in Avrutch (Ovruch), and the youngest son Rabbi Shmuel (1834-1882), continued the Chabad dynasty in Lubavitch. 1834–1882. See Naor, p. xxxi-xxxii.

15. Some date his birth to 1804. See Rabbi Shalom Ber Levin, *A History of Chabad in Czarist Russia* (Heb.), (New York: Kehot, 2010), p. 168.

16. For a biographical sketch see Lesches, *Rabbi, Mystic, Leader,* pp. 1-6*ff.* For an example of a discourse (together with more biographical details), see Rabbi Yeshoshua Mondshine, *Pardes Chabad,* issue 8 (Kfar Chabad), *Tishrei* 2002.

    In his childhood, Rabbi Baruch Shalom had enjoyed a relationship with the founder of Chabad, Rabbi Shneur Zalman, and he accompanied him, sleeping in the same room, as Rabbi Shneur Zalman fled from Napoleon at the end of his life. Rabbi Baruch Shalom was born with a deformed, fingerless right hand, which presented a *halachic* question about the correct way he should don *tefilin* (see *Shu't Tzemach Tzedek Orach Chaim,* sec. 5). Just before Rabbi Shneur Zalman passed away, he said to *Tzemach Tzedek,* "Mendel, ask me!" but *Tzemach Tzedek* was unsure what his grandfather was intimating. Only after Rabbi Shneur Zalman had passed on did it dawn on *Tzemach Tzedek* that his grandfather wanted him to ask about the issue of Baruch Shalom's hand and *tefilin.* (See Rabbi Yehoshua Mondshine, *Ha-Masa Ha-Acharon* (Russia: Knizhniki Publishing Houses, 2012), p. 151.)

17. Rabbi Baruch Shalom's other children were Rabbi Mordechai Schneerson (c1835-1907), chief

Rabbi of Vitebsk; R' Yehuda Leib Schneerson of Kremenchug; Rivka, who married Rabbi Meshullam Reich (d. 1909), and another daughter who married Rabbi Dan Segal Landau (Levin, *Czarist Russia*, p. 167).

18. Baruch Shneur Zalman's older brothers were Rabbi Avraham and Rabbi Menachem Mendel, who served as Rabbi in Chernikov. Rabbi Menachem Mendel's son Rabbi Shneur Zalman Schneerson, was later a rabbi in Paris (from 1935-1960), at the same time his cousin, the future Seventh Rebbe, lived there. Rabbi Menachem Mendel's daughter, Yehudit, married Shneur Zalman Butman.
19. Published in *Reshimat ha-Rabash* (New York: Kehot, 2001).
20. Reb Levik's younger siblings were Shmuel (1888-1944), and Shalom Shlomo (d. 1926). Shalom Shlomo's daughter was the famous Israeli poet, Zelda Schneurson-Mishkovsky (1914-1984). For more on Zelda see Marcia Falk (trans.), *The Spectacular Difference: Selected Poems of Zelda* (Hebrew Union College Press, 2004).
21. See Rabbi Shalom Ber Levin, *Treasures from the Chabad Library: Rare Volumes, Manuscripts, Letters, Documents, Sacred Objects, Marriage Contracts, Portraits and Photographs selected from the Central Chabad Lubavitch Library and Archive Center* (New York: Kehot, 2009), p. 71 (Hebrew section).
22. For more on Rabbi Yanovsky see Tilles, *A Mother in Israel*, pp. 205-213; Meir Shlomo Yovetzky, *Toldot Meir Shlomo* (New York, Talmidei Yeshivat Tomchei Temimim Hamerkazit, 2009).
23. Most notably, *Beit Aharon* (1850), an exhaustive index to Talmudic, Midrashic and Zoharic sources which cite Biblical verses; *Kav Naki* (Warsaw, 1868), a Rabbinic guide to divorce procedure, (the 1951 Kehot edition contains a biographical sketch of the author penned by the Seventh Rebbe); a new edition of the Chabad Siddur, *Torah Ohr*, with sources and commentary, *Sha'ar Ha-Kolel* (Vilna 1896). See also Tilles, *A Mother in Israel*, pp. 197-204.
24. Chana Schneerson Memoirs, installment 29. There his daughter, Chana, recalls: "As soon as he would receive his monthly salary as a Rav, he immediately made a reckoning of how much he needed for his sisters, brother-in-law and brother. There was always someone who needed assistance. First he deducted what had to be given to them, leaving only a small portion for his family. Consequently, it was always necessary to obtain loans to cover our family's expenses for the month. That was how my father conducted all facets of his life."
25. Rabbi Shalom Ber Levin (ed.), *Igrot Kodesh, Admor Shalom Ber Schneersohn* (New York: Kehot, 1982), vol. 1, pp. 251-2 (henceforth "*Igrot Rashab*"); Tilles, *A Mother in Israel*, pp. 210-212.
26. 11th November (3rd Kislev) 1904. Records of Jewish Community of Nikolayev. See http://col.org.il/חדשות_חרד_ג_כסלו_יום הולדת אחיו_של_הרבי_79091.html. See also Chana Schneerson Memoirs, part 37.
27. 3rd May (21st *Iyar*) 1906. His birth certificate was discovered in 2012 by Rabbi Shalom Gotblieb, Chabad Rabbi in Nikolayev. See http://www.shturem.net/index.php?section=artdays&id=2896
28. Letter dated 17th *Tevet* 5665, *Igrot Rashab* vol. 4 (New York: Kehot, 1986), p. 85.
29. Letter dated 5th *Elul* 5666, to Ya'akov Halbreich in Rabbi Shalom Ber Levin (ed.), *Kovetz Chaf Menachem Av, Shishim Shanah* (New York: Kehot, 2004), p. 10.
30. Letter from Rashab to Reb Levik, 5th Day of Chanukah 5667, ibid. p. 12.
31. Menachem Mendel Schneerson, *Sichot Kodesh* 5710-11 (New York, 1985), p. 278. See *Likutei Sichot*, vol. 9 (New York: Kehot, 1975), p. 91, for an account of one of the *halachic* questions posed to Reb Levik and his innovative response which met with Reb Chaim's approval.

    Reb Levik also was awarded *semicha* from Rabbi Eliyahu Chaim Meizel of Lodz (1821-1912) and other non-Chasidic luminaries, presumably during the same period.
32. Letter from Rashab dated 10th *Nissan*, 5667 in Levin ibid.
33. In 1910 there were 69,000 Jews in Yekatrinoslav, 30% of the city's total population.
34. See article of Dr. Shmaryahu Levin (1867-1935) in Harkavi and Yaakov Goldburt,

Dnepropetrovsk Memorial Book (Jerusalem and Tel Aviv: Yekatrinoslav-Dnepropetrovsk Society, 1973), pp. 48-49; Chana Schneerson Memoirs, installment 30.

35. Rabbi Yehuda Leib Levin, *Rabbis of Yekatrinoslav* in Harkavi and Goldburt, p. 113.
36. Memoir of Rabbi Nachum Goldshmidt, printed in *Kovetz Yud Gimmel Iyar* (Tzefat: Va'ad Chalei Beit David, 1999), p. 5, citing his father, who was active in the dispute.
37. Chana Schneerson Memoirs, installment 30. See also Tilles, *A Mother in Israel*, pp. 12-13; Lesches, *Rabbi, Mystic*, pp. 19-20.

    Sergei Pavlovitch was born as Shmarayu (Shmeryl) Paley, the only son of a Chasidic family. He received a traditional Jewish education and only shifted to a secular lifestyle in adulthood after attending a prestigious engineering school in Petersburg, where he was the only Jew. A brilliant engineer, he participated in the design of a bridge across the Dnieper River, one of the largest such structures in Russia at the time. While he was far from observant, he retained a nostalgic admiration for traditional Jewish scholarship.

    Pavlovitch, always doubting and suspicious, did not unquestioningly accept Rashab's recommendation of Reb Levik (letter dated 6th *Adar* I 5668, *Igrot Rashab*, p. 248) and informed the Chasidic community that he wished to assess their candidate in person. The meeting lasted from 9 pm until 4 am. Reb Levik was grilled on, among other issues, the relevance of Kabbalah and Chasidut, and the issue of assimilation. Pavlovitch was so impressed, that he promptly resigned from the Zionist party, a tremendous blow to the movement, and promised that he would do everything within his power to assure Reb Levik's appointment (Memoirs, installment 30-31).
38. Article of Rabbi Yehuda Leib Levin in Harkavi and Goldburt, pp. 113-15. Four years later, with the passing of Rabbi Zakheim, there was a reshuffling of territory. Rabbi Gelman was assigned to Rabbi Zakheim's area and Reb Levik to Rabbi Kozevnikov's prior district (ibid.). In 1921, Gelman tragically passed away at the age of 41, leaving Reb Levik in full control of the city's Rabbinate.
39. See Posner, *Tzemach Tzedek*.
40. Chana Schneerson Memoirs, installment 32.
41. *Torat Menachem—Hitva'aduyot* 5745, vol. 3 (New York: Va'ad Hanachot Lahak, 1986), pp. 1482-3. For another account see Chana Schneerson Memoirs, installment 33.
42. See, for example, Chana Schneerson Memoirs, installment 14, 19, 22; Lesches, *Rabbi, Mystic*, p. 39; Tilles, *A Mother in Israel*, p. 131-2.
43. See Hagit Halperin, *The Maestro: The Life and Works of Avraham Shlonsky* (Tel Aviv: Sifriat Poalim, HaKibbutz Hameuchad Publishers, 2011), chapters 1-2.

    Tziporah's unrelenting disdain for her husband's spiritual leanings gradually drove the couple apart. For their twentieth wedding anniversary, in 1915, Tuvia wrote a loosely fictional parody of their own relationship, which he dedicated to his wife. It was the story of a young Jewish couple, Hillel and Pearl, who love each other dearly and marry on 13th *Tammuz* (Tuvia and Tziporah's own wedding anniversary). Pearl is a modern woman, who is drawn to Hillel precisely because he is not like the "ordinary" Chasidim. A few weeks after their wedding, Hillel decides to make a pilgrimage to the Lubavitcher Rebbe, to the great disappointment of his wife. When he finally arrives home, weeks later than expected, Pearl is determined to stamp out his Chasidic inclinations, and for the next twenty years her loving husband reluctantly accedes to her demands. But the whole time his Chasidic soul burns inside and he is unhappy. Ultimately, he regrets that his wife has clipped his wings for so long, and confesses that he no longer loves her.
44. Interview with Verdina Shlonsky in *Ma'ariv*, 25th March 1977.
45. Halperin, *The Maestro*, p. 50
46. Ibid. p. 49.
47. See Rabbi Michael Zeligson, *Our Heroes: Reb Schneur Zalman Vilenkin*, http://crownheights.info/something-jewish/43952/our-heroes-reb-schneur-zalman-vilenkin/.

48. Rabbi Mordechai Menasheh Laufer, *Yemei Melech,* vol. 1, (Kfar Chabad: Kehot, 1991), p. 136.

49. Halperin, *The Maestro* p. 50; Laufer. p. 144

50. Tilles, *A Mother in Israel,* p. 11. In adulthood, the Rebbe had a command of eight languages: Hebrew, Yiddish, English, French, Russian, German, Latin and Italian. He was unfamiliar with Spanish, Portuguese and Polish, and his office had to hire translators for correspondence received in these languages. (Interview with Rabbi Yehudah Leib Groner, 24th May, 2009).

51. Verdina Shlonsky interview.

52. *Igrot Kodesh,* vol. 26, (New York: Kehot, 2003), p. 353.

53. Halperin ibid.

54. Numerous theories have circulated as to what Berel suffered from, a condition which apparently prevented him from getting married: trauma from the pogroms or his arrest, a psychiatric condition, or chronic intestinal disease. See Chabtai Y. Coen, *De Nikolaïev à Brooklyn* (Paris: Kehot, 2012), p. 26; Rabbi Yosef Y. Kaminetzky, *Kitzur Toldot Chabad* (Kfar Chabad: Hamayan Hachasidi, 2004), p. 340; Halperin, p. 49.

    In the early 1920s Reb Levik, accompanied by Menachem Mendel, took Berel to the Ukranian town of Kharkov for a medical consultation. Since there was a Lubavitch Yeshiva in the town, Menachem Mendel and Berel spent some time there, learning with the Rabbinical students. See *Kfar Chabad,* issue 711; Laufer, *Yemei Melech,* pp. 159-160; *Early Years,* volume 1.

    The only documented evidence of Berel's illness that has surfaced so far is Reb Levik's 1939 interrogation by the Soviet authorities, in which he stated that he was unable to travel to the Holy Land in the 1930s because "the illness of my son Berel prevented me from traveling" (Lesches, p. 122). For more on Berel, see Leshes, p. 91.

55. Goldshmidt memoir. (The memoir is partially reproduced in Laufer, *Yemei Melech,* pp. 133-35). For more on Goldshmidt see Yosef Ashkenazi, *Otzar Chasidim—Eretz Hakodesh* (Israel: Chazak, 2012), pp. 125-138

56. Ibid. pp. 83-4; Goldshmidt memoir. Curiously, in his later sermons of the 1970s and 80s, the Rebbe made numerous references to the way he was taught in *cheder.* A common thread of many of the recollections is his later realization of how the *melamed* had played on the children's innocence and taught them something that was not entirely true. For example, when the *melamed* did not know the meaning of a text, instead of pleading ignorance, he would say "when you grow up, you will understand." (For this, and numerous citations from the later sermons, see Laufer, *Yemei Melech,* vol. 1, pp. 126-133)

57. Interview in JEM, *Early Years,* volume 1.

58. See Chana Schneerson Memoirs, installment 2. In 1990 the Rebbe noted: "I wish to point out an astonishing fact. The vast majority of my father's published works are taken from manuscripts that he wrote while in exile. By Divine Providence, these writings have been made public, while the vast majority of his writings (thousands of pages!), which he wrote while serving as a rabbi in his community, have not reached us" (*Torat Menachem- Hitvaaduyot* 5750, vol. 4, p. 150, fn. 51.)

59. A striking feature of his written work was various attempts to explain different historical phenomena, including his own life events, according to Kabbalistic theosophy. Such interests are highly unusual, to say the least, in an accomplished Talmudic scholar, and perhaps it would not be an exaggeration to say that Reb Levik even introduced his very own genre of Rabbinic discourse. For a series of articles on Reb Levik's thought see *Mayanotecha* (Israel: *Torat Chabad Livnei Hayeshivot*), issue 34, *Menachem Av* 2012.

60. Lesches, p. 86; Laufer, *Yemei Melech* p. 153.

61. *Haggadah Shel Pesach im Likutei Minhagim ve-Ta'amim* (New York: Kehot, 1946). For more on the Rebbe's Haggadah see my introduction to *The Kol Menachem Haggadah* (New York: Kol Menachem, 2008), p. xxiii-xxv.

62. Menachem Mendel Schneerson, *Likutei Sichot,* 39 volumes (New York: Kehot 1962-2001).
63. Menachem Mendel Schneerson, *Sefer ha-Ma'amarim Melukat,* 6 volumes (New York: Kehot, 1987-1992).
64. *Hayom Yom* (New York, Kehot 1990). See facsimile in *Teshurah Cohen-Blau, Tammuz,* 2013, p. 105. (Archives of *Teshurot* cited here, unless otherwise referenced, are available at http://www.teshura.com/teshurapdf/).
65. Laufer, p. 147, citing Goldshmidt. See also Ashkenazi, *Otzar Chasidim,* p. 133.
66. This approach, of showing the necessity of a number of solutions based on various merits and flaws of each argument, later became a hallmark of the Seventh Rebbe's teaching. See Rabbi Tuvia Blau (ed.), *Klalei Rashi,* expanded edition (Kfar Chabad: Kehot, 1991), p. 67 and chapter 4, ibid.
67. Goldshmidt memoir; interview with Rabbi Mordechai Ashkenazi in *Early Years,* volume 1. See also Laufer, p. 154, note 30.

    Rebbetzin Chana recalled how Menachem Mendel, Leibel and Reb Levik would sometimes have in-depth Torah discussions together. While the material was often beyond her, Chana did discern that each of the three Schneersons had a tendency towards a different mode of intellectual expression. Reb Levik always drifted to the Kabbalistic understanding of a concept, Leibel would interpret things with pure logic and Menachem Mendel preferred the terminology of Chabad *Chasidut* (Rabbi Yoel Kahn in *Teshurah mi-ma'amad Chagigat Siyum ha-Rambam* (Kfar Chabad), p. 9.)
68. He was appointed in 1890 and continued until his death in 1933.
69. *Torat Menachem—Hitva'aduyot* 5749, vol. 4, p. 354*ff.*
70. Daughter of Rabbi Yitzchak Pushnitz who was Rabbi in Dubrinka from 1854 until his death in 1904.
71. *Torat Menachem—Hitva'aduyot* 5750, vol. 1 p. 239.
72. Tilles, p. 11.
73. *Torat Menachem—Hitva'aduyot* 5745, vol. 1 pp. 138-9. See also Laufer, p. 141*ff; Early Years,* vol. 1.
74. Tilles, p. 14.
75. Goldshmidt memoir; Laufer, *Yemei Melech,* p. 152.
76. *Sichot Kodesh* 5735, vol. 1, p. 378.
77. Sermon of 20th *Av* 1979 (*Sichot Kodesh* 5739, vol. 3, p. 566). See also *Sichot Kodesh* 5732, vol. 1, p. 593.
78. Tilles, p. 11.
79. Laufer, p. 159; Harkavi and Goldburt, p. 119.
80. Laufer, *Yemei Melech,* vol. 1, p. 144; *Early Years,* supplement.
81. See Tilles, p. 11; *Early Years,* supplement; Laufer, *Yemei Melech,* p. 145; Sher Memoir, in note 83. For Reb Levik's interest mathematics see Chana Schneerson Memoirs, installments 14, 20; Lesches p. 67. Reb Levik was also knowledgeable in astronomy and geography (Lesches ibid.).
82. Interview with Yonah Kesse on Morashah program, Israeli Television, 16th *Kislev* 5733 (cited in Yehiel Harari, *The Secret of the Rebbe* (Heb.), (Tel Aviv: Yedioth Ahronoth and Chemed Books, 2013), p. 300, note 30).
83. Memoir of Yeshayahu Sher in *Kfar Chabad* issues 938-9; interview with Sher by Shaul Avigdor in 1995.
84. Harkavi and Goldburt, pp. 54 and 119.

CHAPTER 2: ENTERING THE COURT

1. See Menachem Mendel Schneersohn (*Tzemach Tzedek*), *Derech Mitzvotecha—Ta'amei Ha-Mitzvot* (New York: Kehot, 2006), p. 107b.
2. See Rabbi Shalom Ber Levin, *A History of Chabad in Soviet Russia* (Heb). (New York: Kehot, 1989).
3. See, for example, A. Litvin (a pseudonym of S. Hurwitz), *Der Letzter Litvisher Guter Yid*, in *Yiddisher Neshamos*, vol. 2 (1917), p. 368*ff*, available at http://ia600301.us.archive.org/15/items/nybc203766/nybc203766.pdf
4. According to one recollection it was on 10th *Shevat*, the very day on which Rayatz would pass away twenty-seven years later, and on which Menachem Mendel would formally ascend to the "throne" the following year.
5. Rabbi Shalom Ber Levin (ed.), *Igrot Kodesh Admor Yosef Yitzchak Schneersohn* (vol. 15 (New York: Kehot, 2010), p. 31 (henceforth "*Igrot Rayatz*").
6. Althaus memoir (for details of the memoir see: Rabbis Boruch Oberlander and Elkanah Shmotkin (eds), *The Rebbe's Early Years—Excerpt* (New York: Jewish Educational Media, 2012), p. 259-260.
7. *Igrot Rayatz* vol. 15 (New York: Kehot, 2010), p. 31.
8. N. Ben Yochanan, *Di Yiddishe Heim*, *Kislev* 1963, p. 5.
9. For detailed family trees of the major Chasidic dynasties see Yitzchak Alfasi, *Chasidut mi-Dor le-Dor* (Jerusalem 1995: *Da'at Yosef*), 2 volumes.
10. Including Rabbi Yisrael Meyer Kagen, the Chofetz Chaim (1838-1933), Rabbi Moshe Soloveitchik (1879-1941) with his son Rabbi Joseph Ber (1903-1993), Rabbi Chaim Ozer Grodzenski (1863-1940), Rabbi Isser Zalman Meltzer (1870-1953), Rabbi Yitzchak Ya'akov Rabinowitz (1854-1918), Rabbi Avraham Dovber Kahana Shapira (1871-1943), as well as the Rebbes of Rachmastrivka, Skver, and Turisk.
11. Letter dated 12 *Shevat* 5744 (my archive).
12. Letter dated 12 *Tammuz* 5720, printed in Rabbi Nissan Mindel (ed.), *The Letter and the Spirit: Letters by the Lubavitcher Rebbe, Rabbi Menachem M. Schneerson*, vol. 1 (New York: Kehot 1998), p. 452.
13. Sermon of 13 *Tammuz*, 5692. In *Sefer ha-Sichot* 5702, p. 154, Rayatz states that there were nine disciples and he was the tenth.
14. In 1922, Rayatz established the Committee of Rabbis in Moscow, out of the conviction that a centralized Rabbinic leadership was now crucial for the face of Russian Jewry. He soon emerged as the committee's dominant leader by virtue of his youthful energy and organizational skills, and now positioned as the official leader of Russian Jewry, he began the work of international fundraising. His initial efforts did not bear much fruit, until 1924, when Rayatz developed ties with Dr. Joseph Rosen at the Moscow branch of the American Joint Distribution Committee. Each subsequent year, until after he was forced to leave the country in 1927, Rayatz's Committee of Rabbis received a huge influx of funds from the "Joint," to the sum of around $50,000 per year, which vastly exceeded the amounts which he had raised from Lubavitch supporters in the United States until that point. These funds were used to support religious institutions in individual communities and major institutions of Torah learning. A centralized legal office offered support to teachers who had been noticed by the authorities, and huge budgets were allocated for Passover relief each year. For details of Rayatz's work in the Soviet Union see Levin, *Soviet Russia*. For a summary in English see David E. Fishman, *Preserving Tradition in the Land of Revolution: The Religious Leadership of Soviet Jewry, 1917-1930*, in Jack Wertheimer (ed.), *The Uses of Tradition: Jewish Continuity in the Modern Era* (New York 1992, Jewish Theological Seminary of America), pp. 85-118.
15. Chana Schneerson Memoirs, installment 34.

16. Hertzog attended the University of London and earned degrees in law, classics, the humanities, sociology and Oriental languages. Later, in Paris, where his father served as a Rabbi, he decided to become an archeologist and studied at the Sorbonne. In 1913 he completed a doctoral thesis on the Biblical dye *techelet* used in *tzitzit*, later published as *The Royal Purple and the Biblical Blue* (Jerusalem: Keter, 1987), Ehud Spanier (ed.). For correspondence between the Rebbe and Rabbi Hertzog on issues of science see *Igrot Kodesh*, vol. 13, p. 142*ff.*
17. *Igrot Rayatz* vol. 5, p. 284.
18. Handwritten diary of Yeshayahu Sher, published in part in *Kfar Chabad* no. 939 (15th *Shevat*, 5761), p. 76.
19. Rabbi Yisrael Jacobson recalls seeing him there the following week (Rabbi Shalom Ber Levin (ed.), *Zikaron Livnei Yisrael* (New York: Kehot 1996), p. 100).
20. Rabbi Yosef Yitzchak Schneersohn, *Sefer Ha-Ma'amarim* 5685 (New York: Kehot, 1986), p. 196.
21. Rabbi Shneur Zalman of Liadi, *Shulchan Aruch Admor ha-Zaken, Orach Chaim* 585:10.
22. Somebody instead stood at the side and merely pointed to the order of the notes printed in the prayer book. He recalled this years later, in 1968 (Laufer, *Ha-Melech be-Mesiboh* vol. 1, p. 235).
23. Kehot (New York, 2006). Some of these *minhagim* originated in the writings of Rabbi Isaac Luria (1534-1572), who established a new system of Jewish esotericism in his time which became a foundation for most subsequent developments in Jewish mysticism. In the Kabbalah, a *mitzvah* is not seen merely as a commemorative ritual, it is understood to have power to influence, perhaps even to "manipulate," the spiritual realms and, ultimately, to affect life here on earth, since it is understood that all of life's good things flow from celestial spiritual influences. In order for the *mitzvah* to have the desired effect, the worshipper must have the correct *kavanah* (pl. *kavanot*) or "spiritual address" in mind when performing the act, and he or she must also carry out the command according to the precise nuances dictated by the Kabbalah. The Chasidic movement dropped the emphasis on *kavanot* for the average person but retained the detailed attention to Kabbalistically attuned nuances of *minhag*. Among the Chabad Rebbes, many of these practices had been carefully preserved by personal transmission from Rebbe to Rebbe, back to the founder of the Chasidic movement, Rabbi Yisrael Baal Shem Tov (1698-1760).
24. Years later, at the end of Rayatz's lifetime and during the beginning of his own leadership, the Seventh Rebbe would devote much energy to refining, clarifying and publishing *minhag* Chabad as it relates to a vast range of Jewish observances. To this day, one cannot underestimate the cohesiveness and spiritual vigor this brings to the movement. Each Chasid takes pride in observing Jewish law in a particularly Chabad fashion, feeling that if he closely approximates the Rebbe's style of worship, even if only externally, his own worship will be more meaningful and will be invested with some of the same spiritual energy and its cosmic influence. In the 1940s the Rebbe (Menachem Mendel) first publicized many Chabad customs in his *Hayom Yom* (1943), and as supplements to Rayatz's discourses which were published periodically. In 1966, he published a book-length reference guide *Sefer ha-Minhagim Chabad* (see, especially, the introduction to this work). In later years, a more exhaustive treatment of Chabad *Minhag* relating to the festivals was published by Rabbi Yehoshua Mondshine, *Otzar Minhagei Chabad* (Jerusalem: Heichal Menachem, 1995-96), 2 volumes. In Rabbi Eliyahu Yochanan Gourary's *Chikrei Minhagim* (Kfar Chabad: Machon Oholei Shem, 1999-2006), the author traces the background and possible sources for various Chabad customs in a broader range of Rabbinic literature.
25. Rabbi Bentzion Shemtov recalls that this was the first *farbrengen* when Menachem Mendel was present (Laufer, *Yemei Melech*, vol. 1, p. 163). Presumably Menachem Mendel returned home after *Tishrei*, otherwise he would have been present at the *farbrengen* of *Yud Kislev*. See *Sefer ha-Sichot* 5680-7, p. 51 (New York: Kehot, 1992). In *Yemei Melech*, vol. 2, p. 893 (Kfar Chabad: Kehot, 1991), Laufer raises a "slight doubt" as to whether Menachem Mendel's first

farbrengen might have been the following year.

26. See *Igrot Rayatz*, vol. 3. p. 411. See ibid. pp. 412-3 for an explanation of the well known saying, "What a farbrengen can achieve, even the angel Michoel could not achieve."
27. Rabbi Michael Yehudah Leib Ha-Kohen, printed in Levin, *Soviet Russia*, p. 55.
28. Ibid.
29. Genesis 1:28.
30. *Sefer ha-Sichot* 5680-87, p. 56.
31. The Seventh Rebbe would repeat the aphorism countless times publicly and in correspondence, attributing it to his father-in-law in the name of "Chasidim of the Alter Rebbe" (Rabbi Shneur Zalman of Liadi), or alternatively, to the Alter Rebbe himself. See, for example, *Torat Menachem—Hitva'aduyot* 5714, vol. 2, p. 196. For more references see Rabbi Michoel Seligson, *Sefer ha-Mafteichot le-Sichot Kodesh* 5695-5752 (New York, 2011), pp. 883-4. For more details of the insight's origin see Menachem Mendel Schneerson, *Reshimat Ha-Yoman* (New York: Kehot, 2006), p. 237.
32. Shemtov recalls that "the listeners thought that these words [of Rayatz] were directed at him [Menachem Mendel]" (Laufer ibid.), but there is a strong possibility that this is a dramatization which developed later.

CHAPTER 3: SCHOLAR-IN-RESIDENCE

1. See at length Shneur Zalman Berger, *The History of Chabad in Petersburg* (Heb.), (Israel, Kfar Chabad: Kehot 2010). For a general Jewish history of the period see Mikhail Beizer, *The Jews of Leningrad* (Heb), (Jerusalem: Zalman Shazar Center for Jewish History, 2005).
2. See at length Naftali Loewenthal, *Communicating the Infinite: The Emergence of the Habad School* (Chicago and London: University of Chicago Press 1990).
3. See Rabbi Yosef Yitzchak Schneersohn (Zalman Posner trans.), *On the Study of Chasidut* (New York: Kehot 1997), *On Learning Chasidut*, chapter 5.
4. *Torat Menachem—Hitva'aduyot* 5712 (vol. 5, p. 173).
5. Undated Hebrew draft of letter from Rayatz to Barchenko, circa. 1926: "the correspondence with... the learned Mr. M. Schneerson (who has been elected as the secretary of our scientific team)."
6. Rabbi Shemaryahu Noach's father was Rabbi Yehuda Leib Schneersohn (1811-1867), the second oldest son of *Tzemach Tzedek*, who set up court in Kapust (Kopys, Belarus) after his father's passing. Sadly, he passed away just six months into office, and was succeeded by his oldest son Rabbi Shlomo Zalman Schneersohn (1830-1900). Rabbi Shlomo Zalman was a contemporary of his uncle, Rabbi Shmuel Schneerson, the Fourth Lubavitcher Rebbe, and was just four years his senior. The two Rebbes had been his study partners in their youth and maintained good relations. Rabbi Shlomo Zalman had a long "reign" of over three decades, and his Chasidic discourses were published in *Magen Avot* (Berdichev 1902, 2 vols.). After his passing, his younger brother, Rabbi Shalom Dov Ber (1834-1908), who was a Rabbi in Reziza (Rechytsa) near Minsk, continued the Kapust dynasty. Rabbi Yehuda Leib's third son was Rabbi Shemaryahu Noach, who, from 1872, established a successful Chasidic court in Babroisk, functioning as a Rebbe for over fifty years. For a period after his brother Rabbi Shalom Dov Ber's passing, he relocated to Kapust to continue the court, but he later returned to Babroisk. See Chaim Meir Heilman, *Beit Rebbe* (Berdichev, 1902), part 3, chapters 8-9.
7. The Third Chabad Rebbe, *Tzemach Tzedek*, had seven sons, and after his passing the movement splintered, with four of the sons setting up court as Chabad Rebbes. Rayatz was descended from Shmuel, *Tzemach Tzedek's* sixth son, whose court remained in Lubavitch; but the other brothers also developed successful courts for a period of time, with a significant following.

8. Rabbi Shemaryahu Noach had two daughters and one son, Rabbi Menachem Mendel, who had managed the Yeshivah in his father's lifetime but did not manage to re-establish the court. See also Litvin ibid for speculation on why the Kapust dynasty failed to renew itself.
9. Zevin received ordination from luminaries such as the Gaon of Rogatchov (Rabbi Yosef Rosen, 1858-1936) and Rabbi Yechiel Michel Epstein (1829-1908), author of the popular *halachic* compendium *Aruch ha-Shulchan.* During Zevin's time in the Lithuanian Yeshiva of Mir, his study partner had been Rabbi Yechiel Ya'akov Weinberg (1884-1966), who later became an important *posek* (*halachic* decisor), authoring Responsa *Seridei Aish.*

   Later, after relocating to Israel in 1935, Rabbi Zevin would pioneer the *Encyclopedia Talmudit,* an exhaustive multi-volume treatment of Talmudic Law.
10. Menachem Mendel Schneerson, *Torat Menachem—Hitva'aduyot* vol. 2, p. 766. Rabbi Zevin later became a close confidante of the Seventh Rebbe, though he differed with the Rebbe on a number of issues, such as Zionism. For more on Zevin, see: Rabbi Shalom Wolpo, *Shemen Sason Mechaveirecha,* vol. 2 (1998, private publication), pp. 68-110.
11. Laufer, *Yemei Melech* vol. 1, pp. 163-4.
12. *Torat Menachem—Hitva'aduyot* 5712 ,vol. 4, pp. 259-260.
13. A facsimile of the *semicha* document is reproduced in Rabbi Chaim Rapoport, *The Afterlife of Scholarship* (Oporto Press, 2011), p. 192.
14. *Igrot Rayatz* vol. 1, p. 626
15. See recollection of Rabbi Yisrael Jacobson in Levin, *Zikaron,* pp. 98-99.
16. *Igrot Rayatz* ibid. For more on the building see Mikhail Beizer, *The Jews of St. Petersburg: Excursions Through a Noble Past* (Philadelphia. Jewish Publication Society 1989), p. 154.
17. From diary note of Rayatz printed in *Sefer ha-Ma'amarim* 5725, p. 349. Rayatz had another similar vision a week later (ibid).
18. Yosef Ashkenazi, *Otzar Chasidim—Eretz Hakodesh* (Israel: Chazak, 2012), p. 133. See also Laufer, *Yemei Melech* p. 165.
19. Printed in *Hayom Yom* from this date onwards. For the Rebbe's handwritten edits see: *Teshurah Cohen-Blau* 2013, p. 108, http://www.teshura.com/teshurapdf/Cohen-Blau%20-%20Tamuz%20 13,%205771.pdf.
20. Recounted by Rabbi Yoel Kahan in 2007, http://shturem.net/index.php?section=news&id=14950.
21. See also above p. 29 for an account of how the Rebbe predicted a solar eclipse during January while at home.
22. *Igrot Kodesh* vol. 21, p. 1. The letter was signed with the pseudonym "Mark Gurari," to avoid the likely censorship of anything bearing the name Schneerson. See Rabbi Shalom Ber Levin, *Avodat ha-Kodesh* (New York, 1995), chapter 11.
23. See Menachem Mendel Schneerson, *Teshuvot u'Biurim* (New York: Kehot 1987), p. 273, where the Rebbe testifies to the Rogatchover's influence on his approach to Torah study.
24. For example, most Biblical *mitzvot* (commandments) are action based, but in a conceptual study we might enquire: What, exactly, does the law require? The action itself (e.g. to put on *tefilin*), or the action's result (that *tefilin* should be put on)? This might seem like a pointless abstraction, but masters of the conceptual approach will always find a *nafka mina,* a "practical ramification," to demonstrate how the matter is actually relevant. In our case, if the *mitzvah* is the action (*peulah*) itself, then the command of *tefilin* would be fulfilled in an instant, when one straps the *tefilin* on the arm or the head. If, on the other hand, the Torah is interested in the result (*nifal*), then one would fulfil the *mitzvah* every moment that they are in place.

   How can we tell which of these conceptions is correct? The Rogatchover points us to a brilliant *nafka mina.* A person is compelled to don *tefilin* very early in the morning when it is still dark, before the *halachically* mandated time for this *mitzvah.* A short while later, when the obligation to put on *tefilin* actually begins, Jewish law requires that one jostle the hand *tefilin* a little (and make the correct blessing for this *mitzvah*), in order to fulfill, at least minimally, the act of "putting on" the *tefilin* in the right time (BT *Menachot* 36a). There is, however, no requirement to jostle the head *tefilin*. Here we see, posits the Rogatchover, that with regard to the hand *tefilin* the mandate is to perform the act of laying *tefilin*, whereas the desideratum of the *mitzvah* of head *tefilin* is that the *tefilin* shall be in place: hence there is no need to jostle the head *tefilin* as the result-*mitzvah* has already been achieved; the *tefilin* are on the head! (See Rabbi Yosef Rosen, *Tzafnat Paneach al ha-Rambam, Laws of Tefilin* 4:4, p. 70d).

In *Likutei Sichot* vol. 39, p. 24ff., the Rebbe suggests that this distinction of the Rogatchover may be alluded to in Scripture itself. In reference to the hand *tefilin*, the verse states, *"bind them as a sign upon your arm"* (*Deut.* 6:8), suggesting that the *mitzvah* here is the action of binding. The verse then continues, *"and let them be ornaments between your eyes,"* indicating that the *mitzvah* of head *tefilin* is the result, to "let them be" on one's head.

25. The conceptual model revolves around a variety of abstract questions: Does the Torah require a *mitzvah's* action (*peulah*) or its result (*nifal*)? Is a *halachic* measure (*shiur*) a single unit (*atzmi*), or is it a composite of smaller pieces (*mitztaref*)? Does a *mitzvah* devolve on the *substance* (*chomer*) of an object, or on its *form* (*tzurah*)? Does the Torah require positive action (*chiyuv*), or to refrain from inaction (*shlilah*)?

    For an anthology of more than a dozen of these principles from the Rogatchover's writings see Rabbi Menachem Mendel Kasher, *Mefaneach Tzefunot* (New York, 1960). For a study of the Rogatchover's influence on the Rebbe, see Rabbi Yehoshua Menachem Newhouser, *Ha-tzafnat Pane'ach be-Mishnat ha-Rebbi* (New York: Va'ad Le-Hafatzat Sichot, 2002). For a general discussion of the conceptual approach to Torah study see Yosef Blau (ed.): *The Conceptual Approach to Jewish Learning* (New Jersey: Ktav Publishing House Inc., 2006)

26. Sermon of the day of *Simchat Torah* 1975.
27. See sermon of 7th April 1979. Rabbi Yosef Engel does follow this path to some extent, but the Rebbe felt that the Rogatchover was far more daring and profoundly innovative. See sermon of last day of Passover 1979.
28. Noach Zevuloni in journal *Turei Yeshurun* 1975. (Zevuloni spent a year with the Rogatchover in 1932-3).
29. See Dovid Zaklikowski, *A Letter to the Rogatchover* in *Ami* Magazine, March 28, 2012, p. 42*ff.* The 1925 letter also refers to previous correspondence. Only eight letters between the Rebbe and Rogatchover (between 1925 and 1932) have survived the Holocaust. The 1925 letter was sold at auction in 2012 to private collector Alan Stern of Los Angeles for close to $40,000. See Zaklikowski ibid.
30. See *Sichot Kodesh* 5738, vol. 1, p. 603. The Rogatchover resided in Leningrad at the same time as Rayatz until January 3, 1925. For a sketch of the Rogatchover's relationship with the Chabad Rebbes, see Rabbi Shalom Wolpo, *Shemen Sason Mechaveirecha* vol. 4 (2009, Private publication), pp. 169-187.
31. BT *Beruchot* 62a, Megillah 28a; *Zohar Tzav*, 28a
32. Published in *Sefer Ha-Ma'amarim* 5685 (New York: Kehot 1986).
33. *Igrot Rayatz* ibid.
34. Levin, *Zikaron*, p. 100.
35. Two of Yisrael Jacobson's great-uncles had emigrated some sixty years previously—something extremely rare at the time due to the challenges of remaining religiously observant in the New World—and they managed to find work as *shochetim*. Years later, they facilitated the emigration of two of their nephews, Yisrael's uncles, who, despite family pressure to stay, left Russia due to the inability to find income and to avoid being drafted into the army.
36. Of Rayatz's thousands of Chasidim, only a handful of families managed to escape Russia during the next decade, mainly to the United States and Israel. The remainder were almost all either killed by Stalin or lost to assimilation.

37. In his French citizenship application of 1937, the Rebbe affirmed that he had studied at the University of Dnipropetrovsk from 1923-6. In the absence of any other corroborating documents, it is difficult to verify this statement. Firstly, the dates on the visa application follow the Rebbe's legally documented birthdate of 1895 (and not the real birthdate of 1902), so an additional seven years of his life needed to be reasonably explained. Secondly, a visa application would clearly have been prepared in order to satisfy strict immigration criteria, and is not a particularly reliable source of historical fact. The Rebbe did once make reference to having studied at university in Russia (see following chapter, note 2), but this probably refers to studies in Leningrad. Yona Kese and Yeshayahu Sher, both residents of Dnipropetrovsk who knew the Rebbe during this period, independently referred to him as "self-taught" in secular wisdom (Kese in *JEM The Early Years,* volume 1; Sher in 1995 interview with Shaul Avigdor). For an analysis of the reliability of the visa application as source of historical fact see Rapoport, *Afterlife,* p. 128.
38. That year was the "Blessing over the Sun," an event that takes place only once in 28 years. In 1981 the Rebbe recalled that he had not been present with Rayatz and did not know whether this blessing was recited in Leningrad (*Sichot Kodesh* 5741 vol. 3, p. 466).
39. *Kfar Chabad* no. 850 (8th *Nissan,* 5759), p. 41
40. See above that Rayatz sought such documents in Leningrad to provide an alias to the GPU about his fund-raising activities.
41. For more about Althaus see p. 25.
42. Althaus description of the event appears in *Likutei Dibburim* (Hebrew), vol. 5, pp. 1375-1377. It is found in English translation in Rabbi Alter B. Metzger, *The Heroic Struggle* (New York: Kehot, 1999), pp. 279-281.
43. While in university, Barchenko had been strongly influenced by the occult and eastern wisdom, which was in vogue during the "Silver Age" (1880s-1918), leading him to seek scientific explanations for paranormal phenomena. (In one series of experiments he had placed aluminum helmets linked by a copper wire on the shaved heads of volunteers, attempting to achieve telepathic transmission, of which he reported some success!) Barchenko also had strong political beliefs that were influenced by his esoteric convictions. He maintained that the decadence of human society was only a few millennia old and had been preceded by a peaceful human cohabitation, guided by spiritual eastern-like wisdom.
44. For all of the above and a detailed account of Barchenko's life and work see Andrei Znamenski, *Red Shambhala: Magic, Prophecy and Geopolitics in the Heart of Asia,* (Illinois: Quest Books, 2011).
45. Letter cited in note 5. Barchenko sent Rayatz a large sum of money to cover the expenses of the research work, but fearing later incrimination, Rayatz returned it (Althaus memoir). This proved to be a very wise move, as when Rayatz was arrested in 1927, he was interrogated about his relationship with Barchenko (Metzger, p. 321).
46. Memoir of Chana Schneerson in *Di Yiddishe Heim* no. 19 (New York: Kehot), *Adar* 1964.
47. *Igrot Rayatz* ibid. Namely, to guide "the chosen of all creations, those gifted with intellect, to the blessed *Ayn Sof* (Infinite One)." In a most unusual formulation for a Chasidic Rebbe, the usual parochial reference to Jews as the "Chosen People" is inflected here on humanity in general, who are "the chosen of all creations" by virtue of their superior intellect. Their common purpose is to commune with G-d (*Ein Sof*).

    Rayatz proposed a six-point system for non-Jewish, Torah-based spirituality: 1. "Avoid evil," which includes minimizing worldly pleasures. 2. Expand the mind through intellectual contemplation. 3. Observe the Torah's commandments (i.e. Noahide Laws) with utter dedication, disregarding all obstacles. 4. Pray to G-d with sincerity and still devotion, that G-d should have mercy and expand the worshipper's mind. 4. Set aside specific times for self-evaluation, to determine if one's thoughts are pure or impure; if one's talk is devoid of lies and slander; if one's actions are unquestioningly in accordance with Torah law. 6. One's thoughts should be, as much as possible, bound with the living G-d with simple faith and without thoughts of reward.

48. Znamenski, p. 231. As of this writing, Barchenko's son, Sviatozar Barchenko, is still alive and resides in Moscow (Personal communication with Andrei Znamenski, September 2013).
49. Such autobiographical fragments in the Rebbe's sermons are quite rare and immediately striking.
50. *Sefer ha-Sichot* 5748 (1988), vol. 2 (New York: Kehot 1989), p. 629 and note 54 ibid.
51. Interview with Chana Schneerson in *Di Yiddishe Heim,* no. 19 (Adar, 5724), p. 6.
52. Interview with Bat-Sheva Althaus, *Kfar Chabad,* issue 280, pp. 12-3.
53. Comment of Rayatz to Rabbi Shmuel Levitin, Yosef Ashkenazi, *Otzar Hachasidim—New York* (Israel: Chazak, 2013), p. 124. See also recollection of Rabbi Yoel Kahan, ibid. p. 67. While these statements were made in 1941, Rayatz appears to have made a similar comment at Menachem Mendel's wedding (Laufer, *Yemei Melech,* vol. 1, p. 273, note 33). For other comments from Rayatz about Menachem Mendel's genius see sources collected in Rapoport, *Afterlife,* pp. 74-8.
54. See Rapoport p. 82, note 216 for multiple citations where Rayatz refers to Menachem Mendel as a *gaon* and, in the same sentence, does not use the same appellation for his other son-in-law, Rashag.
55. *Igrot Rayatz* vol. 5, p. 368.
56. Court proceedings, United States District Court, Eastern District of New York, Case CV 85 2909, page 1859.
57. Althaus ibid. makes this assertion. There is a similar anecdotal report in the name of Rabbi Chaim Lieberman who is said to have eavesdropped on the conversation between Chana and Rayatz from behind a closed door. See Binyamin Lipkin and Yosef Yitzchak Elitov, *In All My House He Is Faithful: The life of Rabbi Shneur Zalman Gurary* (Heb.), (Kfar Chabad: Machon Razag, 2011), p. 207.
58. It is also extremely unlikely that Rashag would have made his bid for the leadership if he had heard from Rayatz's mouth that Menachem Mendel had been chosen as successor.
59. See sources collected in http://www.sichosinenglish.org/books/eternal-joy-2/05.htm.
60. See *Igrot Rayatz* vol. 2, introduction, p. 9.
61. See *Igrot Rayatz* vol. 16, p. 198.
62. Interview with Rabbi Shaar Yashuv Cohen, grandson of Rabbi Chanoch Henich Hetkin (http://www.chabad.org/multimedia/media_cdo/aid/295122/jewish/Shaar-Yashuv-Cohen.htm — accessed October 2013). Rabbi Cohen did not recall any date, remembering only that it was after Menachem Mendel's engagement for a period of seven months. This must have been during the spring/summer/fall of 1926, which is the only such extended period during the Rebbe's engagement when we have no other clear record of his footsteps. The fact that Rayatz was also in Luga during the Summer is also significant. See also *Kfar Chabad,* issue 362, cited in Laufer, *Yemei Melech,* vol. 1, p. 213.
63. *Igrot Rayatz,* vol. 15, pp. 33.
64. Ibid. p. 35.
65. Ibid. p. 33.
66. Ibid. p. 35.

CHAPTER 4: LEAVING HOME

1. For details of Rayatz's relations with the Leningrad community see Beizer, *The Jews of Leningrad* ch. 5; Fishman, *Preserving Tradition,* pp. 108-111; Memoir of Rabbi Eliyahu Chaim Althaus in Metzger, *Heroic Struggle* p. 261*ff;* Berger, *A History of Chabad in Petersburg,* ch. 14; Levin, *Soviet Russia,* ch. 19-20. For Rayatz's own memoir see *Igrot Rayatz* vol. 1, p. 616*ff.*
2. See source in following note. In his 1937 petition for French citizenship, the Rebbe lists Rayatz's home as his address during this period, but, based on Nimoytin's testimony, this

was probably only used as a legal address for mail and official paperwork.

It is unclear why the Rebbe relocated to Leningrad. He may have enrolled in the university or another school, but documents have not yet surfaced. In a private audience in the 1960s the Rebbe recalled, "I was a college student in Russia" (http://www.chabad.org/therebbe/article_cdo/aid/112228/jewish/What-Is-Judaism.htm—accessed October 2014), probably referring to this period. See also the brief biography of the Rebbe in *Challenge: An encounter with Lubavitch-Chabad* (Lubavitch Foundation of Great Britain, 1970), p. 57: "He also took courses at the Universities of Leningrad and Berlin and at the Sorbonne in Paris."

3. *Kfar Chabad* issue 491, p. 18, cited in Rapoport p. 132, note 339.
4. See *Torat Menachem—Hitva'adut*, vol. 7, p. 336.
5. Althaus Memoir (Metzger, p. 292).
6. Metzger p. 295-7.
7. Ibid.
8. The date was not noted, but the visit from a supporter "from outside the country" (5740 account, see following note), apparently refers to the meeting of Rayatz with Mr. Felix M. Warburg, American representative of the JDC, in Moscow in the spring of 1927. See *Igrot Rayatz*, vol. 1, p. 634.
9. Sermon of 20th *Shevat* 5730, (*Sichot Kodesh* 5730, p. 469). See also sermon of *Shabbat Parshat Mishpatim* 5740 (*Sichot Kodesh* 5740, p. 177*ff*).
10. *Likutei Amarim*, ch. 12, 17.
11. For the following see Yosef Yitzchak Schneersohn, *Likkutei Dibburim*, installments 34-36. English translations are found in Metzger pp. 27-129. and in Uri Kaploun (trans.), *Likkutei Dibburim: An Anthology of Talks by Rabbi Yosef Yitzchak Schneersohn of Lubavitch*, vol. 4 (New York: Kehot 1997), pp. 141-218. Further details are found in *Di Yesurim fun Lubavitchen Rebben in Soviet Russland* (Riga 1930)—Hebrew translation in Glitzenstein, pp. 1403-55 (partially adapted by Metzger, pp. 131-167). A further short memoir penned by Rayatz published in *Sefer Hasichot* 5680-7 (New York: Kehot, 2004), pp. 263-74
12. Lieberman was a Jewish bibliographer *par excellence* and began working for Rayatz in 1925 as a personal secretary and librarian. A Lubavitcher Chasid by birth, he had studied at Chabad Yeshivot and acquired Rabbinic ordination. For two years, he had studied medicine at the University of Odessa, but was forced to leave due to a famine which was ravaging the area.
13. Recounted by Rebbetzin Moussia to Rabbi Berel Junik (Rabbi Mishael Aronson, *And the Living Shall Take it to Heart* (Heb. Private publication, 2009), p. 29).
14. Althaus memoir, Metzger pp. 301-2.
15. Recollections of Rabbi Chaim Lieberman in 1983, printed in Rabbi Shalom Ber Levin, *History of Chabad in Czarist Russia* (Heb.), (New York: Kehot, 2010), p. 339, note 24.
16. Soviet Interrogation file #898 of Mr. Chaim Lieberman, cited by Beizer, ibid.
17. Metzger, p. 53. Lieberman told the authorities that the two men visiting him were drunks who had lost their way (Levin ibid.).
18. Ibid. pp. 53-4.
19. Levin, ibid.
20. See Metzger p. 61, note 8.
21. Congressional Record Volume 140, Number 74 (http://www.gpo.gov/fdsys/pkg/CREC-1994-06-14/html/CREC-1994-06-14-pt1-PgS44.htm).
22. Metzger pp. 142-4; Bryan Mark Rigg, *Rescued from the Reich: How One of Hitler's Soldiers Saved the Lubavitcher Rebbe* (Yale University Press, 2004), p. 30.
23. ibid, p. 147 from *Yesurim* ch. 10.
24. Lieberman file (Beizer, ibid).
25. Metzger, p. 145, 147, 308.
26. The full speech is translated in Metzger, pp. 152-4.

27. Metzger, p. 157.
28. Aronson, p. 33.
29. Ibid p. 157. Laufer, *Yemei Melech* vol. 1, p. 211. Court deposition of Moussia Schneerson, 11-12-1985. Rayatz was not officially allowed home until the following day, as the 12th was a legal holiday.
30. *Igrot Kodesh* vol. 20, p. 285. Apparently, the Seventh Rebbe had further significant involvement in the affair, details of which he requested not to be publicized (see Metzger p. 149, note 13).
31. For a more detailed account, see Metzger, chapter 11.
32. Chana Schneerson Memoirs, installment 34.
33. The passport was published by Rabbi Yehoshua Mondshine in *Derech Hamelech* (New York, 2001).
34. *Di Yiddishe Heim* (New York: Kehot), *Kislev* 1964, and *Adar-Iyar* 1962.
35. Most of Rashab's library had been detained in Moscow and was not available to Rayatz, though he did have numerous writings and other books. In 1925, to expand his collection, Rayatz purchased the library of Shmuel Wiener, Librarian of the Jewish Division of the Asiatic Museum in Leningrad, numbering some five thousand volumes.
36. Rigg p. 34. To facilitate the trip Rabbi Yisroel Jacobson raised four thousand dollars from Sam and Avraham Kramer, Chabad supporters in the United States. (Jacobson refused to leave the Kramers' office until the money had been wired to Riga!) See Rigg ibid. and Levin, *Zikaron*, pp. 151-2.
37. *Igrot Rayatz*, vol. 2, ibid.
38. Friedman, *A Mother in Israel*, pp. 15-16.
39. *Di Yiddishe Heim*, *Kislev* 1964.
40. Harari, *Secret*, p. 90.
41. Lesches p. 221.

CHAPTER 5: NEW BEGINNINGS

1. Latvia did serve as an excellent political asylum—Jews lived relatively safely in an independent republic—but, for Rayatz, Latvia was too small to serve as a platform for his work. There were no more than fifty thousand Jews in Riga, and one hundred thousand in the whole country—a far cry from his prior home in Russia which still had one of the largest Jewish populations in the world, numbering some 2.6 million in 1926. Latvian Jews were also more provincial and did not think big—hardly the ideal constituency for an international visionary like Rayatz. It is no wonder, then, that throughout his period in the country the Rebbe's notepaper read "Rabbi Joseph I. Schneersohn, *temporarily* in Riga, Latvia." Rayatz was in search of the best locality to replant the Chabad court, and he was certain it was not Latvia.
2. *Igrot Kodesh* vol. 3, p. 155.
3. See previous chapter, note 7.
4. No documents have surfaced that answer these questions conclusively. We can only conjecture what might have been the motivating factors based on the larger context of his life and circumstantial details.
5. It has been suggested that he was deterred from the Rabbinate by Jewish pietistic teachings which discourage a person from making a living from the Torah (see Maimonides, Laws of Torah Study chapter 3, law 10), but we lack any clear indication that this was the case.
6. See *Igrot Rayatz* vol. 4, p. 377. *Tzemach Tzedek* interest in *handasah* more likely refers to expertise in mathematics and geometry. See Rapoport, *Afterlife*, p. 54, note 144.
7. See Rabbi Menachem Mendel of Lubavitch (*Tzemach Tzedek*), *Derech Mitzvosecha* 104b.

8. Detractors of the Seventh Rebbe, most notably his nephew Shalom Ber (Barry) Gourary and the historians whom he influenced (Shimon Deutch, Samuel Heilman and Menachem Friedman), have painted the Rebbe's attendance at university as a symptom of a weakening Chasidic attachment. However, as Chaim Rapoport has shown, there is no documentary evidence to support this claim. Gourary himself was only a small child of seven years when he spent time with his uncle in Berlin, and all his later claims need to be viewed in the context of their soured relations, beginning in 1950 and climaxing in the unfortunate and bitter dispute that erupted over the Chabad Library in 1985. (Gourary himself never suggested that Menachem Mendel ever lapsed in Orthodox observance. He recalls that in Berlin the future Rebbe covered his head, wore a beard and attended synagogue).

   We know that Rayatz supported Menachem Mendel and Moussia financially throughout their college years, indicating that he was at least sympathetic to, if not encouraging of, their secular studies. Even before Menachem Mendel met Rayatz, he had considerable knowledge of secular wisdom, and the Sixth Rebbe clearly saw this as an asset to the movement, affectionately referring to his future son-in-law as his "Education Minister" (see above, p. 35). The period in Berlin and Paris is therefore in continuum with Menachem Mendel's previous life and interests, and does not, in itself, indicate any radical departure or shift.

   In my view, besides Gourary's general inclination to disparage his uncle, he dramatized this supposed "shift" to make his own candidacy for leadership of the movement viable, despite the weakening of his own Chasidic attachments from the late 1940s onwards. Even if Gourary never seriously desired to be Rebbe, it seems that he felt, as Rayatz's only male descendant, it was his right. Since it was unacceptable that a person with his modern lifestyle might become a Chasidic Rebbe, he overstated the Seventh Rebbe's university attendance as a "departure" so as to provide a precedent for his own possible return. But in the light of Rayatz's financial support of the young couple and the numerous documents from that period which have surfaced in recent years showing Menachem Mendel's sustained interest in Chasidic life and Torah study, the notion of a radical shift or major period of disenchantment is untenable.

9. Interview with Rabbi Chaskel Besser in *The Early Years* vol. 1.
10. Rabbi Levi Yitzchak Schneerson, *Michtavei Hachatuna* (New York, 1999), p. 29.
11. See the Rebbe's 1953 letter on evolution printed in *Likutei Sichot*, vol. 30, pp. 259-263 which cites extensively from German academic literature from the 1920s and 1930s. There are no references, however, to any literature from the 1940s.
12. See Rabbi Adin Steinsaltz, *My Rebbe* (Jerusalem: Maggid Books 2014), p. 38. See also interview with Dr, Meir Shochetman, a fellow student with the Rebbe in his Paris years, in Laufer, *Yemei Melech* vol. 1, p. 373: "He [Menachem Mendel] was hungry for knowledge. He would visit museums, read and study a lot, though his main occupation was with the Sciences."
13. Interview with Rabbi Ezriel Zelig Slonim in *Kfar Chabad*, issue 66. Slonim states that they were *tefilin* of *Rabenu Tam* (an extra pair that many individuals don, in addition to the *tefilin* required by Jewish Law, which follow the opinion of *Rashi*), though the Rebbe's father, Reb Levik, only instructed his son to begin donning *Rabenu Tam tefilin* immediately prior to his wedding, which was not until the following winter (see *Likutei Levi Yitzchak* vol. 3, pp. 206-7). See also interview with Uri Metzner (Jewish Educational Media), for another account of how a person delivering a letter to the Rebbe's apartment one afternoon saw him in *tefilin* studying the Jerusalem Talmud.
14. Laufer, *Yemei Melech*, vol. 1, p. 273, footnote 33.
15. "It is forbidden to occupy oneself with secular wisdom, as the verse implies, '[And these words, which I command you this day] and you shall talk *of them*' (Deut 6:7). You should not mix other matters in with them (*Sifri, Va'etchanan*). And even a person who has already learned the entire Torah, perhaps he will say, 'I have learned Jewish wisdom, now I will go and learn the wisdom of the nations?" In response to this, the Torah teaches us (*Sifri* ibid.),

'You shall guard my laws to walk with them' (Leviticus 18:4)—you never have permission to exempt yourselves from them" (Rabbi Shneur Zalman of Liadi, *Laws of Torah Study* 3:7).

16. See sources cited in letters in following note.
17. *Igrot Kodesh* vol. 3, pp. 122-6 and pp. 167-171, also printed in *Likutei Sichot* vol. 12, pp. 197-199. The letter was written to Rabbi Alter Hilbitz (1906-1994). English translation of first letter available at http://www.sichosinenglish.org/books/letters-rebbe-4/084.htm. For a full treatment of the letter and other sources from the Rebbe pertaining to the study of secular wisdom see: Rabbi Shalom Wolpo, *Limud Chochmot Chitzoniyot be-Mishnat Admor mi-Lubavitch* in *Techumin* vol. 19, (Israel: *Machon Zomet,* 1999), pp. 419-38. For more about Rabbi Hilbitz and his relationship with the Rebbe see Rabbi Shalom Wolpo, *Shemen Sason Mechaveirecho* vol. 1 (1995, Private publication), pp. 165-7.
18. Maimonides, Responsa *Pe'er Ha'dor (*Amsterdam, 1765), section 41.
19. Obviously, Rabbi Shneur Zalman is speaking of exceptional individuals who had first mastered the normative Jewish texts of Scripture, Mishnah, Talmud and Midrash, before engaging in secular study.
20. While there is an obvious anachronism here to applying a 1949 letter to a 1928 decision, the insight is, in fact, already found in brief in *Notes on Tanya* (on this passage in Chapter 8, p. 73, *s.v. ha-Rambam*—accessible at http://lahak.org/pdf2/reshimos-tanya/T-1-perek-08.pdf), which were penned by the Rebbe in his college years. It is likely then, considering that *Tanya* chapter 8 would have been a text which Menachem Mendel pondered deeply before pursuing secular study, that the above discussion was part of his decision-making process. Even if this is not the case, we can at least appreciate in hindsight that Menachem Mendel's secular pursuits, while highly unusual for a Chasid, did fall, according to his own evaluation, within the guidelines of the *Tanya.*

    Later he would oppose college study for Orthodox youth in America (see p. 238).
21. See Shochetman interview: "When Chasidim interrogated him [Menachem Mendel] about his studies in university, he replied that this was important to be a perfect Jew so as to be in a position to 'Know what to answer [the heretic]' (*Avot* 2:14)."
22. Court proceedings, United States District Court, Eastern District of New York, Case CV 85 2909, page 1859.
23. See *Igrot Rayatz,* vol. 4, p. 377.
24. For the above see Rabbi Shalom Ber Levin, *A History of Chabad in Poland, Lithuania, and Latvia, 1790-1946* (Heb.), (New York: Kehot 2011), p. 51.
25. Minutes of the meeting were published in the journal *Degel Yisrael* (New York), in *Adar* of that year (reproduced in Levin, *History of Chabad in the U.S.S.R.,* pp. 108-11).
26. *Brachot* 5:1.
27. *Brachot* 32b.
28. *Pnei Moshe,* ibid.
29. *Rashi,* ibid.
30. *Sichot Kodesh* 5735, volume 1, p. 472-3, edited and reworked in *Likutei Sichot* vol. 16, p. 374*ff.* The Rebbe also repeated the story in public in a 1982 sermon (*Torat Menachem—Hitva'aduyot* 5742, p. 535). For more on this topic see *Likutei Sichot,* vol. 16 (New York: Kehot, 1980), p. 373*ff;* letter to Rabbi Abraham Hecht, printed in *Teshurah mi-simchat nisuin Groner-Pinson,* 9th *Kislev* 5774, p. 5.
31. *Likutei Sichot,* ibid.
32. Mondshine, *Derech Hamelech,* pp. 7-8.
33. *Agudat Yisrael* was an alliance formed between German neo-Orthodoxy, Hungarian Orthodoxy, and the Orthodox Jewries in Poland and Lithuania. While all factions were strongly committed to Orthodoxy, they differed in political and social outlook, and in cultural and organizational matters. Major divergences included: the attitude to general European culture, separatism of the Orthodox community and the importance of spoken Yiddish.

34. Published in *Kfar Chabad*, issue 967, pp. 24-5.
35. Dr. Menachem Rottenberg, one of the leaders of *Agudat Israel* in England.
36. Rabbi Mordechai Zev Gutnick (1898-1931) was one of the students of *Yeshivat Tomchei Temimim* in Lubavitch, and emigrated later to Tel-Aviv. Upon Rayatz's instructions, he relocated to London and held a Rabbinic position there. See *Kfar Chabad*, issues 835-6.
37. Proceedings of the convention were later published in the 28 page pamphlet: Palaestina-Centrale der A.J. (issue 3), *Die Palaestina-Konferenz der Agudas Jisroel in Berlin am 2. und 3. Teweth 5688 / 26. und 27, Dezember 1927* (Frankfurt, *Die Hermon Druckerei* 1928).
38. Letter of Rabbi Shmuel Schneerson, dated 15th *Shevat* 5688 is preserved in the library of *Agudat Chasidei Chabad*, along with its translation into German, submitted to the university. Whether or not Menachem Mendel actually attended the school at Yekatrinoslav is unclear. As an interesting comparison, Rabbi Joseph B. Soloveitchik's gymnasium diploma, presented as part of his application to the University of Berlin, was not authentic and the Rav never attended the school. See Aaron Rakeffet-Rothkoff, *The Rav: The World of Rabbi Joseph B. Soloveitchik, Volume 1* (New Jersey: Ktav, 1999), p. 68, note 9.
39. His responsa are collected in *Seridei Aish* (Jerusalem: *Mosad Harav Kook*, 1961-69), 4 volumes.
40. Menachem Mendel Schneerson, *Reshimot* (New York: Kehot, 1994-2001), installments 127-8. The editors of the 1999 edition of Rabbi Weinberg's Responsa *Seridei Aish* subsequently included the *Reshima* as an addendum.
41. See Rabbi Zusia Wolf, *Admorei Chabad ve-Yahadut Germania* (Kfar Chabad: Kehot, 2007), p. 103-4, from an interview with Rabbi Avraham Abba Weingort, a close confidant of Rabbi Weinberg. Prof. Marc Shapiro, Weinberg's biographer, confirmed with me that Weingort's testimony is reliable, and Shapiro later made the point known on his blog. See http://seforim.blogspot.com/2009/09/marc-b-shapiro-responses-to-comments.html. For more details see: http://www.chabad.org/news/article_cdo/aid/2112908/jewish/Details-of-the-Rebbes-Rabbinical-Ordination-Authenticated.htm.
42. From *Adar* 16th until *Iyar* 6th (Mondshine, *Derech Hamelech* p. 8).
43. See letter to Prof. Marc Shapiro from Berlin University in 1995, (reproduced in Deutch, *Larger than Life*, vol. 2, p. 76) confirming that the Rebbe was registered as an "occasional student" (Gasthörer).
44. For current regulations see http://www.hu-berlin.de/studies/beratung/merk/guest_students
45. While Albert Einstein headed the department of physics during the period the Rebbe was in Berlin University, no reliable evidence has surfaced of any personal encounters. For discussion see Rabbi Yehoshua Mondshine, *The Rebbe, the Rogatchover and... Einstein*, http://www.shturem.net/index.php?id=1101§ion=artdays (accessed Feb 2014).
46. See http://www.manfredlehmann.com/news/news_detail.cgi/110/0.
47. Later published as Abraham Joshua Heschel, *The Prophets* (New York, Harper Collins, 2001). For more on the doctorate see Heschel, *Moral Grandeur and Spiritual Audacity*, (Farrar, Straus and Giroux, 1997) p. xi.
48. Interview with Dr. Yaakov Hanoka (JEM).
49. Laufer, *Yemei Melech* vol. 1, p. 245 citing testimony of a Mr. Tzifel of Milan whose father-in-law was the *mikvah* attendant. Interview with Rabbi Sholom Kowalsky (1920-2007), spring 2006, citing Rabbi Joseph B. Soloveitchik, accessible at http://www.chabad.org/therebbe/article_cdo/aid/529444/jewish/The-Rebbe-and-the-Rav.htm. See also interviews with students of Rabbi Soloveitchik in Jewish Educational Media, *The Early Years* volume 1; interview with Uri Metzner, accessible at http://www.chabad.org/therebbe/livingtorah/player_cdo/aid/1491011/jewish/A-Chassid-in-Berlin.htm.

50. For a biography of Rabbi Slonim see Rabbi Shalom Wolpo, *Eved Melech* (Private publication, 2008).
51. Rabbi Tuvia Blau in *Kfar Chabad* issue 66, p. 9, reproduced in Laufer, *Yemei Melech*, vol. 1, pp. 245-7. See also Wolpo, *Eved Melech* pp. 123-5.
52. *Reshimot*, installment 33 contains a draft of two letters from Menachem Mendel to the Rogatchover, and one reply from the Gaon. The final version of the second letter is printed in *Igrot Kodesh* vol. 1, p. 1.
53. Ibid. The date of this journey is unclear but one possibility is that Menachem Mendel accompanied the Rogatchover back to Dvinsk by train after Rayatz's general meeting in Riga, October 1927.
54. Ibid., letter dated 22nd *Shevat*.
55. *Likutei Levi Yitzchak, Likutim al Pesukei Tanach U'ma'amarei Chazal; Igrot* (New York: Kehot 1972), pp. 197-423.
56. This refers to the *gematria* (numerical values) of the words ibid. pp. 197-8.
57. Ibid. pp. 199-200.
58. Ibid. pp. 201-2.
59. The letter is printed in Wolf, *Admurei Chabad* pp. 101-2.
60. On seeing Menachem Mendel dance for hours after Rosh Hashanah, Rabbi Eliyahu Chaim Althaus commented to Rayatz, "*Mazal tov*. Today the Rebbe has a new Chasid. They couldn't hold your Mendel back from the dancing." See Laufer, *Yemei Melech*, vol. 1, p. 251.
61. Althaus memoir. For a compendium of sources relating to the wedding see Rabbi Shneur Zalman Hertzl, *Nisuai Hanesi'im* (New York 1996, private publication), pp. 117-192; Laufer, *Yemei Melech* vol. 1, p. 257*ff*; *Reshimat Ha-Yoman*, p. 440*ff*. For an excellent collection of sources in English, see Oberlander and Shmotkin, *Early Years—Excerpt*.
62. Althaus memoir. See also *Reshimat Ha-Yoman* pp. 149-150.
63. Althaus memoir.
64. Ibid. Only around ten Chasidim of Rayatz from Riga were able to leave Latvia and join the wedding celebrations (ibid.).
65. *Igrot Rayatz* vol. 16, p. 277.
66. For details about the Warsaw Yeshivah see Levin, *A History of Chabad in Poland*, pp. 83-199.
67. Except for the wedding of Rayatz's oldest daughter, Chana, to Shmaryahu Gourary, which took place after leaving Lubavitch.
68. *Reshimat Ha-Yoman*, p. 443.
69. Althaus memoir.
70. Spiritual manual written by Rabbi Eliyahu de Vidas (1518-1592). The passages referring to the sanctity of marital relations (*Sha'ar ha-Kedushah* chapters 15-17) are traditionally studied by a groom prior to his wedding. See *Igrot Kodesh* vol. 5, p. 129.
71. *Haynt* newspaper, issue 279, 16th *Kislev*, reproduced in Laufer, *Yemei Melech* vol. 1, p. 278.
72. Published in Rabbi Ari Solish (trans.), *The Majestic Bride* (New York: Kehot, 2008)
73. Althaus' memoir ends at the *chupah*. The remaining account is based on *Reshimat Ha-Yoman*, p. 443*ff*, and Laufer, ibid. pp. 306-8.
74. *Torat Menachem, Hitva'aduyot* 5714 vol. 10, p. 200.
75. Laufer, *Yemei Melech* vol. 1, p. 273. While not citing this exact text, Menachem Mendel later made reference to this statement of Rayatz in a letter to his father. See *Michtavei Hachatuna* p. 15.
76. *Sichot Kodesh* 5731, vol. 2, p. 41. The book was a collection of the Lubliner Rav's halachic responsa, entitled *Ohr ha-Meir*.
77. *Sefer Hasichot* 5688-5691, p. 58.
78. *Likutei Levi Yitzchak* ibid. pp. 203-6.
79. *Di Yiddishe Heim* no. 22 (*Kislev* 1964), p. 37.

80. *Likutei Levi Yitzchak*, ibid. p. 207.
81. *Michtavei Chatuna*, p. 13.
82. *Memoirs of Rebbetzin Chana*, installment 10.
83. *Di Yiddishe Heim* no. 22 (*Kislev*, 1964), pp. 22, 37. Accounts of the celebrations are also detailed in letters from Reb Levik and his brother Shmuel to Menachem Mendel in *Michtavei Chatuna*, in which the following details appear.
84. *Torat Menachem, Hitva'aduyot* 5714, vol. 10, p. 206.

CHAPTER 6: STRADDLING WORLDS

1. Official documents cite multiple different addresses and host families during this period. Mondshine, *Derech Hamelech* (the Rebbe's passport and Latvian visas) pp. 16-29, cites five different addresses from 1930 to 1932. University records from 1928 to 1929 cite three further addresses. Since the university semesters took up only seven months of the year it was presumably not worthwhile renting an apartment.
2. *Modern Judaism*, volume 34, number 1 (February 2014), pp. 127-9.
3. See index to *Reshimot*. A number of undated *Reshimot* are probably from this period.
4. See *Igrot Rayatz* vol. 15, pp. 114-5.
5. Published decades later as part of *Sefer Ha-Mafteichot le-kamah mi-sifrei u-ma'amarei Chasidut Chabad* (New York: Kehot 1966). In his introduction, the Rebbe writes: "The indices were written in different times under different conditions, both in comfort and in distress, so they do not have a unified approach."
6. See Levin, *Czarist Russia*, p. 338.
7. Published in installments by *Va'ad Hanachot Lahak* (New York), from 1995 onwards, accessible at http://www.lahak.org/ReshimosTanya.aspx.
8. Letters from this period are found in *Likutei Levi Yitzchak* vol. 3, pp. 208-258, and ibid. 308-321.
9. Letter to Rogatchover from the winter of 5689, printed in *Reshimot*, installment 159. Letter to Rogatchover dated 7th *Av* 5692, printed in *Igrot Kodesh* vol. 1, p. 14. The Rogatchover's reply is found in *Reshimot* installment 104. Reply to Rogatchover dated 27th *Av*, in *Reshimot*, ibid.
10. See below, section VI of this chapter.
11. Facsimile in Rabbi Shalom Ber Schapiro (ed.), *Sparks of Chasidut for Young and Old* (New York: Nissan Mindel Publications, 1999), pp. 137-141.
12. The letter was written to nuclear physicist Herbert Goldstein (1922-2005), later professor of nuclear science and engineering at Columbia University. He was at the time president of the *Association of Orthodox Jewish Scientists*).
13. Much of the archives of the Rebbe's personal correspondence, however, has still to be published (see note 27).
14. This is not uncharacteristic as the Rebbe spoke or wrote very little about himself.
15. We do, however, have numerous oral testimonies, such as those related below, p. 92*ff*.
16. I.e., in Berlin. Concerning his attendance at university in Paris we have many more details, as related in the following chapter.
17. One undated *Reshima* (installment 3), which discusses the religious lessons to be learned from Pascal's Law of Hydrostatics and Geometry, appears to have been penned by the Reb-

be in the 1940s, in the USA, since it is found in the second volume of his notebook, containing the later *Reshimot.* For an adaptation of the *Reshima* in English see Rabbi Joseph Ginsburg and Prof. Herman Branover (Arnie Gotfryd trans.), *Mind over Matter: Teachings of the Lubavitcher Rebbe on Science, Technology and Medicine* (Jerusalem: Shamir, Association of Religious Scientists and Professionals from the former Soviet Union and Eastern Europe, 2003), p. 219*ff.*

18. Portion of (undated) letter in Rabbi Nissan Mindel, *Moreh Le-dor Navuch,* vol. 3 (Kfar Chabad: 2005), p. 131. The letter was originally written in English but, since only a Hebrew translation was available to me, I have attempted to render it back into its original language.
19. *Sefer Ha-Ma'amarim Melukat,* vol. 4 (New York: Kehot, 1991), p. 276, note 48. See also *Likutei Sichot,* vol. 30 (New York: Kehot, 1992), pp. 194-7.
20. Schapiro, *Sparks,* pp. 67-8.
21. Ecclesiastes 1:4. The Talmudic Rabbis accepted the sun's motion around the earth unquestioningly. See BT *Berachot* 59b; *Pesachim* 94b, JT *Rosh Hashanah* 2:5; *Shemot Rabah* 15:22.
22. Reichenbach had attended Albert Einstein's lectures on the Theory of Relativity in Berlin from 1917 to 1920, and subsequently published four books on Relativity's philosophical import, during the period from 1920 to 1928. (Einstein was obviously impressed with these works, as he was influential in Reichenbach's appointment as Assistant Professor at the physics department at the University of Berlin, in 1926). Reichenbach's *Philosophie der Raum-Zeit-Lehre* (*Philosophy of Space and Time*), published around the time of Menachem Mendel's arrival in Berlin in 1928, argued that, in the light of Relativity theory, the notion of a "stationary point" in the universe was totally arbitrary.

> "The relativity theory of dynamics is not a purely academic matter, for it upsets the Copernican worldview. It is meaningless to speak of a difference in truth claims of the theories of Copernicus and Ptolemy; the two conceptions are equivalent descriptions. What had been considered the greatest discovery of western science, compared to antiquity, is now denied its claim to truth.... The Theory of Relativity does not say that the conception of Ptolemy is correct; rather it contests the absolute significance of either theory" (Hans Reichenbach (Maria Reichenbach and John Freund trans.), *The Philosophy of Space and Time* (Dover Publications, 1957), chapter 3, section 34).

The Copernican view, of planets orbiting the Sun, had only been accepted as "true" from a certain worldview, that of motion and dynamics. If one accepted Ptolemy's (and the Torah's) argument that the Earth lies in the center, then the resulting planetary and solar orbits would be extremely messy. This would be uncomfortable from a Newtonian *dynamic* worldview, but not in Einstein's universe which was seen through the eyes of *gravitational pull.* As Reichenbach explains:

> "Newton decided in favor of Copernicus from the point of view of dynamics. It was only for this particular world description that his theory of gravitation offered a *mechanical explanation.* The complicated planetary orbits of Ptolemy, on the other hand, did not fit into any explanation. If we wish to establish the equivalence of both world conceptions, we must find a theory of gravitation sufficiently general to explain the Copernican and also the Ptolemaic planetary motion as a *gravitational phenomenon.* Herein lies the great achievement of Einstein.... Einstein has indeed found such a comprehensive theory of gravitation; and it is with this discovery, which places him on the same plane as Copernicus and Newton, that the problem of the relativity of motion has been brought to a conclusion" (ibid.).

23. See Nissan Mindel (ed.), *The Letter and the Spirit: Letters by the Lubavitcher Rebbe* vol. 2 (New York: Nissan Mindel Publications, 2013), pages, 239, 281, 290-2, and 318. See Ginsburg and Branover, *Mind over Matter,* p. 69.
24. Letter dated June 30, 1975, to Rabbi Feivel Rimmler, printed in *Teshurah mi-simchat nisuin*

Rimler-Schneider, 1995.

25. Mindel, *The Letter*, ibid. p. 290. The Rebbe had in fact already made a public statement about his views in a letter to the editors of the *Jewish Press*, on 9th Iyar 5724 (1964), ibid. p. 239.
26. Ibid. pp. 291-2. Surprisingly, the Rebbe does not makes specific mention of Reichenbach in any of his correspondence (to my knowledge). Perhaps he felt that the argument stood on logic alone and did not wish to present it as the particular view of one scientist. See overview by Prof. Herman Branover (Ginsberg and Branover, p. xiv.), who spent many hours in conversation with the Rebbe about scientific matters, and attributes the Rebbe's source to Reichenbach.
27. Letter, dated 23rd August 1964 in Mindel, p. 244. Green was Professor of Public Health and Microbiology at the University of Minnesota and a participant in NASA's exobiology program, searching for life on Mars. (For similar sentiments see letters in Mindel, p. 281, 292 and 318-9.)

    It is important to note that the Mindel archive contains only draft copies of letters composed by Mindel without final edits from the Rebbe's hand. The current letter is a case in point. A facsimile of the actual letter received by Prof. Greene (reproduced in *Professor Greene, Greetings and Blessings* (Heb.), Central Beit Chabad, Bet Sheva, 2011, pp. 84-6) indicates clearly that Mindel's copy did not contain the Rebbe's handwritten amendments. Other drafts in the Mindel archive were never actually sent by the Rebbe. However, the Mindel archive is still an extremely valuable source since it contains countless letters that are not reproduced elsewhere, though it is necessary to bear in mind that the contents may not represent a final, perfectly accurate articulation of the Rebbe's views.
28. Letter to the *Association of Orthodox Jewish Scientists*, 1971, printed in Ginsberg and Branover, p. 109.
29. Ibid, p. 110. In breaking free from apologetics, the Seventh Rebbe made a bold and intellectually daring move. Many illustrious Rabbinical figures had deemed this path an effective and necessary method of winning over Jews who had been disillusioned by apparently outdated positions of Judaism, or by clashes with thought systems that were in vogue. Rabbi Yisrael Lipschitz (1782–1860), author of an important commentary on the *Mishnah*, *Tiferet Yisrael*, had penned a well received and highly influential apologetic treatise on the topic of evolution. The apologetic posture could, in fact, be traced back to one of Judaism's most celebrated rabbis, Maimonides, who offered non-traditional readings of Torah texts, palatable to the Jews of Moslem Spain who had absorbed the Aristotelean world view.

    In a 1953 letter, the Rebbe himself lamented Maimonides' apologetic tendencies: "What greater example do we have than Maimonides, of whom our great leaders declared, 'From Moses to Moses there is none like Moses.' From a careful reading of his *Mishneh Torah* one can see how many of his interpretations in the *Guide for the Perplexed*, especially when clarifying the rationales for the commandments, did not represent his own Torah outlook" (*Likutei Sichot* vol. 30, p. 260).

    For more on apologetics see *Igrot Kodesh*, vol. 7, p. 133; vol. 15, p. 60 and p. 133. Ginsburg and Branover p. 98*ff.*
30. For a summary of the Rebbe's scientific positions with relevant citations see *Science and Technology in the works of the Lubavitcher Rebbe* in my *Rambam: Thirteen Principles of Faith—Principles 8-9* (New York: Kol Menachem, 2007), p. 364*ff.*
31. See sources collected in Rabbi Shalom Wolpo, *Shemen Sason Mechaveirecho* vol. 3 (2003, private publication), pp. 162-166
32. See above, pp. 8-9.
33. It is not clear to what extent the Rav's study in Berlin was condoned by his father. See lecture of Rabbi Aaron Rakeffet-Rothkoff, 24th October 1995, http://www.yutorah.com/lectures/lecture.cfm/709605/Rabbi_Aaron_Rakeffet-Rothkoff/1995-10-24_Berlin_-_R_Chaim_Heller___24-Oct-95.
34. See Rabbi Soloveitchik's eulogy for Rabbi Moshe Dovber Rivkin (d. 1977), *Rosh Yeshiva* of

Brooklyn's *Mesivta Torah Vodaath* and Chabad Chasid, delivered in Congregation Moriya, NY, December 14, 1976 (printed in Rabbi Ya'akov Leib Altein (ed.), *Heichal Ha-Besht*, issue 32, *Tishrei* 5772, pp. 215*ff*).

35. See Rakeffet, *The Rav*, pp. 23-4. See Kowalsky interview, that the Rav also learned Rabbi Schneur Zalman's *Likutei Torah*.
36. Lecture on 24th October 1995, available at: http://www.yutorah.com/lectures/lecture.cfm/709605/Rabbi_Aaron_Rakeffet-Rothkoff/1995-10-24_Berlin_-_R_Chaim_Heller___24-Oct-95 (accessed October 2013). For more on the Chabad influences on Rabbi Soloveitchik see Dov Schwartz, *Chabad Thought: From Beginning to End* (Israel: Bar Ilan University Press, 2011), pp. 367-385
37. See the Rav's own autobiographical note, appended to his doctorate, published in David D. Possen, *J. B. Soloveitchik: Between Neokantianism and Kierkegaardian Existentialism* in Jon Stewart (ed.), *Kierkegaard's Influence on Theology, Tome III: Catholic and Jewish Theology* (Ashgate Publishing, 2012), p. 191.
38. Josef Solowiejczyk, *Das reine Denken und die Seinskonstituierung bei Hermann Cohen* [The Epistemology of Pure Thought and the Construction of Being according to Herman Cohen], (Berlin: Reuther and Reichard, 1932). The Rav had originally wanted to write a doctorate on the influence of Greek philosophy on Maimonides, but there was no professor in Berlin sufficiently knowledgeable in Maimonides to supervise the dissertation. The work on Cohen is devoid of references to Jewish sources and largely reiterates the views of Rabbi Soloveitchick's supervisor, Heinrich Maier.
39. Interview with Juilus Berman in Jewish Educational Media, *The Early Years*, vol. 1.
40. Letter to Rabbi D. M. Rabinowitz in *Igrot Kodesh Rayatz*, vol. 5 (New York: Kehot, 1987), p. 368. See also letter to Rabinowitz in ibid. vol. 6, pp. 178-9, where Rabbi Yosef Yitzchak expresses his "great pain" at the inappropriate treatment of the Rav. For more details see Seth Farber, *An American Orthodox Dreamer: Rabbi Joseph B. Soloveitchik and Boston's Maimonides School*, (Brandeis University Press, 2004), pp. 62-63.
41. Interview with Rabbi Sholem Kowalsky (1920-2007), spring 2006 (JEM); Interview with Rabbi Fabian Schoenfeld, *Early Years* vol. 1.
42. Kowalsky interview. See also interview with Rabbi Chazkel Besser (1923-2010), *Early Years* vol. 1. In the Dunner interview, the Rebbe was remembered as wearing a grey hat and modern suit, and his beard was kept neatly. See also interview with Rabbi David Hollander (1913–2009), who recalled Rabbi Yechiel Ya'akov Weinberg telling him that Menachem Mendel remained religiously "unscathed" by his university encounters (*Early Years, Supplement*).
43. Facsimile in *Teshurah misimchat nisuin shel* Baruch Shneur and Chaya Krinsky, 15th *Elul* 5770, p. 20, accessible at: http://www.teshura.com/teshurapdf/Krinsky-Schmukler%20-%20Elul%2015%205770.pdf. Rabbi Soloveitchik also commented to Zalman Shazar, President of Israel, in 1973, that he and the Rebbe had been "close friends in Berlin" (report of Rabbi Efraim Wolf to the Rebbe about meeting with Shazar, dated 21st *Shevat* 5733, in Rabbi Zusha Wolf (ed.), *Yemei Temimim*, vol. 6, (Kfar Chabad: Kehot, 2009), p. 96).
44. Kowalsky interview; Rabbi Eliyahu Reichman, *Kfar Chabad* issue 662; interview with Rabbi Chaim Ciment, accesible at http://shturem.org/index.php?section=artdays&id=1901. See also Rabbi Nissan Mindel (ed.), *The Letter and the Spirit: Letters by the Lubavitcher Rebbe* vol. 1 (New York: Nissan Mindel Publications, 1998), introduction page xvii-xvii, where the editor, who served as a secretary of the Seventh Rebbe, notes his personal observation that the Rebbe was able to dictate the response to a letter while simultaneously reading the next letter, and connects this unusual skill to the above anecdote.
45. Interview with Rabbi Chaim Ciment (JEM, *Living Torah*, vol. 46, episode 184).
46. See Kowalsky interview; Ciment interview.
47. Interview with Rabbi Zevulun Charlop. June 16th, 2010 (*Kol Menachem* archive).
48. His edition of Maimonides *Sefer ha-Mitzvot* was hailed as a revolutionary work and became a standard edition. It was praised by Rabbi Israel Meir Ha-Kohen (the Chafetz Chaim), and is

cited by the Rebbe numerous times.

49. For an interesting depiction of Rabbi Chaim Heller's character and talents, especially with regard to the refutation of Biblical criticism, see Dr. Aaron Rosmarin, *Reb Chaim Heller—One in Generations*, in *The Jewish Criterion* (Pittsburgh), September 15, 1944. For a brief biography and list of his published writings see Moshe D. Sherman, *Orthodox Judaism in America: A Biographical Dictionary and Sourcebook* (Connecticut: Greenwood Publishing, 1996), pp. 89-91. For Rabbi Soloveitchik's outstanding eulogy of Rabbi Heller see Joseph Epstein (ed.), *Shiurei Harav: A Conspectus of the Public Lectures of Rabbi Joseph B. Soloveitchik* (New Jersey: KTAV, 1994), p. 46*ff.*
50. Interview with Rabbi Pinchas Pinter, accessible at http://www.chabad.org/therebbe/living-torah/player_cdo/aid/1264768/jewish/Two-Lions.htm.
51. Rakeffet lecture.
52. Surprisingly, there is no published correspondence between Rabbi Heller and the Rebbe during the two decades they both lived in America. We do find, though, that Rabbis Heller and Soloveitchik visited Seven-Seventy to comfort the mourners after the passing of the Rebbe Rayatz. (See Yosef Yitzchak Greenberg and Eliezer Zaklikowsky, *Yemei Bereishit: Historical Biography—1950-1951* (New York: Kehot 1993), p. 86.)
53. See, for example, sources cited in Rabbi Tuvia Blau (ed.), *Klalei Rashi*, expanded edition (Kfar Chabad: Kehot, 1991), chapter 20.
54. Blau sources this methodology extensively, citing some 389 principles of Rashi's methodology proposed in the Rebbe's *sichot*. I am sure that a close reading of the *sichot* would yield many more. See also my essay, *Did Rashi Lack a Scientific Method* in *Algemeiner Journal*, August 11, 2005, accessible at http://www.algemeiner.net/generic.asp?id=426.
55. *Likutei Amarim, First Versions, based on earliest manuscripts* (New York: Kehot, 1982), multiple editors.
56. *Mishneh Torah Mehadurat Shabatai Frankel*, 14 volumes (Hotza'at Shabse Frankel, 1973-2007). When the first volume appeared, the Rebbe brought it into the synagogue with him, and was seen perusing it avidly.
57. See Rabbi Mordechai Laufer (ed.), *Klalei ha-Rambam* (Kfar Chabad: Kehot 1991).
58. Letter to publishers of *Chumash Shay Lamorah* (Jerusalem 2003), in *Igrot Kodesh*, volume 29, pp. 192-3. See, by way of example, *Likutei Sichot* vol. 27, p. 95 where the Rebbe defends the validity of the *girsa ha-nefutzah*, despite the fact that it is absent from most early editions of *Rashi*.
59. See *Sichot Kodesh* (5731, vol. 2, p. 466), where after suggesting a correction to a printed comment of *Rashi*, the Rebbe states, "But that is how the printers have arranged it, and I do not wish to take issue with them."
60. He argued that the latter authorities—such as Rabbi Yosef Caro (1488-1575), author of the halachically normative *Shulchan Aruch*—had not merely deferred to Maimonides' rulings; they had, in fact, contemplated his words deeply, and finding themselves in agreement with his conclusions, they had ruled accordingly. It is therefore irrelevant whether or not they had the correct text of Maimonides, since their rulings represented their own opinion, and it is *they* whom we follow. See *Sichah* of 15th *Tammuz* 5746—*Al Davar ha-Mahadurot de-Sefer ha-Yad le-ha-Rambam* printed in *Torat Menachem—Hitva'aduyot* 5746, vol. 4 (New York: Va'ad Hanachot Lehak, 5750), pp. 94-7. See also Rabbi Baruch Oberlander, *Iyun Be-Mahadurot ha-Chadashot shel ha-Mishneh Torah le-ha-Rambam* in *Ohr Yisrael* issue 23, *Nissan* 5661, p. 215*ff.*
61. Rabbi Samson Raphael Hirsch (1808-1888) did not actually favor *Wissenschaft des Judentums*, but he was a pioneer of German Neo-Orthodoxy that attempted to synthesise traditional Torah values with the prevailing intellectual currents of the day. For an interesting letter by Rayatz on Hirsch's approach see Ginsburg and Branover, pp. 126-131.
62. http://crownheights.info/general/8538/the-rebbe-the-nature-of-american-jewish-students/.
63. The Rebbe was observed by Rabbi Yosef Tzvi Dunner (1913-2007), who studied in the Semi-

nary from 1932 to 1936—as reported to his grandson, Rabbi Pini Dunner. See http://seforim.blogspot.com/2008/03/pini-dunner-unknown-picture-of-late.html; *Early Years, Supplement*, vol. 5. Professor Menachem Ben Sasson of the Hebrew University claimed that his father-in-law, Israeli politician Yosef Burg (1909–1999), who studied in Berlin from 1928 to 1931 did not recall seeing the Rebbe at the seminary (Avirama Golan, "Messiah of Flesh and Blood, Piecing Together the Rebbe's Secret Years," *Haaretz*, 20th April, 1998). If this observation is correct, it is possible that the Rebbe only frequented the seminary in 1932.

64. Interview with Naftali Rubin, Jewish Educational Media.
65. A number of prominent Jewish figures from the second half of the twentieth century studied in Berlin at the same time as the Rebbe, but no evidence has surfaced as to whether they were acquainted with each other at that time. These include Rabbi Abraham Joshua Heschel (1907-1972), Rabbi Yitzchak Hutner (1906-1980), Yeshayahu Leibowitz (1903-1994), and Nechama Leibowitz (1905-1997). In Heschel's biography (Edward Kaplan and Samuel Dresner, *Abraham Joshua Heschel: Prophetic Witness* (Yale University Press, 1998), pp. 138-9), there is an account of a public argument between the Rebbe and Heschel about *halachic* conversions, but the authors themselves question whether the story is true. No information has surfaced about a relationship between Heschel and the Rebbe, even in the United States. Rabbi Shalom Ber Schapiro, curator of the Mindel archive, disclosed to me that the Rebbe wrote a number of letters to Heschel, but chose not to send them. Rabbi Hutner did have a relationship with the Rebbe in the United States, as we shall see later. Nechama Leibowitz stated that she was not acquainted with the Rebbe in Berlin (See Yael Unterman, *Nehama Leibowitz: Teacher and Bible Scholar*, (Jersualem and New York: Urim Press, 2009), p. 29).
66. For a biography of Rabbi Besser see Warren Kozak, *The Rabbi of 84th Street: The Extraordinary Life of Haskel Besser* (New York: Harper Collins, 2004).
67. Interview with Rabbi Besser in *Kfar Chabad*, issue 650, and *Early Years*, volume 1. I have added details from Rabbi Chaim Schneerson's recollection of the event, as reported in Rabbi Shalom Wolpo, *Shemen Sason Mechaveirecha* vol. 4 (2009, Private publication), pp. 206-7.
68. Wolpo ibid. p. 212. *Siach Sarfei Kodesh* p. 389. For more on Rabbi Aharon Rokeach see Yisrael Klapholtz, *Admorei Belz*, vol. 4, (Bnei Brak, 1977). Rayatz was influential in saving the Belzer Rebbe's life from Nazi-occupied Europe. See Wolpo, ibid, p. 200; Rigg, *Rescued* p. 164 and note 32.
69. Rayatz stopped in Berlin in the Summer of 1929 on his way to Israel, and the summer of 1930, on his way home from the United States.
70. These trips had a number of motivating factors. Rayatz was seeking to move from Riga, and both America and the Holy Land were major Jewish centers. The American trip was largely connected with fundraising, and the trip to Israel was in order to visit "holy sites" such as the graves of saintly Rabbis, since it was no longer possible for Rayatz to visit the graves of the previous Chabad Rebbes in Russia. Undoubtedly, these trips provided a refreshing break for Rayatz from Riga, which was a community too small for his desired activities and vision. For details of the Israel trip see Dov Zev Rottenberg, *Masa ha-Rebbi be-Eretz ha-Kodesh* (Kfar Chabad: Aishel, 1999). For the trip to America see Rabbi Shalom Ber Levin, *History of Chabad in the U.S.A—1900-1950* (New York: Kehot, 1988), p. 37*ff*.
71. See *Igrot Rayatz*, vol. 15, p. 93.
72. Harkavi and Goldburt, p. 119.
73. *Igrot Rayatz* vol. 15 (New York: Kehot, 2010).
74. Letter of 18th *Shevat* 5690, ibid. p. 74.
75. Letter of 6th *Adar* 5690, ibid. p. 77.
76. Letter of 2nd *Nisan* 5690, ibid. p. 78.
77. Ibid. p. 88.
78. Letter of 25th *Adar* 5690, ibid. p. 83.
79. Letter of 23rd *Adar* 5961, ibid. p. 103.
80. Letter of *Erev Chag Ha-Sukkot* 5690, ibid. p. 66.

81. Ibid. p. 81. See also p. 105,
82. Letter to Moussia, 5th *Elul* 5689, ibid. p. 60.
83. Letter of *Erev Chanukah* 5690, ibid. p. 71.
84. Letter to Menachem Mendel, 5th *Elul* 5689, ibid. p. 59.
85. Letter of 26th *Tevet* 5690, ibid. p. 74.
86. Letter of 18th *Shevat* 5690, ibid.
87. Letter of 25th *Adar* 5690, ibid. p. 82. Emphasis added.
88. Letter of *Erev Chanukah* 5690, ibid. p. 70.
89. Letter of 9th *Tevet* 5691, ibid. p. 101.
90. Letter of 11th *Shevat* 5692, ibid. pp. 114-5
91. Letter of 26th *Menachem Av*, 5689, ibid. pp. 63-4. Rayatz's reply is ibid. pp. 62-3.
92. Letter of 24th *Kislev* 5691, ibid p. 101.
93. Letter of 4th *Shevat* 5691, ibid.
94. We have seen, at the very least, he had visited the Chortkov Rebbe, the Belzer Rebbe and prayed in the synagogue of the Dombrova Rebbe.
95. Menachem Mendel's letter of request is not printed, but the question is repeated by Rayatz at the introduction to his response (see following note).
96. The full response is printed in *Igrot Rayatz* vol. 2, pp. 361-377, and was initially publicized just a few years after Menachem Mendel received it, in the Chabad journal *Hatamim* (vol. 2, pp. 150-159). It appears in English translation in Shimon Neubort (trans.), *Branches of the Chassidic Menorah* vol. 1 (New York: Sichot in English, 1998), pp. 137-162.
97. Letter of 2nd Shevat 5692, *Igrot Rayatz* vol. 15, p. 112. In English, Neubort p. 163. See also *Reshimot* installment 138.
98. *Igrot Rayatz*, ibid.
99. Ibid. p. 69.
100. Ibid. pp. 84-5;
101. Ibid. p. 86. Rabbi Yehudah Eber (1901-1940), who escaped Russia in the winter of 1930 and was later appointed as *Rosh Yeshivah* at *Yeshivat Tomchei Temimim* in Warsaw-Otwock, from 1932 to 1939. Menachem Mendel replied that Rabbi Eber had a localized (rather than a comparative) style of Talmudic analysis. He was more impressed, though, with Eber's apparent lack of arrogance and ego, which Menachem Mendel described as "extremely rare" (ibid. p. 87). The fact that Rayatz turned to his twenty-eight-year-old son-in-law as an advisor in this capacity demonstrates that he held Menachem Mendel's evaluation of scholarship and character in high regard. For more about Rabbi Eber see Levin, *Poland*, p. 471.
102. Ibid. p. 94.
103. Ibid. pp. 96-7.
104. Ibid. pp. 121-3, pp. 126-8. Rayatz also enlisted Menachem Mendel's brother Leibel for some of these tasks.
105. Sermon of 19th *Kislev* 1976, printed in *Hemshech Ayin Bet* (*Be-sha'ah She-hikdimu 5672*, vol. 3, (Third Edition: New York, Kehot 1992), addenda p. 11*ff*). The Seventh Rebbe justified his actions, from a *halachic* point of view, based on the law that if a written text is deposited for safekeeping with a Torah scholar it is permitted for him to read it and copy it, since this kind of activity would ordinarily be expected from a scholar. The owner of the text must have expected this to transpire and therefore, it has his implicit permission (*Shulchan Aruch, Choshen Mishpat* ch, 292, par. 20 and *Rema*, ibid). Some commentaries justify this even in an instance where the lender stipulates explicitly that the scholar may *not* make a copy (see *Siftei Cohen* ibid. See also *Sh"ut Tzitz Eliezer* vol. 18, responsum 80).
106. In 1929 Rayatz was in America, but he was joined by Menachem Mendel for *Nisan* and *Tishrei* in 1930, 1931 and 1932. For Tishrei of 1931 Rayatz visited the Lubavitch Yeshivah in Warsaw, joined by Menachem Mendel, while Moussia remained with the family in Riga. For the exact dates of his travels between Berlin and Riga, see Mondshine, *Derech Hamelech*.

107. *Torat Menachem—Reshimat Ha-Yoman* (New York: Kehot, 2006).
108. Ibid p. 3
109. Ibid. p. 7.
110. Ibid. p. 46. For more on this meeting see Stanley Schneider and Joseph Berke, "Sigmund Freud and the Lubavitcher Rebbe" in *Psychanalytic Review*, 87(1), 2000; and Berke, *Freud and the Rebbe* (2012), accessible at http://internationalpsychoanalysis.net/wp-content/uploads/2012/09/BerkesPaperFreud.pdf. Berke has a forthcoming book on the subject, entitled *Sigmund Freud and the Lubavitcher Rebbe* (Karnac Books, May 2014).
111. Polen, ibid.
112. While all authorities agree that *tefilin* contain the same four scriptural passages, what is disputed is the *order* in which these four passages should be arranged. The views are also mutually exclusive: according to *Rashi* (Rabbi Shlomo Yitzchaki, 1040–1105), one does not fulfill the mitzvah with *tefilin* arranged according to the opinion of *Rabeinu Tam* (Rabbi Jacob ben Meir, 1100–1171), and vice-versa. The final consensus, decided by *Shulchan Aruch*, is that the law follows *Rashi*, though it is nevertheless recommended to follow both opinions (i.e. to don two pairs of *tefilin*) due to the doubt that remains (*Shulchan Aruch, Orach Chaim* 34:2). For more sources on the importance of *Rabbenu Tam tefilin* see *Likutei Sichot* vol. 2, p. 507, note 39. For the origins of the dispute see my *Rambam, Principles of Faith: Principles 8-9* (New York: Kol Menachem, 2007), pp. 100-101.
113. Rabbi Abraham ben David of Posquières (1125-1198). For his life and thought see Isadore Twersky, *Rabad of Posquières, A Twelfth-Century Talmudist* (Cambridge, Massachusetts: Harvard University Press, 1961).
114. *Halachic* treatise on *tefilin* from the period of the Geonim (589-1038 C.E), of unknown authorship. Printed in the standard Vilna edition of the Bablylonian Talmud at the end of Tractate Menachot.
115. See Rabbi Moshe Zacuto (1610- 1698), *Igrot Ha-Ramaz*, sec. 5: "The *tefilin* of *Shimusha Rabah*... require an untainted body, and pure and clean thoughts." Rabbi Menachem Azariah of Fano (1548–1620) writes, "These *tefilin* plumb such deep mysteries that permission was barely granted to use them" (Responsa, sec. 107). Rabbi Naftali Hertz Bacharach (17th Century) writes: "There is no one who can put on those *tefilin*... no man can put them on" (*Emek HaMelech, Sha'ar Kiryat Arba*, sec. 68).
116. *Reshimat Ha-Yoman*, p. 296.
117. *Likutei Sichot*, ibid.
118. Ibid. p. 294, entry from 12th *Kislev* 5693.
119. For this and the following see Althaus memoir.
120. The custom of the Chabad Rebbes, dating back to Rabbi Shneur Zalman of Liadi, was to extend their personal prayers on the first night of *Rosh Hashanah* well beyond the communal services. Rashab and Rayatz sometimes prayed for as long as three, four or sometimes five hours. (See accounts collected in Rabbi Yehoshua Mondshine, *Otzar Minhagei Chabad, Elul-Tishrei* (Jerusalem: Heichal Menachem, 1995), pp. 71-73). This is not a practice which the Seventh Rebbe publicly continued in later years, so his extended prayers here in the Althaus account are particularly striking.
121. *Reshimot* installments, 115-7
122. Ibid, installments: 7, 110, 153-4, 163, 165, 176, 178.
123. Ibid., installment 15. Rayatz later asked Menachem Mendel to repeat to him, in brief, the content of this *farbrengen*. See *Reshimat Ha-Yoman* p. 266.
124. Menachem Mendel Horenstein (1906-1942), was a first cousin of Rayatz, the second son of Rashab's youngest sister, Chaya Mushka. In 1891, eight years after the passing of her father, the Rebbe Maharash (who lived only until the age of 48), she married Moshe Horenstein (1869-1941), son of the wealthy Boyaner Chasid, Zalman Shaul Horenstein, who owned the largest sugar factory in Russia. (The match was arranged by Rashab and his older brother, Zalman Aharon). Moshe established a woodcutting business in Yelna in White Russia. In

1922, the family relocated to Poland, initially to Warsaw, then Otwock, where they purchased a beautiful villa, surrounded by pine trees. Moshe ran an orphanage in the town, which was funded by the *Joint Distribution Committee*, and he was remembered as having a "noble" character. The Horenstein home was a central hub of the local Chasidic community and was frequented by, among others, psychologist Professor Fishel Schneerson (1887-1958), and poet Zalman Shneur (1887-1959). Little has been written about Menik Horenstein's childhood and youth. By the age of twenty-two, it seems, he was studying in university during the week and returned home for the Sabbath. He travelled to Riga in 1929 and 1930 for the festive month of *Tishrei*. From 1932 he assisted with the running of the Lubavitch Yeshivah in Otwock, receiving funds and other materials from Rayatz. For a collection of biographical details see Eliyahu Shevicha, *Toldot HaRav Menachem Mendel Horenstein*, in *Teshurah Misimchat Nisuiun Eliyahu ve-Chaya Shevicha* 2012.

125. For a brief account of the wedding see *Reshimat Ha-Yoman* p. 239-40. More details are found in Shweke, *Horenstein*, pp. 58-62. Since the huge crowds at Menachem Mendel and Moussia's wedding in Warsaw had been so chaotic, Rayatz chose to make this a smaller affair, in the vacation resort of Landvarvov outside Vilna, then in Poland (Laufer, *Yemei Melech*, p. 349).
126. Ibid.
127. See *Yemei Melech* vol. 1, p. 354-5; interview with Mordechai Sharfstein in *Early Years* vol. 5.

CHAPTER 7: THE QUIET YEARS

1. Marienbad was a popular Jewish resort and had its own culture. See at length Mirjam Zadoff (William Templer trans.), *Next Year in Marienbad, The Lost Worlds of Jewish Spa Culture* (University of Pennsylvania Press, 2012).
2. Letter of Rayatz, 18th *Tammuz* 1938, *Igrot Rayatz* vol. 4, p. 370.
3. Moussia Schneerson, Court Testimony; Rigg, *Rescued from the Reich*, p. 37.
4. *Sichot Kodesh* 5738, vol. 1 (New York, 1986), p. 133. For more on the Rebbe's view not to be perturbed by a negative prognosis, see Rabbi Sholom B. Wineberg, *Healthy in Body, Mind and Spirit*, volume 1 (New York: Sichos in English, 2005), chapter 6.
5. *Igrot Rayatz* vol. 15, p. 130. See also ibid. vol 11, p. 209.
6. Letter of Yechezkel Feigin, printed in editor's introduction to *Igrot Rayatz* vol. 2, p. 28.
7. Ibid.
8. *Igrot Rayatz* vol. 4, ibid.
9. *Igrot Rayatz* vol. 15, p. 177. For more on the relocation see Levin, *Poland*, chapters 16 and 30.
10. A conventional doctor by training, Gerson followed what we would call today a holistic approach to healing, searching for ways to treat the entire person and not just one or two of his many parts. Gerson had chanced upon diet as a powerful tool in healing after realizing that his own migraines were alleviated when he avoided certain food triggers. After twenty years of professional practice in Germany, he achieved a considerable reputation—although he was often ridiculed by the mainstream medical practitioners—for treating migraines, *lupus vulgaris*, some forms of tuberculosis, rheumatoid arthritis and even cancer. His life took a sudden turn in 1933, on a journey to Vienna, when he witnessed Nazi Stormtroopers raid his train and pull off all the Jewish passengers. While his life was spared, he decided that Germany was too unsafe a country for Jews and did not return home, instructing his family to join him in Vienna.
11. *Igrot Rayatz* vol. 3, p. 287. For the term "chief doctor" see ibid, introduction p. 29. For details about Max Gerson see Howard Straus and Barbara Marinacci, *Dr. Max Gerson: Healing the Hopeless* (Ontario: Quarry Health Books, 2002).
12. See editor's note to *Igrot Rayatz* vol. 15, p. 195. For a facsimile of a letter written by Rayatz on the sanitorium's notepaper, see ibid, introduction p. 17.

    Rayatz religiously observed the "Gerson Diet"—low in fat and animal proteins; rich in plants and fruit, with abundant fluid from vegetable soup and juices. All preserved foods, alcohol, coffee, tea, white flour and refined sugar were forbidden.

During the first two months the Rebbe experienced only a slight improvement, but he improved more significantly by the fourth month (*Igrot Rayatz* vol. 3, ibid.). While he was encouraged to speak as little as possible, one activity which was permitted by the doctor was writing, and Rayatz took the opportunity to pen an extremely rich, two-hundred-page historiographic letter to Moussia, tracing the origins of the Chasidic movement from the times of the Baal Shem Tov. (Dated 16th *Shevat* 5695, in *Igrot Rayatz*, ibid. pp. 156-279. English translation in Shimon Neubort (trans.), *The Making of Chassidim* (New York: Sichos in English, 1995)).

The diet is mentioned in Max Gerson M.D., *Dietary considerations in malignant neoplastic disease; preliminary report.* Rev. Gasroenterol 1945-11/12;12:419-425.

Interestingly, with the shift towards holistic therapies in recent years, Dr. Gerson's approach has enjoyed a resurgence. For a contemporary guide to his method see Charlotte Gerson and Morton Walker, *The Gerson Therapy* (New York: Kensington Books, revised edition 2006).

13. Personal communication with Charlotte Gerson Straus, 5th December, 2013.
14. See Levin, *Poland*, chapters 16 and 32.
15. Rayatz's presence, however, was not welcomed by all his colleagues. In a 1974 sermon, the Seventh Rebbe compared Rayatz's situation in Poland to the Biblical account of Joseph and his brothers, where, *"his brothers envied him"* (Gen. 37:11). See *Likutei Sichot* vol. 18, p. 304; *Sichot Kodesh* 5734, vol. 1, p. 345.
16. In 1935 one of Max Gerson's wealthy patients from France invited him to relocate to Paris. As an incentive, the patient offered Gerson a charming, newly purchased hotel some ten miles to the east of Paris for use as a clinic. Fearful of the rise of Nazi sympathizers in Austria, Gerson accepted the offer and made the move.

    Dr. Gerson's "Le Parc" clinic in Ville-D'Avray was a graceful, 35-room hotel, surrounded by tall trees, lawns and a beautiful garden. Each room had its own bath, and there was plenty of space for relaxation and recreation. See *Igrot Rayatz* vol. 3, p. 556; vol. 4, p. 371; vol. 15, p. 231; Straus, p. 147.

    Rayatz had wanted to make the trip earlier in the year, but it was delayed due to problems obtaining a visa. He visited other doctors in Vienna during the winter, but they were not helpful. By the spring, Rayatz's secretary wrote that the trip to Paris was now "essential"—see *Igrot Rayatz* vol. 3, editor's introduction, p. 29. For a facsimile of a letter written by Rayatz in Hotel Le Parc, with the assistance of Menachem Mendel as his secretary, see ibid. p. 11.

    After two months of treatment, Rayatz's health improved "a bit," but he regretted that he was unable to stay any longer in Paris for treatment (*Igrot Rayatz* vol. 3, p. 571.). His secretary, Rabbi Yechezkal Feigin, was "devastated" to see that there had been no significant improvement in the Rebbe's mobility or speech (ibid., introduction, p. 30.).
17. Shevicha, *Horenstein*, p. 64; interview with Bernard Lax (d. 2010), in *JEM Early Years III.*
18. *Igrot Rayatz* vol. 15, pp. 232-3.
19. Rayatz was accompanied to Vienna by his daughter Chana, and met with Menachem Mendel there on 14th *Tevet.* (ibid. pp. 238-9).
20. In autumn of 1936, Rayatz lost his doctor when, due to the fear of rising anti-Semitism, Max Gerson left Paris and moved to London. Rayatz's new doctors found that his health had improved and they agreed that he should stick with the Gerson diet and regimen, with an extended stay at a clinic twice a year. *Igrot Rayatz* vol. 3, p. 371.
21. Ibid. vol. 15, p. 241*ff.*
22. *Igrot Rayatz* vol. 15, p. 290.
23. *Igrot Kodesh* vol. 13, p. 337; *Reshimat Ha-Yoman*, pp. 395-6.
24. For a complete account of all Rayatz's trips for treatment during this period see editor's introductions to *Igrot Rayatz*, vols. 3 and 4.
25. On 15th *Adar* (Affidavit for French Citizenship 1937).

26. Meir Shochetman was the son of Rabbi Mordechai Shochetman, who was a functionary at the Rabbinic Court (Beth Din) of Paris. Meir's memoir is found in Laufer, *Yemei Melech,* vol. 1, p. 373 and 380. See also interview with his son Professor Eliav Shochetman in *JEM Early Years.* Meir Shochetman left Paris and emigrated to Israel in 1936.
27. 119½ absences in 1933-4; 105 absences in 1935-6; and 81 absences in 1936-7.
28. Note on Menachem Mendel's 1936-7 transcript at ESTP, dated 26 July, 1937.
29. Letter dated 25th Tammuz 5698, *Igrot Rayatz,* vol. 4, p. 381.
30. Affidavit for French Citizenship, 1937.
31. See Levine, *Kovetz Chaf Menachem Av,* pp. 56, 64.
32. Student records, Sorbonne University. Besides his enrollment during these two years, which noted his expertise in differential calculus, no further academic records have been found of his studies during this period, though they may have been destroyed during the student riots of 1968. For a testimony that the Rebbe attended lectures at the Sorbonne, see *Early Years III.*
33. See editor's note in *Igrot Rayatz* vol. 15, p. 154.
34. Levine, *Kovetz Chaf Menachem Av,* p. 64.
35. *Igrot Rayatz* 15, p. 212. According to one recollection, he also declined a position in Manchester, England (Laufer, *Yemei Melech,* p. 394).
36. *Sichot Kodesh* 5737, vol. 1, p. 524.
37. Interview with Rabbi Asher Heber in *Early Years III,* heard from his father Rabbi Leibish Heber, who accompanied Menachem Mendel to meet Rabbi Herzog. Rabbi Herzog served in Paris from 1911-34, after acting as Rabbi in Leeds, England. His son was the celebrated Rabbi Yitzchak Herzog, Ashkenazic Chief Rabbi of Israel
38. Besides enabling him to keep a low profile, and the attraction of lower rent (see Lax interview), the apartment in Rue Boulard, to the south of Paris, was near enough the ESTP campus in Cachan that Menachem Mendel could walk home, if necessary, on a Friday afternoon in around one hour. It was also ideally located on the Paris Métro Line 4, which connects directly with the Latin Quarter where the other ESTP campus was located, and also runs close to the Jewish Quarter at the "Pletzl." On the Sabbath he would have been a thirty-minute walk from the Chasseloup Laubat Synagogue in the 15th Arrondissement, or a fifty-minute walk from the Synagogues at the Pleztl.
39. See Shochetman memoir.
40. See interview with Bernard Lax in *Early Years III,* who recalls seeing Menachem Mendel there.
41. See David Zaklikowski, *Inventor's Friendship with the Rebbe,* accessible at http://www.chabad.org/therebbe/article_cdo/aid/691380/jewish/Inventors-Friendship-with-the-Rebbe.htm; interview with David Bezborodko in *Early Years.* For more on Bezborodko see his *An Insider's View Of Jewish Pioneering In The Glass Industry* (Jerusalem, Israel: Gefen Limited, 1987).

    For the Rebbe's insight into the Torah/Science conflict regarding the age of the world see: Aryeh Carmel and Cyril Domb (eds.) *Challenge: Torah Views on Science and Its Problems* (The Association of Orthodox Jewish Scientists in association with Feldheim Publishers, 1976), p. 142; Nissan Mindel (ed.), *The Letter and the Spirit: Letters by the Lubavitcher Rebbe* vol. 2 (New York: Nissan Mindel Publications, 2013), pp. 235-7 264-5, 276, 280, 304, 307-8, 323-6, 328-9.
42. Mindel, *The Letter and the Spirit,* ibid. p. 240. For more on the Rebbe's view on spontaneous generation see *Igrot Kodesh* vol. 19, p. 239; Ginsburg and Branover, *Mind over Matter,* p. 56. For a comparative study with other Rabbinic viewpoints see Rabbi Chaim Rapoport, *Shitat Rabenu ziya bi-davar harigat kinim be-shabbat bizman ha-zeh* in *Ha'arot u'Biurim Oholei Torah,* 11th *Nissan* 2004, pp. 84-94. See also Rabbi J. David Bleich, *Survey of Recent Halakhic Periodical Literature: Piscatorial Parasites* in *Tradition, a journal of Orthodox Jewish Thought* 44:1, Spring 2011 and 44:4, Winter 2011.

43. See Laufer, *Yemei Melech* p. 463-4; *Early Years III*
44. Meir Shochetman's son, Professor Eliav Shochetman, recalled that during the three-and-a-half years that Meir and the Rebbe both resided in Paris they studied together in the Schneerson apartment almost every day, and completed tractate Pesachim and half of Tractate Zevachim.
45. *Igrot Kodesh* vol. 22, p. 149.
46. Interview with Bernard Lax (*JEM Early Years*).
47. Steinsaltz, *My Rebbe*, p. 47.
48. Shochetman memoir; Lax interview.
49. *Reshimot* installments 66 and 48 (Sukkot), 125-6 (Chanukah). The Chanukah lecture was delivered in the Chabad Synagogue at 17 Rue de Rosiers.
50. Interviews with Moshe Zev Ra'atzer and Eliav Shochetman (*JEM Early Years*).
51. *Igrot Rayatz* vol. 15, p. 172
52. See Moussia's letter after moving apartments in 1938: "My younger sister and brother-in-law... continue to be not far from us. For us, this is important." Levine, *Kovetz Chaf Menachem Av*, p. 64.
53. *Igrot Rayatz* vol. 15, p. 134. See also ibid. p. 146.
54. Ibid. p. 335.
55. Ibid. vol. 12, p. 153. Yekutiel Ya'akov Yosef Lis was born in 1935 to Menik Horenstein's younger sister, Sarah, from her second marriage with celebrated singer and poet Kalman Lis (1903-1942).

    Kalman Lis was born in Kovel, Wolin. He studied in a traditional *cheder*, then in a Polish gymnasium, and in Vilna and Warsaw high schools. He specialized in the care of children with special needs. From 1937 until his death, he was in charge of the Tsentos Institution for Special Needs Children in Otwock. He was a popular Yiddish poet, and many of his poems were published, some in book form. He was awarded the I. L. Peretz Award for Young Poets from the Yiddish Pen Center in Warsaw. He was wounded during the bombing of his Children's Institution on September 1, 1939. He recovered in a Warsaw hospital, then returned to the Otwock Children's Institution. When it was attacked by Germans in 1942, he and some of the children ran away. His hiding place was discovered, and he was shot and killed, together with the children. It is uncertain whether he was killed by Nazis or by Poles.
56. *Likutei Levi Yitzchak, Igrot Kodesh* p. 325. See also ibid p. 422 where, in one of his last letters to his son (dated *Erev Yom Kippur* 5699), Reb Levik repeats his blessing for a child.
57. Interview with Mendel Notik in *Early Years*.
58. Rebbetzin Chaya Mushka to Rabbi Berel Junik, 25 Adar 5746. Jewish law requires that milking be supervised to ensure that no milk from a non-kosher animal is added to the cow's milk (See *Shulchan Aruch, Yoreh Deah* 115:1). Some Jews rely on Rabbinic leniencies that permit reliance on government supervision of milk production (though this is not accepted in Chasidic communities).
59. *Sefer ha-Sichot* 5752, vol. 1, p. 182, note 43.
60. *Igrot Rayatz* vol. 15, p. 133-360. Menachem Mendel's responses, if they have all survived, were in most instances not included in this volume, though a few are printed.
61. This was done on the condition of anonymity, and Menachem Mendel's name did not appear on the publication. See *Igrot Rayatz* ibid. p. 208. He prepared the material which was based on writings of Rayatz, namely the "*Igrot Kodesh*" (correspondence) and *History of Chasidism* sections.
62. Ibid, p. 217.
63. Ibid. p. 236.
64. Ibid. p. 268.

65. Ibid. p. 245.
66. Ibid. p. 346. The treatise, published in 1998 as *Reshimat Ha-Menorah* (Kehot) with editor's elucidations, fills some 140 printed pages.
67. An acronym for *sheyichye l'orech yamim tovim aruchim* (*"may he live many long and good days"*), the term is often used to imply that the person is a rabbi of importance. See *Igrot Rayatz* ibid. p. 244.
68. Ibid. p. 178.
69. Ibid. p. 258. See also ibid. p. 318.
70. p. 331-399.
71. *Likutei Levi Yitzchak, Igrot* pp. 298-423
72. *Reshimot* installments 105-9, dated 2nd *Nisan* 1937. Reb Levik acknowledges receipt of the *Reshima* on 7th Iyar in *Likutei Levi Yitzchak*, ibid. p. 388*ff.*
73. Letter dated 19th *Tevet* 1936, ibid. p. 358.
74. Levine, *Kovetz Chaf Menachem Av*, pp. 56-7.
75. "If B.P. [Bonaparte] wins, the wealth and power of the Jewish people will increase, but their hearts will separate and become distant from their Father in heaven; and if A. [Alexander] wins, even though poverty will increase amongst the Jewish people and their power will decline, nevertheless, their hearts will become united, joined and bound to their Father in heaven" (Letter to Rabbi Moshe Meizlish, printed in Chaim Meir Heilman, *Beit Rebbe* (Berdichov, 1902), p. 47a; *Igrot Kodesh* of Rabbi Shneur Zalman, p. 150-151).
76. *Sefer ha-Sichot* 5752, vol. 1, pp. 177-8
77. Ibid. p. 181. In note 38 the editors make it clear that the Rebbe was referring to his own stay in France during the 1930s.

CHAPTER 8: SURVIVAL

1. Levine, *Poland* ch. 54. For the following see ibid. ch. 63; Rigg, *Rescued from the Reich;* Rachel Altein and Eliezer Zaklikovsky, *Out of the Inferno: The efforts that led to the rescue of Rabbi Yosef Yitzchak Schneersohn of Lubavitch from war-torn Europe in 1939-40* (New York: Kehot 2002); Rabbi Shimon Raichik, *From Poland to the United States: The harrowing tale of Rabbi Shmuel Dovid Raichik's journey from war-torn Europe to freedom* (Memento from the wedding of Moishy and Rivka Raichik, May 2013)
2. *Igrot Kodesh,* vol. 1, p. 30. (A facsimile of the letter, which was written in French, is reproduced in introduction p. 24.)
3. Ibid. pp. 34-5.
4. Including: Senator to New York, Robert F. Wagner; Democratic congressman and Chairman of the House Rules Committee, Adolph J. Sabath (Illinois); Chairman of the Foreign Affairs Committee, Sol Bloom (New York); Justice Louis Brandeis, the first Jewish member of the Supreme Court; Attorney General Benjamin Cohen, one of Roosevelt's close advisors; and, most importantly, assistant Chief of the State Department's European Affairs Division, Robert T. Pell and his boss, Secretary of State Cordell Hull (whose father-in-law was Jewish).
5. Chief of the *ba'alei batim* and key partner in the campaign to save the Rebbe was Sam (Yekutiel) Kramer (1894-1986). The brothers Sam, Hyman and Abe Kramer were Americanized, clean-shaven sons of Lubavitcher immigrants, who had retained their Orthodoxy (a rarity at the time) and formed the backbone of *Agudat Chasidei Chabad*, generously giving their time and money to the cause. Sam Kramer graduated from New York University in 1915 and was admitted to practice law in New York State in 1917. After the first World War, he opened a law firm at 1133 Broadway, in Manhattan, and succeeded in winning some of the largest real estate interests in the city.

   In October, Sam Kramer connected Rabbi Jacobson with the man who would prove to be the mastermind of the rescue efforts: Washington lawyer and lobbyist Max Rhoade. Rhoade, who had been a lobbyist for the Zionist Organization of America in the 1920s, obviously felt some sympathy for the Rebbe's plight, but he was only convinced to take on the case due to his friendship with Kramer and on condition that he would be paid handsomely.

The crucial link between the Americans and the Germans was a close relationship between Chief of European Affairs Division, Robert Pell and Helmut Wohlthat (1893-1982), an expert in international industry and economics within the Nazi Party. (The two men had met at a conference in 1938 and had retained a working relationship.) On 3 October 1939, Pell requested the American consul general in Berlin to contact Wohlthat and see if he would be willing to assist in saving "one of the leading Jewish scholars of the world." Since U.S. relations with Germany were strained, and this request emanated from a very high office, Wohlthat welcomed the opportunity to restore some goodwill.

Helmut Wohlthat was one of a number of "ambivalent" Nazis whose hatred of Jews was imperfect and would occasionally come to their assistance. Another such German officer was Admiral Wilhelm Canaris (1887-1945), head of the Abwehr, a small department of the war ministry which worked independently from the SS. Canaris, demoralized by Hitler's invasion of Poland, felt it was the beginning of the end of Germany. While he continued to work for the war machine, his doubts regarding Hitler no doubt opened him to be more sympathetic to the Rebbe's case.

6. Bloch's search for Rayatz was naturally complicated by the fact that no Jew was willing to tell a Nazi where the Lubavitcher Rebbe was to be found. On 25th November, Bloch finally found the correct apartment, but the person who opened the door denied any knowledge of Rayatz's whereabouts and the officers departed. The Rebbe, however, intuited that Bloch was to be trusted and told his family that if the officer returned they should cooperate with him. Bloch knew that he could not waste time; if the SS found the Rebbe first, the results would be disastrous. Convinced that he had found the correct apartment, Bloch returned with some soldiers and entered forcefully, breaking down the door. Knowing that the Jews had virtually no food, Bloch brought the Schneersons cheese, bread and sausages, and was offended and confused when his non-kosher gift was rejected.

   Bloch was quite unprepared for Rayatz's insistence that he save an entire entourage—his wife Nechama Dina, son-in-law Rashag, daughter Chana, grandson Shalom Ber, his mother, Shterna Sara, and his secretary Rabbi Yechezkel Fegin. The German officer had been under the impression that he was going to escort one Rabbi. Negotiations ensued between Wohlthat, Pell and Rhoade, and despite the greater risk and complications, Wohlthat eventually agreed to save the whole group.

7. According to the Kramers, this was a huge sum of $75,000 (Milton E. Kramer, *The Kramers: The Next Generation* (Kramer Family Centennial Committee, 1995), p. 17).
8. *Igrot Rayatz*, vol 5 (New York: Kehot, 1982), p. 2.
9. Ibid. vol. 15, p. 361. Rayatz had successfully transported the *kotavim* with him, but all the other possessions he brought with from Otwock were destroyed in Warsaw. His library remained intact in Otwock. For details of the library's rescue see Rabbi Shalom Ber Levine, *The Lubavitch Library: a sketch of its history based on letters, documents and recollections* (Heb.) (New York: Library of Agudat Chasidei Chabad, 1993), chapters 8 and 11.
10. Letter from Rabbi Yechezkel Fegin to Rabbi Yisrael Jacobson 29th January (9th *Shevat*) 1939 (Levin, *America*, p. 167).
11. See Rigg, p. 229, note 8.
12. Toledo Blade, "Senator Borah dies; state funeral Monday," *Associated Press*, 20th January 1940.
13. Memoir of Rabbi Yisrael Jacobson in Altein and Zaklikovsky, p. 293. In a cable dated 21st December 1939, Jacobson mentions the figure of $50,000 annually as the budget for the support of Rayatz's court (ibid. p. 171).
14. Letter reproduced in Harari, p. 135, from *Kfar Chabad* issue, 671 (24th *Sivan* 1995).

15. See Memo of Conference, Thursday, November 23, 1939, in Altein and Zaklikovsky, p. 110.
16. For the extensive correspondence see Altein and Zaklikovsky, pp. 164-270; Rigg, chapter 8 and 12.
17. Letter of Rabbi Yechezkel Feigin to Rabbi Shalom Posner, 21st February (12th *Adar* I), 1940, (ibid. p. 10); *Igrot Rayatz* vol. 15, pp. 364-5.
18. Some time between February 8th and 13th. See Altein and Zaklikovsky, p. 257, 262.
19. Leibel Zisman (1930-2013), and his father Shraga Feivel Zisman, (1898-1944?)—a wealthy Chasid from Kovno, Lithuania—had been in private audience with Rayatz the last night before he departed from Riga. In his memoir, Leibel recalled the chaos surrounding the Rebbe's departure.

    > People were begging him to stay because so many people were waiting to see him and be blessed by him.... He told his secretary that his father—the Rebbe Rashab who had passed away some twenty years before—would not allow him to stay. He did not explain if his father came to him in a vision or a dream, but he insisted on leaving immediately with his whole family despite his mother's poor medical condition.
    >
    > My father organized a human shield to keep back the crowd, as the ambulance pulled up to the building to take away the Rebbetzin [Shterna Sarah] on a stretcher. Everyone was crying, fearful they would never see the Rebbe again, and it was a very chaotic scene. (Leibel (Leo) Zisman, *I Believe: The Story of One Jewish Life* (New York: GJCF, 2011), p. 56.)

20. Joining the Rebbe on the boat were a number of VIPs: silent movie star, Anna Quirentia Nilsson (1888–1974); Russian aristocrat, Prince Serge Constantinovitch Belosselsky (1867-1951); and Finnish architect Alvar Aalto (1898–1976)—*New York Times*, 20th March, 1940.

    The passage was fraught with danger. German submarines operated in the North Sea and the North Atlantic had already sunk hundreds of boats, including numerous passenger liners. Moments of uncertainty included: an overnight docking to fix mechanical problems, heavy fog, and inspection by two German submarines.
21. A diary penned by one of the travellers recalled, "The Rebbe *shlita* ascended to the upper deck, where he delivered a short speech thanking the captain and his crew for their gracious service. The pier and the entire area in front of the pier was filled to capacity with men and women. As soon as the Rebbe appeared, shouts of *Shalom Aleichem* could be heard, along with sounds of people reciting the blessing of *Shehechiyanu* and the clicking of dozens of cameras" (The anonymous diary, which documents the trans-Atlantic trip in detail, appears in *Sefer Ha-Sichot, Kayitz* 5740, pp. 179-180.)

    The following day, the *New York Times* reported that Rayatz "was met by Investigations Commissioner William B. Herlands, State Senator Philip M. Kleinfeld of Brooklyn, a committee of twenty-five Orthodox Rabbis and about 500 persons, who greeted him enthusiastically."
22. Sheina Matla (Mania) Lotz (1917-1992). In 1949 she married Yitzchak Rosin. See Eliezer Zaklikovsky, *Mekadesh Yisrael: Talks and Images at Wedding Celebrations* 1943-1963 (New York: Kehot, 2000), p. 44; *Igrot Kodesh* vol. 28, p. 314.
23. Mindel's wife was in England at the time. See *Crown Heights Community Newspaper*, July 11, 2008, p. 4.
24. Rigg, p. 141.
25. When Rayatz was still trapped in Warsaw, activists in New York had already been working on attaining visas for the Rebbe's entire family. To facilitate the application in the absence of birth certificates, Menachem Mendel had sent Yisrael Jacobson legal birth dates and places of himself, Moussia and the Horensteins on 11th October 1939 (*Igrot Kodesh* p. 30).
26. Affidavit of Rabbi Yisrael Jacobson, March 21, 1940 (Altein and Zaklikovsky, p. 32). These figures may have been exaggerated for political reasons (see Rigg, p. 225, note 18). On the other hand, if we bear in mind that there were some two million Russian Jewish immigrants to the United States in the thirty years before the Bolshevik Revolution, and that Chabad had been

a dominant force in Russia, the numbers may be realistic.

27. *Agudat Chasidei Chabad* was formed in 1924, for details see Levine, *America* ch. 4, 23. For a memorandum of affiliated congregations see ibid. ch. 26. For the history of the Kramer family's involvement with Chabad see Milton E. Kramer, *The Kramers.* The Kramers had also played a major role in coordinating American efforts for the rescue of Rayatz from Russia in 1927, and in arranging funds from the *Joint Distribution Committee* for Rayatz's work in the 1920's.
28. See at length the Jacobson affidavit. Despite the extreme difficulty in obtaining visas for Jewish refugees at the time, which had been vastly curtailed by the 1924 Immigration Act, the authorities accepted the petition. In principle, the U.S. government granted permission for all the Schneersons to immigrate, but the visas needed to be ratified through consulates abroad, and this posed a number of obstacles. Rayatz had experienced a small delay from his petition being tentatively approved by the U.S. government to actually receiving his visas in the embassy in Riga (approval was cabled from Washington to Riga on January 12th or 13th (ibid. p. 231), but visas were only issued some time between February 8th and 13th.) but this was insignificant compared to the difficulties experienced by his children in Paris and Otwock.
29. The application was supported by an affidavit from Mr. M. B. Hartan and prepared by the New York lawyers, promising financial support to the couple until Menachem Mendel would find a position as an engineer.
30. Clause 4(d) stated that the quota did not apply to, "an immigrant who continuously for at least two years immediately preceding the time of his application for admission to the United States has been, and who seeks to enter the United States solely for the purpose of, carrying on the vocation of minister of any religious denomination, or professor of a college, academy, seminary, or university; and his wife, and his unmarried children under 18 years of age, if accompanying or following to join him." The quota for Russian immigrants in the original 1924 act was a mere 2,248 visas per year.
31. *New York Times,* 28th May, 1940.
32. *Igrot Rayatz* vol. 13, p. 274. Rayatz also petitioned that Menachem Mendel should not be called to fight in the French army, with which he had registered. See also *Igrot Rayatz* vol. 5, introduction p. 21.
33. Goodwin, Doris Kearns *No Ordinary Time. Franklin and Eleanor Roosevelt: The Home Front in World War II* (Simon & Schuster, 1994), p. 173. For the full memo see: http://www.pbs.org/wgbh/amex/holocaust/filmmore/reference/primary/barmemo.html. For a biography of Long examining his role in immigration restrictions see: Neil Rolde, *Breckinridge Long, American Eichmann??? An enquiry into the character of the man who denied visas to the Jews,* (Solon, Maine: Polar Bear & Company, 2013).

    In his afterword to Robert Rosen's *Saving the Jews: Franklin Roosevelt and the Holocaust* (New York: Harper Collins, 2007), Harvard law professor Alan Dershowitz writes, "Roosevelt's failure to fire Breckinridge Long, who was instrumental in delaying visas and causing the deaths of so many Jews, seems inexcusable to me, even in retrospect" (p. 499).
34. Altein and Zaklikovsky, p. 329.
35. See *Brief Sketch of the Rescue of the Rebbe and Rebbetzin* in *Kovetz 28 Sivan, Jubilee Anniversary* (Kehot: 1991), p. 12; interview with Mendel Notik (*Early Years* IV).
36. Renee Poznanski (Nathan Bracher trans), *Jews in France During World War II* (Tauber Institute for the Study of European History and published in association with United States Holocaust Memorial Museum, Brandeis, 2001), p. 24. Approximately one third of the Jews who fled later returned to Paris,
37. Interview with Rabbi Shalom Ber Levine (*Early Years* IV).
38. See Poznanski, p. 27.
39. Poznanski, p. 24. Jews of all stripes flooded to the synagogues, not necessarily out of a fervent religiosity, but more in search of a sense of stability in these turbulent times. The synagogue

also provided a superb place to network and find out information which might be crucial to survival. Along with the other Paris Rabbis, Rabbi Zalman Schneerson (1898-1980) also fled to Vichy and he set up a small synagogue where his cousin Menachem Mendel now prayed and delivered Torah lectures. One lecture particularly impressed a Belgian refugee, Rabbi Aharon Gershon Sungolowsky (1901-1975), who went home and told his family excitedly about it. Aharon Gershon struck up a friendship with Menachem Mendel, and their two wives would journey together to Cusset, a village outside Vichy, to supervise the milking of cows so as to obtain *chalav yisrael.* Menachem Mendel's implicit trust of his Belgian friend came to light a year later when, in the absence of available wine for Passover, the future Rebbe relied on raisin wine prepared by Aharon Gershon. This was significant as the dietary laws of Passover are some of the most stringent in Jewish law (Interview with Joseph Sungolowsky (b. 1929) on *Early Years IV).*

40. *Reshimot* installments 49, 50, 102-3, 51, 13 and 23.
41. Levine, *America,* chapter 35; Rabbi Zusha Wolf and Rabbi Shimon Gopin, *Beit Chayenu 770* (Jerusalem: Heichal Menachem, 2004), section 2.
42. Personal communication with Arthur Brainson, 30th December 2013.
43. The 1920 building boasted a magnificent sanctuary, a large gymnasium, ladies' and men's social rooms, a banquet hall, dining and lounge areas, classrooms, a swimming pool and even a bowling alley. The synagogue appealed to the local community who were making huge sums of money in real estate, business, law and medicine, and wanted to develop an exclusive circle. The ethos was, "to show the world that one might be a Jew and enjoy life at the same time." (Samuel P. Abelow, *History of Brooklyn Jewry* (Brooklyn: Scheba Publishing Company, 1937), p. 73.) For more on the Brooklyn Jewish Center see David Kaufman, *Shul with a Pool: The "synagogue-center" in American Jewish History,* (Hanover, New England: Brandeis University Press, 1999), p. 247*ff.*
44. This is the stated use on the building's Certificate of Occupancy, dated 15th December 1938.
45. See *Reports of cases heard and determined in the Appellate Division of the Supreme Court of the State of New York,* Volume 254 (1938), p. 798; John Harlan Amen, *Report of Kings County Investigation,* 1938-1942, p. 70; Charles R. Ashman, *The Finest Judges Money an Buy, and other forms of Judicial Pollution* (Los Angeles: Nash Publishing, 1973), pp. 89-90; *Brooklyn Daily Eagle,* 27th January 1937 and 28th July 1938; *New York Times,* 14th and 28th March 1939.
46. *Igrot Rayatz* vol. 13, p. 303.
47. Levine ibid.; Wolf and Gopin ibid; Rabbi Avraham B. Hecht, *My Spiritual Journey: An Autobiography* (New York: Private Publication, 2006), p. 104; Ashkenazi, *Otzar Chasidim—New York,* pp. 201-6.
48. The move took place some time between 17th August (13th *Av*), the date of Menachem Mendel's last *Reshima* (installment 13), and 30th August (26th *Av*), when Rashag wrote to Chabad immigration attorney Henry Butler, informing him that the couple had relocated to Nice (*Kovetz 28th Sivan,* p. 13). The couple's visa application was subsequently transferred to the consulate in Nice (ibid.).
49. Back in July, the Chief Rabbi of France, Isaïe Schwartz (1876–1952), had been banned from his usual privilege of broadcasting on the radio, and was warned that measures against the Jews were in the making. Still, it remained inconceivable to many that the French government, which had been so good to the Jews for centuries, would turn against them. Even after Rabbi Schwartz was refused an audience with Chief of State Marshal Philippe Pétain in August, Schwartz still believed that the Marshal was "above suspicion" and that it would be "unjust to say that we are dealing with a deliberate policy of hostility" towards Jews. These naive hopes were finally put to an end when, on 3rd October, the Vichy government passed its first discriminatory laws, the *Statuts des Juifs,* banning Jews from the army, the press, and from commercial and industrial jobs.

    Fleeing to Nice, Menachem Mendel and Moussia placed themselves in a thirty-mile demilitarized zone, occupied by the Italians (following their attack on France in June). While the Italian government was allied with Hitler, and had also passed anti-Jewish legislation in 1938, the implementation of these laws was lax, as Mussolini was far less anti-Semitic than Hitler, possibly due to the presence of many prominent Jews in Italy. Nice was therefore the safest option for Menachem Mendel and Moussia as they waited for Chabad lawyers to persist with the visa application.

50. Interviews with Yeshaya Gertner and David Bezborodka (*Early Years IV*).
51. Letter to Mr. Dov. Padover, dated the third day of Chanukah, 5705, in *Igrot Kodesh* vol. 2, p. 14.
52. Lentshin Chasidut was founded in 1821 by Rabbi Yitzchak Isaac, a disciple of Yaakov Yitzchak Horowitz, the "Seer" of Lublin (1745-1815).
53. Interview with Yeshayah Gertner. For a letter from the Lubavitcher Rebbe to Rabbi Yechiel Gertner, see *Igrot Kodesh*, vol. 8, p. 184. Rabbi Yechiel's daughter married Rabbi Menashe Klein (1923-2011), who became an important postwar *posek* in America and enjoyed a close relationship with the Rebbe.
54. See *Reshimot* installments 1, 20, 144 and 150.
55. Interview with Joseph Sungolowsky (JEM, *Early Years*).
56. According to one testimony, Menachem Mendel traveled to Italy to fetch an *etrog* from the district of Calabria, which, according to Chabad custom, is considered the choicest source. Before Passover, he managed to obtain *shmurah matzah* from the Schmerling family in Switzerland through the assistance of David Bezborodka, who was permitted to travel abroad for his work, something extremely rare during wartime. (Bezborodka manufactured mirrors for use in French submarines.) See interviews with Rabbi Menachem Tiechtel and David Bezborodka (*Early Years* IV). Tiechtel recalls the Rebbe being in Vichy for Sukkot 5701, when, in fact, he was in Nice.
57. For the following see *Kovetz 28th Sivan*, pp. 10-15; Altein and Eliezer Zaklikovsky pp. 328-331; Levine, *Poland*, pp. 347-353.
58. For more on HICEM see Donna F. Ryan, *The Holocaust and Jews of Marseille: The Enforcement of Anti-Semitic Policies in Vichy France* (University of Illinois Press, 1996), pp. 137-40.
59. While in Marseille, Ramash *farbrenged* for students of a makeshift Yeshivah on 15th *Shevat*. Reb Zalman Shachter-Shalomi (b. 1924), who was present at the gathering, recalls the content of Ramash's talk in *Yishmru Daat: Chassidic Teachings of the Fourth Turning* (Ohalah, 2009), p. 7*ff.* See also his interview in *Early Years IV.* For a further recollection of the Marseille visit see interview with Aharon Noach Blasbalg (ibid.)
60. Box 212.
61. *Igrot Rayatz* vol. 13, p. 331.
62. After Italy had declared war on the Allies in 1940, all Italian shipping routes had been closed and only three companies from neutral countries maintained transatlantic routes, two in Portugal and one in Spain. The Lisbon *Serpa Pinto,* which would later achieve iconic status for saving refugees, was an 8,000-ton Portuguese transport ship sailing under the command of Captain Americo dos Santos. With a capacity of 600 passengers, the 150-meter vessel made regular trips to Rio, New York, Philadelphia and Baltimore, saving some 7,800 refugees during the war.
63. Babylonian Talmud, *Sanhedrin* 98a.
64. Interview with Rabbi Leibel Bistritzky (1926-2013) in *Kfar Chabad* issue 1510 (2013).
65. Remarkably, while the vast majority of Polish Jews did not survive the Holocaust, many students of the Yeshivah in Otwock *did* manage to escape. At the outbreak of war, Rayatz encouraged the Yeshivah students to flee across the Lithuanian border, which still remained open, to the Lubavitcher Yeshivah in Vilna. A record of students from January 1940 from the Vilna Yeshivah lists forty-three names, most of whom had arrived from Poland. Rayatz and Rashag spent much energy seeking for an escape route for these students, and by the fall he had secured fifty-two U.S. visas for students in Vilna and Riga. By the winter a further seventy-two visas had been obtained. The planned escape route was via Japan, traveling through Russia, where the visas would be collected at the American consul in Moscow.

Ultimately, only thirty-eight of the students managed to reach Kobe, Japan in the spring of 1941. On arrival, they discovered that their American visas had been revoked as part of Breckinridge Long's campaign to restrict immigration; but all but one of them survived—some reaching Canada later that year, some to America after the war, and one student to Israel. Rayatz also managed to save his secretary, Rabbi Moshe Leib Rothstein (1900?-1967), who escaped from Warsaw to Vilna and eventually reached the United States via the Japan route, arriving in San Francisco in 1940. See Levin, *Poland* chapters 54-62 and ibid. pp. 357-360.

66. Rabbi Yisrael Alpenbaim, *Yirat Shamayim Otzaro, the Life of Harav HaChasid Rabbi Yitzchak the Masmid* (Heb.), (Kfar Chabad 1996: *Kfar Chabad Magazine*), pp. 277-281. For more on Zuber see Chana Sharfstein, *It Was Evening, It Was Morning: Scandinavia in the Aftermath of World War II* (Devora Publishing, 2012).
67. Letter dated 30th October (9th *Cheshvan*) 1941, *Igrot Rayatz* vol. 6, p. 55. For details of the efforts to rescue the couple see Levine, *Poland,* pp. 354-6.
68. *Igrot Kodesh,* vol. 3, p. 161, 173. This was based on the testimony of Mr. Mordechai Unrad from Warsaw, who wrote to Ramash that he had been in Treblinka with the Horensteins. Unrad indentified the *yahrtzeits* as Chaya Mushka Horenstein, 14th Elul; her son Menachem Mendel Horenstein, 25th *Cheshvan*; and his wife, Sheina (Sheina), the second day of *Rosh Hashanah.*

    See also diary of Rayatz from 1945 in Levine, *Treasures* p. 58.
69. *Likutei Levi Yitzchak* (New York: Kehot, 1970), 4 volumes. Reb Levik's arrest and exile was chronicled by his wife Chana Schneerson in her diaries (Tilles, *A Mother in Israel*).
70. Chana Schneerson Memoirs, installment 16.
71. See *Hayom Yom,* introduction. It is unclear whether he was a patient in the hospital or, like other Jews in the area, he was rounded up by the Nazis and taken to the hospital for execution. See, for example, Joshua Rubenstein, Ilya Altman, *The Unknown Black Book: The Holocaust in the German-Occupied Soviet Territories,* (Indiana University Press, 2008), p. 203.
72. Peter Longerich, *Holocaust: The Nazi Persecution and Murder of the Jews,* (Oxford University Press, 2010), p. 241; Yad Vashem database of murder sites in the occupied territories of the former USSR (http://www.yadvashem.org/untoldstories/database/murderSite.asp?site_id=446). A "page of testimony" filed with Yad Vashem by researcher P. Fazzini in 2009 lists Berel's murder as having taken place on 25th June 1941, whereas the Yad Vashem database of murder sites states that the Igren facility began to be liquidated in October.
73. While we do not know her date of birth, her oldest daughter Chana was born in 1880, so she is likely to have been born around 1860 or earlier.
74. Rabbi Shmuel Kamenetzky, interview with Genia Schneerson in 2007 (http://www.col.org.il/show_news.rtx?artID=28210—accessed December 2013).
75. Letter dated 23 *Shevat,* 5744 (January 28, 1984), published in *L'Chaim,* issue 313 (Lubavitch Youth Organization, 1994).

CHAPTER 9: COMING TO AMERICA

1. These are acronyms for the authors of three fundamental commentaries on the Talmud, printed as an addendum to the standard Vilna edition: the commentaries of Rabbi Yitzchak Alfasi (1013–1103), Rabbi Nissim of Gerona (1320–1376), and Rabbenu Asher (1259–1327).
2. *Likutei Torah* is a volume of seminal Chasidic discourses by the founder of Chabad, Rabbi Shneur Zalman, following the order of the weekly Torah portion. The "cross references" mentioned here are complex scholarly notes that were penned by the third Lubavitcher Rebbe, Rabbi Menachem Mendel of Lubavitch, the *Tzemach Tzedek.*
3. Recollection of Rabbi Shmuel Levitin, in *Ashkenazi, Otzar Ha-Chasidim, New York,* p. 124; interview with Rabbi Yitzchak Groner in *Early Years* IV; interview with Rabbi Mottel Sharfstein (JEM).

4. Interview with Rabbi David Eidelman (*Early Years IV*).
5. Rabbi Mishael Aronson (Rabbi Daniel Goldberg, trans.), *The Rebbetzin: Biography, Reminiscences and Stories about Rebbetzin Chaya Mushka Schneerson* (Private Publication, 2012), p. 152.
6. This could normally be done in privacy after the prayers, but on *Rosh Chodesh*, additional *tefilin* are usually donned in the middle of the service before *Musaf* (Additional Prayer).
7. Groner interview (JEM).
8. Hecht, *My Spiritual Journey*, p. 55.
9. While details of the talk have not survived, much of the material may well have been based on his notes on the topic penned in Vichy, a year earlier. See *Reshimot* installments 102-3.
10. Even since his arrival in New York, Rayatz had suffered bouts of debilitating ill health. See, for example, *Igrot Rayatz* vol. 5, pp. 203, 239 and 347.
11. See *Kovetz 28th Sivan* p. 20-21; interviews with Rabbis Hershel Fogelman, Leibel Posner, and Dovid Edelman (JEM *Early Years IV*).
12. English translation by O. Dunkel and E. R. Hedrick, *A Course in Mathematical Analysis*, 3 vols. (Ginn and Company, 1904-1917).
13. Interview with former Navy Yard employee Milton Fechter, who recalled seeing and interacting with the "Rabbi/Engineer" Schneerson (JEM Living Torah Disc 28, Program 112); interview with Yaakov Hardof (ibid. Disc. 53, Program 210).

    The Brooklyn Navy Yard has confirmed with me that the technical details mentioned by Fechter about operations and staff at the Yard are accurate (Personal communication with Daniella Romano, Vice President of Programs, Research, and Archive at the Brooklyn Navy Yard, 30th December 2013). Mike Weidenbach, Curator of Archives, Collections and Research at USS Missouri Memorial Association, Inc., was also extremely impressed by the interview, describing it as "incredibly illuminating" and ringing with authenticity (Personal communication, 30th December 2013).

    Romano also informed me that 1941 marked the year for integration of the Navy and its civilian workforce to grow the talent pool. Civilians were employed if they passed a civil service test and aptitude tests and were usually required to take a loyalty oath. The total employment figure was, as Fechter correctly states in his interview, 77,000.

    See also interview with Rabbi Leibel Bistritzky in *Kfar Chabad*, issue 1510 (2013).
14. For Rayatz's prior encouragement for Ramash to accept a leadership position see *Igrot Rayatz*, vol. 15, p. 212, cited above, chapter 7, note 35. See also pp. 117 and 125. (See also *Igrot Rayatz*, vol. 11, p. 135-6, for an instance where Ramash declined to address the Lubavitcher Yeshiva in Riga.)
15. As it turns out, of all the Nazi occupied countries, France was one of the better places to live during the war. Less than a quarter of French Jews were sent to the gas chambers, compared with a staggering 97% of Polish Jewry, which was annihilated. Even if Menachem Mendel and Moussia had not escaped France it is likely that they would have survived, as did Menachem Mendel's cousin, Rabbi Zalman Schneerson and his family.
16. Rigg, p. 156. Rayatz requested an audience with the president to thank him in person, which was declined (ibid.).
17. Ashkenazi, *Otzar*, p. 47.
18. Rayatz's plans immediately garnered the attention of the press. "It will be interesting to see," mused an editor of the *American Jewish Outlook* a week after the Sixth Rebbe's arrival, "if any changes will take place in the movement in an American environment, whether Chasidism is primarily a product of conditions in the old world or whether it will grow greatly in the new, whether it is a form of Judaism that calls for compactness of its adherents or whether it can thrive with its followers scattered all over the United States." *American Jewish Outlook*, 29th March, 1940, p. 6. On the rebuilding of Chasidic communities in the United States see Joseph Dan, *Hasidism: The Third Century*, in Ada Rapoport-Albert (ed.), *Hasidism Reap-*

praised, (London: Littman Library of Jewish Civilization, 1997), pp. 415-426.

19. *Sichah* of 10th *Shevat* 5743. Translation based on *Sichos in English* vol. 16 (New York: Sichos in English, 1986.

    It is conceivable that Ramash himself was motivated by similar sentiments, and finding himself one of the few rescued from Nazi occupied France, saw it as Providence guiding him to utilize his Rabbinic and leadership talents in the USA.

20. See Levine, *History of Chabad in Poland, Lithuania and Latvia,* chapters 12-13.
21. See Gershon Scholem's famous essay, "The Neutralization of the Messianic Element in Early Hasidism" in his *The Messianic Idea in Judaism, and other essays on Jewish Spirituality* (New York: Schocken Books, 1971), p. 176*ff.*
22. See, for example, *Likutei Amarim, Tanya* chapters 36-37.
23. Jewish Messianism essentially hinges on the belief that renewed commitment to Jewish beliefs, laws and rituals (*teshuvah*) can prompt G-d to redirect the course of history. The normative belief is defined by Maimonides in his legal Code.

    > All the prophets insisted on repentance, since the Jewish people will only be redeemed through *teshuvah.*
    >
    > The Torah has already assured us that, ultimately, the Jewish people will return in *teshuvah* towards the end of their exile and, immediately, they will be redeemed—as the verse states: "*It will come to pass when all these things will come upon you... and you will return to G-d, your G-d.... and G-d, your G-d, will turn your captivity and have compassion on you*" (*Deuteronomy* 30:1-3; *Rambam, Mishneh Torah, Laws of Teshuvah* 7:5, based on BT *Sanhedrin* 97b).

    Situated in New York, Rayatz was now poised for the first time to influence the "New World." The majority of American Jews were immigrants, or children of immigrants who had discarded their observance, and, unlike today's secular Jews, a commitment to "Torah and *mitzvot"* was still in their living memory. The only avenue of opportunity to save all ten million Jews whose lives were endangered in Europe and Russia, Rayatz felt, was to motivate American Jews in *teshuvah* back to their former ways and the ways of their parents. The redemptive power of an American *teshuvah* to release the Jews of Europe and Russia from captivity was a single thread that united all three of Rayatz's constituencies.

24. For the full text of these appeals in English see Steven T. Katz, Shlomo Biderman and Gershon Greenberg (eds.), *Wrestling with G-d: Jewish Theological Responses during and after the Holocaust* (Oxford University Press, 2007), pp. 171-190.

    Rayatz draws heavily on the traditional Rabbinic trope of sin and suffering, which has led some scholars to understand, mistakenly in my opinion, that Rayatz sought to blame the Holocaust on non-observant Jews. Viewed in context of the accompanying activism of *Machne Israel,* the essential point of his message is unmistakably positive and empowering: We are not helpless. There is something we can do about the impending calamities. They can be averted by simple acts of *teshuvah.* As was popular in Rabbinic discourse of the time, the tone is sharp and sometimes borders on the vitriolic, but we need to bear in mind that the readership was largely first- or second-generation immigrants, many of whom bore the guilt of assimilation, and were probably more likely to be receptive to a traditional rebuke-orientated message.

25. Sermon of *Purim* 1987, *Torat Menachem—Hitva'aduyot* 5747, vol. 2, pp. 619-620.
26. Rabbi Abraham Hecht (1922-2013), who was a member of that group, recalled the Yeshiva's humble beginnings. "Benches and tables were dragged down to the basement to service the ten pioneering students. A kitchen was speedily constructed in the homey yeshivah hall, transforming a dingy cellar into a room fit for use. Rabbi Mordechai Mentlik (1912-1987), an acclaimed student of the Yeshivah in Otwock, was chosen as Rosh Yeshivah and our small group became a full-fledged student body." (Hecht, *Spiritual Journey,* p. 103).
27. By 1945, Rashag had already established thirteen *chadarim* (junior schools) in Brooklyn, a major branch of *Yeshivat Tomchei Temimim* in Montreal, and Yeshivot for younger students

(known as *Achei Temimim*, "brothers of the *Temimim*") in Pittsburgh, Newark, Worcester, Rochester, Buffalo, Boston, Philadelphia, New Haven, Bridgeport, Providence, Springfield, and Chicago. At 8 a.m. every day, the "President of the Executive Committee" of the Yeshiva system was typically at his desk, ready for a packed schedule of meetings and conferences with department heads and board members. Rashag would carefully review financial reports received from the many schools and Yeshivot, looking for ways to maximize efficiency. He also travelled extensively, visiting each institution under his auspices at least once a year (*Synagogue Light* (Journal of the Wall Street Synagogue), February 1948).

The educational system ran at a huge deficit, which Rashag offset by tireless fund-raising—a considerable challenge in the 1940s, when American Jews were not especially receptive to Chasidism. Each year he would also arrange a gala dinner, which, health permitting, was attended by the Rebbe Rayatz himself, along with Ramash. (At the first dinner, in 1942, the guest speaker was none other than Ramash's friend from his Berlin days, Rabbi Joseph Soloveitchik). A major building campaign, started by Rashag in 1941, finally reached its goal after five years and the Yeshivah was able to purchase a substantial 39,000 sq. ft. premises on the corner of Bedford Avenue and Dean Street in Brooklyn.

All Rashag's hard work produced impressive results and by 1946 the Lubavitcher Yeshiva system boasted an enrollment of some 3,500 students (*Jewish Criterion*, 29th March 1946, p. 27. For a detailed description of all these activities see Levin, *America* chapters 36-56.). The Chabad Chasidic community in America at the time was still very small, and many of the students at the Yeshivah came from non-Chabad families. Over the course of time, many of these students chose to affiliate as Chabad, and the Yeshivah system acted as a very effective tool in rebuilding the Chabad community in the U.S.A.

28. Outline of activities of *Machne Israel* published in *Hayom Yom* (New York: Kehot, 1943). In his second "Urgent Call," publicized in June 1941, Rayatz encouraged all readers to join the society:

> "Join our *Machne Israel*. It does not come to compete with any movement. It is not for anyone's personal interest. Help us to enlarge the camp and do the work needed at this time for the community of Israel! *Machne Israel* has already quietly accomplished the greatest holy things. We have already saved many Jewish souls...
>
> "Remember, we must awaken the mercies of heaven to avert the terrible troubles that have hit all of Judaism in Europe like a thunder! You cannot rely on your [own power]... Every Jew should join our *Machne Israel*. Together we will become a strong fortress. Through our unity we will influence G-d to shackle our enemies. We call to every Jew, every man or woman, young and old, in every corner of America, no matter which party or movement anyone belongs to. Come closer to sincere Judaism!
>
> "Our united work in the *Machne Israel* will help and benefit all other Jewish activities; it will benefit all those working in all other Jewish areas. We will create a living, conscious, and strong Judaism (Katz, Biderman and Greenberg, p. 177-9).

Since membership and activities were kept strictly confidential, there is no available data of the organization's success; but we can garner some sense of the scope of the activities from the published correspondence of Ramash during the 1940s (published in *Igrot Kodesh* vols. 1-3 (New York: Kehot, 1987). Extensive selections have been translated into English in Rabbi Eliyahu Touger (trans.), *I Will Write it in Their Hearts: A Treasury of Letters from the Lubavitcher Rebbe*, vols. 1-5, (New York: Sichos in English, 1999-2006). In the following citations I will use the reference number of each letter, so that the text may be referenced in the original or in Touger's translation). In a letter before Rosh Hashanah 1941, Ramash appealed that pulpit Rabbis should devote their sermons to the topic of *teshuvah* and redemption (Letter #26). By 1942, Ramash was happy to report, "With thanks to G-d, the activities of *Machne Israel* have spread, as has the membership. People from all sectors of the observant community have joined, without any factional distinction (Letter #34).

Ramash also responded to criticisms about the functioning of *Machne*. One complaint from supporters was that there seemed to be little pressure on members to achieve greater results, and it was relatively easy for a person to "discharge his obligation," with four small good deeds. Ramash responded that the clandestine nature of the society made it virtually impossible to determine whether members were sufficiently eager, and the success of the enterprise depended in any case on the sincere dedication of all members (Letter #35).

Another questioner raised a different issue with the requirement to report four good deeds per month to the central office—an official report, the questioner felt, might lead to members feeling unduly proud of their achievements. Ramash responded that a mere four good deeds per month was not a lot to be proud about, and the reports were necessary so that less enthusiastic members did not slack off completely (Letter #32.).

29. Letters #22 and #63.
30. Students notes from the 1945 lecture have survived and were published in pamphlet form by *Kehot* in 1994, and subsequently reprinted in *Sichot Kodesh Kodem Ha-Nesiut* (New York: Va'ad Chayalei Beit David, 2010), pp. 56-65.
31. See Laufer, *Yemei Melech* vol. 2, p. 662-3, citing from newspaper articles of the period.
32. Letter #159, written to Mr. Tzvi Palmer of New Jersey, 1st *Tammuz*, 1944.
33. The fifteen articles penned by Ramash during these years were collected and published together in *Teshuvot u'Biurim* (New York: Kehot, 1974). They are also reprinted in the *Igrot Kodesh* pertaining to these years.
34. For more on *Machne Israel* and its activities see Laufer, *Yemei Melech* vol. 2, pp. 650-685; Levine, *America*, chaps. 61-63. Until around 1947, Ramash continued to sign off much of his correspondence, "with blessings for *le-alter le-teshuvah, le-alter le-geulah.*" In the 1980s, *Machne Israel* was revived as a fund for an elite group of Chabad supporters.
35. Rabbi Tzvi Yehuda Fogelman, cited in Laufer, *Yemei Melech*, vol. 2, p. 692.
36. Laufer, *Yemei Melech* ibid., p. 704. Rabbi Hecht directed the program until the end of his life, and it continues to this day, under the auspices of the National Committee for the Furtherance of Jewish Education. For a full history of the "Released Time" activities see: Rabbi Yitzchak Naparstek, *Shiurei Limud Hadat: Historical review of the Released Time program of the National Committee for the Furtherance of Jewish Education* (New York: Kehot, 2006).
37. *Igrot Kodesh* vol. 2, p. 358.
38. Letter dated *Erev Purim*, 5737 (March 3, 1977), written in English.
39. Chabad had already carried out pioneering work for girls' education in Riga. See Levin, *Poland* pp. 64-68. For some of the Seventh Rebbe's later reflections on this revolutionary work and its influence on the broader Jewish community, see *Sichot Kodesh* 5752, vol. 2 (New York: Va'ad Kitvei Kodesh, 1992), p. 578.
40. Levine, *America*, chapter 58.
41. Babylonian Talmud, *Bava Basra* 14a.
42. *Sichot Kodesh* 5741, vol. 1, pp. 513-5. For a collection of the Rebbe's statements on this issue see Rabbi Mordechai Menasheh Laufer, *Nitzutei Rebbi* in *Hitkashrut* (Chabad in Israel), issue 499, 21 *Shevat*, 2004; article by Rabbi Peretz Blau, http://www.shturem.net/index.php?section=artdays&id=2097 (accessed 7th January 2014).
43. See Maya Balakirsky Katz, *The Visual Culture of Chabad* (Cambridge University Press, 2010), pp. 135-140.
44. N. Ben Yochanan, *Di Yiddishe Heim, Elul-Tishrei* 1964. Rabbi Chodakov recalled how, back then, he had been impressed with the sincerity with which Ramash recited his prayers.
45. Letter #508.
46. Reprinted in 2003 by *Merkos L'Inyanei Chinuch* in 16 volumes.
47. See Yitzchak Holtzman and Moshe Marinovsky, *Pegishot im Ha-Rebbi* (Kfar Chabad Publications, undated), p. 37*ff;* "Slice of Life" in *L'Chaim* (Lubavitch Youth Organization) issue 238 (23rd October, 1992) and issue 620 (26th May 2000), and http://www.chabad.org/therebbe/article_cdo/aid/375089/jewish/The-Rebbe-and-the-Artist.htm (accessed January 2014).
48. Cohen's letter is reproduced in http://www.meaningfullife.com/torah/parsha/bamidbar/korach/The_Soul_of_a_Conflict.php#_edn17 (accessed 7th January, 2014). Asimov's reply seems plausible, since he responded to over ninety thousand of the one hundred thousand

letters that he received during his professional career. Unfortunately, most of Asimov's correspondence before 1965 has not survived, as he threw it away. If a copy of the Rebbe's letter to Asimov does exist, it is probably in the Nissan Mindel archive, which has not yet been opened to researchers.

49. For the following and a full history of Kehot see Rabbi Zusha Wolf, *Kehot Publications: The History of the Chabad Publishing House* (Heb.) (Israel, Kfar Chabad: Kehot, 2013).
50. See *Reshimot Rabash* p. 25.
51. The *Hayom Yom* had been an anthology of Rayatz's ideas, and after 1950 the Rebbe only edited works prepared by Chasidim but did not pen his own texts.
52. Rabbi Shlomo Yosef Zevin, *Sofrim u'Sefarim* (Tel Aviv: Avraham Zioni, 1959). For more on the Haggadah see my introduction to *The Kol Menachem Haggadah* (New York: Kol Menachem, 2008).

    Ramash also penned a short biography of the Fourth Lubavitcher Rebbe, Rabbi Shmuel Schneersohn, anthologized from Rayatz's writings: *Sefer Ha-Toldot Admor Maharash* (New York: Kehot, 1947).
53. *Igrot Rayatz* vol. 6, p. 386.
54. Letter #170.
55. Chana Schneerson Memoirs, installment 16.
56. Ibid.
57. For the first time in many years, Reb Levik had the joy of being part of an active Jewish community, and he delivered the Sabbath sermon in the synagogue. But as the community grew with the influx of Jewish refugees, Reb Levik's health steadily worsened and he soon was virtually unable to walk. He still managed, though, to attend a local circumcision and deliver his Torah thoughts for over two hours, without a break, as well as engage in a mathematical discussion with some academics. Some of the Lubavitchers in attendance were still not satisfied. "We want more practical inspiration and fewer abstractions," they complained (ibid. part 19-20).
58. Ibid. part 21.
59. Bistrisky interview.
60. See Tilles, *A Mother,* pp. 149-154.
61. For the above see Laufer, *Yemei Melech* vol. 2, pp. 859-873; *Rebbetzin Chana* (JEM).
62. Zisman, *I Believe*, p. 143, 156-7.
63. See Tilles p. 155*ff.*
64. A few notes for the *farbrengens* from this period have survived (collected in *Sichot Kodesh Kodem Ha-Nesiut*), but this represents only a fraction of more than one hundred *farbrengens* which Ramash probably conducted during this period. This changed after the passing of Rayatz, when Ramash's every word was memorized and recorded for the next forty-two years. For a description of the 1940s *farbrengens* see Laufer, *Yemei Melech* vol. 2, p. 558*ff*: interview with Rabbi Leibel Posner (JEM).
65. Posner interview.
66. Notes from this talk, from around 1948, have survived and were edited by the Rebbe for publication many years later, in 1991. Printed in Y. Y. Greenberg and E. Zaklikovsy, *Yemei Bereishit: Historical Biography 1950-1951* (New York: Kehot 1991), p. 338-341.
67. Interview with Ben Zion Shenker (JEM Living Torah, Disc 85, Program 340). Notes of what was probably the first of these lectures which Ramash prepared for publication in 1941, were eventually printed in 1996 as *Hatza'at Tochen Sichah Be-Hitva'adut u-Mesibat Benei Torah, Choveret Rishonah, Shnayim Ochazin be-Tallit* (Kehot).
68. Interview with Rabbi Dovid Edelman, July 2008 (JEM: *Here's My Story,* November 16, 2013).
69. For many hand-written notes that Ramash prepared for his wedding speeches see Zaklikovsky, *Mekadesh Yisrael.* See also notes in *Reshimot* from these years (installments 158-187).

70. Interview with Mendel Feldman (JEM Disc 60, Program 240)
71. Edelman interview (JEM Disc 60, Program 240)
72. See also recollection of Rabbi Yitzchak David Groner about Rayatz's comments, shared by Ramash, after a children's parade in 1942 (JEM).

CHAPTER 10: LUBAVITCH CHOOSES A NEW REBBE

1. After the passing of his mother on 31st January (13th *Shevat*) 1942.
2. From 1942-1945 he did deliver about ten discourses on an informal basis during the course of the Sabbath and Festival meals. This type of delivery, known as a *ma'amar ke'eyn sicha* (discourse resembling a sermon), is said without the formal introduction of a special melody (*niggun*) and with the listeners sitting down (unlike the formal *ma'amarim*, for which they would stand.) The last discourse he delivered verbally was on 23rd June (12th *Tammuz*) 1945.
3. For the efforts to distribute Rayatz's *Ma'amarim* during this period see Levin, *America*, chapter 66. The *Va'ad le-Hafatzat Da"ch* (Committee for the Dissemination of Chasidut) was headed by Rabbi Avraham Paris, who would carefully type Rayatz's handwritten *ma'amarim* and prepare mimeographed copies for the Chasidim. For a letter praising Paris' careful transcriptions see *Igrot Rayatz* vol. 9, p. 370. From the end of 1947 onwards the *ma'amarim* were properly typeset and printed with annotations added by Ramash.
4. *Sefer Ha-Sichot* 5752, vol. 1 (New York: Kehot, 1993), p. 292. The Rebbe, of course, submitted to the Divine will, continuing, "And even though we cannot ask questions of G-d, how He runs His world, particularly with a Jewish leader; and we cannot say how things 'should have been or 'shouldn't have been'—nevertheless, G-d ordained that He only asks from us according to our abilities, and we ought to try and understand things as much as we can." See also *Sichot Kodesh* 5730, vol. 1, p. 455; *Torat Menachem—Hitva'aduyot* 5745, vol. 1, p. 382.
5. With the exception of the discourse of 19th *Kislev* 5708.
6. Rabbi Eliyahu Nachum Sklar (1903-1990) had personally transcribed many discourses from Rayatz's handwritten manuscripts in the 1920s when he worked in the secretariat, and he kept a substantial personal archive. Since many original documents were lost due to Communist and Nazi oppression, Sklar's archive was helpful in preserving many texts of the Sixth and Seventh Rebbes.

   Sklar was born in Zhlobin and learned in *Yeshivat Tomchei Temimim* in Lubavitch, then in Szedrin, Kremenchug, Rostov, Poltava, Nevel, and Charkov. He emigrated to Israel in 1926 and studied in *Yeshivat Torat Emet* in Jerusalem, before moving to the United States in 1930.
7. According to one recollection, this was also the date of Ramash's first visit to the court of Rayatz. See Chapter 2, note 25.
8. The discourse is available in English in Eliyahu Touger and Sholom B. Wineberg (trans.), *Basi LeGani: Chasidic Discourses* (New York: Kehot, 1990). Rayatz's 1923 discourse was later published in *Sefer Ha-Ma'amarim* 5722-3 (New York: Kehot, 1986), p. 168*ff*, and was based on a *ma'amar* of his father, Rashab, delivered in 1898 (*Sefer Ha-Ma'amarim* 5658 (New York: Kehot, 1984), p. 208*ff*).
9. Note of Ramash cited in Yosef Greenberg and Eliezer Zaklikowsky, *Yemei Bereishit: Historical Biography—1950-1951* (New York: Kehot 1993), p. 64 from *Mafteach Sifrei Ma'amarei ve-Derushei Admor Rayatz*, p. 39, note 4.
10. See Hillel Goldberg, *Between Berlin and Slobodka*, (New Jersey: KTAV, 1989), p. 79; Binyamin Lipkin and Yosef Yitzchak Elitov, *In all my house he is faithful: The life of Rabbi Shneur Zalman Gurary* (Heb.), (Kfar Chabad: Machon Razag, 2011), p. 207. Rabbi Hutner expressed his profound appreciation for Chabad Chasidut in a 1977 letter: "The term 'interest' is far too weak to express my attachment to Chabad [Chasidut]. A considerable part of my spiritual world is grounded in Chabad ideas." (*Heichal Ha-Besht*, issue 35, Tishrei 5774, p. 76). Rabbi Hutner had been in Berlin at the same time as Ramash and was probably acquainted with him from this period.

Rabbi Hutner's deep respect for the Rebbe continued, as we see from correspondence even in 1970 regarding the Chabad *tefilin* campaign. See Levine, *Treasures,* p. 88*ff.*

11. Letter of Mordechai Dubinsky in Rabbi Avraham Chanoch Glitzenstein, *Sefer Ha-Toldot Rebbi Yosef Yitzchak Schneersohn of Lubavitch* (Kfar Chabad: Kehot, 1974), p. 129*ff;* diaries of Yoel Kahn and Eli Gross, http://www.yomanim.com. The following is based on these sources and other recollections collected in Greenberg and Zaklikowsky.

    I have followed the time scale in the Dubinsky letter which differs slightly from the letter of 18th *Shevat,* below.

12. Dubinsky's letter.
13. Writing of the Torah scroll had begun in 1942. Ultimately, it was not completed until 1970.
14. See editor's introduction to *Igrot Rayatz* vol. 10 (New York: Kehot, 1989), p. 5.
15. Rayatz's talks from 1945-50 are published in Rabbi Aharon Leib Raskin (ed.), *Sefer Ha-Sichot* 5706-10 (New York: Kehot, 2001).

    In 1950, the community of Chabad Chasidim was small and geographically fragmented, its future uncertain. A large number of its adherents, who had remained in Communist Russia after Rayatz's departure in 1927, had either been murdered by Stalin or lost contact completely. The Chabad communities in Poland, Latvia and Lithuania had been decimated by the Nazis. Most of what remained was a cluster of Chasidim who had made it to America, the thirty-seven students who had escaped from the Yeshiva in Poland (via Japan), and a trickle of Russian Chasidim who managed to escape on false passports in the late 1940s, mainly settling in the new town of Kfar Chabad in Israel. The Chabad Yeshiva system in America and Israel continued to expand, winning new adherents to the movement, but centralized leadership was desperately needed.

16. During his arrest in 1927, before being taken away to prison, Rayatz's thoughts turned to his grandson: "Let us hope that when my grandson grows up he will staunchly tread the path blazed by our holy forebears; that he will stand firm in the cause of Torah and the awe of heaven, undaunted by any obstacle; that he will battle for the preservation of Torah observance and the fear of heaven; and that he will always be of help to those who stand in awe of G-d" (Uri Kaploun (trans.), *Likkutei Dibburim, An Anthology of Talks by Rabbi Yosef Yitzchak Schneersohn of Lubavitch,* vol. 4 (New York: Kehot, 1997), p. 160.

    In the 1930s Shalom Ber (Barry) studied in the Lubavitcher Yeshivah in Otwock and since Rayatz could not be left alone for health reasons, the boy sat with his grandfather during *Yechidut,* hidden by a curtain.

17. This was not uncharacteristic in Chabad, where issues of succession are usually decided by the Chasidim, and not "from above" by the preceding Rebbe. The Fifth Lubavitcher Rebbe, Rashab, did leave a will requesting the Chasidim to consider his son (Rayatz) as Rebbe, but since Rashab had only one son, the will represented more a request for dynastic continuum than the election of a particular candidate.
18. During the week they attended separate prayer services, both desiring to lead the service and say *kaddish* for Rayatz. (According to Chabad custom, one who recites *kaddish* is encouraged to lead the services on a weekday).
19. For more on Rashag's character, see Dalfin lecture in note 30.
20. Ramash's shift to a leadership role, despite his natural introversion, has been described by Friedman and Heilman as him "re-inventing himself." But as Nehemia Polen has astutely noted, "Genuine as opposed to manufactured charisma cannot be conjured by an act of will to buttress a project of self-reinvention.... It is precisely a quality of the numinous, not contrivance or self-presentation, that so many discerning people found in Schneerson and that served to propel his influence.... Charisma depends on being perceived as being closely connected to some central feature of the cosmos and its power" (*Modern Judaism,* volume 34, number 1 (February 2014), pp. 127-8).
21. Rabbi Yoel Kahn served for over forty years as the chief scholar responsible for memorizing the Seventh Rebbe's talks as they were delivered, and ensuring that they were transcribed

accurately. (Jewish law forbids the use of recording devices on the Sabbath and Festivals.) He was also intimately involved with the editing of many of the Rebbe's officially published sermons and discourses, as well as authoring the Chabad Encyclopedia, *Sefer Ha-Arachim—Chabad*, 7 vols. (New York: Kehot, 1970-2009). He has been a mentor and teacher to generations of Chasidim and is revered as one of the leading minds in Chabad. He arrived from Israel in 1950 to see Rayatz and his court, only to discover that the Sixth Rebbe had just passed away. Upon the advice of Rashag and Ramash, he chose to stay in New York and his diary from the period provides a vivid, honest account of the events at 770 during the course of the next two years.

22. Kahn memoir February 20th (3rd Adar) 1950.
23. Ibid, entry for April 19th (2nd *Iyar*) 1950.
24. Letter dated 18th *Shevat* 5710, available at http://pirsumrishon.blogspot.com/2008/08/blog-post.html (accessed January 2014).
25. Letter from Rabbi Eliezer Karasik to Rabbi Moshe Dovber Rivkin, 17th February (*Rosh Chodesh Adar*) 1950. The letter had originally been penned on 1st February (14th *Shevat*), 1950—just four days after Rayatz's passing—and sent to New York by air mail; but it was destroyed in El-Al airplane "Hertzl" which caught on fire at Lod airport on 6th February. After discovering the letter had been lost, Karasik sent another copy on the 17th. The letter is printed, in part, in Shneur Zalman Berger, *Eved Avraham Anochi: The Life and Activities of Rabbi Chaim Eliezer Karasik*, (Israel: Machon Oholei Shem Lubavitch, 2012), p. 221.
26. Berger, *Karasik* pp. 219-220.
27. After Ramash was appointed Rebbe, all loyalties shifted to him, and to admit even privately that one was an erstwhile Rashag supporter would be frowned upon.
28. See editor's introduction to *Igrot Rayatz* vol. 9, pp. 12-13; Rabbi Chaim Dalfin, *Who's Who in Lubavitch II* (New York: Jewish Enrichment Press, 2011), pp. 88-89. On 7th March 1947, the *American Jewish Outlook* reported: "Word has just been received that Rabbi Samarias Gourary... left for Germany last week on a special refugee mission. Under the direction of the Lubavitcher Rabbi, Rabbi Joseph I. Schneersohn, Rabbi Gourary will survey the refugee situation personally and will determine the necessary measures to be taken to expedite and accelerate the rescue of several hundred Russo-Jewish families to the United States of America. These families, through the assistance of the Refugee Aid Committee of the United Lubavitcher Yeshivas, have only recently managed to cross the Russian and Polish borders into the comparatively safer countries of France, Belgium, Holland and Germany's U. S. Zone."
29. *Igrot Rayatz* vol. 10, p. 161.
30. See lecture of Rabbi Chaim Dalfin on Rashag's life at http://www.jli.co.il/go/tc/tags/rashag/, parts 3 and 4 (accessed January 2014).
31. See Kahn diary entry of April 19th (2nd *Iyar*), 1950: "In my opinion, the Chabad community in Israel simply does not know him."
32. See letters from Dubov in Greenberg and Zaklikowsky, p. 199.
33. Letter from 1956 cited in Greenberg and Zaklikowsky, p. 85, note 43**.
34. Greenberg and Zaklikowsky p. 84.
35. Letter dated March 15th (26th *Adar*) 1950, *Igrot Kodesh* vol. 3, p. 260.
36. Belinitzky had maintained a regular correspondence with Ramash on the finer points of Chabad thought. Rayatz had sent Belinitzky's questions relating to the most arcane Chabad doctrines to Ramash to answer (see Berger in following note).
37. The letter is reproduced in Shneur Zalman Berger's biography of Belinitzky, *Yisrael Noach Ha-Gadol* (Israel: private publication, 2006), p. 117. A similar letter was written on the same day to Rabbi Avraham Paris (*Igrot Kodesh* vol. 3, p. 307).
38. Rabbi Shneur Zalman of Liadi, *Tanya, Iggeret Ha-Kodesh*, commentary to Epistle 27. Ramash's talks from this period have been translated into English in Uri Kaploun (trans.), *Proceeding*

Together: The Earliest Talks of the Lubavitcher Rebbe, Rabbi Menachem M. Schneerson, 4 vols. (New York: Sichos in English, 1995-2009).

39. For examples of this exegesis see Kaploun, vol. 1, pp. 23-24, 27-28, 38-40, 78, 113-4, 137-8; vol. 2, pp. 7-8, 24-25, 27, 47-49, 115, 146, 161; vol. 3, pp. 63-7, 141-2, 190-2, 252-7.
40. Kahn diary, entry of April 19th (2nd *Iyar*) 1950. For an academic study of the continued presence of a Rebbe after his passing in Chabad thought, see Shelly Goldberg, *The Spiritual Voyage of the Soul: The Soul of the 'Tzaddik' and the Eternity of the Spirit in Chabad's doctrine* (Israel: Rubin Mass, 2009).
41. Cain has written extensively on the power of introverted leadership and is the author of *Quiet: The Power of Introverts in a World That Can't Stop Talking* (Crown Publishing Group, 2012). The above citation is from her address at the TED Conference, Long Beach California in February 2012 (http://www.ted.com/talks/susan_cain_the_power_of_introverts.html—accessed Jan 2014). Interestingly, Cain attributes much of her insight about introverted leadership to the influence and example of her Rabbinic grandfather, Israel Schorr (1906-2000).
42. Letters of support for Ramash's candidacy circulated from senior Chasidim in England, Rabbis Yitzchak Dubov, Avraham Sender Nemtzov and Ben Zion Shemtov, on 19th February (see Greenberg and Zaklikowsky, p. 104, 116); and senior Chasidim in Israel, Rabbis Shlomo Yosef Zevin, Nachum Shmaryahu Sasonkin and Avraham Chein (ibid.). The extensive efforts to "crown" Ramash are chronicled in Greenberg and Zaklikowsky's volume.
43. See Greenberg and Zaklikowsky pp. 145-6 that on 19th April (2nd Iyar) a delegation of senior Chasidim from New York (including Rabbis Yisrael Jacobson, Eliyahu Simpson and Shlomo Aharon Kazarnovsky) visited Rayatz's grave, asking the late Rebbe to intercede on high that Ramash should accept the leadership. See also Lipkin and Elitov p. 208 for Rabbi Zalman Gurary's decision to back Ramash, despite pressure to the contrary from the old Rebbetzin.
44. See Aronson, p. 159.
45. From letter of Rabbi Ephraim Yolles, 26th February 1950, printed in Wolpo, *Shemen* vol. 2, p. 161.
46. *Igrot Kodesh* vol. 3, pp. 412-2.
47. Letter dated 19th April (2nd *Iyar*) 1950, Greenberg and Zaklikowsky, p. 146.
48. Letter dated 6th June (21st *Sivan*) 1950, ibid p. 173.
49. Memoir of Rabbi Ezriel Chaikin, ibid p. 109. For an example of Ramash's boldness in offering medical advice, see Kahn diary entry of 17th June where Ramash advised an individual not to take an operation which was deemed necessary by a medical professional. See also Gross diary, 15th May (28th *Iyar*).
50. Kahn diary, entry for 18th June (4th *Av*) 1950.
51. Kaploun, *Proceeding Together* vol. 2, pp. 23-4.
52. Greenberg and Zaklikowsky, p. 175-177; Kahn Diary, 12th June (27th *Sivan*), 1950. For the results of the meeting and hand-written list of sixty-four Chasidim who were enlisted to help, see http://www.shturem.net/index.php?section=news&id=68859 (accessed January 2014). See also Lipkin and Elitov, p. 211, that as a result of a weak reaction at the meeting, Ramash's acceptance of the leadership was significantly delayed. See also meeting of 11th *Iyar* 5712 where Ramash (then the Rebbe) declared, "I am not an expert in fundraising." (*Torat Menachem—Hitva'aduyot* vol. 5, p. 186).
53. Kahn diary, 12th June (27th *Sivan*) 1950; Greenberg and Zaklikowsky pp. 182-187.
54. Kahn diary, 16th September (5th *Tishrei*).
55. Ibid., 22nd September (11th *Tishrei*).
56. Letter to Rabbi Shlomo Chaim Kesselman (1894-1971) dated 5th September (23rd *Elul*) 1950. (This hand-written addendum was omitted from the published letter in *Igrot Kodesh* vol. 3, p. 471.) Rabbi Kesselman became one of the venerated *mashpi'im* in postwar Chabad and turned to Ramash immediately after Rayatz's passing. For his biography and teachings see

Rabbi Yisrael Alpenbaim, *Hamashpia Reb Shlomo Chaim Kesselman,* 2 vols. (Israel: Private publication, 2013). For his early attachment to Ramash see ibid. vol. 2, p. 614*ff.*

57. See, for example, Greenberg and Zaklikowsky p. 135; Lipkin and Elitov p. 206.
58. See Lipkin and Elitov, ibid.
59. Kahn diary, 3rd April (26th Adar II) 1951; interview with Mottel Sharfstein (JEM).
60. Ibid. This refers to the period shortly after Ramash accepted the leadership, but arguably reflects her general concern.
61. This is evidenced by Chana and Barry's testimony in the 1985 court case, and from Nechama Dina's will in which she referred to herself as the "last Lubavitcher Rebbetzin."
62. Two separate services were conducted on this day so that both sons-in-law could be honored with *Chatan Bereishit* (see Kahn Diary in following note).
63. Kahn diary, 5th October (24th *Tishrei*), 1950.
64. Kahn diary, 10th December (1st *Tevet*), 1950.
65. Greenberg and Zaklikowsky, p. 344. Text of the letter of *hitkashrut* is on page 346. See also letter of Shmuel Zalmanov on p. 363.
66. The three newspaper articles are reproduced in Greenberg and Zaklikowsky, pp. 348-349.
67. Lipkin and Elitov pp. 209-11. See also Greenberg and Zaklikowsky, p. 351.
68. For this and the following see Greenberg and Zaklikowsky, p. 375ff.
69. The idea is found in *Sefer Ha-Ma'amarim* 5710, p. 105. See also *Sefer Ha-Arachim—Chabad,* s.v. *Ahavat Yisrael,* p. 627ff.
70. *Vayikra Rabah* 29:11.
71. Kahn diary, 25th January (18th *Shevat*), 1951.
72. Ibid., 26th January (19th *Shevat*), 1951.
73. Ibid., 31st January (24th *Shevat*), 1951.
74. Ibid., 26th February (20th *Adar I*), 1951.
75. See Rapoport, pp. 178-180.
76. Letter dated 4th December (5th *Kislev*) 1951, reproduced in Rapoport p. 213.
77. Kahn diary 10th December (11th *Kislev*), 1951.
78. See student's diary that he was present at the *farbrengen* of *Shabbat Bereishit* (29th *Tishrei*) 5713, posted at http://www.yoman770.com//wiki/כ"ט_תשרי_תשי"ג. Kahn's diary entry for 9th April (24th *Nissan*) 1953 also notes that Rashag had "been attending the *farbrengens* for a long time now." For the Rebbe's request for a place of honor for Rashag, see Lipkin and Elitov, p. 214.
79. Kahn diary in previous note. Rashag added: "There is just one condition: Please treat me with respect. Give me the respect that our father-in-law accorded me." See also the account of "one *farbrengen* in 5713" in Lipkin and Elitov ibid., which appears to refer to the same incident (see pp. 359-60).
80. Kahn diary, 8th June (25th *Sivan*) 1953.
81. See the moving letter penned by Rashag in 1971, in Rapoport, p. 183. Rashag's "turnaround" was an impressive act of self-effacement. It is common in Chasidic courts for one who loses a succession battle to set up his own competing court in a different location, or lose interest altogether and pursue business interests.
82. Herbert Weiner, *The Lubovitcher Movement II* in *Commentary,* April 1957.

CHAPTER 11: AT THE COURT OF THE 7TH LUBAVITCHER REBBE

1. Ashkenazi, *Otzar Chasidim—New York,* p. 92.
2. *Torat Menachem—Sefer Ha-Ma'amarim* 5711/2 - 5724, 13 vols. (New York: Va'ad Hanachot Lahak, 2006-10).

3. *Torat Menachem—Hitva'aduyot* vols. 4-40, (New York: Va'ad Hanachot Lahak, 1995-2009). This series contains both the sermons, translated into Hebrew and annotated, and the *Ma'amarim.*
4. Mendel Kalmanson, *Seeds of Wisdom* (New York: Jewish Educational Media, 2013), p. 82.
5. For a chronicle of these visits see Mordechai Lieberman and Eliezer Zaklikovsky, *Bine'ot Deshe* (New York: Kehot, 1993).
6. Interviews with Rabbi Shalom Mendel Simpson, 2007 and 2010.
7. Meeting with supporters of the Yeshivah, 6th December (7th *Kislev*) 1951, in *Torat Menachem—Hitva'aduyot* vol. 4, pp. 151-2
8. Plus a small amount of Russian correspondence.
9. The editors excluded about one-third of the material which was of a personal nature (Simpson interview).
10. Menachem Mendel Schneerson, *Igrot Kodesh,* vols. 5-23. Pastoral letters connected with the festivals are found in *Torat Menachem—Igrot Melech* (Kfar Chabad: Kehot, 1992), 2 vols.
11. Many English letters have appeared in the weekly publication *L'Chaim* (Lubavitch Youth Organization), for many years, and a substantial archive dating back to 1992 exists online at http://www.lchaimweekly.org.
12. Nissan Mindel, *The Letter and the Spirit* (New York: Kehot, 1998), p. xix.
13. Or he would have it opened in his presence. ibid. p. xvii; Simpson interview.
14. http://www.chabad.org/therebbe/article_cdo/aid/1557498/jewish/Local-Is-Global.htm
15. Mindel, ibid. p. xxvii.
16. *Igrot Kodesh* vol. 10, p. 142.
17. Lecture of Rabbi Leibel Groner 2011, http://www.torahcafe.com/rabbi-leibel-groner/the-rebbe-cares-for-all-video_873c613b4.html
18. Ibid. p. xx.
19. Simpson interview; see *Teshurah Tzfasman-Simpson* 8th *Sivan* 2012, p. 15.
20. Interview with Rabbi Yehuda Krinsky in *Mishpacha,* 30th September, 2009.
21. See Uri Kaploun (trans.), *In Good Hands: 100 Letters and Talks of the Lubavitcher Rebbe Rabbi Menachem M. Schneerson on Bitachon, Trusting in G-d* (New York: Sichos in English, 2005), pp. 1-122. An interesting anthology of letters (in Hebrew) is Dov Sinai, and Zev Ginoser, *Ish Emunah* (Tel Aviv: Askilah, 2011).
22. See Rabbi Yosef Yitzchak Havlin (ed.), *Gates of Law and Custom* (Heb.), 4 vols. (Jerusalem: Heichal Menachem, 1993-2001).
23. See Sholom B. Wineberg (ed.), *Healthy in Body, Mind and Spirit based on the Teachings of the Lubavitcher Rebbe, Rabbi Menachem M. Schneerson,* 3 volumes (New York: Sichos in English, 2005-2007).
24. See Yechiel Baruch Oirechman (ed.), *Lema'an Tatzliach: Anthology of directives and advice in earning a living and business* (Heb.), (Kfar Chabad: Eishel, 1998).
25. See Rabbi Joseph Ginsburg and Prof. Herman Branover (Arnie Gotfryd trans.), *Mind over Matter: Teachings of the Lubavitcher Rebbe on Science, Technology and Medicine* (Jerusalem: SHAMIR, Association of Religious Scientists and Professionals from the former Soviet Union and Eastern Europe, 2003).
26. See Rabbi Yosef Yitzchak Havlin (ed.), *Gates of Education,* (Jerusalem: Heichal Menachem, 2007). For an index to letters and sermons on issues of education, see Rabbi Levi Goldstein, *Index to issues of education and guidance* (Heb), (New York: Private publication, 2001).
27. See Sholom B. Wineberg (ed.), *Eternal Joy: A Guide To Shidduchim and Marriage From the works of the Lubavitcher Rebbe, Rabbi Menachem M. Schneerson,* 3 vols. (New York: Sichos in English, 2000-2001).
28. The Rebbe did not know Spanish, Portuguese or Polish, and his secretariat had to hire translators when letters arrived in these languages. In such instances the Rebbe asked that the

names of the correspondents be removed so the translators would not see (Interview with Rabbi Leibel Groner, *Rosh Chodesh Sivan* 2009).

29. See, for example, *Igrot Kodesh* vol. 23, letter 8893, "It is not my business to rule matters of the law." See also vol. 30, p. 109.
30. Meeting with leading *halachic* authority Rabbi Shmuel Wosner on 20th June (22nd *Sivan*) 1976 (Wolpo, *Shemen Sason* vol. 2, p. 15.)
31. *Menuchat Eliyahu* vol. 1 (New York, Private publication, 1965), unpaginated introduction.
32. For a biographical sketch of Rabbi Quint and his involvement with Chabad see Menachem Zigelboim, *Stories from the Rebbe's Room* (Israel: Private publication, 2009), p. 339*ff.*
33. For more on Rothstein see Levin, *Poland*, chapter 65; Zigelboim, p. 349*ff;* editor's introduction to *Igrot Kodesh* vol. 24, (New York: Kehot, 1998), pp. 22-3.
34. See Zigelboim, p. 34*ff.* For his work in Kehot see: Wolf, *Kehot*, references cited in index on page 736.
35. For a biography of Eliyahu Simpson see Shneur Zalman Berger, *Chasid Ne'eman* (Private publication, 2008).
36. Simpson interview.
37. For examples of the Rebbe's edits of this material see *Teshurah Krinsky-Dechter* 5768, ch. 2.
38. Ibid. chap. 3.
39. See *Teshurah Friedman-Grossbaum* 5769, chapter 4.
40. See Krinsky in *Mishpacha;* Harari, p. 152; Zigelboim, p. 203*ff.*
41. See Zigelboim, p. 151*ff.*
42. Memo from *Agudat Chasidei Chabad* in Israel "following instructions from the secretariat of the Rebbe *shlita*," to all directors of Chabad organizations in Israel, dated *Menachem Av* 1977, signed by Rabbi Efrayim Wolf—printed in Rabbi Zusya Wolf (ed.), *Days of the Temimim: Fifty years of activities in building and expanding Chasidut Chabad in the Holy Land*, vol. 7 (Kfar Chabad: Kehot, 2010), p. 175.
43. Recollection of Binyamin Klein in Zigelboim, p. 186; Krinsky interview; Simpson interview.
44. According to one report he generally slept from around 2-4 a.m., and then was awake until around 7:30 am, when he would go to sleep for another two hours.
45. Harari, p. 164.
46. Ibid. p. 174.
47. Transcripts of the Torah discussions at this meal are recorded in Rabbi Mordechai Menasheh Laufer (ed.), *Ha-Melech be-Mesiboh*, 2 vols (Kfar Chabad: Kehot, 1993).
48. Groner lecture.
49. Berger, *Eved Avraham* pp. 234-5.
50. Simon Jacobson (ed.), *Portrait of a Chassid: The Life and Legacy of Rabbi Zvi Hirsh Gansbourg* (New York: GJCF, 2008), p. 105
51. Kalmanson, *Seeds* p. 127.
52. Babylonian Talmud, *Bava Metzia* 38b.
53. Laufer, *Yemei Melech* vol. 3, p. 1225, notes 125 and 128.
54. Besides the First Chabad Rebbe, who also did not commit many of his discourses to writing.
55. From 1952-1964 he delivered over four hundred discourses but edited and published only a handful of them (see Menachem Mendel Schneerson, *Sefer Ha-Ma'amarim Melukat* vol. 1 (New York: Kehot, 1987, pp. 19-86), due to time constraints (see *Igrot Kodesh* vol. 4, p. 104; vol. 8, p. 257). Consistent editing of the discourses by the Rebbe only began in 1986 (see below pp. 383-341). For an account of later efforts to publish the early discourses see article of Rabbi Mordechai Menasheh Laufer in *Hitkashrut* (Israel: Lubavitch Youth Organization), issue 124.
56. See Rabbi Yosef Yitzchak Schneersohn, *Likutei Diburim* vol. 1, p. 390.
57. Published in *Sefer Ha-Ma'amarim* 5643-5680, 29 vols (New York: Kehot, 1974-2003).

58. The *Hemshech* was a genre initially introduced by Rashab's father, the Fourth Lubavitcher Rebbe, Maharash, but developed considerably by the Sixth Rebbe.

59. Chabad scholar Rabbi David Olidort has identified three types of discourse delivered by the Seventh Rebbe, differing in levels of innovation: a.) Elaborations of discourses of his predecessors; b.) treatments of a particular theme, drawing on a range of earlier Chabad sources, synthesizing them into a unit with his own slant; c.) highly original discourses which introduce new modes of understanding (1994 interview with David Olidort, in *Kfar Chabad* issue 617).

60. Wolfson, *Open Secret*, p. 21.

61. This is in contrast to the Fifth and Sixth Rebbes, who delivered *ma'amarim* with their eyes open. See Ashkenazi, *Otzar Chasidim—New York*, p. 283.

62. For more on the structure and content of a *ma'amar* see Rabbi Michoel Golomb (ed.), *Sha'arei Limud Ha-Chasidut* (New York: Kehot, 1994), pp. 43-108.

63. Recollection of Rabbi Yoel Kahn in Ashkenani, *Otzar Ha-Chasidim—New York*, p. 315.

64. Interview with Simon Jacobson, *Ami Magazine*, 1st February 2012.

65. This is in contrast to Rashab who *farbrenged* just three times per year, and Rayatz, whose *farbrengens* were much shorter, less frequent and focused largely around storytelling. The previous Rebbes would deliver *ma'amarim* on a regular basis, but usually without accompanying *sichot*.

66. Harvey Swados, "I Am Interviewed by the Lubavitcher Rebbe," Harvey Swados Papers, University of Massachusetts Amherst Libraries, Box 20:222. For other impressions of a *farbrengen* see: Elie Wiesel, *The Gates of The Forest* (New York: Avon Books, 1966), pp. 187-199; Ellen Koskoff, *Music in Lubavitcher Life* (University of Illinois Press, 2001), pp. 3-15; Bonnie Morris, *Lubavitcher Women*, pp. 58-60; Lis Harris, *Holy Days: The World of a Hasidic Family* (Touchstone, 1985), pp. 121-5; Edward Hoffman, *Despite All Odds: The Story of Lubavitch* (Simon and Schuster, 1991), pp. 29-36; Weiner, *Nine and a Half Mystics*.

67. Those of *Purim*, *Yud Tet Kislev* and *Yud Shevat*.

68. See Zusha Wolf and Shimon Gopin, *Beit Chayenu 770* (Jerusalem: Heichal Menachem, 2004), pp. 195-211.

69. Herman Branover and Avraham Naveh (Mika Tubinshlak trans.), *The Ultimate Jew* (Jerusalem and New York: Shamir books, 2003).

70. Based on Elie Wiesel, *All Rivers Run to the Sea: Memoirs* (Schocken, 1996), pp. 402-4; Ellen Harris, *Elie Wiesel Keynotes Chabad of Solon Opening Gala*, http://www.solonchabad.com/templates/articlecco_cdo/aid/255729/jewish/Elie-Wiesel-Keynotes-Chabad-of-Solon-Opening-Gala.htm (accessed Feb, 2014); 2012 interview with Elie Wiesel by Baila Olidort, http://crownheights.info/something-jewish/44951/in-conversation-with-nobel-prize-winner-elie-wiesel (accessed Feb 2014).

71. Irving Abrahamson (ed.), *Elie Wiesel, Against Silence: The Voice and Vision of Elie Wiesel*, vol. 3 (New York: 1985), p. 63.

72. Polen, ibid.

73. Chana Schneerson Memoirs, installment 36.

74. Weiner ibid.

75. Harris, *Holy Days*, p. 123.

76. Weiner ibid.

77. Interview with Yehuda Krinsky, http://www.chabad.org/blogs/blog_cdo/aid/1128452/jewish/Rabbi-Soloveitchik-Cries-during-Prayers.htm (accessed Feb 2014).

78. Koskoff, *Music*, p. 11-12. Koskoff's experience was from a much later period, but does not seem to differ significantly from earlier depictions, with the obvious exception of the crowd size.

79. Ibid. p. 13.

80. Aryeh Solomon, *The Educational Teachings of Rabbi Menachem M. Schneerson* (New Jersey: Jason Aronson, 2000), p. 50*ff.* For extensive sources for the following, see Solomon ibid.
81. Sotah 3a.
82. See *Likutei Sichot* vol. 2, p. 311-4.
83. Ibid. pp. 350-351; *Tanya* ch. 47.
84. Recollections of Rabbi Yossi Goldstein at http://www.chabad.org/therebbe/article_cdo/aid/984844/jewish/When-the-Rebbe-Climbed-the-Fence.htm and http://www.collive.com/show_news.rtx?id=24423 (accessed Feb. 2014). The detail about Chodakov was conveyed to me by the late Rabbi Immanuel Schochet, who was present on the occasion.
85. Rabbi Shneur Zalman, *Likutei Torah, Leviticus* 41b.
86. The conviction that *every* setback—without exception—is for the sake of progress, is rooted in deep faith, as the Rebbe conveyed in a 1952 sermon.

> G-d's plan for creation is continual progress, and since He is omnipotent, this plan must actually transpire....
>
> Throughout history there are ups and downs.... But each fall and setback is a crucial preparation for the progress which follows.... Since the fall is crucial, it is not really a fall at all, but a phase of progress....
>
> But a person needs to toil in much spiritual work to reach the level where, at the moment of the fall, he not only *believes* or *understands* that he is amid a crucial preparation for further progress, but he actually *feels* it." (Sermon of 14th May (19th *Iyar*) 1952, in *Likutei Sichot* vol. 27, pp. 363-4. The sermon was delivered privately in the week following the death of the Rebbe's brother, Leibel).

Faith can often lead a person to quietistic withdrawal, accepting things as they are without attempts to resist or change them; but in the teachings of the Seventh Lubavitcher Rebbe, faith is configured as a motivational tool. Since G-d cannot fail, neither can we. We just need to recalibrate our perception to a higher vantage point so as to imbibe the message that "every 'descent' is for the sake of 'ascent,'" as a working reality.

87. Ibid vol. 2, p. 351, 954, based on Rabbi Shneur Zalman, *Torah Ohr,* 30a.
88. *Likutei Sichot* vol. 2, p. 452.
89. BT *Shabbat* 31a; JT *Nedarim* 9:4. See also Nissan Dovid Dubov, *To Love A Fellow Jew: The Mitzvah of Ahavat Yisrael in Chasidic Thought* (New York: Sichos in English, 1999).
90. *Likutei Sichot* vol. 1, pp. 94-95; ibid. p. 99-102.
91. See Wolfson, *Open Secret,* especially chap. 1; Moshe Halbertal (Jackie Feldman trans.), *Concealment and Revelation: Esotericism in Jewish Thought and its Philosophical Implications* (Princeton University Press, 2007).
92. See Naftali Loewenthal, *Communicating the Infinite: The Emergence of the Habad School* (Chigago University Press, 1990).
93. For a detailed account of the conflict surrounding the emergence of Chasidism see Mordechai Wilensky, *Chasidim and Mitnagedim* (Heb.), 2 vols. (Jerusalem: Bialik Insitute, 1970).
94. The letter is found in Immanuel Schochet (ed.), *Keter Shem Tov* (New York: Kehot, 2004), pp. 4-5. For a discussion of the authenticity of the letter and its different versions, see Yehoshua Mondshine (ed.), *Shivchei Ha-Besht* (Jerusalem 1982), pp. 229-231; Immanuel Etkes, *The Besht* (Massachusetts: Brandeis University Press, 2005), pp. 272-288. For an anthology of the Rebbe's thoughts on spreading the wellsprings see Mordechai Menasheh Laufer, *Ha-Shlichut* (Kfar Chabad: Kehot, 1987); Zushya Wolf, *Torat Ha-Shlichut: The Task of our Generation in the Lubavitcher Rebbe's Teachings* (Kfar Chabad: Kehot, 2003); Yitzchak Kraus, *Ha-Shevi'i* (Israel: Yedioth Achronoth Books, 2007), chapters 2-4. See also Wolfson, *Open Secret,* chap. 1.
95. See Rachel Elior (Yudith Nave and Arthur Millman trans.), *Jewish Mysticism: The Infinite Expression of Freedom* (Portland: Littman Library, 2007), p. 96.
96. For early sermons on this topic see sources in *Likutei Sichot* vol. 2, p. 706.

97. While his mother-in-law, Rebbetzin Nechamah Dina Schneersohn, was still alive (until 1970), the Rebbe attended all the festival meals (including the *Seder*) in her apartment, in the presence of a number of guests. On Pesach night, Chasidim were able to enter after they had completed their own *Seder* at home.
98. Naftali Loewenthal, *Self-sacrifice of the Zaddik in the Teachings of R. Dov Ber, the Mitteler Rebbe* in Ada Rapoprt-Albert and Steven J. Zipperstein (eds.), *Jewish History: Essays in Honour of Chimen Abramsky* (London: Peter Halban, 1988), p. 492, note 122. See also the account in *Torat Menachem—Hitva'aduyot* vol. 14, p. 133.
99. For an anthology on the spiritual significance of *yechidut* see Avraham Chanoch Glitzenstein (ed.), *Sefer ha-Yechidut* (Kfar Chabad: Kehot, 1989); *Kovetz Yechidut* (New York: Va'ad Talmidei Yeshivat Tomchei Temimim Lubavitch Ha-Merkazit, 2010). From an academic perspective see Zalman Meshullam Schachter-Shalomi, *Spiritual Intimacy: A Study of Counseling in Chasidism* (New Jersey: Jason Aronson, 1991).
100. Liebman, *Orthodoxy*, p. 80; Jonathan Sacks, "In Search of the Soul: Thirty Years of the Lubavitcher Rebbe," *Jewish Chronicle*, 1st February 1980.
101. Ibid.
102. Wiesel (2012 interview).
103. Zalmon Jaffe, *My Encounter with the Rebbe*, vol. 1, (New York: PCL publishing, 2002), p. 23. The twenty-six volumes of Jaffe's memoir, and much of his extensive correspondence with the Rebbe, can be viewed at http://zalmonjaffeencounters.com/ (accessed Feb. 2014).
104. Ibid. pp. 22-23.
105. Swados ibid.
106. Such as Rabbi Avraham Yeshaya Karelitz (1878–1953), author of *Chazon Ish*, Rabbi Yitzchak Zev Soloveitchik (1886–1959), the Brisker Rav, and Rabbi Yisrael Alter (1895-1977), the Gerer Rebbe.
107. Dalfin, pp. 141-6
108. Ibid. pp. 53-60.
109. See Rabbi Yosef Yitzchak Schneersohn (Zalman Posner trans.), *On the Teachings of Chasidus* (New York: Kehot, 1959), chap. 2-3.
110. Dalfin, p. 27*ff.*
111. Letter dated 8th March (24 *Adar* II), 1951 in *Igrot Kodesh*, vol. 4, pp. 222-224.
112. See Chaim Dalfin, *Who's Who in Lubavitch* (New York: Jewish Enrichment Press, 2003), p. 192*ff*; *L'Chaim* (Lubavitch Youth Organization), issue 190.
113. Liebman p. 80.
114. Jacques Lipchitz (with H. Harvard Arnason), *My Life in Sculpture* (Viking Press, 1972), p. 204.
115. 1961 interview with William Berkowitz in *The Reconstructionist* (vol. XL/*Shevat* 1974).
116. *Challenge*, p. 273. For more of Lipchitz's ongoing relationship with the Rebbe see Dovid Zaklikowski, *How Jacques Lipchitz Found G-d*, http://www.chabad.org/therebbe/article_cdo/aid/1025813/jewish/How-Jacques-Lipchitz-Found-G-d.htm (accessed Feb. 2014).
117. Interview with Yaakov Hardof (JEM *Living Torah*, disc. 53, episode 210).
118. Krinsky interview in *Mishpacha* ibid.
119. See Yosef Y. Jacobson, *The Psychiatrist and The Lubavitcher Rebbe*, http://www.algemeiner.net/generic.asp?id=6613 and *The Rebbe and Victor Frankl* http://www.algemeiner.net/generic.asp?id=6634 (accessed Feb 2014); interview with Ya'akov Biderman (JEM Living Torah, Living Torah, Disc 115, Program 459).
120. Rabbi Bernard (Berel) Levy (d. 1987), who acted as an unofficial representative for the Rebbe at *Moetzet* meetings, recalled from a *yechidut* in the early 1960s an explanation offered by the Rebbe why he chose not to attend. Rashab, the Rebbe noted, *did* attend such Rabbinic meetings, but in the light of his large following in Russia, his words carried considerable weight. When Rayatz left Russia, and his following was considerably diminished, he chose not to

attend such meetings where his voice would inevitably be weaker, and exerted influence instead through direct contact with important Rabbinic figures. "I do like my father-in-law," the Rebbe told Levy (interview with Rabbi Don Yoel Levy, JEM *Living Torah*, Disc 99, Program 394).

121. Of these occasions, discussions have been recorded from the Rebbe's visits to Rabbi Yehudah Aryeh Leib Perlow (1877-1961), the Novominsker Rebbe, in 1954; Rabbi Yoel Teitelbaum, the Satmar Rebbe (1887-1979), in 1953; and Rabbi Avraham Yehoshuah Heschel (1888-1967), the Kapishnitzer Rebbe, in 1954. For transcripts of these discussions see *Siach Sarfei Kodesh* (Jerusalem 1998: *Machon Oholei Tzadikim*). More details are found in Wolpo, *Shemen Sason*.

122. *Kol Menachem* archives.

123. See Rabbi Riskin's account of an "empowering" 1964 *yechidut* in Shlomo Riskin, *Listening to G-d: Inspirational Stories for my Grandchildren* (Jerusalem: Maggid Books, 2010), pp. 140-141.

124. See interview with Rabbi Hollander in Dalfin, *Conversations* pp. 71-89.

125. See Mordechai Staiman, *Diamonds of the Rebbe* (New York: Otsar Sifrei Lubavitch, 1998), chapter 16.

126. JEM, *Here's My Story*, August 10, 2013; *Living Torah*, Disc 5, Program 204.

127. Wolfe Kelman, *Moshe Feinstein and Postwar American Orthodoxy*, in William Frankel (ed.) *Survey of Jewish Affairs 1987* (New Jersey: Associated University Presses, 1988), p. 183.

128. For Green's extensive correspondence with the Rebbe see Levi Yitzchak Shaikowitz (ed.), *Professor Green, Greetings and Blessings* (Beit Chabad of Beer Sheva, 2011).

129. Hanoka's thoughts on the age of the universe, influenced by the Rebbe, are published in his *A Time For Everything* (Private publication 2012).

130. For Block's thoughts on philosophy, influenced by his Chabad encounter, see his *G-d, Rationality and Mysticism* (Marquette Univ Press, 2008).

131. Rabbi Yehuda Krinsky explained in 1964 to Samuel Kaplan, the publisher and editor of the *Jewish Western Bulletin* of Vancouver, Canada: "The Rebbe always took a neutral position not only in general political matters but also concerning political issues within the Jewish community, in order to enable persons of every persuasion to approach him for guidance and seek personal acquaintance with him." http://lubavitch.com/news/article/2028658/The-Rebbe-in-1964-On-Jewish-Education-Community-Responsibilty.html (accessed Feb 2014).

132. See http://www.collive.com/show_news.rtx?id=4432 (accessed Feb 2014).

133. *New York Times*, 2nd October, 1964

134. *Ma'ariv*, 18th December 1964.

135. *New York Times*, 22nd May 1963. For an extensive chronicle of the Rebbe's relationship with Shazar see Shmuel Kraus, *Nasi ve-Chasid* (Kfar Chabad: *Agudat Chasidei Chabad*, 1999).

136. Sermon of 15th January (10th *Shevat* 1962), *Torat Menachem—Hitva'aduyot*, vol. 33, p. 30.

137. Sermon of 3rd October (*Simchat Torah* 1961), *Torat Menachem—Hitva'aduyot*, vol. 32, p. 154.

138. Ibid. p. 155-6.

    Besides his general critique of materialism in the local Chabad community, the Rebbe was often also outspoken about specific issues such as: the excessive consumption of alcohol at Chasidic *farbrengens*, overspending on extravagant weddings and unnecessarily long summer vacations.

139. Lipkin and Elitov, p. 308.

140. Ibid. p. 309.

141. Letter of executive committee of *Agudat Chasidei Chabad* in Israel, 28th June (24th *Sivan*) 1951, *Igrot Kodesh* vol. 4, p. 346.

142. Ibid.

143. Letter to executive committee of *Tzeirei Agudat Chabad* in Israel, 10th September (9th *Elul*) 1951, *Igrot Kodesh* vol. 4, p. 463.

144. Babylonian Talmud, *Megillah* 31b.
145. *Igrot Kodesh* ibid. pp. 461-2.
146. *Torat Menachem—Hitva'aduyot* vol. 14, p. 64.
147. Ibid. vol. 18, p. 61*ff.*
148. Rabbi Shneur Zalman, *Likutei Torah,* Leviticus p. 48a.
149. Babylonian Talmud, *Sotah* 49b.
150. Following Isaiah 60:22.
151. *Hitva'aduyot* ibid.
152. Lipkin and Elitov, p. 307.
153. Weiner, ibid.
154. Genesis 28:14.
155. Charles S. Liebman, "Orthodoxy in American Jewish Life," in *American Jewish Year Book,* vol. 66 (1965), pp. 79–92.
156. Jonathan Sacks, "The Man Who Turned Judaism Outwards—A Personal Tribute to the Lubavitcher Rebbe," in *Chabad Journal* (Albany, June 1994).
157. *Ha-Admor he-Hadash mi-Lubavitch* (anonymous editorial), *Ha-Pardes* (25,2) *Iyar* 5711 (1951), p. 24.
158. Yitta Halberstam Mandelbaum, *Holy Brother: Inspiring Stories and Enchanted Tales about Rabbi Shlomo Carlebach* (New Jersey: Jason Aronson, 2002), p. xxix-xxx.
159. 1994 interview with Shlomo Carlebach, *Sha'ah Tova* magazine, November 2009.
160. *Sha'ah Tova* ibid.
161. Ibid. See also Natan Offenbacher, *Rabbi Shlomo Carlebach: Life, Mission, and Legacy* (Urim Publications, 2014), p. 71.
162. 1993 interview in *Practical Wisdom from Shlomo Carlebach, Tikkun Magazine,* Fall 1998.
163. This is how the story is recounted in *Igrot Rayatz,* vol. 1, p. 610. For the 1957 sermon see *Likutei Sichot* vol. 1, p. 100; ibid. p. 225. This message, the Rebbe also argued, is implicit in the *Mishnah's* call to *"love all folk and bring them close to the Torah"* (*Avot* 1:12). The *Mishnah* is suggesting, we ought to engage in outreach ("bring them close to Torah"), but it is the people we must bring closer to the Torah, and not the other way around.
164. This was part of a hugely successful operation of Chabad in Morocco, which had been initially envisioned by Rayatz, to service the 265,000 Jews who inhabited the country after World War II, many of whom were refugees. Chabad established some 70 educational institutions in the area, servicing over 5000 students. However, due to mass emmigration to Israel, by 1967 only 60,000 Jews were left in the country, and Chabad activities were considerably curtailed. See *Challenge: An Encounter with Lubavitch Chabad* (Lubavitch Foundation of Great Britain, 1970), p. 130-131; and, at length, Baruch Sabag, *The Rebbe and Sefardic Jewry* (Heb.), (Israel, 2007).
165. In the case of exceptional Torah scholars, the Rebbe applied the same argument in reverse. For example, the Rebbe advised Rabbi Shlomo Yosef Zevin not to seek a Rabbinic position and complete his *Encyclopedia Talmudit,* since it was "a commandment which cannot be performed by others." See Wolpo, *Shemen Sason* vol. 2, p. 95, 102.
166. Menachem Mendel Schneerson, *Likutei Sichot,* (New York: Kehot, 1990), vol. 23, p. 443.
167. Undated letter from 1964.
168. Weiner ibid. For a collection of the Rebbe's thoughts on college attendance see Menachem Mendel Goldberg, Shalom Heidingsfeld and Bentzion Pape (eds.), *Dem Rebbin's Kinder* (New York: Oholei Torah and Igud Ha-Temimim, 2001), pp. 208-225.
169. The Rebbe was referring to the classic Rabbinic teaching in *Ethics of the Fathers: "Anyone whose fear of sin precedes his wisdom, his wisdom will endure. And anyone whose wisdom precedes his fear of sin, his wisdom will not endure"* (*Avot* 3:9).

170. "Justice shall be the girdle of his loins, and faithfulness the girdle of his waist—eulogy for Rabbi Menachem Mendel Schneerson, the Lubavitch Rebbe," in *Alon Shevut le-Bogrei Yeshivat Har Etzion*, 4th *Tishrei* 5755 (1994), p. 101.

171. Letter dated 10th March (*Rosh Chodesh Adar* II), 1978.

172. Despite the Seventh Rebbe's rejection of "superficial" labels, they nevertheless remained a powerful reference point for American Jews that needed to be reckoned with. If the lines between Orthodox movements, which accepted traditional *halachah*, and others, which did not, would become blurred, "a repentant Jew who wants to 'return' would not know what there was to return to" (Weiner's 1957 interview).

Consequently, the Rebbe chose to embrace the 1956 ban on shared platforms with Conservative and Reform Rabbis, commenting that the issue "strikes deeply at the roots of true Judaism" (Letter dated 21st July (15th *Tammuz*) 1959); but only in instances where Orthodox participation would bring public and formal legitimacy to non-Orthodox groups. Private and informal contact with non-Orthodox Jews, even non-Orthodox Rabbis, was to be encouraged.

"It is necessary to make a distinction between individuals and movements," he clarified in one letter. "For, as an individual Jew, even if he sins, he is a Jew, and it is necessary to do everything *be'ahavah* [with love] to help him back on the right path (see *Tanya*, Chapter 32, *lev* [=heart]). On the other hand, movements and ideologies which are against the Torah must be opposed and exposed" (Letter dated February 24th (22nd *Adar* I) 1965).

It remained important not to be overzealous about imposing distance from Conservative and Reform institutions. In contrast to some Orthodox Rabbis who issued a blanket prohibition on visiting a Conservative or Reform Temple, the Rebbe advised that each situation needs to be judged from both angles. "With regard to your question whether you should visit a Reform institution," he wrote to one questioner in 1960, "generally speaking, in such a question the first consideration is to be careful that one's act will not be misunderstood as an expression of one's personal approval of the institution in question. If there is no basis for such a misunderstanding, the suggestion should be considered" (Letter dated 4th December (15th *Kislev*) 1960).

Thus, in 1962, when the Orthodox Rabbinate in Liverpool, England refused to provide kosher food for a Reform function, the Rebbe expressed his disappointment. "I cannot see on what basis a Jew should be denied *kashrut* facilities, since all Jews, without exception, are bound to observe all *mitzvot*, including *kashrut*," he wrote (Letter to Zalman Jaffe, 30th July, (28th *Tammuz*), 1962, in *Mr. Manchester: Forty Years of Correspondence from the Lubavitcher Rebbe*, (Private publication, 2003), p. 105).

173. Weiner (ibid.). In official correspondence the Rebbe usually made the less ambiguous reference to "the undisputable *halachic* decision formulated by *Rambam* (*Hilchot Teshuvah* 3:8), according to which the doctrines and ideology of the Conservative and Reform movements can only be classed in the category of heretical movements" (Letter dated 21st July (15th *Tammuz*) 1959).

174. A recording of the meeting with Lautenberg is available at http://www.chabad.org/therebbe/article_cdo/aid/551695/jewish/5732-Yechidus-Frank-Lautenberg.htm.

175. Menachem Mendel Schneerson, *Torat Menachem—Hitva'aduyot* vol. 7 (Brooklyn, 2009), pp. 116-7. For further encouragement of the organization see also vol. 11, pp. 64-66; vol. 16, p. 352.

176. See, for example, *Igrot Rayatz* vol. 4, letter 873.

177. *Torat Menachem—Hitva'aduyot*, vol. 9, p. 102.

178. See sermon to the 1958 convention in *Torat Menachem—Hitva'aduyot* vol. 22, p. 316. For a collection of letters to the first twenty-five conventions see *Letters By The Lubavitcher Rebbe shlita, Rabbi M. M. Schneerson To N'shei u'Bnot Chabad 1956-1980* (New York: Kehot, 1981).

179. See *Torat Menachem—Hitva'aduyot*, vol. 18, p. 191. For letters defending this position see *Igrot Kodesh* vol. 8, p. 173; vol. 19, p. 415.

180. For tens of references to such talks in the 1950s see *Sefer ha-Mafteichot le-Torat Menachem—Hitva'aduyot* 5710-9 (New York: Kehot, 2004), entry *nashim*, p. 162-4.

181. For example, expounding upon the verse *"a woman shall encircle a man"* (Jer. 31:22), the Kabbalah had long predicted a reversal of the male-female gender hierarchy, with women surpassing men in the Messianic Era. However, this concept, echoed frequently even in the first generation of Chabad thought, was deemed of no practical significance in pre-Messianic times. This changed with the Seventh Rebbe, who often used the idea to influence contemporary perceptions of womanhood. A striking early example can be found in a 1952 letter to a man who, apparently, had complained to the Rebbe about his wife. After citing the familiar Talmudic instruction to honor one's wife more than oneself, the Rebbe offered a practical insight based on the Kabbalistic trope. "Especially when you consider that we are standing at the end of the Exile, and the perfect Redemption is near, when *'a woman shall encircle a man'*—this alone ought to bring on a sense of respect and care for your wife."

    The exegetical turnaround is so subtle here that it could be easily missed. The teaching that *"a woman shall encircle a man"* was traditionally invoked to illustrate how women will *not* surpass men in the foreseeable future, so long as the Messiah has not come. By rendering the phenomenon as exclusively Messianic, the idea served more to preserve patriarchal dominance than to uproot it. But the Seventh Rebbe, through coloring the current period as "the end of the Exile" when "Redemption is near," blurred the sharp line separating Redemption and Exile, rendering what were previously considered futuristic themes as having contemporary relevance. In a most tangible application, Jewish men ought to have a newfound respect for their wives and for women in general, amid the humbling awareness that in the near future male dominance was to end when *"a woman shall encircle a man."*

    Another striking example of a feminine-positive exegesis is found in a sermon from the summer of 1962, concerning the Matriarchs. In a typically Chasidic paradigm, the sermon depicts both the Patriarchs and Matriarchs not only as historical progenitors of the Jewish people, but, more importantly, as having endowed special soul-powers to all of their descendents. Citing a familiar Kabbalistic characterization of men as tending towards the transcendent, and women as being drawn to the tangible, the Rebbe suggests that all Jews—even men—inherit an invaluable talent from the Matriarchs: the power to maintain awareness of G-d amid tangible, daily life. In a highly unusual feminization of Jewish values, the primary focus of Judaism—which has always been geared towards the sanctification of the physical world, and the practical implementation of spirituality—is depicted as a predominantly female quality. When G-d told Abraham, *"Whatever Sarah tells you, listen to her voice"* (Gen. 21:12), the Rebbe boldly suggests, He was calling upon all Jewish men to nurture their feminine side, a process which is crucial for the destiny of the people of Israel. (Menachem Mendel Schneerson, *Likutei Sichot*, vol. 4 (New York: Kehot, 1964), pp. 1068-9.

    For the above see Ada Rapoport-Albert, *From Woman as Hasid to Woman as Tsadik in the Teachings of the Last Two Lubavitcher Rebbes* in *Jewish History* (2013) 27:435-473. For more examples of the Rebbe's feminine-positive exegesis see Uri Kaploun, *A Partner in the Dynamic of Creation, Womanhood in the Teachings of the Lubavitcher Rebbe, Rabbi Menachem M. Schneerson* (New York: Sichos in Enlgish, 1995); Rabbi Zusya Wolf, *To Jewish Women and Girls: The Jewish Mother, Wife and Daughter in the Thought of the Rebbe* (Heb.) (Kfar Chabad: Kehot, 1996). For an overview of the role of women in Chabad see Eldad Weil, *The Beginning of the Women's Era: Women and Womanhood in the teachings of the Lubavitcher Rebbe* (Heb.), in *Akdamut* 22 (1999), pp. 61-85.

182. Simon Jacobson, *Toward a Meaningful Life, New Edition: The Wisdom of the Rebbe Menachem Mendel Schneerson* (New York: William Morrow, 2004), p. 188.

183. Interview with Yosef Weinberg, February 2010. As early as 1953 Rabbi Pinchas Teitz (1908-1995) conducted Talmud classes over the radio. See Rivkah Teitz Blau, *Learn Torah, Love Torah, Live Torah: HaRav Mordechai Pinchas Teitz, the Quintessential Rabbi* (New Jersey: Ktav, 2001), chapter 10.

184. In one particularly memorable address, he responded to critics from the Satmar community who had argued that radio was a force of evil. "It is impossible for evil to create even the tiniest thing," said the Rebbe, citing proofs from the Talmud (Babylonian Talmud *Sanhedrin* 67a; Jerusalem Talmud *Sanhedrin* end of ch, 7.). Radio, he argued, was a neutral force which could be used for good or bad, and its widespread use for impure matters has not contaminated the medium itself. As always, the Rebbe sought proofs from classic Jewish texts to buttress his point.

    The *Mishnah* states, *"The elders in Rome were asked, 'If He [G-d] has no desire for idolatry, why does He not abolish it?' They replied: 'If people would worship something unnecessary to the world, He would abolish it; but they worship the sun, moon, stars and planets. Should He destroy His universe on account of fools?'"* (*Mishnah, Avodah Zarah* 4:7.). Similarly in our case, just because there are "fools" who employ the power of radio for negative purposes, why should this preclude its positive use?

    Still, people protest: The use of radio is not comparable to the above *Mishnah.* The sun and moon, the purpose of which is to give light, were created *before* fools began to worship them; therefore it makes sense that G-d should not destroy His world on account of fools. But radio was *originally* used for secular and even profane purposes.

    The question, however, stems from ignorance of Jewish sources. The *Midrash* teaches, *"The world was not worthy to use gold. Why, then, was it created? For the sake of the Tabernacle."* (*Genesis Rabbah* 16:2.). Gold first came to light in the six days of Creation and was immediately in evidence, as the verse states, *"The gold of that land is good."* (Genesis 2:12). Yet from creation to the Tabernacle there were twenty-six generations, during which time gold was an object of idol worship.

    Similarly, while the earliest use of radio was for impure purposes, this should not preclude its use for holy purposes, the purpose of its creation. (*Torat Menachem—Hitva'aduyot* 5744, vol. 2 (New York: Va'ad Hanachot Lahak, 1993), pp 1040-1043).

185. JTA, October 10, 1963.

186. Letter dated 14th May (29th *Iyar)* 1953 in *Letters from the Rebbe* (New York, 1998) vol. 4, p. 6.

187. Letter dated 2nd July (23rd Tammuz) 1956, in *Igrot Kodesh,* vol. 13, letter 4555. In a number of letters (cited ibid.), the Rebbe encouraged Rabbi Shlomo Yosef Zevin to press upon the Chief Rabbinate to issue a ban on travelling on the boats.

188. The *Tevet* 5717 issue of *Ohr Ha-Mizrach* publicized a 1954 ruling of Rabbi Frank that travel on the boats was permitted. Upon the Rebbe's request he was visited by a delegation of Chabad Rabbis in the summer of 1957, whereupon Rabbi Frank clarified that he did in fact maintain that travel on the boats was forbidden. The published sanction was an exceptional case, which he requested should no longer be publicized since it would lead to confusion. See *Nitzutzei Rebbi* by Rabbi Mordechai Menasheh Laufer in *Hitkashrut* (*Tzeirei Agudat Chabad* of Israel), issue 872 (2011). See also article by the same author in issue 254 (1999).

189. Rabbi Feinstein had ruled that traveling on the boats was permissible. The Rebbe mailed Rabbi Feinstein a copy of the 2nd July letter sent the Chief Rabbis of Israel, and received a reply written on 16th July (8th *Av*) 1956 (printed in *Igrot Moshe,* vol. 1, p. 150), in which Rabbi Feinstein defended his position. The Rebbe subsequently penned a lengthy response on 22nd July (14th *Av*), printed in *Igrot Kodesh,* vol. 13, letter 4624.

190. *Igrot Kodesh* vol. 15, p. 289.

191. H. Yustos, *Is it Permissible to Travel in an Israeli Liner?* (*Ma'ariv,* 7th August, 1957). The article also reported Rabbi Frank's retraction.

192. *Ha-Pardes* Year 32, Issue 10 (July 1958), pp. 5-10.

193. *Ha-Pardes* Year 33, Issue 5 (February 1959), p. 2. One significant authority who issued such a ruling based on the Rebbe's clarification of the matter, was Rabbi Yitzchak Ya'akov Weiss (1902-1989), in *Minchat Yitzchak,* vol. 3 (New York, 1990), responsum 39.

194. *Letters from the Rebbe* ibid. pp. 12-13.

195. Letter to Marilyn Bell, 11th February (21st *Shevat*), 1958.
196. An influential 1952 article in *Commentary,* Will Herberg argued back that a softer stance on separationism would benefit all Americans, and Jews in particular. "The American Jew must have sufficient confidence in the capacity of democracy to preserve its pluralistic character," he wrote, "without any *absolute* wall of separation between religion and public life." Criticizing Jews for adopting a position which was "extreme and basically secular" he urged them to, "rid themselves of the narrow and crippling minority-group defensiveness." (Will Herberg, *The Sectarian Conflict Over Church and State* in *Commentary* 14 (November 1952), pp. 450-462)
197. Another important proponent of religious aid was Rabbi Moshe Sherer, executive vice-president of the Orthodox *Agudath Israel of America,* who lobbied in favor of the legislation at a hearing of the House Subcommittee on Labor and Education on 29th March, 1961. See http://www.jta.org/1961/03/30/archive/jewish-representatives-testify-on-federal-aid-to-religious-schools (accessed Jan 2014).
198. A Biblical prohibition, see Leviticus 19:14.
199. Maimonides, *Mishneh Torah, Laws of Idol Worship* 9:4.
200. *Shulchan Aruch, Orach Chaim* end of chapter 156. In a 1953 discourse the Rebbe cites several more sources on this issue, see *Torat Menachem—Hitva'aduyot* vol. 7, p. 296, Hebrew note 7.
201. *Likutei Sichot* vol. 8 (New York: Kehot, 1974), pp. 302-4.
202. *Jewish Forum,* May-June, 1962; *New York Times* 20th September and 17th November 1962.
203. pp. 12-13.
204. While the majority of Jews still opposed the legislation, the Rebbe's voice did form part of a growing sympathy for parochial aid, both in the Jewish community and beyond. The *American Jewish Year Book* of 1962 noted that "especially strong support for the Catholic position appeared within the Jewish community, especially among the Orthodox."

    The campaign, as we know, never achieved its goals, but one contemporary author has argued that the special edition of the *Commonweal* permanently redefined the contours of American religious politics. Until that time, the Christian majority had perceived the Jewish community as a single, monolithic unit. In the absence of multiple Jewish voices, the Jewish position on each issue was guided by a strong element of prudence—"Will this upset the Christian world?" was a huge consideration. In 1962, the Jewish community took the bold decision to back, for the first time, a piece of legislation which Christians deeply opposed—the issue of prayer in public schools, which we will soon discuss—and it almost resulted in a collapse of Jewish-Christian relations. Breaking from the mood of harmony which had prevailed since the war, a September 1962 editorial in the Jesuit *America* magazine, warned of a "heightened anti-Semitic feeling."

    The special edition of the *Commonweal,* featuring Jewish thinkers, was groundbreaking as it showed the Christian world that important figures within Jewish ranks were willing to speak out against the majority of their colleagues and side with political positions favored by Christians. The Rebbe's vociferous but unpopular view on school vouchers, which received much rebuke from the Jewish mainstream, shattered the Christian impression that *all* Jews opposed them on crucial issues. This, in turn, empowered the Jewish community with a fresh confidence to voice its political opinions without being intimidated by a potential backlash from Christians, since there would inevitably be some Jewish voices that sympathized with policies of the Christian lobby. As a result of "Schneerson's dissent" and the fact that "Schneerson stood firm against liberal Jewish voices," argued Ben Sales in a 2012 *Jewish Journal* article, "ever since, Jewish and Christian groups have periodically disagreed but maintained an open dialogue... The dispute in 1962 marked a shift in Jewish communal priorities... Today, national Jewish organizations do not tailor their voice solely to ensure peace among religious groups, let alone within the Jewish community. Rather, they aggressively advocate controversial causes... regardless of what the Christian majority thinks." In Sale's opinion, the Rebbe's courage to publicly voice a dissenting opinion from the majority, opened the doors to greater political freedom for the Jewish community for decades to come (Ben Sales, JTA, May 24, 2012).

205. See Proverbs 20:12.

206. Letter dated 8th April (26th *Nissan*), 1964, in *Letters From the Rebbe* vol. 4, pp. 64-74.

In an earlier brief, penned shortly after the Supreme Court decision, the Rebbe offered a detailed response as to why he deemed a non-denominational prayer to be of immense value from a Jewish perspective:

> 1. According to all our authorities, it is a positive commandment to pray to G-d daily.... The Regents Prayer is a valid prayer, especially as it contains two basic elements of prayer: acknowledgment (praise of G-d) and request.
>
> 2. Recognition of the Divine Authority and obedience to it is also one of the imperatives of the Torah, which is to be fulfilled every day. This is the basic purpose of our daily reading of the *Shema*.... Those Jewish children who do not recite the Shema daily could, at least, fulfill that part of it which expresses recognition of the Divine Authority—by means of the Regents Prayer.
>
> 3. The Regents Prayer, expressing as it does the acknowledgment of, and dependence upon, G-d, and that the welfare of this country and of the parents, children and teachers depends on G-d's benevolence, offers in many cases the only opportunity for the children to make some personal "contact" with G-d every day.
>
> 4. The hope expressed in some quarters, that the banning of the Regents Prayer will somehow be compensated eventually by the introduction of more religion into the home, is very doubtful, in the light of the prevailing parental attitude in those circles as mentioned above, towards religion...
>
> 5. As for the argument that the Regents Prayer has little religious value because it would tend to become mechanical and would not reach the heart of the child reciting it, the same argument can be used, and with greater justification, in the case of adults and in regard to any daily prayer in any place....
>
> 6. Those circles which identify themselves with the opposition to the Regents Prayer are quite naturally placed in the same camp with the secularists. There is thus an obvious case of *Chilul Hashem*, the Profanation of G-d's Name, and also to the good name of the Jewish people (that is, *Chilul Hashem* in the eyes of the gentiles).
>
> 7. There is an additional point to be considered: The responsibility which the Jewish religion imposes upon its adherents towards the non-Jew in the matter of dissemination of the belief in G-d. (Letter dated 21st November (24th *Marcheshvan*) 1962 (ibid. p. 42-49)).

207. Jan Feldman, *Lubavitchers as Citizens: A Paradox of Liberal Democracy* (Ithaca and London: Cornell University Press, 2003), p. 45. Feldman offers an astute insight into the Rebbe's approach to American politics, which was already evident in his 1962 positions:

> The Rebbe did not strategize the way public figures usually do; he did not care whether his position won or lost or was popular or unpopular. Public opinion figured not at all in his reasoning. He wanted Lubavitch to be the conscience of American politics. While he voiced tremendous respect for the Constitution and demanded that his followers be scrupulously law abiding, he proposed openly that if the Constitution prohibits school prayer, then the Constitution ought to be changed.
>
> The key to understanding the Rebbe's political positions is to understand his application of Torah to contemporary issues. It was his strong conviction that the Torah could not be at odds with the public good, and therefore, that advocating the *halachic* or Jewish Jaw position on any given policy issue could only benefit all Americans. Because of this, Lubavitch, which might otherwise be described in terms of interest group politics, falls through the cracks of this model, at least at the national level. Here, Lubavitcher initiatives are always intended to pro-

mote the common good and often have no particular, concrete relevance to the Lubavitcher community at all....

The Rebbe's political positions are coherent only when viewed in the context of Torah. Against the standard measure of political coherence employed by Americans, that is, left and right or liberal and conservative, Lubavitch political positions could easily appear inconsistent or contradictory (ibid., pp. 46-7).

In one of his discourses, the Rebbe mentioned an insight from his father-in-law, Rayatz, to clarify this point: "On one of his journeys, he encountered several men who were arguing and expressing differing opinions about the relationship of Torah to political systems, and debating with which system the Torah agreed. Each one of them brought forth as proof a source from Torah in support of his ideology. When they asked the Rebbe for his opinion on this question, he answered: The Torah, since it is the absolute perfection of truth and goodness, contains within itself all of the best ideas which one may find in all ideologies.'" Menachem Mendel Schneerson, *On the Essence of Chassidus* (H. Greenberg and S. Handelman trans.), (New York: Kehot, 1986), p. 12.

208. Notes from conversations with the Rebbe, 1952. http://www.chabad.org/therebbe/article_cdo/aid/664336/jewish/What-is-the-Purpose-of-Life.htm (accessed January 2014).

209. Ibid.

210. Conversation with Hillel Directors, 27th August 27, 1959. http://www.chabad.org/therebbe/article_cdo/aid/987922/jewish/Educating-the-Next-Generation-of-Jews.htm (accessed January 2014).

211. Meeting with Hillel students 7th March 1960. http://www.chabad.org/therebbe/article_cdo/aid/392177/jewish/The-Rebbe-Speaks-to-Hillel-Students.htm (accessed January 2014). He initially cites the analogy in reference to the Ba'al Shem Tov, but later clarifies that it refers to the role of a Rebbe in general.

212. Herbert Weiner, "Farewell, My Rebbe: Thoughts On Leadership" in *New Jersey Jewish News,* June 2, 1994. The full letter is printed in Chaim Dalfin, *Conversations with the Rebbe, Menachem Mendel Schneerson* (Los Angeles: JEC publishing, 1996), pp. 203-6.

213. Weiner, *Nine and a Half Mystics,* ibid.

214. Meeting with Hillel students 7th March 1960.

215. Yehuda Avner, *The Prime Ministers: An Intimate Narrative of Israeli Leadership* (New Milford, Connecticut: The Toby Press, 2010), p. 445. Letter of Nissan Mindel dated Pesach Sheini, 5730, http://crownheights.info/something-jewish/433805/letter-and-spirit-in-defense-of-the-rebbe-and-chabad/. There he adds: "On one occasion, when asked by a student about his helping people in a 'miraculous' way, the Rebbe replied that any Jew who is observant of Torah and *mitzvot* is capable of performing such miracles by virtue of his attachment to the Giver of the Torah and *mitzvot.*"

216. Cited in Rabbi Mordechai Menasheh Laufer, *Machshevei Rebbi* (Private publication, 2000), p. 12.

217. Letter dated 8th April (26th *Nissan*) 1964 in *Letters From the Rebbe* vol. 4, pp. 64-74.

218. Letter dated 11th September (22nd *Elul*) 1963, in *Likutei Sichot* vol. 38, p. 169.

219. Letter dated 20th November (12th *Kislev*) 1961 in *Igrot Kodesh,* vol. 22, letter 8258.

220. Letter dated 2nd *Menachem Av* 1952, in *Igrot Kodesh,* vol. 6, letter 1753.

221. Dalia was educated in London and in 1972 married Avner Rothman, with whom she had two sons: Ariel, in 1975, and Daniel Yehoshua in 1978. The marriage ended in divorce. She has resided for many years in Rechovot, Israel, where she worked in the Weizmann Institute of Science.

222. His death certificate states that he was forty-three, but this follows his false passport in the name of "Mark Gurari" with which he left Russia. His actual birthdate was 3rd May (21st *Iyar*) 1906, which places his death between his secular and Hebrew birthdays. Leibel's body

was taken by boat to Haifa, where it was received by a delegation of sixty Chasidim, who accompanied the deceased to Tzefat, where he was buried (letter of Rabbi Eliezer Krasik to the Rebbe, eve of 15th June (22nd *Sivan*) 1952, in Berger, *Eved Avraham* p. 314). The Rebbe did not attend the funeral, and thanked the participants in a letter (ibid. from *Igrot Kodesh* vol. 6, p. 87).

223. By 1954 the news of Berel's passing had not reached her, though she did fear that he may have been killed (see Chana Schneerson Memoirs, installment 37).
224. Facsimile of some of these signatures is in Levin, *Treasures*, p. 79
225. Chana Schneerson Memoirs, installment 34.
226. Ibid.
227. Ibid. entry of 27th *Tammuz* 1952
228. Ibid. entry of eve *Tisha B'Av* 1952.
229. Ibid. installment 37, entry of 2nd *Menachem Av* 1957.
230. Ibid. installment 36 and 37.
231. Ibid. 3rd day of *Chol Hamo'ed Sukkot* 1953.
232. Ibid. entry of 11th *Tishrei* 1957.
233. Jaffe, *My Encounter* p. 105.
234. For details of the terrorist attack see *Yediot Achronot*, 5th May 1957; Wolf, *Days of the Temimim*, vol. 2, p. 224, ff; Berger, *Eved Avraham* chapter 15; Kraus, *Nasi ve-Chasid*, chap. 18; Moshe Yosef Rubin, *A Father to So Many Chassidim: The Story of Reb Avrohom Drizen Mayorer* (New York: Geder Avos Jewish Heritage Group, 2010), pp. 179-180; editor's introduction to *Igrot Kodesh* vol. 13.
235. *Igrot Kodesh* ibid., p. 41.
236. Ibid. p. 167.
237. See details of the trip in Wolf, pp. 230-243.
238. Rubin, *A Father*, ibid.
239. Sermon of 2nd day of *Shavuot* 1956, in *Likutei Sichot* vol. 12, p. 258.
240. See Zeligson, *Vilenkin*.
241. JTA 14th September, 1964; diaries of Menachem Mendel Wolf, Yisrael Yoel Sosover, and Meir Freiman, available at http://yomanim.com/ (accessed Feb 2014).
242. For notes from these conversations see *Siach Sarfei Kodesh* p. 485*ff.*
243. *American Jewish Yearbook* 1965, p. 82.

CHAPTER 12: RIDING THE COUNTERCULTURE

1. "Rabbi Avraham Lipskier: Fifty Years of *Kiruv*," *Hamodia*, November 8, 2012.
2. For more on Beit Chana see Lynn Davidman, *Tradition in a Rootless World: Women Turn to Orthodox Judaism* (University of California Press, 1991); Edward Hoffman, *Despite All Odds: The Story of Lubavitch* (New York: Simon and Schuster, 1991), chapter 4. For more on Machon Chana, see Branover, chapter 22.
3. Despite earlier opposition, by the early 1970s the Orthodox world outside Chabad was showing openness to the idea of outreach and the nurturing of *ba'alei teshuvah*. Rabbi Noah Weinberg (1930-2009), the son of a Slonimer Chasid, originally met the Rebbe in 1958 to discuss outreach ideas. "In those days everyone who wanted to get involved in *kiruv* (outreach) sought the Rebbe's advice and blessing," he later recalled. While Weinberg had Chasidic blood, he was educated in Lithuanian-style Yeshivot and was uncomfortable with the Rebbe's suggestion to incorporate Chasidic teachings into his outreach efforts (http://www.chabad.org/library/article_cdo/aid/834580/jewish/The-Rosh-Yeshivah-and-the-Shliach.htm—accessed Feb 2014). He chose to work independently, and after a few fledgling efforts, co-founded *Yeshivat Shema Yisrael* for *ba'alei teshuvot* in 1970. Within a few years, he broke

away from that institution—which was later named *Ohr Somayach*—and founded *Yeshivat Aish Hatorah*, in 1974. Both *Yeshivot* were hugely successful and were soon imitated by a variety of other institutions, resulting in the *ba'al teshuvah* becoming a ubiquitous phenomenon in nearly all branches of Orthodoxy. Figures from the first-year attendance in *ba'al teshuvah Yeshivot* in Israel illustrate the trend: 1,200 men and women in 1977; 3,060 in 1987 and 4,180 in 1999 (David Greenberg And Eliezer Witztum, *Sanity and Sanctity: Mental Health Work Among The Ultra-Orthodox In Jerusalem* (Yale University Press, 2001), p. 141).

In America, too, the Lithuanian Yeshivot slowly began to embrace outreach to secular Jews, reversing their earlier opposition to the idea, in what has been dubbed the "Chabadization of American Orthodoxy... a worldview reorientation from a formerly sectarian direction toward a more inclusive, outreach posture" (Adam S. Ferziger, "From Lubavitch to Lakewood: The Chabadization of American Orthodoxy," *Modern Judaism*, Volume 33, Number 2, May 2013, pp. 101-124).

4. Stephanie Wellen Levine, *Mystics, Mavericks, and Merrymakers: An Intimate Journey among Hasidic Girls* (New York University Press, 2003), p. 34. One author has estimated that by 2000, *ba'alei teshuvah* represented fifty percent of the Israeli Chabad community (Adam Jacob Szubin, "Why Lubavitch Wants The Messiah Now" in Albert Baumgarten (ed.), *Apocalyptic Time* (Leiden, Netherlands: Brill, 2000), pp. 218). Even if these rough figures are exaggerated, there is no doubt that returnees represent a huge chunk of the Chabad movement, far greater than in any other Jewish group.
5. Undated letter published in *L'Chaim*, issues 674-5 (Lubavitch Youth Organization, 2001).
6. Babylonian Talmud, *Brachot* 34b.
7. Maimonides, *Laws of Repentance* 7:4. A further advantage possessed by the returnee follows the Talmudic principle that *teshuvah* can actually transform previous sins into merits (Babylonian Talmud, *Yoma* 86b.), a feat which the observant Jew does not have the opportunity to accomplish. These merits, which were once sins, are of a far superior quality to regular *mitzvot*, since they rescue sparks of holiness which have fallen and become captives to the forces of evil (*Derech Mitzvotechah* 191a; *Likutei Sichot* vol. 17, p. 187; *Sefer Ha-Ma'amarim Melukat* vol. 1, p. 56; vol. 2, p.70; vol. 4, p. 140 note 60. See also *Tanya* chapter 7).
8. With all the idealism, transition from a secular existence to an observant one is fraught with considerable challenges: hostility from parents; ridicule from friends; the need to become familiar with a vast range of complex rituals and Jewish texts, as well as new languages such as Hebrew, Aramaic and Yiddish. During the adjustment period, which usually spans several years, the *ba'al teshuvah* needs to remain focused, and can easily be derailed—as the Rebbe explained to one individual:

> "The transition from one mode of living to another, is fraught with trials and tribulations. Therefore, the sooner this critical period is over, the better. It requires determination and fortitude, and where these are not lacking (they are certainly not lacking potentially, and need only be brought to the surface), the difficulties will turn out to be much less insurmountable than they had loomed at first. It may sometimes require an initial leap to break away from the past, but then slowly but surely the going becomes increasingly easier. One must try to shorten the birth pangs of the transition and all the sooner emerge into the newfound world of Torah and *mitzvot*, which holds the key to inner harmony and peace, true fulfillment and happiness....
>
> "You write about the clash between your original decision to follow what you know as the right way and your parents' reactions. But even from the parents' viewpoint, surely their first and ultimate desire is to see their children happy. Whatever their ideas of happiness may be, they surely realize that without inner harmony and peace of mind, life is a very dismal thing. Looking at the situation from their viewpoint, if you act under pressure and accept a life of compromise, it is possible that for a time friction will be avoided. But one must think in terms of a lifetime, not of immediate expedience; and, as outlined above, and as clearly

indicated in your letter, this is the kind of life with which you will not be able to make peace. Sooner or later your parents will notice, or instinctively feel, that they had defeated their own objective" (Letter in *L'Chaim* ibid.).

We also find a number of letters written by the Rebbe to troubled parents whose children were on the path of *teshuvah*. Here, understandably, the Rebbe tended to employ an argument of psychological wellbeing, rather than one of religious imperative. For example, to one mother who was concerned at her son's growing a beard, the Rebbe wrote, in 1966:

"He is in transition from youth to maturity, a time of life that entails considerable strain. During the sensitive period of adolescence, it is particularly important not to do anything that might aggravate the strain.... It is obviously the sacred duty of every near and dear one, and especially of parents, to do everything that may be conducive to the teenager's peace of mind and to make his struggle easier, and certainly to avoid anything which might weaken his willpower to resist the influences of the street, *etc.*

"Inasmuch as your son has adopted a particular approach to the question of shaving, and has done so despite the fact that this makes him different from many young people of his age, including some of his own friends—yet he desires to adhere to this practice, this is clear proof of the importance which he attaches to it as part of his outlook and religious conduct. Therefore, any attempt, to try to discourage him from this would be like trying to dislodge a brick in the structure which your son has built up for himself, an act which could bring down the entire structure. As already asserted, this would be inadvisable under any circumstances, and in any environment, and especially here in the United States of this day and age. For this is not a question concerning a difference between an extreme attitude and a moderate one, but is directly related to the inner peace of the individual" (Letter dated 1966).

9. Personal communication with Shneur Zalman Gafni.
10. See *Sichot Kodesh* 5740, vol. 3, pp. 102-3.
11. Letter dated 13th October (2nd day of *Rosh Chodesh Cheshvan*) 1977, in Rabbi Mordechai Menasheh Laufer (ed.) *Heichal Menachem* vol. 2 (Jerusalem: Heichel Menachem, 1995), p. 76.
12. Lubavitcher Rebbe Memorial Lecture, Logan Hall, London, September 11, 1994.
13. Isi Leibler, *The Case for Israel* (Melbourne: The Executive Council of Australian Jewry, 1972), p. 60.
14. Ibid. p. 18.
15. Ariel Sharon (with David Chanoff), *Warrior* (New York: Simon and Schuster, 1989), p. 182.
16. Telegram to Yehudah Leib Ives, Shmuel Menachem Mendel Langsam, Shmuel Rodel, and Shlomo Shwartz in *Igrot Kodesh* vol. 24, p. 332.
17. Ibid. p. 333.
18. Ibid.
19. Ibid.
20. *Ha'aretz*, *Hatzofeh*, *Ma'ariv* and *Yediot Achronot* 25th May 1967; *Davar* 26th May 1967; *She'arim*, 30th May 1967.
21. Reported in *Ma'ariv* 19th May 1967.
22. Diary of Rabbi Avraham Gerlitzky, 23rd *Iyar* 1967 (http//www.yomanim.com, accessed February 2014).
23. *Esther Rabah* 9:4.
24. *Likutei Sichot* vol. 7, p. 333.
25. Gerlitzky diary.
26. *Hitkashrut* (Chabad Youth Organization, Israel), issue 94 (1996).
27. Gerlitzky diary.

28. *Ha-Melech Be-Mesiboh* vol. 1, p. 181. The full verse reads: *"If you go out to war against your enemies, and see a horse and chariot, a people more numerous than you—you should not be afraid of them! For G-d is with you."*
29. Wolpo, *Shemen Sason* vol. 3, p. 220.
30. Gerlitzky diary. Gerlitzky himself writes, "I don't know if the story is true."
31. See Exodus 13:9, 16; Deut. 6:8, 11:18.
32. Babylonian Talmud, *Menachot* 44a.
33. Ibid. *Berachot* 6a, referring specifically to the head *tefilin.*
34. *Sichot Kodesh* 5727, vol. 2, p. 126.
35. Boston Globe, 24th November, 1967. See also editor's introduction to *Igrot Kodesh* vol. 24.
36. See *Ma'ariv,* 26th July 1967.
37. Letter to Ariel Sharon 17th October (13th *Tishrei*) 1967, *Igrot Kodesh* vol. 28, p. 4.
38. Rabbi Yosef Karo, *Shulchan Aruch, Orach Chaim* 38:4.
39. See Rabbi Yoel Teitelbaum, *Al Ha-Geulah ve-al Ha-Temurah* (Brooklyn, 1967), p. 101, 104-5. The attack was reported in the Israeli press—*Ma'ariv,* 29th November 1967.
40. *Sichot Kodesh* 5728, vol. 2, p. 139.
41. *Likutei Sichot* vol. 6, p. 273. See ibid. pp. 271-5 for a response to several complaints about the campaign.
42. See Levin, *Treasures* p. 88.
43. Reproduced in Wolpo, *Shemen Sasson,* vol. 1, p. 234. See also ibid. p. 235, for a similar declaration of support for the Rebbe's campaign for young girls to light Shabbat candles, in 1974, signed by twenty leading Rabbis.
44. See Mindel, *The Letter and the Spirit* vol. 1, pp. 251-252; *Igrot Kodesh* vol. 19, pp. 444-445.
45. See Mindel, *Letter* p. 324*ff.*
46. Interview with Ephraim Ilin in JEM, *Here's My Story* August 31, 2013. "This plant could be the foundation for all of Israel's industry," the Rebbe told Ilin, pushing him to invest in Israel after Ford had pulled out due to the threat of Arab boycott.
47. See *Sichot Kodesh* 5729, vol. 1 p. 486.
48. 1985 letter in *Heichal Menachem* vol. 1 (Jerusalem: Kehot Publication Society, 1994), page 158*ff.*
49. See *Igrot Kodesh* vol. 11, pp. 167-8; p. 253, p. 385. See *Hitkashrut* (Chabad Youth Organization, Israel), issue 95.
50. See *Igrot Kodesh* vol. 13, p. 293; Mindel, *Letter,* 244; *Likutei Sichot* vol. 23, p. 337.
51. See *Sichot Kodesh* 5736, vol. 2, p. 633*ff; Igrot Kodesh* vol. 24, pp. 404-405; vol. 29, pp. 37-38; 62-63.
52. See JTA, 5th July 1974; *Maariv,* 17th August 1976, p. 4; Harari, p. 230.
53. For an anthology of the Rebbe's teachings on these topics see Menachem Mendel Schneerson (Yosef Yitzchak Havlin, ed.), *Sha'arei Eretz Yisrael* (Jerusalem: Heichal Menachem, 2002). See also Mindel, *Letter,* pp. 231-345.
54. Rabbi Zusya Wolf (ed.), *Days of the Temimim: Fifty Years of Activities in Building and Expanding Chasidut Chabad in the Holy Land,* 8 vols. (Kfar Chabad: Kehot, 2008-2010).
55. He would often repeat to them the teaching of *Tzemach Tzedek* "make here into the land of Israel" (see *Igrot Rayatz,* vol. 1, p. 485). The notion of a Holy Land, he argued, was a vehicle for Divinity, and therefore, entry into the land in the spiritual sense can be achieved even outside of the land. "Israel" can be made in any place where a person makes use of the physical things a vehicle for the holy. See, for example, *Torat Menachem—Hitva'aduyot* 5742, vol. 3, p. 145.
56. Lecture by Ariel Sharon in Kfar Chabad, 29th November 1969.

    In a 1960 letter concerning the expansion of Kfar Chabad II, Ben Gurion showed a profound appreciation for the efforts of Chabad to settle in Israel. "I am pained by your comment," Ben Gurion wrote to Mapai leader Abraham Hartzfeld (1888-1973), "that you are in doubt whether the establishment of Kfar Chabad II will actually transpire. Why not? There is something special about having Jews such as these settle... Meanwhile, there is no hope from the Zionists, but Chasidim... come and settle here. They also have the advantage of having many children. Why would you not give them permission to establish the Kfar?" (Letter from David Ben Gurion to Abraham Hartzfeld, 14th September 1960, http//www.col.org.il/68378_חדשות_חבד_יום_העצמאות_חתונה_ללא_חתן_טור_נוקב.html, accessed Feb 2014).

57. See *Hitkashrut* ibid.

58. The Rebbe received much criticism from those to his religious right, who deemed his close ties with secular Zionists and positive support of Israel highly inappropriate. Most vociferous was Rabbi Yoel Teitelbaum, the Satmar Rebbe, who was harshly critical of what he termed "otherwise righteous Jews" who sought to "embrace and cleave to the wicked" (*Al Ha-Geulah*, p. 31, 118-19). Rabbi Teitelbaum argued that Zionism was theologically odious, representing a deeply misguided human attempt to usurp the Messianic prerogative. In his sustained, vitriolic polemic, Rabbi Teitelbaum painted those who have political or institutional ties with the State of Israel as treacherous opportunists. In the 1950s, relations between the Lubavitcher and Satmar Rebbes had been respectful, and Rabbi Teitelbaum had reportedly praised the Rebbe as having a "once-in-a-generation memory," and as being "no less a zealot than us, just in a different way" (Wolpo, *Shemen* vol. 2, p. 136). While Satmar had always been disapproving of Chabad outreach efforts, tensions escalated after the Six Day War victory, which the Rebbe declared was a miracle from G-d for which we ought to show our gratitude (See sermons of 12th *Tammuz* (par. 6) and *Shabbat Parshat Masei* (par. 2) 1967). "To Satmar this was totally unacceptable," one observer noted. "To them he was taking the depths of evil and bringing it up" (Jerome Mintz, *Hasidic People: A Place in the New World* (Cambridge, Mass: Harvard University Press, 1992), p. 53).

"One shouldn't talk about miracles done by the *sitra achrah* (forces of evil)," the Satmar Rebbe argued in one of his many sermons on the topic. "Even if there were real miracles, we need to conceal this fact and describe events in natural terms as much as possible, out of the concern for negative consequences. Unfortunately due to our great sins, the opposite is done. There is talk and publicity about miracles of Satan which in fact have no basis in reality. They are nothing more than phony miracles that have been produced to fool the masses and to attract them to heresy and rebellion against G-d and His holy Torah. All Jews must avoid talking about these miracles so that they do not have a portion in the denial of G-d and His holy Torah" (Rabbi Yoel Teitelbaum, *Divrei Yoel*, vol. 7 (Brooklyn, 1980), p. 415).

The Lubavitcher Rebbe responded privately to these claims in response to a Satmar sympathizer who had asked in a letter, "How could this be a Divine miracle? Would G-d show a miracle through those who oppose Him?"

The Rebbe wrote: "Certainly, the salvation of 2.5 million Jews in the Holy Land (including Yeshivot etc,), is a miracle from Heaven. If not, 1) Why and for what purpose was there a directive in Williamsburg to say *Tehillim*? 2) What was achieved through this?" The Satmar leadership, which was centered in the Williamsburg district of Brooklyn, had encouraged followers to recite *Tehillim* (Psalms) during the war, to beseech G-d for mercy. Such a directive is indicative of a conviction that a huge salvation was necessary, which could only come from G-d.

As for the fact that the miracle occurred through secular Zionists, the Rebbe noted that, "Dr. Kastner was one," referring to Rudolf Kastner (1906–1957), an Austro-Hungarian activist who helped Jews escape Nazi-occupied Hungary, "and nevertheless he [the Satmar Rebbe] was saved through his assistance"—an event for which Rabbi Teitelbaum made a "feast of gratitude" on 21st *Kislev* each year (Undated letter from the summer of 1967 in *Igrot Kodesh* vol. 24, p. 405. See also Wolpo, *Shemen* vol. 3, p. 140).

On another occasion, when asked by Rabbi Menachem Benzion Wilhelm, why Chabad reaches out to secular Zionists, the Rebbe pointed to a similar Satmar inconsistency. "The

Senator of New York is seated next to the Satmar Rebbe, at the head of the table... yet everyone knows he is a non-observant Jew who publicly desecrates the Sabbath" (ibid. p. 137).

59. See Aviezer Ravitzky (Michael Swirsky and Jonathan Chipman trans.), *Messianism, Zionism, and Jewish Religious Radicalism* (University Of Chicago Press, 1996), chapter 1.
60. Rayatz met with Shazar in Israel in 1929 and was not in further contact until a week before the call, when he had written a letter to Shazar, on 10th November, asking to discuss the possibility of immigration of refugees to Israel (*Igrot Rayatz,* vol. 13, p. 450-1).
61. Speech of Zalman Shazar in 1960, printed in Y. L Maimon, *Sefer Ha-Besht* (Jerusalem: Mosad Harav Kook, 1960), p. 106; and in Zalman Shazar, *Ohri Dorot* (Jerusalem 1971). See Kraus, *Nasi* pp. 85-88 for multiple accounts of this story. Shazar joined the *Yud Tet Kislev farbrengen* at 770, on Monday 1st December, at which Rayatz spoke publicly about the First Chabad Rebbe's involvement with settlements in the Holy Land (See Yosef Yitzchak Schneersohn, *Sefer Ha-Sichot* 5706-5710 (New York: Kehot, 2001), p. 181). In a 1960 sermon (cited in note 10 ibid), the Seventh Rebbe noted the connection between Rayatz's comments at the *farbrengen* and the idea of Kfar Chabad which was initiated at that time
62. *Igrot Kodesh,* vol. 16 pp. 215-216; vol. 26, p. 143*ff,* p. 167*ff.*
63. *Igrot Kodesh,* vol. 12, p. 414; ibid. vol. 13, p. 76*ff.* Similarly he advised his followers to avoid activities which showed formal support of the State's ideology, "since Lubavitch is active in all locations, we have adopted the policy not to become entangled in any matter of factionalism.... since the defining purpose of Chabad is nothing other than unadulterated Torah and *mitzvot,* devoid of any factional ideology" (Letter to Rabbi Shnuer Zalman Serebransky, dated 14th *Elul* 1957). See also *Igrot Kodesh* vol. 11, p. 28.
64. *Yechidut* of 12th August 1967, reported in *Ma'ariv,* 5th September 1967.
65. Interview with Moshe Peled (Professor Moshe Pelli, b. 1936) in *Haboker* 25th September 1957.
66. *Yechidut* with Rabbi Moshe-Zvi Neria (1913-1995), 2nd *Kislev* 5728, in Wolpo, *Shemen* vol. 3, p. 134.
67. The Rebbe believed that even secular Israel was fertile ground for increased Torah observance. In this vein, he endeavored to utilize his connections in the echelons of Israeli society and government towards this goal. In a 1959 letter to Ben Gurion, the Rebbe made his vision clear.

> It was once fashionable in certain circles to suggest that the Jewish religion and religious observances were necessary for those living in the Diaspora—as a shield against assimilation. But for those who can find another "antidote"—in the place of religion, particularly for those living in *Eretz Yisrael,* within their own society, where the atmosphere, language, etc., (apparently) serve as ample assurances of national preservation, the Jewish religion was superfluous—what need had they to burden themselves with all its minutiae in their daily life? But the trend of developments in *Eretz Yisrael* in the last seven or eight years has increasingly emphasized the opposite view: That however vital the need for religion amongst Diaspora Jewry, it is needed even more for the Jews in *Eretz Yisrael.* One of the basic reasons for this is that it is precisely in *Eretz Yisrael* that there exists the danger that a new generation will grow up, a new type bearing the name of Israel but completely divorced from the past of our people and its eternal and essential values, and moreover, hostile to it in its world outlook, its culture, and the content of its daily life; hostile—in spite of the fact that it will speak Hebrew, dwell in the land of the Patriarchs, and wax enthusiastic over the Bible...
>
> The thirst of the youth of our eternal people will certainly not be quenched by rationalizations and theories that are the product of contemporary mortals, which will share the fate of those ideologies which made their debut only yesterday and which are no more today. Here is the place for the Law of Moses and Israel, the Oral and Written Law, our independent values dating from the day the

Jewish people stood before G-d, our G-d, at Horeb, and the great voice was heard which did not stop: *"I am G-d your G-d... You shall have no other gods..."*

Needless to say, I do not speak here of a theoretical religiosity which serves only as a purely philosophical world outlook, or as the subject of lectures at weekends and holidays. I speak of a pervading and practical way of life, which includes the weekdays too, and all such matters which are usually termed "secular." Our faith is, after all, essentially one of practical deeds.

Now is the ideal opportunity to transform the whole canvas of life in *Eretz Yisrael* and direct it into the abovementioned channels. This opportunity is knocking at your door, for you have been granted the ability and privilege to use it to the best advantage, a privilege and opportunity which are not given to every man, and the likes of which have not presented themselves for many decades.

It is more than likely that the aforementioned lines will astonish you. Do I really imagine that by means of this letter I can change or influence an outlook many decades old, and in particular, the outlook of a man who has seen the fruit of his labors? But, since in my opinion the situation in *Eretz Yisrael* is as described above—the situation in itself, the essential truth of the idea, the unique and most wonderful opportunity granted you—it is they which speak, appeal and demand (Letter to David Ben Gurion, 17th February (9th *Adar* I), 1959).

68. For an elaboration of the *Atchalta De-Geulah* position see: Rabbi Menachem Mendel Kasher, *Ha-Tekufah Ha-Gedolah* (Machon Torah Shleima, 1968); Ravitzky, chapter 3.

69. Undated letter (facimile in Wolpo ibid p. 10).

In a number of sermons and letters the Rebbe vehemently rejected the argument, pointing to what he felt were its undesirable consequences. The following excerpt from a 1968 letter is typical.

It is clearly explained both in the Written Torah, as well as in the Oral Torah, that insofar as Jews are concerned, *Galut* (Exile) comes not as a result of military circumstances, namely an outnumbered army, nor as a result of economic pressures necessitating submission to a stronger power, etc. Rather it has amply been explained again and again... that if Jews had always adhered to the Torah and *mitzvot*, they would have never been banished into Exile....

In the light of the above, the true test of events, to see if they herald the *Geulah* (Redemption) or not, is to see whether there has been an essential change in the causes which have brought about the *Galut* in the first place, namely, a new tendency in the direction of stronger adherence to the Torah and *mitzvot*.

The normative Jewish ruling on the matter, in the Rebbe's view, was Maimonides' Code, which, he proceeded to cite, with some elaborations.

"And when a king of the House of David will arrive, dedicated to the study of the Torah and observance of the mitzvot like his father David, according to the Written and Oral Torah, and he will compel all the Jewish people to walk in it and strengthen its fences, and he will fight the wars of G-d, he is assumed to be the Mashiach." (Note that this is not yet a certain sign of the *Geulah*, for all this can still take place in a state of *Galut*. However) *"If he did so and has succeeded* (in the above matters, namely having won all battles and impelled all the Jewish people to study the Torah and to mend its fences, we are still not sure and require a further sign, namely), *and built the Holy Temple in its place* (clearly in the holy city of Jerusalem, indicating that there would be a large Jewish population in that city, yet we are still not certain of the end of the *Galut*, so a further factor must be fulfilled, namely), *and he gathers in the dispersed ones of Israel—then he is certainly the Mashiach...."* (Maimonides, *Laws of Kings* 11:4).

> It is clear from the above ruling of the Rambam that before there can be an ingathering of exiles and the rebuilding of the Holy Temple in its place, there has to be a full and complete return to the Torah and *mitzvot* while Jews are still in the *Galut*, and it is this that is the prelude and preparation for the *Geulah*.

In a concluding passage, the Rebbe highlights what he deemed to be the danger implicit in the belief of *Atchalta De-Geulah*.

> It is simply painful to contemplate how misplaced the concern is of some well-meaning individuals.... Firstly, it is simply a deception of Jews to believe that there can be any other way of *Geulah* than that which G-d had specified, and secondly, while engaged in other ways and means in futile effort to end the *Galut*, they cannot engage fully in the true battle against the *Galut* in terms of the ruling of the Rambam" (Letter dated 15th August (21st *Menachem Av*) 1968 in *Letters from the Rebbe*, vol. 2 (New York, 1997), pp. 69-73).

70. The correspondence, which dates to the early 1980s, is reproduced in Peter Kalms, *Guidance From the Rebbe 1961-1993, Personal Recollections* (London: Lubavitch Foundation , undated), appendix 1.

Insisting that the issue was one of security and had nothing to do with the special sanctity of the Land, the Rebbe cited *halachic* proof—from a ruling that the Sabbath may be transgressed to protect border towns surrounded by non-Jews, even when they have not shown hostility:

> *"When it is a city close to the border, then, even if they want to come only for the purpose of taking straw and stubble, we desecrate the Sabbath because of them; otherwise they may conquer the city, and from there the land will be easy for them to conquer"* (*Shulchan Aruch, Orach Chaim*, chapter 329, par. 6,7).
>
> The said ruling, deals with a situation where gentiles besiege a Jewish border-town, ostensibly to obtain 'straw and chaff,' and then leave. But because of the possible danger, not only to the Jews of the town, but also cities, the *Shulchan Aruch* rules that upon receiving news of the gentiles (even only preparations), the Jews must mobilize immediately and take up arms even on *Shabbat* — in accordance with the rule that "*pikuach-nefesh* (danger to life) supersedes *Shabbat*."
>
> I have repeatedly emphasized that this ruling has nothing to do with the sanctity of *Eretz Yisrael*, or with 'days of Mashiach,' the *Geulah*, and similar considerations, but solely with the rule of *pikuach-nefesh* (Kalms, ibid.).

The Rebbe did, however, maintain a strong conviction that the Land of Israel belonged to the Jewish people, and would often cite *Rashi's* comment at the opening of his commentary to the Torah, that the entire Book of Genesis was written to repudiate gentile claims against Jewish ownership of the Land.

The underlying problem behind the willingness to make concessions, the Rebbe felt, was a lack of Jewish pride, as he explained in a 1973 letter:

> As for the practical thing which Jews everywhere can do to help the present situation... is that every Jew must strengthen his bonds with the Torah from Sinai, when G-d made us the "chosen people." This is also something of which we need not be ashamed, for contrary to those who misunderstand or misrepresent this in terms of privilege which smacks of chauvinism, this chosenness is primarily a matter of duty and obligation to be a model people for the whole world to emulate, a people where form takes precedence over matter, the spiritual over the material, and the soul over the body, a people which was destined to be *"a light unto the nations"* (*Isaiah* 42:6, *etc.*). It is this kind of life and conduct which the Torah describes that also stimulates right thinking and the proper outlook on life.

It is this kind of life that also strengthens the self-confidence of every Jew wherever he may be, and enables him to shed any inferiority complex and the readiness to be impressed by a non-Jew, or by an idea which comes from a non-Jew, or actually non-Jewish ideology. It is sad indeed when, instead of being a model and a living example for non-Jews to emulate, some Jews fall over themselves to emulate non-Jews, rejecting the "spring of living waters," the Jewish Torah and Jewish tradition, etc....

When the adversary sees that his opponent is spiritually and psychologically strong and self-confident and certain of his just cause and not prone to be impressed by the adversary or any non-Jew due to the inferiority complex mentioned above—this is the best way of preventing wars, not only major wars, but even wars of attrition. It is hardly to be expected that a Jew, who in his personal life is afraid to show that he is a proud Jew, whether at home or outside, who prefers to stack his library with non-Jewish volumes and authors, etc., and who makes sure to bring up his children in a way that when they walk in the street they should show no signs of being Jewish, yet this same Jew should draw the line and take a different posture when he meets a political adversary and engages in political negotiations with representatives of other countries. Could such a Jewish representative truly consider himself at least equal to the gentile adversary in such a confrontation, having tried all his life to emulate and follow slavishly the gentile world and way of life? And whatever pretense and facade he might make, will surely not convince the adversary (Letter dated 26th December (*Rosh Chodesh Tevet*) 1973).

71. Levi Groner and Moshe Karishovsky (ed.), *Karati V'en Oneh*, (Jerusalem: M.L. Publications, 2002). The title, a citation from Isaiah 50:2, was employed by the Rebbe himself in a 1970 talk, during which he cried bitterly (ibid p. 13). For the reference to screaming when in pain, see sermons of 19th *Kislev* 5743, *Shabbat Parashat Miketz* 5744, and *Zot Chanukah* 5746. For a written version, see *Me-Otzar Hamelech* (Brooklyn, 2005), p. 219.

    For selections from the Rebbe in English on the topic of territorial integrity see Mordechai Sones and Yankel Koncepolski: *When Silence is a Sin: The Obligation to Protest and The Obligation to Settle the Entire Land of Israel* (New York: Sichos in Engish, 2005); Eliyahu Touger, *Eyes Upon The Land* (New York: Sichos in English, 1997). For full-length treatments of the Rebbe's view see Rabbi Shalom Wolpo, *Da'at Torah Be'inyanei Ha-Matzav B'Eretz HaKodesh* (Kiryat Gat: Private Publication, 1981), *Shalom Shalom V'Ein Shalom* (Jerusalem, Private Publication, 1982); Rabbi Yosef Yitzchak Gutnick, *Shleimut Ha-Aretz* (Private Publication, 1996).

72. *Yechidut* with Rabbi Chaim Gutnick, 12th August 1967, printed in *Kuntres Tzadik Le-Melech* vol. 6, (New York 1993), p. 179. The *Yechidut* was reported, in part, in *Ma'ariv*, 5th September, 1967, p. 10.

73. *Igrot Kodesh* vol. 25, p. 2*ff.* Gansburg's autobiography from 1927-1964 has been published in *Chayal Be-Sheirut Ha-Rebbi* (New York, 2000).

74. Diary of Rabbi Leibel Groner (http://yomanim.com/images/4/4c/_27%ר_-_תמוז_תשכ"ח_יהודה_לייב_גראנער.pdf).

75. *L'Chaim* issue 666 (2001).

76. Interview with Rabbi Zev Segal, JEM Living Torah, Disc 41.

77. Interview with Rabbi Jean (Yehoshua) Kling in *Kfar Chabad*, issue 685. If this account is accurate, it obviously could not have occurred at the June 19th, meeting since the plane was hijacked on July 23rd. Segal, however, mentions that Sharon came "to say goodbye" to the Rebbe, so Kling's account might have transpired at a shorter visit en route to the airport.

78. Letter to Ariel Sharon dated 5th September (12th *Elul*) 1968, in *Igrot Kodesh* vol. 25, p. 227*ff.*

79. Lecture by Ariel Sharon in Kfar Chabad, 29th November 1969.

80. Interview with Ariel Sharon 2000, JEM.

81. Letter to Rabbi Immanuel Jakobovitz in Kalms ibid.
82. Letter dated 11th November (16th *Cheshvan*) 1973, in *L'Chaim* (Lubavitch Youth Organization), issue 676 (2001). For more on the summer campaign see editor's introduction to *Igrot Kodesh* vol. 28, pp. 10-13; *Likutei Sichot* vol. 13, p. 166*ff.* vol. 14, p. 261*ff.*

    For a detailed account of the Rebbe's public statements preceding and during the war, see Chaim Brook, *To Still the Enemy and Avenger: Forty Years since the Miracles of the Yom Kippur War* (Heb.), (New York, 2014).
83. Babylonian Talmud, *Shabbat* 119b.
84. *Igrot Kodesh* vol. 28, p. 358; *Likutei Sichot* vol. 13, p. 268.
85. Rashi to Genesis 45:18
86. Sermon of 9th October (13th *Tishrei*) 1973, *Likutei Sichot* vol. 14, p. 404.
87. 1973 letter cited above.
88. Notes of *yechidut* penned by Ran Pekar (*Kol Menachem* archive).
89. Letter dated 1980 to editors of *B'nai Brith Messenger,* Los Angeles, California. For more on Camp David see sermons of *Motzoei Shabbat Parshat Ha'azinu,* 13 *Tishrei,* 5739; *Motzoei Shabbat Parshat Chaye Sarah,* 5739; *Shabbat Parshat Sisa,* 5740; 24th *Tevet* 5742; *Shabbat Parshat Mikeitz,* 5744; *Purim* 5745; and *Zot Chanukah* 5746. For a summary of the Rebbe's position see Rabbi Yosef Loebenstein, *An Analysis of the Camp David Peace Process* (http://www.sichosinenglish.org/essays/17.htm, accessed Feb 2014). For a handwritten note that the Rebbe penned to Menachem Begin on the issue, see *Teshurah Avtzon-Simpson* 3rd *Shevat* 5765 (2005), p. 17.
90. Sermon of 24th *Tevet* 5742.
91. Meeting with Moshe Katzav, then Transportation Minister of Israel, 15th January 1992, in Sones and Koncepolski, Appendix E.
92. While the main body of the letter was brief and to the point, the Rebbe appended a lengthy postscript adding some reasoning to the matter:

    > All that follows now is merely an additional postscript, written with the intention of emphasizing that even if the following is not accepted, either in part or in full, this does not detract at all from the finality of the opinion I have outlined above....
    >
    > a) The question of registration, or however it may be described, is not a matter confined to Israel alone. It goes without saying—as explained in your letter—that no one may raise a barrier between the Jews of Israel and those of the Diaspora. On the contrary, all our brethren, wherever they may be, have constituted one people, from the moment of their emergence, in spite of their dispersion in all the corners of the world. Consequently, the solution to the problem must be one that is acceptable to all members of the Jewish people everywhere, that is, capable of forging and strengthening the bonds of unity of all Jews, and certainly not one that would be cause, even the remotest, of disunity and dissension. Accordingly, even if you may argue that the present conditions in *Eretz Yisroel* call for a special study of the abovementioned question, these conditions do not restrict the problem to *Eretz Yisroel,* but, as noted, constitute a matter of common concern to every Jew everywhere.
    >
    > b) The belonging to the Jewish people was never considered by our people as a formal, external matter. It has always been defined and delineated in terms of the commitment of the whole being of the Jew, something intimately linked with his very essence and innermost experience. Accordingly, any movement which disregards or belittles any of the procedures in this connection degrades the feeling of belonging to the Jewish people and cannot but be detrimental to the serious and profound attitude toward the Jew's inner link with his people.

c) To ease the conditions of transition and affiliation to the Jewish people—particularly in the special circumstances of *Eretz Yisroel*, surrounded by countries and peoples unsympathetic towards it (that is an understatement)—is to endanger considerably the security of *Eretz Yisroel*.

d) What emerges from the above points is that even if an attempt is made to avoid the proper solution to the problem by a compromise, such as substituting for the word "Jew" a word of completely secular connotations, this will not constitute a way out, since the damage would remain both with respect to strengthening the bonds of unity with Jews everywhere, as well as from the point of view of inner strength and security.

e) Of course, no argument can be adduced from the cases of persons who have been converted in the proper manner and have nevertheless caused harm to the Jewish people. The demand for the due conversion procedure is likewise not negated by the fact that there are "non-Jewish saints" who, as the description implies, are for all that, still "non-Jews."

f) In the frame of reference in which the question was put, the matter of discrimination was mentioned. Discrimination can, however, only apply to granting or withholding of rights, or meting our punishments; it can have no relevance to the question of registration which has to do with existing reality. Let me conclude with the hope and expectation that *Eretz Yisroel* in all its aspects, both present and future, should constitute a factor uniting Jews everywhere, both Orthodox and non-Orthodox of all trends, by attuning itself in all its affairs more and more to the name by which it is known among all the peoples of the world—"the Holy Land" (Letters from the Rebbe vol. 1, pp. 124-6; See also *Igrot Kodesh* vol. 18, p. 123, where the Rebbe encourages other Rabbis to respond to Ben Gurion's letter).

93. The other respondents were later disclosed: Shmuel Yossef Agnon, Alexander Altmann, Henry Baruk, Shmuel Hugo Bergmann, Isaiah Berlin, Yehuda Bourla Haim Hermann Cohn, Louis Eliezer Halevi Finkelstein, Felix Frankfurter, Solomon B. Freehof, Shlomo Goren, Aryeh Leib Grossnass, Meir Lew, Abraham Rappoport, Meir Halevy Steinberg, Morris Swift, Zecharya Hacohen, Shalom Yitzhak Halevi, Hayim Hazaz, Yitzhak Isaac Halevi Herzog, Abraham Joshua Heschel, Joseph Shlomo Kahaneman, Yossef Kappah, Jacob Kaplan, Mordecai Menahem Kaplan, Yekhezkel Kaufmann, Aaron Kotler, Dante Lattes, Saul Lieberman, Yehuda Leib Hakohen Maimon, Moshe Maisels, André Neher, Salomon Rodrigues Pereira, Chaim Perelman, Simon H. Rifkind, Yecheskiel Sarne, Joseph Schecter, Shalom Joseph Shapira Shalom, Moshe Silberg, Akiva Ernst Simon, Leon (Arye) Simon, Joseph Dov Soloveitchik, Chaim Heller, Alfredo Shabtai Toaff, Elio Raffaelo Toaff, Ephraim A Urbach, Yekhiel Weinberg, Harry Wolfson, Aaron Zeitlin, Shlomo Y. Zevin. For the full correspondence see Eliezer Ben-Rafael, *Jewish Identities: Fifty Intellectuals Answer Ben Gurion* (Leiden: Brill, 2002).
94. For more details of Ben Gurion's involvement with the Law of Return see Ariel L. Feldestein, *Ben-Gurion, Zionism and American Jewry 1948-1963* (New York: Routledge, 2006), chapter 8.
95. See Suzi Navot, *Constitutional Law of Israel* (Netherlands: Kluwer Law International, 2007), pp. 188-190.
96. *Likutei Sichot* vol. 21, p. 411.
97. "The Oracle of Crown Heights," *New York Times Magazine*, 15th March 1992.
98. For a detailed list of sermons on the topic, see Rabbi Michoel Seligson, *Sefer ha-Mafteichot le-Sichot Kodesh* 5695-5752 (New York, 2011), pp. 569-584.

While he had no direct representation in the Knesset, the Rebbe galvanized all the influence he could muster to campaign for the 1970 enactment to be amended. Key Chabad activists in Israel, such as Rabbis Shlomo Maidanchik (1924-2004), Berke Wolf (1944-2000), and Shmuel Chefer, worked tirelessly to sway Knesset members from both the right and the left. Chefer recalled long telephone calls to Rabbi Chodakov during which the Rebbe was on the line. "The Rebbe gave detailed instructions to whom to turn, how to approach them, how to speak with them," he said.

An interesting example of how the Rebbe gained personal contact with government officials is the case of Avner-Hai Shaki (1926-2005). In 1970, Shaki entered the Knesset as a Mafdal member and in September of that year, he was appointed Deputy Minister of Education and Culture. When Shaki made known to the Mafdal leadership that he was in favor of amending the Law of Return to require *halachic* conversions, he was advised to "abstain or be absent" when it came to a vote on the law. After Shaki resisted, he was warned, "Why do you need problems? You have a luxury apartment and a respected position and you'll lose it all in a moment if you vote for the amendment of the law." Shaki, however, remained strong to his convictions and, after submitting his vote, immediately wrote a letter of preemptive resignation.

A few days later, at 2 a.m., there was a knock on the door of Shaki's apartment. Initially fearing for his safety, Shaki was relieved to see Yechiel Gartner, an old friend from law school. Gartner apologized for intruding at such a late hour, and explained that he had promised the Lubavitcher Rebbe, whom he had just met in America, that as soon as he landed in Israel he would visit Shaki right away to convey a personal message. "The Rebbe wants to congratulate you for your vote," Gartner said, repeating additional words of blessing from the Rebbe. Shaki, who had no connection with the Rebbe or Chabad, was deeply moved.

A month later Avner-Hai Shaki was in New York in *yechidut* along with his wife, in a meeting which lasted three hours. (He later described the Rebbe as "without doubt, the most interesting, charming, fascinating, and comprehensive person that I have ever met.") After discussing the Israeli political landscape in depth, and encouraging Shaki to complete a legal study of the Law of Return, the Rebbe offered some words to lift his spirits. "An athlete takes a few steps back before he leaps forward," the Rebbe observed. "Now, you are in the stage of a few steps backward." The Rebbe encouraged Shaki that he would eventually return to the government as a respected minister. In the following years Shaki proved to be a great ally in the campaign of *Mihu Yehudi*, especially after he was re-elected to the Knesset in 1984, and appointed *Minister without Portfolio responsible for Jerusalem Affairs* in 1988.

99. Moshe Ishon in a 1971 article published in *Hatzofeh*, reprinted in Avraham Chanoch Glitzenstein, Adin Steinsalz and Berke Wolf (eds.), *The Rebbe: Thirty Years of Leadership* (Israel, 1980), vol. 1, p. 174; Interview with Moshe Ishon 2012.

In numerous press reports the Rebbe censured the religious parties, demanding that they offer their resignation if they could not successfully amend the law—as Mafdal had done in the times of Ben Gurion (see, for example, *Ma'ariv* 25th May 1970; *Davar* 3rd August 1972, 3rd April 1973 and 7th March 1983.). In one letter he argued that if the religious politicians were unable to change the law, "then they are *obliged* to leave the government since their presence there is a *clear* sanction... as representatives of the Jewish religion" (undated handwritten note in *Me-Otzar Ha-Melech* (New York, 2005), p. 99.).

The criticism was not taken well. In 1973, Interior Minister Yosef Burg (1909-1999) attacked the Chabad movement for what he considered "propaganda," by insinuating that Cabinet ministers were failing in their religious duties. Burg told the 22nd Mizrachi-Hapoel Hamizrachi Convention that ministers were not "stuck to their Cabinet seats" and were not fearful of being unemployed (JTA 15th January 1973). Even Prime Minister Golda Meir, who previously shared a warm relationship with Chabad, voiced her discontent at the Rebbe's steering Israeli politics from abroad (*Davar* 25th February 1974; JTA 26th February 1974).

100. *Hitkashrut* (Chabad Youth Organization of Israel), issue 292.

101. Zalmon Jaffe, *My Encounter With The Rebbe*, 6th Installment.

After two decades, the issue became so damaging for Chabad and so hopelessly incorrigible that, in a 1989 sermon, the Rebbe advised his followers to completely refrain from any further discussion of the issue which had brought about "many disagreements among the Jewish people." Instead, they ought to focus exclusively on promoting Judaism in their own particular locations (Sermon of 24th *Tevet* 1989, in *Torat Menachem—Hitva'aduyot* 5749, vol. 2, p. 196-201). In a clarification penned after the sermon, he wrote, "This issue has no *practical* relevance *at all*—since we are speaking of a law and conduct of more than *forty years* in Israel. Only, there are those who wish to *enter* into even more arguments, and by participating in any discussion it will assist them." One exception was noted, "If the other side say that they *only* wish to know the truth, then one could send them references to the *Code of Jewish Law etc.*" (handwritten memo in *Teshura Groner-Pinson* 9th *Kislev*, 5774).

102. *Nachalat Har Chabad* in Kiryat Malachi, which today is home to hundreds of families and several educational institutions, was founded by the Rebbe in 1969, in response to a new waves of immigrants from Russia, Uzbekistan and Georgia. By this time Kfar Chabad was unable to handle the volume of new settlers and the Israeli government proposed that they be scattered around the country. The Rebbe was unhappy with this plan and enlisted the assistance of Rabbi Binyamin Gorodetzky (1905-1995), Chief Chabad representative of Europe and North Africa, who was deeply involved with the settlement of refugees. Gorodetzky successfully negotiated a plot in Kiryat Malachi which was capable of housing the six-hundred families that were expected to arrive. Early in 1969, the Rebbe instructed that ten young Chabad couples should relocate to the new settlement before the new immigrants landed, so as to provide a communal infrastructure, support and guidance. The name, *Nachalat Har Chabad* was chosen by the Rebbe himself—*har* ("mountain"), alluding to the bedrock of faith required by new immigrants to settle into a traditional Jewish life—and he continued to be heavily involved in the details of the settlements for a number of years, personally sending them a Torah scroll. His correspondence with the leaders of the new settlement from 1969-1974 fills over a hundred pages (Rabbi Zusha Wolf, *The Founding and Expansion of the Nachlat Har Chabad Community* (Kfar Chabad, 2008)).

103. In 1973 by Rabbi Aryeh Leib Kaplan (1947-1998). In a final *yechidut* before his departure, Kaplan received a lengthy briefing. "Do you speak Hebrew well?" the Rebbe asked him. When Kaplan replied that his Hebrew was "average," the Rebbe smiled and replied, "That's good. It's better not to speak Hebrew too well because then they might think you are an Israeli. I don't know why, but over there they have a huge respect for Americans."

    The Chabad settlement in Tzefat, later named *Kiryat Chabad*, began with the opening of a synagogue and *Kolel* (Advanced Talmudic academy for married students). At a *yechidut* towards the end of the year, the Rebbe encouraged his new *shliach*, "Tzefat is going to expand enormously. But you don't need to announce that there is going to be *Ufaratza*. It will be step by step." From 1976-1978 the Rebbe sent three groups of young, talented Chabad men and women as *shluchim* to Tzefat, providing a foundation to the new community. Today it is home to more than six-hundred families, most of whom are graduates from the numerous Chabad educational institutions founded in the city. Tragically, Rabbi Kaplan was killed in a car crash in 1998.

    For the above and over 150 pages of correspondence with the Rebbe about the development of the Tzefat community see: Rabbi Zusha Wolf, *The Founding and Expansion of the Kiryat Chabad in Tzefat* (Kfar Chabad, 2009).

104. An anthology of these sermons, filling some 600 pages, is Rabbi Zusha Wolf (ed.), *Diedushka: The Lubavitcher Rebbe and Russian Jewry* (Moscow: Committee of Shluchim of the Soviet Union, 2006).

105. For example, the sermon of *Lag B'Omer* 1980.

106. Sermon of 10th *Shevat* 1970 in Wolf, *Diedushka* pp. 127*ff.*

107. Personal communication with Rabbi Meyer Gutnick, 2nd March 2014. For more on the *Lishkat* and a list of its organizers and other participants see ibid. p. 489-495. See also ibid. pp. 499-529 for details of other organizations formed by the Rebbe to assist Russian refugees, *Shamir* (*Shomrei Mitzvot Yotzei Russia*) and *Friends of Refugees of Eastern Europe* (F.R.E.E). For more on *Shamir* see Peter Kalms, *A Place of Their Own: The Founding of Shamir* (London, 2005).

108. This was coupled with an ongoing campaign, throughout his leadership, for the construction of *mikvaot* (ritual baths). For the contemporary revival of *taharat ha-mishpacha* see Rivkah Slonim (ed.), *Total Immersion: A Mikvah Anthology* (Urim Publications; 2nd revised edition, 2006); Sue Fishkoff, *The Rebbe's Army: Inside the World of Chabad-Lubavitch* (New York: Shocken, 2003), chapter 8.
109. For an anthology of the Rebbe's sermons and other sources pertaining to these campaigns see Rabbi Shmuel Bistritzky, *Ha-Mivtza'im Ke-Hilchatam* (Israel: Private publication, 2009).
110. See editor's introduction to *Igrot Kodesh* vol. 28, p. 13.
111. 1967 *yechidut* with Rabbi Moshe Zvi Neria (1913-1995) in Wolpo, *Shemen Sason* vol. 3, p. 134.
112. Rabbi Shneur Zalman, *Tanya, Likutei Amarim* chapter 35. For a deeper insight into the virtue of practical commandments, see *Likutei Sichot* vol. 16, pp. 41-46. See also Rabbi Faitel Levin, *Heaven on Earth: Reflections on the Theology of Rabbi Menachem M. Schneerson* (New York: Kehot, 2002), chapter 13; Wolfson, *Open Secret*, pp. 74-5.
113. *New York Times*, 27th March 1972.
114. http://www.chabad.org/therebbe/article_cdo/aid/1567954/jewish/The-Rebbe-Cared-Deeply-for-My-Dying-Daughter.htm (accessed March 2014).
115. Written response dated 22nd November (27th *Cheshvan*) 1973 in *Igrot Kodesh* vol. 29, p. 30 (facsimile reproduced ibid., introduction p. 19). The other suggestions were: 1. Perhaps some details of the laws of family purity may not have been observed correctly; 2. Many individuals, including leaders of the Jewish people, had been born only after a miscarriage; 3. Perhaps the couple had voiced strong reservations about the pregnancy or about the observance of the laws.
116. Letter dated 8th April, 1977.
117. http://www.chabad.org/therebbe/article_cdo/aid/461848/jewish/The-Rebbe-and-President-Ford.htm (accessed March 2014).
118. See Wolf and Gopin, *Beit Chayenu 770* p. 212ff.
119. Edward S. Shapiro, *Crown Heights: Blacks, Jews and the 1991 Brooklyn Riot* (Massachussets: Brandeis University Press, 2006), p. 73.
120. Sermon of the last day of Passover 1969, *Likutei Sichot* vol. 6, pp. 350-356.
121. Letter dated 25th *Iyar* 1969 *Ha-Pardes, Sivan* 5729.
122. Shapiro pp. 76-77.
123. *Algemeiner Journal*, 21st January 1977.
124. See sermon of Rabbi Yoel Teitelbaum in *Divrei Yoel* vol. 5, (Brooklyn 1977), p. 122, which refers to the contemporary efforts to spread the wellsprings of Chasidut as "the opinion of fools."
125. Jaffe, *My Encounter with the Rebbe*, 9th installment.
126. http://www.chabad.org/blogs/blog_cdo/aid/1731964/jewish/The-Rebbe-and-The-Volunteer-Ambulance-Organization.htm (accessed March 2014).
127. For details see *A Chassidisher Derher*, Issue 2(39), *Shevat* 5772, pp. 28-37.
128. Jaffe, installment 7.
129. *Kovetz Yechidut*, p. 14. According to one account (ibid.) this was due to strain on the Rebbe's health from staying up three nights per week. This may also be connected with a report from the Seligson family that the Rebbe suffered a minor heart-attack on or around 9th December 1962 (Personal communication with Rabbi Michoel Seligson, 5th March 2014. Seligson's father was one of the Rebbe's personal physicians).
130. Sermon of 6th *Tishrei* 5734 (ibid. p. 18).
131. Sermon of *Shabbat Bereishit* 5735 (ibid. p. 21).
132. Jaffe ibid.
133. Solomon, *Educational Teachings*, p. 335.
134. Interview with Rabbi Leibel Groner, 17th *Iyar* 5769.

135. From 2005 onwards *Jewish Education Media* (JEM) initiated an extensive series of video interviews with individuals who attended *yechidut* or were otherwise touched by the Rebbe. As of this writing some 800 interviews have been conducted, segments of which are publicized weekly in their video "magazine," *Living Torah.*

136. JEM Living Torah, volume 119, program 475.

137. Lautenberg was at the time president of the United Jewish Appeal and later Senator of New Jersey. For a transcript see http://www.collive.com/show_news.rtx?id=25549. A full recording of the meeting is available at http://www.chabad.org/therebbe/article_cdo/aid/551695/jewish/5732-Yechidus-Frank-Lautenberg.htm (accessed March 2014).

138. Kraus, chaps 34, 39 and 42.

139. http://www.chabad.org/therebbe/article_cdo/aid/523714/jewish/The-Rebbe-and-Rabin.htm (accessed March 2014).

140. http://www.collive.com/show_news.rtx?id=20949&alias=peres-divulges-meeting-details (accessed March 2014).

141. Solomon ibid.

142. Transcripts of these discussions are reproduced in *Siach Sarfei Kodesh.*

143. Interview with Mordechai Tendler in *The Jewish Voice and Opinion*, April 2011, p. 44; Wolpo, *Shemen Sasson* vol. 4, p. 36. Rabbi Feinstein had conducted a wedding ceremony outside 770 and met with the Rebbe privately afterwards for about an hour.

144. Letter dated 20th March (*Rosh Chodesh Nissan*) 1977 in Wolpo ibid. p. 37.

145. In sermons of the eve of *Shavuot* 1976 (*Sichot Kodesh* 5736, vol. 2, pp. 241-260) and Second day of *Shavuot* (ibid. pp. 268-274, 286-298); subsequently (in part) in *Likutei Sichot* vol. 16, pp. 211-222.

146. Jaffe, installment 8, chapter 7.

147. "A visit to the Lubavitcher Rebbe" in *Ha-Ma'or* (The Light), vol. 15, nos. 2-3 (September 1977), pp. 24-30, reproduced in Jaffe, installment 9, introduction. I have rendered Hebrew terms into English.

148. This refers to the two Chasidic discourses delivered, printed in *Sefer Ha-Ma'amarim* 5736 (New York: Va'ad Kitvei Kodesh, 1994), pp. 226-236.

149. This probably refers to the combined length of the two *farbrengens*. An audio recording of the *farbrengen* of the eve of *Shavuot* indicates that it lasted two hours.

150. Address at Logan Hall, London, September 11, 1994.

151. Jonathan-Sacks extended CV, September 2013; lecture to Annual Conference of *Shluchim*, November 20, 2011; personal communication with Shneur Zalman Gafni.

152. Jonathan Sacks, *A Letter in the Scroll: Understanding Our Jewish Identity and Exploring the Legacy of the World's Oldest Religion* (New York: Free Press, 2000), p. 210-211.

153. 2011 lecture, ibid.

154. For the above see Israel Meir Lau (Jessica Setbon and Shira Leibowitz Schmidt trans.), *Out of the Depths: The Story of a Child of Buchenwald Who Returned Home at Last* (New York: Sterling Press, 2010), pp. 193-204.

155. Interview with Dr. David Luchins, who was present at Chisholm's 1983 speech, JEM *Living Torah*, disc 39, program 153.

156. Herman Branover, *Return: The Spiritual Odyssey of a Soviet Scientist* (Israel: Shamir, third edition 2002), pp. 91-2, 118-9, 168-9; Dalfin, *Conversations*, pp. 6-15; Herman Branover, *The Connection between Science and Faith* (2002).

157. *"Rashi"* is an acronym for Rabbi Shlomo Yitzchaki (1040-1105), author of a highly popular fundamental running commentary on the Bible and Talmud.

158. In *Likutei Sichot* vols. 5-39, a significant proportion of which are *Rashi Sichot.* For a skeletal Hebrew summary of the edited *Rashi Sichot* see: Rabbi Alter Eliyahu Friedman (ed), *Biurim le-Perush Rashi al Ha-Torah*, 5 vols. (New York: Kehot, expanded edition 1993). Appended to this

edition is an index of the other *Rashi Sichot* which were not edited by the Rebbe, and remain in transcript form (ibid. vol. 5, p. 316-343). In my *Chumash Kol Menachem* 5. vols, (New York: Kol Menachem, 2002-2005), I have adapted selections from several hundred *Rashi Sichot* into English. For full translations of a small selection of *Rashi Sichot* into English see Rabbi Eliezer Danziger (trans.), *Studies in Rashi*, 3 vols. (New York: Kehot 2011-2014).

159. Some of the better known super-commentaries on *Rashi* commentary to the Torah were penned by Rabbi Eliyahu Mizrachi (1450-1526), Rabbi Ovadiah of Bartinuro (1450-1576), Rabbi Chaim ben Betzalel (1520-1588), Rabbi Yehudah Loew of Prague (1525-1609), Rabbi Mordechai Jaffe (1535-1612), Rabbi David ben Shmuel HaLevi (1586-1670), Rabbi Yisachar Ber Eilenberg (published 1624); Rabbi Yaakov Slovik (published in 1642); Rabbi Shabetai ben Yosef Bass, (1648-1718) and Rabbi David Pardo (1718-1790).

160. *Rashi* to Genesis 3:8.

161. *Mishnah, Avot* 5:22.

162. For example, in his commentary to Genesis 3:8, *Rashi* quotes the Talmud's teaching that Adam and Eve "sinned in the tenth hour." The Talmud's intention, which can easily be gleaned by looking up the source, was that the sin occurred in the tenth hour *on the day Adam and Eve were created.* However, the Rebbe argues that *Rashi's* intended readership is unfamiliar with this detail from the Talmudic source, and is not even able to look it up. What *Rashi* has done is to borrow the Talmud's statement and transplant it to a different, literal context—clarifying scripture's reference to the position of the sun at the time the sin occurred (*"in the direction of the day"*). Accepting the Talmud's interpretation that "the direction of the day" refers to the tenth hour, when the sun is in the west, does not force us to accept the broader context of the Talmud's interpretation *not cited by Rashi*, that the sin occurred on the first day Adam and Eve were created. On the contrary, a literal reading of scripture would lead us to believe otherwise. It is written earlier (1:31) that Adam and Eve's creation day was declared by G-d as "very good," hardly the most calamitous day in the history of mankind. The placement of the sin narrative here in chapter three of Genesis also suggests that the events transpired some time after the creation story in chapter one. Logically, too, one would also expect Adam and Eve not to have been devoid of moral caliber, and it is likely to have taken the Serpent some time to convince them to sin. Sermon of *Shabbat Parshat Bereishit* 1988, adapted in *Chumash Kol Menachem, Genesis* p. 22-25.

Unlike the world of Rabbinic hermeneutics whose rules have been expounded upon exhaustively, the underlying principles of the purely logical and non-traditional universe of *peshat* (literal interpretation), have been largely neglected in Rabbinic literature. If *Rashi* really was a literalist, he must have had a precise and rigorous method through which he analyzed *Talmud* and *Midrash* and reconfigured these teachings to the different set of concerns which dominate the school of literal interpretation. In the process of deciphering *Rashi*, the Rebbe sought to uncover his method, and in almost every one of the *Rashi Sichot*, the Rebbe proposes a new *klal*—a sweeping hypothetical principle of *Rashi's* methodology.

It is one thing to interpret a few lines of text with expertise, but a *klal* must be demonstrably consistent throughout the tens of thousands of lines of *Rashi's* commentary. In his 1991 compilation, Rabbi Tuvia Blau identified some 389 principle of *Rashi's* methodology which had been suggested throughout the years of *Rashi Sichot*, concerning a host of issues, such as: the logic behind *Rashi's* instances where *Rashi* offers multiple interpretations of a verse; the precise boundaries of literal interpretation; *Rashi's* extreme precision in scriptural citation; the sequential development of *Rashi's* ideas; the logic behind *Rashi's* occasional and selective citation of sources; *Rashi's* choice of scriptural and Rabbinic proofs; *Rashi's* selective citation of *Targum Onkelos*, and *Rashi's* use of old French—to name but a few (See Rabbi Tuvia Blau, *Klalei Rashi* (Kfar Chabad: Kehot, expanded edition 1991).

163. The essay was developed from a sermon delivered on 13th December (19th *Kislev*) 1965, and published as an introduction to the first volume of the Chabad Encyclopedia *Sefer Ha-Arachim* (New York: Kehot, 1970), and the following year as a separate pamphlet, entitled

Inyana shel Torat ha-Chasidut. In 1978 it was translated into English by Rabbi Y. H. Greenberg and Susan Handelman as *On the Essence of Chasidut.*

164. These lectures are collected, in Hebrew translation, in David Feldman (trans.) *Torat Menachem—Tiferet Levi Yitzchak,* 3 vols. (New York: Kehot, 1990). Some were edited by the Rebbe and published in *Likutei Sichot* vol. 39, pp. 51-160.
165. Collected, in part, in *Likutei Sichot* vol. 39, pp. 161-228.
166. Summarized in Rabbi Alter Eliyahu Friedman (ed.), *Biurim le-Pirkei Avot* 2 vols, (New York: Kehot, 4th edition 1996).
167. *Sichot Kodesh* 5725, vol. 1, p. 392.
168. *Sichot Kodesh* 5735, vol. 1, p. 405.
169. With the exception of a break in 1972.
170. Over the years the editors of *Likutei Sichot* included: Rabbis Yoel Kahn, Leibel Schapiro, Nachman Schapiro, and Leibel Altein.
171. A sketch of her life was penned the following summer by Rabbi Shmuel Zalmanov, in *Bitaon Chabad, Menachem Av* 5731.
172. *Yediot Acharonot,* 24th March 1972
173. "A meeting between faith and song," *Ma'ariv,* 25th March, 1977.
174. Letter dated 19th March (11th *Adar* II), 1970, in *Igrot Kodesh* vol. 26, (New York: Kehot, 2003), p. 353.
175. In thanks for good wishes received from Shlonsky by the Rebbe on his own 70th birthday (Levin, *Treasures,* p. 99).
176. Letter dated 5th June (23rd *Sivan*) 1972 *Igrot Kodesh* vol. 27, p. 425. Shlonsky passed away less than a year later, on 18th May 1973.
177. Vol. 22, pp. 119-149 (1978), by Mark Gurari (Leibel's legal name from the false Russian passport he used to flee the country).
178. For the above see Eliyahu Touger, *To Know and To Care* volume 2 (New York: Sichos in English, 1996), chapter 1; Shimon Silman, *Scientific Thought in Messianic Times* (New York: 2010), pp. 151-155. A recording of the Rebbe's discussion with Rosenbloom at the *farbrengen* can be seen in JEM *Living Torah,* Disc 35, Program 138.
179. http://www.col.org.il/show_news.rtx?artID=38164 (accessed March 2014).
180. Jaffe, installment 7.
181. *Yechidut* with Rabbi Shmuel Levitin, 10th December (5th *Tevet*) 1964, in *Sichot Kodesh* 5725, vol. 1, p. 532.
182. Sermon of 11th *Nissan* 1972 (*Sichot Kodesh* 5732, vol. 2, p. 113*ff*). See *Bitaon Chabad* issue 38-39, p. 94. For an account of the activity the campaign inspired in Israel see article of Chanoch Glitzenstein in *Shearim,* 11th *Nisan* 1973. Breaking from the mold that Chabad institutions were required to be funded completely independently, the Rebbe offered to cover ten percent of the costs of establishing these new institutions.
183. Resolution of the Ninety-Fifth Congress of the United States of America authorizing "Education Day, U.S.A," April 17th 1978.
184. *New York Times,* 27th March 1972.
185. This is Rabbi Krinsky's recollection. According to Dr. Glazman, it was his own idea to call Weiss, whom he had noticed in a cover story in *Time* magazine. (Weiss had appeared in the 14th July 1967 edition of *Time*).
186. Dr. Lawrence Resnick (1948-2004) continued the Rebbe's care after Dr. Weiss returned to Chicago.
187. Interview with Ira Weiss, by Baila Olidort, March 2013; JEM interview with Ira Weiss; diaries of Leibel Groner and Michoel Seligson; interview with Yehudah Krisnky in *Mishpacha,* 30th September, 2009; lecture by Dr. Mordechai Glazman at Lubavitch Yeshivah of Toronto, November 2002.

CHAPTER 13: THE REBBE'S ARMY

1. Private *yechidut* was replaced with "group *yechidut*," (*yechidut klalit*) which took place in the synagogue at 770, where a number of guests would be welcomed together with the Rebbe sitting behind a table, and a short sermon would be delivered. Group *yechidut* was available for visitors from abroad; bar-mitzvah boys and their fathers; couples before their wedding; *yeshivah* students who were embarking on, or returning, from a *shlichut* abroad; and for supporters of the *Machneh Israel* development fund, with their *shluchim*. Group *yechidut* took place seven times each year, around the time of festivals or dates in the Chasidic calendar when many guests were present.

   Private *yechidut* did continue very occasionally for special guests of importance, such as leading Rabbis, a handful of other individuals. (For more details see *Kovetz Yechidut*.)
2. A possible indication of the reduced volume of correspondence can be seen from the published letters to Rabbi Efraim Wolf, a leading activist in Israel, in the series *Yemei Temimim:* Letters from 1950 to 1980 fill seven volumes (around half of which is devoted to the 1970s), whereas those from 1981-1988 are contained in just one volume.

   While the Rebbe's letters from this later period have not yet been published systematically in the series *Igrot Kodesh*—which as of this writing dates up to 1975— many hundreds of letters from 1976 onwards have been published in the thirty-nine volumes of *Likutei Sichot* and in a host of various other Chabad publications. Over the last twenty years it has also been popular for Chabad families to share letters which they received from the Rebbe in a souvenir journal (*teshurah*), distributed at weddings and other special occasions. Many of these have been archived online at http://www.teshura.com/ (accessed March 2014).
3. This is evident from simply perusing the 93 volumes of unedited transcripts of the *sichot* from 1950-1992. During the 1950s a year's *sichot* would generally fill one volume; during the 1960s and most of the 1970s, there are two volumes per year; for 1979 and 1980, three volumes each year; and from 1981 onwards, there are four volumes per year, peaking at five volumes in 1985.

   The *ma'amarim* (Chasidic discourses), however, while still a regular fixture, grew shorter during this period, and were often delivered without the formalities of a preparatory melody and standing congregation.
4. Rabbi Menachem Mendel Schneerson, *Hayom Yom* (New York: Kehot, 34th edition, 2013), pp. 22-39.
5. Sermon of 8th November (*Shabbat Parshas Toldot*) 1980, (Sichos in English, volume 7).
6. Sermon of 8th March (*Shabbat Parshat Ki Tissa*), 1980 (Sichos in English, vol. 5).
7. Sermon of 30th September (13th *Tishrei*) 1982 in *Torat Menachem—Hitva'aduyot* 5743, vol.1, pp. 145-6. (My translation follows the audio recording of this sermon.) For the response to the request for a photo, see *Davar Melech* (Israel, Kfar Chabad, 1992), p. 54.
8. The English transcripts were published in *Sichos in English*, 51 volumes (New York, 1978-1992).
9. See *Teshurah Krinsky-Stazakovsky*, 6th June (28th *Sivan*) 2013, chapter 2.
10. See *Teshurah Krinsky-Dechter*, 14th October (2nd *Cheshvan*) 2007, chapter 5.
11. http://www.col.org.il/show_news.rtx?artID=78555 (accessed March 2014).
12. Resolution dated 18th April 1978, signed by Thomas Phillip O'Neill, Speaker of the House of Representatives, Walter F. Mondale, Vice-President of the United States and President of the Senate, and President Jimmy Carter. The proposal was carried by a two-thirds majority in the House of Representatives and by unanimous vote in the Senate. Since "Education Day U.S.A." follows the Rebbe's birthday on the Hebrew Calendar, its date on the American calendar varies each year. Since 1992 the annual proclamation has been referred to as "Education and Sharing Day U.S.A."

    Following his usual practice of demurring from personal honors, the Rebbe declined Carter's invitation in 1979 to attend the White House on Education Day, and even passed the opportunity to receive a congratulatory telephone call from the President. See Fishkoff, *The Rebbe's Army*, pp. 193-4

13. *Washington Post*, 28th September 1979.
14. Letter to President Jimmy Carter, 9th February 1979.
15. Address of 17th July 1997 in Washington D.C. honoring the third anniversary of the Rebbe's passing, cited in part in Fishkoff, p. 192. See JTA 21st July 1997.
16. Letter from Stuart E. Eizenstat to Rabbi Menachem M. Schneerson dated 17th April 1980; JTA February 1, 1980.
17. Letter dated 2nd April, 1982.
18. Sermon of 11th *Nissan* 1982
19. Letter dated 18th April (25th *Nissan*) 1982.
20. Sermon of 24th January (10th *Shevat*) 1983.
21. Ibid.
22. Sermon of 24th November (19th *Kislev*) 1983.
23. http://www.presidency.ucsb.edu/ws/index.php?pid=40205 (accessed March 2014).
24. Sermon of 28th January 1984, *Sichot Kodesh* 5744, vol. 2, (New York: Va'ad Hanachat Ha-Temimim, 2000), p. 278-280.
25. JTA 6th June 1985.
26. *Mishneh Torah, Laws of Kings* chapter 12. This is in addition to the political restoration of a Torah-based state in the Land of Israel, the reconstruction of the Temple etc., which pertains to the Jews in particular. See Maimonides ibid. 11:4.
27. See Chaim Chavel (ed), *Kitvei Ha-Ramban* (Jerusalem: Mosad Harav Kook, 1964), vol. 1, p. 154-5. This is also the view of Rabad of Posquières in his gloss to Maimonides, ibid. 12:1. For Chabad's embrace of Nachmanides' position, see sources cited in *Torat Menachem—Hitva'aduyot* 5748, vol. 3, p. 147, note 76.
28. *Likutei Sichot* vol. 27, pp. 191-206, based on sermons delivered during the month of *Nisan* 1973.
29. Maimonides (ibid 11:3) states that Mashiach is not required to perform any supernatural activity.
30. This follows BT *Sanhedrin* 98a, which argues that if miracles occur in the future it will be as a result of special "merit." The Rebbe argues that, even according to Maimonides, there will inevitably come a time, even in a totally natural redemption, where sufficient merit will accrue to precipitate some miracles. That is why even Maimonides accepts that the dead will ultimately be revived, which is clearly supernatural (and in his *Epistle on Resurrection* ch. 6, he writes that the absence of miracles in the future is not absolutely clear to him). However, this, and all other supernatural activity, is totally incidental to the goal of Jewish messianism, as defined by *halachah*, which is the perfection of nature and history (see *Likutei Sichot* ibid.)
31. *Hayom Yom* identifies this date as the initiation of the campaign, though a number of sermons in the preceding years already highlighted the issue.
32. See my *Rambam: Principles of Faith, Principles 8-9* (New York: Kol Menachem, 2nd edition 2008), Principle 8, Lessons 3 and 11.
33. For examples of the latter, see ibid. pp. 384-395.
34. Babylonian Talmud, *Sanhedrin* 56a.
35. In its precise formulation, this law is the prohibition against eating a limb torn from a living animal (*aver min ha-chai*). As a category, it represents a requirement to have compassion on animals and humans in general. See *Torat Menachem—Hitva'aduyot* 5744, vol. 2, p. 984.
36. Maimonides, *Mishneh Torah, Laws of Kings* chapters 9-10. For a detailed analysis see Rabbi Moshe Weiner, *Sefer Sheva Mitzvot Hashem*, 3 vols. (Pittsburgh: Ask Noah International,

2008-2013). The first volume has been translated into English as *The Divine Code* (second edition, 2011).

37. Maimonides ibid. 8:10. Gentiles who observe the Code are promised eternal bliss, "a share in the World-to-Come" (ibid. 11).

38. *Likutei Sichot* vol. 26, p. 132*ff.*, adapted from sermons delivered the previous year. For a review of many sources on the topic in English see Rabbi Michael J. Broyde, *The Obligation of Jews to Seek Observance of Noachide Laws by Gentiles: A Theoretical Review*, at http://www.jlaw.com/Articles/noach2.html. For an anthology of many of the Rebbe's sermons on Noachide Law talks see Rabbi Chaim Miller (ed.), *Kol Boi Ha-Olam* (New York: *Va'ad mi-Golah le-Geulah*, 1999).

39. On 7th October 1986 the Rebbe said to Chabad supporter David Chase, "I'm very occupied now with spreading the Seven Noahide laws" (JEM Living Torah, Disc 31, Program 123).

40. See response of the Rebbe from 1991, reproduced by Rabbi Yosef Simcha Ginsburg in *Hitkashrut* vol. 464 (2003).

41. Presidential Proclamation of National Day of Reflection, 3rd April 1982.

42. Letter dated 18th April (25th *Nissan*) 1982. See also *Torat Menachem—Hitva'aduyot* 5745, vol. 3, pp. 1840-1842.

43. Letter dated 6th September (12th *Elul*) 1987.

44. *Torat Menachem—Hitva'aduyot* 5747, vol. 3, p. 67.

45. *Likutei Sichot* ibid. p. 143.

46. Letter to Israel Drazin, 31st October 1986.

47. See sources cited in *Likutei Sichot* vol. 25, p. 192, note 56. The Rebbe also argued that Christians today do not understand the Trinity and that it therefore borders on the theologically benign (*Torat Menachem—Hitva'aduyot* 5743, vol. 3, p. 1386).

48. See, however, *Teshurah Lipskar-Krinsky* 2013, p. 19, that the Rebbe rejected a draft press release stating that Americans should "worship G-d freely, each in accordance with his or her beliefs," protesting that, "Christianity is idolatrous, contravening the Noahide Code."

    To reconcile this with his comments cited in *Likutei Sichot* in the previous note, it appears the Rebbe maintained that Jews should not *actively* promote Christianity as an acceptable monotheism, even though many *halachic* authorities deemed it to be so, since other authorities do not (notably Maimonides). In the absence of a clear consensus, we need to take all authorities into account.

    For more of the Rebbe's views on Christianity see *Teshurah Simpson-Zajac* 2th *Cheshvan* 5771 (2010), p. 9

49. Letter to David Chase, 16th April 1981.

50. Interview with David Chase (JEM *Living Torah*, Disc 61, Program 241). The Rebbe later recounted the story at a *farbrengen*, omitting the detail about church attendance (Sermons of 11th *Nissan* and Last Day of Passover 1983).

51. See *Likutei Sichot* ibid. p. 192. For more on Chabad acosmism see Rabbi Shneur Zalman of Liadi, *Tanya, Likutei Amarim* chapters 20-21 and *Sha'ar Ha-Yichud veha-Emunah*; Rabbi Menachem Mendel Schneersohn (*Tzemach Tzedek*), *Derech Mitzvotecha—Ta'amei Ha-Mitzvot* (New York: Kehot, 2006), p 59b*ff;* Norman Lamm, *The Shema: Spirituality and Law in Judaism* (Philadelphia: Jewish Publication Society, 1998), chapter 7; Rabbi Yoel Kahn, *Shiurim Be-Torat Chabad* (Israel: Mayanotecha, 2006), pp. 152-165; Wolfson, *Open Secret* pp. 46-47, 93, 105; Rachel Elior, *The Paradoxical Ascent to G-d: The Kabbalisitc Theosophy of Habad Hasidism* (Albany: State University of New York, 1993), chapters 11-12; Jay Michaelson, *Everything is G-d: The Radical Path of Nondual Judaism* (Boston and London: Trumpeter Books, 2009); Dov Schwartz, *Habad's Thought: From Beginning to End* (Heb.), (Ramat Gan: Bar Ilan University Press, 2011), chapter 1; Jacob Gotlieb, *Rationalism in Hasidic Attire: Habad's Harmonistic Approach to Maimonides* (Heb.), (Ramat Gan: Bar Ilan University Press, 2009), pp. 55-59.

52. Letter from Israel Drazin to the Rebbe, 22nd October 1986.
53. Letter to Drazin ibid.
54. For many examples see Menachem Kellner, *Maimonides on Judaism and the Jewish People* (State University of New York Press, 1991).
55. See Svante Lundgren, *Particularism and Universalism in Modern Jewish Thought* (Academic Studies in the History of Judaism, 2000), pp. 169-181.
56. For the roots and development of this idea see M. Hallamish, *The Attitude of the Kabbalists to Non-Jews* (Heb.), in Hallamish and Kasher, *Filosophia Yisraelit,* pp. 49-71; Shaul Magid, *From Metaphysics to Midrash: Myth, History, and the Interpretation of Scripture in Lurianic Kabbala* (Bloomington and Indianapolis: Indiana University Press, 2008), pp. 143-149.
57. For an extensive discussion see Rabbis Yoel Kahn and Chaim Shalom Ber Lipskier, *Sefer Ha-Arachim Chabad,* vol. 2 (New York: Kehot 1972), pp. 266-277.
58. *Likutei Sichot* vol. 21, p. 107.
59. The idea, which is a Chasidic elaboration of a Midrashic teaching (*Shemot Rabah* 12:3; *Tanchuma, Va'era* 15), is discussed extensively in the Rebbe's discourses. For a seminal treatment see *Likutei Sichot,* vol. 15, p. 83. For an overview of the idea see Kahn, *Shiurim* pp. 76-92; Alon Dahan, *Dirah ba-Tachtonim* (PhD dissertation, Hebrew University 2006), pp. 89-111.
60. Maimonides, *Laws of Kings,* end of chap. 11; *Likutei Sichot* vol. 23, pp. 172-181.
61. As was usually stressed in prior Chabad thought. See Kahn and Lipskier, pp. 273-7.
62. Nevertheless, there will remain a difference between the Jew and the non-Jew in the *mechanism* by which this disclosure will take place, thereby preserving a distinctiveness to the Jewish people (*Likutei Sichot* ibid. and vol. 12, p. 74, note 30).

    For more on the topic of non-Jewish spirituality in Chabad thought see Wolfson, *Open Secret* chapter 6. Wolfson argues that to perceive the Noahide campaign as weakening of the traditional ethnocentrism is "apologetic," since the Rebbe did not recoil from the prior teachings of Chabad and repeated them often. In my view, there are a number of instances where the Rebbe considerably "narrowed the gap" separating Jew and non-Jew in what appears to be a significant shift from, though not an outright rejection of, the prior Chabad position, such as the sermons I have cited here.
63. See *Sichot Kodesh* 5736, vol. 2, p. 146*ff;* 199, 347 and 428.
64. In Jewish law, children's observance is seen only as a preparative phase for actual worship which begins at the age of bar- or bat-mitzvah (13 years for a boy and 12 years for a girl).
65. Sermon of 5th day of *Sukkot* 1980.
66. For an anthology of sermons to children, see *Der Rebbe Redt Tzu Kinder*, vol. 5, (New York: Tzivot Hashem, 2005).
67. *Souvenir Journal Celebrating the Wedding of Aron and Dinie Rabin,* 20th *Elul* 1999, p. 19.
68. Ibid. p. 49.
69. Letter dated 21st January (26th *Tevet*), 1982 in *L'Chaim* (Lubavitch Youth Organization), issue 494 (1997).
70. Jaffe, 16th installment.
71. Letter in *L'Chaim* ibid.
72. The Rebbe's directives and results of the campaign are documented extensively in the album *Letter in a Torah Scroll* (Heb,), (Kfar Chabad: Va'ad Le-Ketivat Sefer Torah Shel Yaldei Yisrael, 2009).
73. Response penned on night of 29th July 1978, http://www.col.org.il/חדשות_חבד_מה_ענה_הרבי_לאימו_של_הילד_שניגב_מצחו_בסירטוק_של_הרבי_77904.html (accessed March 2014).
74. Shulamith's letter and the Rebbe's response, dated 1st October (6th *Tishrei*) 1981, are reproduced at http://crownheights.info/chabad-news/425410/new-document-shows-the-rebbes-coded-message/ (accessed March 2014).
75. Sermon of 7th February (*Shabbat Parshat Terumah*), 1981.

76. See *Torah: The Beauty of the Elderly* in *Sichos in English* vol. 6, from sermons of *Shabbat Parshat Eikev*, 20th Av; *Motzoei Shabbat Eikev; Shabbat Parshat Re'eh* and *Rosh Chodesh Elul* 1980.
77. Jaffe, 14th installment.
78. Sermon of 11th Nissan 1982.
79. *Sichot Kodesh* 5734, p. 195*ff.*
80. "Roundup of Chanuka Activities," JTA 24th December 1976.
81. Ibid.
82. "Chanukah Menorahs to Light Up Cities," JTA 22nd December 1978.
83. Letter dated 25th April 1978, in Jonathan Sarna and David Dalin, *Religion and State in the American Jewish Experience* (Indiana: University of Notre Dame Press, 1997), pp. 291-2.
84. Ibid.
85. Ibid. pp. 293-4.
86. Ibid. p. 296.
87. Archive of *The American Presidency Project* http://www.presidency.ucsb.edu/ws/?pid=31848 (accessed March 2014).
88. Letter to President Jimmy Carter, 31st January 1980.
89. Letter to JCC of Teaneck dated 9th December (13th *Kislev*) 1981.

    After receiving a request to clarify his views further, the Rebbe penned a detailed response, explaining why he favored a more publicly visible Judaism even in a predominantly Christian country.

    > 1. To begin with, it should be noted that when it comes to a relationship between two different ethnic or religious groups, which aims at delineating their respective concerns, *etc.*, it is not enough when one of the parties resolves to follow a certain policy in the hope of avoiding an undesirable reaction on the part of the other party, for, obviously, it has no control over the other party, which may react in one of three ways: favorably, unfavorably, or indifferently. Thus, there is no assurance that the policy which may be well intended to call forth a favorable reaction may actually turn out to be counterproductive.
    >
    > 2. Since the time of the dispersion of our Jewish people, following our exile from our land, Jews have lived as a minority among the nations, often a very small minority. The problem of coexistence has thus always been present in the Diaspora and most of the time in an acute form.
    >
    > Although circumstances varied from time to time, and from place to place, requiring policy adjustment on the part of the Jewish minority as to how to relate to the non Jewish majority, there has also been a common denominator which has been a decisive consideration at all times and in all places of Jewish dispersion. This has been the regrettable, but unavoidable, fact that the gentile majority, especially one that did not fully live up to the prescriptions of the Divine moral precepts (the so-called "Seven Noahide Laws," with all their ramifications, which G-d ordained for the descendants of Noah, i.e. all humanity, after the Flood, as stated in the Torah, Gen. 9:1,17)—has generally considered itself entitled to everything, while anything it granted to the minority was considered as an act of grace. So much so that it came to regard the minority as having fully acquiesced in this relationship, even if the minority called its requests "demands" of privileges it considered itself entitled to.
    >
    > 3. Under such circumstances, if the minority voluntarily gives up certain privileges which it once enjoyed, not to mention if it voluntarily forgoes a certain right which the same minority enjoys elsewhere—it is bound to be regarded as a sign of weakness and an admission that it is not really entitled to it at all. Many illustrations could be cited, but there is no need to expand on this in a letter, especially in

a situation which is assumed to be of a local character, requiring a local approach.

4. There is, of course, the directive in Torah not to "taunt" an adversary, but the emphasis is on "taunting"; it does not mean at all that we have to surrender positions we have won over the years.

5. Even if a "low profile" or concessionary tactic has been followed by a community and it seemed to have worked for a time, with the other side refraining from asserting itself, there is no assurance that this policy will always be effective. In a democratically free country like the U.S.A., with periodic elections, one can never know who the next public officials or community leaders will be, and what their policy will be.

With the above prefatory remarks in mind, let us now consider the practical implications of the issue under discussion.

The Jewish community in the U.S.A. is as old as the U.S.A. itself. We know the problems it faced, and the actual discriminations it suffered, until it has won its place in this country. Yet, even in this day and age prejudice and anti-Semitism exist, not only latently, but also overtly. Under these circumstances we must not relax our alertness to any sign of erosion of our hard-won positions.

One of these positions is the annual lighting of a Chanukah Menorah in public places. As mentioned in my previous letter, such Chanukah Menorahs have been kindled in the Nation's capital (in Lafayette Park, facing the White House), in Manhattan, Albany, Philadelphia, Chicago, and in many other cities of the Union. There has been no opposition to their being placed on public property from non-Jewish quarters. Regrettably, there have been some Jews who did raise objections in several places out of fear that kindling a Menorah on public property, would call attention to the fact that there are Jews living in that city; Jews who would apparently be willing to forgo the claim that the public place belongs also to them, as part of the public.

I also pointed out that in Washington, D.C. the President personally participated in the ceremony, that in New York City the Attorney General of the State of New York personally participated in the ceremony, and elsewhere public officials and dignitaries were on hand at this public event. There is no need for any stronger evidence that the Chanukah Menorah—with its universal message, which is especially akin to the spirit of liberty and independence of this nation—has won a place not only in Jewish life, but also in the life of the American people.

In light of the above, when a Jewish community in the U.S.A. publicly raises objections to placing a Chanukah Menorah in a public place—on whatever grounds, and however well intentioned—it is thereby jeopardizing the Jewish position in general. It is also undermining its own position in the long run, as mentioned above. With all due respect to the claim that hitherto this policy has resulted in a "steady reduction of all Christological elements in public life," I doubt whether these have been eliminated completely. But granted, for the sake of argument, that this is the case, it would be most exceptional and unnatural in American life, since by and large the American people is Christian....

Now, to come to the essential point; Why is it so important for Jews to have a Chanukah Menorah displayed publicly? The answer is that experience has shown that the Chanukah Menorah displayed publicly during the eight days of Chanukah, has been an inspiration to many, many Jews and evoked in them a spirit of identity with their Jewish people and the Jewish way of life. To many others, it has brought a sense of pride in their Yiddishkeit and the realization that there is no reason really in this free country to hide one's Jewishness, as if it were contrary or inimical to American life and culture. On the contrary, it is fully in keeping with the American national slogan *e pluribus unum* and the fact that American culture has been enriched by the thriving ethnic cultures which contributed very much, each in its own way, to American life both materially and spiritually.

Certainly, Jews are not in the proselytizing business. The Chanukah Menorah is not intended to, and can in no way, bring us converts to Judaism. But it can, and does, bring many Jews back to their Jewish roots. I personally know of scores of such Jewish returnees, and I have good reason to believe that in recent years, hundreds, even thousands, of Jews experience a kindling of their inner Jewish spark by the public kindling of the Chanukah Menorah in their particular city and in the Nation's capital, *etc.*, as publicized by the media.

In summary, Jews, either individually or communally, should not create the impression that they are ashamed to show their Jewishness, or that they wish to gain their neighbors' respect by covering up their Jewishness. Nor will this attitude insure their rights to which they are entitled, including the privilege of publicly lighting a Chanukah Menorah, a practice which has been sanctioned by precedent and custom, as to become a tradition.

I also must point out that I do not think that a Jewish community can disregard its responsibility to other Jewish communities in regard to an issue of this kind, which cannot remain localized, and must have its impact on other Jewish communities and community relations (Letter to JCC of Teaneck, dated 29th December (3rd *Tevet*) 1981.).

90. Yosef B. Friedman (ed.), *Let There Be Light: Thirty Days in the Lives of the Chabad Lubavitch Lamplighters* (New York: Kehot, 1986).

91. *...And There Was Light: A photographic chronicle of the Public Chanukah Menorah celebrations sponsored by Chabad Lubavitch around the world* (New York: Kehot, 1987).

92. *Teshurah Lipskar-Krinsky* 2013, pp. 18-20. Though the Supreme Court ruling set an important precedent, it did not prevent future disputes about the issue with Chabad, occasionally losing regional court battles.

93. JTA 5th December 2006.

94. Commentary to *Exodus* 25:32.

95. As depicted in a diagram drawn by Maimonides himself (reproduced in *Commentary to the Mishnah* (Kapach 1967), *Kodashim* p. 79, and in hand-written manuscripts of *Mishneh Torah, Laws of the Chosen House* 3:10). Rambam's son, Avraham, also confirmed that this was his father's opinion (commentary to *Exodus* ibid.).

96. *Likutei Sichot* vol. 21, pp. 168-171. Since there is no traditional *Jewish* source that maintains that the Menorah branches were curved, the Rebbe argued that we are consequently forced to reject the validity of any historical or archeological findings that are in conflict with our tradition. (Ibn Ezra's statement that the branches were in a "semi-circle" (Exodus 27:21) refers not to round branches, but to straight branches that are arranged to encircle the central column. *Zayit Ra'anan* does entertain the possibility that the branches might have been curved, based on a statement in *Sifri Zuta* (cited in *Yalkut Shimoni*, beginning of *Parshat Beha'alothca*) but he rejects the conclusion as "tenuous"). The image on the Arch of Titus is also inconsistent with Jewish tradition in that: a.) It contains engraved images, including that of a dragon (which is, in fact, a symbol of idol worship—BT *Avodah Zarah* 42b). b.) It has no legs, which were present according to Jewish tradition (BT *Menachot* 28b).

In the same period, the Rebbe also reiterated his view, expressed by the *Merkos* logo from the 1940s, that the Tablets of the Covenant ought to be depicted without rounded tops, another image derived from a non-Jewish source. See Sermon of *Shabbos Parshas Ki Sisa* 5741; Sermon of the day of *Simchat Torah* 5742; Discourse of *Shabbat Parshat Behar-Bechukosai* 5748. For more on the above see also *Ha'arot u-Biurim Oholei Torah* (Brooklyn), issue 770, p. 35ff.; *Kovetz Ohr Yisra'el* (Monsey), issue 19, p. 146ff.; ibid. issue 22, p. 194.

97. Interview with Abraham Twerski in Dalfin, *Conversations* pp. 179-180.

98. Memorandum dated January (*Tevet*) 1978. http://portraitofaleader.blogspot.com/2007/10/needless-to-say-on-my-part-i-will-do.html (accessed March 2014).
99. Letter to Yehuda Landes dated 30th March (21st *Adar II*), 1978
100. Letters from Yehuda Landes to the Rebbe dated 22nd March, 10th April and 7th June 1978.
101. Kaplan subsequently authored a number of influential books on the topic: *Meditation and the Bible* (York Beach, Maine: Samuel Weiser, Inc., 1978); *Meditation and Kabbalah* (York Beach, Maine: Samuel Weiser, Inc., 1982); *Jewish Meditation: A Practical Guide* (New York: Schocken Books, 1985); Abraham Sutton (ed.), *Inner Space: Introduction to Kabbalah, Meditation and Prophecy* (Jerusalem: Moznaim Publishing, 1990).
102. Letter to Yehuda Landes, dated 16th June (11th *Sivan*) 1978.
103. Letter to Yehuda Landes, dated 5th July 1979.
104. For the above see: Dr. Natan Ophir, *The Lubavitcher Rebbe's Call for a Scientific Non-Hasidic Meditation*, (B'or Ha'torah, vol. 22, 2013, pp. 109-123).
105. Sermon of 8th July 1979.
106. Sermon of 26th August, 1978.
107. Sermon of Shabbat, 7th January 1984.
108. Diary of Rabbi Aharon Kornet at http://yomanim.com (accessed March 2014).
109. Letter from Rabbi Moshe Feinstein, reproduced in Wolpo, *Shemen Sason*, p. 38.
110. Letter from 1982, ibid. p. 37
111. Rabbenu Jacob ben Meir Tam (1100-1171) disagreed with his grandfather, Rabbi Sholmo Yizchaki (*Rashi*–1040-1105), as to the order in which scriptural passages are to be inserted into the *tefilin*. The dispute is significant as the opinions are mutually exclusive: each one maintains that, according to the other, one does not fulfill the commandment at all. The Jewish community has long accepted *Rashi's* view as authoritative, but the respect for Rabbenu Tam's opinion is so great that many pious Jews don two pairs of *tefilin*. This is, in fact, recommended by the *Code of Jewish Law* (*Orach Chaim* ch. 34): "A G-d fearing person should fulfill both opinions by procuring two pairs of tefilin and donning both of them." In his sermon of Purim 1976, the Rebbe also stressed the importance of this custom in particular for Rabbis and Torah scholars whose very profession demands that they be "G-d fearing."
112. Letter dated 15th February 1980, in *Igrot Moshe*, vol. 6, pp. 11-14.
113. *Kfar Chabad*, issue 252. The scribe was Rabbi Eliezer Zirkind.
114. *Kovetz Hadrat Melech*, published in honor of the first *Siyum Ha-Rambam* (New York: Kehot, 1985).
115. Rabbi Shach objected vehemently to most of the Rebbe's outreach campaigns including those of: *Neshek* (Shabbat candles), *Tefilin*, *Rambam* study, children's parades on *Lag B'Omer*, and the Noahide Laws. See Elazar Shach, *Michtavim v'Ma'amarim* vol. 1, p. 15, 19; vol. 3, pp. 100–102; vol. 4, p. 69, 71; vol. 5, p. 137, 139.
116. Sermon of 19th May 1980 (*Sichot Kodesh* 5740, vol. 3, p. 194). The Rebbe did not mention Rabbi Shach by name in the sermon though it was clear to whom he was referring.
117. Lecture by Benjamin Netanyahu at 92nd Street Y, New York, 29th September 2009, http://www.youtube.com/watch?v=GvMIk_-CRj0 (accessed March 2014). See also Ira Weiss interview for his recollection of the visit.
118. Lecture by Benjamin Netanyahu to U.N. Assembly, 24th September 2009.
119. 29th September lecture.
120. Weiss interview.
121. Lipkin and Elitov p. 375.
122. Ibid. p. 374.
123. Ibid. p. 372. A comparable patient was subsequently found in Boston, and she was brought to New York to converse with the Rebbetzin.
124. Weiss interview.

125. *Agudas Chasidei Chabad Of United States v. Gourary No.* Cv-85-2909. The following is based on court documents and personal accounts of: Rabbi Yehuda Krinsky (*Mishpacha,* 30th September, 2009), Rabbi Avraham Shemtov (*Kfar Chabad,* December 2006), Rabbi Shalom Ber Levin (*Mishpat Ha-Sefarim—Didan Naztach,* undated, http://www.chabadlibrary.org/books/pdf/didannatzach.pdf), Rabbi Moshe Bogomilsky (*Hei Teves—Didan Notzach: The Victory of the Sefarim,* private publication, fourth impression 2012), Rabbi Zalman Gurary (Lipkin and Elitov pp. 429-441), Rabbi Chaim Baruch Halberstam (http://www.yomanim.com/index.php?title=אירועי_ה%27_טבת_-_ר%27_חיים_ברוך_הלברשטם), and Nathan Lewin (Dalfin, *Conversations* pp. 99-111). General accounts are found in Edward Hoffman, *Despite All Odds: The Story of Lubavitch* (New York: Simon and Schuster, 1991), chapter 9; Mintz, *Hasidic People,* chapter 24, and Binyamin Lipkin, *Cheshbono Shel Olam* (Israel: Machon Ha-Sefer, 2000), chapter 5.
126. For the history of Rayatz's library see Rabbi Shalom Ber Levin, *The Lubavitch Library* (Heb.), (New York: Library of Agudat Chasidei Chabad, 1993), chaps. 6-9.
127. Levin, p. 6
128. Likfin and Elitov, p. 214.
129. See Levin, *Library,* chap. 10.
130. Facsimile of Levin's letter and the Rebbe's handwritten response in Levin, *Mishpat Ha-Sefarim* p. 5.
131. Ironically, Chaskind had been the first individual to publicly call "Ramash" to the Torah as "Rebbe" (see p. 184).
132. See memoir of Rabbi Zvi Hirsh Gansbourg from 1958, Simon Jacobson (ed.), *Portrait of a Chassid: The Life and Legacy of Rabbi Zvi Hirsh Gansbourg* (New York: GJCF, 2008), p. 134.
133. Barry later claimed that Rebbetzin Moussia *had* given her consent in a phone call to his mother, but, from the actual conversation, as related in her sworn deposition of 11-12-1985 (see p. 363), it is clear that she did not give willing consent.
134. Pp. 6-7.
135. See, for example, Jaffe's memoir from 1974: "I had a nice experience the following day. A sleek Cadillac drew up to '770.' At the same moment, the Rebbetzin's sister came down the drive. I assumed, correctly, that this was Rebbetzin Gourary, because she looked very much like our own Rebbetzin. I dashed forward to open the door of the car for her.... I was then astonished to notice that the driver whom I thought was a young girl of eighteen, was our very own Rebbetzin. She is, of course, very petite and she looked very chic and smart. The Rebbetzin gave me a wave, a glad smile and drove off."
136. Moussia Schneerson, videotaped court deposition of 11-12-1985.
137. By the time Chabad obtained a restraining order against Barry on 29th July 1985, he had extracted 550 books from the library, of which he had sold around 100, for a total of $169,000. The cost to Chabad of re-purchasing the book sold was $433,000 (Bogomilsky, p. 56). Privately, Barry was approached by some Chabad adherents offering a substantial financial settlement, on condition he relinquish any rights to ownership of the library, but he declined.
138. Levin p. 7. The Rebbe spoke publicly about the issue on 1st July, 4th July and 13th July.
139. Sermon of 13th July. These two arguments played a central role in the subsequent court case.
140. This did, in fact, deter at least one future purchaser. See Bogomilsky pp. 36-7.
141. BT *Shabbat* 105b.
142. Sermon of 13th July 1985, reproduced in Shmuel Lieberman, *Hey Teves Story* (undated), p. 19, http://www.teshura.com/teshurapdf/Hey%20Teves%20Story.pdf (accessed March 2014).
143. Court testimony of Chana Gourary.
144. In private, he reputedly told Rabbi Zalman Gurary that the case represented a challenge "*oif dem benkel*" to the seat of Chabad leadership (cited in Bogomilsky, p. 7, note 4). In all likelihood, this did not mean to imply that Barry desired to lead Chabad—he had surely given up

any such hopes by this point—but that his actions in liquidating Rayatz's library represented a *de facto* dismissal of the Rebbe's leadership.

145. See sermon of 13th January (12th *Tevet*) 1987 (*Torat Menachem—Hitva'aduyot* 5747, vol. 1, p. 238, note 31 and pp. 243-4 citing *Leviticus Rabah* 24:3)

146. Interview with Nathan Lewin in Lipkin and Elitov p. 436. In Dalfin's interview, Lewin recalls that it was Krinsky who initially contacted him.

147. Rabbi Piekarsky was a pre-eminent scholar who, although not from a Chabad background, was appointed *Rosh Yeshivah* of 770 in 1951. For more on him and his relationship with the Rebbe see Wolpo, *Shemen Sasson* vol. 4, pp. 49-61.

148. See Rabbi Moshe Feinstein, *Igrot Moshe, Choshen Mishpat* vol. 2, responsum 12.

149. Dalfin, p. 101-3; Bogomilsky p. 29, 69. This account is based on Lewin's recollection in Dalfin ibid. A 1988 article on the case in *Newsday* similarly reported that "Gourary confirms that he rejected going to a rabbinical court" (Bob Liff, *Theft Or Inheritance? A $460,000 Question*, 16th May, 1988).

    Barry also enlisted the support of the Satmar community, whose antagonism to Chabad had climaxed in 1983 with violent outbursts (ibid.). On 27th May 1983 Rabbi Pinchas Korf was attacked by a group of young men and his beard was cut. On 29th June 1983, a Satmar group forced Lubavitcher Rabbi Mendel Wechter into a van and cut off his beard. Wechter, an astute scholar, had "defected" from Satmar to Lubavitch a few years earlier. (*New York Times*, 21st June 1983. See *Kfar Chabad* issue 103; Mintz, chapter 14).

150. Bogomilsky, p. 35, 59. See Levin pp. 30-33.

151. Levin, p. 8. Facimile on p. 23.

152. Diary of Noach Vogel (www.yomanim.com).

153. Dalfin, pp. 105-6; Shemtov memoir.

154. Excerpted from Dalfin p. 108.

155. Court decision, CV-85-2909 by Judge Charles Sifton, 6th January 1987.

156. Dalfin p. 106; Shemtov memoir.

157. Krinsky in *Mishpacha;* Shemtov memoir.

158. Krinsky in *Mishpacha.*

159. Friedman, together with Samuel Heilman, later wrote *The Rebbe: The Life and Afterlife of Menachem Mendel Schneerson* (Princeton University Press, 2010), which was heavily influenced by Barry's views. See above, chapter 5, note 8.

160. Handwritten (undated) note from the Rebbe in Levin, p. 12.

161. Levin, p. 14

162. Court decision, CV-85-2909 by Charles Sifton, 6th January 1987.

163. Wiesel testimony cited in Hoffman, p. 186.

164. "That is, evidence sufficient to persuade the undersigned beyond a reasonable doubt that the Rebbe delivered his library to representatives of plaintiff with a clear and unequivocal 'manifestation of an intention to create it . . . subjecting the person by whom the property is held to equitable duties to deal with the property for a charitable purpose.' A. Scott, The Law of Trusts, §348 at 2768 (3d ed. 1967), *quoting Restatement* (Second) of Trusts" (Sifton decision).

165. Bogomilksy, p. 6, note 3.

166. In a similar vein, Rabbi Shneur Zalman of Liadi was said to refer to the Ba'al Shem Tov as "grandfather," despite the fact that the Ba'al Shem Tov had living biological heirs, out of the conviction that his own formulation of Chasidut represented the spiritual legacy of the movement's founder. (See *Ha-Tamim*, Vol. II, p. 56; *Ha-Yom Yom*, 27th *Iyar*; *Likutei Sichot*, vol. 4, p. 1136.) See also BT *Sanhedrin* 19b: "Whoever teaches Torah to the son of another person is considered as if he fathered him."

167. *Souvenir Journal Celebrating the Wedding of Aron and Dinie Rabin*, 20th *Elul* 1999, p. 6.

168. Sermon of 7th *Tevet* 1992.

CHAPTER 14: FUTURE VISIONS

1. For the above see Lipkin, chapter 2; Lipkin and Elitov pp. 400-409; accounts of Rabbis Leibel Groner, Binyamin Klein and Shalom Ber Gansburg in *Kfar Chabad* (January 2008).
2. Transcripts of discussions of the following Rabbinic visitors at the *shiva* are found in *Siach Sarfei Kodesh* (Israel, Machon Beohalei Tzadikim, 2007): Rabbi Moshe Shalom Ungar, Rabbi Rafael Goldstein of Skolye, Rabbi Shalom Yehudah Gross of Holmin, Rabbi Yisrael Menachem Greenwald of Pupa, Rabbi Yisrael Hagar, Rabbi Pinchas Hirschprung, Klausenberger Rebbe Shmuel David Halberstam, Rabbi Moshe Wolfson, Spinka Rebbe Naftali Weiss, Rabbi Refael Zilber, Alexander Rebbe Yechiel Menachem Zinger, Rabbi Yitzchak Chaim Zeltenreich, Nadvorna Rebbe Shlomo Leifer, Rabbi Aharon Soloveitchik, Rabbi Simcha Elberg, Rabbi Simcha Bunim Ehrenfeld, Rabbi Avraham Pam, Skulener Rebbe Yisrael Avraham Portugal, Novominsker Rebbe Yaakov Perlow, Ratzfert Rebbe Asher Anshel Kraus, Skolye Rebbe Avraham Moshe Rabinowits, Munkatcher Rebbe Moshe Yehuda Leib Rabinowitz, Dinover Rebbe Yaakov Rabinowitz, Rabbi Yisrael Menachem Rottenberg, Karlin-Stoliner Rebbe Baruch Meir Yaakov Shochet, Bobov Rosh Yeshiva Rabbi Moshe David Steinwurtzel, Debreciner Rav Moshe Stern, Kozhnitzer Rebbe of Tel Aviv Yaakov Shimshon Sternberg, Rabbi David Berish Spira, Bluzhover Rebbe Tzvi Spira.
3. See Krinsky in *Mishpacha;* Lipkin pp. 39-44. Facsimile of the will is reproduced in (unpaginated) supplement to Lipkin.
4. *Torat Menachem—Hitva'aduyot* 5748, vol. 4, p. 397*ff.* Only after the Rebbe passed on, in 1994, was the sermon shared with the broader community, in *Kfar Chabad Magazine,* Issue 624.

   For the above, and text of the sermon, see Likfin pp. 45-48.

   During the summer of 1988 the Rebbe also called a number of meetings with Rabbis Chodakov, Mindel and Piekarsky to draft a charter of whom would direct the central Chabad organizations after his passing. The Rebbe's intentions, however, have remained moot in the absence of a signed copy of the document that was prepared. After the Rebbe's passing in 1994, the issue was the source of much internal debate in the movement.
5. *Torat Menachem* ibid. vol. 2, p. 369.
6. Ibid. p. 308.
7. *Likutei Sichot* vol. 29, p. 298.
8. *Torat Menachem* ibid.
9. Levin, *Avodat Ha-Kodesh* p. 28.
10. *Igrot Kodesh* vols. 1-22 (New York: Kehot, 1987-1994), with correspondence up to 1963. In subsequent years a further eight volumes have been published (vols. 24-30), spanning 1964-1975.
11. *Torat Menachem—Hitva'aduyot* 5747, vol. 2, p. 620.
12. This was a theme stressed repeatedly in 1990, the fortieth year of his leadership, when he often cited the Talmudic idea (BT *Avodah Zarah* 5b), that after forty years a student is able to fathom the wisdom of his teacher (see, for example, *Torat Menachem—Hitva'aduyot* 5750, vol. 2, p. 193).
13. ibid 5746, vol. 2, pp. 674-5. This kind of activity was not unusual, as the Rebbe would often maintain a public dialogue with his students through commenting at *farbrengens* on papers published in Chabad journals. For an interesting collection of all the Rebbe's public comments to papers published in one journal, published by the New York Chabad Yeshiva *Oholei Torah,* see Mendel Mishulovin and Levi Raitchik (eds.), *Sefer Ha-Yovel Ha'arot U'Biurim* (New York: Oholei Torah, 2010).
14. Ibid. 5747, vol. 1, p. 579.
15. Ibid. vol. 2, p. 456.
16. Groner interview in *Kfar Chabad.*
17. Weiss interview.
18. http://forward.com/articles/147997/meet-chaya-mushka-again-and-again/ (accessed April 2014).

19. Levin, *Avodat Hakodesh,* chapter 10.
20. *Torat Menachem—Hitava'aduyot* 5752, vol 2, pp. 254-7.
21. From 1989-1990 he delivered just five discourses, and none during 1991-2.
22. During the eleven months of mourning for his wife, weekday services were conducted in his home.
23. From 1951 until 1986 he edited *ma'amarim* very occasionally, and only fifty edited discourses were published during this entire period—later collected in *Sefer Ha-Ma'amarim Melukat,* vol 1, (New York: Kehot, 1986). The discourses he edited from 1987-1992 fill five further volumes—ibid. vol. 2-6. Interestingly, this activity mirrors the last years of Rayatz's life, when he ceased delivering discourses and instead edited them for publication (see p. 168).
24. The materials edited from 1987 to 1992 fill twelve volumes of edited *farbrengens* (*Sefer Ha-Sichot* 5747-5752), ten volumes of *Likutei Sichot* (vols. 30-39), and five volumes of discourses (*Sefer Ha-Ma'amarim Melukat,* vols. 2-6). If we add to that the twenty volumes of *Igrot Kodesh* which appeared during this period, it follows that a staggering forty-seven volumes of edited teachings were published by the Rebbe in the last six years of his active life. This surpassed the twenty-nine volumes of *Likutei Sichot* and one volume of *Ma'amarim* which had appeared during the previous thirty-six years. (Of course, this refers only to the publication schedule of *edited* materials. The non-edited transcripts from 1950-1986 fill seventy-one volumes of sermons and thirty volumes of discourses)
25. Many of the texts handed out were pamphlets of the Rebbe's own discourses, but he also distributed volumes by Rabbi Shneur Zalman, *Tzemach Tzedek, Rashab and Rayatz.* Along with each copy of the text, the Rebbe usually gave $1, $2 or $5 to be distributed to charity. On *Lag B'Omer* of 1990 and 1991 a special commemorative coin was distributed. On Chanukah of 1990 and 1991 he distributed $1 coins.

    The distributions of printed materials were (unless noted, the text was a *ma'amar* of the Rebbe):

    1987: 20th *Cheshvan* (*Kuntres Heichaltzu* of *Rashab*), *Rosh Chodesh Kislev.*

    1989: 11th *Nisan* (*Kuntres Ahavat Yisrael*), eve of *Rosh Hashanah* (summaries of *Tanya* by *Tzemach Tzedek*), 6th *Tishrei* (discourse of *Tzemach Tzedek*).

    1990: 10th *Shevat* (book of Tanya), 11th *Nisan,* 8th *Tammuz* (discourse of *Rayatz*), 20th *Cheshvan* (*Kuntres Etz Chaim* of *Rashab*), 24th *Cheshvan* (discourse of *Rashab*), 19th *Kislev* (book of *Tanya*).

    1991: 10th *Shevat* (discourse of Rashab), 15th *Iyar* (*Dvar Malchut,* a compendium of *sichot*), 28th *Sivan* (pamphlet commemorating fifty years in America), 20th *Cheshvan,* 27th *Cheshvan,* 16th *Kislev* (discourse of *Rayatz*).

    1992: 10th *Shevat* (discourse of *Rayatz*), 22nd *Shevat,* 14th *Adar* I.
26. A selection of these have been published in *Zorea Tzedakot Matzmiach Yeshuot* (New York: Fax a Sicha, 1993). A brief subtitled segment of the video-recordings of dollars distribution appears in the weekly video magazine *Living Torah,* by Jewish Educational Media.
27. Gordon Zacks, *Defining Moments: Stories of Character, Courage and Leadership* (New York: Beaufort Books, 2006), pp. 137-146. In his memoir, Zacks recalls his 1987 discussion with the Rebbe from memory, and I have adjusted it here to the precise exchange as recorded on video (http://www.chabad.org/therebbe/article_cdo/aid/526496/jewish/Increasing-in-Education.htm). I have, however, presumed that the dates of the two encounters as recorded in the memoir are correct, and that the gap between the meetings was not nineteen years, as Zacks said to the Rebbe, but seventeen.
28. Interview with Jackie Mason in Mordechai Staiman, *Diamonds of the Rebbe* (New York: Otsar Sifrei Lubavitch, 1998), p. 11.
29. Interview with Joe Lieberman, ibid. p. 33
30. Meeting of March 27, 1989. While women's issues, especially the need for advanced Torah study by women, had been an ongoing concern for the Rebbe throughout his leadership,

during this period he devoted a major sermon to the topic, in the summer of 1990. *Torat Menachem—Hitva'aduyot* 5750, vol. 3, p. 171*ff.* On this topic see also on *Likutei Sichos* vol. 14, p. 37ff., and its adaptation in Chaim Miller, *Chumash Kol Menachem* (New York: Kol Menachem, 2006), pp. 1195-7.

31. The hundreds of directives from the period 1988-1992 have been collected by Rabbi Levi Stolik in *A Call to Action*, http://ichossid.com (accessed April 2014).
32. See *Torat Menachem—Hitva'aduyot* 5748, vol. 2, p. 460-2.
33. The idea is sourced in a letter of Rayatz (*Igrot Rayatz* vol. 5, p. 106), and parallels other Jewish ideas and practices which were only revealed to later generations (see *Likutei Sichot* vol. 20. p. 386ff). In one letter he describes "the particular relevance of the birthday":

> The *aliyah* to the Torah, on the preceding Shabbat, which is by way of preparation for the birthday, emphasizes that with each birthday the Jew rises to a higher spiritual level. This is indicated also by the word *aliyah* ("going up")....
>
> A person, of course, grows physically and mentally from day to day and from year to year, so that in some respects the person is not exactly the same today as the day before. Certainly in the spiritual sphere the birthday is meant to bring about an essential (not merely superficial) change, since on that day his *mazel* is renewed. By that is meant, as the Gemarah expresses it, *mazelayu chazi* (BT *Megillah* 3a. See also JT *Rosh Hashanah* 3:8.), the "root" of the soul, which remains attached to its Source On High, while only an extension of the soul, as it were, descends into the body and vitalizes it. For, obviously, the soul which is eternal and part of "real G-dliness" could not be "wholly confined" within the body, any more than G-d Himself could be confined within the world He created. And just as G-d is both in the world and beyond it (immanent and transcendent) so it is in regard to the soul and body.
>
> Therefore, when the birthday comes, the Jew is expected to ascend to a higher level in an essential way, namely by strengthening the very root of the soul, when, as a matter of course, the change is felt also in the "lower" aspect of the soul that vitalizes the physical body. Such a change can be achieved only through Torah, which is *"our very life and the length of our days"* (Liturgy, Evening Service).
>
> The second observance—an increase in the actual Torah study—follows the first, but in a more tangible way, namely the study of the Torah with understanding and comprehension, so that it permeates the mind and is reflected in actual living experience in the daily life.
>
> The third item—the giving of *tzedakah*—signifies the giving of oneself, both of body and soul. Since a person consists of both body and soul, his growth and advancement has to encompass both the spiritual and the physical. If the *aliyah* and Torah study primarily reflect the spiritual, the giving of *tzedakah* reflects the physical and material, namely the sweat and toil of earning money, which is then converted into some thing spiritual and sacred, since it is dedicated to a sacred cause (Letter dated 10th November (25th *Cheshvan*) 1974 in *L'Chaim* issue 866 (2005)).

34. The passport incorrectly identifies the Rebbe's date of birth as 2nd March 1895.
35. Audio-recording of talk to Chabad supporters on 19th September 1988. See *Torat Menachem—Hitva'aduyot* 5749, vol. 1, pp. 54-9.
36. For commemorative album celebrating the *Chanukah Live* events see *One Hour, Forty Years* (*Merkos L'Inyanei Chinuch*, 1990). For more details of the broadcasts see *A Chassidisher Derher* issue 14 (*Tevet* 5774), pp. 17-27.
37. Collected in *Sefer Ha-Shlichut* (New York: Kehot, sixth edition, 1990)
38. Note of the Rebbe dated 29th October (21st *Cheshvan* 1991) in *Teshurah Krinsky-Dechter*, 14th October (2nd *Cheshvan*) 2007, p. 36.

39. Ibid. p. 33-34.
40. Sermon of 17th November 1990. See *Torat Menachem—Hitva'aduyot* 5750, vol. 1, p. 332. The color album was published as Yosef B. Friedman (ed.), *Sefer Ha-Shluchim* (New York: Kehot 1991, 4 vols).
41. *Ha-Targil Ha-Masriach,* a term coined by Yitzchak Rabin. See *Dan Kurzman, Soldier of Peace: The Life of Yitzhak Rabin* (New York: Harper, 1998) p. 422.
42. Ari Goldman, "One Brooklyn Rabbi's Long Shadow," *New York Times,* 13th April 1990.
43. "Rebbe's Influence Blamed for Labor's Failure to Form Governing Coalition," JTA, April 13, 1990.
44. G.G. Labelle, "New York Rabbi Emerges as Key in Effort to form Israeli Gov't," *Associated Press,* 12th Apr, 1990; JTA ibid. The Rebbe's direct involvement was also denied by Rabbi Berke Wolff, Chabad spokesman in Israel, and Rabbi Menachem Porush of *Agudat Israel.*
45. For the text of the lecture, which became known as the "Rabbits and Pigs Speech," see *Ha'aretz,* 28th March 1990.
46. Yitzchak Fishel, in *The Jewish Thinker,* 21st January 2013.
47. *Torat Menachem—Hitva'aduyot* 5750, vol. 2, p. 479.
48. Associated Press, 28th December 1990.
49. For a collection of sources see Gershon Greenberg, *Menahem Mendel Schneersohn's Response To The Holocaust* in *Modern Judaism* volume 34, number 1 (February 2014), pp. 86-122.
50. See BT *Shabbat* 68b; *Shavuot* 5a. See also Maimonides, *Hilchot Mamrim* 3:3; *Shulchan Aruch, Yoreh De'ah* 159:3, *Beit Yosef* and *Darkei Moshe,* ibid; *Shulchan Aruch Admor Ha-Zaken, Hilchot Ribbit,* 79, 80. See also Jacob J. Schacter (ed.), *The Orthodox Forum Series: Jewish Tradition and the Non-Traditional Jew* (New Jersey: Jason Aronson, Inc., 2006).
51. Deuteronomy 14:1.
52. Exodus 4:22.
53. Zechariah 2:12.
54. BT *Menachot* 29b.
55. *Shemot Rabah* 5:22.
56. Isaiah 54:7.
57. *Torat Menachem—Hitva'aduyot* 5751, vol. 2, p. 112*ff.*
58. In the press it was widely reported that the Rebbe had predicted the war would end by the festival of Purim (it ended on Purim). This, however, was not stated either in a sermon or in correspondence, and was probably based on a comment made by the Rebbe at Sunday Dollars on 20th January 1991 to Col. Chaplain Yaakov Goldstein that he would not be reading the Megillah on Purim in Saudia Arabia. However, see Goldstein's recollection and understanding of the encounter in *A Chassidisher Derher* issue 16 (Adar I 5774), p. 18. See also *Kfar Chabad* issue 943 (2001), that upon hearing the announcement made in his name in the media, the Rebbe asked Yehuda Krinsky in surprise: "Did I promise that the war would end on Purim?"

    For a collection of responses made during this period at Sunday Dollars and in correspondence, see *A Chassidisher Derher* ibid., pp. 11-21
59. Ibid. p, 18, 20.
60. Steve Fetter, George N. Lewis, and Lisbeth Gronlund, *Why were Casualties so low?* in *Nature,* vol. 361 (28th January 1993), pp. 293–296.
61. Pastoral letter dated 11th March (25th *Adar*) 1991.
62. Edward S. Shapiro, *Crown Heights: Blacks, Jews and the 1991 Brooklyn Riot* (Waltham, Mass.: Brandeis University Press, 2006), p. xi.
63. Ibid. chapters 1-2. See also Mintz, *Hasidic People* chapter 27.
64. Video available at http://www.chabad.org/therebbe/article_cdo/aid/1599198/jewish/The-Rebbe-and-David-Dinkins.htm. The discussion is paraphrased in Mintz, p. 338.

65. JEM, *Living Torah*, Disc 43, Program 171.
66. See *Mishnah, Sanhedrin* 4:5.
67. Letter to Mr. Ardadiusz Rybicki, Office of the President of the Republic of Poland, 23rd October 1991 in *L'Chaim* issue 539 (1998).
68. See New York Times, 9th February 1992; *L'Chaim* issue 214 (8th May 1992).
69. Sermon of 13th February 1992 (*Sichot Kodesh* 5752, vol. 2, (New York: Va'ad Kitvei Kodesh 1992, pp. 730-733).
70. See *Likutei Sichot* vol. 20, p. 430, 456; *Sichot Kodesh* 5741, vol. 2, p. 737*ff.* For academic discussions of the Rebbe's Messianism see Elliot R. Wolfson, "Revealing and Re/veiling Menahem Mendel Schneerson's Messianic Secret," in *Kabbalah: Journal for the Study of Jewish Mystical Texts* 26 (2012), pp. 25-96, and sources cited ibid. note 2.
71. *Likutei Sichot* ibid. p. 234, note 50, citing a predictive calculation by Rabbi Shaul Brach (1865–1940), Chief Rabbi of Kashau (Košice) in Hungary. See *Hayom Yom*, introduction, year 5742.
72. See BT *Sanhedrin* 97b where such activity is sharply censored. However see *Likutei Sichot* ibid. note 51, for the Rebbe's view that this was directed at ordinary Jews, and not *Gedolei Yisrael* (major Jewish leaders), as is evidenced from the fact that many Jewish leaders did involve themselves in Messianic speculation.
73. Commentary to Daniel 7:25, 8:14 (This reference, and those that follow, appear in the Rebbe's original handwritten note).
74. *Letter to Teiman.*
75. Daniel 11:30.
76. *Hadar Zekenim*, beginning of portion of *Vayeishev.*
77. *Sefer Geulah.*
78. Commentary on Megillot ("approximately after 5540 years").
79. *Mayanei Ha-Yeshua*, and a number of other places.
80. Beginning of portion of *Tzav.*
81. Commentary to *Safra d'Tzni'usa.*
82. *Maaseh Oreg* to *Mishnayot* (*Ma'aser Sheini* 5:2).
83. He also cited BT *Sanhedrin* 97b and *Zohar* I 139b.

    (Undated) handwritten response of the Rebbe from the early 1950s, in *Teshurah Avtzon-Simpson*, 3rd *Shevat* 5765 (2005), p. 12.
84. For example Chabad Chasidic thought teaches that, before his death, Moses tried to elevate the people to his level, and that even though this proved not to be possible, the people still benefitted from the experience of having been exposed to a glimmer of Moses' exalted position. See sources in *Likutei Sichot* ibid. pp. 233-4, note 46.
85. Ibid. pp. 233-4.
86. Ibid. (the particular reference here is to the Patriarch Jacob, but is presumably true of all *tzadikim*).
87. BT *Pesachim* 56a; *Rashi* to Genesis 49:1.
88. Ibid. Despite the fact that G-d withheld the "end" from Jacob, his desire to communicate it nevertheless represented a valuable attempt to narrow the gap beween leader and disciple.
89. *Zorea Tzedakot Matzmiach Yeshuot*, p. 149. This was shortly after his "famous sermon" of 1991. See below.
90. The Rebbe was, in fact, careful never to predict Mashiach's coming within a specific timeframe. When asked by a journalist on 4th August (24th *Menachem Av*) 1991, "When is he [Mashiach] coming," the Rebbe replied, "Write about the preparations for his coming." When the reporter persisted, "But when is he coming," the Rebbe said, "When he will come is for him to decide. But what each one of us has to do is to add in Torah and *mitzvot.* That will speed his coming" (ibid. p. 148).
91. A term employed by the *Talmud* (BT Sotah 49b), borrowed from Psalms 89:52, to refer to the period preceding the Messianic coming.

92. "With the footsteps of the Messiah, insolence will increase and honor dwindle; the vine will yield its fruit [abundantly] but wine will be expensive; the government will turn to heresy and there will be none [to offer them] reproof; the meeting place [of scholars] will be used for immorality; Galilee will be destroyed, Gablan desolated, and the dwellers on the frontier will go about [begging] from place to place without anyone to take pity on them; the wisdom of the learned will degenerate; fearers of sin will be despised; and the truth will be lacking; youths will put old men to shame; the old will stand up in the presence of the young; a son will revile his father; a daughter will rise against her mother, a daughter-in-law against her mother-in-law; and a man's enemies will be the members of his household; the face of the generation will be like the face of a dog; a son will not feel ashamed before his father. So upon whom is it for us to rely? Upon our father who is in heaven" (*Sotah* ibid).
93. Letter dated 23rd Adar 1963 in *L'Chaim* issue 1149 (2010).
94. Dalfin, p. 141-6.
95. Written response on letter dated 27th April (30th *Nisan*) 1979 in Tzvi Hirsh Notik, Mordechai Liberov and Eliezer Zaklikovsky (eds.), *Nalchah B'Orchotav* (New York: Private publication, 1996), p. 219. The Rebbe also wrote, "In my opinion, the doctors overestimate their evaluation of the damage caused by obesity," also pointing to the drawback of a narrow vision that isolates one detail (weight) from a broader, holistic picture.
96. For the predicted shift see Rabbi Shmuel Di Uzeda, *Midrash Shmuel* to *Avot* 5:19; Rabbi Shalom Buzaglo, *Mikdash Melech* to *Zohar* I 17b; Rabbi Shneur Zalman of Liadi, *Likutei Torah, Korach* 54b; *Tosafot Chadashim* to *Avot* 1:1.
97. BT *Yevamot* 14a.
98. BT *Eruvin* 13b.
99. *Laws of Kings*, at end.
100. See *Torat Menachem—Hitva'aduyot* 5751, vol. 3, p. 449*ff.*
101. *New York Times* 27th March 1972.
102. The former ("a") narrows the chasm separating G-d and the physical world, by utilizing physical objects for a sacred purpose; and the latter ("b") prepares the mind for the elevated thought patterns of the Messianic Era.
103. The Rebbe seemed to favor the view of *Rashi* (BT *Sukkah*, 41a), the *Zohar* (I 28a), that the Temple would be built by G-d. The requirement of human participation stipulated by Maimonides (*Laws of Kings* 11:4), he argued, could be satisfied through a small gesture, such as attaching a door (See *Likutei Sichot* vol. 9, p. 26*ff*; vol. 11, p. 98; vol. 18, pp. 418-9). In any case, his sermons were devoid of any practical (i.e. non-spiritual) suggestions towards building the Temple.
104. According to Maimonides (ibid.) the "ingathering of exiles" takes place only after the construction of the Temple. See letter in chapter 12, note 69.

    For the Rebbe's thoughts why he did not visit Israel see article of Shlomo Goren in Lipkin (unpaginated supplement).
105. Maimonides states that Mashiach will "fight the wars of G-d," but in *Likutei Sichot* vol. 24, p. 19, note 58, he argues that Maimonides speaks of a "worst-case scenario" and that wars will hopefully prove unnecessary.
106. Ibid.
107. Letter cited in note 104. Citations from Maimonides are in italics. This argument was repeated several times in sermons and letters, and I cite this particular letter since it was originally written in English.
108. See handwritten note of the Rebbe in Lipkin (end of supplementary documents, unpaginated), from *Adar* 1992: "There is no requirement *whatsoever* to determine the identity of Mashiach." See also *Hitkashrut* (Chabad in Israel), issue 100 (1996), that when the editorial board responsible for preparing the Rebbe's sermons for publication submitted a draft text

to him stating that *shluchim* ought to publicize "the identity of Mashiach" the Rebbe crossed these words out.

109. The term, which literally means "Chabad elite" or "super-Chabad" was employed by the Rebbe a number of times in sermons to critique the misplaced convictions and activities of some well-meaning but overzealous Chabad Chasidim. For a collection of some of these statements see *Hitkashrut* (Chabad of Israel), issue 309 (2000).
110. Sermon of 20th October 1984 (*Torat Menachem—Hitva'aduyot* 5745, vol. 1, p. 465). For more background to the sermon see Rabbi Yehoshua Mondshine, *Igeret le-Yedid* (spring of 1992), http://www.shturem.net/index.php?section=blog_new&article_id=127 (accessed April 2014).
111. Sermon of 11th April (28th *Nisan*) 1991 (from video-recording. For an edited transcript see *Torat Menachem—Hitva'aduyot* 5751, vol. 3, p. 119). Employing a Kabbalistic trope familiar to his audience, the Rebbe stipulated that whatever activities would be undertaken, while infused with intense passion (*orot de-tohu*), must be carefully thought out and devoid of any hint of anarchy or chaos (*be-kelim de-tikun*). For the reference to the sermon as the *sicha ha-yadua* see response from 1991 reproduced in *Davar Melech* (Israel, Kfar Chabad, 1992), p. 63.
112. The Rebbe was apparently unimpressed with the response and reputedly commented to Rabbi Zalman Gurary, as he left the synagogue, that the sermon's message had not penetrated the audience in the slightest.
113. Sermon of 12th October 1991, *Sichot Kodesh* 5752, vol. 1, pp. 259-260.
114. Written response to Rabbi Aharon Dov Halperin, editor of *Kfar Chabad* in Lipkin, pp. 142-3.
115. Written response to Rabbi Shalom Wolpo, in Lipkin, p. 143.

    See Lipkin p. 142-6 for further documentation and analysis that throughout the entire period following the 1991 sermon when the Rebbe was still able to communicate verbally and in writing, he did not retract from his 1984 position that public speculation over the identity of Mashiach would be highly counterproductive.
116. *Hitva'aduyot* ibid. p. 164.
117. Yehuda Krinsky in *Mishpacha*, 30th September 2009.
118. Weiss interview.
119. Jaffe, installment 25.
120. *Jerusalem Post*, 20th June 1994.
121. *Ma'ariv*, 13th June 1994, estimated the crowd at 100,000. The *Jewish Press*, 17th-23rd June, put the figure at 50,000. For the above details see *Jewish Press* ibid. and *New York Newsday* 13th June, 1994.
122. Malachi 2:6.

AFTERWORD

1. Speech delivered to American Friends of Lubavitch at the Library of Congress, Washington D.C., March 11, 2002. See also Steinsaltz, *My Rebbe*, p. 212.
2. Aharon Lichtenstein, "Justice shall be the girdle of his loins, and faithfulness the girdle of his waist—eulogy for Rabbi Menachem Mendel Schneerson, the Lubavitch Rebbe," in *Alon Shevut le-Bogrei Yeshivat Har Etzion*, 4, *Tishrei* 5755 (1994), p. 101.
3. Adam S. Ferziger, "From Lubavitch to Lakewood: The Chabadization of American Orthodoxy," *Modern Judaism*, Volume 33, Number 2, May 2013, pp. 101-124.
4. Jack Wertheimer, "The Outreach Revolution," in *Commentary*, 1st April, 2013.
5. Eric Yoffie, Sermon at the Minnesota Biennial, Union for Reform Judaism, 67th General As-

sembly, Minneapolis, MN, 8th November, 2003. http://urj.org/about/union/leadership/yoffie/biennialsermon03.

6. Idem, *Jerusalem Post,* 12th July, 2007.
7. Idem. *Ha'aretz,* 21st April 2013.
8. Dana Evan Kaplan, *Contemporary American Judaism: Transformation and Renewal* (New York: Columbia University Press, 2009), p. 305, 310.
9. Jay Michaelson, *Jerusalem Post,* 10th November, 2005.
10. Tzvi Hersh Weinreb, "The Rebbe's Legacy," *Jerusalem Post,* 18th June 2007.
11. Sarah Maslin Nir, "Jews Make a Pilgrimage to a Grand Rebbe's Grave," *New York Times,* 13th September, 2013.
12. http://www.collive.com/show_news.rtx?id=27310
13. Personal communication with Domenico Lepore, 30th March 2014.
14. Yaakov Brawer, *Eyes that See* (Montreal: Seminary Beis Menachem).

INDEX